THE SPIRIT OF THE HIGH PEAK

THE 20TH CENTURY IN PHOTOGRAPHS

Mike Smith

Published by

Landmark Publishing Ltd,

Waterloo House, 12 Compton, Ashbourne, Derbyshire DE6 1DA England
Tel: (01335) 347349 Fax: (01335) 347303
e-mail: landmark@clara.net www.landmark publishing.co.uk

1st edition

ISBN 1 901522-87-3

© **Mike Smith**

The rights of Mike Smith as the author of this work
have been asserted by him in accordance with the Copyright,
Design and Patents Act, 1993.

All rights reserved. No part of this publication may be reproduced, stored in a retrieval system or transmitted in any form or by any means, electronic, mechanical, photocopying, recording or otherwise without the prior permission of Landmark Publishing Ltd.

British Library Cataloguing in Publication Data: a catalogue record for this book is available from the British Library.

Print: MPG Ltd, Bodmin, Cornwall
Design: Mark Titterton
Cover by James Allsopp

Front cover: Centre-Anna Brindley, 1990 Buxton Carnival Queen; Top left-Celebrating a new play area at Edale; Top right-Princess Diana on a visit to the High Peak in 1990; Bottom-Buxton from the Slopes

Back cover: Top-Market Street, Chapel-en-le-Frith in the early fifties; Middle-Freddie of Freddie and the Dreamers at the Pavilion Gardens Bottom-Lancaster bomber over Ladybower

Title page: Aerial view of Buxton Spa

Contents

Foreword — 4
Introduction — 4
Acknowledgements — 5
Subscribers list — 6
1 A century of change — 7
2 The happiest days of your life — 33
3 White Peak, Dark Peak — 53
4 Flower power — 69
5 On parade — 73
6 High Peak at work — 87
7 High Peak at play — 93
8 War and peace — 111
9 Clubbing together — 121
10 Campaigning zeal — 131
11 Conservation and restoration — 137
12 Weather centre — 153
13 Spa of the Blue Waters — 159
14 For the good of your health — 167
15 Places of worship — 171
16 "999" — 177
17 Enthusiasts — 181
18 Making music — 191
19 Putting on a show — 197
20 Celebration time — 205
21 Animal magic — 209
22 Peak personalities and personalities in the Peak — 215

Foreword

The dramatic changes to all areas of life over the last 100 years would be difficult to match by any other century. This book, however, concentrates on how time has treated our own small area. The photographs are snapshots of time which preserve many familiar characters and places from the ravages of that progress.

The environment around us is changing so quickly that many familiar landmarks disappear without us realising it. In many places the once rural landscape has changed beyond all recognition.

A book like this allows us to stand back and appreciate our heritage but at the same time we can also learn from our predecessors as we build for the future.

By turning the pages, you will find the social, industrial and architectural history of High Peak, and the changing lives of the townsfolk and villagers within it.

Both historically and within this book Buxton has played a major role but the important contributions of many other towns and villages within the surrounding area are not overlooked.

The photographs will help future generations assess the contribution not only of past residents but also our own brief spell of stewardship.

On a personal note it is very strange to see events attended so recently already consigned to the pages of history.

Jason Chadwick,
Buxton Advertiser photographer

Emma Downes,
Buxton Advertiser senior reporter

Introduction

Writing in 1968, the artist Andy Warhol predicted a future in which "everyone will be famous for fifteen minutes". The people who feature in the pages of this publication became famous for at least fifteen minutes when their image appeared in the local newspaper. A few remained in the public eye for a much longer period, but those whose fame was merely fleeting, and the thousands of other local residents who do not appear in these pages, have all made their contribution to the development of the High Peak in the twentieth century. Some of the people featured here have helped to bring about change, because they are the leaders, innovators, shakers and movers of the community, but all the inhabitants of the High Peak have played their part in maintaining the unique traditions of the region and ensuring its continued economic and cultural vitality. The photographic evidence in this publication clearly demonstrates the depth of talent, the wide range of interests, the sense of humour, the capacity for enjoyment, the generosity and the fortitude of Peakland people.

No illustrated book about the Peak District would be complete without photographs of the natural landscape and the towns and villages within it. Accordingly, I have included scenic views from every decade of the twentieth century. They tell of a land of plateaux, edges, cliffs and gorges which has evolved geologically over millions of years, but they also show a countryside whose general appearance and surface patterns are largely man-made. Farmers have tamed and settled the high plateaux, braved the harsh weather, planted clumps of trees to protect their cattle from lead pollution and covered the land with a complex lattice of drystone walls. Quarrymen have made available the gritstones and limestones of the region for re-fashioning into farmsteads, villages and towns, all of which merge deferentially with the natural landscape because they are built of the very stuff on which they stand.

The High Peak is a treasured landscape: famous access battles were fought here by ramblers and it is largely thanks to their efforts that much of the region now enjoys the protection of National Park status. The town of Buxton has one of the finest townscapes and some of the best Georgian and Victorian architecture in England. Its heyday as a spa is well illustrated by photographs from the early years of the century. The place then suffered a slow decline and had almost gone to sleep by the sixties, but perhaps we should be grateful, for Buxton was saved from the disfigurement which could have been caused by thoughtless post-War development and the sort of architectural vulgarities which mar some other spas. The revival of the town from the mid seventies onwards as a cultural, conference and holiday centre is also evident in these pages.

The look of the High Peak and the fabric of its towns and villages changed very little in the twentieth century, but there was a massive change in lifestyle. At the beginning of the century most people rarely travelled far from their homes and the first powered flight had not yet taken place. By the end of the century almost everyone owned a car and most people could also afford to fly off to far-flung destinations. Universal car ownership brought about a profound change in shopping habits with daily visits to corner shops being replaced by a weekly trip to a superstore. One hundred years ago most people got in touch with friends and relatives by letter or by postcard (some of which are used in this publication); today people are able to communicate instantly by fax or e-mail and, through the Internet, they have access to a huge range of information from all parts of the world. Most inhabitants of the High Peak in the early years of the century had been born in the region, lived all their lives there and would die there; many of today's residents are incomers, some commute daily to work in the city, others are only resident at weekends. Very few women had influential roles in the High Peak in the Victorian era, but it is evident from the photographs in these pages that many women now do so. The twentieth century was perhaps above all a century of visual images: the movies arrived, cinemas became enormously popular, fell from favour, closed down in their hundreds, and then began to appear again (but not in the High Peak); television just grew and grew, and photography carried on, but in ever more sophisticated form.

When selecting images of people from the large range of photographs at my disposal, I have largely concentrated on pictures from the second half of the century, in order to give people who are alive at the turn of the millennium a chance to look back on their life in the High Peak during the twentieth century. Wherever possible, I have included names in the text, but I should be delighted to hear from any readers who are able to make additional identifications - extra names could be added to further editions. Every care has been taken to label photographs accurately from the information available, but I offer my apologies in advance for any errors, especially those which may inadvertently cause hurt or embarrassment. Some photographs will evoke treasured memories; others will revive long-forgotten events. In fact, whilst I was selecting photographs for this book, I found an image of myself on a photograph of an event which had escaped my memory.

The pictures in this publication have been selected to illustrate the diversity of High Peak life and to support a text which traces the history of the region over the last one hundred years. Many organisations and individuals are included, but many others equally worthy of coverage are omitted. No slight is intended, for a book of this nature can only offer a snapshot of a very eventful century.

Mike Smith
Sept 2000

Acknowledgements

Many people have helped me during the preparation of this book. I am greatly indebted to Mark Dickens, editor of the *Buxton Advertiser*, for allowing me to select freely from the newspaper's large archive of photographs, and to the Derbyshire Library Service for giving me permission to use pictures from their own collection and images passed on to them by the *Buxton Advertiser*. It would not have been possible to produce this book without the enormous contribution made by Jason Chadwick, staff photographer at the *Buxton Advertiser*. Jason took most of the photographs which cover events in the last twelve years and he very generously gave his time to help me identify many of the places and people depicted. As a photographer on a local newspaper, Jason is obliged to take many commemorative group shots and photographs of individuals receiving outsize cheques, but he is also highly skilled in capturing the moment of most dramatic action, the atmosphere of an event and the character of an individual. I have been greatly privileged to use his pictures.

The staff of Buxton Library were most helpful to me during the time I spent preparing for this book: they put research facilities at my disposal and generously gave their time to ferret for photographs and respond to requests. The staff of New Mills Library also gave me help in accessing material. Keith Holford very kindly allowed me to use a considerable number of images from his impressive archive of photographs and freely shared with me his vast knowledge of local history. I am also indebted to the following people and organisations who loaned photographs for use in this publication: Sandy Broadbent, Baz Brown, Rev. Bob Davies, Joyce Hall, Graham Harper, Ada Hitchens, Donna Kadzewska, Roger Marshall, Barbara Matthews, John Stirling, Pauline Whitelegg, Combs Sailing Club, New Mills Local History Society, Federal Mogul Ltd, Chapel-en-le-Frith Parish Council and Cavendish Golf Club.

Last, but not least, I am indebted to my wife Jo-Ann and my daughter Charlotte for tolerating the many hours I spent in front of a computer screen during the preparation of this book.

Subscribers list

RB Baldry	Buxton
Sue Barber	Tideswell
Robert R Barratt	Chapel-en-le-Frith
Olive Bowyer	New Mills
Mr C Brown	NewMills
Prof & Mrs RM Bryant	New Mills
Malcolm Cawthorn	Chapel-en-le-Frith
Chapel-en-le-Frith High School	Chapel-en-le-Frith
Russell Crompton	Whaley Bridge
Mr DO & TM Evans	Chapel-en-le-Frith
First Chapel-en-le-Frith Company The Boys Brigade	Chapel-en-le-Frith
Andy & Honor Fraser	Buxton
Trevor George Gilman	Buxton
Jacqueline Goddard	Chapel-en-le-Frith
Peter J Goddard	Chapel-en-le-Frith
Megan Hollinrake	Chapel-en-le-Frith
Maureen Howe	Buxton
Mr J Humphreys	New Mills
Mr Lomas	Chapel-en-le-Frith
Donna D Kadzevska	Chapel-en-le-Frith
V Needham	Chapel-en-le-Frith
New Mills School & Sixth Form Centre	New Mills
D & JG Prime	Chapel-en-le-Frith
Frank Redfern	Chapel-en-le-Frith
Mrs K Shepherd	Buxton
Mr Allan Smith	Buxton
Mr David M Smith	Buxton
Mrs I Wibberley	Derby
Mr L Walton	Chapel-en-le-Frith

Chapter 1 – A century of change

These two photographs, separated by a century, are worlds apart. The two Victorian ladies standing in front of the Crescent are dressed in a style popularised by Queen Victoria and they almost look like pastiches of the band umberella which is in front of them. The heavy covering of their apparel is a reflection of the repressed position of women in Victorian society, whereas the far less modest clothing worn by models at a fashion show held in 1990 reflects the more emancipated state of women in the late twentieth century. The show was staged by Next of Buxton for Children in Need. Models gave their services for free and, at the last minute, young model Mark Holland was joined on the cat-walk by his sister Louise.

Going, going, gone

The Industrial Revolution came early to some of the valleys of the High Peak, but almost all the buildings associated with early industrialisation have either disappeared or been converted to new uses. Jason Chadwick's fine sequence of photographs shows the demolition of Slacks chimney at Hayfield in 1990. Fred Dibnah did the ground work for the demolition, but 6 year old Ben Lonsdale pressed the button which started the action. A sweepstake took place on the time taken for the chimney to fall, in order to raise money to support a world-wide appeal for bone marrow for Ben who had a rare blood disorder.

Minus its chimney, Clough Mill at Little Hayfield (previous page) has now been converted to accommodate up-market housing

Little Hayfield's Park Hall outdoor pool (below), with its classical statues and idyllic location, was once a highly popular venue on a sunny summer day. This splendid facility no longer exists.

Lost Landmarks

Herbert Frood began manufacturing brake linings at Gorton in 1897, but moved production to Chapel-en-le-Frith in 1902. He named his firm "Ferodo", an anagram which combines his surname with the initial of his wife Elizabeth's Christian name. The Ferodo factory (pictured below), which was a major source of employment for local people throughout the century, is still producing brake blocks, but is now owned by the Federal Mogul company. Twin 100ft chimneys, one built in 1925 and the other 28 years later, have also disappeared, the last one being demolished, brick by brick, in 1997, when a state-of-the-art heating system was introduced.

By the end of the nineteenth century Buxton had all the trappings of a major inland spa. Optimism about the tourist potential of the town was reflected in the building, between 1901 and 1903, of the massive and luxurious Empire Hotel, at a cost of £130,000. However, the Empire was not a commercial success and traded as a hotel for only 11 seasons. The building was subsequently put to a number of temporary uses: as a hospital and as a demobilisation unit for Canadian troops in the First World War; as a facility for the Sherwood Foresters and the Royal Engineers and as a refuge for families made homeless by the bombing of Sheffield in the Second World War. Talk of the High Peak College being housed in the hotel came to nothing and the Empire was finally demolished in 1964. The fate of the building is

almost a metaphor for Buxton's failure to establish itself as a major rival to Bath. The fabric of the hotel suffered from severe erosion because it was rather pretentiously constructed in Bath stone, a material which was incapable of withstanding Buxton's harsh weather conditions. The pretensions of a Pennine town at an altitude of 1,000ft to be a health spa have always seemed a little preposterous too!

Hair and hats

These two photographs, separated by a quarter of a century, are an essay in changing hairstyles. The 1953 picture of the Buxworth team which won the Reporter Cup dates from the era of "short back and sides", but the 1977 picture of the Buxton College team dates from a time when men wore their hair as long as women. Now, a quarter century later, it is fashionable for footballers to shave their heads completely!

It is said that universal car ownership killed mass hat manufacture. People protected from the elements by a car roof do not regard the hat as a necessity and anyone wearing a hat finds it rather difficult to climb in and out of a car, particularly if it is a Mini. However, as our photographs from 1990 illustrate, the hat lives on for specialist wear and as a fashion accessory. In the course of their research into Scottish industry, pupils from Buxton College each donned a traditional chef's hat to prepare a salmon sent by Alting Seafood of Lerwick, and the ladies of Whaley Bridge topped their outfits with splendid headgear for their annual trip to Ascot. Chefs (left to right): Andrew Flanagan; Matthew Humphrey; Daniel Noble; Nigel Lingley (Palace Hotel chef); James Barber. Ascot ladies (left to right): Florence Bond (landlady of Jodrell Arms); Ann Fletcher; Stephanie Bond; Caroline Hall; Sue Longden; Sandra Woodward; Sandra Pearson.

Entrance to the church

April 1994 saw the completion of new facilities at Town End Methodist Church in Chapel-en-le-Frith. These included a coffee bar, a meeting room and a new entrance way. The new addition is thoroughly modern in design, but styled to be in sympathy with the architecture of the Victorian church. High Peak Mayor John Francis, Rev. Malcolm Willey, who served here from 1984 to 1990, and his wife were special guests at the opening ceremony. Rev. Colin Smith, the minister in 1994, is at the top right of the picture.

These "before and after" photographs of Buxton's Church Street tell a sad story of decline. The upper picture, taken in 1933, shows a charming and picturesque street of old cottages. The lower photograph, taken 32 years later, shows the same street with Victoria Cottages due for demolition.

Pavilion Pleasures

The two photographs shown here illustrate a revolution in musical tastes. Visitors to the Pavilion Gardens in Victorian times were entertained by the Gardens Orchestra which played twice daily throughout the year. In summer months, there were also organ and pianoforte recitals. By 1965, the "Merseybeat" had swept the country and Freddie, of Freddie and the Dreamers, was singing to an appreciative Pavilion Gardens audience, with female admirers packing the front row.

The Pavilion Gardens is home to many contrasting activities. The earnest expressions on the faces of people in the queue for the 1965 Antiques Fair reflect the serious mission of treasure seekers. The expression on the face of the lady who has just caught sight of Giant Haystacks on his way to the ring sums up the impact made by the flamboyant wrestler on audiences in the seventies.

From horses to horseless carriages

The change from horse-power to internal combustion engine is well illustrated in this trio of photographs. The busy scene with carriages loading up outside the Crescent dates from the turn of the century; the photograph of the Quadrant was taken in 1925, a time of limited car ownership; the photograph of Castleton was taken three quarters of a century later when car ownership was virtually universal.

There is no sign of motor vehicles in this picture of Chapel-en-le-Frith's Market Street taken in the fifties. Two horse riders are happy to occupy the middle of the carriageway and the children taking a ride on the milk cart have no worries about their safety. 30 years later, vehicles were proving a considerable hazard in many Peak settlements and by-passes were being built to take traffic away from narrow and steep village streets. Ironically, Hayfield's by-pass, pictured here, has itself been the scene of a number of serious accidents.

Bikes and Trains

The twentieth century saw the rise and fall of the railways as a means of mass communication. Our view of the steam train passing through Chinley Station is a magnificent sight from the great age of the railways. Nearby Buxworth station is now used as an outward bound centre, but it was operational as a railway station in 1930 when our photograph was taken. This picture has further historical significance for this was the year when the village of Bugsworth was re-christened Buxworth after a campaign by villagers to shed their centuries-old "ugly" name. The change of name on the station signs left each of them with a blank, redundant letter space!

Two-wheel transport also suffered fluctuating fortunes during the twentieth century, including a period of popularity for motor cycle and side-car combinations and a later period when motor scooters were all the fashion, but motorbikes have been used for sport throughout the century. The illustration shows John Shirt proudly showing off his bike, his girlfriend Ruth Crowther, and his third successive Manx Sword of State, awarded for victory in the two-day trial championship.

The communication revolution

As the twentieth century progressed, the main access road from the Manchester conurbation to the Peak District brought increasing volumes of traffic to Whaley Bridge and Chapel-en-le-Frith. The construction in 1987 of a four-mile by-pass not only brought some relief to these settlements, but also gave tourists entering the Peak District a magnificent first view the hills. Local people were given preview rides before the road was opened to general traffic.

Another communication revolution took place in the twentieth century. In the early decades most long distance verbal communication was by letter or postcard, but the art of letter writing suffered a decline when telephone ownership became almost universal. Written communication then experienced a revival with the advent of the internet and e-mail. Our lower picture shows Chapel High School pupils Corrie Jones and Beth Holder sampling a range of communication equipment when Barry Walker brought a "technology bus" to the school in 1995. Our upper picture shows Buxton's main post office in the Quadrant, at a time when customers had to join different queues for different services. The facility is now housed in supermarket in Spring Gardens. Will post offices still be part of Britain's high street landscape at the end of the twenty first century?

Do you remember when ....?

At the time when mass television ownership was becoming a reality it was fashionable to forecast the death of the book; obituaries were written again when computers came on the scene. In fact, the book lives on and has even gained new vitality. Libraries are a particularly valuable resource, making it possible, as Alan Sillitoe has said, for "anyone in England wanting to become knowledgeable or cultured, no matter what their income or status, to do so freely and at little cost". Do you remember when the Buxton branch of Boots contained a library and do you remember when the town's public library was housed under the beautiful Adam-style ceiling in the Crescent?

The cinema, which was hugely popular in the middle years of the century, went into decline with the advent of television. Our photograph of Buxton's Spa Cinema, taken in 1985 when the theatre was showing, rather symbollically, *Against All Odds*, shows a picture house on its last legs, with Bingo being used as a replacement source of revenue. The incongruous white building in Chapel-en-le-Frith's Market Street (lower photograph) is the former Empress Cinema, which once had three different programmes showing each week. It too turned to Bingo before being demolished.

Chinley changes

The lower photograph shows the Squirrels Inn before it was demolished to make way for the Princes Hotel, depicted in the upper photograph. The name of the hotel eventually reverted to the Squirrels, and the recreation area in front of the building was christened Squirrel Green as the result of a naming competition involving local school children.

The three Chinley locations shown here have all undergone change. Even local residents may have difficulty recognising the terrace of houses on Green Lane (top photograph). The fenestration pattern on the first floor remains unchanged but the attractive ground floor bay windows have been replaced by a continuous line of shop frontages. The perimeter wall has also disappeared but its foundations are still visible. The entrance to Lower Lane (centre) has undergone much less change: the arcading on the right was restored in the last decade but the Cooperative Society building on the left is now occupied by a carpet shop and a homecare agency. The Hayfield Turnpike, which passed by the door of the Lamb Inn (lower photograph), has now been re-aligned, leaving the public house in a cosy hollow below the carriageway.

Developments that have changed our lives

The upper photograph shows electricity cables being laid in Buxton in 1900. The new supply was quickly installed in the Pavilion Gardens and the Concert Hall. The development of gadgets powered by electricity grew exponentially in the twentieth century, culminating in the computer. It was computer technology that made possible the introduction of a smoothly operating National Lottery in 1994. The Lottery has increased our optimism that we might "get rich quick" but only marginally increased our chances of doing so. However, Lottery money has transformed our country by subsidising many ambitious projects. Our picture shows Charles Hendry M.P. buying one of the first Lottery tickets at A & J Stewarts on Lightwood Road. 400 were sold in the shop on the first day.

Every school now has its computers and virtually all members of the younger generation are computer literate. These computers were in use at Whaley bridge primary school in 1983. Computers have caused an information and communication revolution, but universal car ownership has brought about a shopping revolution which has seen the disappearance of many corner shops and small retail outlets. Most people now supply their weekly needs by one-stop shopping in a superstore. Our photograph shows the construction of the Safeway superstore on the perimeter of Buxton in 1992.

There no more

In 1840, Samuel Grimshawe, a wealthy industrialist, built himself a grand mansion in the Goyt Valley. The Grimshawes lived in great style, employing a staff of 20 to run the house and grounds, a resident Catholic priest and a Spanish aristocrat, Dolores de Bergrin, to teach the estate children. Their home was crammed with books and the grounds were planted with 40,000 azaleas and rhododendrons brought back from travels in their ocean-going

yacht, the *Marquita*. The hall was demolished in 1930 when Fernilee reservoir was constructed and its gaunt ruins now stand as a romantic reminder of a former way of life. Errwood reservoir was added in 1968, to complete a pair of reservoirs that normally supplies 8 million gallons per day to North West Water. Supply was reduced by half when this picture was taken during the great drought of 1995, the driest summer since records began.

In the Industrial Revolution, the great Torrs gorge at New Mills was chosen as the ideal location for cotton mills. Torr Mill (seen above), adjacent to the Union Road viaduct, was one of a number of huge factories constructed in the valley. The viaduct and the lower level bridge remain, but the mill has disappeared and the site is now used by walkers rather than workers (see lower picture)!

Bridge that gap

Torr Vale Mill has survived as the longest-working cotton mill in the country. The factory occupies a bend in the river Goyt and confronts a massive gritstone railway retaining wall on the other bank. This section of the Goyt was inaccessible to walkers until the construction of

a 500ft Millennium Walkway, partly supported on stilts and partly cantilevered from the retaining wall. The bridge forms the last link in a path which runs from the French Riviera to Stranraer (Channel crossing excepted). Pupils in Pauline Whitelegg's class at St Mary's R.C. School enjoyed a picnic of jam and cheese spread butties on the bridge, to celebrate the 18th birthday of one of their student helpers (bottom picture).

Chapter 2 – The happiest days of your life

This delightful photograph, taken by Jason Chadwick, shows a happy beginning to the school day. A pupil of Whaley Bridge Primary School embraces school patrol warden Joan Swindells on her last day at work. Mrs Swindells, who retired at the age of 70, spent 32 years as a crossing patrol warden and missed only two days due to sickness in 32 years. She was given a long service medal, as well as expressions of thanks from parents, pupils and staff.

Changing times

The looks of horror on the faces of pupils at Whaley Bridge Primary School as their headmaster Rick Heys swishes the cane (during a Victorian Day) tell the story of schooldays in the bad old days. There was also some apprehension on the faces of children at Fairfield Infants' School when a Dalek came to visit in 1966, and I well remember my own children watching Daleks on television whilst half-hidden for safety behind the sofa.

The pupils in an old class photograph from Hardwick Square Junior School look decidedly glum-faced, but the children taking part in a High Peak Community Arts event organised in 1991 by Alison Bowry of New Mills look very much happier.

All our yesterdays

Cavendish School for Girls, which opened in 1906, finally closed its doors in 1990, when the girls' and boys' secondary schools in Buxton merged to form Buxton Community School and moved to new buildings on a single site. The former pupils shown here returned to have one last look at their old school.

Let us hasten to point out that the ladies in our photograph on the left are not old enough to remember the scenes in these photographs taken at Cavendish School in 1920, but they will have vivid memories of the locations shown here.

Aspects of the curriculum

Since the last war, Technology has been one of the fastest-changing subjects on the school curriculum, with "design and make" acting as a motto for the new approach. Debra Thomson, Amy Hulme, James Beresford and Brett Greaves of Taxal and Fernilee School won their heat of the 1990 Granada Power Game after designing and making an electronically powered buggy that could negotiate an assault course. A more traditional form of creativity is represented in our lower picture: three young artists from New Mills School, Lesley Downs, Jane Seddon and Samantha Copestake, won prizes in a Milk in Action painting competition in the same year.

A considerable proportion of educational experiences now takes place outside the classroom. The upper picture shows a group of Buxton College students setting off for France in 1961. Jackets, ties, carefully buttoned collars and general smartness of appearance were obviously still in vogue at the time! The happy group of New Mills students in the lower picture consists of award holders from the Duke of Edinburgh Award scheme, a character—building programme that has proved very popular with secondary school and college students. Pictured here are: Suzy Bingham, Lucy Jackson, Jayne Cole, Claire Barber, Graham Thackrah, Cara Jones, Suzy Farrell, Stephanie Livermore, Tim Longson, Matthew Pattison, Kate Waterhouse, Claire Pickles and Joanna Kendall.

More aspects of the curriculum

Children are less inhibited these days. Involvement in Drama lessons at school may well have contributed to their confidence. 13 year old Ben Ward had problems keeping hold of all the awards he had just picked up at the Hazel Grove festival of Peak Drama in 1994. Ben won all five classes for which he entered.

Under the rules of the National Curriculum, all schools must now provide dedicated daily sessions for the teaching of literacy. Chapel pupils had the subject brought to life when a real-life author, Berlie Doherty, gave them an insight into professional writing. There has been much debate about the time left for school sport in the face of statutory demands on the curriculum, but there is plenty of evidence of healthy sporting activity in this picture of the Chapel High School's Y10 netball team which won the Derbyshire Schools' Championship in 1994. Pictured from left to right are: Vicki Hallam; Michelle Benstead; Louise Taylor; Gemma Hallam; Claire Thomas and Michelle Lowe. Captain Katie Hamps has taken up the reclining position.

Annual events

Although some schools have abandoned their annual Speech Day and Prizegiving ceremony, many retain the ritual as a proper means of publicly rewarding effort. The secret of making the event bearable for the audience is to invite an entertaining speaker. On the evidence of the attentive audience for Cavendish Grammar School's 1969 Speech Day, Virginia Wade was one such speaker.

Sports Day is another annual event which is dreaded by many pupils but gives the athletically gifted a chance of glory. The girls of Cavendish Grammar School attacked the hurdles with great gusto during their 1970 Sports Day and both the prizewinner, whose name I do not have, and the prize presenter, High Peak Mayor Miss E. I. Heathcote, showed tremendous enthusiasm in this delightful photograph taken at Buxton College's 1964 Sports Day.

Running, jumping and standing still

The girls in this 1963 Music and Movement class at Cavendish Grammar School seem to be intent, not on movement, but on keeping one student in a steady elevated position. The boys in the 1967 Buxton Schools' cross-country race obviously have differing views on the best way to tackle a stone wall obstacle. Some jump the wall; others head for the stile.

The young gymnasts of Whaley Bridge School have contorted themselves into a nice symmetrical formation in preparation for the 1990 Inter schools Gymnastics Competition. The pupils are Nicola Tim, Paula Clitheroe, Rebecca Sherwood, Emma Jones, Gina Holden, Emma Yates, Melanie Taylor, Tristan Lee and William Gardener. Pupils taking part in the Junior Fun Race in the 1995 New Mills Summer Festival look full of running as they leave the grounds of the secondary school.

Classes

These two jolly photographs would seem to prove that schooldays are indeed the happiest days of your life. The upper photograph was taken in the late fifties at Chapel-en-le-Frith Infants' School; the lower photograph was taken in the early sixties at St Anne's R.C. School.

These two pictures illustrate pupils hard at work, at least for the benefit of the cameraman. The upper photograph was taken at Fairfield Junior School in 1969 and the lower photograph was taken at St Anne's Primary school in 1965.

Doing their bit

The pupils of St Anne's R.C. Primary School employed various catchphrases, as well as a photograph of Morecambe and Wise, in a 1974 attempt to persuade us to "Keep Britain Tidy".

In 1970, the children of Hardwick Square Junior School knitted lots of squares and combined them into patchwork blankets which they then sent to the victims of an earthquake in Turkey. The sixth formers of New Mills School have long-standing arrangements for entertaining and visiting local pensioners.

Presentation time

Once upon a time, the villages of Chinley and Buxworth had a number of clocks fitted to lamp-posts, but these were removed in 1985. In 1993, Cllr Colston fitted one of the old clocks to the wall of Buxworth School.

Headmaster Mike James of New Mills School is seen accepting a splendid painting of his school from one of his students, artist Michael Bingham. The pupils of Fairfield Junior School gave a presentation to Mr Hooley in 1970 in recognition of his 30 years' teaching at the school. At the ceremony they were asked to hold their hands up and count their digits three times, in order to gain some idea of the length of Mr Hooley's service.

The end of school

Pupils with school phobia may well have expressed a wish on at least one occasion that their school would burn down, although one suspects that most pupils hold their school in considerable affection. The fire shown top left took place at Hardwick School in 1930. Pupils and staff of Chapel Infants' School had no sooner celebrated the 150th anniversary of their Victorian school (top right) than they moved to brand-new premises at the other side of town. Pupils at the Silverlands site in Buxton held a massive balloon launch (lower picture) to celebrate the closure of their school in 1990, when four Buxton schools amalgamated to form the new Community School.

Chapter 3 – White Peak, Dark Peak

There are two Peak Districts: the Dark Peak, with its expanses of high moorland and its gritstone edges, and the White Peak, a gently undulating pastel-green plateau, covered by a network of limestone walls and scored by deep gorges with fast-flowing streams. The High Peak sits at the junction between the two regions. The upper photograph, taken by F.B.Hills, an evacuee who came to live in Chapel-en-le-Frith, shows the old Turnpike as it leaves New Smithy for its journey over the Dark Peak to Glossop. The lower photograph of the White Peak shows the unique field strips that run at right angles from Chelmorton's main street. Thirteen parallel stone walls subdivide a former medieval open field.

Light and dark

The road from Buxton to Chapel-en-le-Frith runs along the boundary between gritstone and limestone before it takes a right angle turn through the wooded valley of Barmoor Clough (spelt "Barmore" on the caption to this old photograph). The track which runs by the roadside is the route of the Peak Forest Tramway, which closed in 1926. Pedestrians would not dare to stand on the carriageway today, because the road forms part of the A6, a busy cross-Pennine route. When the A6 leaves Buxton for Bakewell it twists and turns with the river Wye along the deep limestone gorge of Ashwood Dale (lower photograph). The natural contours in this old picture are little altered, but it would be very difficult nowadays to take a photograph featuring an empty carriageway!

Stones from the limestone quarries near Buxton were once carried by the Peak Forest Tramway to the canal basin at Bugsworth and thence by barge along the Peak Forest Canal. Our photograph shows the canal at Whaley Bridge where there is a surviving grade II* listed warehouse, but it is pleasure boats, including the *Judith Mary*, which is available for cream tea cruises, champagne breakfasts and the like, which now use the canal. Despite its name, the Peak District contains very few peaks, but South Head, to the north of Chapel-en-le-Frith, is a notable exception. This shapely hill, which rises from the centre of the ridge in our lower picture, taken in the fifties, is the first prominent landmark encountered by motorists entering the Peak District from the Manchester conurbation.

Royal Forest of the Peak

A vast area of the Peak, bordered by the rivers Goyt, Etherow, Derwent and Wye, was once a Royal Forest used as hunting reserve by the Norman kings. In 1225, the Earl of Derby gave a group of foresters permission to build a chapel in the forest (a "chapel-en-le-frith"), and the town that grew up around the new church quickly became a market and administrative centre for the forest. The Olde Stocks Cafe, which stands near the Cromwellian stocks on Chapel-en-le-Frith's Market Place, contains a mural by Claire Taylor which depicts a cattle market day in 1897. The nearby churchyard contains a tombstone known as the Woodcutter's Grave, a simple slab with a depiction of an axe. Some claim that the grave dates from the days of the Royal Forest.

A remarkable feature of the parish of Chapel-en-le-Frith is its very high concentration of country houses. The grand gritstone halls and their estates could date from the days of the Royal Forest when "burgages" were granted in exchange for services to the Crown. When the Sheffield Turnpike was constructed right through the garden of old Slack Hall (in our upper photograph), a new hall was built in the valley below. Nearby Ford Hall is the ancestral home of the Bagshawes, most famous of whom is William Bagshawe, the "Apostle of the Peak", who held secret non-conformist services here after being expelled from his Ministry at Glossop in 1662.

Beauty spots and carbuncles

The Victorians, being great romantics, loved Peak District scenery. The Cat and Fiddle inn, 1690ft up on the moors and the second highest inn in England, was a popular destination for excursions from Buxton. For two shillings a head, tourists could take a two hour coach ride to the inn and back. Limestone gorges were also popular with the Victorians. A deep cleft in Ashwood Dale (lower photograph) was given the romantic name "Lovers' Leap".

The hills of the Peak District rarely exceed 2,000ft in height but there is often an illusion of mountain scenery, despite the modest real dimensions. The eye is deceived by mountain-shaped hills like Mam Tor and pass-shaped gorges like the Winnats only if man-made intrusions in the landscape are deferentially small. Large constructions act as yardsticks and reduce apparent height to its real scale. The 400ft chimney of Earl cement works (upper photograph) stands in the Hope Valley like Gulliver in Lilliput. As our aerial view of Dove Holes (lower photograph) demonstrates, large-scale quarry working has left vast open sores in the landscape, but one fascinating feature in this area has managed to survive unscathed: the circular earthwork known as the Bull Ring (middle right of photograph), which is the site of a former Neolithic stone circle.

Village life

The twentieth century saw radical changes in living and working habits, including a marked drift from countryside to town. Some remote villages became depopulated, only to be re-born as weekend and holiday retreats for city dwellers or dormitories for city-workers. Despite the changes, traditional village life has survived wonderfully well in the Peak District, as demonstrated by our photographs of a crowded fun fair at Hayfield and maypole dancing at a P.T.A. Summer Show at Chinley School.

Whitehough is a picturesque hamlet of attractive inns and old houses, gathered around its Old Hall and situated in the Blackbrook Valley below Chinley Churn. A miniature monument at the centre of the village carries the legend "Pax Vobiscum". In fact, the peace of the valley, so evident in our lower photograph, has been disturbed by the construction of a four-mile by-pass. The gentleman on the cycle in the picture is Mr Prescott, the village schoolmaster who, together with the local vicar, Rev. Towers, conducted a successful campaign in 1930 to change the name of Bugsworth, a village just down the road from Whitehough, to Buxworth.

The Hope Valley

From "Surprise View", above Hathersage, there is a superb view of the beautiful Hope Valley. The road from Sheffield runs through the villages of Hathersage, Hope and Castleton to the head of the valley at Mam Tor. Sheffield could so easily have spread its tentacles along this dale but for the establishment of the Peak National Park in 1951. The upper photograph, from years gone by, is an idyllic view of Hope; the more recent picture shows the village of Castleton. The cafe, the smart shops and the double yellow lines indicate the popularity of the village in an age of mass tourism.

Since the collapse of the Mam Tor road, which has always suffered from chronic subsidence, motorists have had to leave the Hope Valley via Winnats Pass which climbs a narrow 1 in 4 road between towering peaks. When the National Trust acquired the gorge, the line of telegraph poles, which had the effect of reducing the apparent height of the flanking limestone pinnacles, was removed. At one point, the gorge came under renewed threat with a proposal to widen the carriageway but, thankfully, the plan was dropped and the narrow, winding road through the gorge survives to emphasize the vertical scale. From the summit of Winnats Pass, one road leads to the unspoilt Edale Valley (lower picture) with its backcloth of the Kinder Scout plateau. Albert Finney contemplated this magnificent panorama when he drove into Edale in the film *Charlie Bubbles* and thousand of walkers use the village of Edale as the starting point for a three-week trek to Scotland on the 270 mile Pennine Way, opened in 1965.

England's highest town

This superb aerial view of Buxton, taken in 1961, shows the Market Place with a collection of half-cab buses, the Town Hall with open arcading (now gone), and the spa town in the valley beyond. The whole picture is a composition of complementary curves: the arcs of Eagle Parade, the Crescent and the Quadrant, and the circle of the dome of the Devonshire Royal Hospital. The Palace Hotel, built when the railway finally reached Buxton in the 1860s, sits above and beyond the Crescent.

There is some dispute as to whether Alston, in Cumbria, or Buxton, in the Peak District, is the highest market town in England. Whatever the truth, Buxton's stall market certainly occupies a very lofty site which is exposed to extreme weather conditions. However, the hardy traders made such a success of their Saturday market that a Tuesday market, first introduced as an experiment, has now become a permanent fixture. The road from Buxton to Ashbourne leaves the town for the even higher land of the White Peak, a limestone plateau which is tamed and settled with enclosures, but also exposed to harsh weather. The night shot of the curving road at its exit from the town makes a splendid composition.

Towns on the edge of the Peak

New Mills developed in the Industrial Revolution as a town of great cotton mills. The mills have largely gone now, but the town is very proud of its past. The Heritage Centre, at the head of Union Road, contains a magnificent model of New Mills and the Torrs as it would have appeared in 1884, as well as a mock mine and an urban study centre. The town itself retains a solid, grey appearance in keeping with its origins and its gritstone surroundings.

Glossop and Whaley Bridge both stand at the limit of the Manchester conurbation. Some of their Victorian terraces bear similarities to those in the old Lancashire mill towns, but they are built of stone rather than brick. There is also a backcloth of Dark Peak hills, indicating that the metamorphosis of urban sprawl into the wide open spaces of the Pennines has begun. Our pictures show Glossop and the Nab from times gone by (above) and the main street of Whaley Bridge, by-passed by the A6 since 1987 (below).

Cul-de-sacs

The cul-de-sac village of Bagshaw (shown above), situated in the high hills of the Dark Peak, is now a conservation area. Its gritstone houses and farms, which date from the eighteenth and nineteenth centuries, flank a sinuous road which falls steeply with the contours. The White Peak hamlet of King Sterndale is set around a village green which marks the termination of a narrow lane running from the Buxton-Ashbourne road; the green contains a portion of an old "butter cross". King Sterndale Hall (below) was the home of the Pickford family for over 200 years. Miss Dorothy Pickford, seen below at a 1961 open day, was a descendant of the Pickfords of Prestbury who founded the famous haulage business.

Chapter 4 – Flower Power

The Derbyshire custom of well-dressing began 650 years ago in the village of Tissington, perhaps as a thanksgiving for a supply of water during the Black Death, perhaps as an expression of gratitude for a productive well during a period of drought. Well-dressing harnesses local talent, fosters community spirit and draws in the tourists, so it is not surprising that more than 70 towns and villages in the Peak District area now hold an annual dressing of the wells. Jason Chadwick's photograph shows Christine Bould of Buxton demonstrating the art of well-dressing at a "Woman's World" exhibition at the Palace Hotel.

Making and blessing the wells

Well-dressing is traditionally governed by strict rules: only natural materials, such as petals, leaves, bark and stones, may be used to create the pictures. The decorations are produced by pressing the materials onto a thick layer of wet clay which is contained in wooden boards. The clay is prepared by a process of "puddling" - trampling the wet clay to give it the correct consistency. The upper photograph shows Brian Aries, Chairman of Chapel-en-le-Frith Amenity Society, in the act of puddling. The lower photograph shows Margaret Coleman hard at work on the panels for the 1990 Buxton well-dressing. That year, St Ann's Well was based on the theme "England's Green and Pleasant Land", in recognition of the 75th anniversary of the Women's Institute and their theme song *Jerusalem*.

When the boards have been dressed and hoisted into place, they are ready for the blessing ceremony. Our illustration shows the blessing of the Higher Buxton well in 1984. As can be seen, it is customary for a fair to be held in the same week as the well-dressing, so producing a cacophony of sound and colour on the Market Place. The wells are usually left on display for at least a week, and they draw large crowds of admirers. Princess Elizabeth and Prince Phillip made an inspection of St Ann's Well in 1949.

Flower pictures

Well-dressings often have a religious content, as shown in the tableau at St Ann's Well in 1931 (top left), but there is a wide variety of other themes. The 1999 Town Well at Chapel-en-le-Frith (top right) celebrated the re-opening of the Bugsworth Basin to canal traffic after a splendid restoration project, and the Wormhill well of 1994 marked V.E. Day anniversary celebrations by depicting Bayeux Cathedral, the first cathedral to be liberated by the Allies after the Normandy landings.

Chapter 5 – On parade

The people of the High Peak love putting on a show. Many towns in the area stage carnivals in addition to well-dressing weeks, although the two events often coincide. A local girl is chosen as Carnival Queen, her proud parents decorate their home with paper flowers in celebration, many other buildings are also covered in bright paper decorations, bunting is strung across the road and a grand procession takes place through the town. The Carnival Queen undertakes various public duties during her one-year reign and she also attends all the other carnivals in the area. Jason Chadwick's stunning photograph, taken at the 1990 Buxton Carnival, shows Anna Brindley, a particularly radiant Carnival Queen.

Crowning glory

The crowning moment of Carnival Day is the placing of the crown on the head of the new queen. The upper picture shows Tanya Furness, the 1994 Dove Holes Queen, being crowned by her predecessor Emma Burns. The lower photograph shows Donna Heather, Chapel-en-le-Frith Queen for 1937, crowning the 1938 Queen, Iris Harrison.

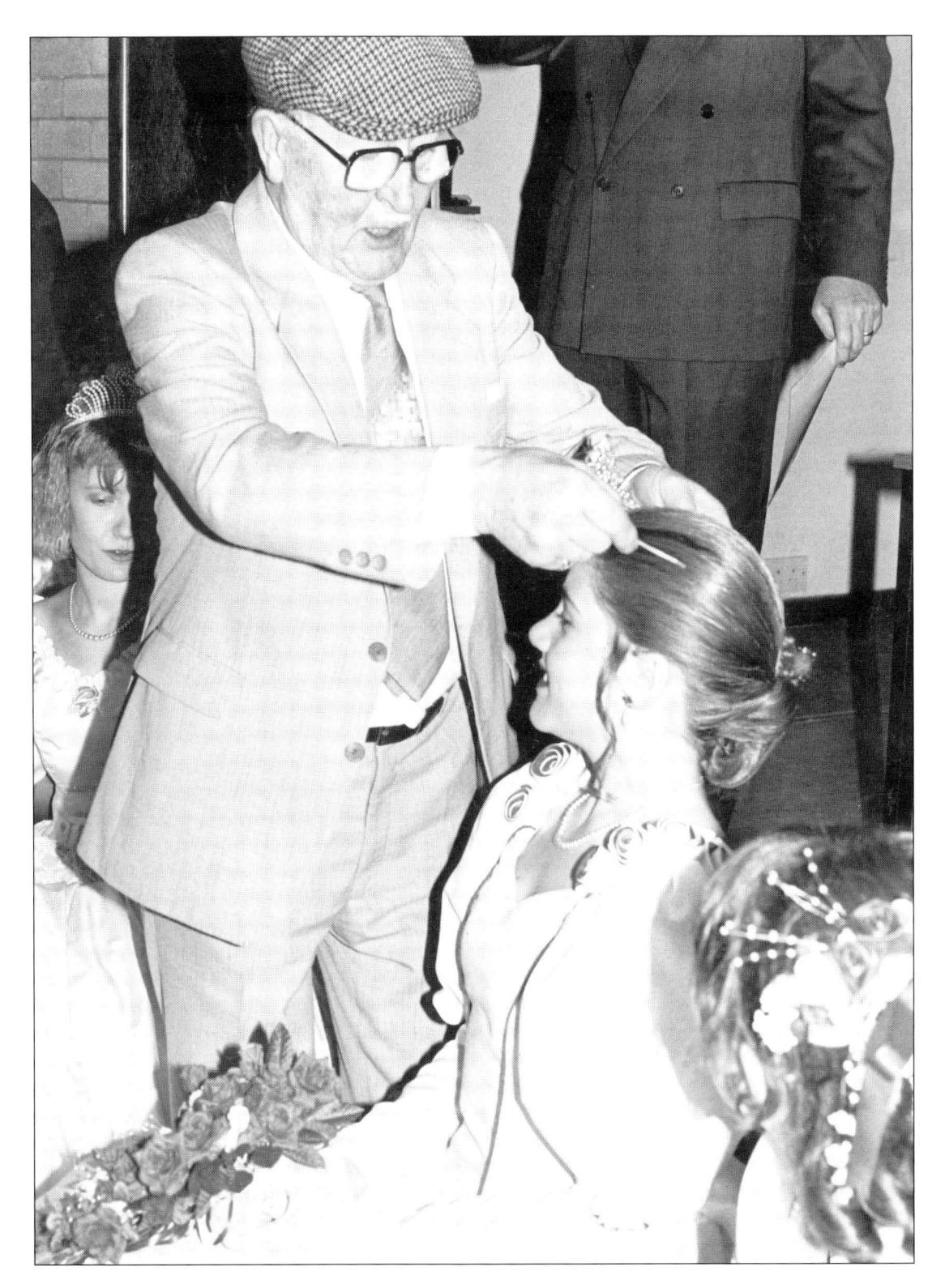

The crowning of the new queen is not always carried out by the retiring queen: a personality is sometimes brought in to perform the task. Percy Sugden, himself crowned with a flat cap, placed the crown on the head of the 1993 Dove Holes queen Emma Burns.

The procession

The procession of the queen and her attendants is always a splendid sight. The parade of the Kettleshulme queen Helen Davis (aged 14), her crown bearer Ian Sanderson, her lady-in-waiting Victoria Coward and her attendants Katherine Adams, Ivy Taylor, Victoria Greenwood and Jessica Coatsworth, makes an archetypal village scene. The procession of the 1955 Chinley and Buxworth queen and her retinue is a particularly fine illustration of "putting on a brave face". High Peak carnival processions often have to contend with adverse weather conditions but their spirit is rarely dampened.

In the village of Hayfield it is customary for the retiring queen to enter the arena through a Guard of Honour. Retiring queen Sarah Robinson made her way through a line of Beefeaters in 1995.

Floating by

A great deal of effort goes into the preparation of carnival floats. This magnificent streamlined float featured in a Chapel-en-le-Frith carnival in the fifties and the Tipsy Pheasant float took part in the 1990 Hayfield carnival.

Children who join a carnival float have a wonderful opportunity to let their hair down and also cajole the spectators to throw money at them. The young warriors in our upper photograph and the football team in our lower photograph were both taking part in the 1995 Chapel-en-le-Frith carnival.

Promenaders

Troupes of majorettes are a common feature of carnival processions, and for many years no High Peak carnival has been complete without the presence of Bill Weston's Billerettes, splendidly macho female impersonators who have become increasingly sophisticated in the performance of their routines. In fact, grown men in silly costumes always raise the biggest smiles at carnivals. Our lower picture, from the 1991 Whaley Bridge carnival, features a novel little cart with a cute passenger.

No carnival procession would be complete without at least one band. The people of the High Peak have a passion, not only for brass bands, but also for jazz. Our upper photograph shows the New Orleans-style Heritage Jazz Band blowing their way through Buxton and our lower photograph shows the Thornsett Brass Band playing their way with equal gusto through the streets of Hayfield.

All the fun of Carnival Day

Dressing up for Carnival Day is great fun for people of all ages. Rachel Saxby looks a little bewildered, but suitably splendid, in her flower-decked surroundings in the 1993 Chapel-en-le-Frith Carnival, and two young outlaws, Frankie Golden and Adrian Graham, made a delightful addition to the Fairfield Carnival of 1961. They later blew their horns to announce the arrival of the queen elect.

Some very strange creatures appear on the streets on Carnival Day, not least this colourful, and rather long-legged, caterpillar which slithered its way through Buxton in 1975. All is not as it seems in our lower photograph of the 1991 Dove Holes procession: the carnival was being replayed for the benefit of a Channel 4 television crew. The re-enactment was actually bigger than the original event!

Beauty Parade

The people of the High Peak love a pageant, especially when it involves pretty girls. The young ladies (and one young man) of Tideswell were not frightened to show a leg in their 1976 parade and the finalists in the 1979 Miss High Peak College contest cared little for political correctness as they lined up to be judged.

Three more High Peak College girls feature in our photograph of the three finalists in the 1976 contest. Victoria Ann Rains, the very pretty young lady in our upper photograph, was taking part in an Easter Bonnet Parade at the Pavilion Gardens in 1963.

Joining in the fun

The joy of Carnival Day is well illustrated by the two photographs on this page. Emma Bennett, Charlotte Smith and Hannah Lord make the most of the bouncy castle in the Memorial Park on the day of Chapel-en-le-Frith's carnival and the people of Buxton line the streets on a glorious Carnival day in 1990.

Chapter 6 – High Peak at work

The latticework of stone walls which covers the High Peak results from the Enclosure Acts of the eighteenth and nineteenth centuries and the general appearance of the countryside has been fashioned by the working of the land over the last 10,000 years. The upper photograph of sheep farming presents an idyllic picture of rural life, but the reality is more disturbing. In the later years of the twentieth century farmers began to experience considerable difficulties brought about by the B.S.E. crisis, the effects of the strong pound and the reform of the Common Agricultural Policy. Many challenges lie ahead for members of the Young Farmers group, seen at their meeting in Chelmorton. Charles Hendry, who was guest speaker, contrasted the life of an M.P. with that of a farmer. Harry Swindell, local poet and Chelmorton personality, is also seated at the table.

Quarryworkers, dyers and wire-workers

Quarrying has long been an important part of the High Peak economy, but the nature of the industry changed greatly during the twentieth century. The old quarrymen helped to enhance the appearance of the Peak by making its stone available for re-fashioning into the farmsteads and villages which blend so well with the natural landscape. Scars were left by this cosmetic operation but they have healed because the quarries were worked on a small-scale, but the modern trend is for a few enormous quarries and most of the stone extracted from them is now used by the chemical industry and for road-making, rather than for local building. Quarries create work for local people and satisfy national needs, but they have an adverse effect on the landscape and hence the tourist potential of the area; reconciling these demands is a difficult task. The old stone quarries at Buxworth, seen above, were the source of a beautiful pink stone which is a feature of many older local buildings in the locality. The exhibition of quarrying equipment at Hillhead quarry is the largest show of its kind in the world.

The site of John Welsh & Sons (Bleachers, Dyers and Finishers) is now used for P.V.C. manufacture. This change of use reflects a twentieth century chemical revolution brought about by the introduction of synthetic polymers. The upper photograph was taken in the dyehouse in the mid-thirties. The Britannia Wire Works in Chinley had contracts for springs with British Leyland and for the QE2. This photograph was taken before the dramatic decline in the British motor and shipbuilding industries. The driver is Bill Lomas.

Workers and onlookers

Chapel Coat of Arms "One Working T'others Watching"

A popular postcard from the early years of the twentieth century featured a man hard at work in his garden and a group of rather more idle onlookers. The card carried the slogan "Chapel-en-le-Frith Coat-of-Arms: one working; t'others watching". Female workers labouring on repetitive tasks was a feature of the twentieth century until changes were brought about by automation and the drive for equality in the work place. Our photograph shows workers at Cooper's corset factory in Buxton. A housing estate now occupies the site of the factory.

There is a considerable and understandable look of apprehension on the faces of the dignitaries who are about to tour the underground tunnels of the new mushroom farm at Harpur Hill in 1964. High Peak Mayor E.I. Heathcote and her sister, the Lady Mayoress, were being shown around by Graham Griffiths of the Wrington Vale Group, who had put to good use the eleven tunnels constructed by the Air Ministry for bomb storage in 1938.

Marketing the spa

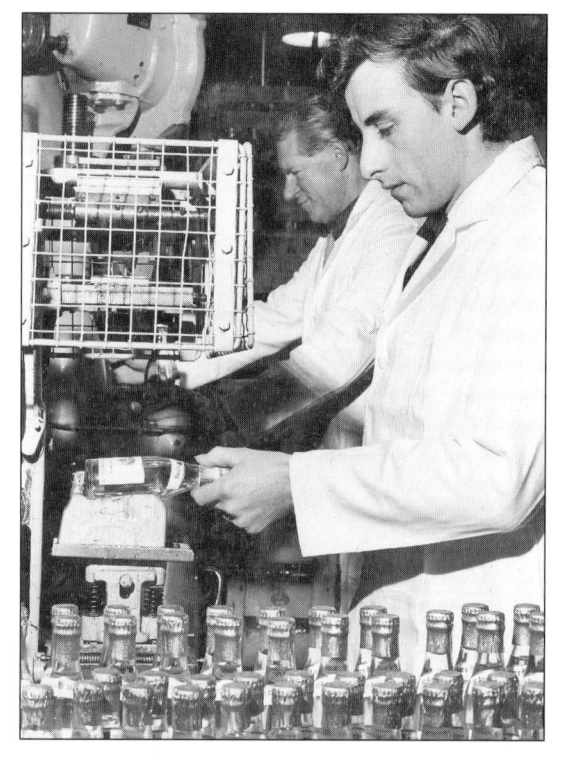

Publicity from the spa era claimed that Buxton's waters have the power to wash away gout, rheumatism, neuralgia, skin disorders and heart conditions. The daily procession of people filling their water containers at St Ann's Well indicates a continuing faith in the beneficial effects of the liquid that emanates from the town's springs. Buxton spa water is now bottled and sold widely. The Chamber of Commerce staged a marketing exercise with a difference in 1978 when they held a Romany Market on the forecourt of the Crescent.

Chapter 7 – High Peak at play

Sport plays a large part in High Peak life. There are many long-established and well-supported sports clubs in the area covering a wide range of outdoor team games, and some of their pitches are in idyllic locations. The High Peak also boasts some of the highest golf courses in England. The Duke of Devonshire is seen here taking careful aim with a putter under the watchful eye of club captain Derek Price (kneeling) and president Walter Chatterton, when he opened the new club house at Chapel-en-le-Frith Golf Club in 1995. The speaker at the club's dinner that evening was comedian Jimmy Tarbuck.

Sailing centres and sports centres

The High Peak does not contain any natural sheets of water, but there are several man-made lakes, including the reservoirs at Combs and Todbrook, which were built to service the Peak Forest Canal. Sailing clubs operate on both lakes. Our photographs show a regatta at Todbrook in the early sixties, sailing at Combs in the fifties and two of the founder members at Combs, "Jumbo" Clarke and Philip Carpenter. The Combs club once had a rule about a fixed proportion of members living within three miles of the Hanging Gate pub, but Philip Carpenter nicely got round this restriction by claiming he lived "just 2.9 nautical miles", from the pub. The Combs club carried on sailing throughout the eight years when water levels in the reservoir were drastically reduced as a precaution after a landslip took place on the retaining wall.

The Fairfield Sports Centre was opened in the late sixties. The upper photograph shows construction nearing completion in 1968. The second picture was taken in the harsh winter of 1979. At first sight, it appears to show squash rackets about to be used for snow clearing, but is actually designed to demonstrate that the centre stayed open for squash and other activities thanks to the hard work of the caretaker, Ron Warren, who cleared a path.

Making a hit

When the Buxton Amateur Boxing Association held their annual dinner at the Pavilion Gardens in 1994 they staged some fights as part of the evening's entertainment. Jason Chadwick's photograph shows Simon Leighton on the defensive against Karl Birds. Swimmer Alan Rapley made a hit in a different way by representing his country at two World Student Games and in the Atlanta Olympics. He also captained the swimming squads at both the student games and the Olympics. He still holds a number of records at Buxton's swimming pool, but much of his training was done with the University of Arkansas Swimming Team in the U.S.A.

Peter Harrison, retiring Director of Housing and Planning, and Graham Sisson, Borough Treasurer, were hoping to make some successful hits with the new golf clubs presented to each of them in 1990, in recognition of their twenty five years service with High Peak Borough Council. The two men joined the council within a few days of each other.

American golfing sensation 'Babe' Zaharias was a big hit at Cavendish Golf Club in 1951 when she came with five other lady American golfers to play an exhibition match. On the first tee she encouraged the other lady players to "loosen your girdles and let it ride". Our picture shows left to right: Babe Zaharias, Betty Jameson, Betty Bush, Peggy Kirk, Betsy Rawls, Patty Berg. Back: Fred Corcoran, unknown, G.Q. Henriques, Mrs F. Gaertner, R.A.C. Johnson, T. Frangopulo

Stamina

The Buxton Half Marathon, run over a gruelling "up-hill-and-down-dale" course, has attracted many runners over the years. Andy Wilton, pictured here, had a persistent habit of winning the event, even after recent injury, as in this particular year.

The photograph of Monyash's 1979 tug-of-war team is a splendid essay in determination and stamina. These qualities were also needed by riders competing in a cycle race around New Mills organised in 1990 by Chafes Solicitors, to celebrate 100 years of business and to raise money for the Goyt Valley Minibus appeal.

Champions

Champions from a variety of sports are shown here. Reading clockwise, they are: Chapel High School pupils selected for the County Athletics Team (Left to right: Mark James; Katie Amps; Vanessa Willerby; Andrew Chaddock; William Gardener; Matthew Ball); multiple medal-winning tug-of-war champion Ian Hulme of Dove Holes (three Golds and a Bronze at the National Championships and a Gold in the 1992 World Championship); synchronised swimmer Kirsty Pearson, who won consecutive gold medals at the Northern Counties Championships; darts champions Barry Goodwin (Herald Cup) and Pat Bishop (Samuel Smith Trophy).

Two cup-winning football teams are shown here: the Kents Bank team of 1968, a set of likely lads who look like a team of eleven Norman Hunters; and the Buxton Football Club who won the Phillips Cup in the famous footballing year of 1966. One young supporter looks as if he is running off with a part of the trophy!

Fun sports

The chariot race organised in 1994 by the 1st Chinley Scout Group to raise money for the renovation of Victory Hall may have been a fun-run, but the look of determination on the faces of the competitors is there for all to see. Badminton with a constantly shifting court was played throughout the 1978 Buxton carnival procession.

A friendly match between British and French teams took place in 1977 when Cote Heath Juniors took on a team of visitors from Oignies, Buxton's twin town. The locals won 15-2! The Oignies exchange celebrated its 25th anniversary in 1993 by holding a mini-Olympics which included shot-putting the balloon. The Buxton Advertiser reported that the result of this event was the same as that at Waterloo in 1815 - a victory for the English!

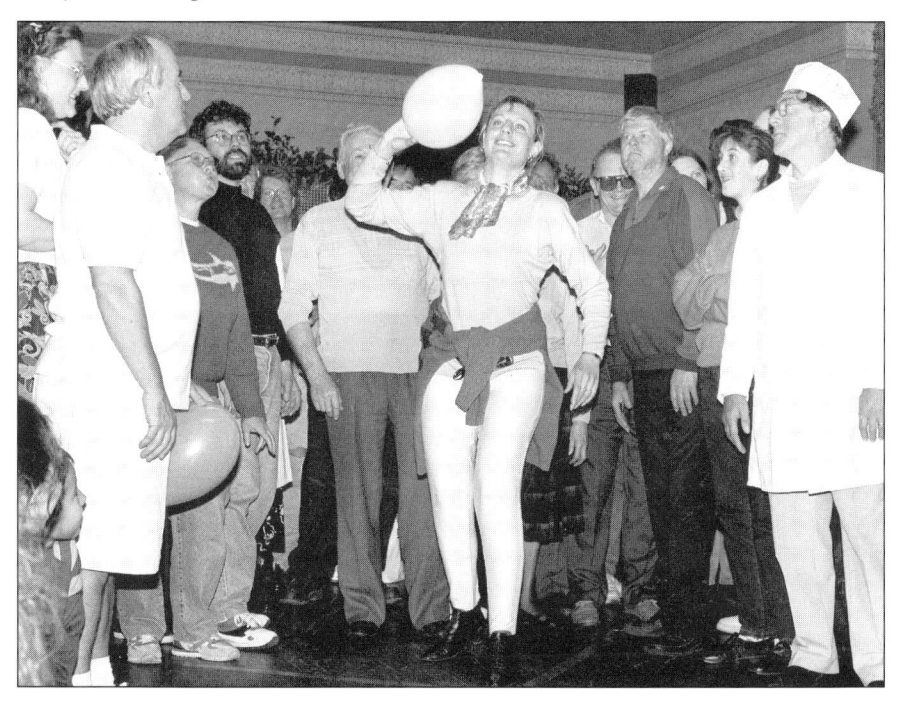

At the wicket

Buxton's cricket ground was formerly a superbly scenic venue for County matches. Our upper photograph shows the wicket being prepared for the Derbyshire v Somerset game in 1968. However, frequent interruptions due to adverse weather over the years culminated in the famous occasion in June 1975 when "snow stopped play" in a game between Lancashire and Derbyshire. The game is also remarkable for other reasons: Clive Lloyd (seen here) scored an unbeaten 167, the highest individual score made at the ground, and Lancashire made 477 for 5, the highest team score made at Buxton. The umpire was none other than Dickie Bird. The ground is no longer used for County matches.

The upper photograph shows a cricket match between Chapel-en-le-Frith and Buxworth taking place in an idyllic High Peak setting. Batsman Alan Johnson is shown surviving an appeal for a catch. The lower photograph shows the successful Chapel-en-le-Frith ladies' team of 1942, captained by star player Connie Pink (with bat in hand). Marion Bagshawe of Ford Hall is standing on the top right of the group.

For town and village

Two Buxton teams are shown here: the junior cricket team of 1970 and the ladies' hockey team of 1984.

Two village teams feature on this page: the Dove Holes football team of 1980 and the Buxworth cricket team from the fifties. Buxworth off-spinner Les Gagen (bottom right) played competitive cricket for thirty years. In 1959 he took 88 wickets for 581 runs (an average of 6.6) in glorious summer conditions that were not supposed to suit his bowling!

Keeping it in the family

Three Winterbottoms played in the same Bugsworth football team: Jack, the centre forward; Fred, the goalkeeper; and Billy, the outside right.

Harry Holford Senior and Harry Holford Junior both played for Hadfield's cricket team at Whitehough. In 1908, Harry Senior was awarded a medal for the best batting averages, presented by Albert Profumo, a relative of Jack Profumo, the Minister for War who became embroiled in the Christine Keeler scandal of the sixties.

Play areas

In our upper photograph the children of Edale are seen celebrating the opening of their new play area in 1990. The grounds were opened by High Peak Mayor Cllr Peter Coakley. Mrs Coakley and Mike Loader, the chair of the Community and Leisure Committee, were also in attendance. Our lower photograph, in contrast, shows young members of the Chinley's Saturday morning sports club protesting at the likely closure of their club resulting from high charges for using Chapel High School's premises.

Chapter 8 – War and peace

Many local men volunteered for service when war broke out in 1914. The Buxton Advertiser reported their exploits in detail throughout the Great War and also recorded their periods at home on leave. As the war progressed, and casualties mounted, the pages of the newspaper made increasingly grim reading. Tragically, the Great War was not the predicted "war to end all wars" and more casualties were suffered by High Peak families in World War II. 45 years of relative peace has not dimmed the respectful memory of High Peak people for those who died. Our picture shows four year old Luke Pountley, who thankfully has no experience of war, trying out a wartime air-raid siren during Peaklands Nursery School VE Day celebrations.

Before and after

Our photographs show recruits from Chapel-en-le-Frith making their way to the station in 1914. The War Memorial in Chapel's Market Place is unusual in listing the names of all the 599 Chapel men who served in the First World War. Crosses mark the names of the 78 men who were killed.

The peace of 1918 was understandably received with great jubilation after a war of terrible carnage. The impressive bearded figure who dominates these pictures of Buxton's peace celebrations in 1919 is Josiah Taylor, the first Town Clerk of Buxton.

Practising

The 200 year old target wall in Chapel-en-le-Frith was built by the Volunteers, who merged with the Sherwood Foresters in 1804. The wall was used for target practice in the Boer war and in both world wars. The structure, which was 20ft high and 50ft wide, was reduced to rubble by a J.C.B. in 1991. Jason Chadwick's picture shows Cllr Malcolm Cawthorn, Chairman of Chapel-en-le-Frith Parish Council, and Graham Harper, who is shown holding a cup presented to Fred Nichols in 1901 in recognition of his shooting expertise.

The Derwent reservoirs were used as a practice area by crews training for the famous Dam Buster raid on Germany. When the only operational Lancaster made a commemorative fly-past on the fiftieth anniversary of the "bouncing bomb" raid some 100,000 spectators turned up to watch. The group of Buxton Army Cadets, pictured in 1970 with an array of weaponry, look as if they mean business, but there is another aspect to Cadet activities: in 1981, Christopher Penistone of Buxton joined other cadets on an 80 mile walk to raise money for a lift walker at Cressy Fields Hostel in Alfreton. The lift helps wheelchair-bound people to walk again.

Reactions to war

On Remembrance Day, services are held throughout the High Peak. All of them are conducted with solemnity in due respect for the people of the High Peak who died in the terrible wars of the twentieth century. Our photographs show a 1978 Remembrance Day march on the slopes in Buxton and also the Whaley Bridge Royal British Legion Drumhead Service in 1965.

At the height of the Cold War, when the nuclear arms race had run out of control, fears were raised that a nuclear holocaust could be triggered either by a nation making a pre-emptive first strike or by a hasty reaction to a few misleading blips on a radar screen. This small meeting of the Buxton branch of the Campaign for Nuclear Disarmament took place in 1980. The considerable police presence hardly seems warranted. By 1995 the Cold War had wound down and the threat of another world war had receded, so this group of Dove Holes revellers in World War II costumes (lower picture) could afford to be jolly.

Celebrating the victory and remembering the dead

The atmosphere of V.E. Day was recreated at a Pavilion Gardens party and dance to celebrate the fiftieth anniversary of the end of war in Europe. Age did not deter the participants from entering fully into the spirit of the occasion.

The photographs on this page show both young and old remembering those who died. The upper photograph shows a solemn procession on the Slopes on Remembrance Day 1974, and the lower photograph shows Remembrance Day on the Market Place in Chapel-en-le-Frith in 1976.

The regimental ram

The Sherwood Foresters made a rare march through Buxton in March 1997. The regimental ram headed the procession, crowds lined the streets, and Union Jacks were flown from many buildings.

Chapter 9 – Clubbing together

Americans who use Eugene Fodor's guidebooks for their trips to Europe are warned that the British have a predilection for exclusive clubs, designed to accommodate groups of people with similar tastes, outlook and interests. The High Peak has a plethora of clubs and organisations catering for people of all ages and tastes. A few of them are represented in the following pages. This photograph, taken on the 70th anniversary of 1st Taxal Scouts shows Les Wheeldon, the oldest member, and 11 year old Christopher Whitney, one of the youngest members.

Scouting for boys

It would seem that both grand country houses and modest huts have a part to play in scouting provision. Our upper photograph shows scouts from St Peter's, Fairfield attending a jamboree on the Chatsworth estate in 1974, whilst our lower photograph shows Furness Vale scouts at the opening of their new hut in 1980.

Cubs from St Peter's, Fairfield posed for this picture in 1965. The cubs on the back row look as if they are about to sing Auld Lang Syne! Our lower picture shows a group of enthusiastic scouts taking part in a cart-pull along Broad Walk in 1994. The event is organised by the Rotary Club of Buxton to raise funds for good causes.

Brownies and brigades

Our upper picture from 1974 shows Buxton Brownies taking part in an energetic sponsored skip. The Brownies gave a further demonstration of their athletic activities in 1978 when they participated in a "mini-Olympics".

The photographs on this page feature members of Chapel-en-le-Frith Boys' Brigade The upper picture shows David Helps, Dale McNicholas and Jonathan Hall manning one of the fun stalls at a Christmas Fayre held in 1991. The lower picture shows the band of the Boys' Brigade leading members of the company on a march down Chapel-en-le-Frith's Market Street in the same year. Peter Goddard, nearest to the camera, is now Brigade leader.

Digging in

There is a look of apprehension on the faces of the guests at the 1974 St Andrew's Night dinner of Buxton and District Caledonian Society as Rev. Macduff Cooper, the Chieftain of the Society, digs into the haggis. Digging of a different kind took place in 1970 when the Society of Business and Professional Women opened a garden for the use of blind people.

Members of the Rotary Club of Buxton, who organise many worthwhile events and money-raising ventures in the town, look eager to dig into their meal at their 1969 annual dinner at the St Ann's Hotel and members of Combs and District Women's Institute are seen digging into their 21st Anniversary celebration cake.

Well organised

Everyone seems to be enjoying the Christmas party at Chapel-en-le-Frith's Memorial Club in 1974 and members of Sparrowpit Women's Institute look justifiably proud of the food they have prepared for their produce sale in 1990.

Buxton has had a highly successful twinning arrangement with the French town of Oignies for over a quarter of a century. In 1978 the new mayor, Cllr Harold Littlewood (3rd right) went along to meet members of the organising committee for the twinning. Thanks to Keith Holford, I am able to name all the members of Buxworth Over Sixties Group who embarked on a trip to Trentham Gardens in the fifties. Back row: Mr Proctor, Mr Proctor, Mr Bennett, Mrs Barnes. Next row: Mrs Goddard, Miss Plant, Mrs Walton, Mrs Wilson, Bower's driver, Mrs Cooper, Mrs Lowe, Mrs Carrington, Mrs Wright, Miss A Hibbert, Mrs Cain, Mrs Holford, Mrs Bennett, Miss L Winterbottom. Front row: Mr and Mrs T Winterbottom. Miss E Hibbert, Mrs Waterhouse, Miss Tissy Barnes, Miss A Huges, Mrs Bennett.

The Ancient Order of Foresters

When roof repairs took place at the Pack Horse inn in Hayfield, a locked box was found in the rafters. When licensee Harold Clarke opened the box he found a silk and hand-painted banner for the Ancient Order of Foresters. The upper photograph shows one of the builders, Graham Hadfield (kneeling), and Richard Rowbotham, who works in the pub. The lower photograph shows members of the ancient order, all in their regalia, at their annual dinner in 1975.

Chapter 10 – Campaigning zeal

The willingness of British people to contribute to charities and to fight for worthwhile causes has been demonstrated many times. The people of the High Peak are as zealous as anyone else in their efforts to raise money and in their battles for justice. They also show an uninhibited willingness to make fools of themselves as a means of raising money. For example, Chapel High School teacher Mike Walker allowed fifth former Karen Knowles and others to "gunge" him at a £2-a-go, in order to raise funds on Red Nose Day in 1991.

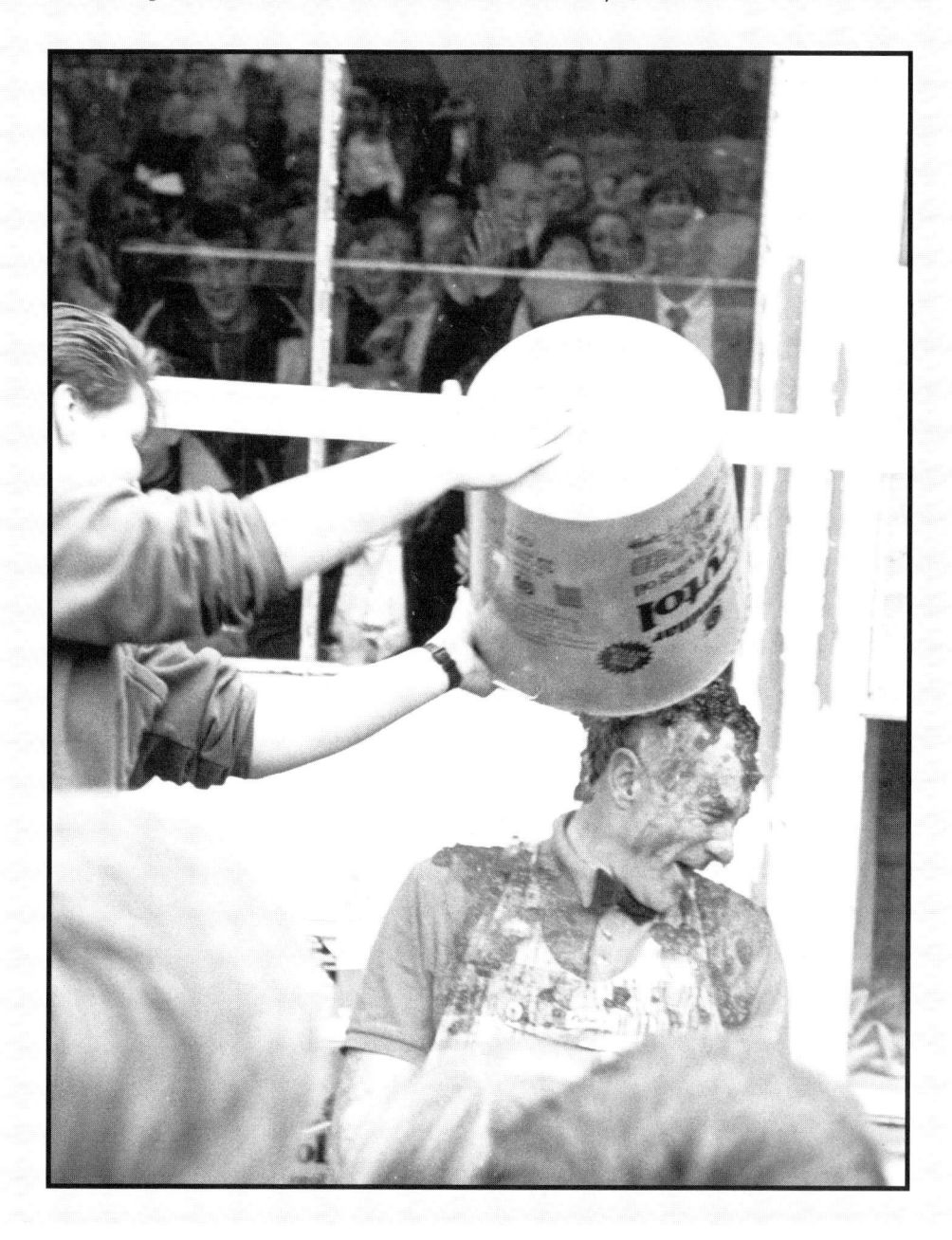

In your face

In 1994, Warmbrook School headteacher John Smith raised £150 by agreeing to have his beard of twenty years shaved off by local hairdresser George Cossidinos. Pupils John and Stuart Else and Lisa Williams seemed to have some doubts about the wisdom of the operation as they inspected the newly clean-shaven face of their headteacher. Voluntary worker Colin Floyd subjected himself to the same operation at the hands of Jean Hayes in a money-raising venture at Fairfield Sports Centre.

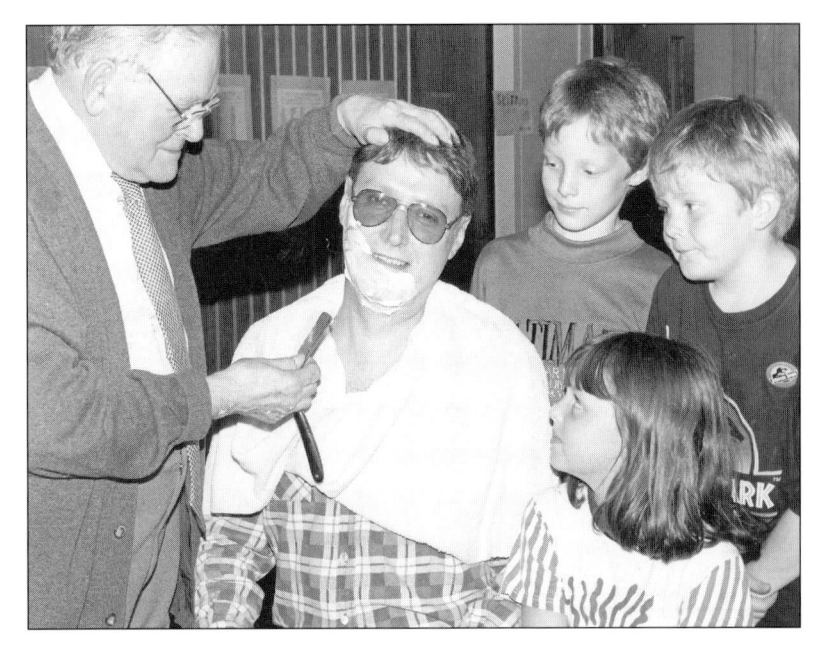

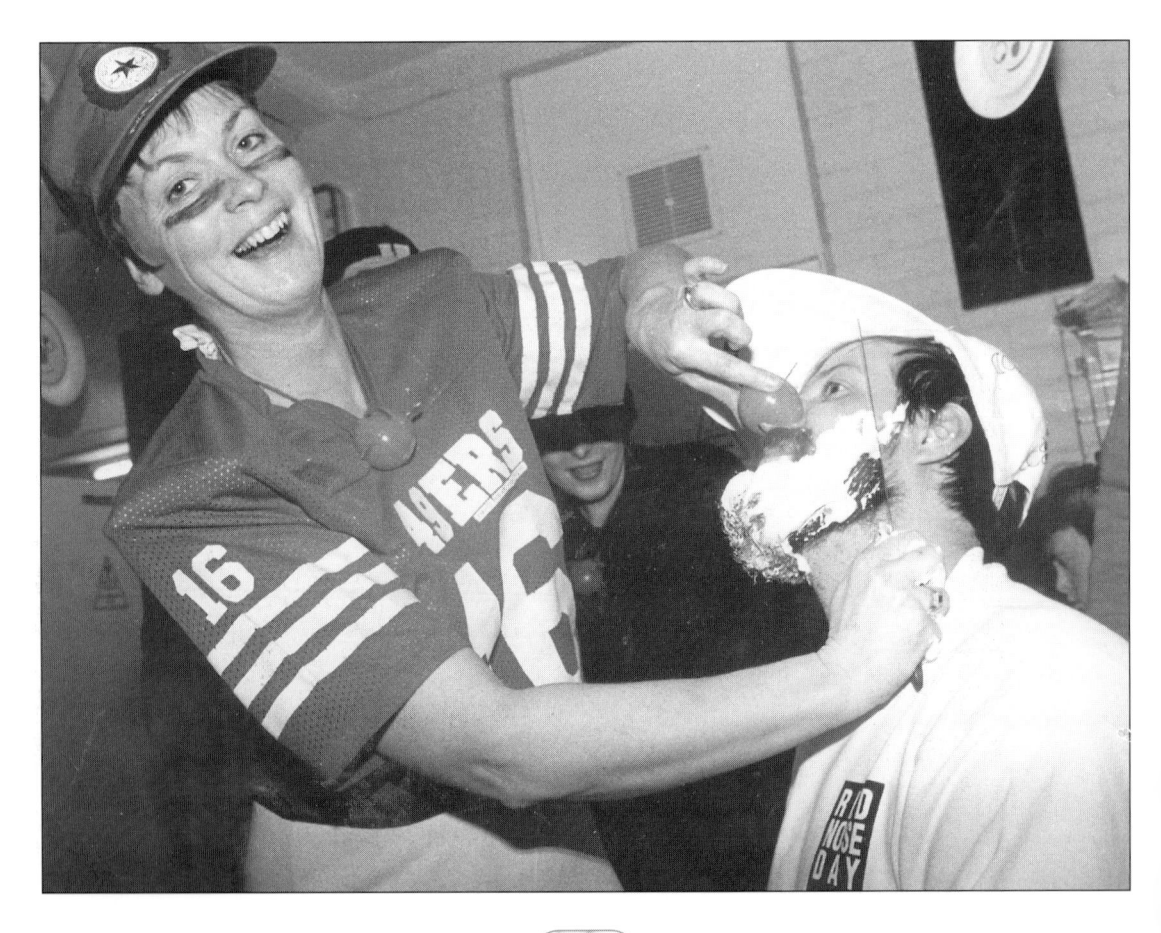

High Peak M.P. Charles Hendry bravely put his head in the stocks at Chinley 's Fun Day to raise money for the renovation of Victory hall - something of a risk for a politician, one would have thought! Bill Weston's rather burly majorettes put on yet another in-your-face display to raise money in the 1993 Buxton carnival. The onlookers outside the Baker's Arms certainly seemed to appreciate the efforts of the Billerettes.

Surprise, surprise

High Peak Conservatives were anything but conservative when they tried their hand at tossing pancakes on their stall in 1977 , and Princess Margaret walked into an exotic setting when she attended Barnardo's Royal Ball in 1975. The local paper reported " a Caribbean stmosphere in the high hills of Derbyshire on a cold winter's night". The guest was described as "a vision in gold with diamonds sparkling brilliantly from her necklace and matching earrings". Alison Barclay, in contrast, wore an Hawaian grass skirt for her meeting with the princess.

The Duke of Devonshire sportingly joined a sponsored walk in aid of orthopaedic research in 1993. He was accompanied by Arnold Howe of Horwich End, who had received two hip replacements.

Getting the message across

The main road through Dove Holes looks quiet enough in this early photograph of the High Peak village, but the carriageway, which now forms part of the A6, has become increasingly choked with cars and heavy goods vehicles. Traffic noise levels in Dove Holes are very high and the dangers to pedestrians are considerable. Cllr Brian Millward campaigned tirelessly for a by-pass, which never materialised, and for safer crossing arrangements for pedestrians as an interim measure. When a crossing was finally installed after a five year campaign, Cllr Millward, shown here, was far from satisfied. He claimed that the new traffic lights did not stay on red long enough to allow people to cross safely.

Chapter 11 – Conservation and restoration

Since 1951, much of the High Peak has enjoyed the protection of National Park status, but this does not make conservation a simple matter, because British National Parks, unlike the original American models, are not untouched areas of wilderness and natural beauty, but lived-in landscapes. 40,000 people live and work in the Peak Park and there is further pressure from the 22 million visitors who come into the Peak annually. The towns of the High Peak, with their solid stone buildings which are so in tune with the natural environment, lie outside the National Park, but they are no less worthy of preservation. The grand and elegant spa town of Buxton, which is also outside the Park, poses particular problems, because new uses have to be found for buildings whose original function is obsolete. The following pages highlight just a few aspects of conservation in the region. We begin with the efforts of Edale Primary School in Plant-a-tree Week in 1995. Headteacher Peter Irwin, with spade in hand, Peak Park Ranger Gordon Miller and farmer Cedric Gilbert joined the pupils for this commemorative picture.

The Civic Association

Buxton Civic Association has had an enormous part to play in the conservation and enhancement of Buxton and its environs. The society has campaigned hard for the landscaping of areas to the south of the town which bore the scars of quarry working, fought against further quarrying operations, developed one of the country's first Country Parks and managed many other areas of woodland around the town. Our photographs show Sir Hugh Molson addressing a meeting of the Buxton Civic Association in 1968 and members of the association setting a good example by cleaning the windows of a shop housing their display in 1965.

Poole's Cavern, a spectacular show cave, had been closed for 11 years when it was acquired by the Buxton Civic Association in 1976 as the focus of their new Country Park. Dave Allsop, the first warden (shown here), installed 100 electric lights along the 320m underground route and did much to publicise the cavern. The land beyond the Country Park was badly scarred by old quarry workings until Derbyshire County Council carried out a three-year landscaping operation in the early eighties, which included the imaginative conversion of the old quarry into a caravan park.

The Opera House

Buxton's delightful Edwardian Opera house was designed by the famous theatre architect Frank Matcham. The upper photograph shows the Opera house in 1937 and the lower photograph shows the magnificent interior with its painted ceiling, which is a restrained riot of delicate decoration.

In 1977, a publicity campaign was launched to promote the restoration of the Opera House. The upper photograph shows Cllr Mrs Millican, Mayor of the High Peak, Cllr Ray Walter, Chair of the Amenities Committee, and Mrs Helen O'Neill, a P.R. freelance, at the Opera House in 1977. Three years later, Mrs Millican was able to attend a production by a Gala Performance by the D'Oyly Carte Opera Company in the newly restored theatre.

Destruction and renewal

The fire at the Pavilion Gardens in 1982 turned out to be a blessing in disguise. During rebuilding, a superb ceiling was exposed when a false roof was removed, and a second tier was added to the lounge to allow customers a splendid panoramic view over 26 acres of landscaped gardens. Not all Buxton's worthwhile buildings have been saved. The United Reform Church was demolished in 1980, but at least its windows (shown below) were preserved and installed in the United Reform School Rooms in Hardwick Square.

Buxton's magnificent Crescent, designed in 1780 by John Carr and the first crescent to be built outside Bath, has been empty for some years. It was described in the *Guardian* as "the most notorious Grade I listed building at risk in England" and drastic action was needed by the late eighties to prevent irreversible deterioration. Restoration work on the exterior was completed by 1996 (see lower picture), but much work remains to be done on the interior and the building still awaits a new occupant. The upper photograph shows a concerned group visiting the building at the start of the English Heritage restoration project. Members of the group include High Peak M.P. Charles Hendry and Housing Minister Sir George Young

Chapel changes

The old Hearse House, a Grade II listed building of 1818 with a distinctive porthole-like upper window, was formerly used to house the parish hearse - the hirer provided the horse. Chapel-en-le-Frith Amenity Society carried out a careful restoration of the building which was opened as a visitor centre by the Duchess of Devonshire in 1992.

The stocks on Chapel-en-le-Frith's Market Place could well date from the Cromwellian period. The wooden slats and seat have been replaced many times, but the stone uprights are said to be original. One upright was knocked 45 degrees out of the vertical by a charabanc in 1920, but the renovated stocks now stand on a protected dais and are surrounded by paving which quarantines them from traffic.

Hill towns

The oldest part of Chapel-en-le-Frith, set on a ridge below Eccles Pike, clusters around its parish church, founded in 1225. The Old Town has something of the air of a French *village perché* and Church Brow, the steep, cobbled street which runs from the church to Market Street, is Derbyshire's answer to Gold Hill in Dorset, famous as a setting for a Hovis commercial. Some houses have been rendered in recent years, but the contours of the street have not changed in the half century that separates these photographs.

Sparrowpit is an isolated, linear settlement set along a high ridge. The hamlet is unusual in that almost all its houses are set on one side of the street. Thankfully, no development has taken place since the early photograph was taken and the terrace of lead miners' cottages has been well preserved. The whole of Sparrowpit has now been designated a Conservation Area.

A basin full

The High Peak Tramway once carried stones from the quarries near Buxton to Bugsworth Basin, where they were loaded onto barges for transportation along the Peak Forest Canal. The basin, which once saw 600 tons of lime a day being loaded on to 40 barges, was closed in 1925.

A long, painstaking restoration of the Bugsworth Basin has seen the clearing of the canal, the restoration of its perimeter, the reinstatement of stone foundations on a stretch of the tramway and, finally, the reopening of the basin to boats. Our picture shows High Peak Mayor Joyce Brocklehurst cutting the tape at the re-opening of the Bugsworth Basin in 1999.

Waste disposal

Litter is one of the curses of our country. As a nation, we are not good at clearing up our waste. If matters are to improve, education must start with the young, and it is good to report that considerable efforts have been made in this direction in High Peak schools. In 1995, pupils from Hayfield Primary School decided to purchase a new litter bin whose design would not allow birds to get at the litter and scatter it. The pupils are Heather Winfield, Richard Kindred, Emma Burgess, Grace Hallam and Leigh Rogers

Whaley Bridge Guides and Brownies took part in a National Spring Clean organised by the Tidy Britain campaign in 1994, by tidying up the car park and canal basin in Whaley Bridge. Litter picking on a much bigger scale saw the removal of the vast Bibbington tip (seen in our lower photograph, centre right). The waste heap was a long-standing eyesore on the A6 between Buxton and Dove Holes.

A job well done

Celebrations of jobs well done are featured here. Castleton Youth Hostel warden Alistair Boyd presented certificates to Castleton Junior school pupils in recognition of the plans they had drawn up for a wildlife garden in the grounds of the hostel. Headteacher Alan Jackson was also present. The shrine to Our lady of the World on Long Hill, originally built in his spare time by S.B.Foxton, a member of the Peak Park Board's planning office staff, was possibly the first shrine to be erected on public land since the Reformation. The shrine was renovated in 1994 after being damaged by a vehicle. The Rector of Buxton, Canon John Tomlinson, and Father Higgins of St Anne's R.C. Church are seen at the rededication ceremony.

Chapter 12 – Weather centre

There is a strange paradox about Buxton: the town established a reputation as a health resort, but it could be argued that only the fit and healthy can withstand its climate. Buxton stands 1,000ft above sea-level and on many days in the year it is the coldest place in England. Meteorological records between 1928 and 1954 indicate that the town has an average of 38 days of snow and 211 days of rainfall per year. Needless to say, Buxton people are used to dealing with adverse weather conditions. Our upper photograph shows Mr Mosley and Morton's Dairy horse Tom battling through dreadful conditions in 1965. Buxton's market traders have to deal with appalling weather conditions on an almost weekly basis, but even they gave up the struggle in March 1979 when the market was reduced to a couple of stalls

Casualties of the weather

November 1969 saw snowfalls which brought chaos to the exposed Ashbourne Road (upper picture): many cars were left stranded on the verge and some were even abandoned on the carriageway. The heavy snowfalls in the winter of 1963 caused havoc at Batham Gate (lower picture) where this car was well and truly anchored in the snow. Incidentally, the abandoned car, a Vauxhall Victor, dates from a brief period when wrap-around front and rear windows were an automotive fashion.

Two very different casualties of the High Peak weather are illustrated here. Cows were killed by lightning at Shepley Farm in 1960 and a coach came to grief in the snow on Long Hill in the winter of 1979-80.

Snowfalls often cause chaos for travellers but they also bring joys for children, as illustrated by the two photographs on this page. Cousins Rebecca and Laura Turner and Gareth Ashby are certainly enjoying themselves on the slopes of Cavendish Golf Club in 1997 (upper photograph), as are the tobogganists on the same stretch of hillside in 1962.

The High Peak is beautiful at all times of year but snow-covered fields and buildings take on a very special magic. Our photographs show the little hamlet of King Sterndale under snow in the eighties and Hayfield Road, in Chapel-en-le-Frith, covered in snow in the nineties.

Flood tide

Snow is not the only weather hazard in the High Peak. Rainfall in the region is heavy and it can often arrive in great downpours. Ashwood Park has had its share of flooding over the years (lower picture) and traffic has often had to splash through water on Ashwood Dale where the river Wye bursts its banks under the slightest provocation. The scene in our upper photograph dates from 1965.

Chapter 13 – Spa of the Blue waters

Writing in the nineteenth century, Dr Thresh attempted a scientific explanation for the healing properties of Buxton's waters: "the presence of nitrogen and carbonic acid, in their nascent state, and the recent demonstration by Lord Rayleigh of the presence of argon and helium, and by Lord Blythswood of radium, may explain the action of these waters. The molecular activity of radium is the most powerful of any known body: and it is probable that, in combination with the above gases, it sets up a corresponding activity in the peripheral nerve endings of the tissues of the skin which is thence communicated throughout the whole system". Mary Queen of Scots certainly believed in the power of Buxton water and Victorians came in droves to take the Buxton Cure. The demise of the Pump Room, or St Ann's Well, illustrates modern scepticism about the curative powers of spa water.

BUXTON, ST ANN'S WELL.
WITH CONSTANT FLOW OF WARM RADIO-ACTIVE WATER

Spa town

The slogan "Spa of the Blue Waters", which was used to market Buxton for many years, can be seen clearly on the roof of the Thermal Baths in our upper picture. The baths, which provided immersion and vapour treatment, closed in 1963 and the building, now re-roofed with a glass dome, currently houses a shopping arcade. The aerial photograsph of Buxton, taken in 1967, shows a spa town of fine buildings which would not be out of place in the Black Forest. The domed Devonshire Royal Hospital and the chateau-like Palace Hotel dominate the picture.

These old photographs show the Pump Room, or St Ann's Well. The facility was built at the suggestion of the sixth Duke of Devonshire and opened by the seventh Duke in 1894. Visitors could pay for a glass of spa water, pumped here from St Ann's Well, and sit and enjoy it in elegant surroundings

Perambulating

Broad Walk is a wide promenade, lined on its south side with grand villas and bordered on its north side by the Pavilion Gardens. A baby in a pram is the centre of attention in our lower photograph and an elaborate glass and iron projecting roof is the eye-catching feature of our upper photograph, taken at the eastern end of Broad Walk. The projection is attached to the double-gabled house which was occupied by J. C. Bates, the proprietor of the *Buxton Advertiser*.

The area known as the Slopes was planned by Sir Jeffrey Wyatville in 1818 on the cliff above the Crescent which he criss-crossed with paths of fairly gentle gradient to allow invalids to reach the summit without undue exertion. Upon reaching the summit, they could enjoy a magnificent bird's-eye-view of the spa town in its High Peak setting. The Slopes have a much greater tree covering these days and an uninterrupted panoramic view can now only be obtained by climbing to the top of the tower of the Town Hall, which is situated at the head of the Slopes. Facilities for less strenuous promenading were provided at the Pavilion Gardens. Our photograph shows the glass and iron range of the pavilion of 1871 and the octagonal Concert Hall of 1876.

Spa hotels

The Palace Hotel was built between 1864 and 1866 and further wings and a ballroom were added in 1887. The construction of a hotel on the grand scale reflects the confidence of the spa era and also the benefits which came with the arrival of the railway. The building still operates as a hotel and retains an atmosphere of Edwardian elegance as evidenced by this interior shot taken in 1994.

The two photographs on this page reflect the refinement and elegance which visitors expect in a spa town. The upper picture was taken at the Buckingham Hotel in 1985 and the lower, much older picture was taken in the dining room of the Buxton Crescent Hotel which formerly occupied the eighteenth century Crescent. Diners ate beneath the Adam-style ceiling and the glittering chandeliers.

Photographic licence

This view of Buxton was widely used in guide books published in the fifties. The photograph has been cleverly doctored by the superimposition of a limestone cliff in the bottom right hand corner, so giving a clear, but completely misleading impression that a dramatic view of the town in its setting may be obtained from the summit of a precipitous rock above Terrace Road!

Chapter 14 – For the good of your health

Having received a commission from the fifth Duke of Devonshire to design a crescent for Buxton spa, architect John Carr was also asked to design a stables block to service the expected influx of visitors. The block, which was constructed around a large central exercise yard, became obsolete when the railway arrived. Despite the objections of Dr Robertson, who complained that, "no human creatures could be healthy where horses had lived", the stable complex was converted into a hospital "for the sick poor", and the central exercise yard was covered in 1880 by the largest unsupported dome in the world. The Devonshire Royal Hospital maintained a fine record of expert and specialist treatment until the end of the twentieth century, when maintenance costs and moves to centralise services forced its closure. When Eartha Kitt visited the hospital in 1970, she offered some "old-fashioned" treatment to male patients!

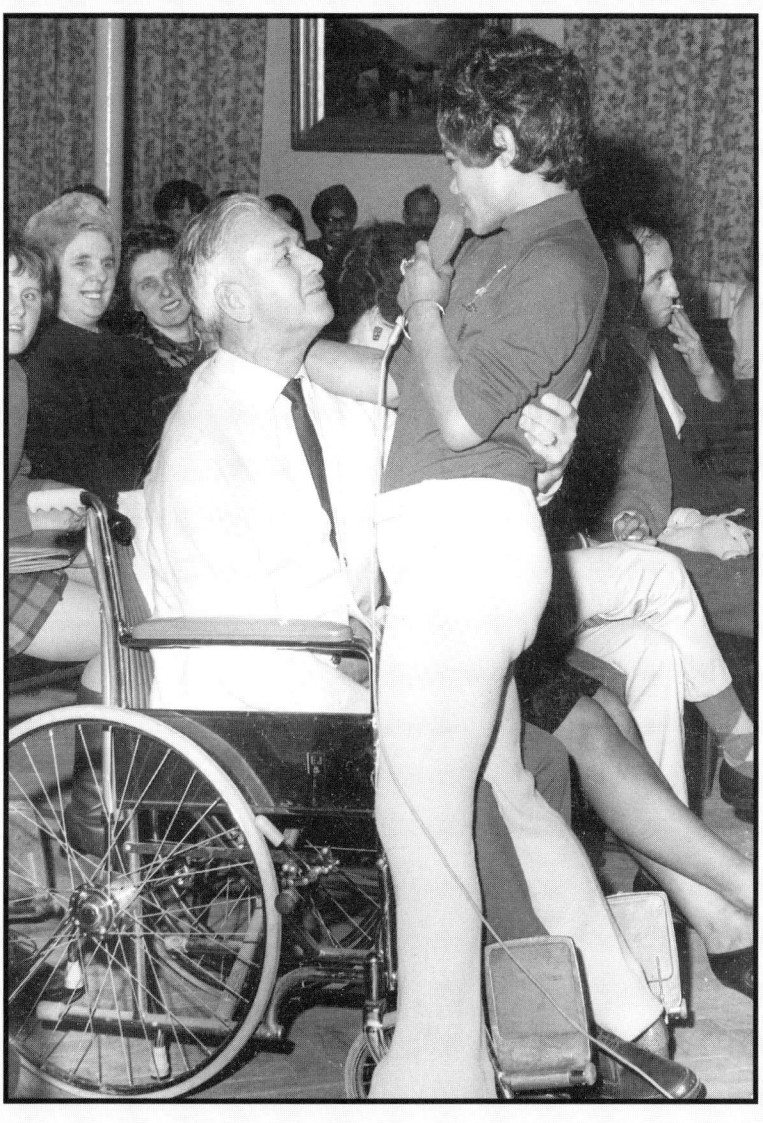

Care old and new

Entertainer Jimmy Saville, who has a big reputation for supporting hospitals, paid a visit to the Devonshire Royal Hospital in 1962 and brought some cheer to patients. In this shot he appears to be saying to camera: "How's about that, then ?" The Devonshire's dome is the most distinctive feature in Buxton's skyline and the building is one of the town's most important pieces of architecture. As the century ends and the hospital closes, hopes have been raised that Derby University may find a use for the buildings - Buxton may yet become a university town of "dreaming domes".

Treatments old and new are represented by the photographs on this page. Mr Brown, pictured above, was the last driver of the horse-drawn fever van. The fever hospital, at Hayfield Road in Chinley, now houses the offices of High Peak Borough Council. Eccles Fold, in nearby Chapel-en-le-Frith, began life as the Elms workhouse, but evolved, in 1984, into a new complex with sheltered housing and a day-care centre. As the century ended, a new hospice was being constructed on an adjacent site. Our photograph shows Theresa Hawksworth, Iain Parker (appeal patron) Dr Simon Cocksedge, Jane Inglefield (High Peak Mayor), and David Close (both Hospice Care Diectors). The group is inspecting a model of the proposed hospice.

Bath time

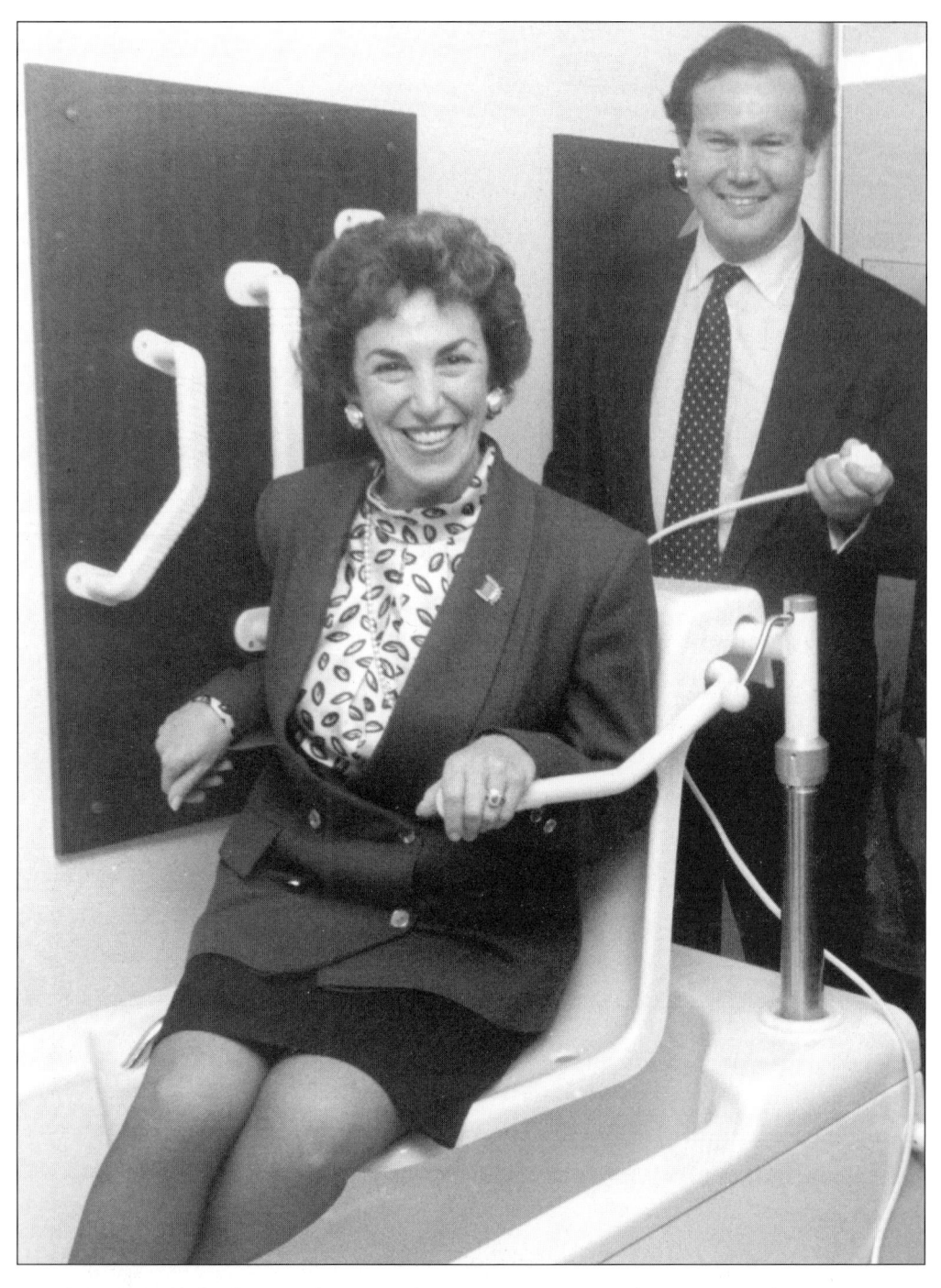

Local Tory M.P. Charles Hendry joined former Junior Health Minister Edwina Currie in the bathroom on a 1995 visit to open new headquarters of Invadex in Chapel-en-le-Frith. The incident didn't make it into the tabloid press as both Members of Parliament were fully clothed! Invadex manufactures household fittings for the disabled.

Chapter 15 – Places of worship

The typical High Peak church is solid, bold and unfussy, but there are some notable exceptions to this rule. The Church of St John the Baptist was provided for visitors to Buxton spa in 1811 by the fifth Duke of Devonshire. The church, designed in an eclectic Classical style, has a distinctive, faintly Italianate tower, no aisles, the tiniest of transepts, and Tuscan pilasters. The building originally had a portico, but this was filled in to create extra accommodation. A ramp to the south door provided access for Bath chairs.

Old and new

The Church of St Mary the Virgin, on Dale Road, Buxton, is a product of the Arts and Crafts movement. It was designed in 1916 by Currey and Thompson, the angels on the corbels were carved by the Hunstones of Tideswell and a horse called Fanny transported the building stone from Nithen End Quarry. The building has now been re-clad in stone and given a very individual external appearance with an array of mixed architectural elements. Little St Ann's, in Higher Buxton, is the oldest church in town. Originally constructed in 1625, it was restored in the mid-nineteenth century. As can be seen in our lower photograph, the succession of tie-beams is very low-slung and there is no demarcation between nave and chancel.

An architect charged with adding an annexe to an old church has a difficult task. The simplest, but least imaginative solution is to slavishly copy the style of the original building. A more difficult approach involves designing something that is both modern in style but in sympathy with its older surroundings. Two successful examples of this approach are shown here. The upper photograph shows Buxton Methodist church's new vestibule, which is part of an annexe containing meeting rooms, serving facilities and an administrative centre, all designed to open up the church to the community. The extension to Town End Methodist Church in Chapel-en-le-Frith was designed for a similar purpose and it too successfully combines old and new architecture.

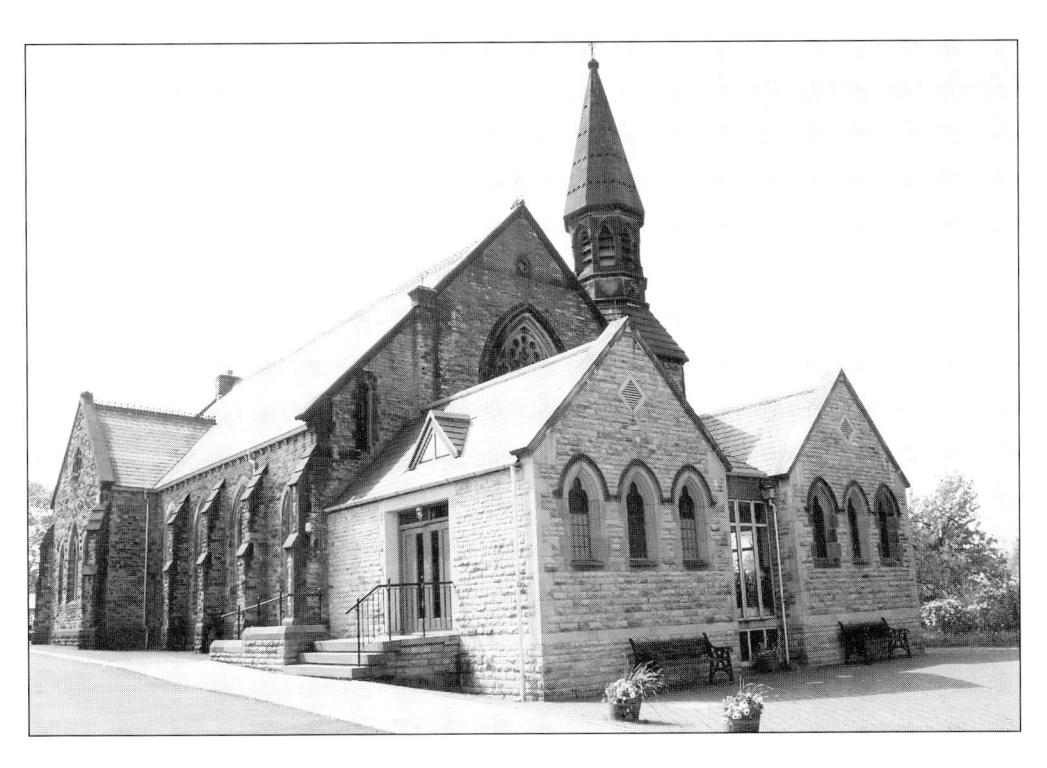

Celebrations

Rev. Betty Packham, a former Deputy Head at Buxton Girls' School, was one of the first women priests to be ordained in the Diocese of Derby. She described her ordination as "the greatest moment in my life". After being curate in the Parish of Buxton and Harpur Hill, Rev. Packham was given her own parish at Chinley and Buxworth where she is pictured with Stan Jones, a churchwarden. St Peter's, Fairfield celebrated local artistic talent by holding an Arts Festival in the nave of their church in 1980 (see below).

Chapel-en-le-Frith church was founded in the Royal Forest of the Peak in 1225. Its 700th anniversary, in 1925, was celebrated in somewhat bizarre and gruesome fashion by the holding of an ox-roast in the Market Place. Local children took turns at rotating the spit, having paid a penny each for the privilege. A ceremony of a different kind took place when a new cemetery was opened at Thornsett. Rev. John Minor, Father Jim Norton and Father Jim O'Hanlon gave a collective blessing of the new burial ground.

Roundhouse

The grand Italianate mansion in the Goyt Valley where the Grimshawe family lived in considerable style is now a scattering of ruins, but there are plenty of reminders of the family and their life style in the grounds. 40,000 azaleas and rhododendrons still burst into flower each June, a little family cemetery occupies a promontory above the house and, in a far-flung corner of the grounds, there is a round shrine to St Joseph which also celebrates the life of Miss Dolores de Bergrin, a Spanish aristocrat who taught at the private school run by the Grimshawes. Miss Dolores died on a visit to Lourdes in 1889.

Chapter 16 – "999"

Thankfully, the High Peak is not an area with a high incidence of crime but, like all other areas, it does have its fair share of emergencies. The twentieth century saw a shift in policing styles with officers in cars replacing friendly "bobbies on the beat". There may have been good operational reasons for this approach, but people began to feel less secure as a result. In 1979, Spt. Bartram of Buxton Central Division tried an experiment. Realising it is easier for the public to comminicate with a policeman on a bike rather than an officer in a Panda car, he decided to bring his force closer to the community. Our photograph shows Constable Birch on his brand-new bicycle.

To the rescue

The emergency services came to the rescue in 1974 when a lime spillage caused havoc on Ashwood Dale. The Eagle Squadron came to the rescue in 1977 when they were delegated to stand in for striking firemen. When the airmen patronised the Eagle Hotel they were presented with white T-shirts bearing the words "The Eagle, Buxton". Our picture shows Carol Lomas and Ann Woodman with the emergency firefighters and their "green goddess" engine. Meanwhile Derbyshire N.U.M. gave £100 and 100 per cent support to the striking firemen.

A damsel in distress was recued by High Peak firemen in a realistic demonstration at Buxton Fire Station in 1974 (upper photograph). Youngsters at Buxton Community school Playgroup were made aware of dangers in the home and on the streets in a Playsafe Fortnight in 1994. Leading firefighter Gordon Critchlow gave some of the youngsters some hands-on experience.

Safe driving and safe keeping

Ambulance drivers have to be capable of combining fast driving with safe driving. Our upper picture shows safe driving awards being presented to ambulance drivers in 1970. Public safety of a different kind was catered for in 1994 when cells were constructed in the new police station at New Mills. Constable Peter Harrison tried them out by locking up High Peak Mayor John Francis.

Chapter 17 – Enthusiasts

Some southerners have a tendency to stereotype people who live in northern hills as Philistines. The reality is very different: the range of interests and talents shown by inhabitants of the High Peak is enormous: clubs and organisations flourish, many people have a profound knowledge of local history and Peaklanders characteristically pursue their hobbies with great enthusiasm. Although the high altitude of the region makes for difficult growing conditions and a short season, gardening is a very popular activity in the High Peak. Jason Chadwick's photograph shows Chairman Les Checkey and Secretary Gordon Bellfield with an impressive display of marrows at the Buxworth and District Gardening Show.

A growing hobby

The region's top gardeners and allotment holders hardly need prizes to motivate them, but it is nice to see the best practitioners receiving some public recognition. Our upper picture shows Chapel Parish Council Chairman Ann Young presenting prizes to Roy Milner (keeper of the best allotment in the parish) Melvin Cross (best allotment in Chapel-en-le-Frith) and David More (winner of the Dove Holes section). The lower picture shows a carnival atmosphere in a Hayfield presentation to successful growers with May Queens doing the presentation.

Gardening enthusiasts in the area were given some expert advice when the B.B.C.'s *Gardener's Question Time* was recorded in Buxton in 1965. The New Mills and District Chrysanthemum Society, which has members from all areas of the High Peak, also sought expert advice when they visited top growers Fred and Les Waining at Bradwell. Our picture shows Bernard Gould, Fred Waining, John Bould, John Webber, Gerald Shirt, Glynn Hill and Les Waining.

Steam enthusiasts

Workers at Dorothea Restorations at Whaley Bridge put tremendous effort into a £30,000 restoration of *Sans Pareil* ("Without Equal"), a replica of an engine that competed with Stephenson's *Rocket*. The steam engine had been damaged in a derailment in County Durham.

The look of intense concentration on the faces of these schoolboys at Buxton and District Model Railway Exhibition in 1968 illustrates the fascination of steam trains for young people even in an age of diesel engines. Many adults retain this enthusiasm as is evidenced by the regular steam fairs held in the High Peak. On the evidence of the lower picture, the phrase "traction engine" is an appropriate label for even the smallest of vehicles!.

Art and science

The region has many talented artists. The upper photograph shows High Peak Mayor David Lomax presenting Dee Stone of Hayfield with the 1997 Artist of the Year Award at the High Peak Artists' annual exhibition. Dee's superb acrylic painting *Blue Jug with Fennel* can be seen hanging on the gallery wall. Although the two New Mills students in our lower photograph are pictured in front of works of art, it was their ability as scientists and mathematicians that won them places at Cambridge in 1993. Kate Carpenter was given an offer to read Pharmacology and Lesley Bott to read Mathematics.

The Art department at the newly-formed Buxton Community School quickly gained a reputation for high quality work. Exhibits at the school's 1991 exhibition included this life-size sculpture. An examiner claimed the work of the students was the best in Derbyshire and Head of Department Tom Brown felt some of the students had produced pieces of degree standard. Drawing from life is one of the most difficult and concentrated tasks an artist has to undertake. Cllr Littlewood wore his full regalia when he posed as a model for a group of Buxton artists in 1979, but one wonders if the electric fire visible in the picture is for the benefit of the regular models, who are usually unclothed.

Recorded happenings

One evening, Mike Langham and Colin Wells sat in the bar of the 19th Hole, a public house just outside Buxton, and mused about the lack of books about the history of their town. Having resolved to fill the void themselves, they have gone on to produce an impressive collection of works about the development of Buxton, including the very popular *Pictorial History* (shown here) and a thoroughly researched biography of Robert Rippon Duke, an architect who did so much to shape the town. After completing their draft manuscripts, the two authors always turn to Oliver Gomersal, a Buxton mam with a vast store of local knowledge. Oliver, a former Senior administrative Officer at the Town Hall is seen here being presented with a canteen of cutlery by Trevor Brooks (Works Director) on the occasion of his retirement in 1979, after 39 years service with High Peak Borough Council. Oliver's wife Marjorie is also in the photograph.

A B.B.C. poll showed that one person in ten thinks they could write a book and one in fifty has already done so. Sadly, only a small proportion of these works is ever published, but budding authors in the High Peak are lucky to have in their midst an enterprising Methodist minister who runs a small publishing house, *Church in the Market Place Publications*, for the benefit of local writers. Bob (left) is seen here with local M.P. Tom Levitt and author Jenny Nicholson with her book *Where Heather Blooms on Ladylow*, which tells the story of Dove Holes village. Local author Terry Lamsley (below) does not chronicle local historical facts, but writes ghost stories set in actual locations in and about the town. Terry, who has won a number of international prizes for his writing, says: "Why do I have this compulsion to fill an innocent, harmless little town like Buxton with all kinds of horrors? Better not to ask, I guess".

Peak poet

Retired dairy farmer Harry Swindell won a literature prize at school when he was 11 years old. Although he has written poems and some prose pieces for local magazines throughout his life, Harry was only really "discovered" as a writer at the age of 88 when Rev. Bob Davies published Harry's first book of poems *In his Grass Roots*. A succession of other books of poetry and reminiscence has followed. As the century ends, Harry, now aged 94, is still writing splendidly evocative verse and prose about life in the High Peak.

Chapter 18 – Making music

Music plays a large part in High Peak life. Concerts are well attended and many people make music through their membership of bands or choirs. The demands of the National Curriculum and the ending of free instrumental tuition for schoolchidren could well have reduced the strength of musical education and so threatened the continuing vitality of music in the area, but all the region's schools seem determined to maintain their strong musical traditions. Our photograph shows a group of students from New Mills school, all of whom have performed creditably in their instrumental grade examinations. The student musicians are: Chris Etchells, Rachel Sumner, Rachel Eary, Lizzie Sumner and David McCartney (front).

Instruments and voices

The upper photograph shows conductor Sir John Barbarolli looking the very epitome of a musical maestro as he conducts the famous Halle orchestra, when they played at the Derbyshire Festival of Music in 1961. The lower picture shows 80 young musicians rehearsing with the High Peak Youth Orchestra in 1993 at a concert organised by north-west Derbyshire music centres. The occasion had particular significance for this was the first concert to be staged after the discontinuation of free music lessons in schools.

Spice Girls eat your hearts out! The girl group from Fairfield Venturers pre-dates the famous all-female pop group by a quarter of a century. An all-male choir has been in existence in Chapel-en-le-Frith since 1920 when it was formed by servicemen returning from the Great War. The commemorative Millennium photograph below shows current members, who are drawn from a wide area of the Peak District, with their conductor Harry Redfern and their accompanist Karen Dexter.

Brass and blues

There is a very strong tradition of brass bands in the High Peak with long-established, high quality bands in most towns and villages. Our upper photograph depicts the Fairfield Band in classic big band pose and our lower picture shows the Dove Holes band on the move.

The Dove Holes Community centre may seem an unlikely venue for a northern rival to Ronnie Scott's Club, but Roger Marshall has been organising highly popular jazz nights at the centre for many years. Roger's network of connections in the jazz world has enabled him to attract leading bands from many countries. Our picture shows "Sir" Alan Bradley playing at Dove Holes. Hayfield was formerly another great centre for jazz. An annual jazz festival held in the village in the late seventies and early eighties attracted bands from all over the world. Unfortunately, the event also attracted people who treated the occasion as an excuse for rowdy and drunken behaviour, with the result that villagers voted to put a stop to the event. The evocative picture below was taken at the Hayfield Jazz Festival in 1980.

Matcham theatre

The Buxton Opera House and its surroundings of arcaded buildings and grand, eccentric architecture almost look like a set for an operetta and so make a perfect venue for an annual Gilbert and Sullivan festival. The Opera House was designed by the prolific architect Frank Matcham who was responsible for some 150 theatres. Sadly, only 19 Matcham theatres remain. This photograph was taken on the occasion of a visit to Buxton's Opera House by a party from Wakefield where the centenary of Matcham's Theatre Royal and Opera House was being celebrated. The Wakefield group would like to establish a national "Matcham Trail". The group on the balcony comprises: High Peak Deputy Mayor Cllr David Lomax; his wife Hilary; Wakefied Centenary Chairman Arthur Starkie; Wakefield Deputy Mayoress Margaret Bolland; Deputy Mayor Ken Bolland; Judith Christian.

Chapter 19 – Putting on a show

The High Peak is teeming with thespian talent. Amateur theatre groups abound and many other organisations put on shows. The Buxton Amateur Dramatic and Operatic Society (BADOS) has a long tradition of staging highly polished productions. Our photograph shows the large cast for a production of *Oliver* at the Buxton Opera House in the sixties.

Thespians

Chinley Amateur Dramatic Society (above) celebrated their fiftieth anniversary in 1995 by presenting excerpts from their productions over the last 20 years, including *Cabaret* and *Allo, Allo*. The New Mills and District Amateur Operatic and Dramatic Society staged a production of *Half a Sixpence* (see below) at the New Mills Arts Theatre in the same year.

School productions are often very ambitious and require the combined voluntary efforts of a number of school departments, especially when musicals are chosen. Whaley Bridge Primary School put on a production of *Oliver* in 1995 and Buxton Community school staged a production of *Grease* in 1993. The car was supplied by Gardner Scrap Limited of Dove Holes.

As a former headteacher, I am all too aware of the enormous time and effort which staff and pupils put into school productions. The dress designers for the 1963 production (seen in our upper picture) at Buxton College must have put in some considerable unpaid overtime and the student actors seen below rehearsing for a 1960 production at the College look well prepared to face an audience.

The girls of Silverlands Secondary School mounted a production with a difference in 1965 when they staged an ambitious *Son et Lumiere*, and the pupils of Buxworth Primary School slipped into Old Tyme Music Hall mode for their 1990 production. The young actors are: Karen and David Pawlock, Christopher Collins, Kirsty Persey, Katy Amps, Vanessa Saunders, Lianne Gardner, David Brocklehurst, Samantha Tamson, Sarah Scowcroft and Michael Hancock.

Feet first

Red Nose day always provides an excuse for people to let their hair down or, as in this case, put their feet up. Adults, in wartime costume, had plenty of fun in 1993 and the children of Burbage School put their feet first in this March 1993 effort to raise money for Children in Need.

Two High Peak versions of "showing a leg" are shown in these photographs. The upper picture depicts members of the Towmnswomen's Guild performing a routine from their 1964 revue *Ring out, Wild Belles*. The lower photograph shows Chelmorton's version of the Can-Can, performed at their Shrove Tuesday concert in 1972. Both these performances could well have caused as big a stir in the High Peak as Angela Rippon's dance on the *Morecambe and Wise* show did nationally!

These two members of Chinley Amateur Dramatic Society are certainly getting into character through costume and by expression. Mike Tetley is the dame and Tom Goodfellow is the cleric

Chapter 20 – Celebration time

People in the High Peak are particularly good at celebrations. A number of towns and villages stage organised bonfires on Guy Fawkes Night, giving parents and children a safe option. The annual Round Table bonfire and firework display in Buxton always attracts large crowds. This photograph, taken in 1978, shows the Buxton sky being lit up in spectacular fashion.

Cause for celebration

The organised Guy Fawkes Night celebrations in the High Peak offer more than just a fire and a firework display. The upper photograph, taken in 1978, shows the torchlight procession which accompanies the Round Table bonfire in Buxton. The organising committee of the Dove Holes bonfire usually invite a local personality to spark off their celebrations. The lower photograph shows B.B.C. presenter Alister Macdonald stoking up the bonfire.

85 year old George Hudson celebrated 70 years as a regular at the White Hart, Whaley Bridge with two of his drinking companions, Lawrence Kelly, 85 and Glen Garlick, baby of the party at 73. The streets of a number of High Peak towns and villages are festooned with electric lights and illuminated trees over the Christmas period. The lower photograph shows Christmas at Whaley Bridge in 1990.

Jubilees

The Queen's Silver Jubilee in 1977 was celebrated enthusiastically in the streets, on the greens and in the village halls of the High Peak - people were not so sceptical about the monarchy in those days. The villagers of Peak Dale (shown above) celebrated in fine style. Ian Green (below) was given a celebration cake in 1995 to commemorate his sixty years service as an organist at St Thomas Becket Church, Chapel-en-le-Frith. Ian, a retired solicitor, now spends much of his time helping out in local schools, so it was appropriate that pupils Zoe and Sophie Buxton and Thomas Hibbert should help him cut the cake.

Chapter 21 – Animal magic

British Brown Bears once roamed the hills of the High Peak. This particular specimen roars loudly at visitors to Buxton Museum as they wander through the *Wonders of the Peak* exhibition which won a Museum of the Year Award for the town's museum in 1990.

Dogs, ducks and donkeys

Dennis Hill, of Chapel-en-le-Frith, drove off without his whippet Jenny one day after walking in the Derbyshire Dales. The dog, which is hardly equipped to survive the High Peak winter, went missing for 8 months, but was eventually spotted by Mr Hill when he was driving through Eyam. There was a public outcry and also an expression of sympathy in the form of a makeshift grave when High Peak Borough Council carried out the killing of 100 ducks in 1993. The council had taken this action beacause the ratio of mallards to female ducks had become so high that females were drowning as a result of incessant mating!

Television and theatre producer John Stirling once wrote a play for Patricia Hayes about an eccentric lady who owns 12 donkeys, each named after an Apostle. In the course of his research, he became aware of the suffering and neglect experienced by so many donkeys and he resolved to set up a sanctuary in the High Peak. Thanks to his theatre and T.V. connections, John has been able to gather a team of active, high profile patrons, including Kathy Staff, better known as Nora Batty.

On show

Pet shows are always popular in the High Peak. Our photographs show scenes from the 1964 King Sterndale pet show (above), a long-running annual event, and the 1962 dog show run by the Cannine Association, when table top dogs became top dogs!

The Buxton Archaeological and Natural History Society had a lecture with a difference in 1962 when an array of exotic birds and animals was displayed to members at Terry's Cafe. "Captain", a macaw from Peak Pets, Fairfield, was put through his paces by actor Glyn Edwards when he auditioned for a role as understudy in a production of *Treasure Island* at Buxton Opera House. The first choice bird was suffering from stress after a fire at another theatre!

Watch the birdie

Michael Boal and Charlotte Potts of Chapel-en-le-Frith Infants' School did their bit for our feathered friends when they built this bird box for their school garden.

Chapter 22 – Peak Personalities and Personalities in the Peak

Princess Diana, the "People's Princess", paid a visit to the High Peak in 1990. Her whirlwind tour took in New Mills, Whaley Bridge, Dove Holes, Gamesley and Charlesworth. People who met her were struck by her beauty and approachability, and the Princess is reported to have said at one stage on her journey: "Whaley Bridge is wonderful".

How tickled I am

Stuart Hall came along to present the awards at 1974 Bride of the Year contest. The winner, judged on her personality, was Mrs Susan Burbridge. In the same year, the "Fenn Street Boys", including "Duffy" and "Frankie Abbott", made a presentation to J. Gregory, Buxton and District Darts and Dominoes Champion.

Ken Dodd had great fun with his "tickling stick" in 1968 when he was a guest at the 1968 Buxton Chamber of Trade Exhibition. Mayor Cllr Beadle, Mayoress Mrs Shaw and Chamber President Mr Vale joined in the laughter as Doddy used his trademark implement to good effect!

Special delivery

It seems that many people in the High Peak do not really believe in giving up work at the recognised retirement age. Connie Allpress (a highly appropriate surname) finally retired from her position as the Devonshire Library's newsgirl in 1980. She was 82!

The Miller family have delivered Sunday papers in the Hayfield area for sixty years. Mary Miller, shown here, made her deliveries on foot or by motorbike.

Big impact

Our upper picture shows the present Duchess of Devonshire greeting Dr Wilfrid Jackson on the occasion of his 90th birthday. Dr Jackson's daughter Alicia is also present.. The Duchess is a very popular figure in the High Peak and is always willing to lend her support to local causes and events. Dr Jackson worked under Dr Boyd Dawkins for many years and was an expert in conchology. He "retired" to Buxton in 1945 but carried on lecturing and publishing papers for the next 33 years - he was still leading an annual Presidential Tour for the Buxton Archaeological Society when he was 96! Another High Peak man who made a big impact was Sam Longson, Chapel-en-le-Frith's self-made businessman and long-serving President of Derby County Football. Sam is seen here with Bill Winterbottom, Chairman of the High Peak Supporters Club, and manager Tommy Docherty who was attending Chapel's Memorial Club for a question-and-answer session.

Pasteur once said: "Chance favours the prepared mind". Herbert Frood's mind was certainly prepared when he spotted some discarded oil-soaked belts at his father-in-law's belting factory. Frood, who had become alarmed at the inadequate brakes on wagons crossing the hills of the High Peak, found that the discarded belts had surprising friction properties. After experimenting in his garden shed at Combs (pictured above), Frood set up the Ferodo company to manufacture his revolutionary new brake blocks. The rest is history! Another High Peak resident who made his mark through a highly original production, but of a very different kind, is Tim Brooke-Taylor, one of the three members of the highly innovative *Goodies* T.V. series. Tim is seen here returning to his roots for a Buxton event in 1976.

Politicians in all their guises

Two formidable female politicians are seen here. Shirley Williams, one of the founder members of the Social Democratic Party (S.D.P.), which broke away from the Labour Party, is seen here addressing a group of Buxtonians on the forecourt of the Crescent in 1983. Muriel Bradbury (below) received an Honorary Townsmanship of Chapel-en-le-Frith in 1991 in recognition of her 26 years of continuous service as a parish councillor. Pictured with Mrs Bradbury are: Colonel Peter Hilton (Lord Lieutenant of Derbyshire); Glynne Jones (Clerk to the Parish Council); Peter Harrison (Chairman of the Parish Council); Malcolm Cawthorn (Vice-Chairman). Mrs Bradbury was later awarded the M.B.E.

The Father Christmas figure pictured here in 1993 looks remarkably like Tom Levitt, the current Member of Parliament for the High Peak.

Royal appreciation

Princess Anne looked suitably impressed by the superb Adam-style ceiling in Buxton's Crescent when she paid a visit with Ald. J.W. Trippett in 1972. The room had just been renovated for use by the divisional library. At the turn of the century, the room and the rest of the Crescent are empty and awaiting a new tenant. It is to be hoped that a new use can be finally found for the Crescent, for it is not only the best building in Buxton, it also one of the finest examples of Georgian architecture in England.

lonely planet

EPIC
BIKE RIDES
of AUSTRALIA &
NEW ZEALAND

Explore Australia and New Zealand's most exciting cycling routes

CONTENTS

INTRODUCTION	04

AUSTRALIAN CAPITAL TERRITORY, NEW SOUTH WALES & QUEENSLAND — 06

Destination Cape York	08
Lake Burley Griffin Circuit	14
Canberra's Centenary Trail	20
Gears & Beers at Wagga Wagga	26
Top to Bottom in the Blue Mountains	32
The Atherton Tablelands	38
The Sandstone Wilderness Outback Adventure	44
Minjerribah Island in Winter	50
A Bikepacking First on Brisbane Valley Rail Trail	56
The Central West Cycle Trail	62

NORTHERN TERRITORY, SOUTH AUSTRALIA & WESTERN AUSTRALIA — 68

The Tour of Margaret River	70
Rocks & Crocs in the Top End	76
The Mawson Trail	82
The Munda Biddi Trail	88
Tailing the Tour in Adelaide	94
A Myponga Beach Loop	100

TASMANIA & VICTORIA — 106

Stories of the City: the Melburn-Roobaix	108
Finding Serenity on Flinders Island	114
Take a Peak Inside Tasmania	120
Australian Alpine Epic Trail	126
Along the Acheron Way	132
Bikepacking on the Goldfields Track	138
On the Road to Nowhere	144

© Mark Watson

Easy Harder Epic

🚲 Murray to the Mountains	150
🚲 Victoria's Otway Odyssey	156
🚲 The Bay of Fires Trail	162
🚲 The Silver City of the Western Wilds	168

NORTH ISLAND, NEW ZEALAND 174

🚲 The Hauraki Rail Trail	176
🚲 Overnight on the Moerangi Track	182
🚲 Mountains to Sea Explorer	188
🚲 Pakihi Circuit on the Motu Trails	194
🚲 Whakarewarewa Forest Loop	200
🚲 Remutaka Cycle Trail Loop	206
🚲 The Heart of the Octopus	212
🚲 A Northern Coromandel Loop	218
🚲 Touring Hawkes Bay Wineries	224
🚲 The Timber Trail	230
🚲 Kōpiko Aotearoa	236

SOUTH ISLAND, NEW ZEALAND 242

🚲 The Molesworth Muster	244
🚲 The West Coast Wilderness Trail	250
🚲 The Old Ghost Road	256
🚲 The Queen Charlotte Track	262
🚲 Otago's Central Rail Trail	268
🚲 Paparoa & Pike29 Memorial Tracks	274
🚲 Touring the Wakatipu Ranges	280
🚲 The Heaphy Track	286
🚲 The Coronet Loop	292
🚲 Canterbury's Banks Peninsula	298
🚲 Alps 2 Ocean Cycle Trail	304
🚲 The Old Dunstan Trail	310

INDEX 316
ACKNOWLEDGMENTS 320

© Sam Rice, Matt Beaver, Daniela Tommasi, courtesy of the Tour of Margaret River

- EPIC BIKE RIDES OF AUSTRALIA & NEW ZEALAND -

INTRODUCTION

What makes for a great bike ride? Compiling this collection of cycling stories from Australia and New Zealand offered a few answers.

Awe-inspiring scenery is a given out here. Riding through the Nevis Range in New Zealand or around Tasmania's Flinders Island provides a backdrop the match of anywhere in the world. But even on less rugged rides, you are often surrounded by Oceania's unique plants and wildlife. Routes in this book reach deep into forests to find the world's largest trees, such as the kauri, karri and mountain ash. Crocodiles, wallabies, wombats, emus, echidnas, parrots and possums are just a few of the creatures you're very likely to see, and the birdlife of both countries is inescapable, particularly if you're being swooped on by a protective magpie. We know the benefits of being in nature for our mental health – couple that with the physical exercise of cycling and it's clear that these rides do wonders for our wellbeing. Just slow down and appreciate the golden blooms of wattle or autumn's russet colours.

Challenging your own fears and trying something outside your comfort zone, such as a solo ride into the Outback like Sarah Pendergrass's 700km (435-mile) Queensland adventure, rewards riders with a sense of personal growth. Bike rides also allow us the time to reconnect with family and friends, away from daily life. Peter English persuaded his family to embark on an ambitious expedition along South Australia's Mawson Trail and they all survived. And of the group rides described in this book, the Kōpiko Aotearoa adventure across New Zealand undertaken by Sam Elworthy and his motley crew probably had the most things going wrong but it all still turned out okay in the end.

But great bike rides are not always just about us. Pedalling through a place is a valuable opportunity to learn about local history and culture because it's often easier to meet and talk to people when travelling at a slower pace. Māori oncologist George Laking introduces the ancestral connections of the Motu Trails in New Zealand. In Australia, the Goldfields Track is a way to explore the mining history of northwest Victoria.

Finally, let's not forget just how fun riding a bike should be. A healthy sense of playfulness, which Iain Treloar captures in the chaotic Melburn-Roobaix ride or is evident at the annual Gears and Beers event in Wagga Wagga in which Georgina von Marburg flies through fields of yellow canola, is more precious now than ever.

Since Lonely Planet published the first book in this series – Epic Bike Rides of the World – in 2016, a lot has happened. There was a global pandemic. Unable to travel internationally, more people bought bicycles with which to discover what lay on their doorsteps. And regional and national organisations have created more official routes since 2016, meaning that bikepacking – basically, backpacking on a bicycle – has come of age. The rides in this book cover everything from road racing in Margaret River to mountain bike parks in New Zealand, but there's a greater number of adventure routes than ever. Many of these use rail trails or other traffic-free paths (not least because the standard of driving by other road users in Australia and especially New Zealand is notably poor – be warned).

In an era of increasingly extreme weather events, driven by a changing climate, cycling remains the most sustainable mode of travel there is. And it's still reasonably low cost. There's really no better or more responsible way of experiencing Australia and New Zealand than on a bicycle.

HOW TO USE THIS BOOK

The main stories in each chapter of the book feature first-hand accounts of fantastic bike rides in that region. Each includes a toolkit to help plan the trip – when is the best time of year to ride, how to get there, and what to take. On the contents page, the rides have been colour coded according to their difficulty, which takes into account not just distance but also logistics and local conditions. Some rides can be completed in single day, others over several weeks. Many are signposted and safe for novice cyclists to attempt but a few require a degree of experience and expertise. And the 'more like this' section following each story, offers other ideas along a similar theme.

© Matt Beaver; Sam Rice; Matt Munro / Lonely Planet

Clockwise from left: watch out for wildlife wherever you're riding in Australia and New Zealand; descending the Old Ghost Road in New Zealand; the Gears and Beers ride in Wagga Wagga, Australia

Opening spreads from left: riding New Zealand's epic Nevis Range; a bridge crossing on the Timber Trail; sharing stories at Gears and Beers; the Tour of Margaret River

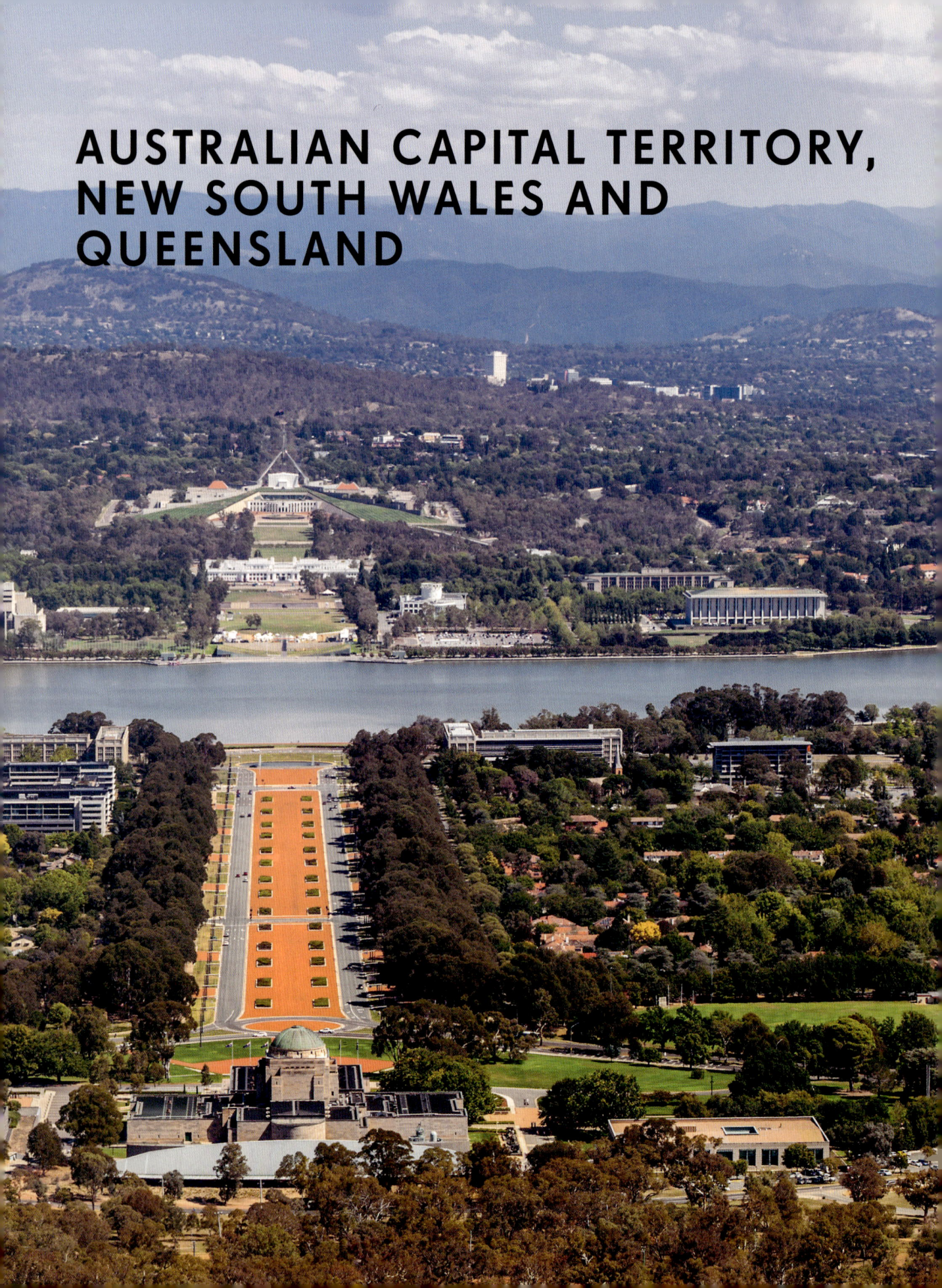

AUSTRALIAN CAPITAL TERRITORY, NEW SOUTH WALES AND QUEENSLAND

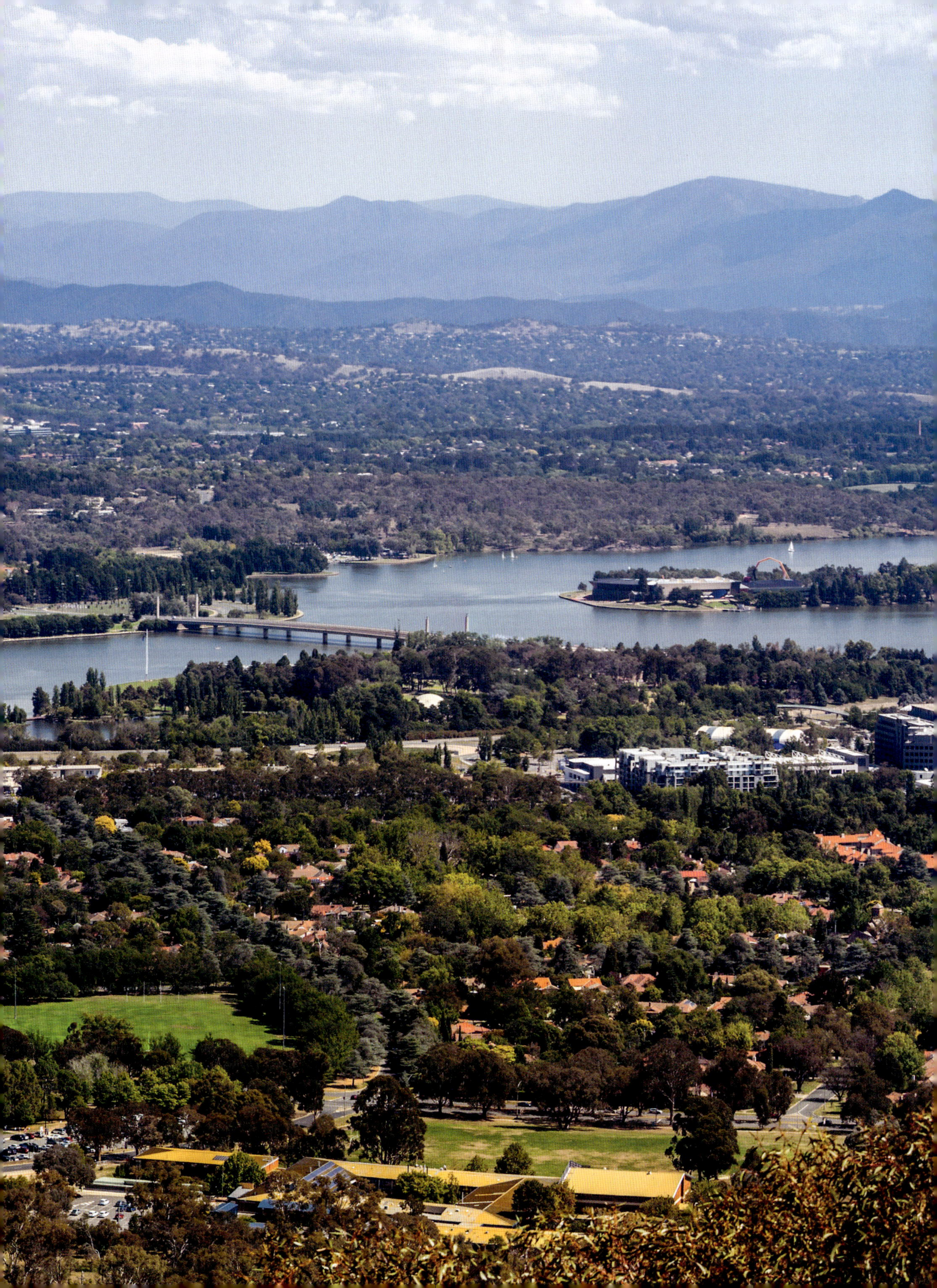

DESTINATION CAPE YORK

Tackle one of Australia's most notorious outback road trips by cycling to the country's northernmost point on a remote ride for highly experienced bike tourers.

On the road north of Cape Tribulation, I'm taking my bike for a walk. The gradient on the Bloomfield Track has suddenly ramped up to 33% and I make it about 100m (330ft) along the climb before I'm off and pushing my bike, something I will be doing for most of this prolonged ascent and for long periods in the days ahead. This one hill is just the first great obstacle along one of the most committing bikes rides possible in Australia.

I'm cycling to Cape York, the Australian mainland's northernmost point, with five friends. Even by the outback's severe standards, this long haul to the top is considered one of the final travelling frontiers, where riders battle roads notorious for sand, dust, corrugations and crocodiles. Few cyclists venture here, and we hear the phrase 'rocks in your head' almost daily, though the only rocks are those on the road.

It's a journey almost entirely on unsealed roads, although it begins on a highway heading north from Cairns, passing the resort town of Port Douglas and rolling on to the Daintree River. Although this will be the easiest part of the journey, we cycle short days to prepare our bodies for the challenge ahead – and also to savour the beauty of this rainforest-draped coastline.

The Daintree River is notoriously a crowded pool of crocodiles, but the real things with bite are the hills beyond. Two ranges separate us from Cape Tribulation, where the bitumen road ends. It's also here that the biggest climb of all awaits, as we set out on the Bloomfield Track. Built despite environmental protests in the 1980s, this rough and rugged 4WD track slows us to a walk – in one long day we'll cover just 40km (25 miles) into Ayton.

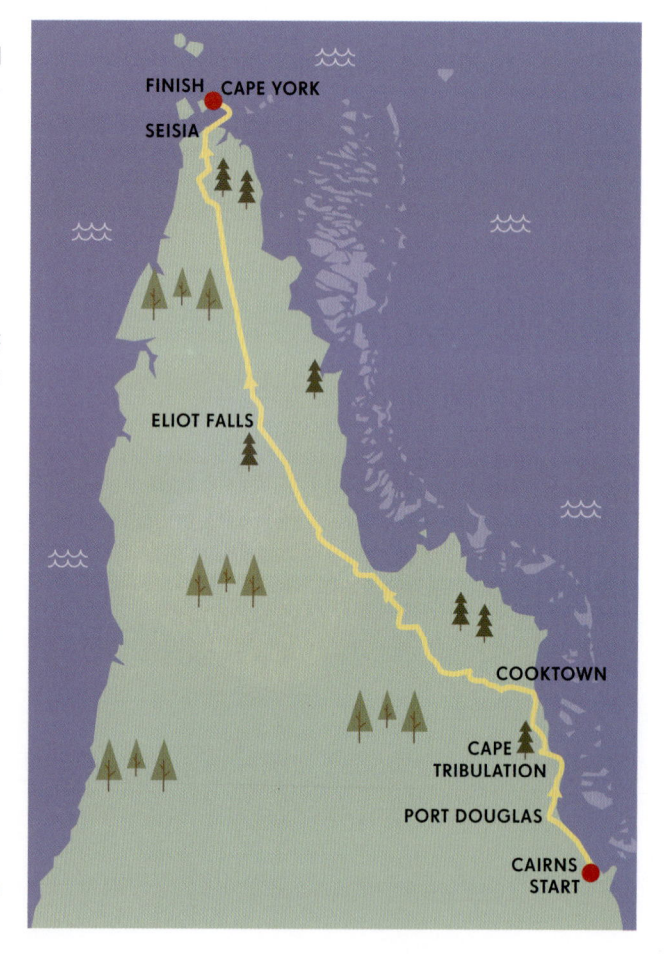

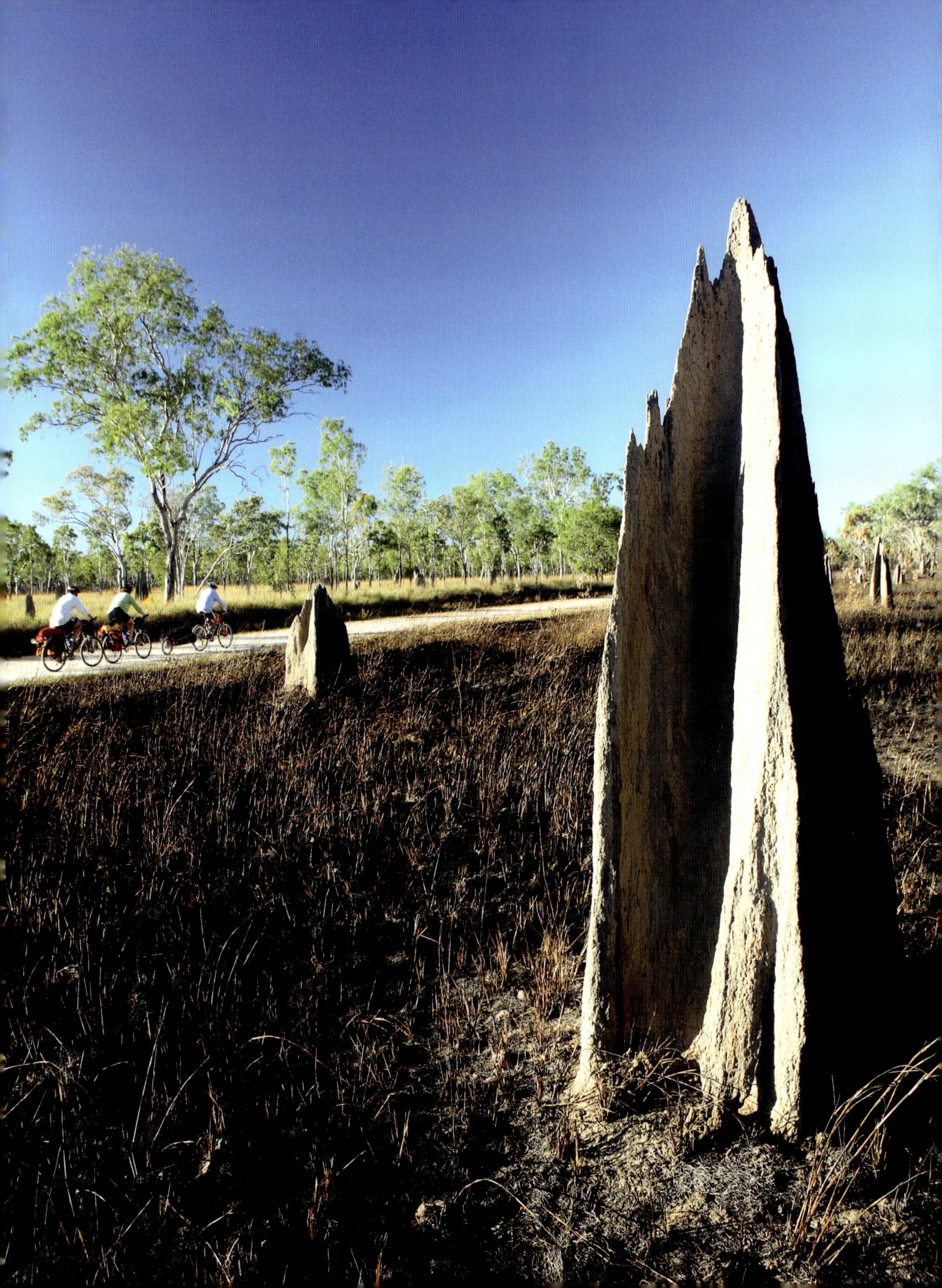

> "The hard work is tempered by the track's beauty as the forest closes around us, then splits open into heathland and the orange glow of grevillea flowers"

'How were the hills?' asks one resident with a knowing smirk. 'Some cyclists who've come through have needed two people pushing each bike to get through those hills.'

Another day of riding beyond is Cooktown, the final town of any size on the peninsula, and despite the challenges of the four days already behind us, it somehow feels like our true beginning. Beyond here, Cape York's reputation goes from scenic to savage, and we now face 270km (168 miles) of sand, corrugations and crocodiles through Rinyirru (Lakefield) National Park just to get to the next roadhouse. The rainforest falls behind, replaced by the sparse savannah woodland that covers so much of northern Australia.

Through the national park, the road becomes a sand pit, and hours pass without sight of another vehicle. These days are glorious and secluded, but at night the corrugations continue to reverberate through our arms. A sign beside the murky Normanby River announces: 'Lost: Brown and White Dog' – it's not hard to put one and one together to equal crocodile. Even our own plans to camp near water are foiled when a crocodile appears in the Laura River beside our camp one night. The next evening we pitch far from water, on the gloriously empty and treeless Nifold Plain, sleeping among tombstone-like termite mounds.

By the time we reach the Peninsula Development Rd, we're halfway to Cape York and only now have we encountered its major road. Our plan has long been to avoid this road as much as possible, for it has no designs on being scenic, only in carving the shortest possible route to the tip.

For the four days we're on the Peninsula Development Rd, we pedal hard in the cool of each morning, pumping out 30km (19 mile) stints between breaks, keen to be off this road and onto the beautifully lonely prospect of the Old Telegraph Track (OTT), more than 300km (186 miles) ahead.

Once the only route to the tip, the unmaintained OTT is Cape York at its best, dotted with waterfalls and swimming holes, but also seemingly the place where almost every grain of sand on the peninsula has made its home. Within 1km (0.6 miles) my bike is buried to its rims in sand, and it takes an hour to ride the first 6km (3.7 miles), pushing our bikes as much as riding them.

The hard work is tempered by the track's beauty as the forest closes around us, then splits open into heathland and the orange glow of grevillea flowers. Termite mounds become castles, rising metres above our heads. We pause to camp and swim at the Dulhunty River and again at Eliot Falls, soaking away the effort of our progress. These are the slowest and best days of the journey.

As we cycle on from Eliot Falls, the tip of Cape York is little more than 130km (80 miles) away. Although we rejoin the firmer Development Rd, we slow our pace, no longer keen for this ride to end. Less than 20km (12 miles) from the top, we turn away west, detouring to Punsand Bay for a night in a campground with the ultimate luxury of showers, and seeing ocean for the first time in two weeks. We can also see the tip of Cape York, stretching finger-like across the eastern horizon.

We can delay no more, and the next morning we begin the short ride to Cape York. We hide our panniers in the bush and pedal to the road's end at Frangipani Beach, where mangroves grip at the sand of the continent's northernmost beach. From its edge, a rough and rugged headland stretches on for a few hundred metres to the spot where the country peters out to a rocky finish. Suitably, it's too rough to ride, and we push our bikes to the small sign announcing Australia's northernmost point. It's an end in every sense – the end of the country and the end of our journey. **AB**

SHIP TO SHORE

You've made it to Cape York. Now how the hell do you get back? Why not add to the sense of journey by sailing back on the only remaining cargo ship in Australia that takes passengers? Boarding in Seisia, a small township 50km (31 miles) from Cape York, the MV *Trinity Bay* sails weekly to Cairns. It's a two-day journey inside the line of the Great Barrier Reef, with lingering views along the Cape York coast.

Opposite from top: mission accomplished; dinner at Punsand Bay; overlooking Frangipani Beach. Previous spread: termite mounds and scorched ground in Lakefield National Park

TOOLKIT

Start // Cairns
Finish // Cape York
Distance // 1200km (745 miles)
Duration // 21 days
Getting there // The ride begins in Cairns, 1,700km (1,050 miles) north of Brisbane. There are flights back to Cairns from Bamaga, 35km (22 miles) south of Cape York.
When to go // The dry season, from around May to September, is the only feasible time to attempt this ride.
What to pack // Cyclists on this route need to be totally self-sufficient, carrying full camping gear and the capacity to haul enough food and water between roadhouses and the small sprinkling of towns.
Tours // Cape York Mountain Bike Adventures (www.capeyorkmtb.com.au) runs eight-day trips, riding from Coen (550km/340 miles north of Cairns) to the tip, using your own bike and camping equipment.
More info // www.tropicalnorthqueensland.org.au

Opposite: the lighthouse at Cape Reinga, the most northerly point of New Zealand

MORE LIKE THIS
GEOGRAPHIC EXTREMITIES

CAPE REINGA, NEW ZEALAND

As on Cape York, there's the option of taking to sand when cycling to New Zealand's northern tip. But unlike the soft, laborious sand of the former, Ninety Mile Beach is as hard as a road, providing an approach with a difference to Cape Reinga. You just need to keep an eye on the tides. Start in Whangarei to avoid the traffic and turmoil of Auckland, and make the most of the Northland climate and beauty by taking the slow approach, looping out to the coastline and beaches around Ngunguru and Ōakura before reaching the celebrated Bay of Islands. From here, it's a more direct ride to Ahipara, at the southern end of Ninety Mile Beach. Though a misleading 88km (55 miles) in length, Ninety Mile Beach is officially classified as a highway, and you'll barely sink into the sand before turning off the beach at Te Paki Stream, returning to roads for the final few kilometres to New Zealand's touted northern point (the true northern point is actually 30km/19 miles away at Surville Cliffs).
Start // Whangarei
Finish // Cape Reinga
Distance // 370km (230 miles)
Duration // 5-7 days

COCKLE CREEK, TASMANIA

Although you can't reach Tasmania's southernmost point by bike (and barely even on foot), you can cycle as far as the southern road end at Cockle Creek, almost in sight of the Southern Ocean and thoughts of Antarctica. Setting out from Hobart, there are plenty of ways to avoid the main highway, by hugging the coast through Kettering and Cygnet (and perhaps detouring across to Bruny Island) and then taking to the coast again on quiet roads on the approach to Dover. As the options slim to a lone road beyond Dover, take a side trip to Hastings Caves (and its thermal swimming pool) before the road switches to gravel for the final, beautiful 20km (12 miles) around the shores of Recherche Bay. Crossing a bridge over Cockle Creek, there's suddenly no way further south on wheels in Australia.
Start // Hobart
Finish // Cockle Creek
Distance // 215km (133 miles)
Duration // 3-4 days

BLUFF, NEW ZEALAND

The southernmost point of New Zealand's South Island is Slope Point. But 50km (31 miles) due west of here, and only slightly further north, the peninsula-set town of Bluff feels more of a journey's end: it's the departure point for ferries south to Stewart Island. To cycle here from Dunedin is to throw in the natural beauty of the Catlins region as a bonus. Out of Dunedin, it's a due-south journey to Papatowai and the Catlins coast, where you'll ride pinched between forest and the South Pacific. The terrain is hilly, the feeling is remote, and it's worth lingering to spend time at places such as Porpoise Bay, where Hector's dolphins are often seen surfing the waves, and lighthouse-topped Nugget Point, with its collection of rocky islets gathered around it like chicks. Pull in at Invercargill and make the 60km (37 mile) return pilgrimage to Stirling Point at Bluff.
Start // Dunedin
Finish // Invercargill
Distance // 330km (205 miles)
Duration // 4-6 days

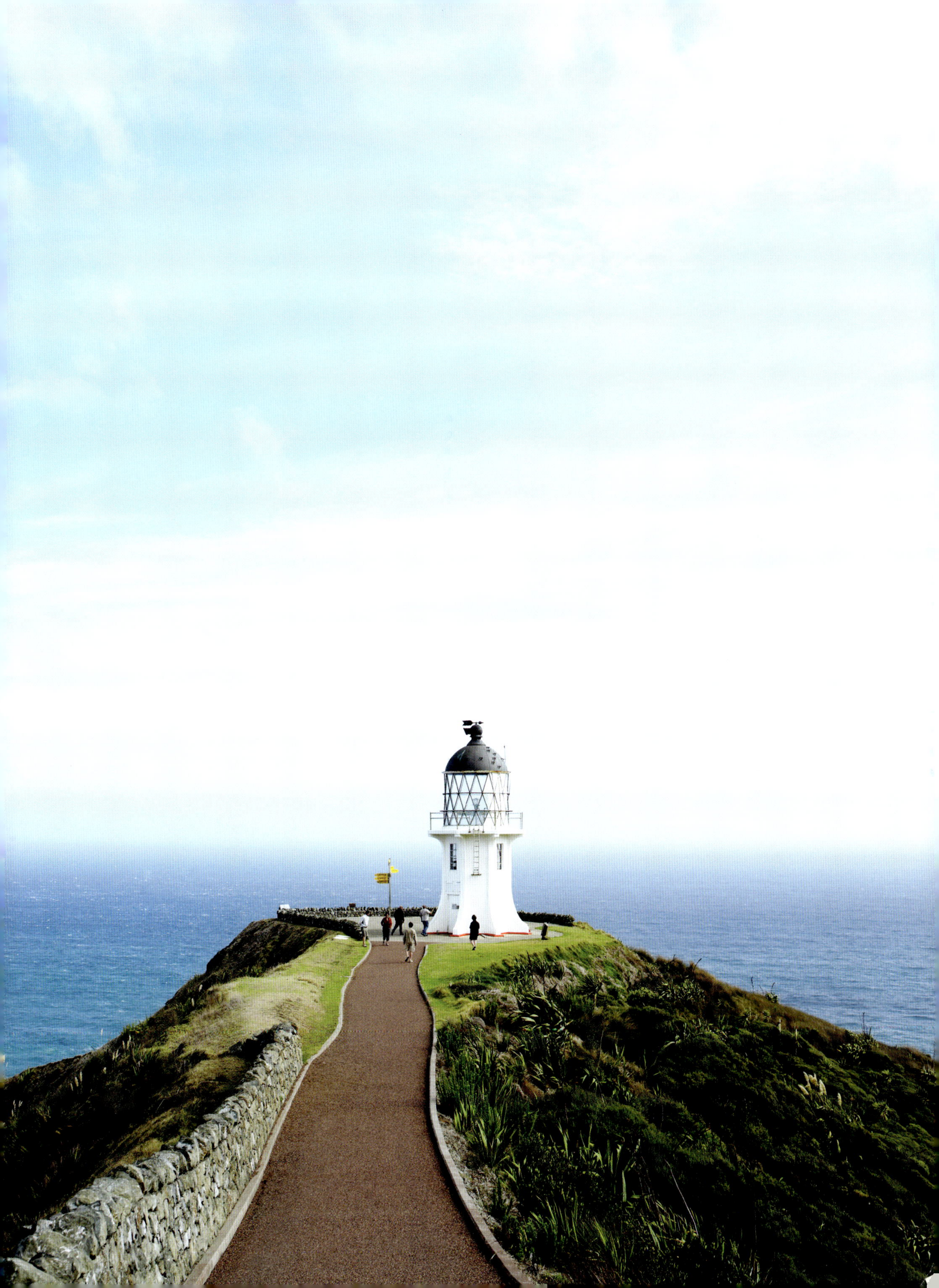

LAKE BURLEY GRIFFIN CIRCUIT

What better way to explore Canberra's museums, art galleries and national monuments than by taking to the car-free path around the lake at the capital's heart?

It's one of those beautiful, crisp autumn days in Canberra, the kind that starts off quite fresh, but then rewards you with a clearing blue sky and not a breath of wind. Finishing off my coffee and brunch at Bean and Table on the Kingston Foreshore, I can't help but feel lucky as I scan my surroundings. The lake is still enough to make perfect reflections of the shoreline buildings, with just the rippled wakes of black swans shimmering in the distance. My day off has started well, and I'm keen to spend it on my bike. For a ride in Canberra to match the occasion, it has to be a circuit all the way around Lake Burley Griffin, with a couple of stops thrown in for good measure.

Today, the lake is the city centre's defining feature, but it wasn't until 1963 – half a century after Canberra was founded – that the Molonglo River was dammed to achieve the vision of the capital's designer, Walter Burley Griffin. The snaking lakeshores where the rising waters finally stopped are bounded closely by bike paths, with only a few necessary inland excursions, like the one around Government House, at the southern end of the Scrivener Dam.

As I begin my clockwise loop, passing under Kings Avenue Bridge, there's a mix of runners, walkers and fellow cyclists passing the resplendent lines of deciduous trees, their

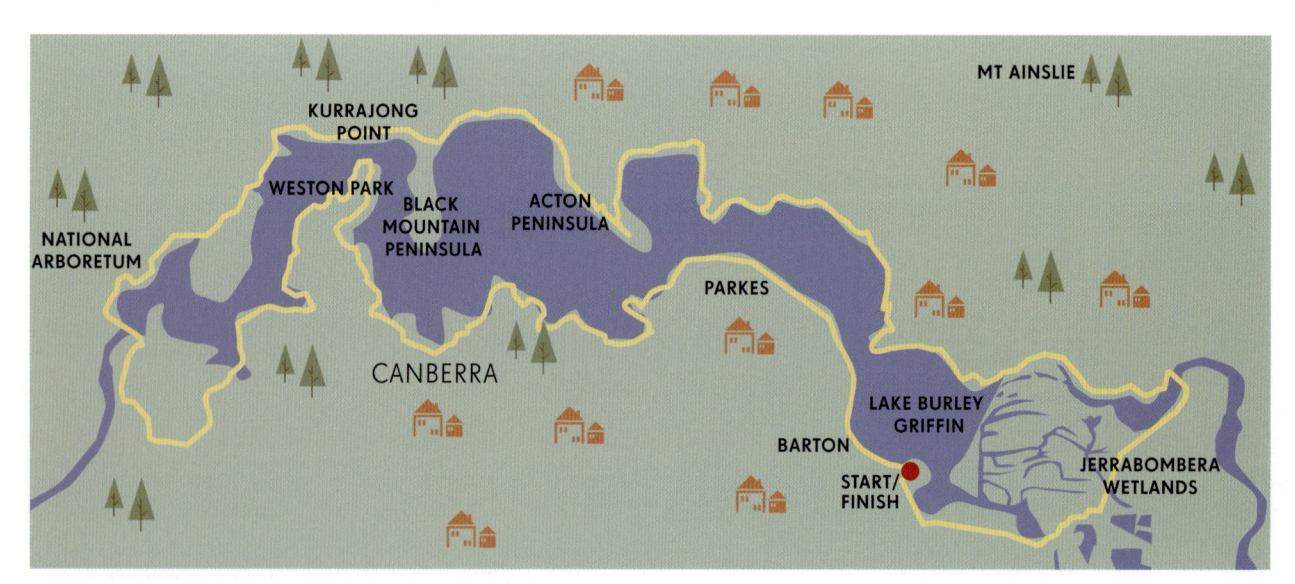

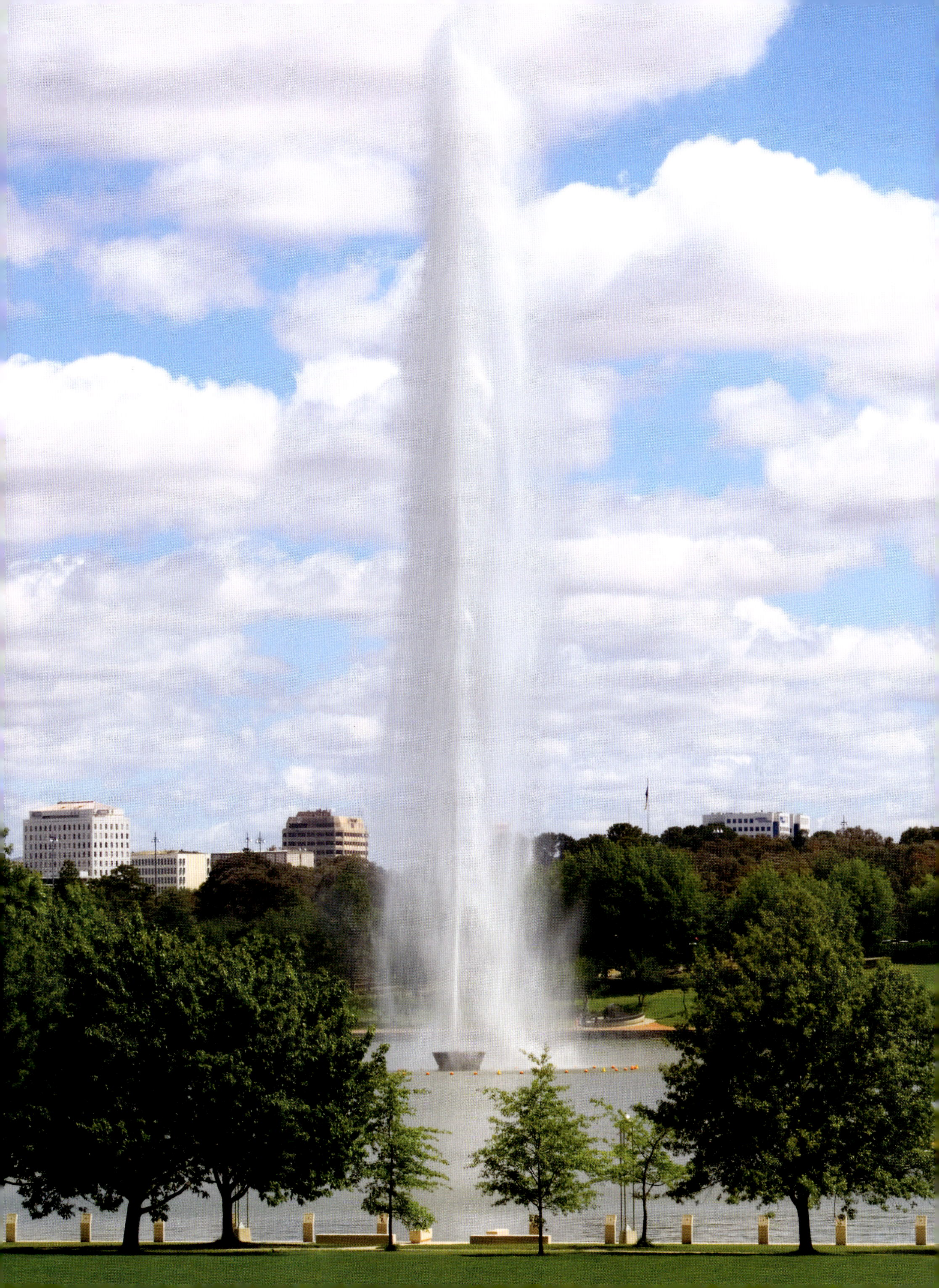

vivid oranges, reds and browns set off against the blue sky. To the left across the lawns is the sparse, white form of Old Parliament House, framed by the National Gallery, National Portrait Gallery and National Library. On the water to my right, a lone kayaker glides along, while across the lake in the distance, I can make out the dome of the Australian War Memorial at the foot of Mt Ainslie.

Passing under Commonwealth Avenue Bridge, I leave behind the formal geometry of the heart of government, to trace more winding paths along Yarralumla's shores, the striking colours of the oak trees to one side, and on the other, the ducks floating between the yachts in Lotus Bay, which look like they could tell a story or two about some of our past politicians.

I'm not here for the yacht club, and hurry on to Weston Park on its promontory. I often think that if ever a visitor to Australia asked me where they could see a kangaroo, this is where I'd take them. They don't disappoint this time: pretty quickly, I spot the small mob of roos that seem to call this section of the park home. The reputation of the 'Bush Capital' is intact. Across the water looms Black Mountain with the unmistakable white Telstra Tower atop it, glinting in the sun. I spare a thought for the cyclists making their way up to the summit; today I'm quite content to be looking at it from a distance.

I reach my favourite section of the cycle path, which works its way between a forest of pine trees, before crossing a clackity wooden bridge. Not far off, golfers are teeing off on the Royal Canberra's course, and on the opposite shore I see the groves of the National Arboretum – only a short diversion from the path, with a wonderful overlook of the city.

The path climbs briefly as it ducks around Government House, then zooms down the other side. I make sure I let off a gleeful 'wheech' noise as I ride through a short underpass tunnel. A cyclist heading the other way smiles and joins in, and I can't help but laugh. Making my way over the wall of the Scrivener Dam, I look downstream to see if I can spot any of the four giraffes from the nearby National Zoo and Aquarium. If I'm lucky, I can just about make out their craning necks.

I rarely stop to take in the view on my rides around Canberra, but I do so this time after another short climb. Looking back on where I've come from, Weston Park seems almost at touching distance, and there's that old wooden bridge. That's one joy of cycling around Lake Burley Griffin: being able to pick out the same landmarks from different vantage points.

– EPIC BIKE RIDES OF AUSTRALIA & NEW ZEALAND –

From the lookout at Black Mountain Peninsula, I get a preview of the large, yellow arch of the National Museum of Australia on the next spur of land along. The cycle path runs right to the front entrance. I park the bike for a bit, engaging with Australia's past in the social history exhibitions – and enjoying coffee, cake and lake views in the sunshine at the museum's outdoor cafe.

The final quarter of the ride, back under Commonwealth Avenue Bridge and east along the lake, takes the morning's reflections and turns them around. There's little time to appreciate the vista up to Parliament House and its flagpole before I feel the mist on skin – carried over from the plume of the Captain Cook Memorial Jet just offshore. Together with another Canberra landmark at the eastern end of Commonwealth Park, the National Carillon with its 57 bells, it makes a pair of 'pillars' framing the curving shore that makes a sublime vantage point for sunrises and sunsets.

I won't be there this time round for close of day – I intend to end the ride before that with a drink and bowl of chips at the Walt and Burley pub back at the Kingston Foreshore – but before I sign off, I have one last stretch of the Lake Burley Griffin to take in. The Jerrabomberra Wetlands, where the Molonglo River opens into the lake, provides an important breeding habitat for birds, but it's another type of animal that draws my attention: a herd of black Angus cows, barely three kilometres from Capital Hill.

Kangaroos and giraffes at one end of the lake, grazing cattle at the other – I've closed the Canberra loop. **BM**

WONDER IN THE WATER

Just as the Jet d'Eau is an icon of Lake Geneva, the Captain Cook Memorial Jet is one of the standout sights of Australia's capital. Opened in 1970 in imitation of its Swiss cousin, Canberra's jet can shoot an impressive six tonnes of water into the air at speeds of up to 260km/h (160mph), reaching heights of 147m (482ft). When a breeze is blowing, the water fans out, creating a spectacular rainbow that falls towards the lake. To see it in action, visit between 11am and 2pm.

Opposite from top: Australia's National Portrait Gallery; a kangaroo in Canberra's Weston Park. Previous spread: the city's Captain Cook Memorial Jet

TOOLKIT

Start/Finish // Kingston Foreshore
Distance // 32km (20 miles)
Duration // 2-3 hours
Getting there // Canberra is a 3-hour drive or 4-hour train ride from Sydney. Alternatively, Canberra Airport is 10km (6 miles) from the city centre.
When to go // Although this is a route you can tackle all year round, it's worth visiting Canberra during autumn or spring to see the city at its best.
Where to stay // Hotels and rentals in the Kingston area allow easy access to the cycle path if you choose to start at Kingston Foreshore.
More info // www.transport.act.gov.au

Opposite: a rainbow sculpture made of shipping containers on the Fremantle Public Art Trail

MORE LIKE THIS
ARTS AND CULTURE

FREMANTLE PUBLIC ART TRAIL, WESTERN AUSTRALIA

A score of artworks are dotted around the streets of Fremantle, a port on the Indian Ocean, 30 minutes from Perth. Down by Fremantle Fishing Boat Harbour you can see tributes in bronze to the fishermen who worked here, as well as to Bon Scott, the lead singer of AC/DC. Begin a little way up the Swan River with a leisurely cycle through the streets of East Fremantle, where some 16 artworks have been picked out on a map, before taking the 7.5km (4.5 mile) Fremantle Highlights cycle trail to stop by the World-Heritage listed Fremantle Prison, and the Fremantle Arts Centre, home to 1500 pieces in a Gothic building from the 1860s.
Start // East Fremantle Town Hall
Finish // Kings Square, Fremantle
Distance // 15km (9 miles)
More info // www.destinationperth.com.au

SILO ART TRAIL, VICTORIA

In the Wimmera Mallee region of western Victoria, the Silo Art Trail counts as Australia's largest outdoor gallery. The plan – conceived in 2006 – to transform otherwise-uninteresting grain silos into canvases for bold murals has morphed into a popular tourist attraction. The full trail from Rupanyup to Horsham runs for 600km (370 miles) to take in 13 pieces of silo art, which each seek to reflect stories from the community where they are located. Themes range from celebrating local Indigenous culture to farming and sport. A more manageable half-day route, best explored on a road bike, incorporates the first three of the giant art installations, at Rupanyup, Sheep Hills and Brim.
Start // Rupanyup
Finish // Brim
Distance // 72km (44 miles)
More info // www.siloarttrail.com

EAST GIPPSLAND RAIL TRAIL, VICTORIA

Opened in 2006, the East Gippsland Rail Trail is a popular car-free route enabling cyclists to explore the diverse landscapes of northeastern Victoria. Trail users now have a new experience to look forward to along the way: a public outdoor art gallery entitled Under The Surface. Local and international artists have created works at five sites, including the large trestle bridge at Nicholson and an old butter factory turned brewery. The pieces were made in collaboration with members of the Gunaikurnai community to help connect rail trail users to the stories of the Traditional Owners of the land.
Start // Orbost
Finish // Bairnsdale
Distance // 96km (60 miles)
More info // www.visiteastgippsland.com.au

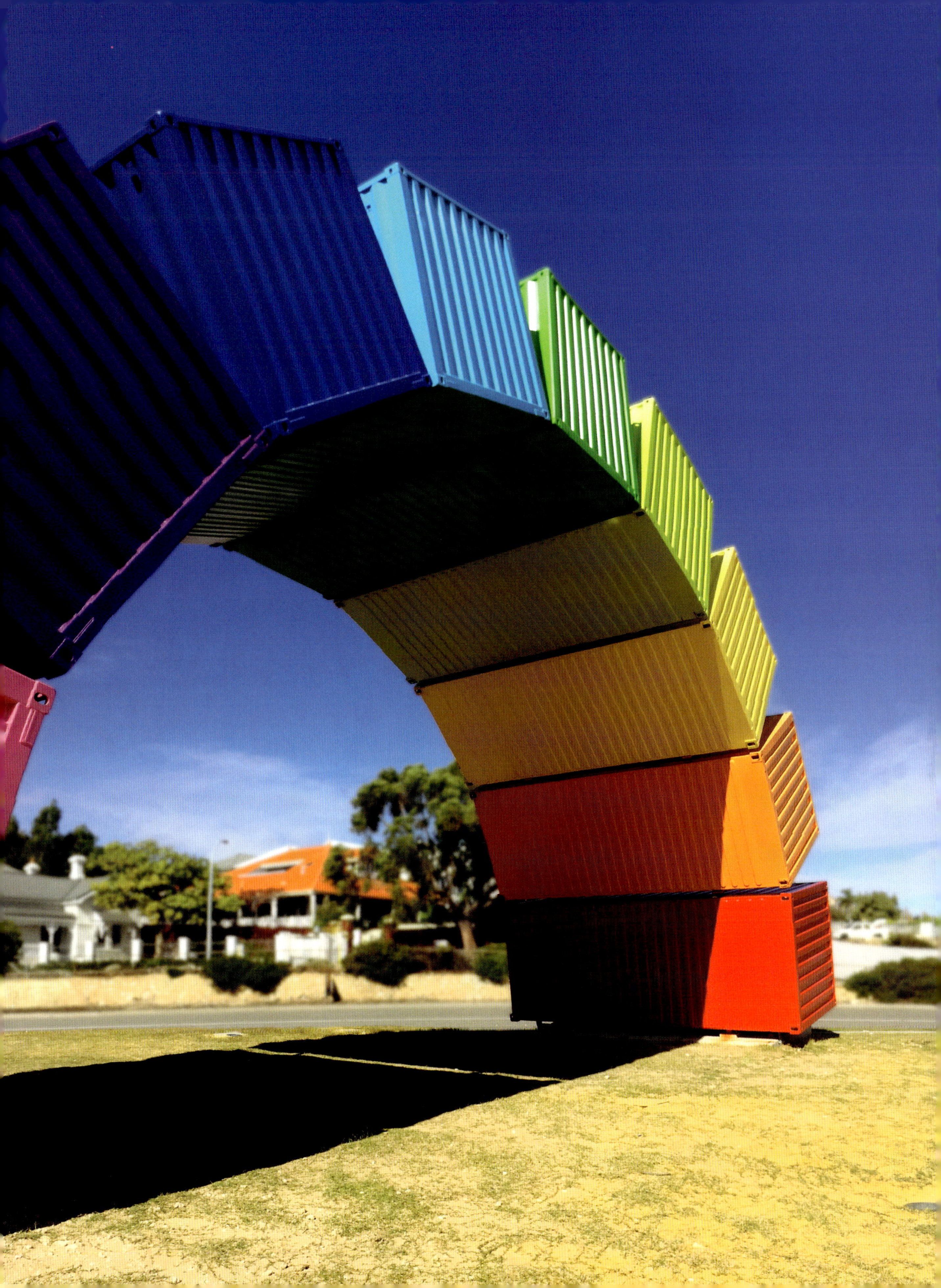

CANBERRA'S CENTENARY TRAIL

Canberra has more nature reserves than government departments, as you'll discover on a view-filled mountain bike ride around the Australian Capital Territory.

An extra big breakfast and a double shot of coffee at Lonsdale Street Roasters: fuel for the long ride ahead of me on the Canberra Centenary Trail. Set up in 2013 to mark 100 years since Australia's new capital was given its name and role, the entire trail – of which I'm planning to explore large portions – is 145km (90 miles) long. This hiking and cycling route pieces together gravel firetrails, dirt singletrack and suburban cycle paths, creating an ultimate lap around Canberra, its varied landscapes and historic sights.

From the cafe in Braddon, I immediately ride towards the trailhead at the base of Mt Ainslie, next to the Australian War Memorial, and map out the day ahead from the information board. My goal is to ride the Centenary Trail anti-clockwise, through Canberra's northern suburbs and then all the way around until Mt Stromlo, a total distance of 90km (56 miles). It's a well-marked route, dotted with official signage showing a logo of twin C-curve tracks on a blue-green background.

This first section runs through Mt Ainslie and Mt Majura nature reserves, two of the 39 that make up Canberra Nature Park. I've been here many times before, sometimes diverting off the firetrail to explore the mountain bike (MTB) trails nearby at Majura Pines. I pass through a bridleway gate and soon enough I'm cycling up the first climb of the day. It isn't long, but some sections are steep. At the top, a glance over my left shoulder travels all the way to the low hills past Gungahlin. After the descent, it's a singletrack run to the Hughie Edwards VC Rest Area, and a quick break in the shade of a tree.

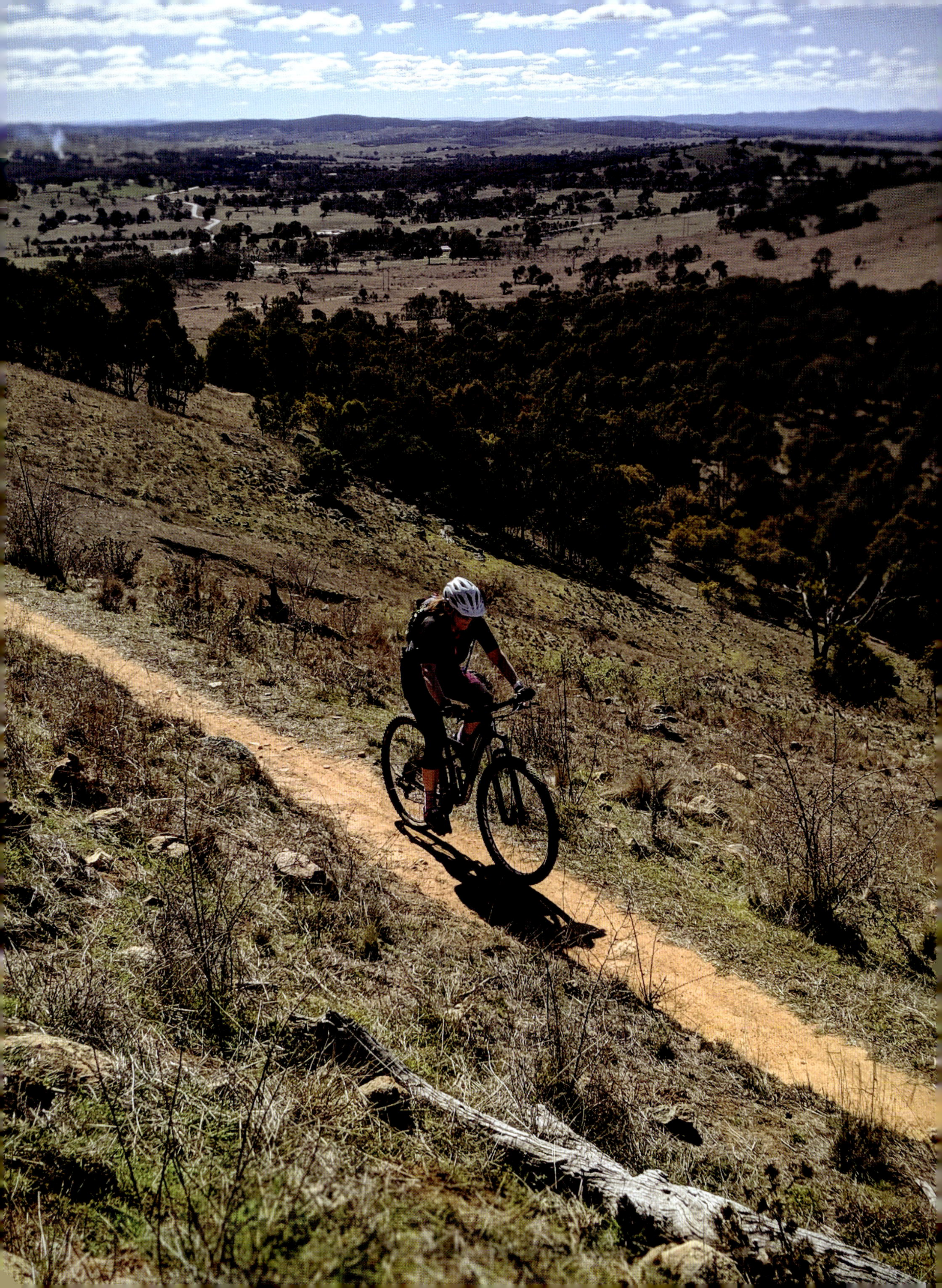

From here the trail leads me safely under the Federal Highway and I enter the Goorooyarroo Nature Reserve. Once again, I'm riding on steeper terrain through the trees, but I know I'll be rewarded with a downhill soon. After a few more kilometres, I reach the Mulligans Flat Woodland Sanctuary and its big, gated fence that keeps the foxes, cats and rabbits from the endangered bettongs and quolls in its box-gum woodland. I stop to take a look at the old corrugated-iron shearing shed here, before continuing towards Forde.

A short ride along the cycle path ensues before the next significant climb on the Centenary Trail – Oak Hill. This section is located on old pasture lands, and I'm afforded sweeping views as I track a fence line that borders New South Wales. Suddenly, the climb begins to bite, and as I get closer to the top, I wonder if I will be reduced to walking. The relief at being able to pedal all the way justifies the photo stop – as does the vista of Canberra's northern districts. A few kilometres on, I reach the Northern Border Campsite.

The next section of the track proves to be my favourite, and I'm grinning from ear to ear while winding in and out of the gum trees. It's not long now before the significant climb of One Tree Hill – at 863m (2831ft), the highest point I'll reach on the trail, and the spot from which the first surveys of the region

"Just a few kilometres away from the city centre, I feel as though I'm deep in the countryside"

were made in 1829. It's a hard effort getting to the top (the last few metres are on foot only), but worth it for the prize views of Canberra's Molonglo Valley. The fast, flowing kilometres that follow lead me to the village of Hall, a rare reminder of the rural communities that existed before the land was given over to the Australian Capital Territory. It's definitely time for some food – I settle for a bowl of chips and a steak sandwich at the George Harcourt Inn.

The post-lunch part of the Centenary Trail uses suburban cycle paths for a faster ride all the way to Belconnen and onwards to Bruce Ridge. This area is home to some fantastic singletrack through the eucalypt forest, but those mountain bike trails will keep for another day. Instead, I continue towards Black Mountain Reserve.

The firetrails here are great fun: some challenging climbs are interspersed with thrilling downhills. Just a few kilometres

MT STROMLO

Stromlo Forest Park is just 15 minutes west of the city centre – a 12sq-km site on the slopes of 770m/2530ft-high Mt Stromlo, with its hilltop observatory. The park has over 50km (31 miles) of MTB trails, suited to riders of all abilities, plus bike hire and a shuttle service to take riders from the lower car park all the way to the top. The area is also popular with trail runners, walkers and equestrian riders, making it Australia's premier multi-use recreational sporting facility.

Left to right: the Australian War Memorial, close to the ride's starting point; the National Arboretum. Previous spread: the Centenary Trail uses dirt tracks

away from the city centre, I feel as though I'm deep in the countryside. It's a thought I've had many times today – though not yet so close to the heart of the capital – and is something I really love about the Centenary Trail.

After linking up with another cycle path, and a fast downhill, I arrive at the National Arboretum. Riding through the hundred-year-old cork-oak forest, I decide to divert off the Centenary Trail. There are so many MTB tracks that weave in and out of the different sections, and it's too good an opportunity to pass up. It's enjoyably easy to incorporate these side trails into my ride – surely what the route designers had in mind when they pieced it all together. I cycle all the way to the top of Dairy Farmers Hill to see the surrounding landscape bathed in the golden light of late afternoon. The panorama lets me see not only where I've ridden from, but also out towards the Brindabella Range and my final destination – Mt Stromlo.

Leaving the arboretum behind, I rejoin the Centenary Trail on a bike path tracking right alongside the Molonglo River. Just 8km (5 miles) remain until I reach my destination – Mt Stromlo Forest Park. Multiple mountain bikers are busy riding some of Australia's premier MTB trails, but I'm ready to cap off my perfect day with a deserved drink under the zigzag awning of the Handlebar cafe. **BM**

TOOLKIT

Start/Finish // Parliament House (for trailhead 1)
Distance // 145km (90 miles)
Duration // 2-3 days
Getting there // Canberra is 3 hours from Sydney by car, and 4 hours by train. Its airport is 10km (6 miles) from the city centre.
When to go // The Centenary Trail is accessible year-round.
Where to eat // There are several good eateries to choose from in the historic village of Hall.
Things to know // Although it's possible to ride the Centenary Trail on a gravel bike, a mountain bike is most people's preferred choice.
More info // www.parks.act.gov.au

Opposite: the Thredbo Valley Track near Lake Crackenback

MORE LIKE THIS
STUNNING VISTAS AND CHANGING LANDSCAPES

THREDBO VALLEY TRACK, NEW SOUTH WALES

The Thredbo Valley Track in the Snowy Mountains is a highlight of the region for cyclists. This mountain bike ride begins at the resort of Thredbo and involves taking a chairlift to the start of the trailhead. From here, the singletrack flows downhill all the way to the Gaden Trout Hatchery. This scenic corridor tracks the Thredbo River in its entirety. Along the way, there are several impressive suspension bridges, allowing riders to cross the river at intervals. Recently, the trail was extended by 15km (9 miles) from the resort of Lake Crackenback to the Gaden Trout Hatchery. This section of trail contains more challenging terrain and is more suitable for intermediate to advanced riders.
Start // Thredbo
Finish // Gaden Trout Hatchery
Distance: 37km (23 miles)
More info //
www.nationalparks.nsw.gov.au

BRISBANE VALLEY RAIL TRAIL, QUEENSLAND

Following the old route of the Brisbane Valley railway line that closed in the early 1990s, this is Australia's longest rail trail, and a great way to explore the history of this part of southeast Queensland. The dirt route is accessible year-round, and its gentle gradients make it suitable for all levels of fitness. Amenity stops are located every 20km (12 miles), which makes planning a multi-day trip easier. Highlights of the trail include the Lockyer Creek Bridge, Bellevue Homestead and the Yimbun tunnel. Well-preserved old railway stations and museums along the route give a hint of its historic significance. Free camping is allowed at several spots along the trail, making it very popular for short bikepacking trips.
Start // Wulkuraka Station, Ipswich
Finish // Yarraman
Distance // 161km (100 miles)
More info // www.tmr.qld.gov.au/bvrt

TASMANIAN TRAIL, TASMANIA

This multi-use trail is the only one of its kind in Tasmania, and traverses the state from north to south. It's composed of gravel trails and forestry roads, and is perfect for exploring on a mountain bike. The long-distance route has been split into sections, which can be completed comfortably over the course of eight days – or less for those seeking a harder challenge. Sign markers are located across 95% of the trail. The landscape changes markedly from fertile river valleys to the open plains of the Central Plateau. Tasmania's unique fauna and flora is on display throughout. For the best experience, ride the trail in the summer months.
Start // Devonport
Finish // Dover
Distance // 465km (281 miles)
More info //
www.tasmaniantrail.com.au

Thredbo Valley Track

Destination	Distance
Bullocks Flat - Skitube	0.5km
The Diggings	2.8km
Ngarigo	7.4km
Bridge 5	8.0km
Thredbo Village	16.7km

Track Rules
- Cyclists give way to walkers
- No riding when track is wet or closed
- Watch out for fallen trees, obstacles or rocks
- Plan your trip - know your ability

for more information on IMBA rules of the trail and track grading go to www.imba-au.com

TRACK OPEN

- EPIC BIKE RIDES OF AUSTRALIA & NEW ZEALAND -

GEARS AND BEERS AT WAGGA WAGGA

A rural town surrounded by canola farms, Wagga Wagga has become the home of Australia's most beloved gravel cycling event.

– EPIC BIKE RIDES OF AUSTRALIA & NEW ZEALAND –

As we rolled out of the motel at 6.30am on an October morning, the spring air was crisp and clear. The sun was gently making its way down the sleepy streets of town and the unmistakeable hum of bicycle wheels echoed around us. It was the morning of the Wagga Wagga Gears and Beers 'Dirty 130' ride, and the town centre was quietly buzzing with hundreds of like-minded gravel grinders.

My friend and I have been nudging each other into different endurance adventures and events since we met, and our pilgrimage to Wagga was no different. The plan was hatched in the depths of winter: ride from my home in Bright to Albury on the first day, then Albury to Wagga on the second, and then ride the Wagga Gears and Beers event on the third. The total trip, including the 130km (81 mile) event in Wagga, covered 350km (217 miles) across rail trails, gravel roads, back streets and bitumen. We carried a change of clothes and stayed at motels along the way – classic credit-card touring.

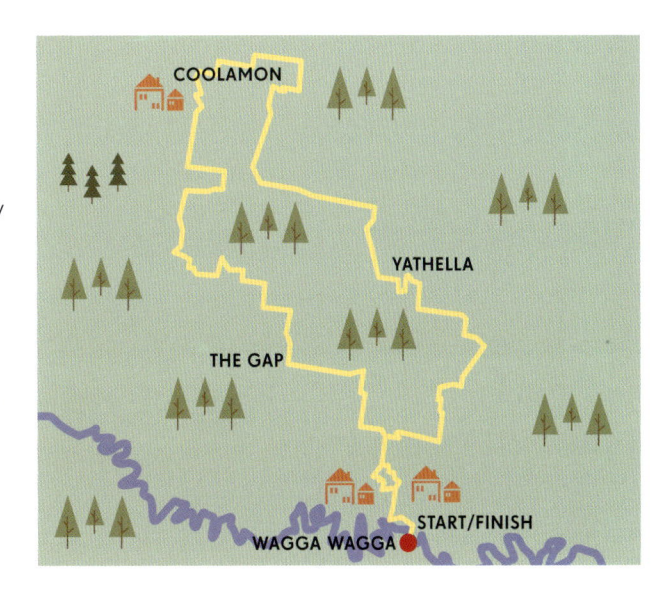

Wagga Wagga is in the middle of New South Wales, and certainly isn't the first town that comes to mind as a cycling destination. But since 2014, the Gears and Beers event has exposed some of the finest dirt roads in Australia. Why the title? First, you churn the gears, and then you enjoy the beers. A craft beer festival featuring regional brewers and live music awaits all riders at the finish line; the ideal Sunday afternoon for any cyclist.

Because of the nature of endurance sports, many gravel events appeal to the competitively minded and dedicated athlete at the expense of the wider community of cyclists. But this is not the case with the Gears and Beers festival. As I will learn, the 130km (81 mile) course is enough to challenge any calibre of rider when tackled at pace. But the smorgasbord of courses surrounding the main event encourage thousands of participants from all walks of life. The 10km (6 mile) 'Strawberry Ride' takes kids and adults alike through cycle paths and strawberry farms before looping back into town; the 'Filthy 50' is a scenic 50km (31 mile) route catering to all bikes, from cheap hardtails to purebred road bikes, with a healthy dose of dusty roads and pinchy hills. And if you feel your fitness lies somewhere in between, there are also 30km (19 mile) and 115km (71 mile) courses to choose.

But back to the flagship event. As an outsider, you'd be confused by the rabble of riders at the start line of the Dirty 130. Some are clearly national-level athletes with logoed jerseys and shiny bikes, while others have rolled out in shorts and a hoodie. Some are repping their local cycling club's kit, while others are dressed in Hawaiian shirts in preparation for post-ride festivities. My friend and I have feet in both camps.

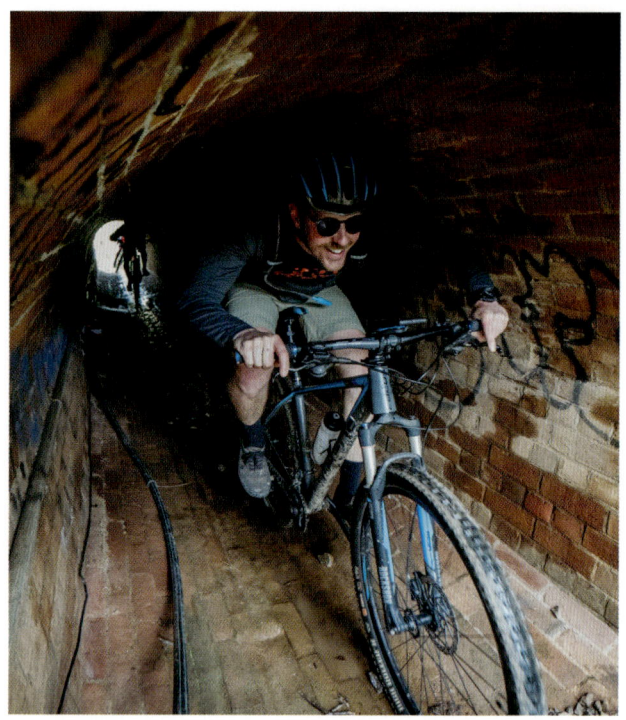

> *"There are no timing chips attached to any bikes, because this is not a race. This is a ride, and you can go as hard or as cruisey as you like"*

After a charismatic spiel by the event organisers, we roll onto the course via the town's main street. There are no timing chips attached to any bikes, because this is not a race. This is a ride, and you can go as hard or as cruisey as you like. Of course, the front bunch will always urge each other to set an impressive pace, and somehow I'm caught in this early rush of enthusiasm. As we enter the first gravel section, the sun is just breaking above the horizon, and the riders in front of me are veiled in a silhouette of dust. The pace quickens again, splitting riders into naturally selected groups. Once I find my group of similarly fit (or unfit) buddies, we settle into a rhythm and prepare for a long day.

Zigzagging through endless farmland dotted with grain silos, I'm reminded of just how good the Wagga gravel roads are. Some are public roads and others are private, but all of them have the smoothest dirt I've ever ridden. Farmers from around the area have opened up their gates and paddocks to allow the event to pass through. They stand on the side of the road cheering with their kids while sitting back enjoying a coffee. Each section of road has its own flavour according to the farmland; some are a deep brown and ready for planting, while others have become pale white from the many hours that trucks and utes have passed over them.

As we enter the halfway mark at Coolamon, I thank my new friends for the tow and pull off to enjoy the generous refreshments waiting at the feed station here. All the event marshals and volunteers are just happy to be there; they're helpful and friendly, and send everyone on their way with a cupcake and hydration tablet. Some riders stay to sip a coffee, while others are keen to hit the road again and beat their mates to the finish. And that's the beauty of Gears and Beers: you ride it how you please.

After some ridiculously fun sections of backroad animal tracks and technical descents, the roads open up again at the 100km (60 mile) mark. I realise that my legs are actually cooked, and a foreboding bonk is beginning to set in. But just as I start counting down the kilometres, the course gives us its last hurrah: a meadow of head-high canola flowers. Suddenly I'm surrounded by a wall of glistening yellow on either side, and any hint of weariness leaves my body. After this brief moment of bliss, it's head down and high gearing across the flat plains back to town.

Slumping on the cool grass at the finish line, I crack open one of the many craft beers on offer. I'm actually more of a wine girl – but on this one day, beer has never tasted better. Through the expanding throng of riders, I eventually find my mate, and he proceeds to tell me all about his epic day up at the pointy end of the peloton. As the live music kicks off and we wipe the dust from our faces with an air of complete satisfaction, we're already hatching goals and plans for next year's Gears and Beers. **GVM**

FLEMISH FIZZ

What is it with beers and cycling? There's as much history as there is marketing to this match made in heaven. Flanders, the home of cyclo-cross and gravel sectors – and arguably where gravel riding originated – is obsessed with the golden liquid. While now sponsored by lotteries and tiling companies, cycling teams from this Belgian region were once backed by breweries. The professional podiums still pay homage to this history with gigantic glasses of beer for the winners.

Left to right: riding out from Wagga in the early light; beer time; the route features unusual challenges; the post-ride party. Previous spread: crossing the famous canola fields

TOOLKIT

Start/Finish // Victory Memorial Gardens, Wagga Wagga
Distance // 130km (80 miles) for the 'Dirty 130,' plus shorter-distance events
Getting there // Wagga is about a 1.5-hour drive from Albury, or 5 hours from Melbourne.
When to go // The event is usually held in the middle of spring, but check the website to confirm dates.
What to pack // While there is a feed station at Coolamon, you will still want to pack an appropriate amount of snacks and water.
Where to stay // There are many accommodation options in Wagga, catering to any taste or budget.
Things to know // Gears and Beers is organised by the Wollundry Rotary Club of Wagga Wagga with 100% of all rider registrations going to charity thanks to the event sponsors and volunteers.
More info // www.gearsandbeers.org.au

Opposite: riding amid the trees on the Great Otways Gravel Grind

MORE LIKE THIS
GREAT GRAVEL CHALLENGES

GRAVELISTA, VICTORIA

If you're seeking a more competitive element for your gravel rides, look no further than this one in Beechworth, Victoria. A recent addition to the gravel calendar, it has already earned a spot in the UCI Gravel World Series with its 120km (75 mile) course, but there's also a shorter one for the less driven. The roads surrounding Beechworth include the magical forests of the Chiltern – Mt Pilot National Park. The landscape is lush and mossy at the time of year this event is held, and provides a scenic tour of the high country outskirts as well as a suffer fest. The undulating terrain is a brilliant mix of tar and 'champagne gravel', before the dauntingly steep climb before the finish line. A tough but rewarding course, the 120km edition is one for the seasoned gravel kings and queens. Beechworth itself is a historic gold-rush era town, but the mines have long made way for flourishing antiques stores, bakeries and restaurants.
Start/Finish // Beechworth, Victoria
Distance // 80km (49 miles) or 120km (74 miles)
More info // www.gravelista.cc

GREAT OTWAYS GRAVEL GRIND, VICTORIA

A little closer to Melbourne, the Great Otways Gravel Grind is a new addition to the longstanding Otway Odyssey mountain bike marathon. The gravel edition of this race occurs the day after the mountain bike event, throwing in a few, fun twists to the typical gravel adventure race. Great Otway National Park has some of the lushest terrain in Victoria, with rolling hills, tall ferns and ancient trees stretching back from the coastline. During the race, the roads are completely closed, with zero traffic hindering your good times. There are also 'time-out zones' so you can wait for your friends to catch up without sacrificing your own results. The closest towns to the event centre are Forrest and Apollo Bay – holiday destinations in their own right. Many riders compete in both the mountain bike and gravel race over the weekend, but regardless of your goals, stay a few days either side to enjoy the Great Otways.
Start/Finish // Forrest, Victoria
Distance // 49km (30 miles) or 97km (60 miles)
More info // gogg.rapidascent.com.au

GIRLS GO GRAVEL, QUEENSLAND

This one's for the girls! Get your team together to ride this intermediate-friendly gravel event over two days on the balmy Sunshine Coast. Girls Go Gravel takes all the best parts of gravel and presents them in a non-competitive and achievable format over the course of a weekend. Think glamping, wine tasting, BBQs and vehicle-supported rides through the hinterland and forest roads of the Sunshine Coast. If that still sounds a little overwhelming, you'll be accompanied by experienced ride leaders to teach you all the tips and tricks of the gravel trade. The July edition of the event is highly coveted among southerners, providing a summery escape in the depths of winter. And the luxury yurts at the Noosa Eco Retreat are the perfect accommodation for such an event, catering to social downtime off the bikes. If you're new to the sport – or just looking for the best hen party ever – the Girls Go Gravel event is an easy way in to multi-day gravel adventures.
Start/Finish // Pomona, Queensland
Distance // 45km (28 miles) on day 1; 40km (25 miles) on day 2
More info // www.ridesunshinecoast.com

© Courtesy of Rapid Ascent

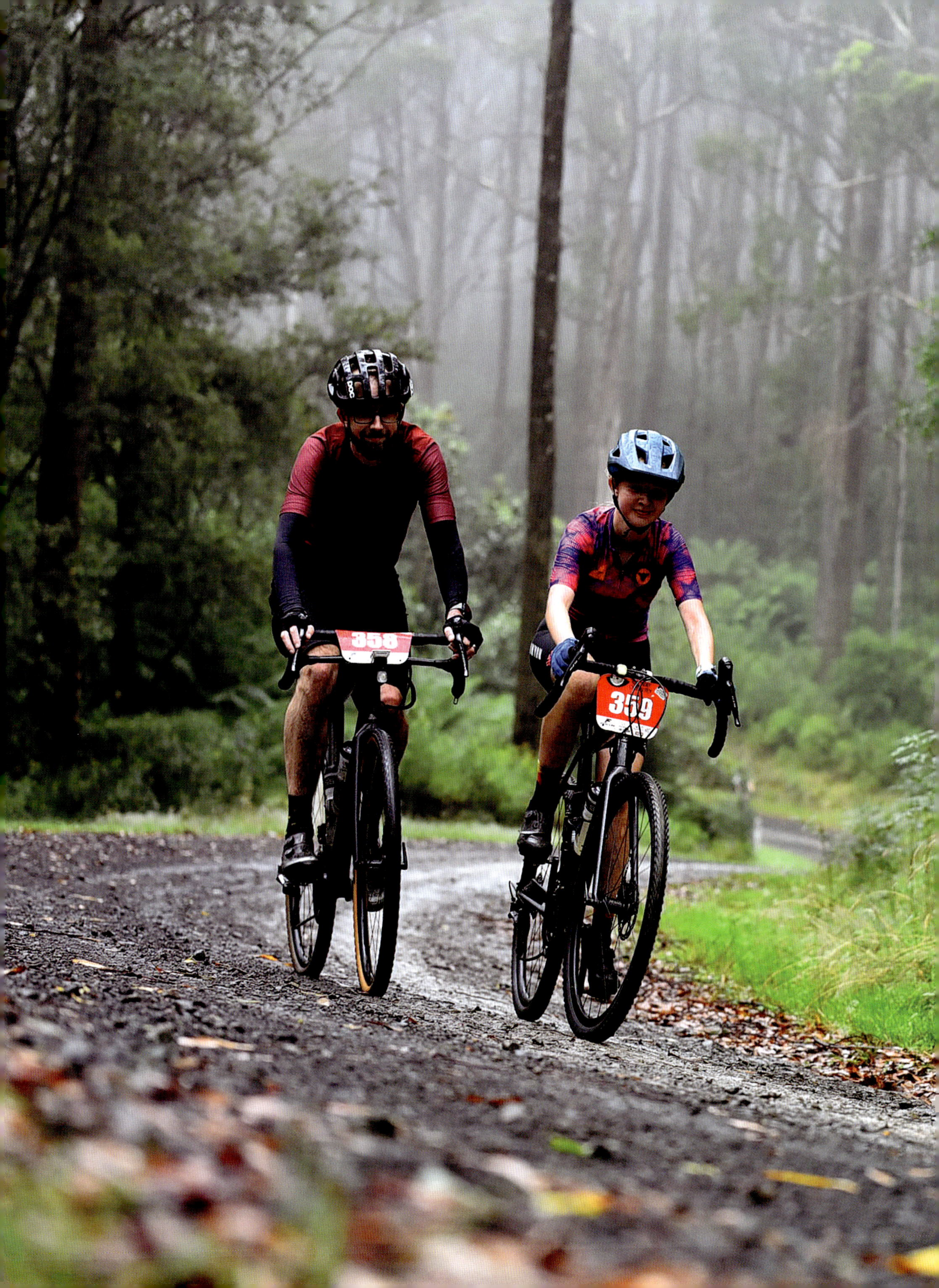
358
359

– EPIC BIKE RIDES OF AUSTRALIA & NEW ZEALAND –

TOP TO BOTTOM IN THE BLUE MOUNTAINS

An adventurous firetrail descent through the gum forests of the Blue Mountains, this train-accessible classic ride makes for a great overnighter or all-day epic.

It's the last hour of daylight on a Friday after work and the light is the colour of a peach bellini. I roll my bike off the train at Wentworth Falls and descend the ridgeline of Kings Tableland Rd. As I do so, the land on both sides falls away into valleys, an undulating canopy of gum trees spreading on and on into the distance.

It's been a long week and I'm grateful for the deep quiet of the deserted road. At the abandoned Queen Victoria Hospital, the pavement ends and the road becomes rough and deeply potholed. I roll on past tall gum trees and a cockatoo regarding me quizzically from a high branch. Some way down the road, I find a disused side trail, so I ride in and string up my hammock – the perfect wild camp.

The night is moonless and the stars wheel brightly above me. When morning dawns, it is bright, clear and warm. I pack up and cycle off down the road. Half an hour later I turn onto the rough dirt of Andersons Firetrail as it undulates through scrub and low woods. A few kilometres later the track enters the tall

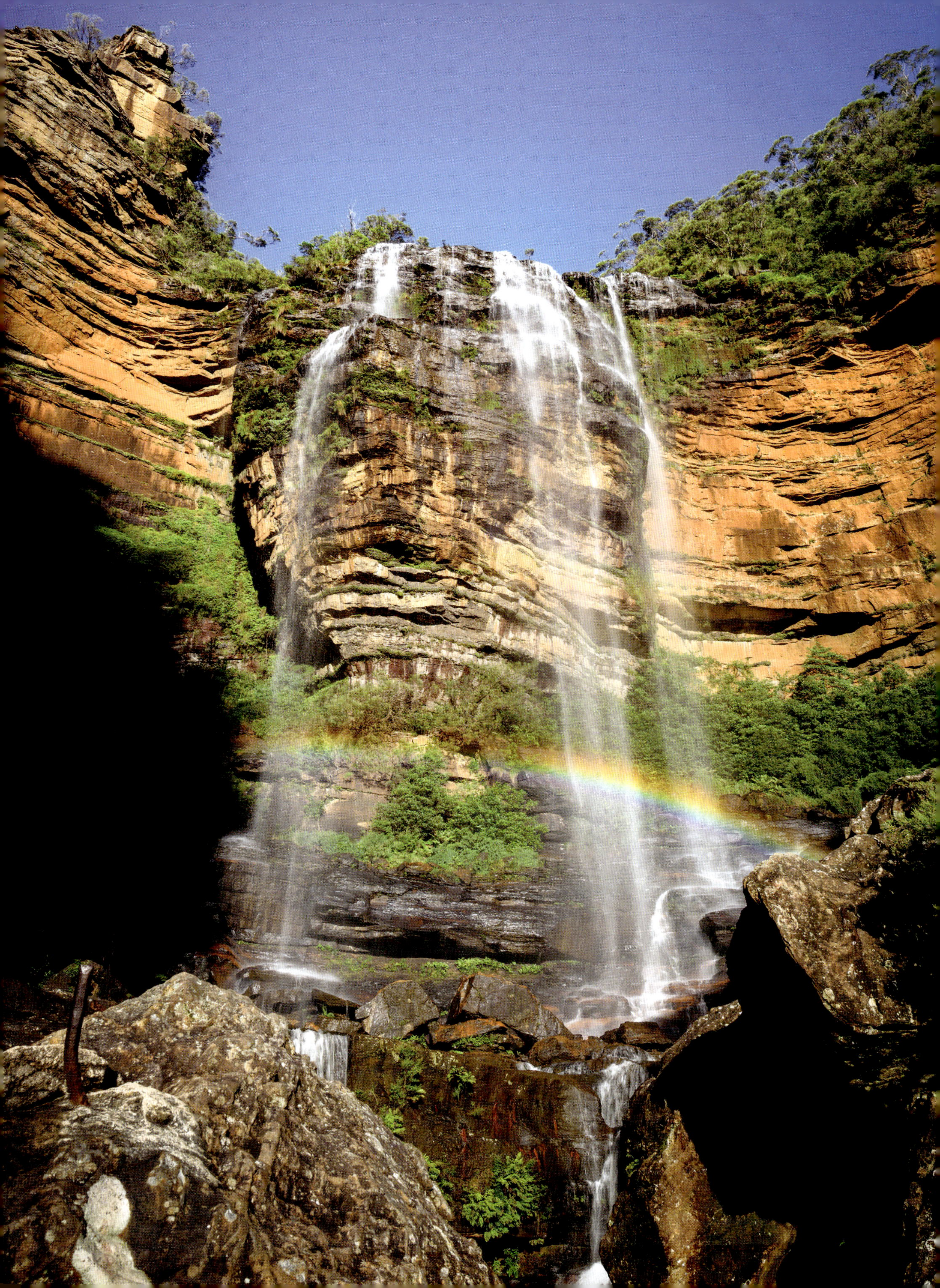

> *"Reaching the bottom, I gleefully crash through the creek as the water fountains in a huge plume around me"*

trees of the mature gum forest, and the air is instantly a few degrees cooler and perfumed with the scent of eucalyptus.

This route drops from nearly 900m (2,950ft) in elevation to just below 100m (328ft) over its 66km (41 mile) length, but that hardly tells the whole story. Because while I'll descend nearly 1,500 vertical metres (4,920ft) overall, there's also the better part of 1,000m (3,280ft) of climbing. And some of those climbs? They're absolutely brutal.

To prove this point, an hour down the trail, the track takes a hard left and descends sharply to Bedford Creek, a screaming descent that I take hanging off the back of the saddle. Reaching the bottom, I gleefully crash through the creek as the water fountains in a huge plume around me. I'd love to celebrate how much fun I'm having, but I already know what's coming next and it isn't pretty.

On the other side, the track immediately begins to climb. Hard. I claw up one steep twisty switchback after another, my lungs and quads burning like they've been filled with battery acid. Eventually, I reach the locked gate at the top of Andersons and the grade mellows out – phew! From here I could turn right for a short detour down to the tall trees of Murphy's Glen campground, but I've decided I'm going all the way. So I turn left and cycle up onto bitumen once again.

Next up after Andersons is the Oaks Firetrail. It starts from the paved residential roads just outside the train station at Woodford, where you can bail out if your legs are cooked, or else start the ride at its halfway point.

I gratefully refill my water bottle from the spigot at the entrance to the firetrail, then start off down the track. The Oaks has been recently regraded and, unlike Andersons, is reasonably smooth going, suitable even for gravel bikes. The track alternates short descents with short climbs, as breaks in the trees provide glimpses of the undulating forested ridges of the lower Blue Mountains. A spiky little echidna waddles across the trail in front of me, and I pass riders churning uphill from Glenbrook, puffing as they climb.

Twelve kilometres (7.5 miles) in, I hit the wide cleared area of the helipad and the start of five continuous kilometres of descent – woohoo! For the next 10 minutes or so, I barely need to think about my brakes as I fly downward past tall trees, wind in my face, catching a bit of air off the occasional waterbar.

Down at the bottom, past the huge grove of lovely old-growth eucalypts known as the Blue Labyrinth, the trail flattens

TURNING THE AIR BLUE

The Blue Mountains are a natural wonder in Sydney's backyard. The country of the Gundungurra and Dharug peoples, the 'Blueies' encompass more than a million hectares of sandstone plateaus, cliffs, gorges and valleys. Named a Unesco World Heritage site in 2000, it shelters an exceptional diversity of eucalypt species, as well as many rare and threatened Australian plants and animals. The mountains' name comes from the blueish haze in the air that comes from terpenoids emitted by the eucalyptus forests.

Clockwise from top: eucalyptus trees in the Blue Mountains; dusty descents; parked up on Andersons Trail. Previous page: Wentworth Falls

out a bit. At the locked gate at its entrance, I get to make a choice: more cruisey firetrail, or a singletrack adventure? I'm loaded up with my camping equipment, but can never resist the lure of the singletrack. I take the left fork of the trail and am soon swooping down a flowing trail full of rocks, roots and ruts, doing my damnedest to avoid bottoming out onto my rims. This section isn't known as 'Pinchflat Alley' for nothing.

After about 5km (3 miles) of singletrack, I get to another fork in the trail: do I head out to the road, or into the MTB park for a few more minutes of fun? Foolishly, of course, I choose the latter. I skip the jumps and drop-offs, but navigate through technical rock gardens and around banked berms. By the time I pop out at the car park, I'm muddy and my fingers are fatigued from working the brakes.

From here, I could head up the road to the superb campground at Euroka, with its resident population of cheeky, larcenous kookaburras, but I'm ready to head home. Down the paved road I go, splashing across the deep water of the Glenbrook Causeway. The end of the ride – the train station at Glenbrook – is only two short kilometres away, but it's 120 vertical metres (394ft) of climbing on steep, twisty pavement switchbacks to get there. After the previous 64km (40 miles), these last two feel the hardest.

I reach the village and pop into the bottle shop for a celebratory beer before catching my train back to Sydney. The shop clerk, looking at my tired, muddy, smiling face, knows exactly where I've been. **MC**

TOOLKIT

Start // Wentworth Falls station
Finish // Glenbrook station
Distance // 66km (41 miles)
Getting there // The route is accessible via the Blue Mountains trainline from Sydney's central station. It's also possible to start or end the ride at its midpoint at Woodford station.
When to go // Any time, although winter nights in the mountains can get below freezing, and Glenbrook Causeway can be impassable after heavy rains. Check the latest warnings before setting out.
What to wear // Layers – weather in the Blue Mountains is very changeable, and you'll appreciate having options.
Where to stay // There are official campgrounds at Murphy's Glen outside Woodford, and at Euroka outside Glenbrook. Wild camping is permitted elsewhere in Blue Mountains National Park where not specifically prohibited.
More info // www.visitnsw.com

Opposite: the limestone caves of Wombeyan in the Southern Highlands

MORE LIKE THIS
TRAIN-ACCESSIBLE ADVENTURES AROUND SYDNEY

THE ROYAL RAMBLE

This scenic mixed route takes you on a tour through Australia's first national park, The Royal. It can be done as a day ride, or completed with a night of camping. You start off with a train to Sutherland station. From there it's on into Royal National Park, where you soon leave the pavement behind. After some quiet forest riding, you'll pop out onto Lady Wakehurst Drive for a few twisty kilometres to Otford, with deep-blue ocean views. Drop down the hill to cross the train tracks, then begin the long, steep climb of Otford Rd. Stop off for a cheeky beer at the pub in Helensburgh, then turn onto the lovely abandoned track of Cawley's Rd, which will lead you to the highway, and then to Waterfall station. If you're not ready for the ride to end, head down 5km (3 miles) of firetrail to the superb campsite at Uloola Falls.
Start // Sutherland station
Finish // Waterfall station
Distance // 51km (32 miles)

NARROW NECK PENINSULA

For sheer views-per-mile, nothing beats a trip out to Narrow Neck. Running the length of a thin, high, isolated plateau stretching between the Jameson and Megalong Valleys, the trail offers arguably the most scenic day ride in the Blue Mountains. Start off with an easy downhill from Katoomba station to the access road onto the peninsula, with great views of Mt Solitary along the way. Once past the locked gate at the start of the firetrail, the trail alternates steep climbs and descents, with incredible vistas over the Wild Dog Mountains and Lake Burragorang. The trail ends at Taros Ladder, a set of chains and steps bolted into the rock that descend to the valley floor.
Start/Finish // Katoomba station
Distance // 31km (19 miles)

MITTAGONG TO WOMBEYAN CAVES

The Southern Highlands – a vast upland 110km (68 miles) southwest of Sydney – not only offer endless opportunities for exploration, but are easily accessible by train. One of the best and most scenic introductions to the region is the ride from Mittagong station to the spectacular karst limestone formations of Wombeyan Caves. The ride starts out on the tarmac of Wombeyan Caves Rd past farmland and wineries, but within an hour you'll be cycling a gravel road through a mix of forest and grazing country, where you'll likely encounter kangaroos. A long, twisting descent drops you to the crossing of the Wollondilly River, and from there you're into the prettiest part of the ride, a deep backcountry passage through mossy, towering rocks. Be ready to be tired out climbing the switchbacks leading to Wombeyan Caves themselves, where there's a campground and the opportunity to rest before reversing the route on the following day.
Start/Finish // Mittagong station
Distance // 134km (83 miles)

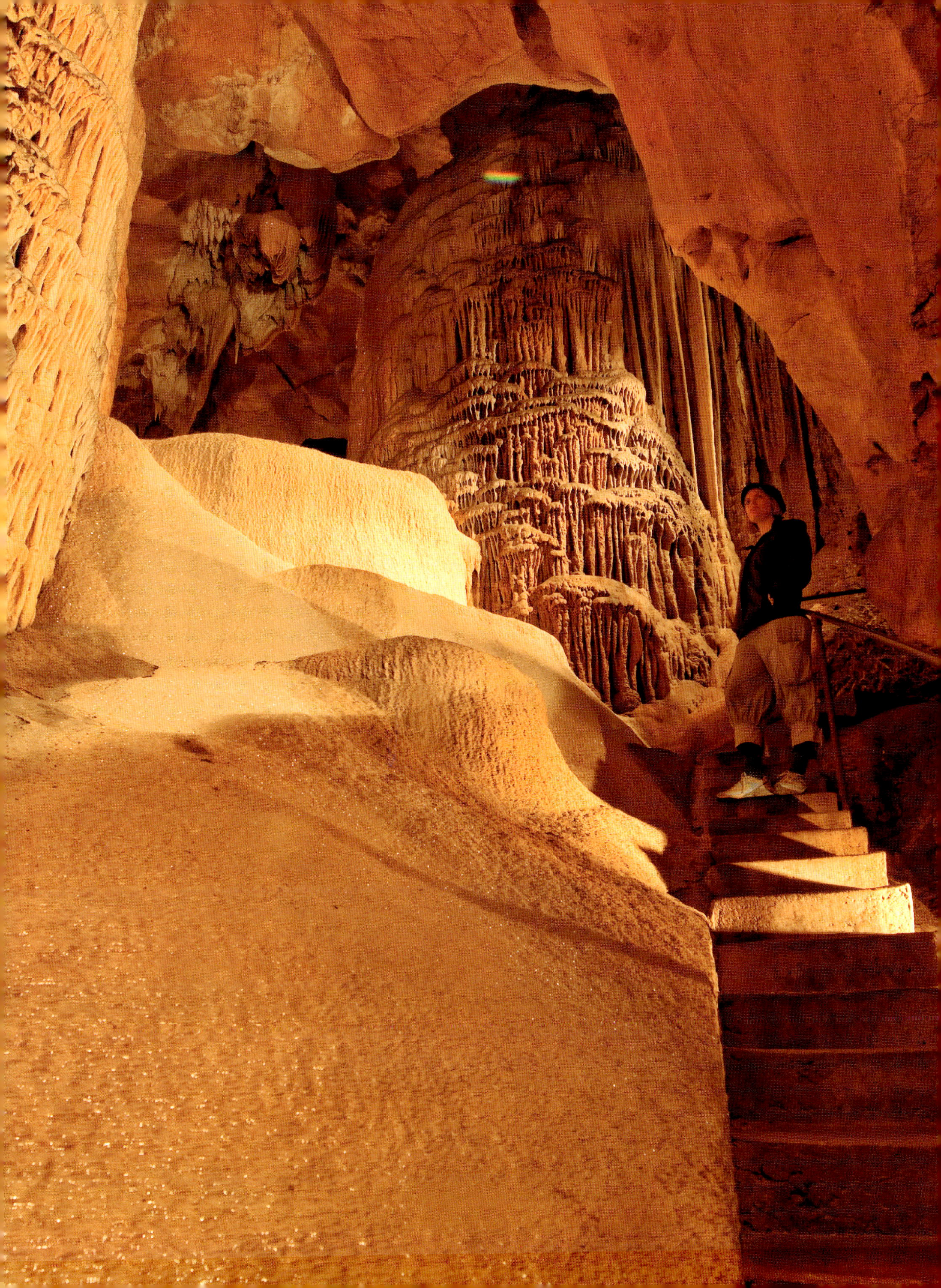

- EPIC BIKE RIDES OF AUSTRALIA & NEW ZEALAND -

THE ATHERTON TABLELANDS

Rolling through rainforests across tropical tablelands that tower above the sun-splashed beaches of Cairns, a sensational suite of mountain-bike trails awaits.

Even the flora is feisty in Tropical North Queensland. I've been bucked from my bike in many colourful ways, but only once has a plant pulled me from the saddle. The triffid attack happened while riding rainforest trails in the hinterland high above the beaches of Australia's Coral Sea coast, when a stray strand of the wicked wait-a-while vine snared my torso with its hooked spine and dragged me down. It suddenly became obvious how this vine got its name.

This is the real Australia: a gritty, wild place, where trails creep past creeks with crocodile warning signs and anything can, and – judging by anecdotes from local cyclists – does, happen. I've even heard tales of a rider being booted off his bike by a cassowary, a primeval-looking, human-sized rooster of a species that stalks the forests of this region like leftover dinosaurs in an Arthur Conan Doyle story.

The riding, however, is sublime. And, just like the aforementioned wait-a-while, this place is hard to shake off once you're hooked. For years I kept returning to ride the Triple-R – Australia's oldest mountain-bike race – and razz around steamy jungle trails at Smithfield, but it took a while to realise that the cream of the North Queensland scene was floating on the top, with the development of a huge highlands hubs-and-links system.

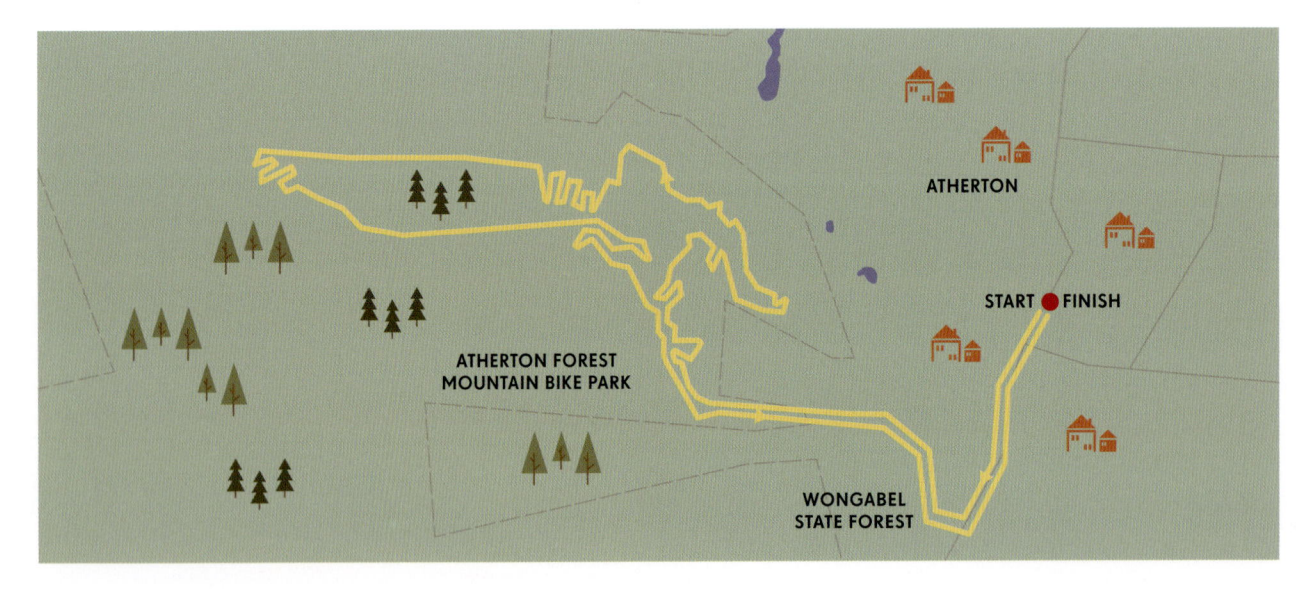

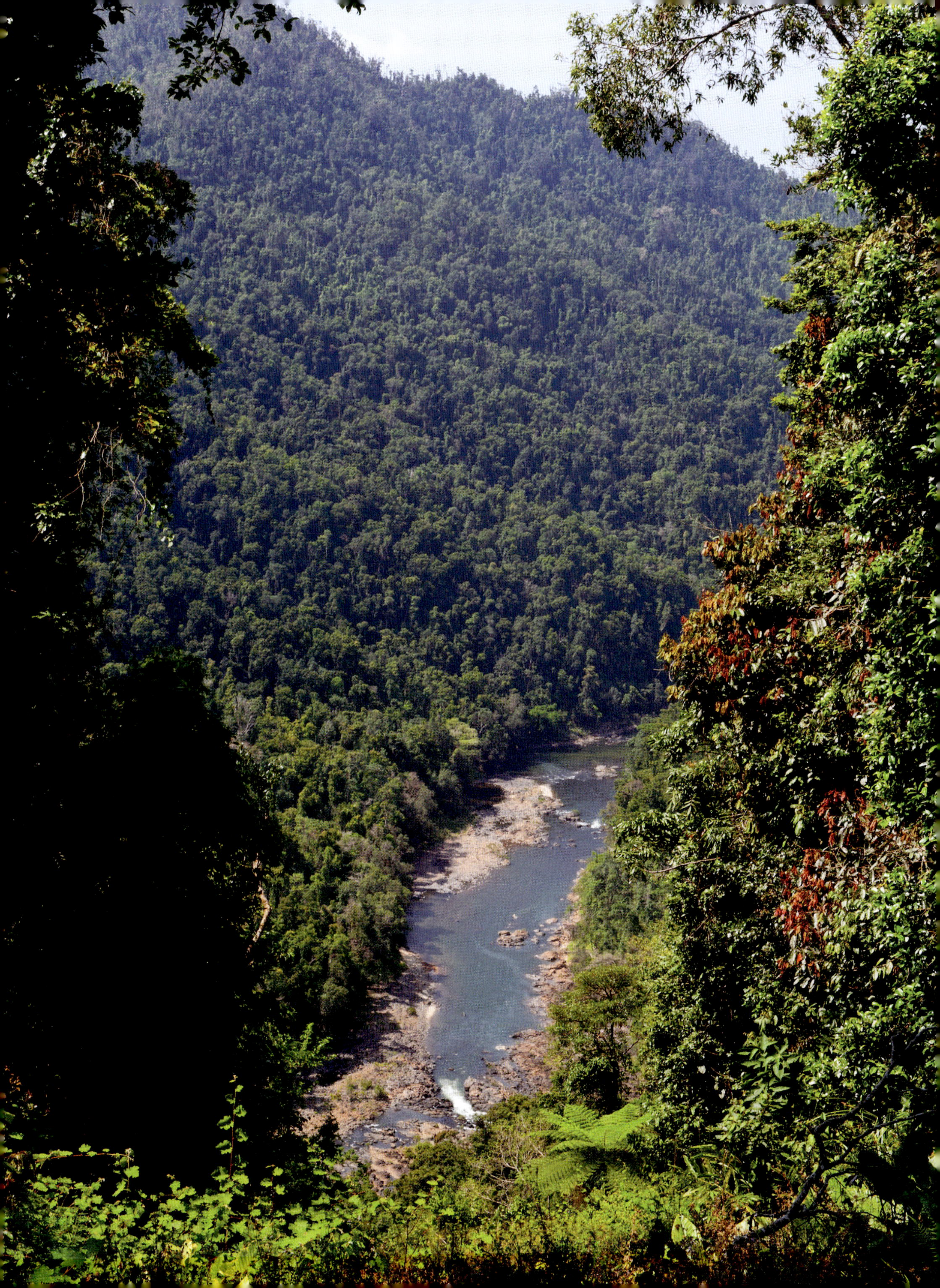

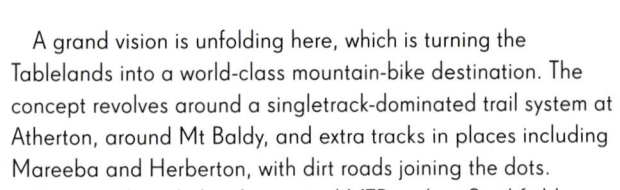

A grand vision is unfolding here, which is turning the Tablelands into a world-class mountain-bike destination. The concept revolves around a singletrack-dominated trail system at Atherton, around Mt Baldy, and extra tracks in places including Mareeba and Herberton, with dirt roads joining the dots.

Between these hubs, the original MTB park at Smithfields and an additional smattering of tracks and trails around Port Douglas, Daintree and the Cassowary Coast, the region boasts more than 700km (435 miles) of documented rideable off-road routes. It's this kind of offering that has attracted mountain-biking's biggest events – the World Cup and the World Championships – to the region. Because these definitely aren't average trails. The tropical tracks slice through great green sweaty swathes of World Heritage-listed rainforest, throwing everything at riders from snarly tree roots to hand-sized spiders. The first dash of the day is a cobweb-clearing ride – not for the faint hearted.

Yet, every morning at 6am, a rotating mob of mountain bikers meet at a cafe in Atherton to ride up Rifle Range Rd and launch themselves into orbit around a still-expanding trail universe, currently comprising 65km (40 miles) of singletrack.

We start on Ridgy Didge, which is Atherton's original professionally sculpted trail, constructed when Queensland Parks and Wildlife began investing in the creation of this mountain biking hub. In Australian slang, Ridgy Didge means 'the real deal' – and this 6.7km (4 mile) loop manages to epitomise everything that's epic about the area.

"This trail turns new mountain bikers into lifelong converts, but it also challenges really good riders"

Climbing around switchbacks bathed in dappled dawn sunlight, we hoon around the route until the arresting view at Leasie's Lookout demands that we take a breather and drink in the verdant vista across the tablelands.

'Atherton is now one of the greatest bike parks in Australia,' enthuses local legend and Mountain Bike Hall of Famer Glen Jacobs, who knows a thing or two about the country's best trails, having created most of them, including this one.

'This is still my favourite Tablelands track,' says Jacobs. 'Partly because it was the first, but also because it has everything, from uphill berms and switchbacks that make the climbing as much fun as the descents, to some really fast and flowy downhill sections. This trail turns new mountain bikers into lifelong converts, but it also challenges really good riders, because if you're not careful you can overcook it.'

Ridgy Didge segues with Bandy-Bandy, a challenging 2.6km (1.6 mile) trail with a technical climb that rewards with another magical outlook. This is one of three tracks named after snakes, which reveals the nature of the local wildlife, but also the feel of the trails, which slide and glide through the trees with serpentine grace, occasionally delivering a viper's nip along the way.

Both circuits pass through the spaghetti junction that forms the network's nucleus, the 'Roundabout', from where trails spin off in all directions. The longest is Stairway to Heaven, which features almost 11km (7 miles) of continuous singletrack, wending around endless eucalypt-fringed elbows, up and over a ridgeline offering amazing views across the Great Dividing Range, and ultimately arriving at Three-ways, where downhill devotees have several options to sink their tyres into.

Ricochet is a fast and furious 1.5km (1 mile) descending trail that shoots towards Rifle Range, bouncing around big berms and serving up many technical treats, including jumps. Yahoo Wahoo is slightly gentler, but it's still gravity assisted for 75% of its 3km (2 mile) length, punctuated by the odd uphill pinch.

Crucially, Atherton has embraced its new incarnation as a magnet for mountain bikers. When we return to the cafe for a post-ride caffeine blast, staff are utterly unfazed by our mud-splattered appearance, even when a leech detaches from my leg and sends a trail of blood across the floor.

The trails are well used for events, including Far North Queensland's notoriously cruel Crocodile Trophy – an eight-stage 650km (404 mile) race, rated among the planet's toughest MTB challenges – which spends two entire days in Atherton. And since 2018, the four-day Reef to Reef has climbed from Smithfields in Cairns to do a Tablelands traverse, ending with a gravity-assisted rampage from Mt Molloy, down the infamous Bump Track, to finish on Four Mile Beach at Port Douglas. Now that's epic. **PK**

WORLD CHAMPS

In 1996, Cairns skidded onto the mountain-biking map by staging the UCI World MTB Championships. Glen Jacobs wasn't solely responsible for this coup, but his revolutionary route designs influenced a still-evolving sport, and the event launched his career as a globetrotting trail architect. When the World Championships returned to the tropics in 2017, Jacobs was back, working on the Atherton trails and redesigning Cairn's Smithfield MTB park.

Left to right: Atherton Tablelands; Yungaburra's Whistle Stop Cafe; mountain biking the Tablelands; Millaa Millaa Falls. Previous spread: view over the Atherton Tablelands

TOOLKIT

Start/End // Atherton
Distance // 24km (15 miles)
Getting there // Access the Atherton Tablelands via Cairns, which has an international airport.
When to ride // June to September offers the best conditions. Temperatures get sticky during the day year-round, so the ideal time for riding is in the early morning and late afternoon.
Where to swim // Cool down between rides in the plunge pool beneath Millaa Millaa Falls, or in the green waters of volcano-created Lake Eacham. Always obey warning signs when swimming in Tropical North Queensland, where killer crocodiles lurk.
What to take // A dual-suspension bike is recommended, with tubeless tyres.
More info // www.ridecairns.com; www.tablelandstrails.com; www.reeftoreefmtb.com

Opposite: Yackandandah's ever-growing trail network

MORE LIKE THIS
MOUNTAIN BIKE TRAIL HUBS

EAGLE MOUNTAIN, SA

On the edge of Adelaide, barely 12km from the Oval and well within pedalling distance of the pie-floater pushers, is Eagle Mountain Bike Park, one of Australia's original mountain-bike trail centres. Spiraling around the edge of Eagle Bowl, an old abandoned quarry, 21km (13 miles) of cross-country trails are etched into the hillside here – mostly technical tracks through trees, characterised by steep rocky descents on loose gravel – plus designated downhill trails for gravity assisted hair-raising fun runs. Don't expect lifts, though, you need to grunt your way back up to the trailheads. There's also a skills development and trials area, and a jumps park. And besides the mapped and graded runs, you can also explore a looser network of trails that flow out across the flanks of the Mt Lofty Ranges, which overlook the city. There are no facilities, so come prepared.
Gateway // Adelaide
Distance // 21km (13 miles)
More info // www.orsr.sa.gov.au > Eagle Mountain Bike Park

MAJURA PINES, ACT

Canberra is surrounded by some of the country's best mountain biking, and the evergreen wooded wonderland to the east of the city boasts some especially sublime singletrack – very different to nearby Stromlo. Here, in magical Majura Pines, you will find over 20km of genuinely world-class trails flowing through the woods, with brilliant berms, challenging drops and seemingly endless tight turns and rooty runs. The routes range from black-diamond nerve janglers to intro-level loops for greener riders and absolute beginners. The whole network is well mapped and marked, plus there's a pump track, and a huge dirt jump park. Rough riders – including some world champs – have been sharpening their skills here for decades, but it was all so very nearly lost to a road development recently. Fortunately the Majura Pines Trails Alliance saved the day and the trails not only survived, but were expanded and improved upon.
Gateway // Canberra
Distance // 20km (12.5 miles)
More info // www.majurapines.org

YACK TRACKS, VIC

A beautiful little former-mining village nestled in verdant northeast Victoria, Yackandandah is not just a pretty face, it's also the gateway to the Yack Tracks, a series of sustainably built mountain-bike trails that roll out from the edge of the hamlet into the scenic surrounds of Stanley State Forest, wending through tall trees and clay canyons, once scoured for gold. The Yackandandah Mountain Bike Track Network, as the new development is more formally known, features a rich mix of well-mapped and clearly waymarked routes, but most are rated green and blue to complement the chilled feel of the place. The longest, Diggers Loop, extends over 18km. Mostly singletrack, there are almost 100km of trails to explore in total, all cross-country and designed to promote continuous flow through the unique landscape, with the mining history incorporated into the journey.
Gateway // Yackandandah, near Wodonga and Beechworth
Distance // 93km (58 miles)
More info // www.exploreyackandandah.com.au

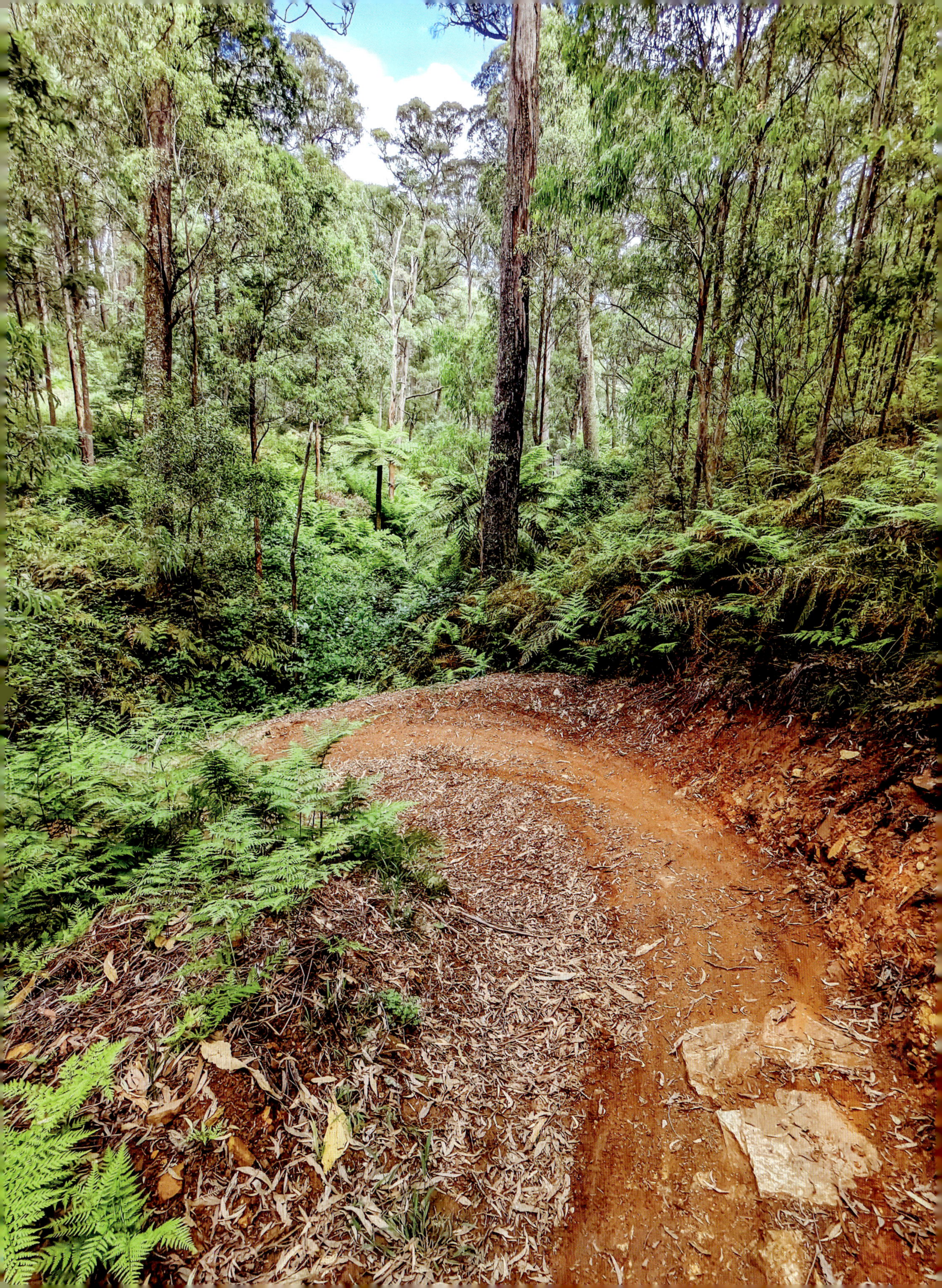

— EPIC BIKE RIDES OF AUSTRALIA & NEW ZEALAND —

THE SANDSTONE WILDERNESS OUTBACK ADVENTURE

A remote, multi-day mission through Queensland's vast inland plains links Emerald and Longreach, with the Spirit of the Outback train helping to complete the loop.

Basking in the deliciously cool waters of a secluded waterhole, surrounded by the vibrant greens of the vegetation sheltering me from the relentless sun, I reflected on the past few days of riding through such a contrasting landscape – traversing vast, dry plains and open, stinking hot stretches of gravel roads under cloudless blue skies.

The decision to map a remote ride across a small stretch of Outback Queensland came about in part out of a desire to visit friends who had relocated to the region's unofficial capital, Longreach. It was also because I was longing for a remote and challenging self-propelled mission in a classic Australian environment. The route name, 'Sandstone Wilderness', was born from the landscapes of the many national parks in the area. A slow love affair grew as I pedalled every day with the sight of rugged sandstone cliffs appearing on the horizon, towering over the vast, barren plains below.

Kicking off the route from the lovingly restored railway station in Emerald, I bid farewell to the town, knowing that the next time I rolled in would be on board the Spirit of the Outback train at the end of my adventure. With the inevitable nerves and excitement that accompany a new mission, my first day of riding was a straightforward 80km (50 mile) stretch to reach

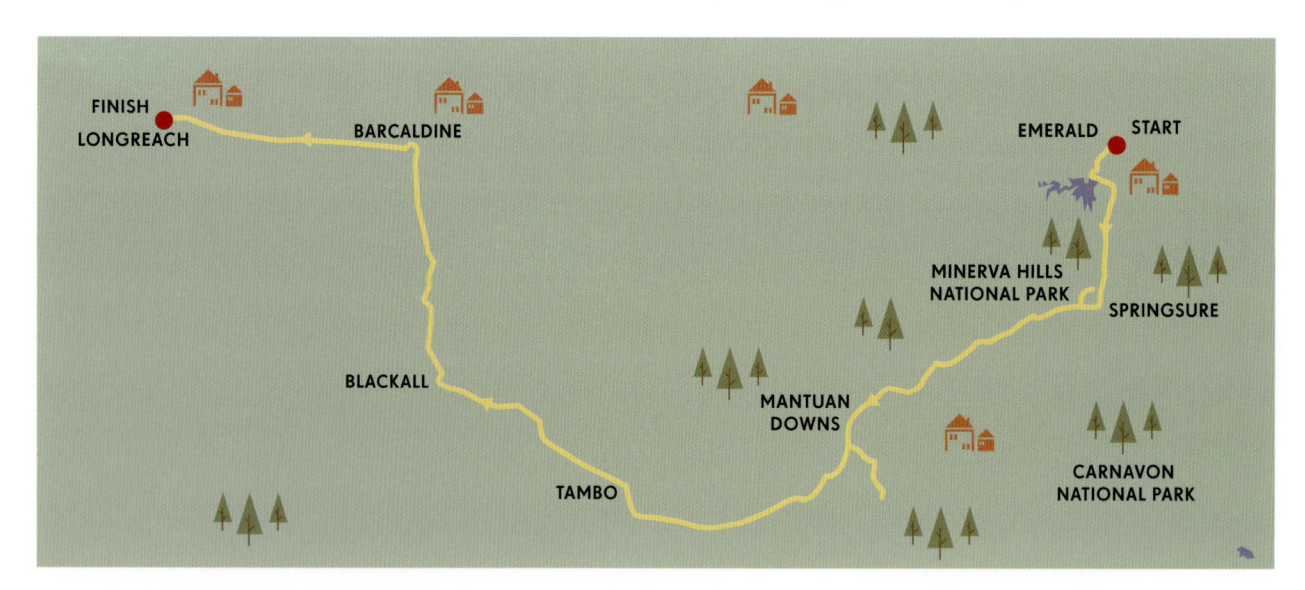

ACT – NSW – QLD

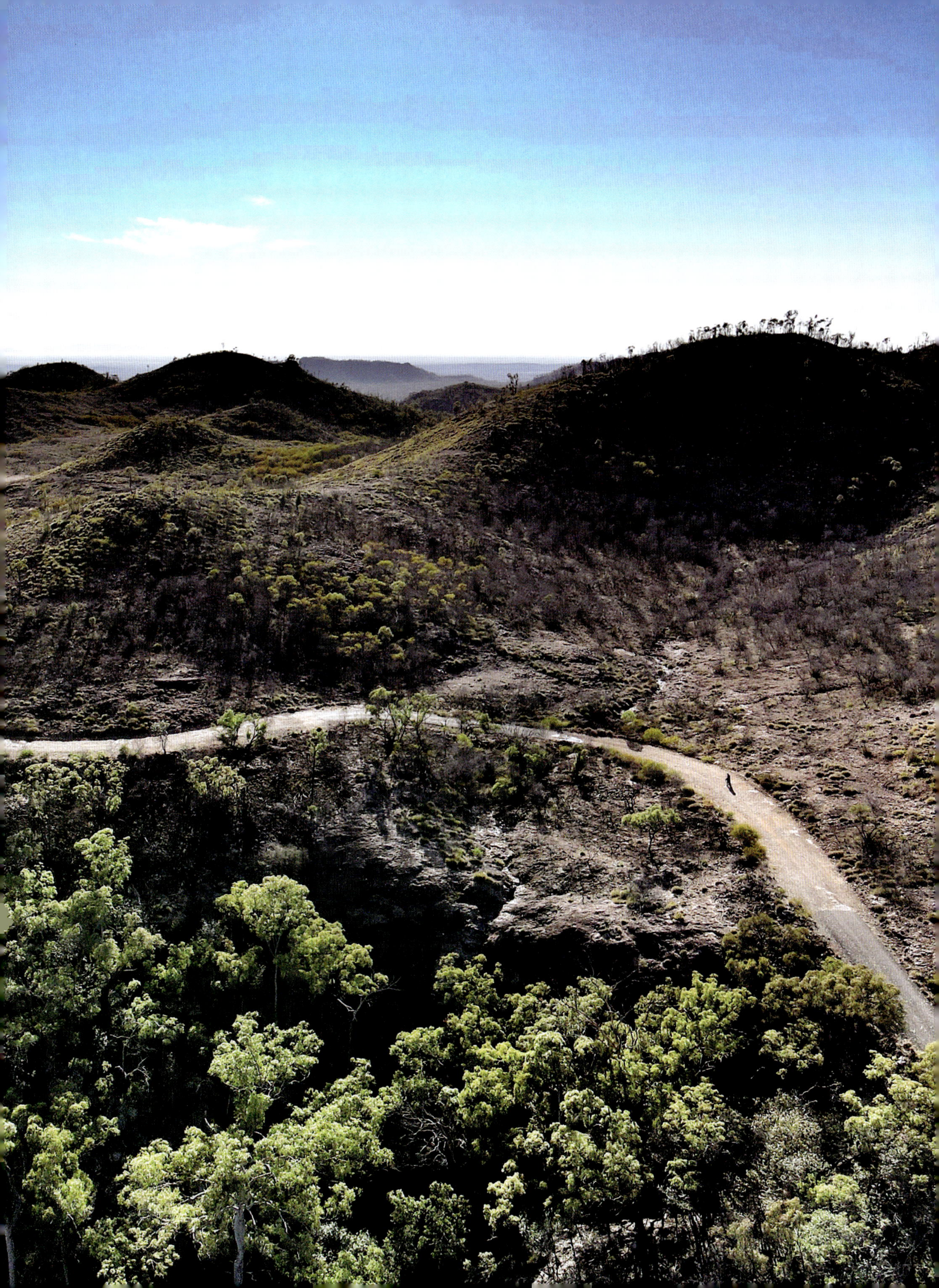

the neighbouring town, Springsure, banked by the looming red cliffs of Minerva Hills National Park.

The next day, exploring Minerva Hills made for a memorable side trip, which included a winding climb up through a moon-like landscape to the rocky summit of Mt Zamia. Riding through stretches of grey-green spinifex, amid the aroma of the eucalypts, with majestic birds of prey soaring high above me, I had the first tangible sense of the outback wilderness I was venturing deep into. With camping not permitted in the park, I enjoyed a fun, breezy descent back down the mountain and into Springsure for my last night with the luxuries of power and running water.

Leaving early the following morning, my bike stocked with water and dehydrated food, I encountered a road sign at the start of the track reading 'Caution'. I ventured on, wondering where caution might need to be exercised, confident I had planned sufficiently to be safe on the adventure ahead.

I had left my ride until late in the year – October – which meant the daytime temperatures were often blisteringly hot, while the nights were marked by that classic desert starry sky chill. The following couple of days were a challenging mission to cover almost 200km (125 miles) to reach the Salvator Rosa section of Carnarvon National Park, where I had booked a spot at the '4WD-only accessible' national park campsite on the banks of the Nogoa River. The thought of cool waters to

"Sighting other humans was rare, typically limited to the exchange of a brief wave"

drink and bathe in spurred me on while I pedalled relentlessly in the fiery heat of the midday sun, looking out for rare spots of shade, sparse in those barren plains.

My main company along the way were cows and conversations with myself. Sighting other humans was rare and typically limited to the exchange of a brief wave as they drove by. A few memorable encounters, however, really made the trip so much richer. When you're riding a push bike alone through the outback, you're bound to look a little out of place and attract snippets of entertaining conversation from curious passers-by. A local cowboy called me 'crazy' and offered me a lift in his ute; while another brought out delicious cold water and fruit from the fridge of his truck – pure, sweet nectar amid the stark hot, dry air I had been inhaling through my chapped lips for hours and hours. These simple gifts were such a treat.

Riding towards the spectacular cliffs of the sandstone escarpment and arriving at Carnarvon National Park was a moment of joy. Enjoying the next day off the bike to explore on foot, I hiked to lush waterholes around ancient rock formations, including the magnificent Spyglass Peak.

Although much of the signage along the 'Wilderness Way' on the next 130km (81 mile) stretch to Tambo related to the lives of the settlers in the region, the area is rich in Indigenous history. As I rode the corrugated tracks, surrounded by deep-red rocky outcrops, I was reminded of a conversation I had enjoyed with a man revisiting his Aboriginal ancestry at Nogoa River. This stranger prompted me to listen to Country, and to thank Country for my safe passing as I pedalled through these vast landscapes, filled with immense gratitude.

Hitting bitumen again after hours of dusty gravel and hearing my phone receive a signal again came with mixed emotions. I was exhausted from a gruelling day in the sun and relieved to be rolling into the tiny town of Tambo, in search of a proper bed for the night and a visit to the quirky and locally famous chicken races, held every night at the town hotel. Sitting on a chair, freshly showered, with a cold cider in hand while a lively crowd cheered for the multicoloured chickens they had backed, was a far cry from the solitude of the wilderness camp the night before.

From Tambo, the adventure returned to the bitumen as I rode long stretches of straight, hazy highway towards my final destination, Longreach. I was fatigued, sunburned, satisfied and deeply grateful for an incredible outback adventure that fitted so fully into my trip mantra: 'Make good choices; there are no rules.' **SP**

OUTBACK ON FOOT

Take a day off the bike to explore the Salvator Rosa section of Carnarvon National Park, with short, sandy, leafy bushwalks accessible from the campsite, across the Nogoa River. Hike through open bloodwood forest, climb Homoranthus Hill for panoramic views across the park's bluffs, and walk the 2km (1.2 mile) loop around Spyglass Peak – a cliff with a magical 10m/33ft-diameter hole through its walls. Spring is also known for its wonderful show of wildflowers across the region.

Left to right: taking a break; Stockmans Hall of Fame and outback heritage centre; Salvator Rosa, Carnarvon National Park. Previous spread: epic vistas in the outback

TOOLKIT

Start // Emerald
Finish // Longreach
Distance // 700km (435 miles)
Getting there // By road it's 2.5 hours from Rockhampton. By train, take the Spirit of the Outback from Brisbane. Flights also operate into Emerald and Longreach from major cities.
When to go // April to September, or spring to see wildflowers.
What to pack // A bike capable of tackling rough off-road sections. Layers for extremes of temperature. Large water-carrying capacity. Tent and camping gear. Emergency radio beacon, ideally.
Things to know // Sections of this ride involve days without resupply of food and water, or phone signal. Full research and experience in wilderness areas is essential.
More info // www.queensland.com

Opposite: admire Uluru from afar

MORE LIKE THIS
OUTBACK EXPERIENCES

MAWSON TRAIL, SOUTH AUSTRALIA

The Mawson Trail is a 900km (560 mile) off-road ride that traverses from the urban landscape of South Australia's capital, Adelaide, through diverse landscapes north to the edge of the South Australian desert at Blinman in the Flinders Rangers. Via undulating hills; vineyards; farmland; forest on unsealed roads and tracks, the route takes riders across a mix of surfaces into the heart of the breathtaking Flinders Ranges. Notorious for its 'peanut butter mud' in sections after heavy rains, the track conditions, and subsequently the ease of riding, vary hugely depending on the weather. With plenty of towns along the trail, accommodation and resupply can be planned relatively easily with some research in advance. Both camping and flashpacking are viable options.
Start // Adelaide
Finish // Blinman
Distance // 900km (560 miles)

RIDE AROUND THE ROCK, ULURU, NORTHERN TERRITORY

Pack plenty of water and sunscreen for this 15km (9 mile) adventure in Australia's precious red centre. The route loops around the base of Uluru, a truly magnificent landmark, and you have the option to take your own bike or to hire from Outback Cycling (seasonally available). The trail is flat, and other than some sandy patches, it's very rideable for all levels of cyclist. This isn't a ride to be rushed – take time to stop and soak in the sights and feelings of this sacred place. The route starts at the cultural centre, where you can support the local community and deepen your understanding of Uluru-Kata Tjuta National Park, learning about Anangu culture and the park's natural environment through exhibits and free presentations with Anangu and park rangers.
Start/Finish // Car park at Uluru-Kata Tjuta Cultural Centre
Distance // 15km (9.5 miles)

ACROSS AUSTRALIA

Yes, people have pedalled across Australia, although (obviously) it's not a trip to be taken lightly since it covers some of the most inhospitable terrain on the planet. The Indian Pacific Wheel Ride (IPWR) travels from Perth to Sydney Opera House, covering around 5500km (3417 miles), including such barren expanses as the Nullarbor Plain. Tragically, in 2017, cycling endurance legend Mike Hall was killed by a driver during the IPWR. The Nullarbor was first cycled way back in 1896, by Arthur Richardson, aged 24, which he did without roads, GPS, maps or gears on his bike. In the 1940s, Wendy Law Stuart and Shirley Duncan were the first women to cycle across the Nullarbor as part of their three-year bike ride around Australia. More recently, several people have cycled from Melbourne (or Alice Springs) to Darwin, which is slightly shorter but no less of an Outback adventure.
Distance // variable

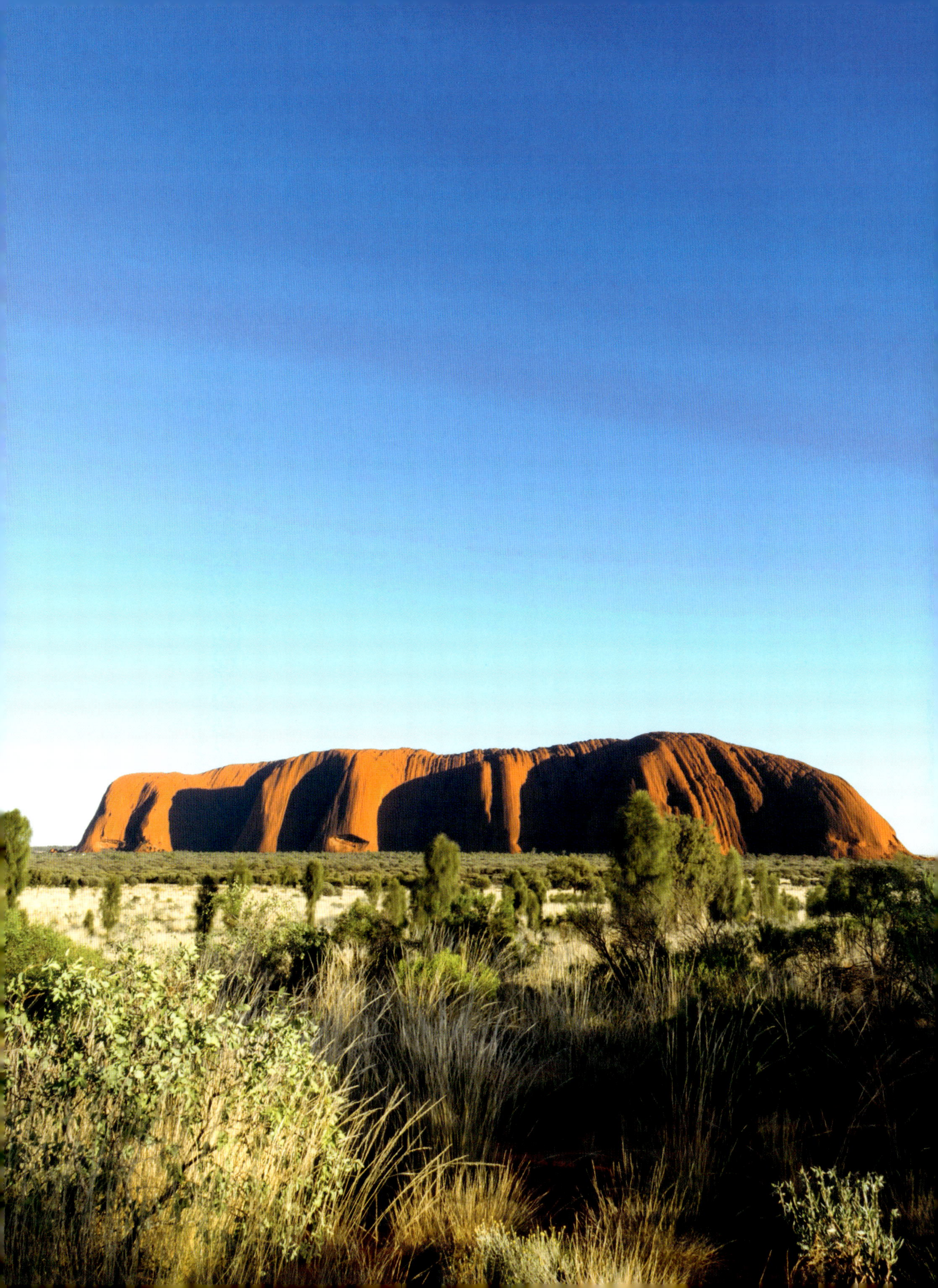

MINJERRIBAH ISLAND IN WINTER

An easy hop from Brisbane leads to a wildlife-rich overnight adventure on a tropical island, filled with beach riding and waterfront camping.

There's something about a leisurely start time and loading a bicycle decked out with camping gear onto a cute little passenger ferry that really raises those good-feeling adventure vibes. And there's something even more exciting when you're voyaging across the waters from the bustle of the city to an island of beautiful sandy beaches and a bounty of native wildlife.

While I'm accustomed to adventuring solo, this weekend adventure was even richer thanks to it being a celebration of a wonderful group of local and interstate bikepackers coming together for the first time. United by a love of riding bikes with chunky tyres in beautiful places and sleeping out under the stars, a motley crew arranged to meet at the ferry terminal at Cleveland for a relaxed weekend of beach riding and camping out. It was instigated by Mattie, who suggested he travel up from Canberra for an overnighter. Then, my southeast Queensland friend and bikepacker Allison put forward the route idea, and soon there we all were, eight of us, many having never met before beyond the world of Instagram.

Winter is an absolutely wonderful time for an adventure like this in Queensland, with the mild temperatures and warm sunshine creating the perfect formula for an easy overnight mission. As the ferry glided across glassy waters to Minjerribah (North Stradbroke Island), Mattie basked in the sun and celebrated feeling 'like he was in the Caribbean', having flown up for the weekend to escape the comparatively harsh Canberra winter.

An hour later, offloading the bikes at the small town of Dunwich, we rolled along for our first essential stop – the bakery – before heading to camp. The planned distances were short and the going was at party pace. The focus was on fun, connection, conversation and time to soak in this breathtaking island and the glorious weather. From Dunwich, we began our ride across to the eastern side, full of laughter and gratitude to be embarking on this adventure together; the memory of the working week already a distant blur. Although we were all content with a conversational pace, Minjerribah is not a flat island, and some of us confessed to feeling the climbs as we made our way on quiet bitumen roads, surrounded by beautiful bushland and lured by the ocean ahead.

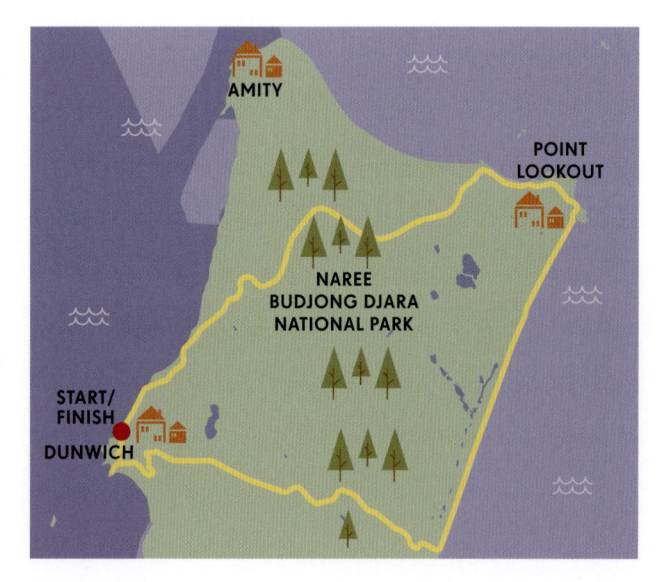

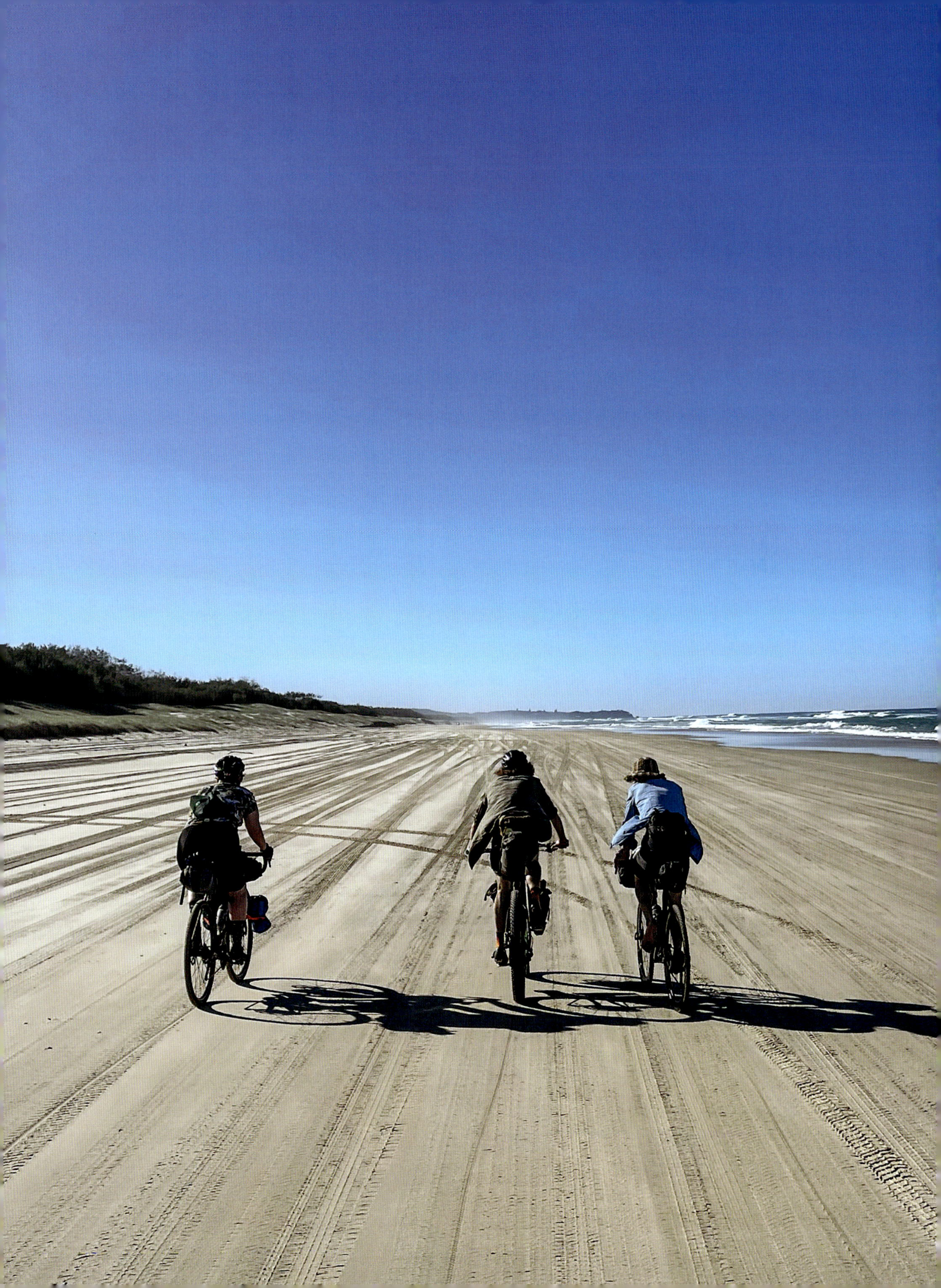

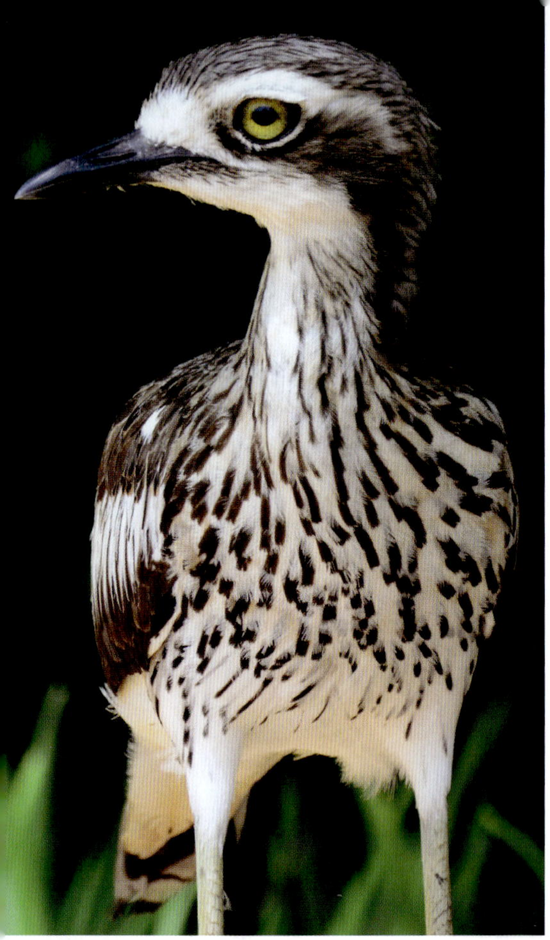

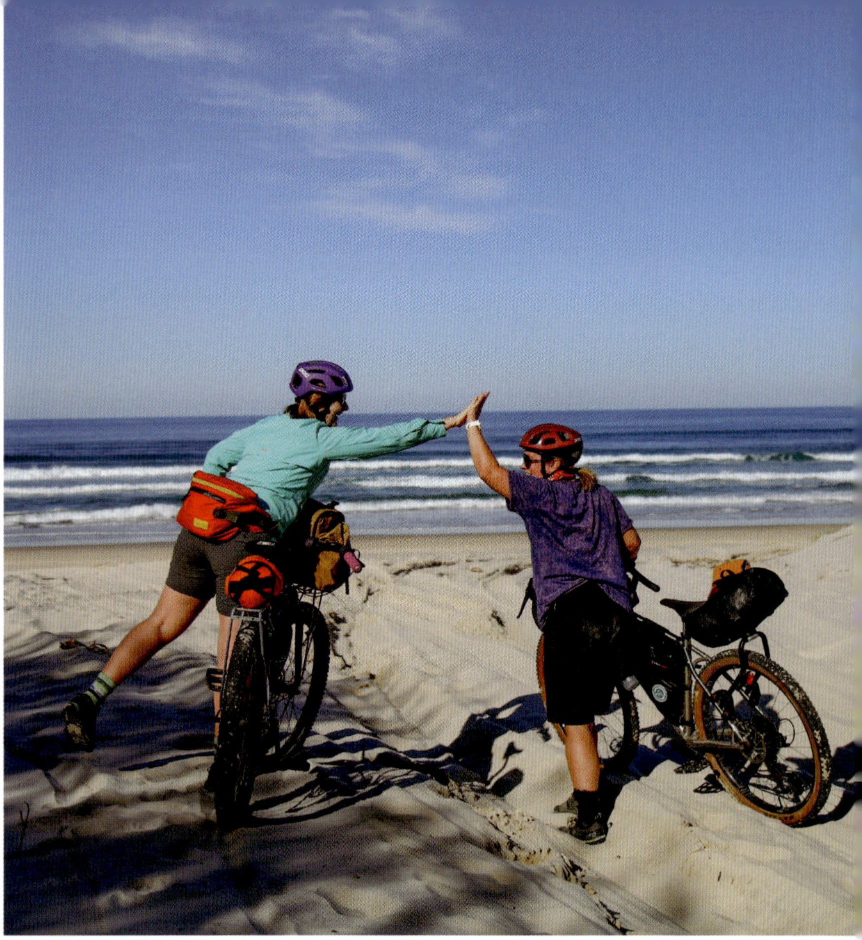

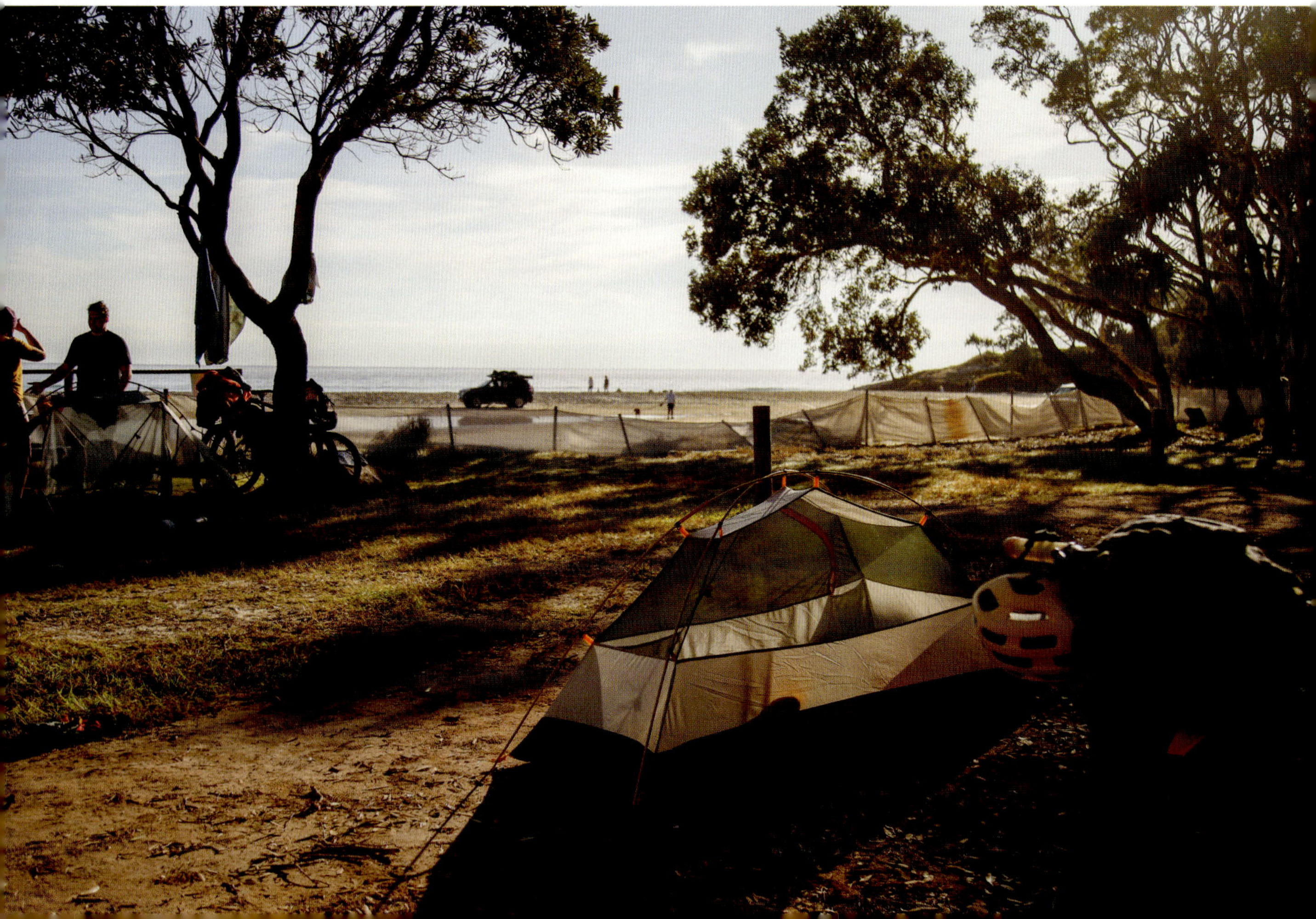

A real gift of visiting Minjerribah in winter is not only the beautiful conditions, but also the fact it is whale season. Riding along the beach, flicking between laughter and shared conversation, while being mesmerised by the playfulness of migrating humpback whales offshore, was a truly special experience. Gleeful shouts of 'this is the life' were shared as we cruised along the enormous stretch of beach on compact sand, beverages in one hand, handlebars in the other, on our way north towards Point Lookout, at the tip of Minjerribah.

While Mother Nature can offer such magnificence, she can also pose challenges. A slight neglect of checking the tide times soon meant that our gleeful cruising came to a halt as the rising tide began to rapidly swallow the rideable part of the beach. One by one, we had to accept there was no choice but to slowly hike our bikes through the remaining miles of deep, soft, seemingly relentless sand. That being said, Main Beach is comprised of mile after mile of clean sand, skirting the eastern side of Minjerribah. Hiking our bikes in the sunshine, while white-bellied sea eagles soared overhead and whales tail-slapped just offshore, can hardly be described as suffering.

On reaching Point Lookout, we all laughed and sighed with relief as we left the sand-wading behind us and cruised along the bitumen, a short ride to our home for the night at Adder Rock Camping Ground. Preferring more solitude and simplicity, I wouldn't typically opt for a caravan park when I'm on my own. However, with its beachfront sites, hot showers and proximity to the pub, this was the perfect spot for a hassle-free stay with a great group of riding companions. Tents were pitched while we took in a spectacular golden sunset over the ocean in front of us. Next stop was a short ride to the local pub up the hill for a good feed before bedtime.

After a peaceful night in my tent, I was the first to wake up the following morning, and took the opportunity to stroll across the beach, up to the headland at first light, just metres from our campsite. The coastline of Minjerribah is both rugged and tropical, and thick with pandanus trees. At sunrise, we all congregated quietly on the sea cliffs; Kate, painting with watercolours; Jake and Keegan, carefully shooting with SLRs; and me, sharing oracle card readings with the sounds of the ocean and the morning chorus of birds surrounding us. These little treats – watercolours, cameras, books and cards – all luxury elements of a relaxed adventure and no need to pack for anything 'light and fast'.

Before breaking down our camp and rolling west back to the ferry to mark the end of our trip, we all jumped into the cool ocean in front of the campsite for one last dip before home. It was a beautifully simple start to the day, feeling energised for a relaxed, undulating road ride back to the boat, full of gratitude for new friendships formed, and for a magnificent winter island adventure shared. **SP**

SUNSHINE ISLE

Minjerribah is the Aboriginal name for North Stradbroke Island, meaning 'Island in the Sun' in the Jandai language. On 4 July 2011, the Federal Court of Australia recognised the Quandamooka People's native title rights over the land and waters on and surrounding North Stradbroke Island, and some islands in Moreton Bay. On Minjerribah, Matthew Burns shares Quandamooka culture through workshops and tours, including smoking ceremonies, dance and didgeridoo.

Clockwise from top: a bush stone curlew; beach rendezvous; camping options range from cabins to no-facility sites on beaches. Previous spread: rolling on sand

TOOLKIT

Start/Finish // Cleveland Ferry Terminal
Distance // 50km (31 miles)
Getting there // The ferry terminal at Cleveland is a 40-minute drive from Brisbane city centre. Rail and bus options are also available. The ferry operates seven days a week, with both a passenger and car ferry option.
When to go // Winter is an ideal time, due to its mild temperatures and whale-watching opportunities.
Where to stay // Camping is available across various sites on the island, along with holiday rental options. There are three townships – Dunwich, Amity and Point Lookout, each around 20km (12 miles) apart.
More info // www.stradbrokeisland.com

Opposite: a resident seal colony at Cathedral Rocks, Rottnest Island

MORE LIKE THIS
ISLAND UNDERTAKINGS

MARIA ISLAND NATIONAL PARK, TASMANIA

No cars are allowed on Maria Island (pronounced ma-rye-ah), other than a few ranger vehicles, so it's a great choice if you're considering your first bikepacking adventure. Catch the passenger ferry with your bike from Triabunna to Darlington, then ride across the island to the campsite at Encampment Cove or set up camp at Darlington, near the ferry pier, and explore from there. The island is home to incredible wildlife, including a huge population of wombats, birdlife and even Tasmanian devils. Enjoy winding gravel roads skirting white sandy beaches and crystal-clear water. Take a detour on foot to visit the Painted Cliffs. There are no shops or cafes on Maria Island, so ensure you come prepared and can be self-sufficient.
Start/Finish // Triabunna Harbour
Distance // About 35km (22 miles)
More info // www.parks.tas.gov.au

WAIHEKE ISLAND, NEW ZEALAND

Stunning Waiheke Island is just a 40-minute ferry ride from downtown Auckland, so hop on a mountain bike and take on a circular loop of its road and trails. Soak up the beautiful beaches and tropical island feeling, and perhaps stop in at one of the island's famous vineyards or olive groves to rest the legs for a while. Don't be lulled into a sense of ease: Waiheke is home to undulating hills, steep climbs and fun descents. Choose to take a tent and camp out under the stars on one of the island's campsites, or book a hotel or rental accommodation in advance if you prefer a little more luxury at the end of the day.
Start/Finish // Downtown Ferry Terminal, Auckland
Distance // 54km (34 miles)
More info // www.tourismwaiheke.co.nz

WADJEMUP/ROTTNEST ISLAND, WESTERN AUSTRALIA

Only 19km (12 miles) from the coast of Fremantle and 33km (20.5 miles) from Perth city centre, Wadjemup/Rottnest Island is an easily accessed and unforgettable island experience. Ferry transfers range from 25 to 90 minutes, leaving daily from Fremantle and northern Perth, and allow you to take bikes on board – or simply hire one on Wadjemup. Arriving at the main jetty in Thomson Bay, the 22km (14 mile) Island Ride awaits, looping around the whole spectacular coastline. Pack snorkel gear and take on the tranquil network of winding roads and paths, exploring this vehicle-restricted island and jumping into the crystal blue waters of the bays to cool off. In this protected sanctuary for native wildlife, keep your eyes peeled for a sighting of a quokka – an emblematic marsupial resident of Wadjemup.
Start/Finish // Ferry terminals at Perth City, Fremantle, North Fremantle & Hillarys Boat Harbour
Distance // 22km (14 miles)
More info // www.rottnestisland.com

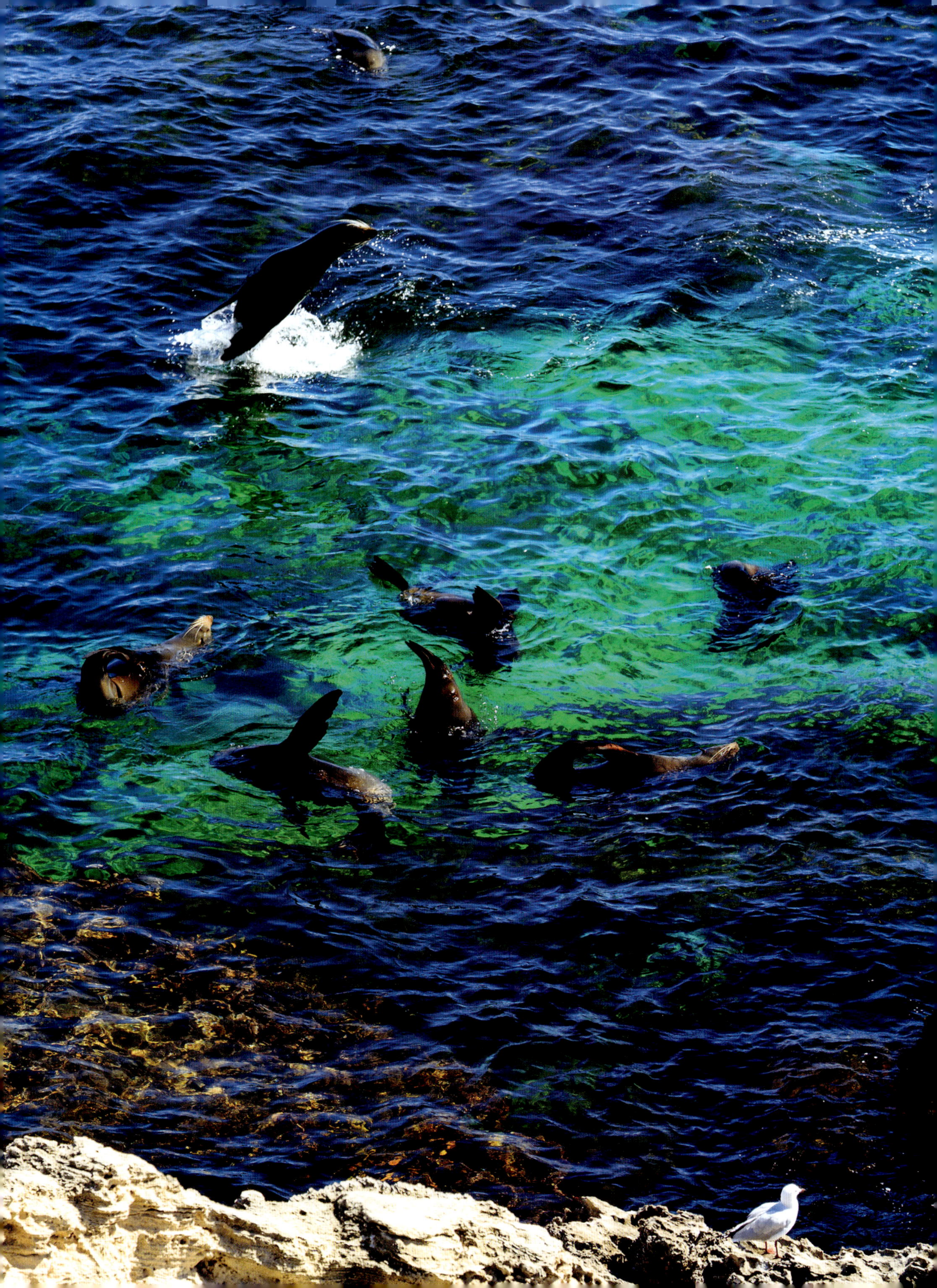

- EPIC BIKE RIDES OF AUSTRALIA & NEW ZEALAND -

A BIKEPACKING FIRST ON BRISBANE VALLEY RAIL TRAIL

A journey along the Brisbane Valley Rail Trail through the southern Queensland countryside is the perfect route for a first-time, point-to-point bikepacking adventure.

Although it's hard to imagine now, there was a time when I had not heard of bikepacking. Many adventures later, bikepacking is now a favourite form of self-propelled adventure. We all have to start somewhere, and the Brisbane Valley Rail Trail, on my first ever gravel bike, is where my bikepacking journey began.

Not being a part of the bikepacking community back then, my awareness of the route came from ultra-running friends. All off-road but not too technical, and with plenty of towns along the way, it seemed like a perfect testing ground for my bikepacking curiosity. The rail trail's website stated: 'Now the longest rail trail in Australia, the 161km [100 mile] BVRT follows the disused Brisbane Valley rail line that commenced construction at Wulkuraka near Ipswich in 1884 and was completed at Yarraman in 1913.' It also mentioned coffee stops every 25km (16 miles) – a firm motivator in my decision making. Winding its way up the Brisbane valley, the BVRT passes through Fernvale, Lowood, Coominya, Esk, Toogoolawah, Moore, Linville, Benarkin and Blackbutt before ending in the small rural town of Yarraman.

As a fan of adventures from my doorstep, I undertook this ride from home on the Sunshine Coast – riding to Landsborough station to take the train to Ipswich. My plan was to break the length of the rail trail into two days of riding, camping along the way, before riding home by road from Yarraman. With the weather forecast looking ominous, I was both excited and nervous – hoping my gear would stay attached to my bike and that there actually would be coffee stops every 25km as advertised.

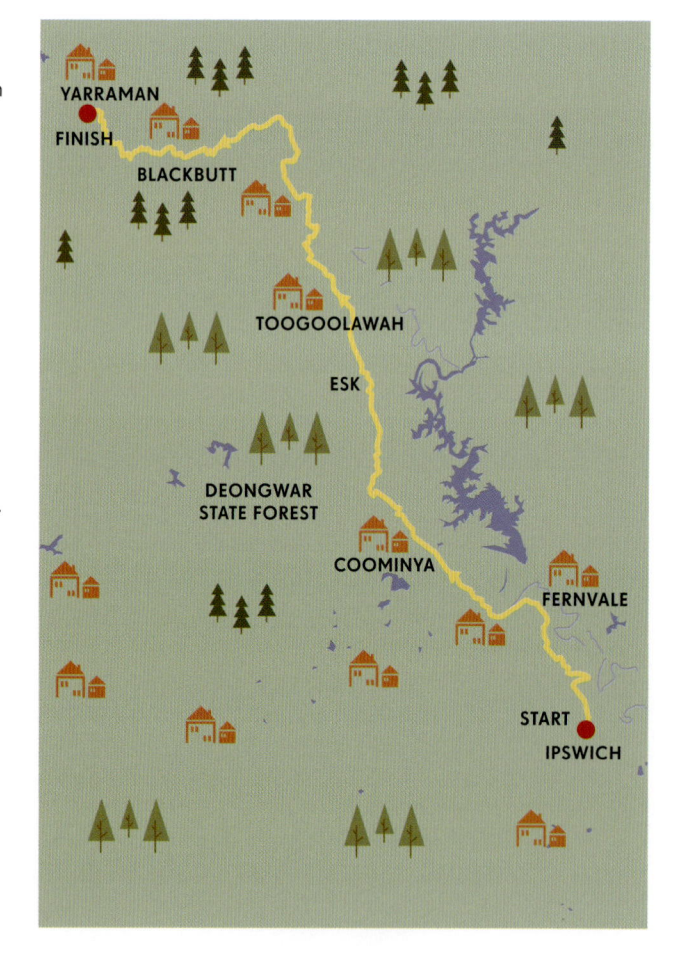

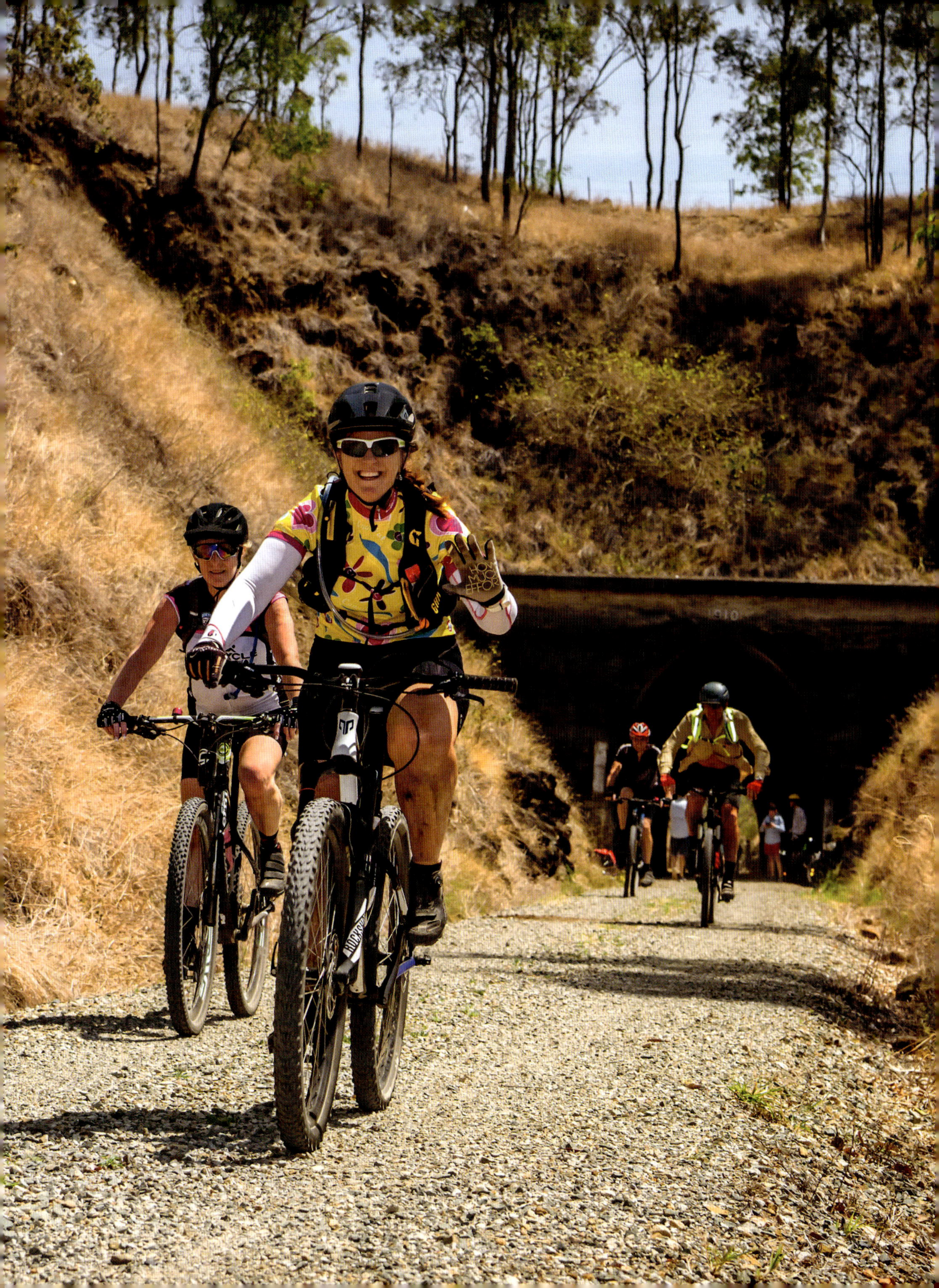

With so many towns along the way, it would be easy to break up the trail into as many days as you like. The towns also mean you have a choice of camping or 'flashpacking', and food logistics are easy thanks to a variety of shops, pubs and cafes. I didn't have a fixed plan when I left Ipswich, other than considering Esk as the potential overnight stop – perhaps because it amounted to almost 100km (62 miles) of riding (roughly 70km/43 miles of that on the BVRT). I took my time along the way and lucked out with blue skies, albeit a little wind; a mix of surfaces from bitumen to gravel to grass; navigating the occasional gate and the odd water crossing. Riding my bike fully laden for the first time felt thrilling. I also came to adore the noise of the wind whistling through the frame as I pedalled across grassy, open flats, with curious cows watching from the surrounding fields.

Come early evening, I was rolling into the lovely township of Esk. The ride so far had been fairly flat and straightforward, with the trail signposted the whole way, along with historical markers and beautiful old trestle bridges. Riding through the different towns and seeing the old stations with their beautifully simple white and black signs and vintage platforms was a nostalgic signifier of the area's past, and the importance the railway line once held.

"Riding my bike fully laden for the first time felt thrilling. I came to adore the noise of the wind whistling through the frame as I pedalled across grassy flats"

The campground staff at Esk were friendly and recommended the town hotel for a pub dinner. I pitched my tent in a grassy area and rode across to the hotel, where I was promptly told that I needn't worry about locking my bike – it was safe there. Fuelled up on calamari and red wine, I rode the short distance back to my tent, not expecting the cold night ahead.

After a chilly, sleepless night, morning finally shone on Esk, and I was both excited and drowsy, packing up a condensation-soaked tent, ready for the next section of trail. Not however, before a coffee stop, where the barista (a lovely older gentleman) gave me an extra biscuit when I said I was riding the 94km (58 miles) to Yarraman that day.

A couple of places stand out in my mind from this day – Blackbutt, because of its famous bakery, which of course warranted a stop. I also rested with a coffee and a snack in

WHERE TENNIS MEETS THE TRAIL

A somewhat unexpected attraction along the way, Blackbutt is home to the Roy Emerson Museum, celebrating the Australian tennis legend. He was a staggering 28-time Grand Slam title winner, ranking Number 1 in the world from 1964 to 1965, and again in 1967. Born in Blackbutt in 1936, Emerson attended primary school at the Nukku State School. The museum houses photos and stories about Roy, as well as a life-size bronze statue situated nearby.

Left to right: directions are clear on the Brisbane Valley Rail Trail; cyclists consult information boards; a koala rests in a gum tree; a marker of progress. Previous spread: pass through repurposed railway tunnels

Moore, where I enjoyed a conversation with the regulars about the area and the trail. Another memorable spot was Linville. The Linville Hotel, right on the trail, looked like a good lunch stop, with an old red train parked up at the original station. There is also a pleasant free camping area here. The trail out of Linville to the north was one of my favourite sections of the ride. It was the first time I felt marginally remote, which I love, and came with rolling ups and downs. The beautiful green, undulating hills were home to hundreds of fluttering butterflies.

As I slowly approached my final destination on the BVRT, Yarraman, I tossed a coin in my mind over whether to head to the campsite and sleep in my soggy tent, or book into the local motel. Motel it was. It was delightful to plonk down onto a real mattress, enjoy a hot shower, and have a warm, dry space to unpack my bike, dry stuff and repack it for the last stretch home. What a satisfying way to end a fun day: completing the full rail trail while riding through friendly towns and countryside alive with wildflowers along the way.

Riding my bike loaded for the first time; the simplicity of bikepacking; the welcoming nature of the BVRT route as a beginner's stomping ground – all had my heart full and my mind content, full of ideas for future adventures. **SP**

TOOLKIT

Start // Ipswich
Finish // Yarraman
Distance // 161km (100 miles)
Getting there // Take the train from Brisbane to Ipswich.
When to go // All year – however spring and autumn are preferable to avoid summer heat in exposed stretches.
Where to stay // The trail passes through many towns, with campsite and holiday rental or hotel/motel options.
Tours // Shuttles are available to transport you back to the start. Out There Cycling provides on-demand shuttles (www.outtherecycling.com.au).
Things to know // North to south, commencing at Yarraman, is deemed easier as there is more downhill in this direction. A range of bikes would suit the BVRT, but given some of the rougher terrain, a gravel bike or mountain bike is the most comfortable choice.
More info // www.tmr.qld.gov.au/bvrt

Opposite: the Kingaroy Peanut Silos can be seen on the Kilkivan to Kingaroy Rail Trail in Queensland

MORE LIKE THIS
RAIL TRAILS

KILKIVAN TO KINGAROY RAIL TRAIL, QUEENSLAND

The Kilkivan to Kingaroy Rail Trail (KKRT) follows an old railway line through peaceful Queensland countryside, between the two towns of Kilkivan and Kingaroy. Stretching out for 88km (55 miles), the route passes through Goomeri, Murgon, Wondai, Tingoora, Wooroolin, Memerambi and Crawford. The KKRT between Kingaroy and Murgon takes in smooth bitumen path which makes for easy riding for all levels. Beyond Murgon, en route to Kilkivan, the trail is unsealed, and depending on weather conditions the gravel and dirt trail can prove to be a little more adventurous and challenging for riders. All sections of the Kilkivan to Kingaroy Rail Trail offer car-free riding and a great opportunity to explore the rural towns through which the trail passes. Free camping is available at Wondai and Wooroolin.
Start // Kilkivan
Finish // Kingaroy
Distance // 88km (55 miles)
More info // www.gympie.qld.gov.au

MURRAY TO THE MOUNTAINS RAIL TRAIL, VICTORIA

With various route options stretching between the classic Victorian towns of Harrietville, Yackandah and Wangaratta, the Murray to Mountains Rail Trail offers more than 100km (62 miles) of sealed and unsealed riding through diverse landscapes. Through natural bushland and rich farmland, with a backdrop of some of Australia's most celebrated mountain landscapes, the trail connects a host of beautiful towns, including Wangaratta, Beechworth, Rutherglen, Bright and Myrtleford. It also skirts Mount Buffalo National Park. Autumn is a fine time of year to adventure by bike through the region, as the crisp air turns the leaves of the mature trees to golden hues. Since the area is also famous for having some of Australia's finest gourmet produce, wines and craft beers, there are plenty of options to turn a bike adventure into a gastronomic experience. With an unexpected climb on the 15km (9 mile) stretch between Everton and Beechworth, just make sure you choose your direction of travel carefully.
Start/Finish // Harrietville/ Yackandah/Wangaratta
Distance // 100km (62 miles)
More info // www.ridehighcountry.com.au

LILYDALE TO WARBURTON RAIL TRAIL, VICTORIA

Since 1996, this popular rail trail has enabled Melburnians to pedal out to the wild Yarra Ranges for a weekend retreat. Catch a train to Lilydale in the northeast suburbs from the city and hop on the signposted trail. Riders pass through rolling countryside before reaching Yarra Junction and then Warburton, which lies at the foot of the Yarra Ranges, surrounded by cool temperate forest along the Yarra River. There plenty of places to stay and eat in the town and you can explore other traffic-free routes in the area, such as the O'Shannassy Aqueduct Trail. Warburton is on the verge of developing into top-notch cycling destination with plans for purpose-built mountain bike trails in the hills. There's an extension to the rail trail to Yarra Glen too.
Start // Lilydale
Finish // Warburton
Distance // 40km (25 miles)
More info // www.yarraranges.vic.gov.au

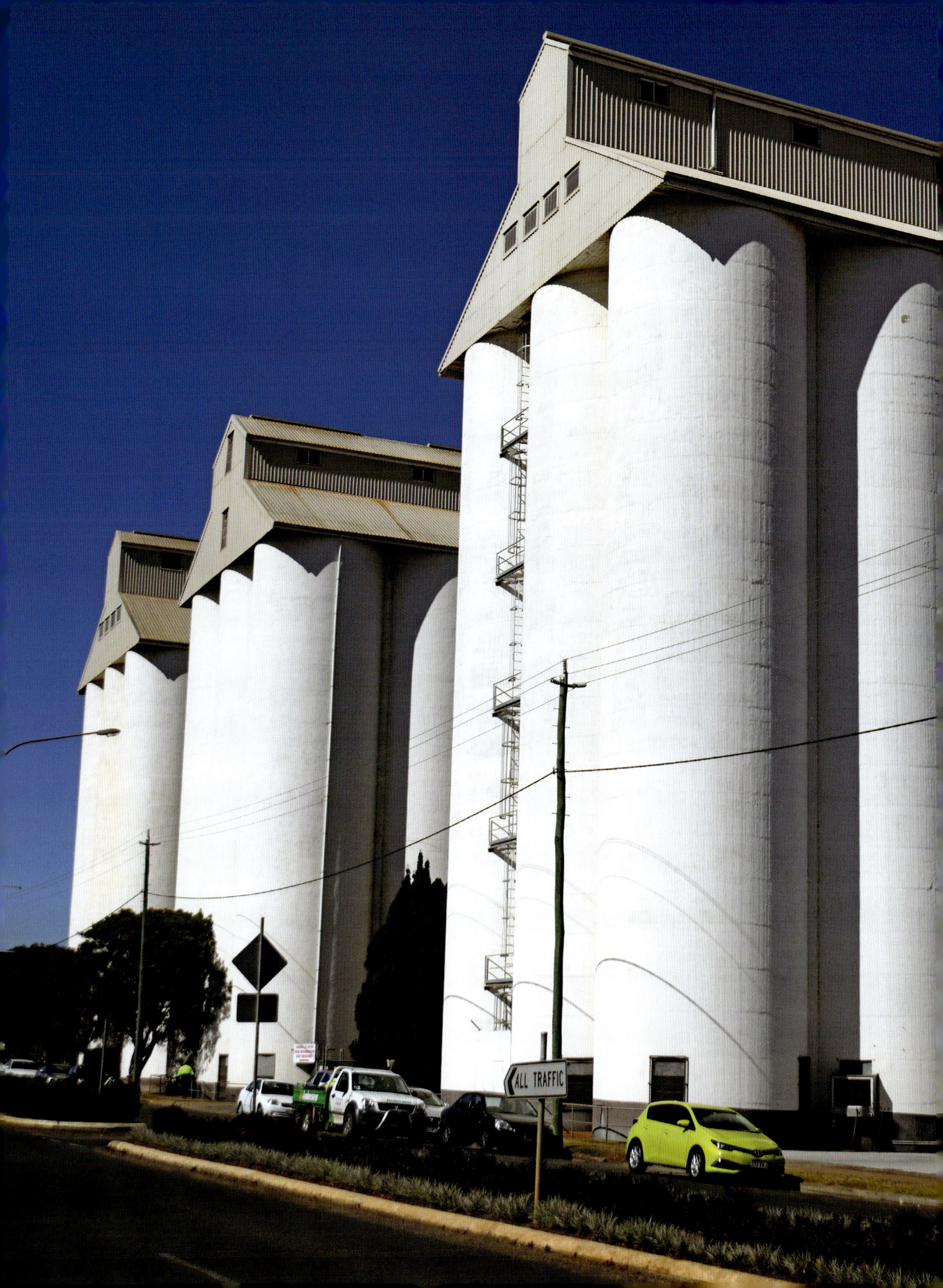
ALL TRAFFIC

- EPIC BIKE RIDES OF AUSTRALIA & NEW ZEALAND -

THE CENTRAL WEST CYCLE TRAIL

A community-led effort has created a five-day route through central western NSW, linking regional towns via quiet dirt roads and tracks through vineyards and carpets of wildflowers.

Everyone who goes cycle touring does it for different reasons, but for me, it's the epitome of 'the journey, not the destination'. The Central West Cycle Trail (CWC) is all about the journey, because it's a loop — you can start and finish wherever you want. This circuit of the central west of New South Wales links the major towns of Mudgee, Dubbo and Wellington, and a handful of smaller ones, including Gulgong, Dunedoo, Mendooran and Ballimore.

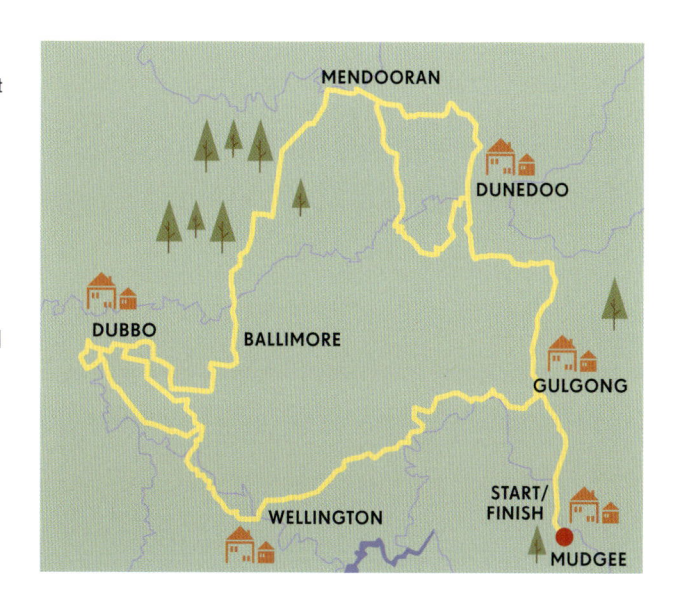

It's unique in NSW as the only marked multi-day trail for cyclists. A group of locals set it up after trying for years to build a rail trail in the district. Sick of battling the bureaucracy, they decided to map out their own trail, putting up yellow markers, and producing a website with downloadable maps. They searched out the quietest country roads and trails through woodlands, farms and conservation areas, so bike-packers could find plenty of variety, with barely a passing car. Each day ends at a town with an Airbnb, pub or camping option available, all pumping money into the local economy. It's perfect for people like me who've cycled in Europe, but haven't done much in Australia, simply because of the lack of options.

Pete and I headed out of Mudgee on the highway. After a few kilometres, we turned off onto back-roads and soon, even quieter gravel. The winter rains had been good and the fields were full of chest-high wheat, interspersed with vineyards, in one of Australia's oldest wine regions.

After 30km (19 miles), we made it to the beautiful little town of Gulgong, and saw our first group of fellow cyclists lingering outside a cafe with a CWC sticker in the window. They were doing the trail too – albeit on alternative routes to challenge their new 29er steel mountain bikes with super-fat tyres. One attraction of the CWC is that the organisers have mapped out various alternative routes, so you can choose your adventure.

After coffee, Pete and I headed back out onto the road, on the main trail, making for the small town of Dunedoo, while our new friends took the backroads via the intriguingly named Slap Dash Creek. Our paths crossed again later that morning. They'd had a ball with their big tyres on a trail suitable for mountain bikes, but told us we'd made the right decision to stick to easier dirt roads on our gravel bikes. While we pushed on, they turned the other way for a date with a farmer, who was offering lunch for passing cyclists. As Barbara Hickson, one of the trail's founders, has said: 'It's helping everyone, all sorts of people: breweries, cheese makers, cafes and farmers.'

> *"The beer we shared that afternoon at the Hair of the Dog hotel, watched by a friendly horse, was well earned"*

We made Dunedoo (population 750) in the mid-afternoon, after 90km (55 miles) and about 600m (1950ft) of climbing – nothing too strenuous, but requiring a good base level of fitness. The next day we set out for Mendooran in woodier country, once again on quiet dirt roads, and for the first time with no mobile phone reception. Only the sheep and cows were around to keep us company. At the end of the day, we fetched up at the Royal Hotel, shared with six more groups of cyclists, some of whom staying in the rooms and others camping out the back. That night we sat on the hotel's balcony, discussing our ride with the others. The universal theme was excitement at being able to tour off-the-beaten-track in Australia.

The next day, between Mendooran and Ballimore, was a joy, riding through Goonoo State Conservation Area on the most challenging but rewarding day of the whole trip. The firetrail was hard going, as we picked our way carefully around rocks and stones, only to hit a sudden patch of sand and slide out altogether. Progress was easier after I let some pressure out of my tyres.

MUDGEE WINES

Mudgee is one of the best food and wine destinations in NSW. Grapes have been grown here since 1858, but in the past few decades, the region has taken off, producing cabernet sauvignons, chardonnays, rieslings and shiraz. Anyone doing the CWC can spend an extra few days in Mudgee or its surrounds to visit some of the wineries. The Mudgee Food and Wine Month in September is a great time to explore the region by bike.

Left to right: Gulgong Pioneers Museum offers a wealth of local history; a river near Dubbo during the dry season; vintage signage in a Gulgong pub. Previous spread: scenes along the way

But there were other glorious stretches among a sea of wildflowers that had exploded after the winter rains. The beer we shared that afternoon at the Hair of the Dog hotel, watched by a friendly horse, was well earned.

The following day we were back on bitumen, under leaden skies that soon gave way to rain. By the time we pulled into the small town of Wongarbon to shelter under the post office awning, we were soaked through. As I pulled some dry clothes from my bag, the door (with a CWC sticker on it) opened, a woman stepped out, and unbidden said, 'I can only offer you coffee and muffins.'

'That'll do,' we replied, and with the hot drinks in us and dry tops on, we began to feel vaguely normal. From Wongarbon, the trail has a 60km (37 mile) side loop west to Dubbo, the largest town in the central west, known for the branch of Taronga Zoo that it hosts, along with all the animals too big for the Sydney site. Still, we decided to stay on the loop and head east for Wellington.

The rain had stopped by now, and the riding was wonderful through the rolling hills, on thankfully quiet bitumen roads, before the climb up Mt Arthur and descent into Wellington. The fifth day took us back to Gulgong, following the picturesque Cudgegong River on good dirt roads, despite the recent downpours. It was a pleasure to return to the same café with its friendly CWC sticker. We were wet and tired after five days of exploring new countryside – but above all, we were happy. **DM**

TOOLKIT

Start/Finish // Mudgee or Dubbo
Distance // 430km (267 miles)
Duration // 4-6 days

Getting there // The easiest way to access the trail from Sydney (the closest big city) is to drive to Mudgee and leave your car there. Trains run from Sydney's Central Station to Wellington or Dubbo with a maximum of four spots for bikes, which must be boxed. You can also catch a train to Lithgow and transfer by coach to Mudgee.

When to go // You can do the trail year-round, but summers can get very hot and winters cold. The best months are March to June and September to November.

What to pack // Keep it light and simple. Take a few pairs of cycling knicks and tops, including a long sleeve version, a jacket and waterproof outerwear. For evenings, take an extra pair of trousers and footwear.

Where to stay // All the towns along the CWC have accommodation at pubs, hotels and private rentals. Most towns and some pubs have areas for camping.

More info // www.centralwestcycletrail.com.au

Opposite: Canyons and caves at Wombeyan

MORE LIKE THIS
NEW SOUTH WALES RIDES

WINDSOR TO GOSFORD VIA WISEMANS FERRY

The sandstone bush country around Sydney is the setting for this ride along quiet roads beside the Hawkesbury River. There are some busy on-road sections at the start of the ride from Windsor train station and at the end going into Gosford, but otherwise it's quiet, with a couple of breaks to cross the river on a ferry. Reward yourself at the end of day one with a dip in the river at Wisemans Ferry and a drink at the pub. Day two begins with more stunning riding along the Hawkesbury before the road leaves the river and climbs Mangrove Mountain. It's a long climb, so have a good rest at the top before winding down into Gosford where you can catch a train back to Sydney.

Start // Windsor train station
Finish // Gosford train station
Distance // 138km (85 miles)
Duration // 2 days

SWALLOW TAIL PASS LOOP

Day one of this ride in the Southern Highlands takes you through rugged bushlands from Mittagong, down to the Wollondilly River, then on to the Wombeyan Caves. It's worth taking the time to explore these caves in the Wombeyan Karst Conservation Reserve. You can camp there or push on for Taralga, where there are a couple of hotel options. Day two is longer, at 120km (74 miles), so be prepared, particularly as tap water isn't available for 85km (53 miles) after Taralga. There's more great riding along gravel and bitumen as you follow the Wollondilly River and then head through the Southern Highlands towns of Exeter, Moss Vale and Bowral to finish back in Mittagong.

Start/Finish // Mittagong train station
Distance // 217km (135 miles)
Duration // 2 days
More info // www.omafiets.com.au

MOSS VALE TO NOWRA

This ride runs from the Southern Highlands down the escarpment to the south coast of New South Wales. You can start at Moss Vale, or add 16km (10 miles) by getting off the train earlier at Mittagong. Either way, it's a doable one-day ride, or a leisurely two days with an overnight stay at the beautiful village of Kangaroo Valley. The highlight is the descent through thick rainforest into Kangaroo Valley, before a climb out and another descent to the coast. Catch a train back to Sydney from Bomaderry, 5km (3 miles) from Nowra.

Start // Moss Vale train station
Finish// Nowra
Distance // 85km (53 miles)
Duration // 1-2 days
More info //
www.visitkangaroovalley.com.au;
www.omafiets.com.au

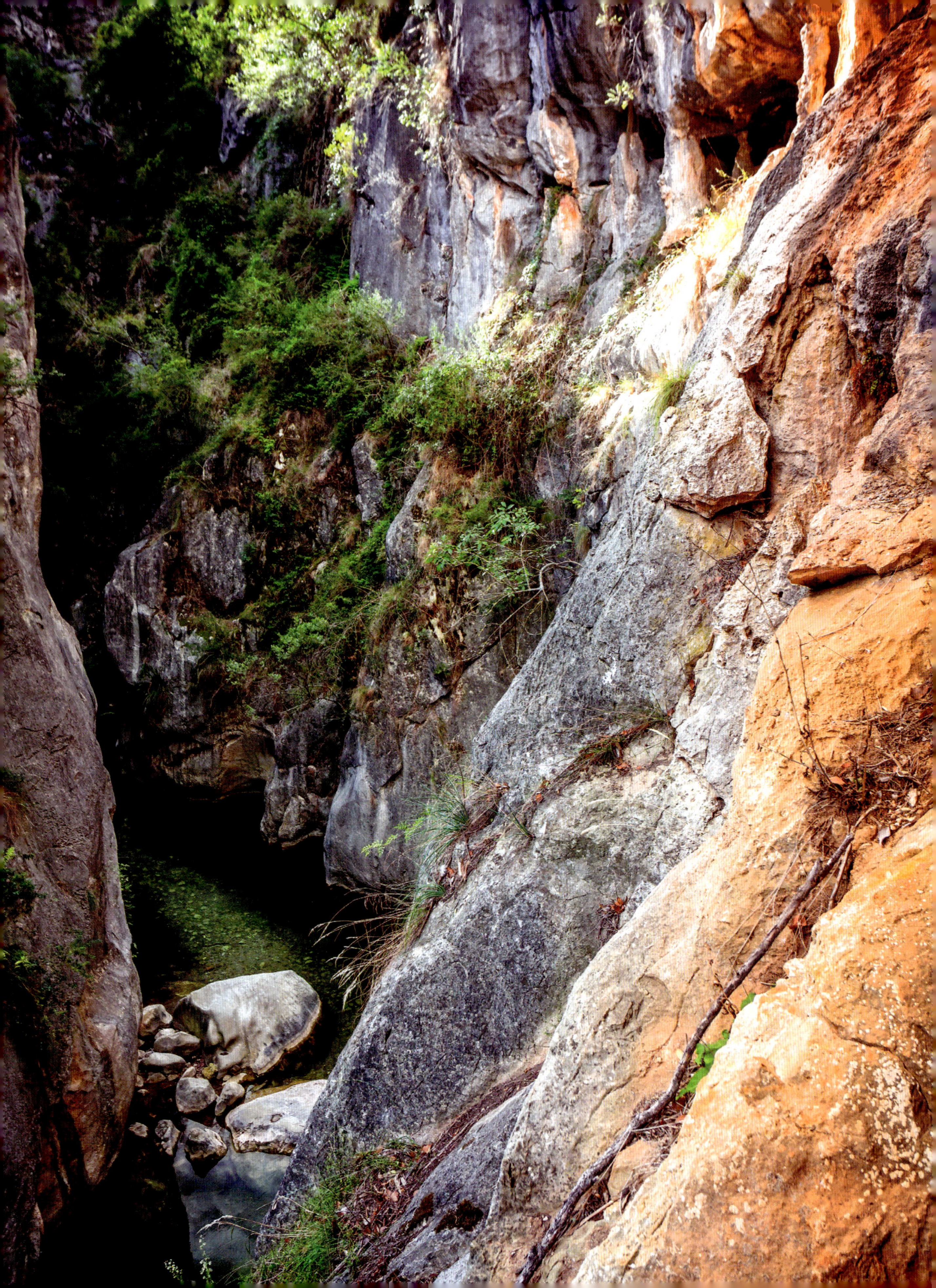

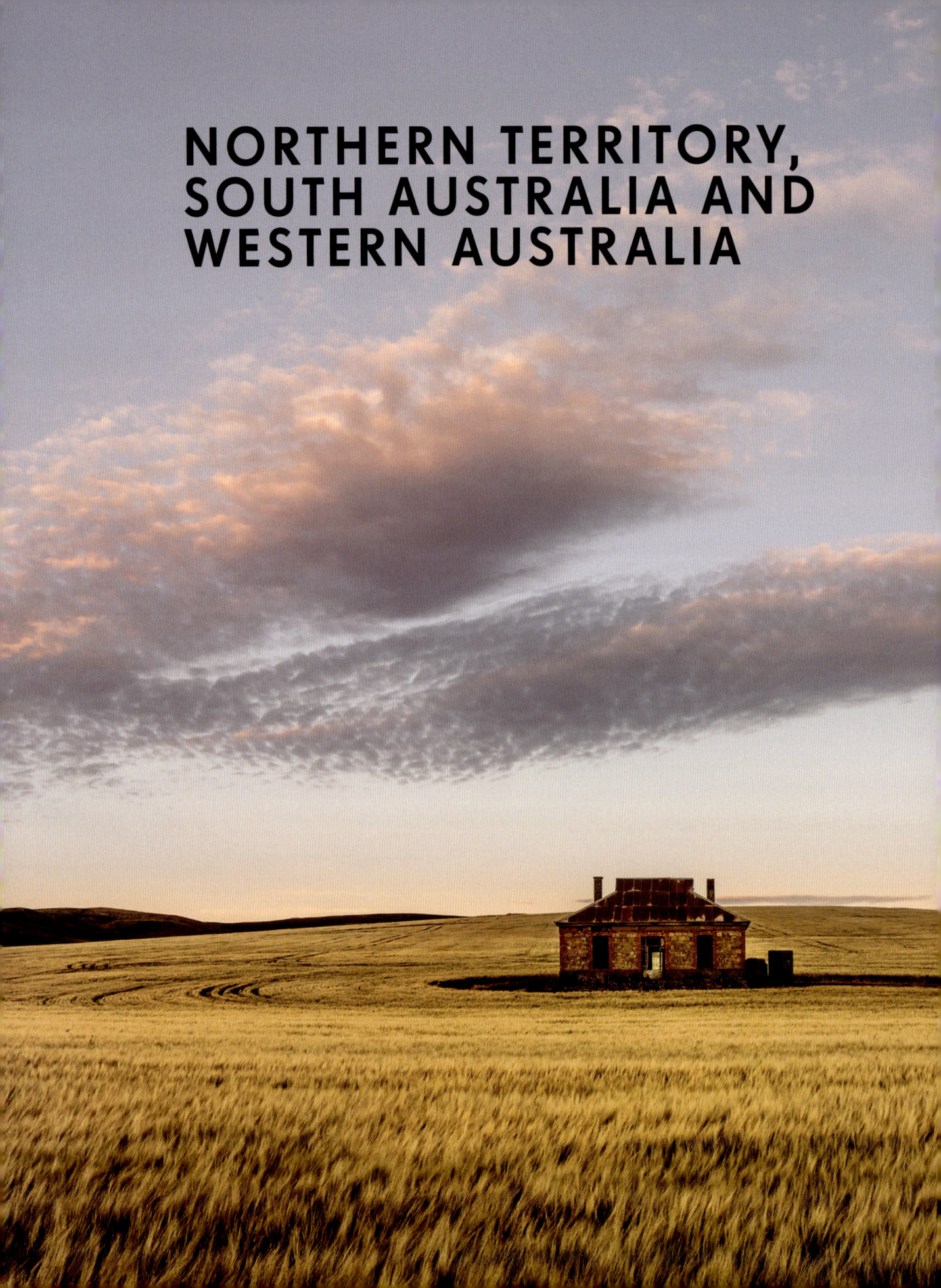

NORTHERN TERRITORY, SOUTH AUSTRALIA AND WESTERN AUSTRALIA

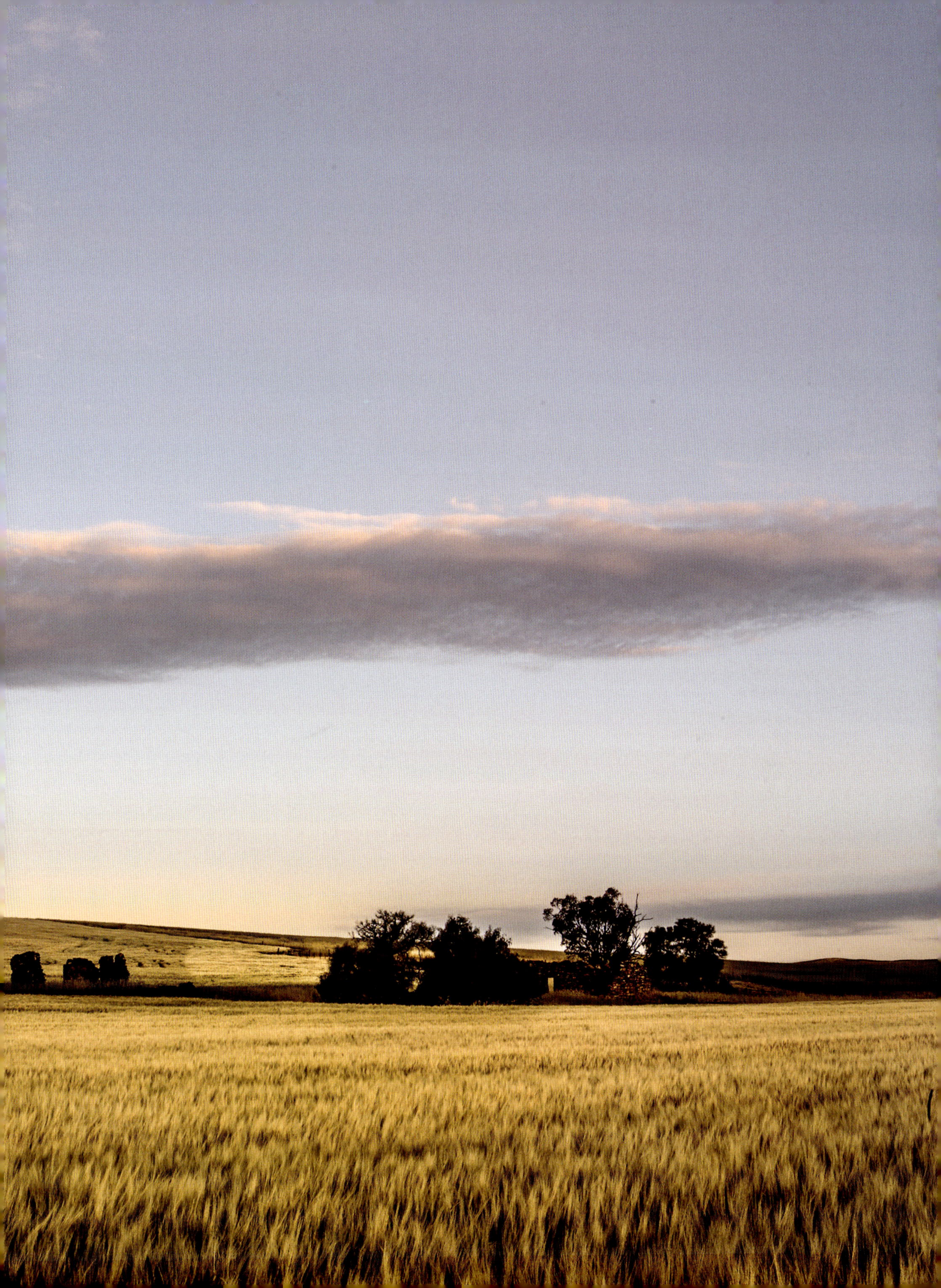

— EPIC BIKE RIDES OF AUSTRALIA & NEW ZEALAND —

THE TOUR OF MARGARET RIVER

Cycling's closest event to a golf pro-am gets you racing shoulder-to-shoulder with world champions along beaches and through the vineyards of Margaret River.

It's an uphill grind from the windswept beach of Yallingup. The air is salt-soaked and, for once this week, not by my sweat. I glance up and see an Orica Greenedge jersey come past, fresh off a season of Grand Tours. It offers a perplexing moment: do I follow that wheel? It seems like an opportunity too good to pass up – how often does a professional cyclist give me a free draft? Or is it going to put me in a world of hurt in another kilometre or two?

How did I get into this situation? I signed up for the Tour of Margaret River, a three-day sportive event with 150 teams of all levels, from corporate and social clubs to national racers, with the added element of invited World Tour professionals among the teams. It's an unconventional race format that surprises and delights, and it's not every day you have Marianne Vos, Annemiek Van Vleuten or Jens Voigt as your domestique.

We arrive for day one, south of Perth in the small Western Australian town of Augusta, where the Indian and Southern Oceans meet. Needless to say, it's windy. As we line up for stage one, we hear our names booming over the loudspeaker, introduced by the English voice of the Tour de France, Matthew Keenan. It just got very real. It's a 6km (3.7 mile) individual time trial, but ridden as a team, the aim is to get our protected rider to the line first, sacrificing ourselves along the way.

Almost as predictable as the wind was me losing contact with my Italian teammates, a feeling I'd become all too familiar with over the next four stages. But as the road empties in front of me, I look up from my stem and appreciate the breeze and the eucalypt forests running to the continent's southwesterly tip.

This is the most exhausted I've ever felt riding 6km. We have two hours before stage two begins, returning to our hire car to rest our feet. Parked next to us is Cameron Meyer. We have a chat over whatever snacks we can scramble together and call lunch. Just as bizarre as the stage formats in this race is the notion of riding shoulder-to-shoulder with world champions, of being called to the line by Matt or Robbie McEwen, or Scott Sunderland directing our race as if it were the Tour of Flanders.

The afternoon brings another time trial, this one ridden as a full team. Stage two leads from Cape Leeuwin, north to

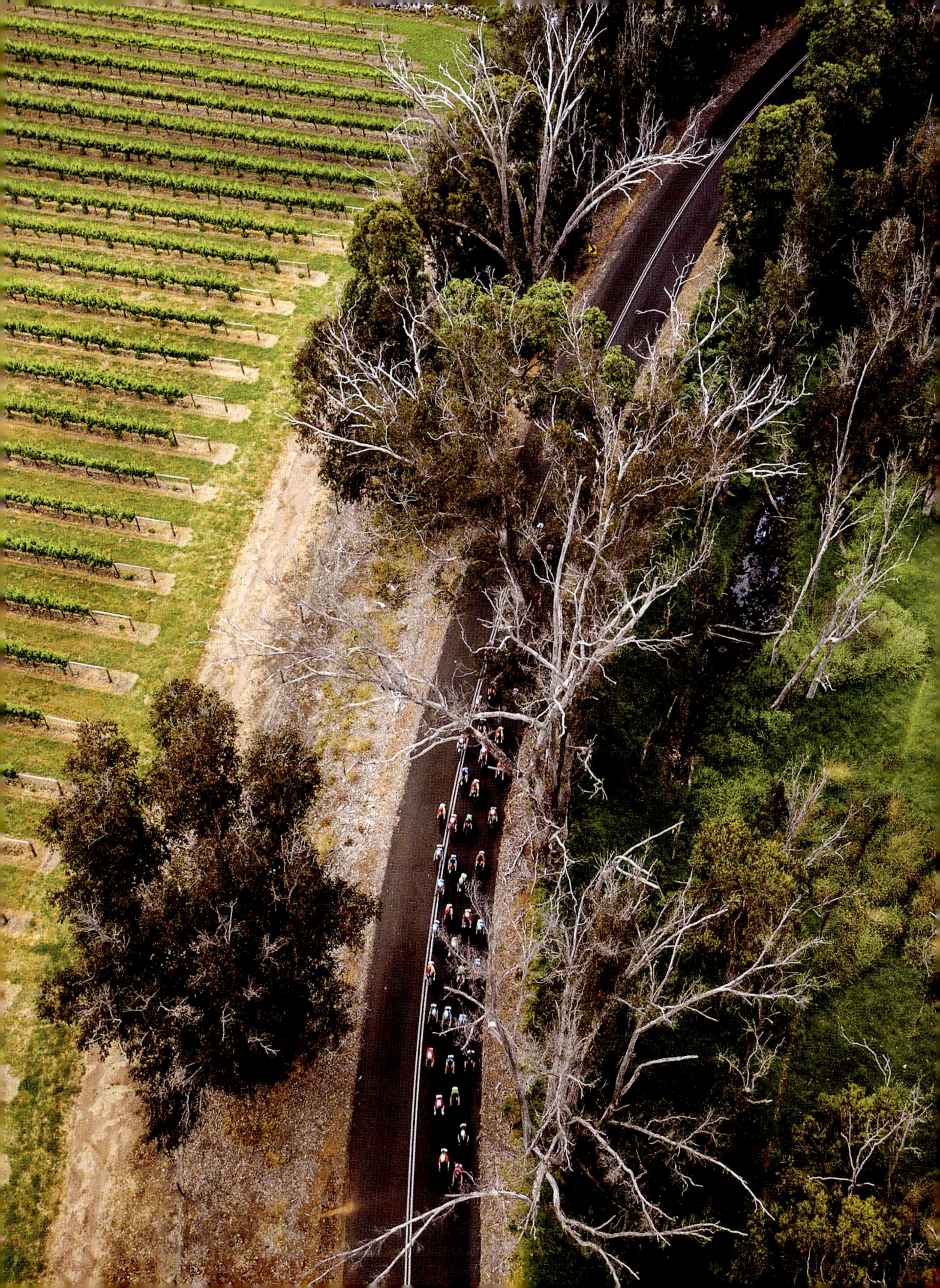

Witchcliffe, a small town on the way to Cape Naturaliste, through the Leeuwin-Naturaliste National Park, Western Australia's most visited. It's on to the iconic Caves Rd and we have it all to ourselves. We ride past the signs to numerous limestone karst systems that hold fossils of Australia's extinct megafauna and evidence of Indigenous habitation dating back nearly 50,000 years.

Maybe I was too distracted by the signs to all the caves and tall trees, because we emerge at an intersection to find pro racer Luke Durbridge and four riders in tow, coming from the other direction. We must have taken a wrong turn. We scramble and attempt to follow them on the winding road through towering karri and jarrah eucalypts. The karris, growing to 90m (295ft), are some of the tallest trees in the world and are only found around the southwest.

The following day we meet stage three, a real challenge, with a 100km (62 mile) loop through pine forests, occasionally opening up to vineyards. This is the furthest we've been from the coast, through places such as Nannup, Dalgarup, Maranup, Balingup – you get the idea. For the Noongar people, 'up' translates to a 'place of'. We start and finish in Nannup, translating to 'stopping place' – or possibly 'place of parrots'. Again, it takes approximately 6km (3.7 miles) before our team disintegrates. I bounce from group to group, eventually finding tempo with some of the women's division favourites. It is an amazing opportunity to be able to tag along on the back of a women's race, and as the dust settles through the afternoon glow, I see a few of them give a lesson in sprinting.

SOUTHWESTERN WINE COUNTRY

Margaret River is known as one of Australia's great wine destinations and also its most isolated. With a population of less than 9,000, yet more than 200 vineyards, it produces 25% of the country's premium wine. The first vines were planted barely 50 years ago, generally Bordeaux varieties. The ridge between Capes Leeuwin and Naturaliste is considered Australia's most marked maritime climate – wet in winter, with onshore winds and mild summers.

Clockwise from top: teams race against the clock on the time-trial stage of the Tour of Margaret River. Previous spread: road racing among the vines

We head back to the coast and have a slow afternoon ride along the beaches near the quiet hamlet of Gracetown and one of Australia's legendary surf breaks at Prevelly. We bump into Robbie McEwen making the most of the quiet roads and long daylight hours after race day has wrapped up, and he advises us it's far safer on the road than in those waters.

Stage four departs from Yalingup, near the tip of Cape Naturaliste, to ride south back to Witchcliffe, thus completing stage two's journey from cape to cape. The Indian Ocean is battering the start line, and if we wait here any longer we'll be shaking sand out of our shoes. The road immediately ramps up and so does the pace. I ping-pong between wheels, catching a draft off Damien Howson, then leapfrog to another group with Steele von Hoff. Caves Road winds through the coastal heath, undulating with occasional glimpses of the sea and a fresh breeze on the small rises. I watch as Luke Durbridge and Robbie McEwen marshal their group for the final few kilometres. I may have just witnessed history: Robbie leading out a sprint.

The day ends in renowned Margaret River style, at a vineyard. The official presentations are held in a casual atmosphere with a bite to eat and a cold glass of a regional favourite as we lie on the lawn watching the trophies being handed out in front of the sunset. Our rider made the podium in a respectable second place, but we didn't quite clinch the victory. We're soon consoled over a beer with Tiffany Cromwell, while Simon Clarke recounts his second place at the Cadel Evans Road Race earlier this season. After three days of fantasy cycling, we feel like we can almost relate. **HSH**

"The Indian Ocean is battering the start line, and if we wait here any longer we'll be shaking sand out of our shoes"

TOOLKIT

Start // Witchcliffe
Finish // Nannup
Distance // 225km (140 miles)
Duration // 4-5 stages over 3 days
Getting there // Margaret River is 270km (168 miles) south of Perth, with its international airport, car rentals and bus services. Alternatively, Busselton Margaret River Airport has direct flights to Melbourne.
When to go // The Tour of Margaret River runs annually in early November.
What to take // A team of six riders, basic spares, any nutrition required and sunscreen.
Where to stay // There's a wide range of accommodation available throughout the small towns and along the coast en route.
Where to eat // Margaret River township has many places where you can grab a bite.
More info // www.facebook.com/tourofmr

Opposite: sun-soaked Perth is a new venue for criterium racing

MORE LIKE THIS
SUPER SPORTIVES

GOLDFIELDS CYCLASSIC, WA

Touted as Australia's richest handicap race, this runs through the Outback 600km (373 miles) inland from Perth, in a region that's home to some of the world's richest gold deposits. Its origins date to 1928, when residents of the booming mining towns wanted to bring distance cycling races to the region. Racing over the red soil takes place over the first weekend in June with a graded handicap each day – 131km (81 miles) from Kalgoorlie to Menzies, and 113km (70 miles) from Menzies to Leonora. As you might expect, the roads are generally flat, flanked by red desert and big skies. For those not competing, the Saturday route also plays host to a non-competitive fondo, ridden as an individual, or team relay.
Start // Kalgoorlie
Finish // Leonora
Distance // 244km (151 miles)
More info // www.cyclassic.com.au

PERTH CITY CRITERIUM, WA

In 2023, crit racing – in which riders sprint hell-for-leather around laps of an urban course – returned to Perth. City streets were closed for the March event, which will hopefully be here to stay. It's an exciting spectator occasion, with plenty of vantage points to view the elbow-to-elbow racing, but if you've got a B, C or D-grade racing licence you can also take part before the elite category take to the streets. Races last about 30 minutes for amateurs and longer for the pros. There are also taster sessions for all sorts of cycling and the public can ride a loop of the 900m (2950ft) closed-road circuit before the racing starts.
Start/Finish // Russell Square
More info // www.westcycle.org.au

THE WEEKENDER, VIC

A new event by the stalwarts of Australian sportives, Bicycle Network, the Weekender celebrates the region of South and West Gippsland, known for its coastlines and vineyards, but never cycled enough. This is a fully supported ride, from the foothills of the Strzelecki Range to the coast and back. It features historic small towns and rolling green hills, with the coastline and open farm vistas the highlight looping south on day one; while the riding is a little higher in the forests and ridges of the Strzelecki Ranges heading north on day two. The whole event is fully supported, with feed stations, mechanical expertise and vehicles, and an event tent village is available for camping accommodation. Both days depart and return to Leongatha, a small country town two hours west of Melbourne.
Start/Finish // Leongatha
Distance // 115km (71 miles); 70km (43 miles)
More info // www.bicyclenetwork.com.au

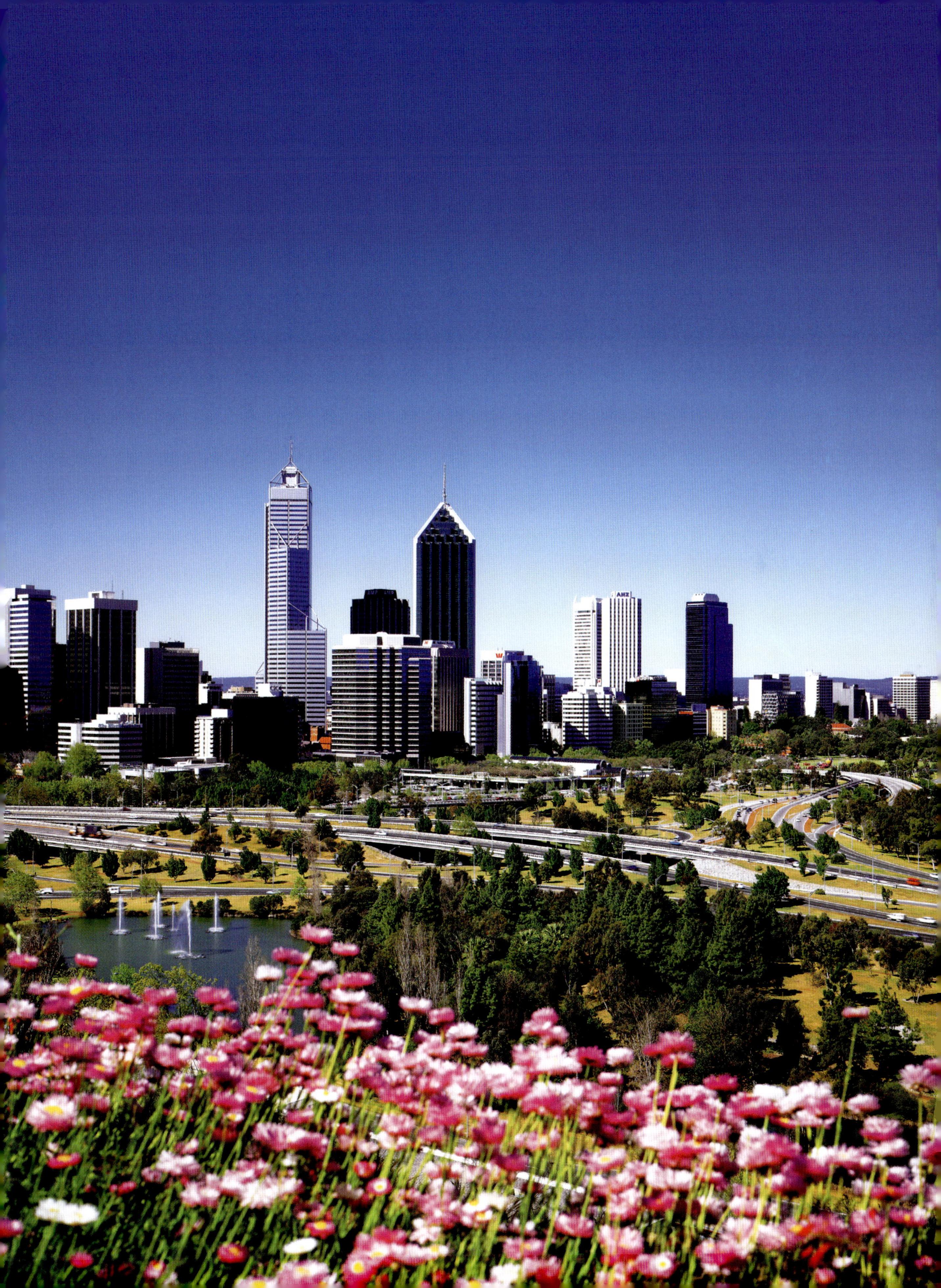

- EPIC BIKE RIDES OF AUSTRALIA & NEW ZEALAND -

ROCKS AND CROCS IN THE TOP END

This adventurous ride takes you through the Top End's land-out-of-time landscapes, with its endless waterfalls, gorges and escarpments, and strong connections to Aboriginal Australia.

The thermometer reads 36°C. I've been out of water for hours, and the next town is still 50km (31 miles) away. Flies swarm in their hundreds, drinking the moisture from my skin. It makes sense – I'm the only water source around. Am I in over my head? I was in over my head hours ago.

The Top End – the locals' name for the Northern Territory's far north – is maybe a questionable location for a bicycle tour. The shocking heat, ever-present crocodiles and sheer remoteness are all arguments for taking it easy instead. Yet the Top End is also exactly the Australia that people so often dream about, where the landscape is wild, the swimming holes pristine and the possibilities for adventure endless.

My week-long ride starts on the ferry at dawn. It's just a short hop across the harbour from Darwin to the Cox Peninsula, and as I wheel my bike off the ferry, the day is already growing hot. The tarmac road is deserted and the red earth is parched. I startle flights of red-tailed black cockatoos from the trees as I pedal past. I spin the day away, and 130km (81 miles) later reach Wangi Falls in Litchfield National Park, where I pitch my tent and swim out beneath its high twin cascades. Litchfield is a wonderland of rock holes and waterfalls, but what I'm

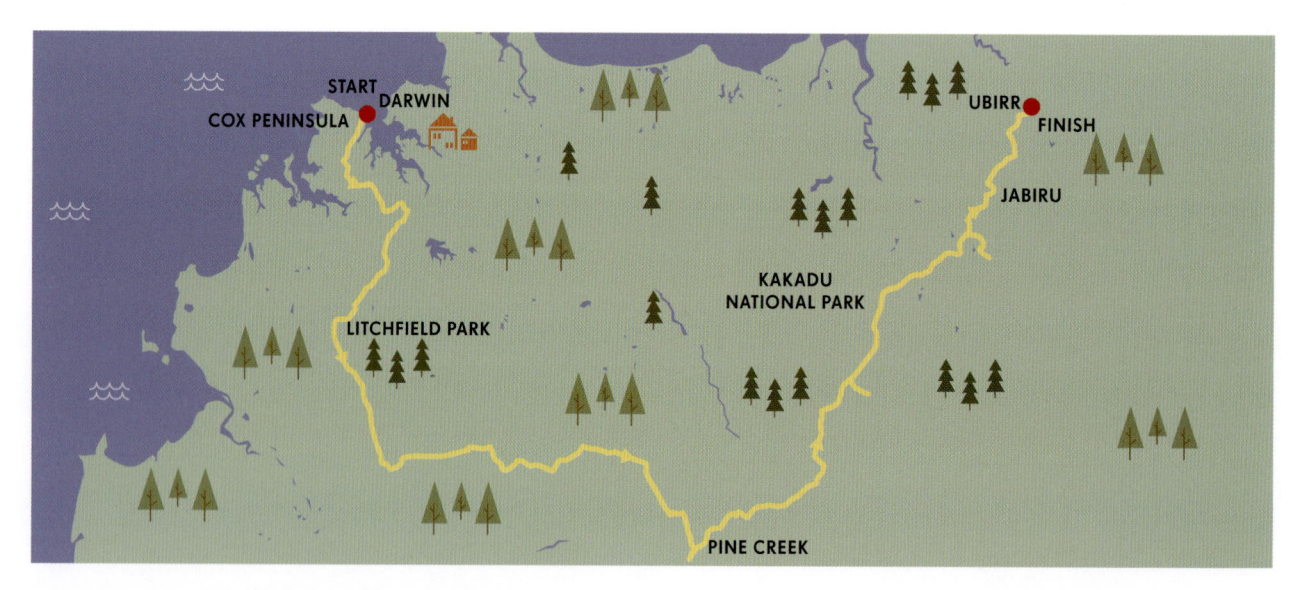

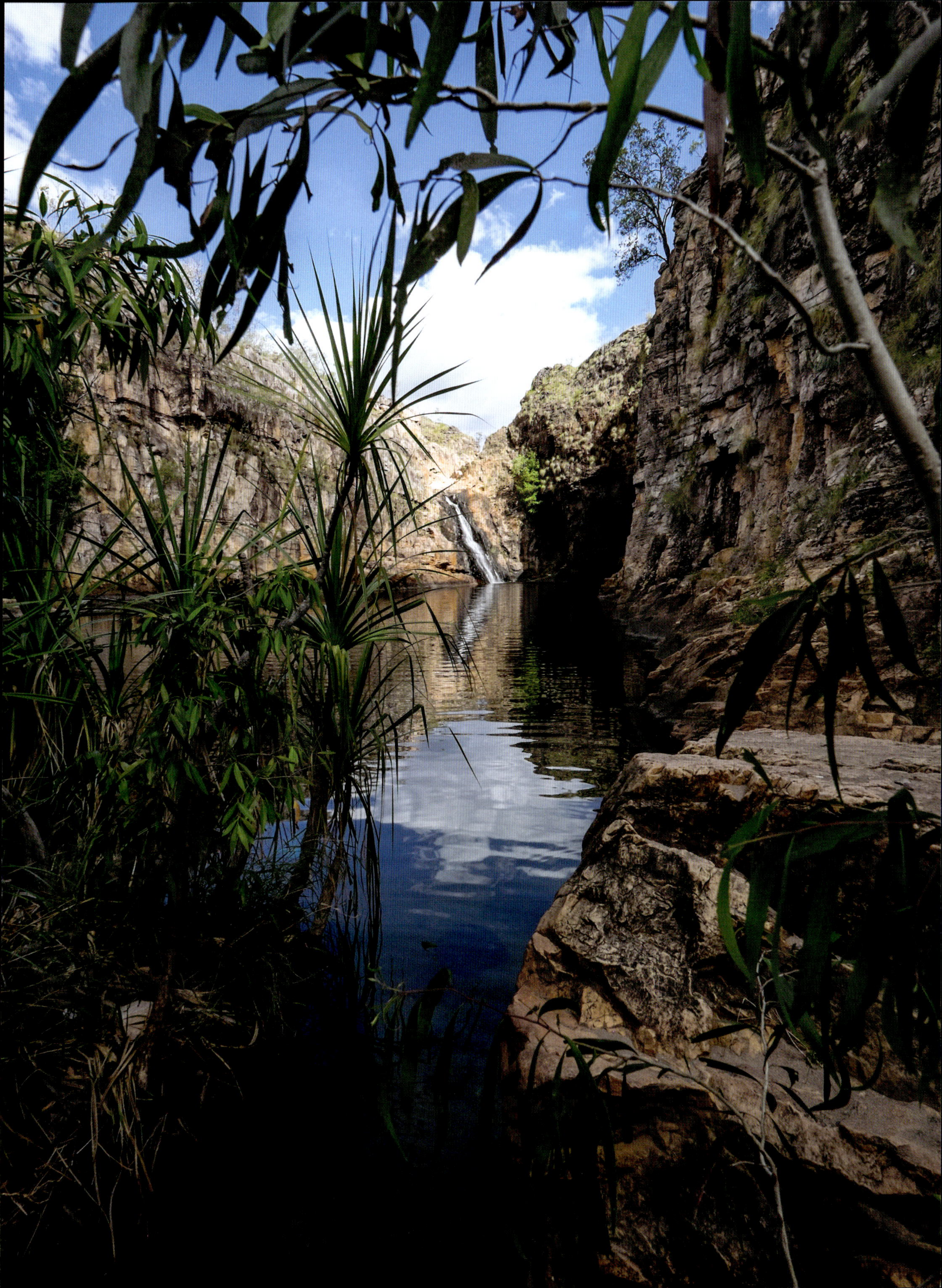

"A dozen huge saltwater crocodiles haunt the water, submerging and surfacing like toothy submarines. I stay well back"

really here for is the Reynolds River Track. It's 44km (27 miles) of remote and gloriously bad road, and I set off on it the next morning. It's good fun churning through loose sand and over deep ruts and baby-head rocks, but the water crossings are another matter. I wade the clear-flowing Reynolds River itself, but hitch across a very croc-y looking swamp with a passing 4WD. The driver merrily drinks a beer in the cab as we plough through the deep, dark water.

On the other side, I cycle over red earth beneath big blue skies. Huge, alien-looking termite mounds dot the grasslands, and lean kangaroos scatter into the bush as I pass. I make camp that night in a grove at Sandy Creek Falls, luxuriating in a cooling swim after a hot and dusty day.

The next morning I emerge onto the Daly River Road, and spend hours stupidly pedalling through the heat of midday. I arrive at the tiny ghost town of Grove Hill, 115km (71 miles) later, with night having fallen. I am nauseous and feel dead in the saddle. Stan, the owner of Grove Hill's now-defunct pub greets me with typical Aussie candour: 'Jesus, mate. You look buggered!'

The next day I get a reprieve. It's an easy 60km (37 miles) of undulating dirt road to the lively little town of Pine Creek; on arriving, I immediately head to the pub. After the past three days, it feels like a holiday. I spend a glorious evening drinking cold beer and yarning with Pine Creek's mix of locals and tourists, Aboriginal folk and whitefellas alike. A park ranger here educates me about the difference between freshwater and saltwater crocodiles thus: 'The freshies, see, they'll just take a bite outta ya. But the salties, they won't just kill ya – they'll stalk ya to kill ya!' He roars with laughter. Duly noted.

The next morning, I turn onto the smooth tarmac of the Kakadu Highway, and into Kakadu National Park itself. It's the largest national park in Australia, and Unesco-listed for its outstanding natural and cultural heritage.

Kakadu also has dozens of official and unofficial side-tracks to explore. At the recommendation of the ranger in Pine Creek, I cycle down a dirt road to the gorge at Maguk, then hike up to the pools hidden above the falls. In the evening I lie back and watch the long, incandescent sunset from my tent.

It's a cool, grey dawn when I set out the next day, stopping at the billabong at Yellow Water for sunrise, and watching magpie geese and huge black-necked jabiru storks take flight from the mirror-like water. The next stage takes me north up the highway to the Aboriginal rock art site at Burrungkuy. There, in the shade of towering rock ledges, I marvel at 20,000 years of visible history, and at the ingenuity of the people who created it.

The day is furnace-like, and though I know I should stop, I am so close to Jabiru, the park's main settlement, that I pedal through the heat, arriving 90 minutes later to a supermarket feast of cheese and fresh fruit. I camp at the town's caravan park, then the next morning ride 40km (25 miles) north to the edge of the park. From the highway, the wild stone country of Arnhem Land rises up to the east like the walls of Mordor. At Cahills Crossing, the causeway across the East Alligator River, a dozen huge saltwater crocodiles haunt the water at low tide, submerging and surfacing like toothy submarines. I stay well back from the edge.

In the afternoon, I pitch my tent at a sandy campsite, and wait for the sunset. As the day's shadows lengthen, I ride up to the sprawling rock-art site at Ubirr, then set off on foot, exploring the hundreds of paintings nestled among its ledges, cliffs and overhangs.

I sigh. The day and the ride are almost over. Above the rocks is a plateau overlooking the broad green floodplain to the west, painted gold by the setting sun. 'Unforgettable' is one of the most overused words in travel, I think. But the Top End? It truly is. **MC**

© Michael Crompton

ROCK ART

This ride – like all activities in Australia – takes place on Aboriginal land, and the thousands of paintings at Kakadu represent an unparalleled historical and cultural record. The work covers a period of 20,000 years, much of it from the 'Freshwater Period' of the past 2,000 years. It includes outstanding examples of 'x-ray art' of local animals such as wallabies and goannas, as well as stories of the Dreaming, and even records of early European contact.

Clockwise from top: a termite mound near Surprise Creek; rock art at Nourlangie in Kakadu National Park; Buley swimming hole in Litchfield National Park. Previous spread: Barramundi Gorge in Kakadu National Park

TOOLKIT

Start/Finish // Darwin
Distance // 630km (390 miles)
Getting there // Darwin has good domestic and international air connections. From Jabiru in Kakadu National Park it's 290km (180 miles) back to Darwin. A bus service (3.5 hours) is available.
When to go // The dry season is from May to October – the landscape can be underwater at other times. Always check the latest road conditions.
What to wear // Light, loose-fitting clothing with maximum coverage for sun protection.
What to pack // Wide tyres (2.4-plus inches) are advisable for the Reynolds River Track, and some side tracks in Kakadu. Have at least 8 litres of water-carrying capacity, plus purification tabs or a filter.
Where to stay // There are good campsites in the national parks, and hotels in Darwin, Pine Creek and Jabiru.
More info // www.northernterritory.com

Opposite: an emu grazes near South Australia's Oodnadatta Track

MORE LIKE THIS
OUTBACK ODYSSEYS

MEREENIE LOOP, NORTHERN TERRITORY

This remote, adventurous, week-long route takes in some of the finest scenery of Australia's Red Centre, including the spectacular West MacDonnell Ranges. Starting at the beehive domes of Kings Canyon, the tarmac ends shortly thereafter, and for the next 200km (124 miles) you're on your own – no food or water resupply. The road is often sandy and wildly corrugated, but the scenery is more than adequate compensation: a way-out tableau of red earth and low broken mountains, with the occasional wild brumby galloping past. After the climb of Tylers Pass (with great views of the meteorite crater of Gosse Bluff), the paved, well-travelled Namatjira Drive leads all the way back to Alice Springs past the wonders of the West Macs. It's worth taking a few extra days to explore the hikes and waterholes here – the climb of Mount Sonder and a swim at Ellery Creek are highlights. You officially need a $5 permit to travel the Loop – buy one in Alice Springs or Kings Canyon.
Start // Kings Canyon
Finish // Alice Springs
Distance // 390km (242 miles)
More info //
www.discovercentralaustralia.com

GIBB RIVER ROAD, WESTERN AUSTRALIA

The Gibb is legendary as the premier dirt route through the heart of WA's Kimberley region. Over the two-plus weeks of the ride (dry season, May–October only), you'll pass through savannah, tropical rainforest and lush river gorges, plus more red dirt than you can shake a stick at. The days when you'd have the Gibb to yourself are long over, but there's still more than enough adventure – and river crossings – to get the heart pumping. The road (mostly flat, but hot) takes in remote cattle stations, classic Aussie roadhouses, and some of the planet's most pristine swimming holes. The Gibb isn't on the way to anywhere, but it does belong on the bucket list.
Start // Kununurra
Finish // Derby
Distance // 700km (435 miles) – tack on another 200km (125 miles) for side trips

OODNADATTA TRACK, SOUTH AUSTRALIA

The Oodnadatta could be called the 'accessible Outback': a roughly week-long trek on good-quality gravel roads through a stark and beautiful desert landscape peppered with curiosities from Australia's past. The track takes between seven and 10 days to cycle, and should only be done in the cooler months from March to November. Over its (mostly flat) length, the Oodnadatta rolls on endlessly beneath big skies, passing natural hot springs at Coward Springs, and a number of fine oasis waterholes. The route also follows the old Ghan Railway and Overland Telegraph lines, and is dotted with countless cast-offs from these decommissioned pieces of infrastructure, including remains of old railway sidings, and crumbling and rusted telegraph stations, plus the odd settler homestead. For those with a bit more time, detours are possible out into the Painted Desert, or the dry inland basin of Lake Eyre.
Start // Marree
Finish // Marla
Distance // 620km (385 miles)

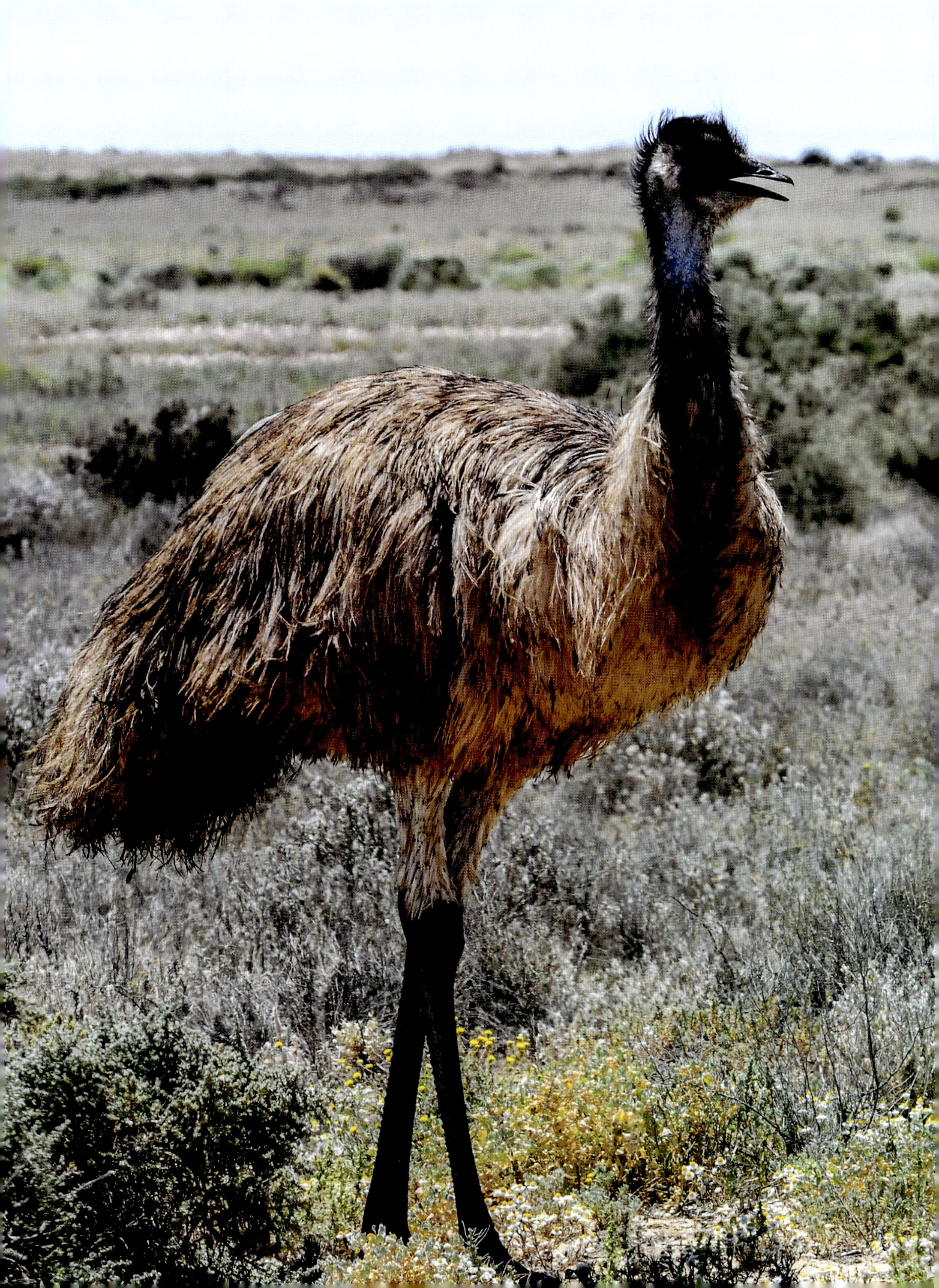

- EPIC BIKE RIDES OF AUSTRALIA & NEW ZEALAND -

THE MULTI-DAY MAWSON TRAIL

This 900km (560-mile) bikepacking odyssey through the Outback, from the Flinders Ranges to Adelaide, mixes gravel, grit, wind farms, wineries and wonder.

'Guess where this guy is taking his kids on holiday?' the service-station mechanic in the tiny town of Hawker shouts to his wife. 'Adelaide... on a bike. Lucky kids!'

I have to laugh. He's just let me pump up four sets of tyres in his workshop, and runs the general store, the first shop we've seen in two sleeps and 144km (89 miles). The joke at our expense is totally worth it.

The daily stages of our 900km (560 mile) Mawson Trail trip were months in the planning, especially over this first week in the Outback when help could be too far away to think about. In the first phase, route length depends solely on the distance between towns or, in their absence, hamlets and campsites with any type of food. After the fresh blast of air at Hawker, we experience our first headwinds as we turn away from the central Flinders Ranges' huge variety of hills towards flatter, dustier country and the pub in Cradock, population 13, with only five full-time residents according to the tourist sign.

Next morning, we start an 85km (53 mile) transition from the wide-open red-and-brown landscape into arid sheep-grazing land. We pass through the ruins of Simmonston, a town that started to be built in the late 1800s but was never finished, because it was too far from anything useful, and have lunch at the grave of the son of an earl, who drowned in a flash flood in 1852.

There's no sign of any water today, until we reach the green farms on the edge of Quorn. It's the first time we all think we might just make it to our destination in Adelaide, having become familiar with the packing and long days of decreasing

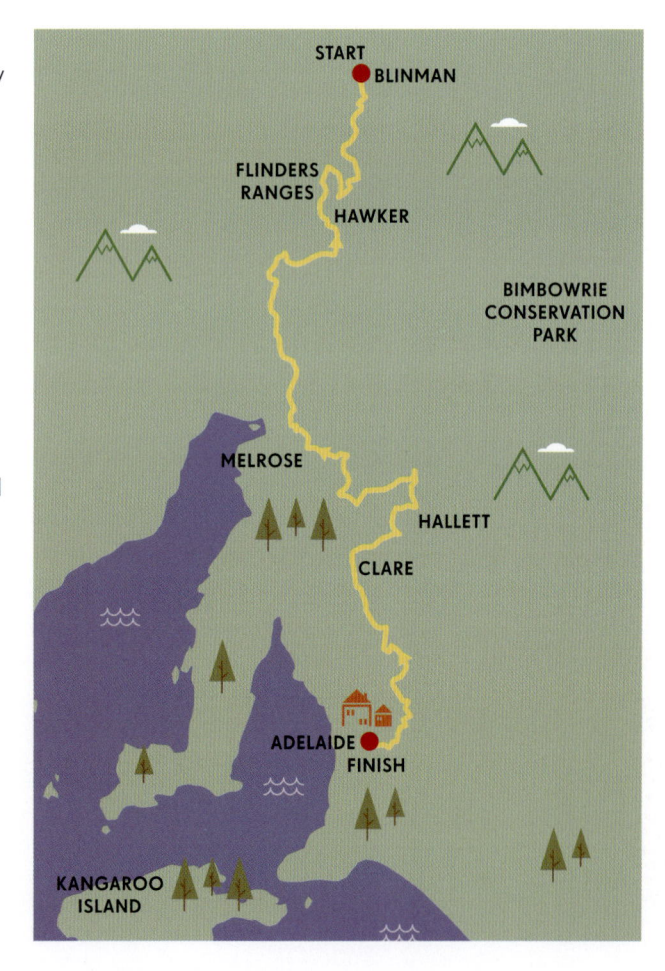

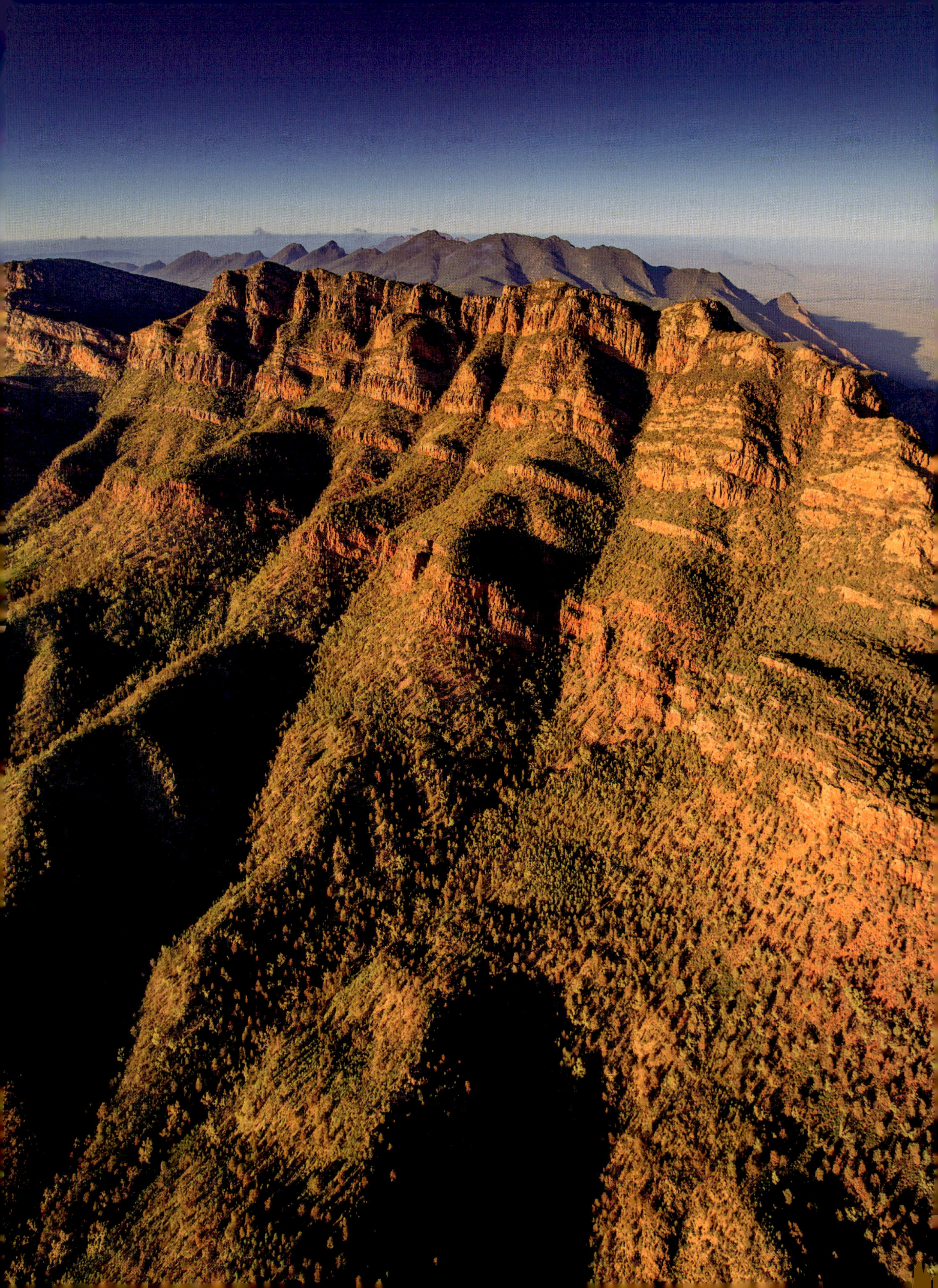

worry and increasing fun. From tomorrow, if we have a mechanical, someone will see us within an hour.

We had started the north-south version of the trail in Blinman, a former copper mine and South Australia's highest town, dug deep into the rugged Outback with the stunningly brutal Flinders Ranges in every corner of the background. Attempting our 15-day version of the route was a way to show our daughter and son, both young teenagers, different parts of the country and open their eyes to new realities – and adventures.

The route is named after Sir Douglas Mawson, an Australian geologist best remembered as a brave Antarctic explorer, and we spotted the first of the many well-placed trail signs near the Blinman Pub. A group of riders who had just finished the south-north route waved us off, and when they tooted their car horns later as we descended towards the first stretch of dirt, we thought of the cyclist camaraderie we'd share over the next few weeks. We didn't see another bike for three days.

Instead, our four-person peloton travelled with wedge-tailed eagles, brown falcons, echelons of emus, and squawks of corellas and galahs through the valleys and gorges. The profile on day one provided some groans from the teens, with 1,100m (3610ft) of climbing over almost 70km (43 miles) into Wilpena Pound, the most elevation until the penultimate day. On the plus side, it had the Bunyeroo Rd, a gravel surface winding down to the base of the Pound, and a mountainous backdrop to the best descent of the trip. It was a shame the tour's Instagram highlight came so early, but if we didn't ride another day we'd already have banked something spectacular.

Each morning begins with a stage overview, often in the mode of Eurosport commentator Carlton Kirby. There are many starts when pretend Carlton can't contain himself, such as the drop from Wilpena Pound into Rawnsley Park on stage 2: 'What a treat we have today, forget the sprinters, take in the vistas.'

Over the first three days there was Outback eye candy everywhere, including on all sides of the Moralana Scenic Drive back to Wilpena Pound, or west to the Elder Ranges. We were glad to be on mountain bikes on the rough trails and often spiky rocks, although this changed for the final two weeks when we wished we owned gravel bikes.

Melrose, where we have our first rest day after six stages and 360km (220 miles), has a dedicated mountain bike park – and a bike shop. After a midday sleep-in, I ask my daughter if her legs are sore. 'Yes.' Where? 'Everywhere.' I can't convince anyone else to try the trails.

Overnight, it rains, and it's still drizzling when we re-start, dreading the upcoming Mawson mud. In a couple of spots, thick gloops of red muck stick onto everything, forcing a cleaning stop every 50m or so, just to get the wheels moving. Nobody is allowed to think of the damage to their components. It's only day eight, and there's still about 500km (310 miles) to go. In a place where water is precious, it takes some courage to ask the caravan park owners in the small town of Laura if we can hose down four bikes. They say yes. They also give us scones with jam and cream.

The Mawson often intersects with the Heysen Trail, a 1,200km (756 mile) walking track named after the artist Hans. The ruined settler cottages dotted across the canola country outside Laura create views that will hang in our memories forever. If you squint at the yellow blossoms, you can imagine sunflowers and riding through a French summer instead of a shivery headwind. The wind farms on the peaks around here are perfectly placed.

Today, the sun is out and we cross the Mount Lofty Ranges for the first time before descending towards Spalding, avoiding our first two snakes, and passing through a gauntlet of gates that make us grumpy. Nobody needs to stop this often near the end of a hilly 80km (50 mile) family ride.

Across the hills to the northeast is Hallett, which has a general store and a cafe. A road sign tells us Adelaide is only 186km (115 miles) away. Sorry kids, on the zig-zagging Mawson there's still double that to go. Our trip motto has been 'adventure, not torture' and so far there's been plenty of the first and not enough of the second to bother either of the teen activists. But it's during another Mount Lofty Ranges crossing that my daughter sums up her version of the tour. 'The hills are nice to look at,' she says, 'but I don't like riding up them.' She never asks if she can give up.

By stage 12, when the scenery changes in the riesling wine region of Clare, both children are realising their fitness gains. 'I'm almost faster than you, Dad,' my boy says as we climb up through more sheep and canola fields in the Camel Hump Range. He was only partly right – sometimes he's quicker. His main daily concern now is whether the next place will have wi-fi.

Happily, the tour has reached the indulgence phase, and we have no doubt we'll make it to the end. This is cycling mini-break territory, and we are only a handful of bumps from the Barossa Valley. Whether a day off spent wine tasting there should be followed by a 74km (46 mile) uphill traipse into the Adelaide Hills is still up for debate.

As we slog up our last real climb, a 250m (820ft) gravel rise through more vineyards, my boy is waiting for everyone again, barely puffing when we reach him. 'I didn't need to stop,' he tells us. While we snuggle at the Cudlee Creek Tavern, I wonder how long us parents will be able to ride with both kids? Will he and his sister still let us?

Adelaide and the promised hotel-with-pool are on the horizon, along with our finish line. We cruise down the appropriately titled Gorge Road, finding the final trail marker, then soft-pedal on a bike path towards the city's North Terrace, where we pose for a treasured family holiday photo in front of the bust of Sir Douglas Mawson. **PE**

BEFORE THE DINOSAURS

Wilpena Pound, in the Ikara-Flinders Ranges National Park, dominates the view at the northern end of the Mawson Trail. A bowl created by a circle of spectacular peaks, the Pound is popular with walkers and wildlife. The area is also a geological marvel, containing fossils dating back hundreds of millions of years to the Ediacaran Period. The Wilpena Pound entrance is almost at the start (or end) of the ride, so it might be best to return another day.

Left to right: Flinders' gravel roads; one of several abandoned cottages; the welcoming town of Laura. Previous spread: Wilpena Pound

TOOLKIT

Start/Finish // Blinman/Adelaide
Distance // 900km (560 miles)
Getting there // Adelaide's airport is a 15-minute drive from the CBD. The official trail starts at the base of Gorge Rd, on the edge of the city. Blinman is roughly 500km (310 miles) by road north of Adelaide.
When to go // Avoid January to March, when the temperatures can exceed 40°C, and there is danger of heatwaves and bushfires.
What to wear // Weather conditions can vary considerably, so be prepared for anything.
What to pack // Long-sleeve hiking shirt, raincoats, thermals, neck warmers, suncream, first-aid kit, GPS emergency beacon, bike tools, pump and spare tubes.
Where to stay // Pubs, motels, caravan parks, cabins, Airbnbs, camp dongas, walking huts...
Things to know // Be prepared to be self-sufficient. Carry extra water, up to 4 litres, in the remote northern sections.
More info // www.southaustraliantrails.com; www.davidhume.net/mawsontrail/maps

Opposite: Kangaroo Island's Remarkable Rocks

MORE LIKE THIS
SOUTH AUSTRALIA FAMILY RIDES

KANGAROO ISLAND

This is a choose-your-own route, not an official trail, but if riders want a memorable experience on Australia's third-largest island, there are many rewards. The highlight is Flinders Chase National Park, tucked in the southwest corner and recovering from the horrendous bushfires of 2020. If there's one stretch to aim for, it's Cape du Couedic Rd, bumping its way through the regrowing bush on the way to cliffs overlooking the Southern Ocean. Watch the seals at Admirals Arch, stare at the lonely lighthouse, and remove your cleats to clamber over the Remarkable Rocks. One idea involves starting at the Penneshaw ferry and looping the island anti-clockwise – 360km (220 miles) in six days of riding. Fun rest-day sights and activities include Seal Bay, Stokes Bay, swimming with the wild bottlenose dolphins off Kingscote, and spotting penguins at night in Penneshaw. This trip is best on gravel, touring, or wider-tyre road bikes, but careful planning is required for the western and southern sides of the island to avoid running out of food.
More info //
www.tourkangarooisland.com.au

LAVENDER CYCLING TRAIL

A useful practice trail if building up to the Mawson, this links the wine region of Clare, through farming land and small country towns, with the plains of the Murray River, Australia's longest. While best ridden over four to six days, the route still requires considerable planning because of the distances between food and accommodation, variable phone reception and the remoteness east of the Mount Lofty Ranges and Barossa Valley. Look out for old farmhouses, grain silos, wildlife and churches along the mostly gravel roads and variable singletrack. The elevation in Clare is almost 400m (1300ft) higher than Murray Bridge, which might be a factor in route selection.
Start // Murray Bridge
Finish // Clare
Distance // 300km (185 miles)
More info //
www.lavendercyclingtrail.org.au

THE RIESLING TRAIL, BAROSSA TRAIL & JACK BOBRIDGE TRACK

Not ready for a multi-day trip but still want to ride with the family on holiday? The Clare and Barossa valleys both have dedicated tracks with lots of distractions. The Riesling Trail is a section of the Mawson, along an old rail route from Auburn to just north of Clare. Pass a string of cellar doors and enjoy the well-packed path with gentle gradients, making it suitable for the whole family. Further south is the Barossa Trail and Jack Bobridge Track, connecting Gawler and Angaston in the heart of the wine region. The sealed path, which has some steep pinches not so suitable for younger children, travels through some of the area's most famous wineries.
Distance // Riesling Trail, 33km (20 miles); Barossa Trail and Jack Bobridge Track, 40km (25 miles)
More info //
www.southaustraliantrails.com

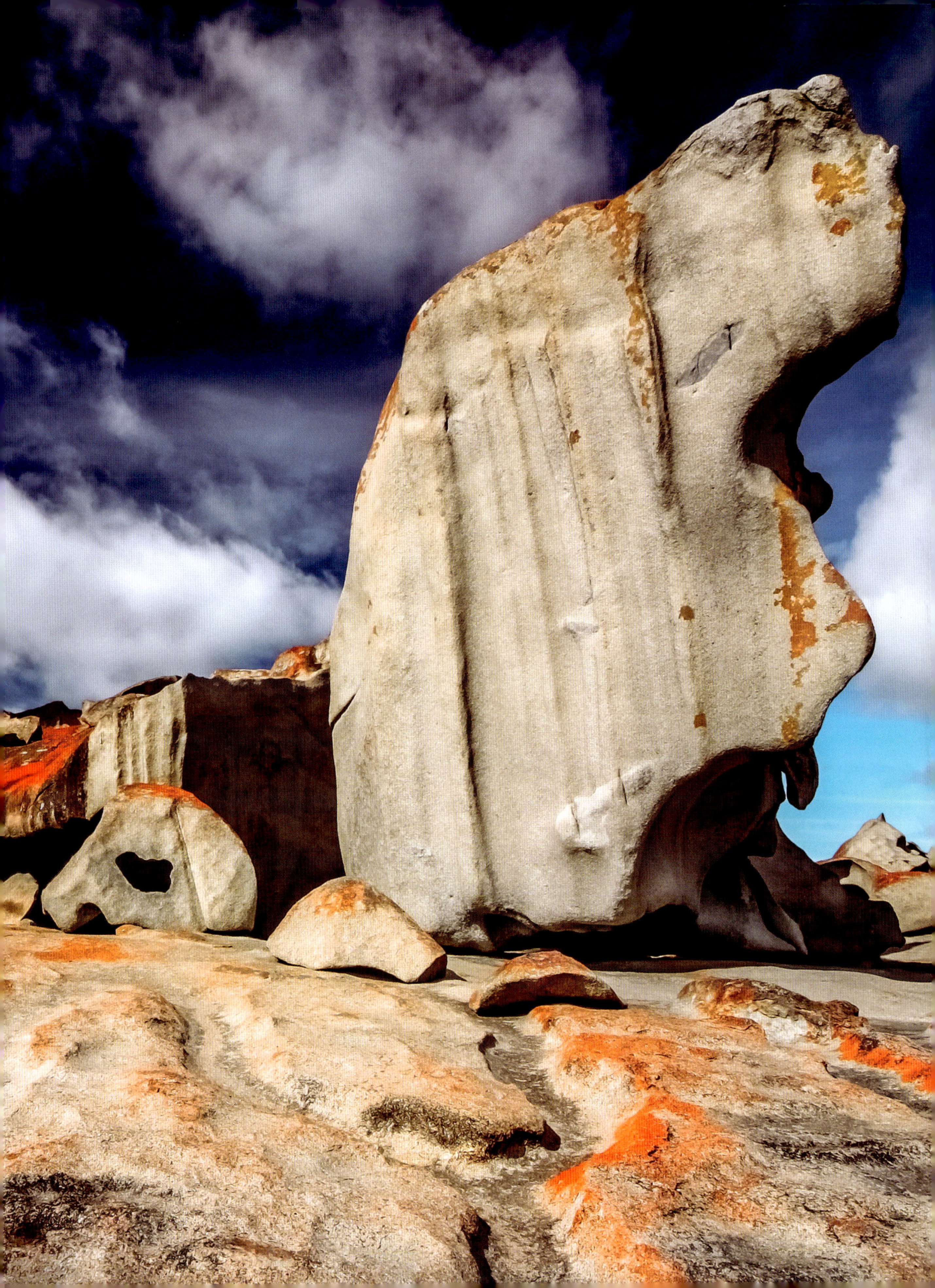

THE MUNDA BIDDI TRAIL

Western Australia's 1000km (621-mile) Munda Biddi Trail is one of the world's longest dedicated off-road cycling tracks – and a challenging wilderness adventure.

It's 8.15am and the air is starting to warm up in this wild and thickly wooded patch of southwestern Western Australia. Shafts of sunlight stream through breaks in the jarrah canopy to illuminate the wildflowers growing alongside the narrow dirt paths that our little convoy has been following for these past five days.

The distant 'kerrreee-kerrreee' calls of red-tailed black cockatoos can be heard through the gum leaves. My morning coffee, brewed on a camp stove, has barely kicked in, but already I am knee-deep in water and clambering across rocks in a shallow but fast-flowing section of WA's Murray River. We are about 5km (3 miles) south of Dwellingup, and I am half pushing, half carrying my mountain bike. My legs are sore for the fourth morning, but I have a big, fat grin daubed across my face.

This is not how I pictured this week turning out, when our team of four set out from Mundaring, east of Perth. From getting lost on badly signposted dirt roads and navigating steep, rutted sections of trail; to climbing constantly undulating hills – frequently leaping into waterholes, rivers, pools and cascades – and just coping with the technical complexity of up to 60km (37 miles) a day of difficult terrain, there has been much more scope for serious adventure than I could have anticipated. The 333km (207 mile) section of Munda Biddi that we were attempting over seven days is – I quickly discovered – seriously hard work.

This northern section of the Munda Biddi ('path through the forest' in one of the local Nyungar dialects) winds over 498km (309 miles) from Mundaring in the Darling Range to Nannup on the Blackwood River. It zips through thick forest and open patches of dry bushland and river valleys, as well as along a massive escarpment that looks out over a 30km (18.5 mile)-wide coastal plain to the Indian Ocean. 'It's a cycling wilderness experience that's probably the best you'll get in Australia,'

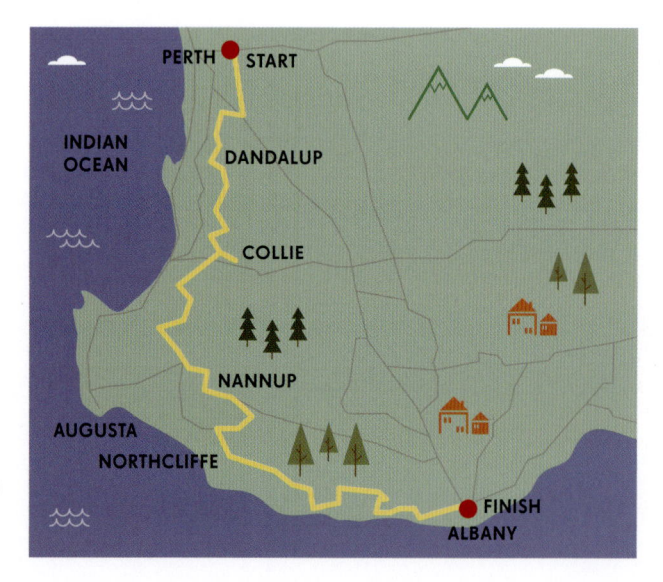

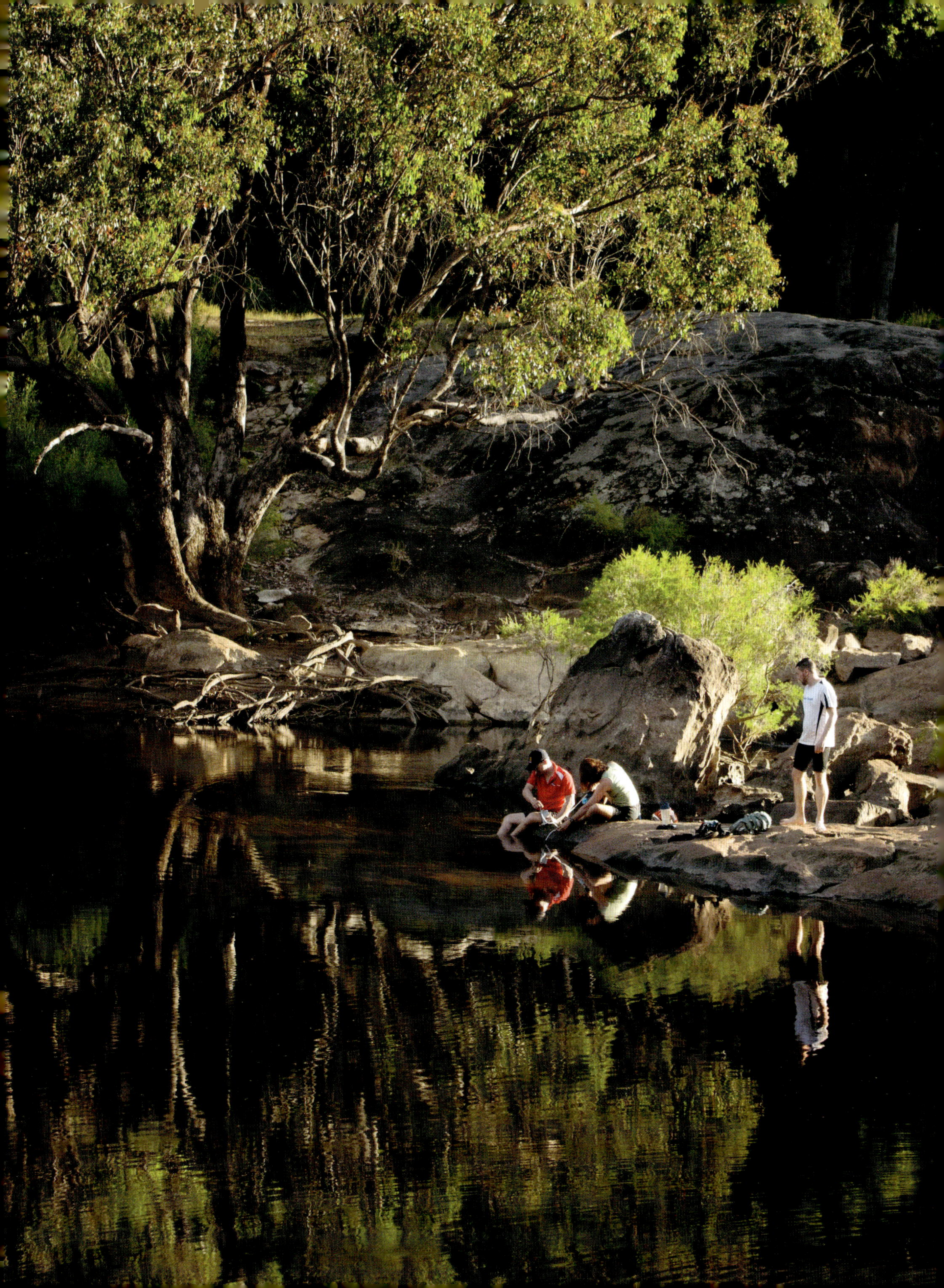

says Munda Biddi Trail Foundation (MBTF) volunteer Stewart Parkinson. 'In some of the state forests, you're going into areas that are totally uninhabited. It's quite primeval.' The complete Munda Biddi Trail wends all the way down through the stately karri forests of the south via Walpole and Denmark to Albany.

'What makes the Munda Biddi unique is that it's one trail, it has got purpose-built huts and it is, effectively, wilderness,' says Ron Colman, chairman of the MBTF. The trail is designed so that every 40km (25 miles) or so, there is either a town or a hut. The idea is that you stop in to restock your food supplies (so you never have to carry more than a couple of days' worth), carry out any repairs (on both bikes and weary bodies), get a shower and sleep in a bed.

At the end of the third day, 137km (85 miles) into our journey, we roll into the Dandalup campsite. On top of a vast escarpment – the Darling Range – and facing the coast, this hut has stunning views along the northern part of the trail. From here you can see across 30km (18.5 miles) of coastal plains to the sea. A charming uphill section of narrow trail twists and turns through open woodland, studded with primitive-looking, multi-headed grass trees. There is a decking area, so we stop to take in the view. Later we watch the sun set over the ocean.

The northern part of the trail up to Dandalup features the greatest concentration of sections graded 'challenging' and 'medium' by the MBTF – meaning they are steep and the trail condition can be poor. But the great thing about the Munda Biddi is that there are many entry points from roads, so you can devise a trip to suit both your fitness levels and your thirst for excitement.

FIRE LOOKOUT TREES

Back in the 1940s, pegs were embedded in eight karri trees (the third tallest species in the world) in the town of Pemberton, which this trail passes by. This was to create nature's own fire lookout towers. Two of these towers – the Diamond Tree and the Gloucester Tree – can still be climbed. The Dave Evans Bicentennial Tree, which reaches a dizzying height of 75m (246ft) with 165 pegs spiralling up the trunk, was made a fire lookout in the 1980s.

Clockwise from top: a cockpit view near Dandalup; a western shingleback; Tom's crossing on the Munda Biddi; waterfalls near Baden Powell Camp

Previous spread: cooling off at Lane Pool Reserve, outside Perth

It's the end of the sixth day of riding – 227km (141 miles) into our journey – and by now I've lost track of the dates or the days of the week. Our lives out here are driven by rhythms: the sun rising, passing across the sky and setting again each day; the packing up of our gear and saddling it to the bike every morning; the wheels and spokes as they spin, and the repetitive crunch of the pea gravel; the constant eating (nuts, chocolate, trail bars, sweets, bread, peanut butter, Gatorade) to fuel the pistons that our legs have become; and the rhythms of the bush, as the rustling and buzzing rises into a crescendo and falls away again each day. At several points I feel totally unplugged from civilisation.

The next day is our last on the trail. The final stretch into the coal-mining town of Collie is more open, flanked by farmland, and even though it's late spring and the wildflower season is waning, there's still a sprinkling of flame peas, Woodbridge Poison, pom-poms, fringe lilies and other blooms. Our convoy makes a sudden stop at one point to avoid two feisty western shingleback lizards sunning themselves on the path and flashing their tongues at us. We are joined later by a large and noisy flock of wheeling red-tailed black cockatoos. It seems as if they've come to bid us goodbye.

'What I enjoy about cycling,' says one of our crew, 'is that you're going fast enough so you're actually going somewhere, but you're also right in the environment, not like being in a car.' I agree and, as we roll into Collie, I'm already thinking about where my next mountain biking adventure might be. **JP**

TOOLKIT

Start // Mundaring, Perth Hills
Finish // Albany
Distance // 621 miles (1,000km)
Where to stay // There's a wide range of accommodation available, from campsites to B&Bs, depending on your budget and preference.
What to take // A mountain bike, or at least a bike with wide, knobbly tyres to tackle the gravel. Be equipped to perform on-the-road bike maintenance, so bring spare chain links, spokes, inner tubes and a puncture repair kit.
When to ride // You'll need about three weeks to do the full 1,000km trail, longer if you take rest days, but most riders just come for a day or two. Summer (January and February) is hot and not ideal for cycling. Spring and autumn are better, while the winter (July, August) is also typically mild.
More info // www.mundabiddi.org.au

Opposite: cross Kosciuszko National Park on the Bicentennial Trail

MORE LIKE THIS
LONG-HAUL TRIPS

BICENTENNIAL TRAIL

Crossing the country from Cooktown in Queensland to Healesville in Victoria, tracing the peaks of the Great Dividing Range and arcing around the hinterland of Australia's east coast, the 5330km (3312-mile) Bicentennial Trail is one of the planet's longest off-road routes. It began as the National Horse Trail, but people pedal it too. Mountain biking the entire route is an arduous undertaking, but the BCT has been broken down into 12 sections. The most enjoyable for cyclists is arguably the 350km stretch from Blackbutt to Killarney in Southern Queensland. For some type-2 fun, start at the southern trailhead in Healesville, 60km northeast of Melbourne, and ride 500km east through gold towns and gorgeous alpine wilderness to Omeo – but beware: after a relatively gentle start, the route turns snarly and gnarly after Big River, beginning with a brutal climb on aptly-named Mt Terrible.
More details // www.nationaltrail.com.au

TANAMI TRACK, NT

An Outback epic, this rusty, dusty, devilishly demanding bikepacking adventure scratches a 1075km line across the Top End, from Alice to the Kimberley. En route, intrepid cyclists can divert 22km to Wolfe Creek National Park to wonder at the world's second-largest meteorite-caused crater. About 200km of the route is sealed, the rest is red earth, compressed and crinkled by road trains and 4WDs – be prepared for wrist-wrecking corrugation. This ride requires very careful planning and shouldn't be taken on lightly or by rider inexperienced in remote regions. Cyclists must carry lots of water (like 25L+). Since Rabbit Flat roadhouse closed, there's a desolate 580km section between Yuendumu and Billiluna with no active settlements. Allow at least 12 days and avoid the Wet/summer season. Camping is not permitted near the Indigenous communities of Yuendumu and Billiluna – otherwise, pitch wherever and enjoy some extraordinary night skies.
Start/Finish// Alice Springs/Halls Creek
Distance// 1075km (668 miles)
More info // www.cycletrailsaustralia.com

KAHURANGI 500, NEW ZEALAND

Arguably the southern hemisphere's most exciting bikepacking circuit, this lovely loop leads riders on a 500km route around Kahurangi National Park at the top of New Zealand's South Island. The multiday off-road odyssey incorporates several iconic smaller routes, including the Rāmeka and Heaphy tracks, and the Old Ghost Road. Most bikers begin in Tapawera and go anticlockwise towards gorgeous Golden Bay, before lapping up the fabulous flowing singletrack trails encountered on the Rāmeka and Heaphy tracks. You have to earn your turns first, however, by sweating up Tākaka Hill. After the Old Ghost Road the route rises over the mountains to reach Lyell, before rolling through Buller Gorge to Murchison and then tracing the Braeburn Track to Lake Rotoroa and closing the circle with a spin up Tadmor Valley to Tapawera. There are campsites and facilities at regular intervals, and plenty of opportunities to plunge into the ocean.
Start/Finish// Tapawera
Distance// 500km (310 miles)
More info // www.nzcycletrail.com

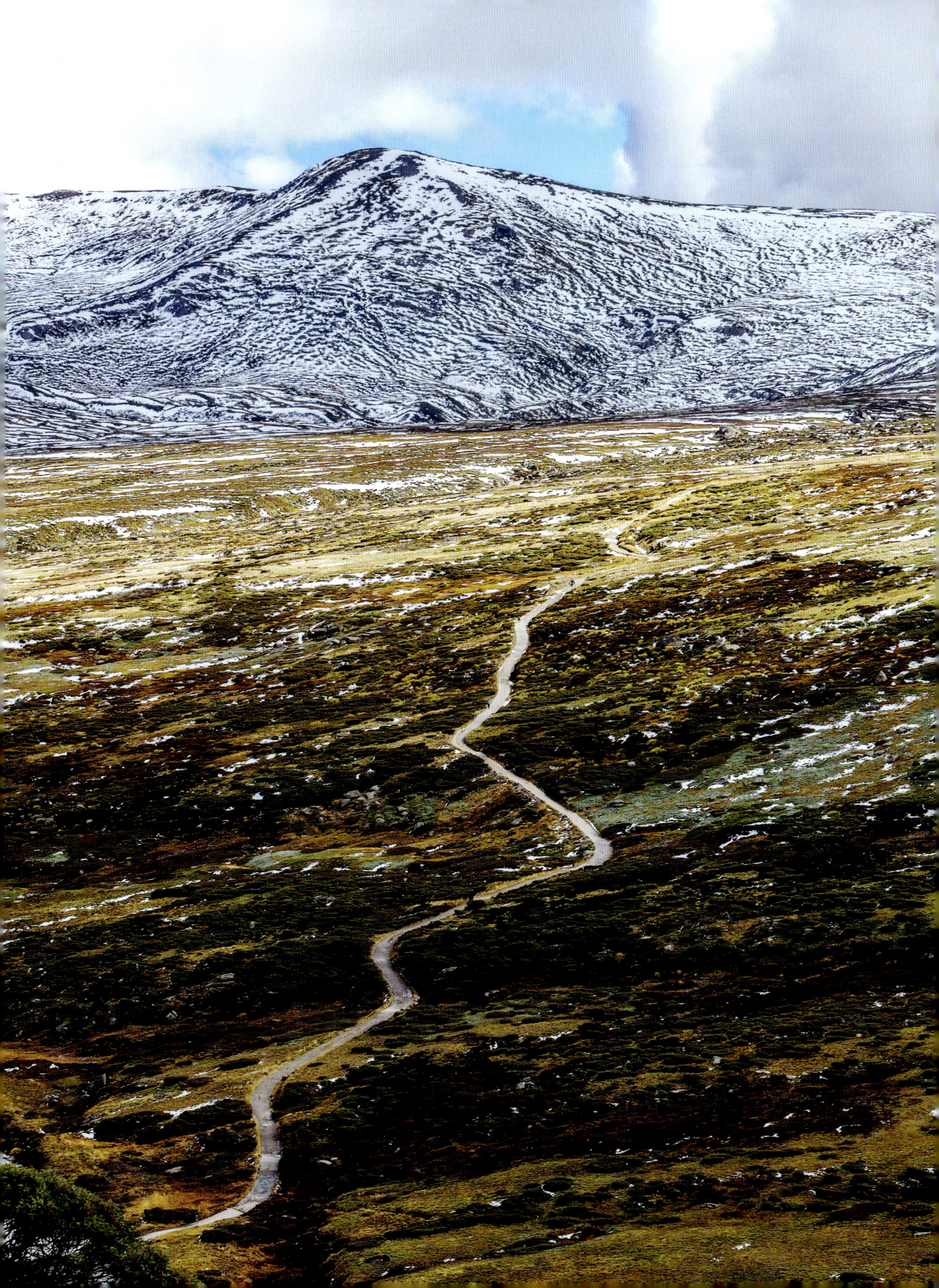

TAILING THE TOUR IN ADELAIDE

During the Tour Down Under, the South Australian capital is a magnet for cycling fans. This short circuit shows off the region's highlights.

We're at one of Adelaide's bustling restaurants, enjoying a glass of wine. The Tour Down Under has the city full to the brim on the night before our group ride. There's some animated discussion about the following day's challenges: the climbing, the descents and the wildlife we might spot.

Some of my fellow riders have come from across the country, while others, like me, have come from different parts of the globe. I've only come from New Zealand, but there are riders from Singapore, Japan, England and Germany. In fact, I'm only one of approximately 40,000 visitors here this week.

The Tour Down Under transforms this sleepy South Australian city with all the fanfare of a European Grand Tour. The nine-day race was first held in 1999, and in 2007 was the first event to gain UCI Pro Tour status outside Europe – guaranteeing all of the world's top professional teams would be present. Indeed, even the once-mighty Lance Armstrong used the Tour Down Under as his comeback race in 2008. Once a year, Adelaide becomes the hottest cycling destination on the planet. I'm eager to see if it lives up to the hype.

The morning dawns clear and warm. I'm mentally checking off everything I need – shoes, kit, sunscreen, snacks, helmet, coffee. Definitely more coffee. Luckily, someone had already thought this through, as the departure point for the ride – The Glasshouse – is also one of Adelaide's top cafes. While the barista works on the fuel we need to kickstart our metabolisms, introductions are made and friends reunited. There is a small mountain of bikes leaning against the wall and still more riders are rolling up. Although there are smiles all round, some are more nervous than others.

I soon see why: the route we have planned is a challenging one. We head straight out for the hills. The city rolls past us and we navigate the outer suburbs along Greenhill Rd towards Mt Osmond, which is the first climb of the day. It seems like only a few miles have passed before the 18% climb has us in its grip. Despite the gradient, a rhythm is surprisingly easy to find and the view that emerges as we approach the top makes the toil worth it. The conversations

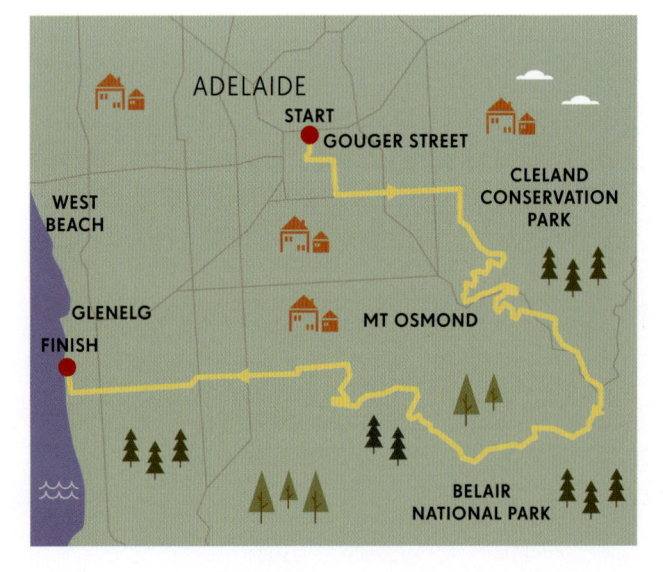

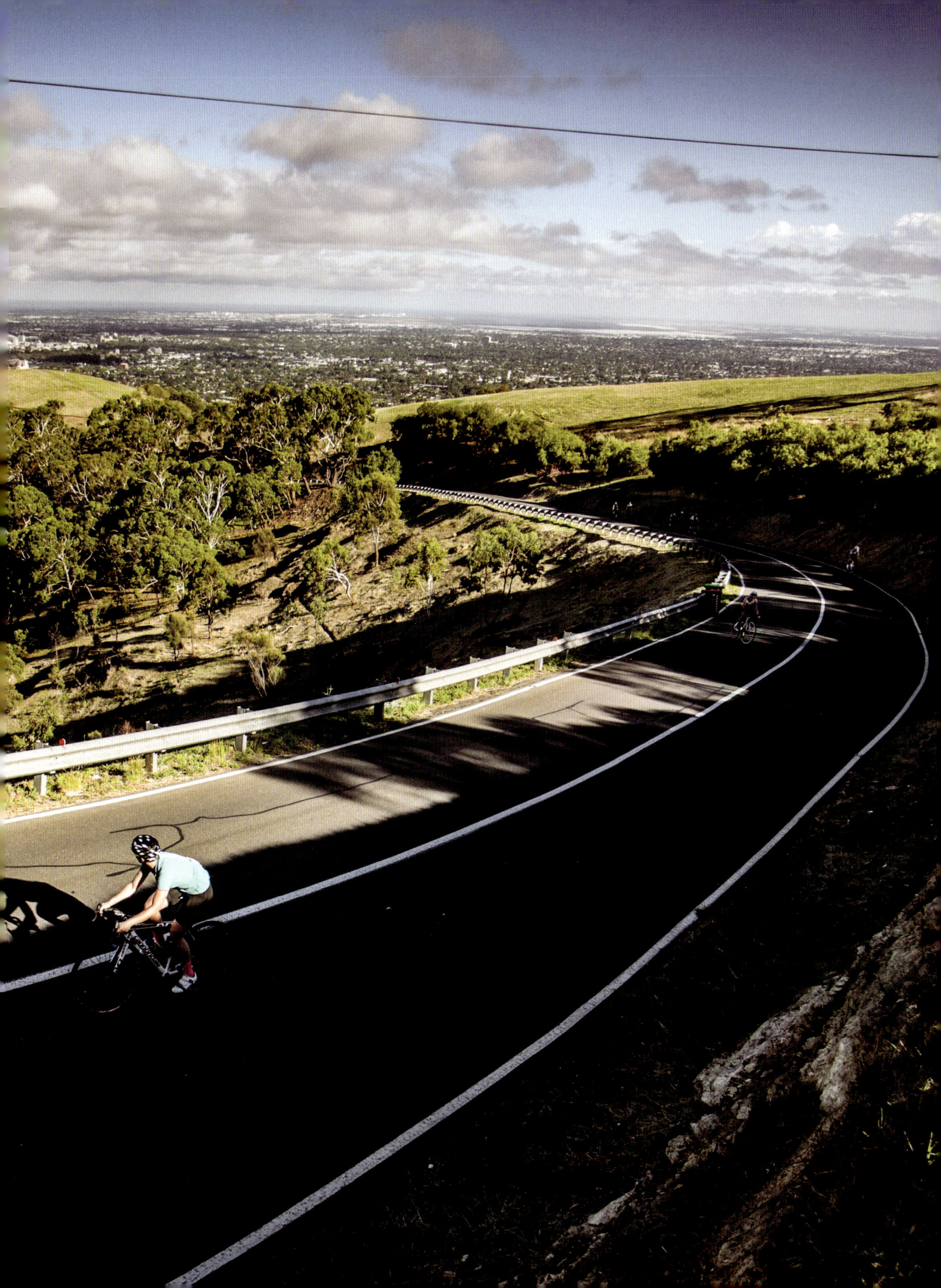

and chatter continue without pause as the road winds skywards. We discuss our favourite riding spots – from the Alps in Europe to the flatlands of Singapore and the remote far north of my own home turf. Local tips, gear selections, best (and worst) riding food, favourite bikes. By the end of the first climb I've added at least three countries and two bikes to my 'must-ride' list.

The road rolls on through the mountainside. The climbs around here are long but beguiling. Whoever carved these roads did a good job. Everyone is in good spirits. There are words of encouragement, the occasional helping hand and celebrations when the road begins to flatten out. A quick stop at the top of the longer climbs gives us some respite and a chance for everyone to regroup.

In the moments of quiet we contemplate the surroundings. From the tops of the climbs we're rewarded with sweeping views over the city and coastline below. Gum trees provide some shade and the smell of eucalyptus wafts on the breeze. We make our way up Mt Barker. This long and steady climb traces a disused section of highway, now closed to car traffic and designated as a bike lane. There are cyclists as far as the eye can see and, without the worry of cars, a chance to absorb the full experience of the Adelaide Hills.

I get overly excited at the sight of two large kangaroos sitting by the side of the road, close enough to touch. The Australians laugh at me. The kangaroos also seem to give a mocking glance. But I feel that I can tick something off my list of touristic achievements.

CAUTION: ANIMALS CROSSING

The Adelaide Hills and surrounding region host an abundance of wildlife. Kangaroos, koalas, snakes, lizards, echidnas, any number of birds and other creatures are easily spotted. Take care, especially when riding down fast descents or on roads with blind corners: an injury from hitting a kangaroo is not something you want to take home. Although they are beautiful to look at, wild animals should never be approached.

Clockwise from top: riding two abreast; a cafe stop before the big ride; Australia's beautiful morning light. Previous page: pedalling into the Adelaide Hills

We roll through Belair National Park, eyes darting between the road and trees as we hope to catch a glimpse of a koala. We had been lucky enough to spot one the day before. The animals probably heard us coming, as they keep themselves well hidden today.

After each of the climbs come the descents. Steep, twisting ribbons of tarmac. Our train of riders flies down them. Pedal, float, lean, repeat. The smiles get even wider.

The weather in Adelaide can be fickle, and halfway through the ride the sky begins to darken and a few spots of rain make an appearance. An unseasonably chilly wind rustles the trees. A gilet would have been a welcome addition at this point. The pace quickens as we try to stay warm.

We're hurtling down Windy Point. Twisting, turning, dropping towards the ocean. There's very little opportunity to savour the view because this road isn't particularly smooth, and a few potholes and cracks in the surface provide an extra challenge on an already fast descent. Remarkably, the clouds have blown over. There are a few sighs of relief and a flat sprint to the finish.

Finally, it's right there: the beach spreads wide in front of us. This is where our ride ends. We roll gently towards the crowds at Glenelg, the flat bike path a welcome relief to protesting legs.

Cerulean ocean to the left, emerald hills to the right. An urban playground behind us and a beachside town in front. It's hard to believe that in one short morning we've experienced such a perfect melange of riding. **EB**

"From the top of the climb we're rewarded with sweeping views over the city and coastline below"

TOOLKIT

Start // Gouger St (King William end)
Finish // Glenelg
Distance // 37 miles (60km)
How to get there // Adelaide International Airport is located 6km (4 miles) west of the city.
Where to stay // There are accommodation options for every budget. Book early for the Tour Down Under week and expect prices to be higher than normal.
Need to know // Usually temperate, Adelaide can experience exceptionally hot weather during the Tour Down Under each January. Be prepared for anything between 20°C and 45°C.
More details // www.southaustralia.com
More rides // There are usually a series of sportive rides before the race. For more details, visit www.tourdownunder.com.au

Opposite: hot-air balloons above Canowindra in New South Wales

MORE LIKE THIS
LEG-BURNING LANDSCAPES

NEWCREST ORANGE CHALLENGE, NSW

A nod to the spring classics, designed to test the legs of even the most seasoned *rouleur*, the Newcrest Orange Challenge loop takes in more than 2,000m (6,560ft) of climbing over 170km (106 miles). The event is run as a fully supported Gran Fondo and riders are given a total of eight hours to complete the journey. However, anyone with strong legs and a keen sense of adventure can follow the route at any time. The loop circumnavigates Mt Canabolos, known to locals as 'The Nob' and passes through Cudal, Canowindra and Mandurama.
Start/Finish // Orange
Distance // 170km (106 miles)

SNOWY VALLEYS CYCLE CHALLENGE, NSW

Hosted by the Rotary Club of Tumut, the Snowy Valleys Cycle Challenge is a sportive that explores the foothills of the Snowy Mountains on the edge of Kosciuszko National Park in New South Wales. Choose from a range of distances according to your fitness, all the way up to the 160km (100-mile) Rosewood and Tumbarumba figure-of-eight loops. Riders have the benefit of food and water at checkpoints along the signposted routes, plus marshalls and support vehicles for repairs. New South Wales' roads are not usually the most welcoming for cyclists so it's nice to ride them in a group. The event takes place every March..
Start/Finish // Adelong
Distances // 16km (10 miles) to 160km (100 miles)
More info // www.snowyvalleyscyclechallenge.com.au

AUCKLAND TO PIHA, NEW ZEALAND

What it lacks in distance, this ride makes up for in leg-draining climbs and breathtaking views. There's a very good reason it has become a yardstick for Auckland cyclists who need to test their form. Piha is a tiny surfing town nestled on the west coast of Auckland's Waikatere Ranges, famous for its pounding surf, rugged coastline and glistening black sand. The aptly named Scenic Drive road to Piha twists and winds its way up through subtropical rainforest before plummeting down a heart-pounding descent to the beach. The road is narrow and challenging, requiring high levels of attention and strong legs, but it rewards riders with postcard-worthy views of the city, coastline and beyond. For an extra challenge, drop down to Karekare beach (as seen in the film *The Piano*) on the way.
Start // Auckland
Finish // Piha
Distance // 40km (25 miles)

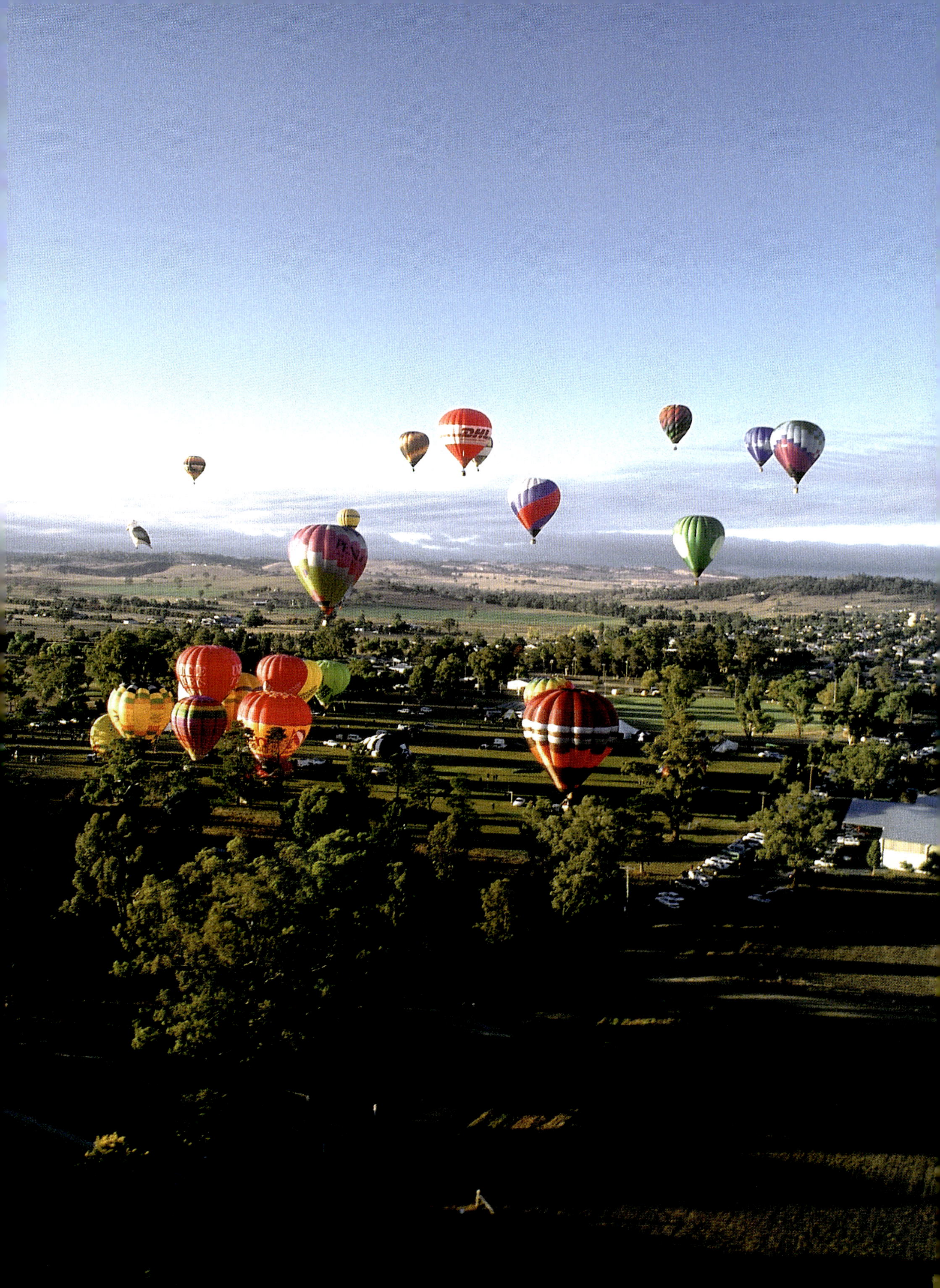
DHL

A MYPONGA BEACH LOOP

Gruelling gravel climbs, outstanding vistas and gourmet delights: this little loop is the best of the Fleurieu Peninsula in a nutshell.

Curling south of Adelaide like the tail of a sleepy seahorse, the Fleurieu Peninsula is a place of gorgeous beaches and weathered ranges. Some of its attractions are internationally renowned – such as the McLaren Vale wine region – while for cyclists it's associated with the famous climb of Willunga Hill, a climactic feature of the Tour Down Under for the better part of two decades. Off the beaten path, however, there are adventures to be had, including gravel roads with stunning views, leg-sapping climbs, soaring descents, and food and drink to reward those efforts.

Our journey begins at the Victory Hotel, a Sellicks Hill institution known for combining honest pub grub with a more elevated dining experience. Although it may be tempting to spelunk the cellar or sink a pint in the beer garden, save that for after the ride. The car park conveniently leads onto the closed gravel road up Old Sellicks Hill, which climbs for 3km (1.8 miles) at around 8%. It'd be a pretty rude beginning to a ride if it wasn't so pretty, with its gullies off the side of the road; sheep tracks written in red dirt across the hillside; the green sea of vineyards towards McLaren Vale over your shoulder; and the sea twinkling in the sun at the bottom of the hill. It's 'gravel' in name only, really, with chunky rocks and loose surfaces demanding close attention and careful lines. But when you hop the gate at the top of the climb, you're onto smoother stuff.

All that climbing earns you a nice roll along the plateau at the top of these hulking hills. There are paddocks of sheep on both sides; to the right you'll see the ranges folding in on

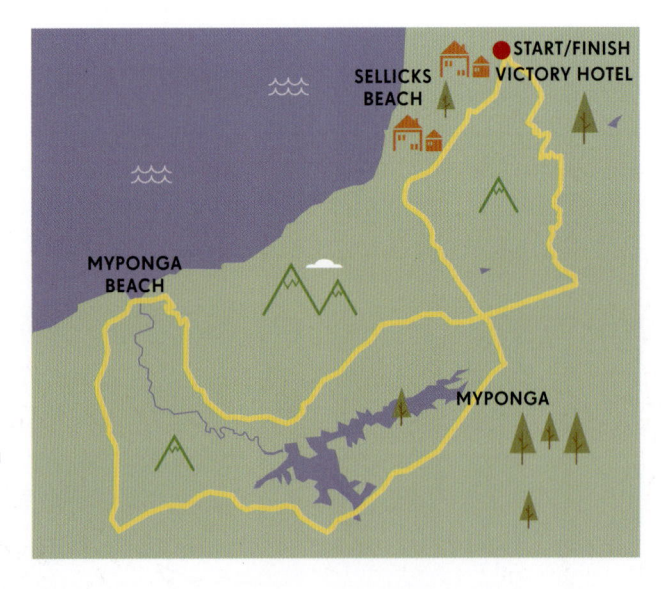

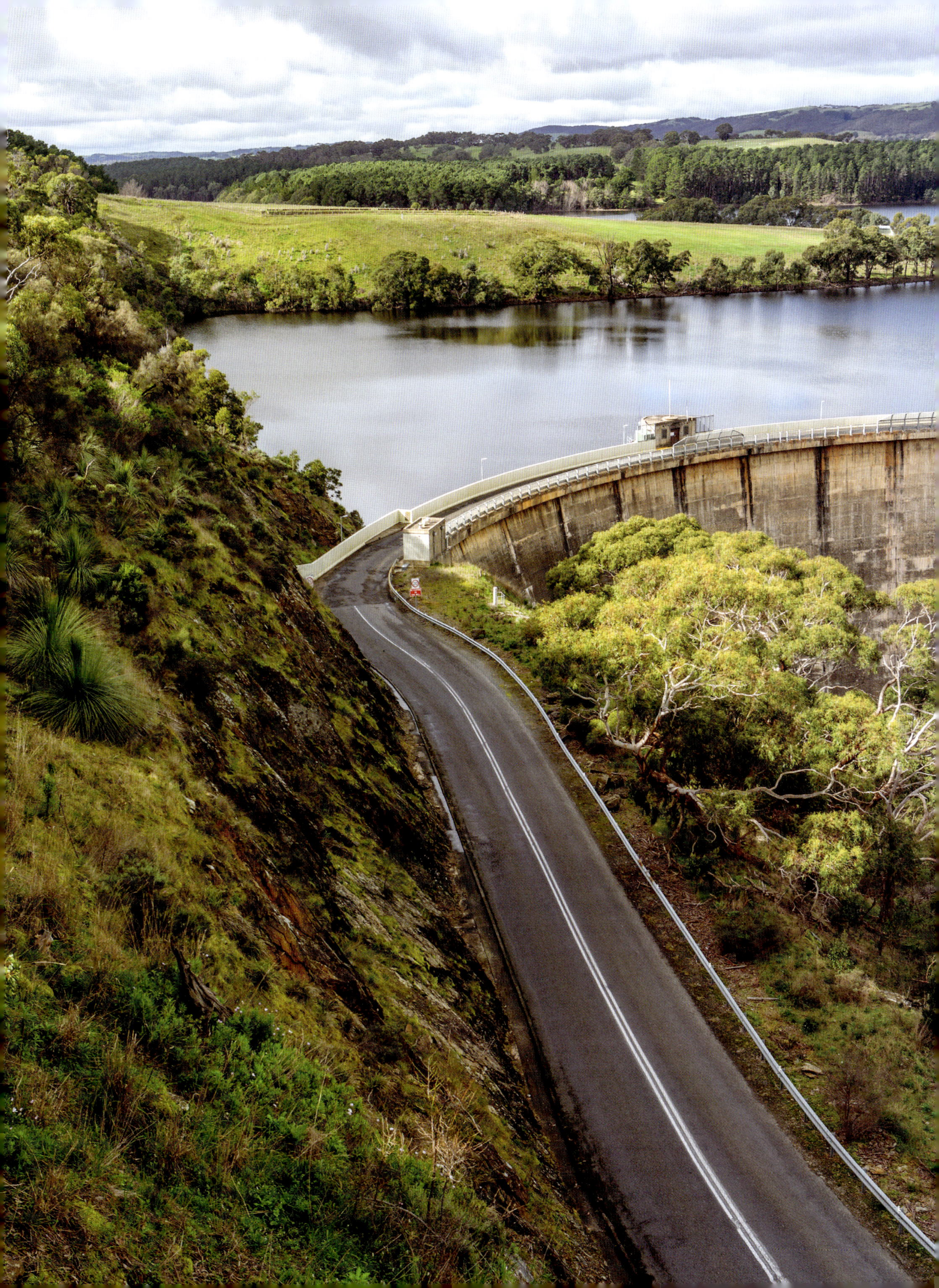

each other into valleys that reach out to the sea. About 300 vertical metres (980ft) below you is beautiful Sellicks Beach – the extreme southern boundary of greater Adelaide – with its pastel cliffs and gentle waters. The next little bay along is where we're headed.

The dirt road pitches downwards through roadside groves of trees, and for a while you'd be forgiven for thinking you're riding the route of Tuscany's Strade Bianche. By the bottom of the descent, though, it's pure Australiana. Turn right onto Sinclair Rd and bounce along between farms until you get to Main South Rd, taking some care as you cross it, and continue straight and up onto Reservoir Rd.

An occasional feature of the Tour Down Under, this straight, short and brutish climb doesn't bother with niceties, taking you back onto the hilltops. A rolling, quiet road awaits. To the right, you can see the coastline stretching back up to Adelaide. You might just be able to hear engine brakes from trucks making the long descent from Main South Rd back in the direction you've come from, but more likely than not it'll just be you, the wind rattling tall grasses, and your thoughts.

The road gets its name from the Myponga Reservoir that it traverses, and if you've got the time and legs for a detour, it's worth going a bit further, if only for the novelty of riding across a dam wall. But for the purposes of this adventure, take the right-hand turn onto Sampson Road for an almost 5km/3 mile-long descent down to Myponga Beach: a tiny, shopless gaggle of beach houses tucked away at the base of a rough gravel road, with a slightly less rough road out (or vice versa, depending on how you want to play it). Watch out for the sometimes-fierce corrugations that will rattle your fillings, and enjoy the drop.

After a paddle around at Myponga Beach, there's nowhere to go but up. Myponga Beach Rd (4.8km/3 miles at 5%) is a bit gentler and better formed than Sampson Rd. As you climb, the dirt road changes colour, from sandy white to pinkish to red. On windy days it can be pretty blustery, but just plug along and – sooner or later – you'll get to the top, back onto the plateau again.

At the intersection with the tarmac of Forktree Rd, swing a left and head back inland. The road rolls along beguilingly, before turning into gravel just after the turn-off to the reservoir. The sometimes-rutted road skirts the boundary of the catchment before it meets with Main South Rd again, where you will take a brief but regrettably traffic-prone spin toward Myponga town.

By this point you've ticked off most of the climbing and all of the gravel, and you're likely to be: a) hungry, b) thirsty, or

ADELAIDE'S GOLDEN FRINGE

Sellicks Beach, just down the hill from this ride's start and end point, is one of the Adelaide area's most photogenic beaches. Looking south, the hills rise up with dramatic cliffs at their base; a mix of ochre, pink and yellow tinges make for a striking palette, especially at sunset. The beach is open to vehicular traffic almost up to the sandstone reef, but a walk further beyond that point takes you along deserted beaches past canyons disappearing into the folds of the hills.

Left to right: cliffs above Sellicks Beach; Myponga town; the peloton hits Sellicks Hill during the Tour Down Under. Previous spread: Myponga Dam

c) all of the above. Myponga is quite small, but it has options. Smiling Samoyed Brewery is just off the main road, serving good woodfired pizza and a decent range of its own beers – and the owners' happy samoyed dogs are floating about like clouds waiting for pats. If coffee's more your speed, the Valley of Yore cafe is worth a visit, offering a welcoming environment, killer coffee and burnt Basque cheesecake.

But you could wait to sate your appetite too. Heading north out of Myponga, you'll fairly shortly roll over a crest and begin a 6km (3.7 mile) descent back to Sellicks Hill and the Victory Hotel where you started off from. There are a couple of scenic lookouts on the way down, where you can survey the sea and the hills that you've been going up and down for the past couple of hours. One such lookout is situated at a long-under-construction temple complex; for years here there's been the frame of a building, cyclone wire, and an enormous Buddha gazing serenely, surreally, out at St Vincent Gulf.

You may or may not have reached enlightenment on this ride, but by the time you roll back to the Victory Hotel, you'll have reached the end of this particular journey – one that has brought you from hilltop to sea level and back again, through some of the Fleurieu's best-kept riding secrets. **IT**

TOOLKIT

Start/Finish // Victory Hotel car park, Sellicks Hill
Distance // 42km (26 miles)
Getting there // Driving along Main South Rd from Adelaide is probably the most straightforward way to arrive. Otherwise, there is a train service as far as Seaford, from where you can take an 18km (11 mile) ride on unappealing roads, or a much more scenic ride of 25km (15.5 miles), with trails along the cliffs from Moana to beautiful Port Willunga, with some road and singletrack to Sellicks Beach and up from there.
What to pack // Be prepared to be self-sufficient in the event of mechanical issues. Although you're not anywhere too isolated, you're unlikely to see too many other people in sections of the route.
What to ride // The route is best suited for a gravel bike with 35mm tyres and upwards.
More info// www.fleurieupeninsula.com.au

Opposite: prized vines in the Adelaide Hills

MORE LIKE THIS
HILLS OUTSIDE THE CITY

WILLUNGA HILLS

If the 'steep gravel climbs and rolling plateau' thing from this ride has piqued your interest, or you want to make a bigger day of it, you can have fun stitching together a route slightly inland from these coastal surrounds. The historic town of Willunga can act as a great starting point to tackle the punishingly steep, barely-a-4WD-track Louds Hill Rd, from which you can continue downhill to Pages Flat Rd, or roll along Range Rd looking across the sea of green towards McLaren Vale. Other highlights in the area include Wakefield Rd, which passes through spinifex grasses and native forest, and the paved Delabole Rd, which is a brute of a climb and a ripper of a descent. If you're feeling peppy, channel your inner Richie Porte and finish it off with an ascent of Old Willunga Hill Rd.
Start/Finish// Willunga

MT LOFTY TO MT OSMOND LOOKOUT

In Adelaide with a gravel bike and a couple of hours to spare? The Adelaide Hills are calling. Head east out of the city towards the suburb of Burnside, hooking onto Waterfall Gully Rd until you reach Burnside Quarry Track. Steadily work your way upwards onto Bartrill Spur Track on gravel, popping out at Cleland Conservation Park. Continue up towards Mount Lofty – there are a number of trails that'll get you there, but Steub Trail is probably the pick of them – before a ripping descent down Spa Track to the leafy suburb of Crafers. A gentle roll along the (paved) Old Freeway path leads you to Old Bullock Track, and back onto the gravel for more descending. Mt Osmond lookout is the prize at the end, where views across the city are glorious. It's the right time to pull out that tinnie that's been rattling around your handlebar bag for the past hour.
Start // Burnside
Finish // Mt Osmond lookout
Distance// 19km (12 miles)
More info//
www.visitadelaidehills.com.au

SUGARLOAF RESERVOIR LOOP

On the north-eastern outskirts of Melbourne, the riverside suburb of Warrandyte makes a good starting point for a hilly mixed-terrain ride with a cameo from a reservoir. Aim for the festively named Christmas Hills, preferably via the scenic Menzies and Henley roads. From there, it's a gravel gala. Skyline Rd circles the southern edge of the Sugarloaf Reservoir, with some steep climbs and descents to keep you on your toes. For the easternmost part of the ride, there are striking views of the Yarra Valley vineyards and Great Dividing Range, before you turn back around the other side of the reservoir. There's a joyful descent in store, down Muir Rd, Ridge Rd and Westering Rd. That's followed by a tamer ride along an old aqueduct to the end of Menzies Rd, from where you can retrace your steps to Warrandyte, where the local bakery beckons.
Start/Finish // Warrandyte
Distance // 42km (26 miles)

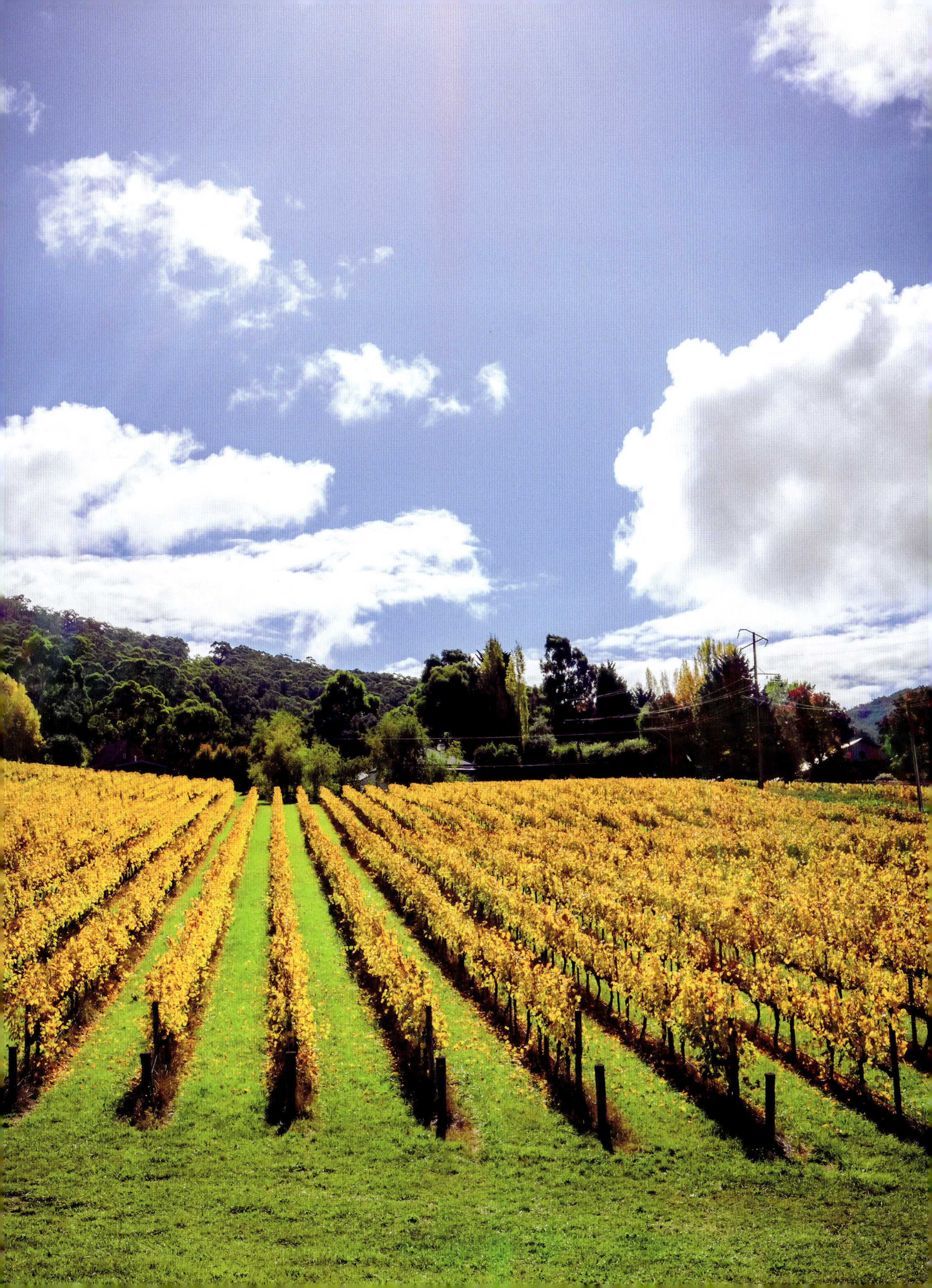

TASMANIA AND VICTORIA

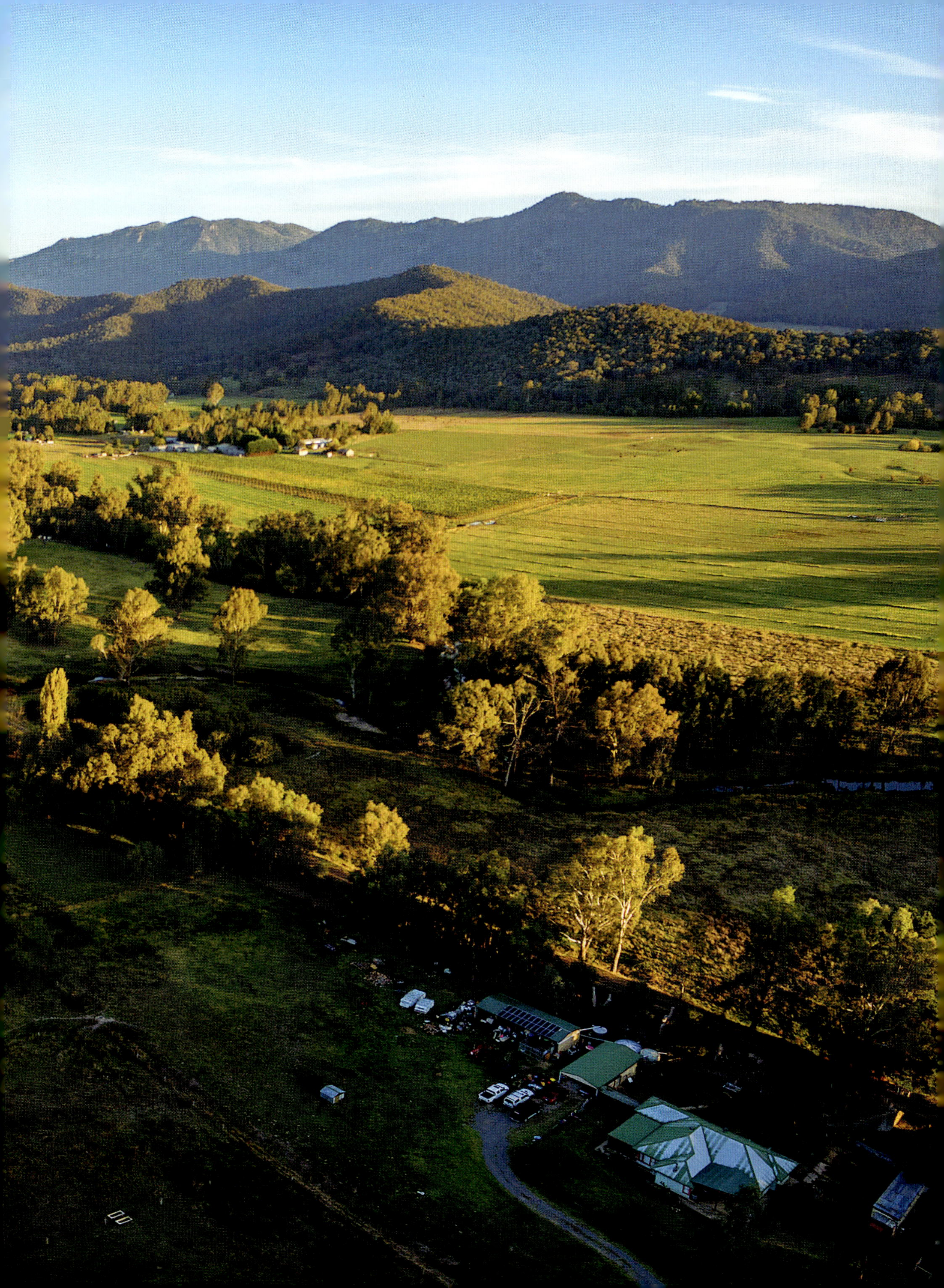

- EPIC BIKE RIDES OF AUSTRALIA & NEW ZEALAND -

STORIES OF THE CITY: THE MELBURN-ROOBAIX

Every winter, through the cobbled laneways of Melbourne, cyclists of all abilities and ambitions embark on a mad, magnificent adventure.

Sometimes a moment of transcendence finds you in the least expected place. Case in point: some anonymous alleyway in Brunswick in the depths of winter. It had been raining most of the day, and the bluestone cobbles, dotted with muddy puddles, were wet and unforgiving. And yet, there we all were, splattered with spray, laughing and smiling, and trying to keep upright.

My friends were behind me and in front of me, and we sped across the wet stones, dodging potholes. Chains clattered against frames. All around us, all day, were thousands of other Melbourne cyclists – roadies, gravel riders, kids in trailers, families in costumed convoys, friends on tandems, nutters on tall bikes. All of us holding onto our handlebars and hoping, because what else is there to do besides hope?

Founded 16 years ago by Melbourne cycling legend Andy White, the Melburn-Roobaix quickly became an institution. This non-competitive alley-cat ride, stitching together segments of bluestone laneways across the inner suburbs, was loosely modelled on the unsanctioned courier races that White had competed in during a former life as a bike courier. In the years since, his event has become a pillar of the cycling community's social calendar, a wintry Sunday circled in the diary every year.

The route changes with each hosting, taking in cobbled and dirt segments with their difficulty graded in a star rating, just like the notorious professional road-cycling classic of Paris-Roubaix. As with that race, you count the segments of Melburn-Roobaix down until you get to a velodrome finish. At day's end, someone heaves a cobblestone trophy over their

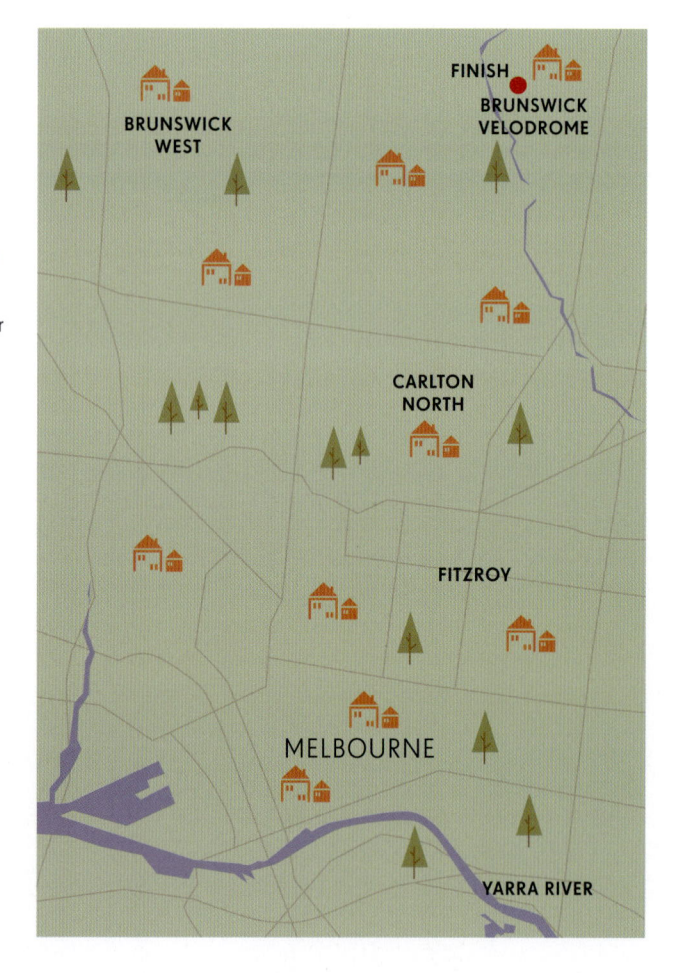

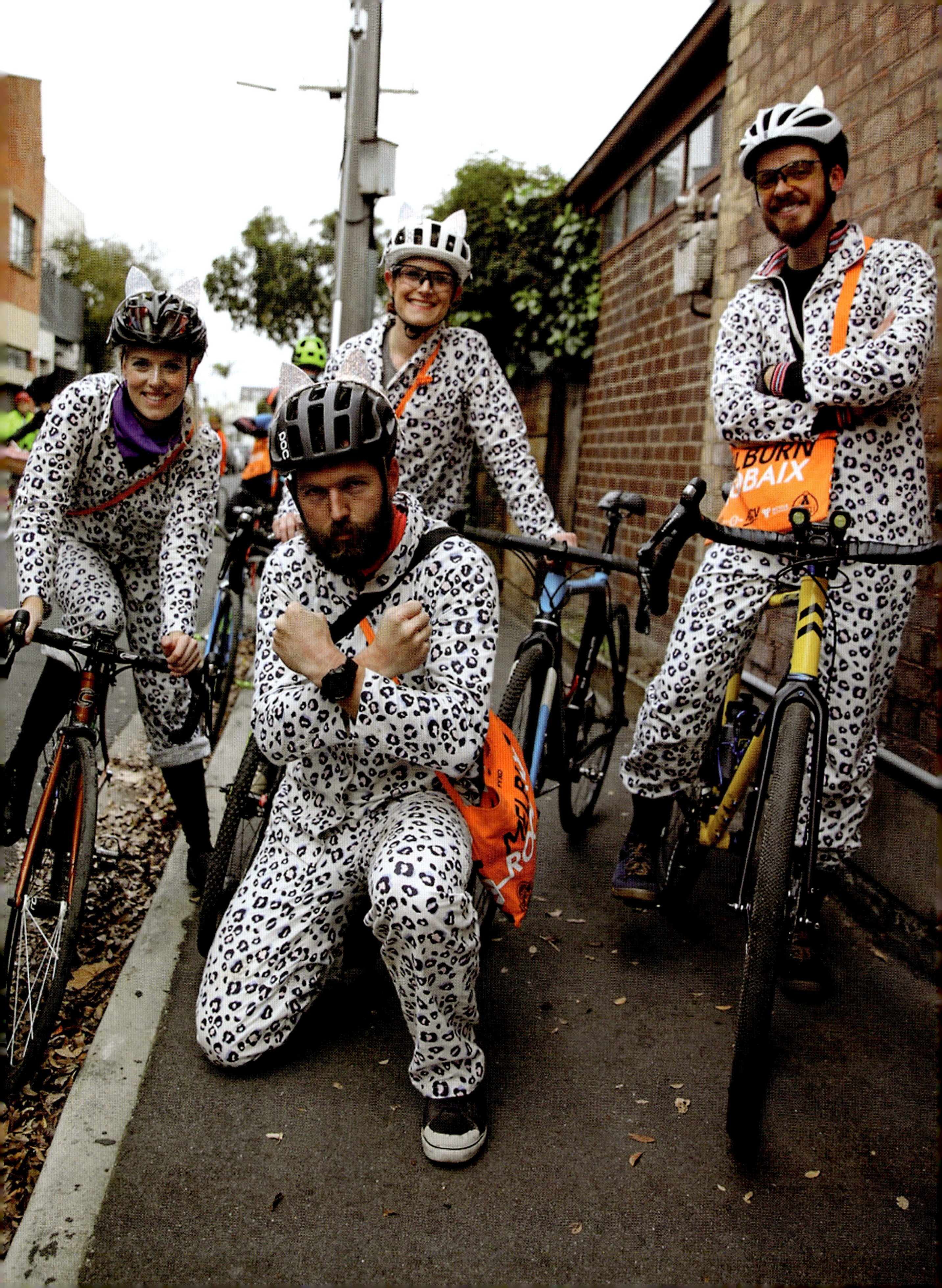

head. But whereas Paris-Roubaix is one of road cycling's most punishing events, Melburn-Roobaix is an inclusive, open-armed embrace of all things bike. 'All these people dressed up – everywhere you look, there are people,' White enthused. 'People on retro bikes, old bikes, cool bikes, wacky bikes, everything. I love the visual spectacle.'

Everyone's a winner at Melburn-Roobaix, just by participating, but there are prizes too – of a sort. Across the day you fill out questions on a ride manifest as you bounce around the city, making it a kind of scavenger hunt. When you get to the velodrome, you slip your manifest into a barrel, where a lucky recipient – drawn at random – scores a gold, spray-painted stone and a pot of jam. Other prestigious classifications include the likes of 'cutest couple', judged by the loudness of crowd applause in the track's grassy infield. To be in the mix, you need to put together a pretty great costume – and in 2022, it was clear that people had spent years scheming.

It had been a long time between rides. The previous Melburn-Roobaix was way back in 2019, before Covid-19

THE BLUES

Melbourne bluestone is a building material woven into the city's fabric. With stones formed from local volcanic basalt, the laneways of Melburn-Roobaix were originally conceived for collection of human excrement. In the post-plumbing age, however, they are a reminder of the city's past – and increasingly popular cultural sites, especially in the CBD, where street artists and restaurateurs refashion old surroundings into something new, and distinctly 'Melbourne'.

From left: roving riders; bluestone cobbles in Hosier Lane; Melbourne's CBD and Yarra River. Previous spread: party!

shut much of the world down. The 2021 edition was cancelled at short notice, due to a reinstatement of distancing measures – a sting in the tail of a hard couple of years for Melburnians, who'd endured one of the world's longest lockdowns, complete with limits on movement, curfews and travel bubbles. I don't think I've ever looked forward to a ride with friends as much as I did Melburn-Roobaix in 2022. It felt like the turning of a page.

To ride Melburn-Roobaix is not a single linear experience; it is hundreds of different stories spread across half a city. That's kind of the point, really – the places you stop along the way, the time spent connecting with friends over a coffee or a pint. And then, back into the pouring rain to keep rambling along laneways and bike paths and creek-side trails. It wasn't much of a day weather-wise, but it was perfect in spite of that – maybe because of that. We were all in it together, just like we had been through the bleakest moments of those many lockdowns.

There was both joy and poignancy after the pause of the past few years, rolling with friends with kids I'd never met; celebrating new relationships and mourning broken ones. Groups split and reformed, navigating by increasingly pulpy paper maps. One sloppy embankment next to a bridge led to a brewery where a muddy horde converged to wolf down hot chips. Another sloppy embankment a few hours later had a marching band playing at the bottom as riders slid their way down, brakes locked up, searching for a line through the ruts. At the end of the day, we lapped the Brunswick Velodrome, hit the photobooth and took the now-traditional black and white photo with the friends we'd ridden with – arms wrapped around each other, broad smiles and muddy faces.

Sixteen years ago, when Andy White had this idea, it was out of a love for bikes and the community that rode them. 'I started putting on events because I remembered how much fun it was, and all the unknowns,' he said. Now it's a family affair – Andy's wife, Melodie, runs it with him, and their daughter pulls winners' names out of the barrel. 'It's a really powerful thing to be associated with someone else's defining cycling memories.'

Most people's conception of 'cycling memories' is about the places you go and what they demand of your body. If you're donning outrageous costumes or welding bizarre bike frames for the day, that's a different beast. Normal cycling events aren't remembered for earnest heart-to-hearts at the pub, or for the way that they provide a conduit to deeper human connection. You'll have cycling memories from the Melburn-Roobaix, but there will be life memories too.

Melburn-Roobaix is the expression of a city's love for bikes and the full spectrum of what that can mean to different people. Euphoria. Catharsis. Escape. Exploration. Not bad for a wet, wintry Sunday spent in anonymous alleyways. **IT**

> *"To ride Melburn-Roobaix is not a single linear experience; it's hundreds of different stories spread across half a city"*

TOOLKIT

Start // Location varies
Finish // Brunswick Velodrome
Distance // About 40km (25 miles)
Getting there // Start and finish locations are close to public transport and major Melbourne bike infrastructure.
When to go // Late June, annually.
What to wear // Your most imaginative costume.
What to take // A sense of fun and a good nose for navigation.
More info // www.melburnroobaix.co

Opposite: find out where Melbourne's Capital City Trail bike path on the banks of the Yarra River leads on your own adventure

MORE LIKE THIS
COMMUNAL FUN RIDES

BEECHWORTH GRANITE CLASSIC, VIC

Set in picturesque, historic Beechworth, this event is a festival of all things gravel cycling. The Beechworth Granite Classic takes place over three days, with a series of short(ish) social rides and events bookending the main show on Saturday. Riders can take in distances ranging from 15km (9 miles) with 220m (720ft) vertical gain, to 115km (71 miles) with 1,400m (4,600ft) vertical gain, all exploring the scenic surrounds of this old gold mining town set in Victoria's high country. In addition to the riding, there's also a handmade bike show held at the popular Bridge Road brewery, and a sit-down dinner hosted by cycling personalities. The community of Beechworth has always been good to cyclists, and this event brings it all together in one weekend.
More info //
beechworthgraniteclassic.com.au

DIRTY DEEDS CX, VIC

A grassroots cyclocross series run by Brunswick Cycling Club, Dirty Deeds takes in courses dotted around the inner suburbs of Melbourne. Depending on which category is competing, the action can be hard-fought or fun-focused and everything in between. Over the years, Brunswick Cycling Club has built a reputation as a family-friendly, inclusive club. In addition to the kids' races, there is also the offshoot Melburn Durt ride collective catering for women, the trans community and gender non-conforming cyclists. Melburn Durt runs Wednesday night CX skills sessions at Brunswick Velodrome, so when Dirty Deeds rolls around, everyone's ready for bikes, banter and beers.
More info // www.facebook.com/
DirtyDeedsCyclocrossSeries/

CREATE YOUR OWN ADVENTURE

Gather a group of friends, choose a theme of your own and set out to find a different side of your city. Maybe you'll opt for a food odyssey, chasing the perfect banh mi or hot jam doughnuts at the local market; maybe you'll set out to explore a suburb you've never ridden in before, just to see what it's like when viewed at the leisurely pace of pedal power; or maybe your adventure follows a creekside bike path that you've always ridden past but never down, filling in the gaps in your mental map. One thing's for sure, the best times on a bike are times shared, and all you need is a bit of imagination and some social connection to make some indelible memories.

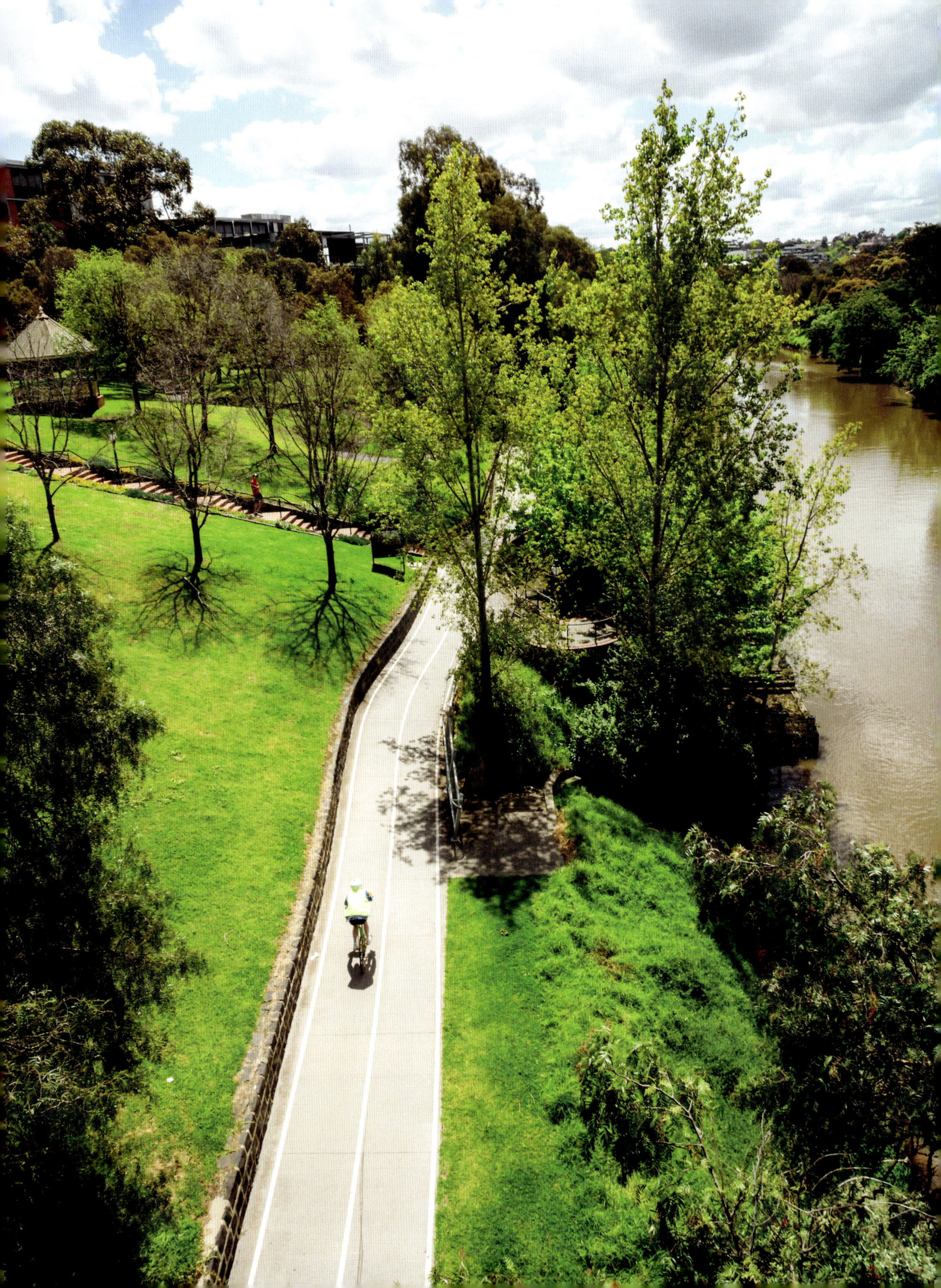

FINDING SERENITY ON FLINDERS ISLAND

When lapping one of Australia's most beautiful islands, parking at beaches and viewing geological oddities, you'll have the company of few people – but abundant wildlife.

In summer, Tasmania's east coast can seem like nothing but a crowd of bicycles, as pelotons of pannier-toting cyclists cruise between Launceston and Hobart along one of Australia's most popular touring routes.

But look slightly to the north, to Flinders Island, and there's rarely a bike in sight, despite the fact that Tasmania's largest offshore island – the high tip of a land bridge that once connected the state to mainland Australia – shares much the same geography: the same frame of granite, the same bright blazes of orange lichen, and the same flour-fine sand. It's also more compact, more manageable and arguably more spectacular.

Here, beaches nestle into the foot of mountains that are 800m (2620ft) high, where wombats, wallabies and Cape Barren geese abound, but vehicle traffic doesn't. As short cycle tours go, it makes for near-on perfection, with the slow pace of cycle travel amply suited to the slow pace of island life.

My cycling plan is to circuit the island in four days, looping out from the main town of Whitemark along the rugged west coast and then through the rural east. The single greatest impediment to cycling here is apparent at a glance, even in Whitemark. Flinders Island straddles the 40th parallel south – the line of the infamous Roaring Forties winds – and the island's tea-tree scrub is combed almost flat by the prevailing westerlies. As I pedal out of Whitemark, the blades of the island's wind turbines are cartwheeling furiously atop Hays Hill.

I've planned a short first day – just 20km (12 miles) south from Whitemark to the island's signature beach at Trousers Point. Eight kilometres (5 miles) out of Whitemark, I turn

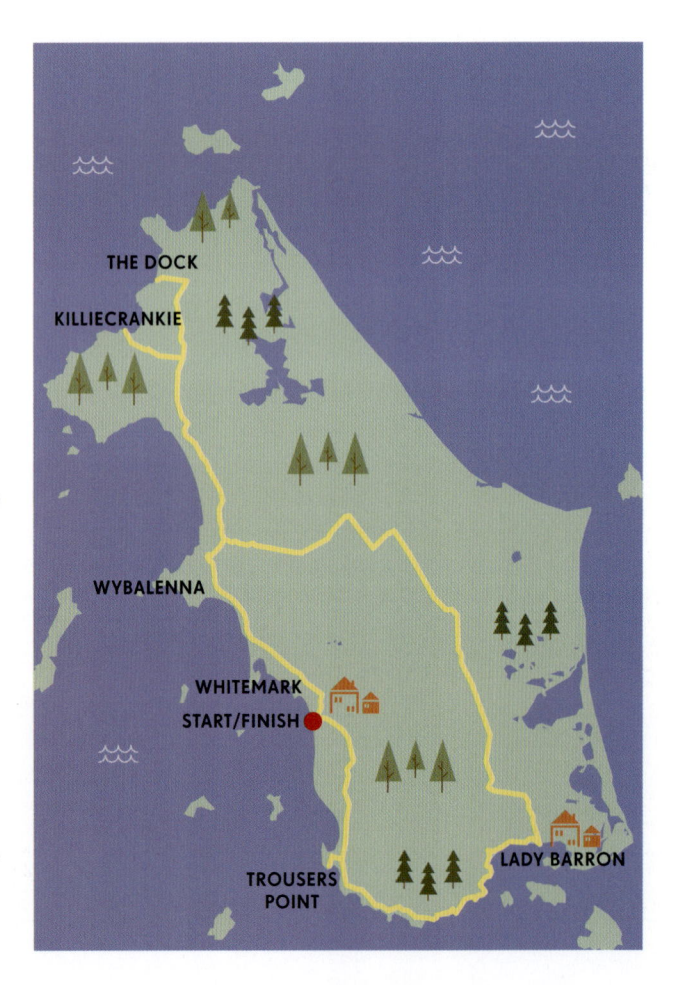

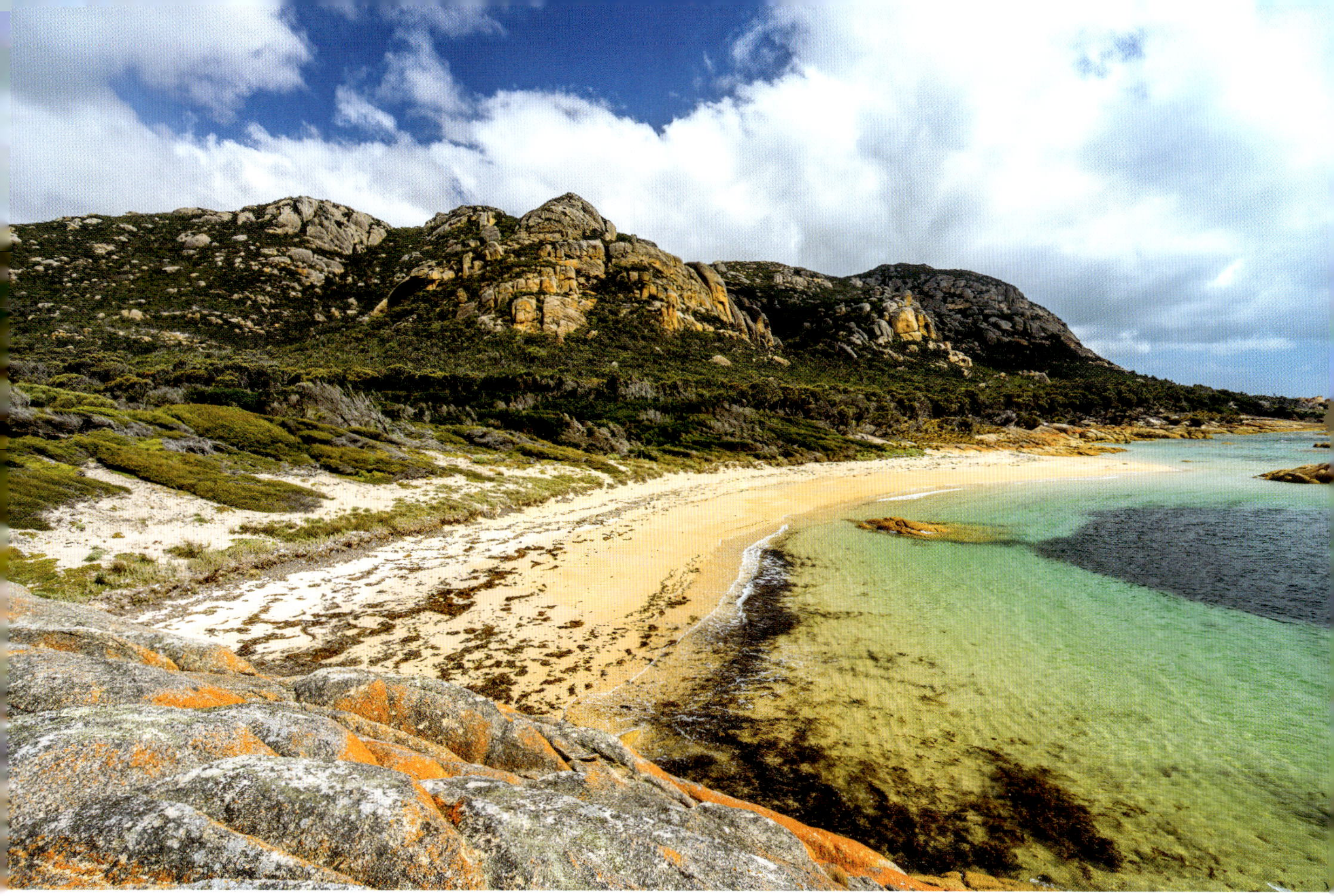

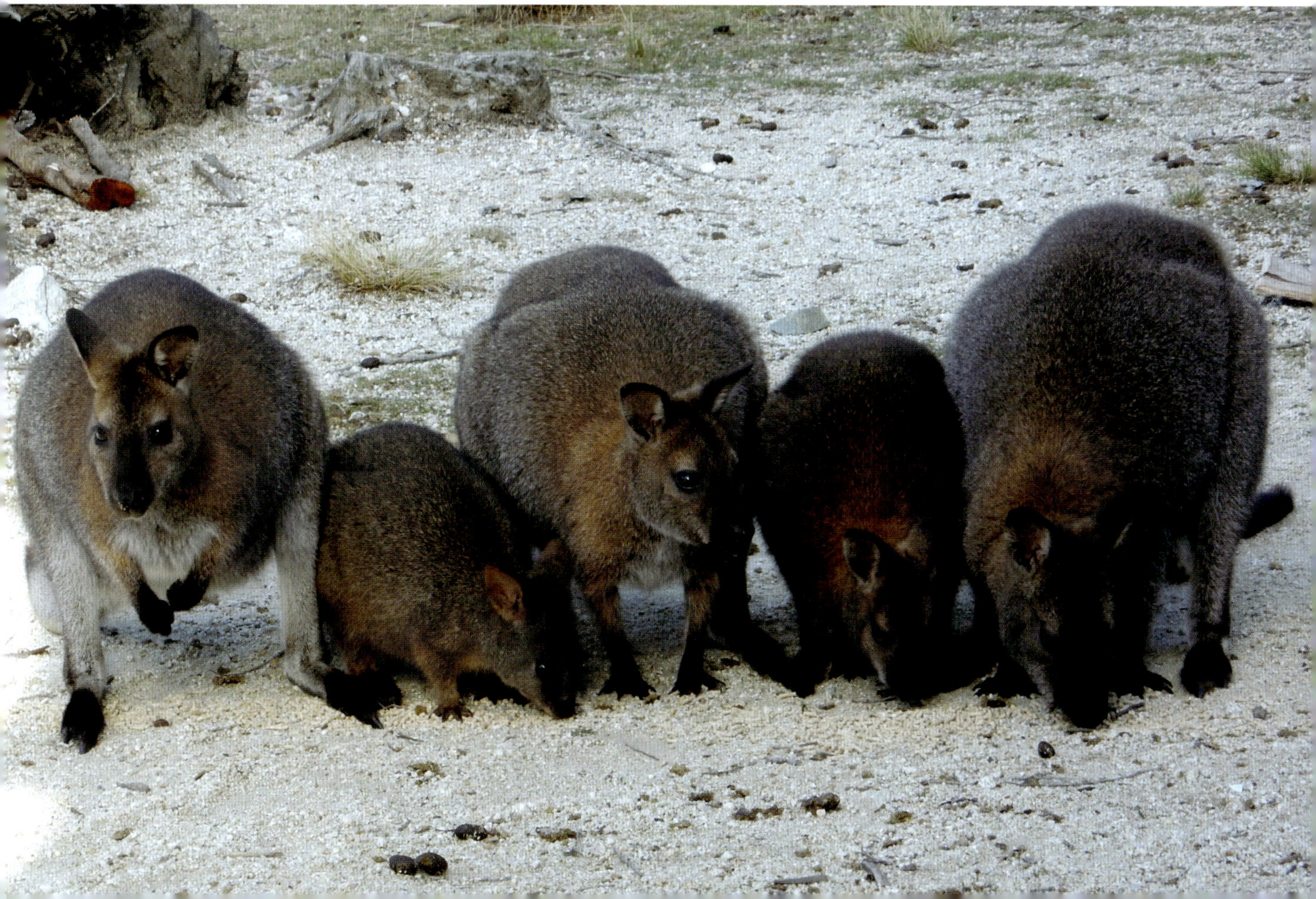

"Side tracks invite exploration, and I spend much of the afternoon ducking down unmarked trails"

off Flinders' main road onto the dirt track to Trousers Point. Immediately the traffic flow drops from a car every five minutes to a car roughly every 30 minutes.

Trousers Point is like Tasmania's larapuna/Bay of Fires without the hype. Gift-wrapped in granite and basted in orange lichen, it's an earthly rainbow of colours. Rising directly behind the beach are the Strzelecki Peaks, a bald-faced and rugged granite massif towering more than 800m (2,620ft) directly out of the sea. If road maps are to be believed, I need to double back to the main road from Trousers Point to reach the island's second town, southerly Lady Barron. But from Trousers Point, a faint, seemingly disused track bumps around the south coast, past a chain of castaway beaches that locals swear pull the pants off Trousers Point.

By Big River, part-way around, the track has deteriorated into a rutted mess, a bumpy mat of bark, sand and fallen trees.

This is terrain for mountain bikes or gravel bikes only. Side tracks invite exploration, and I spend much of the afternoon ducking down unmarked trails. Some reach the coast, some don't. It comes to seem beside the point anyway – the fun is in not knowing.

If the island now feels like an idyll, the reverie has broken by the next morning. Through the night, the wind has grown muscles, and by the time I set out from Lady Barron it's gusting up to 70km/h (43mph) – a customary day on this exposed island. Into this, I plan to ride 80km (50 miles) to Killiecrankie. I'm truly on Flinders Island now.

At times through this day, it feels as though I'm riding a stationary exercise bike, getting nowhere. There are dams that have waves rolling across them, and suitably I cross the 40th parallel midway through the morning. Through scenery that is almost entirely rural, I lean my body into the wind and almost fall over every time the gusts subside.

At one point, an ute pulls alongside my bike, and a farmer grins out at me.

'Where are you riding?' he asks.

'Killiecrankie.'

'You poor bugger,' he laughs. 'In this wind.' Then he drives on. I'm strangely revived by his lack of sympathy.

Near Emita, I rejoin the island's main road. North from here, Flinders is a different place again, with farmland turning into a blanket of scrub that provides a welcome wind break.

For most of the day, the wind has held my average speed to less than 10km/h (6mph), so it's late when I roll into Killiecrankie. It has been worth the effort, for the beach here, backed by a jigsaw of granite on the slopes of Mt Killiecrankie, is as beautifully curved as Tasmania's famed Wineglass Bay.

On my final morning, I continue north from Killiecrankie, even though my end goal – Whitemark – is south, because on the other side of Mt Killiecrankie is The Dock. Once a sleeper favourite among rock climbers in the know, it's now a little-visited beach area awaiting rediscovery.

I swing onto the narrow 4WD track that heads to The Dock, plunging at its end to the coast – I'm sure I will regret this detour when it's time to ride back out. Stepping onto the beach, it's as though every rock on Earth has somehow made its way here: in the sea, along the shores and on the slopes of Mt Killiecrankie. A claw-like rock stands guard above the beach, and the sea is as clear as gin.

As I finally return south, I realise that I've cycled 30km (19 miles) this morning without seeing another vehicle. Couple that with the abundant diversions on this final stretch – the beaches around Emita; the colossal Castle Rock; the haunting chapel at Wybalenna where, in the 1830s, Tasmania's Aboriginal population was exiled and isolated – and it's another flawless cycling day on Flinders Island, especially with the wind now at my back and not in my face. Together, we blow on south. **AB**

WYBALENNA

One of Australia's darkest colonial moments is on show at Wybalenna, a short detour along this ride's final day. Here, in 1833, 134 Tasmanian Aboriginal people were exiled to be (in the words of George Augustus Robinson, who brought them here) 'civilised and Christianised'. By the time the population was transferred from Wybalenna to Oyster Cove in southern Tasmania in 1847, only 47 were still alive. All that remains of Wybalenna, which was returned to the Aboriginal community in 1999, is its chapel and graveyard.

Clockwise from top: a beach break at Trousers Point; navigating a flooded 4WD track on Flinders Island; straddling the 40th Parallel South. Previous spread, from top: the Dock lookout; a family of Flinders wallabies

TOOLKIT

Start/Finish // Whitemark
Distance // 180km (112 miles)
Duration // 4 days
Getting there // Flights to Flinders Island depart from Melbourne, Hobart and Launceston. Bikes can be taken on the flights, though depending on flight loads, they may be transported on a separate flight. There's also a weekly ferry service from Bridport (Tasmania) to Lady Barron at the southern end of the island.
When to go // Take advantage of the many beaches with a summer ride, or wait until autumn, when winds are typically at their lightest.
Where to stay // There are accommodation options in each of the island's small towns and sprinkled along the coast.
More info // www.visitflindersisland.com.au

Opposite, from top: Cape Wickham Lighthouse on King Island in Tasmania; the Bass Coast Rail Trail over Bourne Creek at Kilcunda in Victoria, Australia

MORE LIKE THIS
COASTAL EXPLORATION

KING ISLAND, TASMANIA

Complete the set of Bass Strait bookends by cycling around King Island, at the western end of the strait. With no mountains (the island's highest point is just 162m above sea level) and little traffic, the only cycling foe here is wind – there's a reason all those trees are growing bent. Flights arrive in Currie, midway along the island's west coast, so begin here, heading north to Cape Wickham, the island's northern tip and home to Australia's tallest lighthouse (and one of the country's top golf courses) before detouring out to Lavinia Beach to ponder one of the world's great surf waves. At Reekara, turn east to cross Sea Elephant River, stopping in at tiny Naracoopa and Grassy. As you return across the island towards Currie, detour south to Seal Rocks (the island's highest cliffs) and the Calcified Forest. Excluding the wind, the cycling is easy, but bring a gravel or mountain bike because there are unsealed sections.
Start/Finish // Currie
Distance // 220km (136 miles)
More info // www.kingisland.org.au

BASS COAST RAIL TRAIL, VICTORIA

Victoria's only coastal rail trail is a gentle seaside affair, passing the former coal mines that prompted the settlement of the region and skirting the beach-lined shores around Kilcunda. The highlight of the trail is a 91m-long railway trestle bridge that straddles Bourne Creek high above Kilcunda's surf beach – be sure to wander down onto the sands to get the beach's view of the bridge rather than just the bridge's view of the beach. There are two more smaller trestle bridges to cross as the trail swings inland beyond Kilcunda, passing behind a wind farm and wetlands, and staying faithfully flat (as it does throughout) into Wonthaggi, where the ride ends beside the old railway station. There are plans to extend the rail trail at its western end to the Woolamai Racecourse, 4km beyond Anderson, and eventually on to Nyora, another 25km to the north.
Start // Anderson
Finish // Wonthaggi
Distance // 17km (10 miles)
More info // www.basscoast.vic.gov.au

GEORGE TOWN MOUNTAIN BIKE TRAILS, TASMANIA

Crouched beside the mouth of kanamaluka/River Tamar, 50km (31 miles) north of Launceston, George Town is Australia's third-oldest settlement but it's also one of the country's newest mountain-bike destinations. Launched in October 2021, the two-pronged trail network is framed around grandiosely named Mt George (a 245m-high hill) and the nearby Tippogoree Hills. The bulk of the riding – 57km (35 miles) of trails – is on the latter, though the signature trail is arguably Mt George's Hebe Jeebies, descending through a dolerite rock slab named the Reef (pay no heed to the fact that it's named after a shipwreck; you'll be fine). Mt George has 10 trails, covering 16km (10km) of riding, and runs are short, but that also means that shuttles back to the top take just a few minutes, allowing plenty of descents in a day. Tippogoree is defined by rock, with its slopes armour plated in slabs and boulders – seek out the black-diamond Devil's Elbow for the full rock 'n' roll experience.
More info // georgetownmtbtrails.com.au

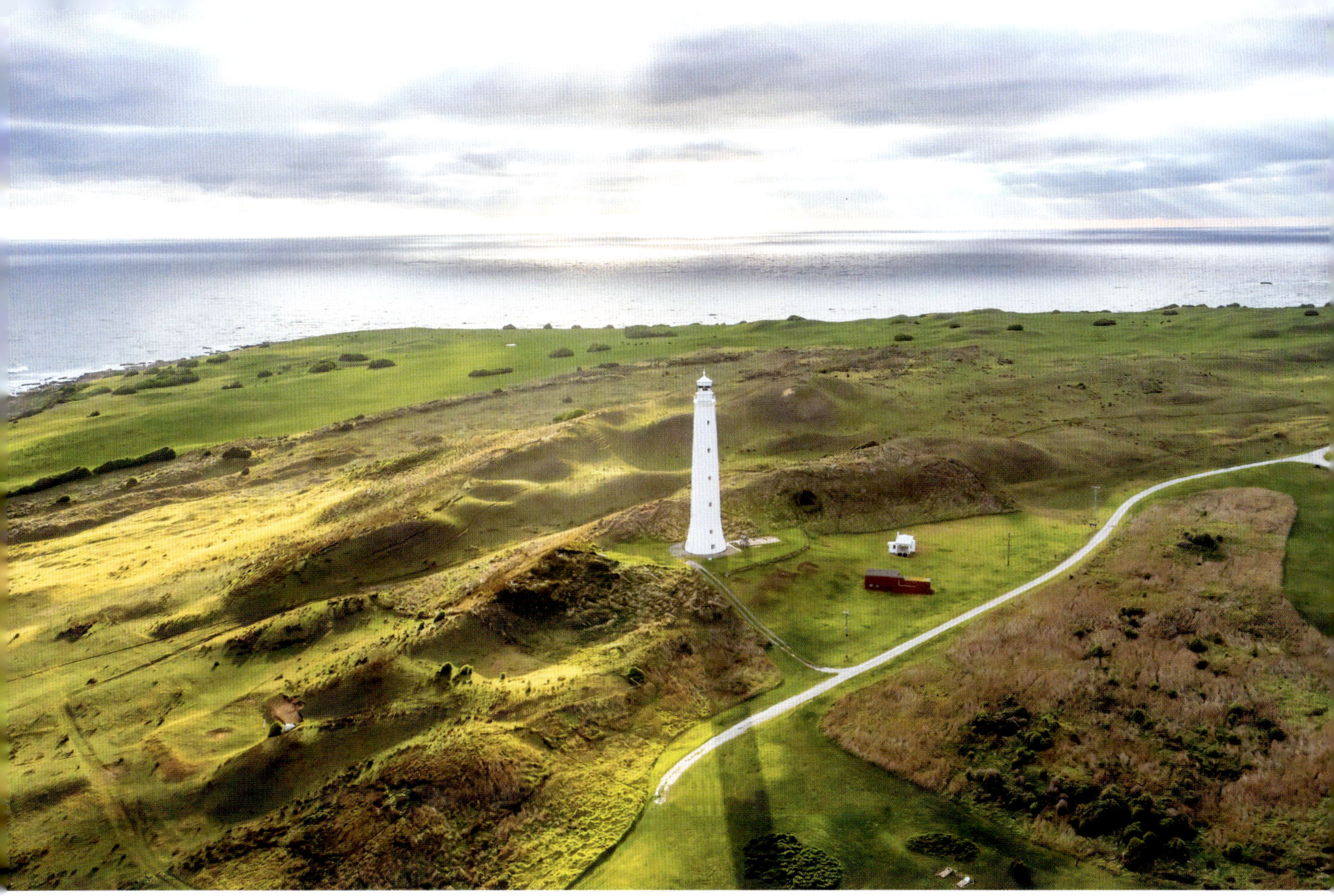

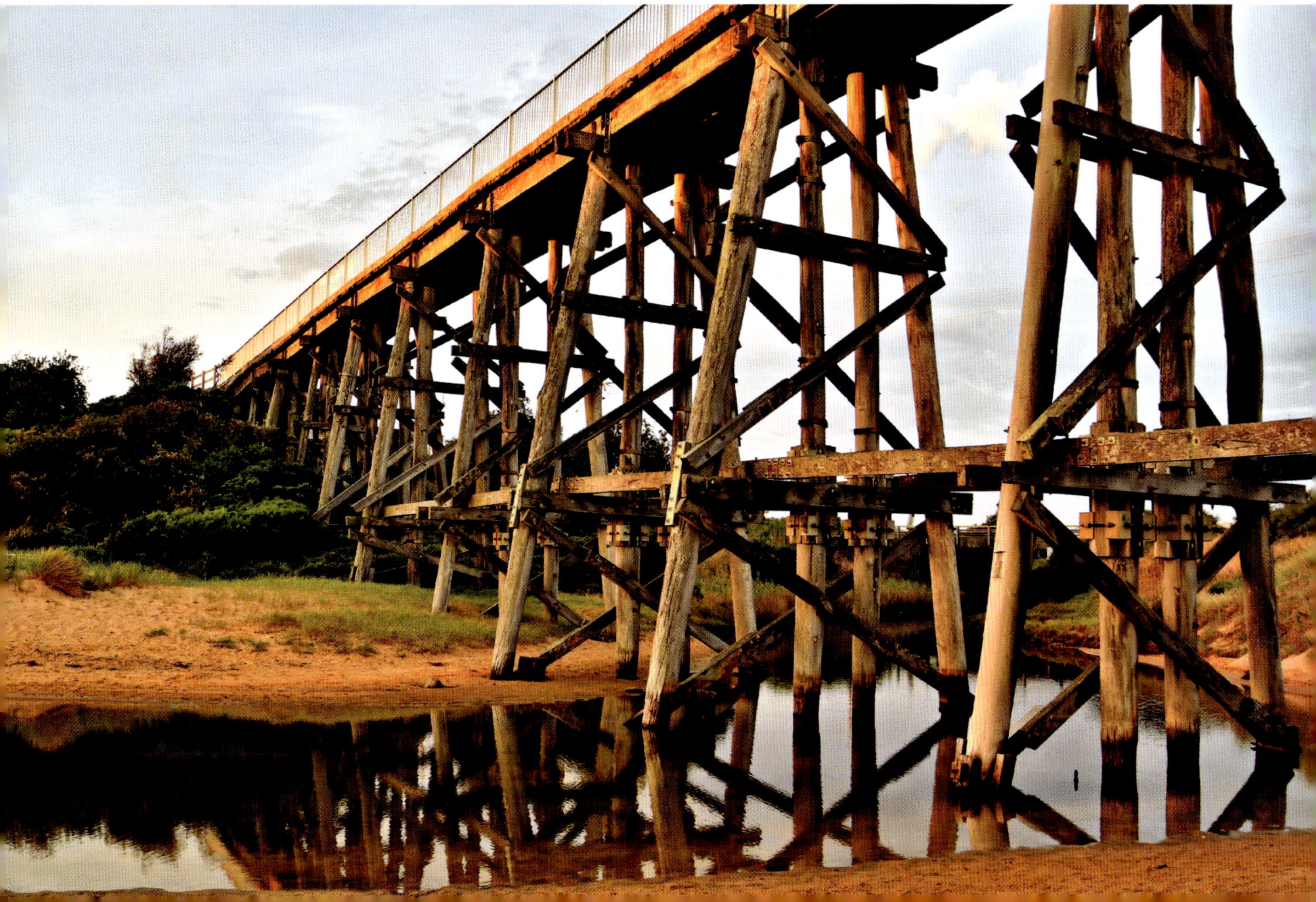

- EPIC BIKE RIDES OF AUSTRALIA & NEW ZEALAND -

TAKE A PEAK INSIDE TASMANIA

Magical mountain views are a Tasmanian speciality, but Ben Lomond and the Barrow are among the most enchanting ascents on the island.

Tasmania is one of those places that seems to hold more than its share of secrets. Its other name, lutruwita – which like all locations in the palawa kani language uses only lowercase letters – reflects an ongoing effort to reconstruct the speech of the people who lived here for tens of thousands of years, all from the scarcest of records.

An island poised to fall off the edge of the map, still untamed in many parts, it has a great deal of potential from a rider's perspective. It encompasses winding sealed roads in the great southwest, gravel backroads to nowhere, and world-class mountain bike trails that end at pristine beaches. Tasmania's 90,000 sq km (34,750 sq miles) makes it Australia's smallest state – less than half the size of the next biggest, Victoria – but that still results in some eight hours of driving from end to end, and, for the bike-based traveller, a need to focus.

It's also proportionally the country's most mountainous state. Indeed, it's been said that the real challenge of riding in Tasmania is finding a truly flat part of the island. To get an honest two-wheeled insight into this southern land, you therefore not only have to put in those vertical metres, but find

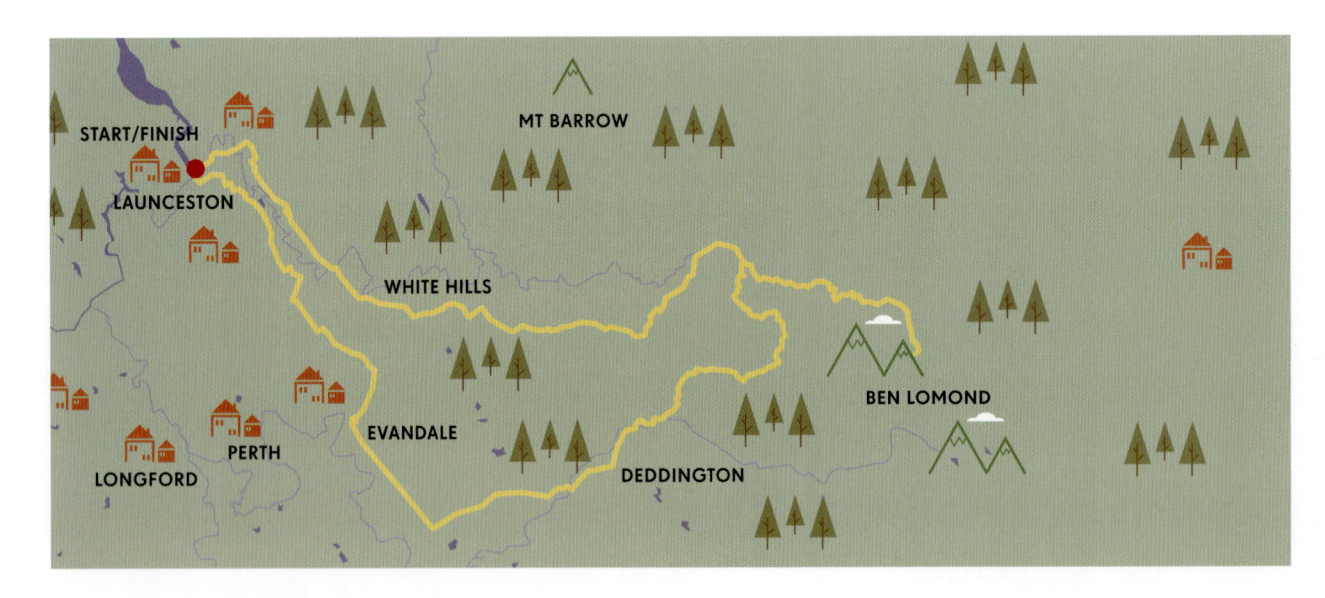

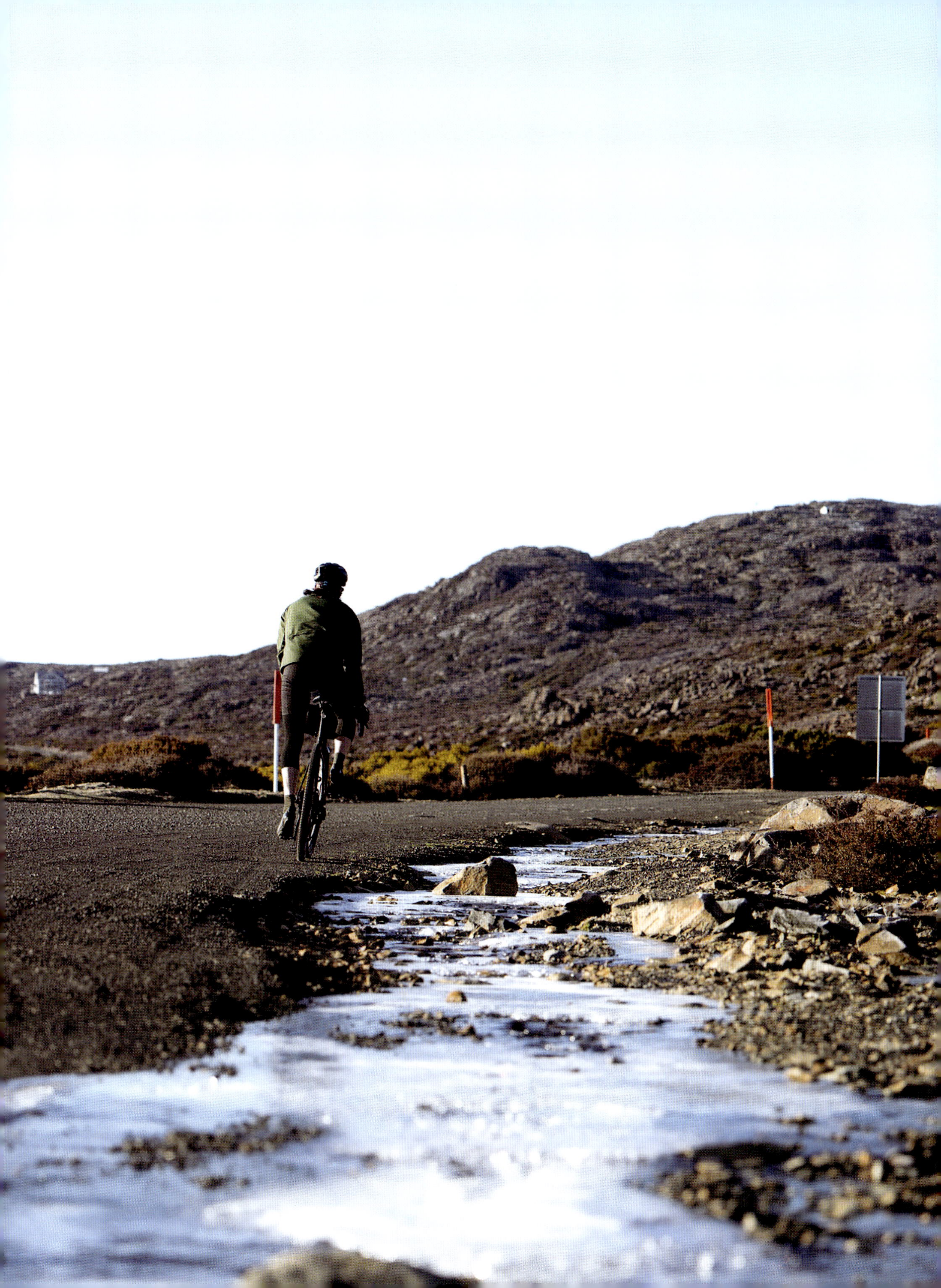

a way not to be overwhelmed by choice when picking from those peaks generously scattered around.

When I refine this selection to create my own 'sneak peak' of Tasmania, I like to concentrate on the gravel roads found in the northeast of the island, with the city of Launceston as the launch point. It's the major regional centre of the northern half of the state, and is also home to a few local secret watering holes. The Ben (turapina) and Barrow (pialermeliggener) are the majestic beauties of my mountain list, within a day's ride (give or take) of each other and also from Launceston – or, as I like to think of it, my front door.

Ben Lomond, or as the locals know it, 'The Ben', is not quite the tallest of Tasmania's mountains, but as the centre of its namesake national park 45km (28 miles) southeast of Launceston, it's one of the best known. With the road reaching up to 1,460m (4,790ft) of The Ben's 1572m (5157ft) height, you experience true alpine conditions when climbing the mountain. When planning my ride, I'm mindful of the weather forecast and prepare clothing for sudden changes in conditions. There are a few ways to access the beginning of the Ben Lomond ascent, but the Sawpit Hill Road brings that special gravel touch. The road ambles from the town of Evandale to Blessington and makes a nice loop from the base of the climb.

The Ben itself has around 17km (10.5 miles) of ascent through state reserve, eventually reaching a national park that is pure gravel climbing joy. The road begins in eucalypt forest, where I spy a couple of hot-pink waratahs growing wild. At this forest-bracketed stage of the ride, glimpses of my surroundings are fleeting, and I must stay patient for the mountain views.

Then, the section that truthfully brings me here: Jacobs Ladder. After the left fork, the road flattens out to circle around the shoulder of the mountain. The trees begin to thin and the cliffs build on the right-hand side. This is all just all scene-setting for the turn that reveals the entrance to Jacobs Ladder. Six hairpins zigzag up through a dolerite amphitheatre. On a good day, you can see the coast 70km (43 miles) to the north, and beyond that to the far-off islands in the Bass Strait. On a bad day, you can't see more than a foot in front of you. It may just be that you get both experiences in the same day.

Summiting over the ladder, I can ease off on the final stretch, which is a relatively gentle amble up a rocky valley filled with highland scrub. Snow poles flank the road, guiding me to the small ski village at the end. My favourite way to do this ride is in the chilly pre-dawn, with a clear sunrise warming my bones, as I make my way up and over Jacobs Ladder, my early rise from bed now proving its worth.

Most gravel-curious riders visiting Tasmania would already know of The Ben, but its slightly smaller yet equally adventurous brother sometimes get overlooked. At 1406m (4612ft), Mt Barrow comes with all the same cautions for riding in the Highlands. Located 25km (15.5 miles) northeast of Launceston, Barrow is accessible as its own ride via the Tasman Highway.

Although there are a few variations off the main sealed drag to add spice to this ride, the real fun and gravel begins when turning onto Mt Barrow Rd. I begin my ascent through farmland at the base of the mountain, and once again, more eucalypts striving for the skies, which dominate these local forest reserves. The road ramps upwards with the trees giving way here and there for glances of surrounding peaks, sunbathed or otherwise. Through a picnic area and a forestry gate, the climb takes on a different persona, as the steady gravel ascent gives way to switchbacks.

The alpine character of the road is revealed at last, as I exit the forest gateway onto an open escarpment of scree and boulder-strewn slopes. Hairpins count their way up to a lookout almost at the top of the mountain, where the road flattens out by a stone bunker – a chance to get out of the seemingly constant Tasmanian breeze (and by breeze, I mean wind). The light of a crisp morning is nothing short of spectacular.

The descent of Barrow is equal to the climb. The switchbacks that I painstakingly climbed at a very slow pace are now launched into like a rollercoaster dive, braking at the last possible moment before disaster over the boulder fields. I take the long straights between the corners at breakneck speed, swerving and hopping the front wheel over a regularly maintained yet often-rutted mixed gravel surface. This is the point of this style of riding.

The Ben and Barrow are two points in a dot-to-dot, to which you could add the town of Mathinna as a waypoint, and use stunning gravel tracks such as Camden Rd or Roses Tier Rd to join the dots. My two chosen peaks have their individual beauty, but with just a little stitching together, they begin to reveal the bigger picture of this island that can feel like a world apart.

Now that we have had a glimpse, let's have a taste. Riding mountains is a great way to make you hungry and thirsty. Not only is Tasmania known for its pristine wilderness, it is just as well known for its fresh local produce and craft. Looking at these rides individually with Launceston as your base provides an opportunity to sample some of this produce. There are two crucial elements required at the end of a big day's riding: hot food and cold beer. It seems fitting given this story's wilderness theme that the Du Cane craft brewery is where we end this little peak. Du Cane was named after a mountain range located in the Central Highlands, forming the region called the Labyrinth. Newly developed in a former outdoors store, Du Cane celebrates the concept of being surrounded by nature. The brewery is flanked by brick laneway and is a perfect place to end this small glimpse of what Tassie gravel has to offer.

If stitching this together as an adventure ride is your thing, one notable place to eat and potentially stay is The Creech in Mathinna, a farmstay surrounded by forests. Its Shearer's Quarters accommodation is warm and inviting, while the food is a paddock-to-plate experience like no other. But if self-supported is your vibe, there are lots of little camping and wild camping opportunities throughout this region. **SM**

THE BEN IN WINTER CLOTHES

In the depths of winter, Ben Lomond is transformed into a skiing village. July and August are the months when the chances of snow are at their highest – the village has several lifts to get you up and down the mountain. During these months, whether on or off Jacobs Ladder, chains are a must for drivers. A climb up the mountain by bike at this time of year has its own magical qualities, but be prepared to be very cold and very dirty by the end of the experience.

Left to right: a waratah in flower; the town of Launceston is a great base for mountain rides; taking a break on the Ben. Previous spread: watch out for ice

TOOLKIT

Start/Finish // Launceston
Distance // Around 145km (90 miles) per loop
Getting there // Launceston is less than a three-hour drive from Hobart, and its airport has domestic flights to many major cities.
When to go // Any time of year, as each season provides its own challenge, although winter snow is a special one.
What to wear // Dress for the season, but carry wind protection for descending regardless of the weather.
What to pack // Pack for a self-sufficient day ride.
Where to stay // Experience urban-rural contrasts at Hotel Verge in the centre of Launceston and The Creech farmstay near Mathinna.
Where to eat // If using Launceston as your base, you'll have a wide choice of eateries. Du Cane is a brewpub in a former outdoors store, with an artisan pizza menu.
Tours // For supported overnight tours of this region, check out www.tasmaniangraveltours.com.au
More info // www.discovertasmania.com.au

Opposite: the glacial gorge of Devil's Gullet

MORE LIKE THIS
HIGHLANDS OF NORTHERN TASMANIA

MT VICTORIA RD

Forming part of the Ben Lomond bio-region, Mt Victoria is a thickly wooded 1213m (3980ft) peak, with a through road running on its northern flanks, which brings access to a rabbit warren of quartz-gravel logging roads that weave their way through the substantial state reserves of northeastern Tasmania. Both mapped and unmapped, this is a great region to explore by bike. Near the 850m (2789ft) high point of the road, you'll find a parking area, from which a 10-minute rainforest walk leads to a viewing platform looking across to Ralphs Falls. This near-100m (330ft) drop off a cliff face counts as one of Tasmania's highest waterfalls. From the falls, you can retrace your route or continue on the loop trail to Cash's Gorge, with the bonus of walking through buttongrass.
Start // Ringarooma
Finish // Pyengana
Distance // 35km (22 miles)
More info // www.parks.tas.gov.au

MT ALBERT RD

A logical addition to the Mt Victoria climb, the Mt Albert Rd runs to the south of the summits of Mt Victoria and her smaller partner, Mt Albert. Although not a peak climb that can be accessed by bike, it's a gravel-riding experience that fills the soul with dusty joy. The quartz squeaks under your tyres as you pass through a vista of mountains and buttongrass plains normally associated with the more remote regions of the central highlands and west coast. The Mt Albert and Mt Victoria roads form the two major climbs of a deep-winter racing classic – the Devil's Cardigan. This is gravel racing with a true Tassie twist, where the temperature isn't likely to get into double figures, and the possibility of snow is ever-present. One hundred kilometres of type-2 fun, all for the price of a bag of Scottsdale potatoes – what's a race without a few jagged edges?
Start // St Helens
Finish // Ringarooma
Distance // 64km (40 miles)
More info // www.devilscardigan.com.au

DEVIL'S GULLET

We're not just talking peaks – here's a 200-million-year-old gorge. Deep in the alpine region of the central plateau is the Devil's Gullet, a plunging glacial gorge formed by 220m (656ft) dolerite cliffs. Looking out over it, you could be forgiven for thinking how insignificant we truly are against the majesty of a landscape that traces its history back to the age of Gondwanaland. The privilege of visiting this natural phenomenon comes courtesy of the Tasmanian hydroelectric scheme. Access to the Devil's Gullet is via the Lake Mackenzie Road, a 21.7km (13.5 mile) ribbon of gravel climbing to 1122m (3681ft) above sea level. It's a further 7km (4.3 miles) past the turn-off to the gorge lookout walk to reach the shore of Lake Mackenzie – two former highland lakes that were dammed to form a single one, but whose original lines can be seen in summer when water levels are low.
Start // Mole Creek
Finish // Lake Mackenzie Dam
Distance // 43km (27 miles)
More info // www.discovertasmania.com.au

© Ryan Hoi/Shutterstock

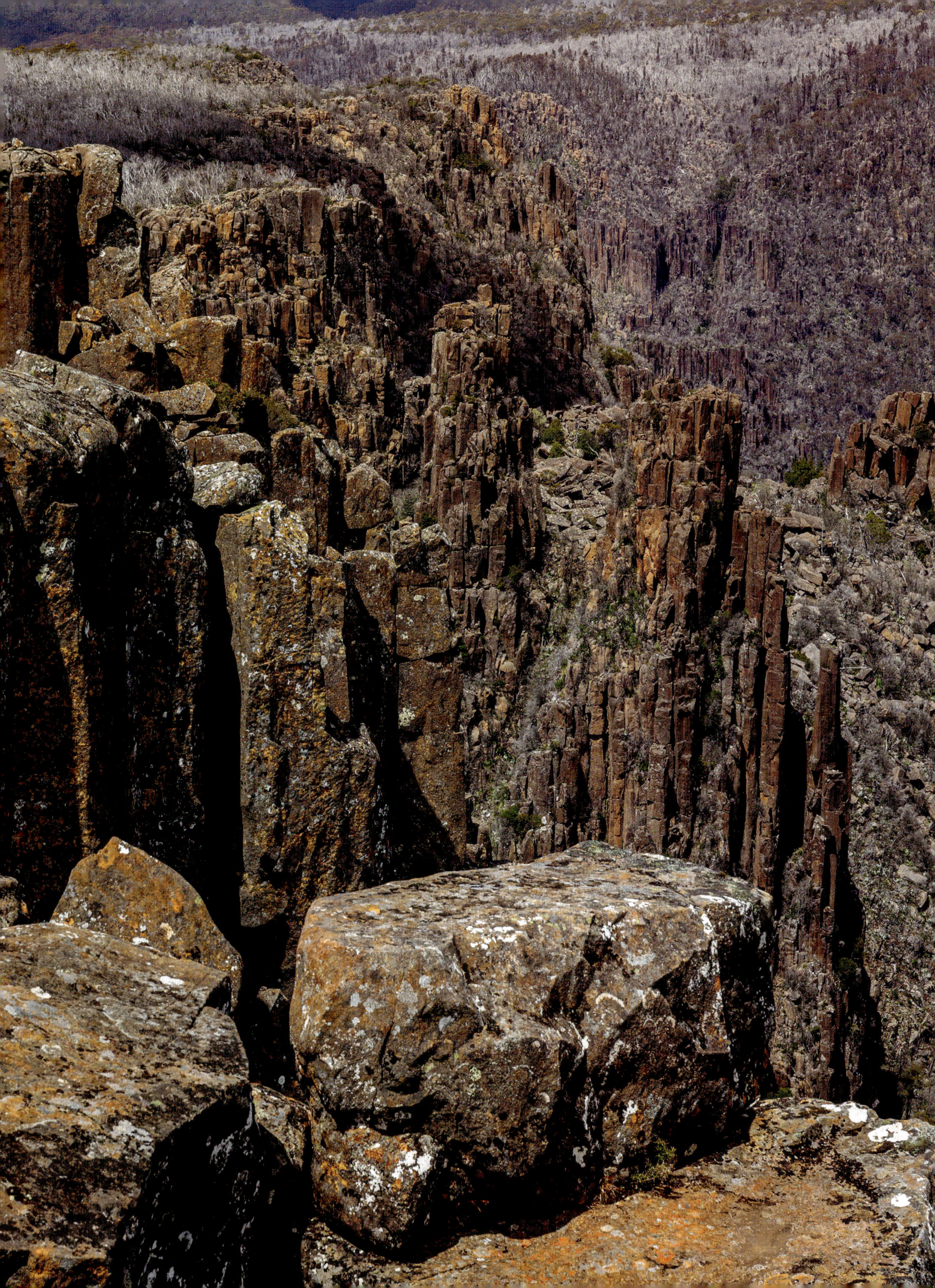

AUSTRALIAN ALPINE EPIC TRAIL

Mt Buller's thrilling trail has set the standard for day-long adventure rides in mainland Australia, with unforgettable scenery and endless descents.

Mountains have the uncanny ability to make us feel both insignificant and herculean at the same time. The heights can humble us with nature's might, yet simultaneously fill us with a sense of achievement while we stand on their shoulders. They offer an experience unlike anything else, and it is an especially rare one in Australia. The alpine area of Australia accounts for only 0.15% of the continent, making these towering peaks an unmissable pilgrimage that's not to be taken for granted.

Pursuing my passion for mountain biking, I moved to the Victorian High Country in 2021 – an unoriginal but understandable life choice. Since then, I've been lucky enough to make a living by photographing and writing about this passion. Several jobs have drawn me to Mt Buller, a 2½-hour drive from my home in Bright. I've had the pleasure of photographing the Contour Works trail builders riding their own creations, as well as several other events at the resort. This time, I've returned to navigate the Australian Alpine Epic Trail.

Mt Buller is home to more than 50km (31 miles) of modern mountain bike trails. The first were opened in 2014, after years of planning, by the esteemed builders at World Trail. One of these trails is the famous Australian Alpine Epic Trail – an unoriginal and self-explanatory name, but a worthy title nonetheless. It is an IMBA-certified cross-country adventure covering 51km (31 miles) of singletrack and firetrail, with 1,200m (3,937ft) of climbing and an eye-watering 2,200m (7,218ft) of descent.

In the ensuing years, Buller was at the forefront of event-hosting, with multiple gravity and cross-country races on its network each year. However, as bike technology changed, the Buller trails were unable to provide the vertical drop and features required to challenge modern mountain bikers.

Action man David 'Danger' McCoombe, from Mt Buller and Mt Stirling Resort Management, has been skiing and riding this mountain long enough to have seen the mountain bike network rise and fall with the times. He has also anticipated its revival. 'Everyone has singletrack now, but a destination like Buller wants a bit more than that,' he says.

In 2021, a government-issued grant enabled the refurbishment of the Buller trail network and brought this

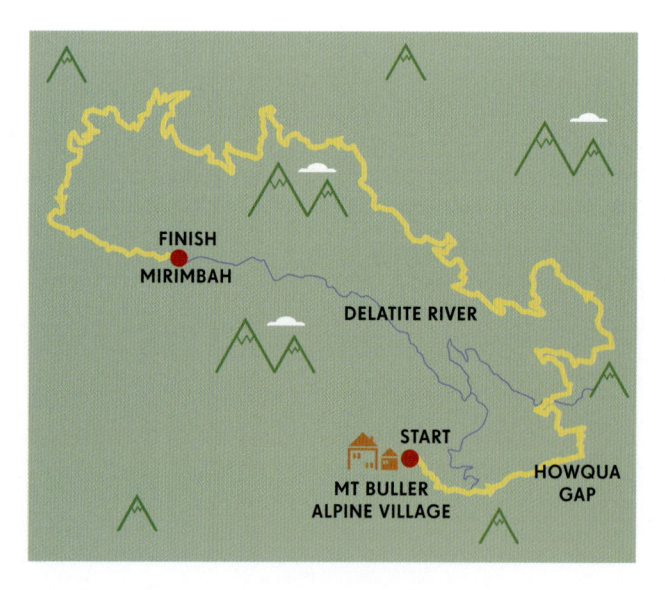

© Georgina Von Marburg

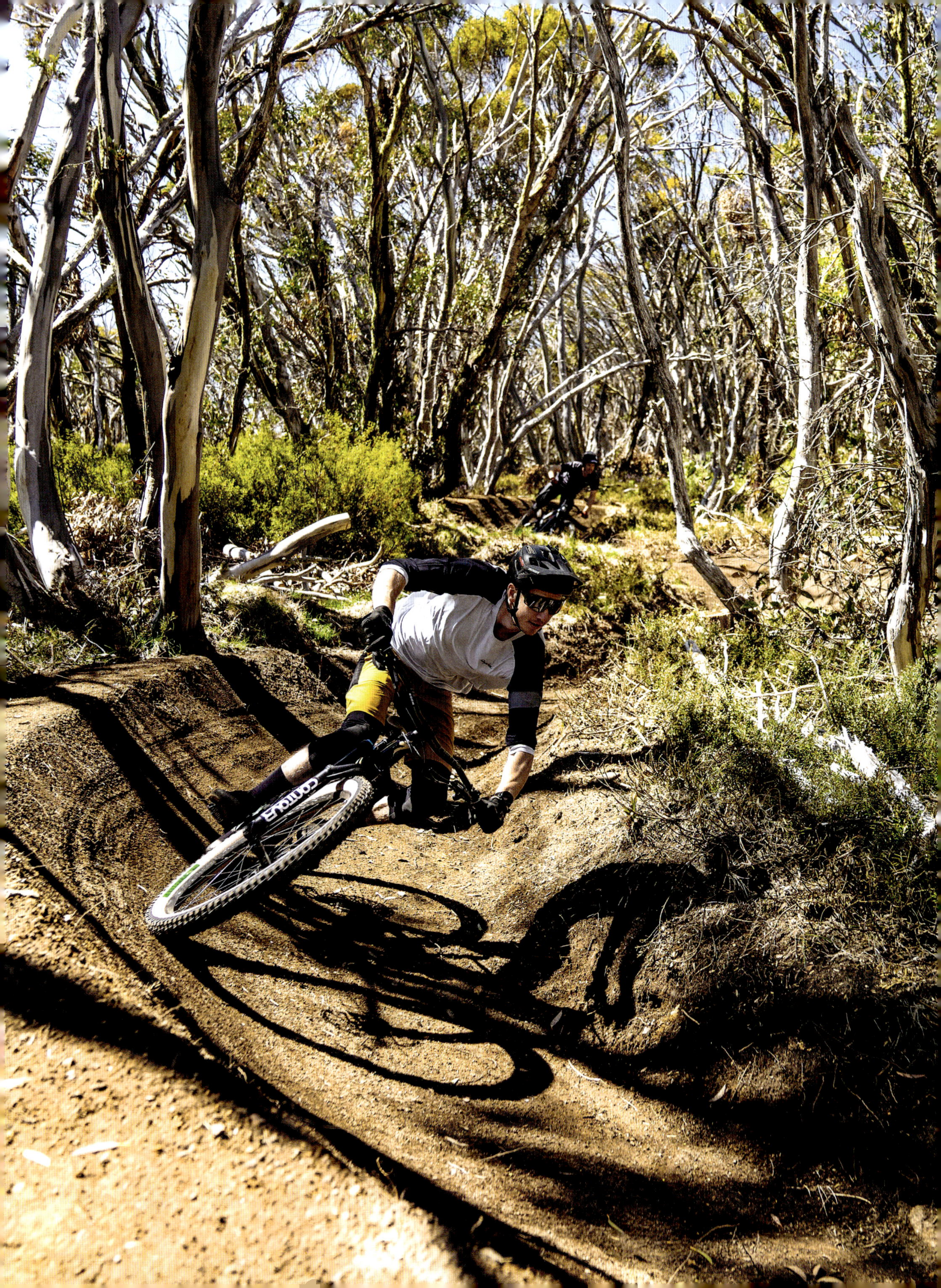

> "Whether I'm ducking beneath ferns or perching on a boulder while surveying the heights of Australia, the Epic Trail makes me feel miles away from civilisation"

famous riding destination back to life. Trail building company Contour Works – led by World Trail graduates Evan Winton and Ryan De La Rue – renovated the Buller trails to create a paradise of sweeping berms, high doubles and progressive flow. After racing several events at Mt Buller in its heyday, I've now revisited the resort multiple times to experience the rejuvenated trails.

And the improvement is evident. 'My favourite trail [before the renovations] was probably Clancy's, but what they've done to it now has made it a hundred times better,' says Danger, relating his enthusiasm. 'It's still Clancy's, but it's got that modern twist that we're all craving.'

But the trail that never ceases to amaze, before and after Contour Works weaved its magic, is the Epic Trail. Beginning with 'Gang Gangs' near Buller's village square, the Epic Trail greets you with a series of perfectly manicured berms and table-tops, before dropping you onto the aptly named Trigger Happy trail. The last time I rode Trigger Happy, it was a slog of a climb, albeit with heavenly views over the ranges. But these days, thanks to Contour Works, this trail is one of the finest descents in the region. Following Danger's wheel, I savour every metre of this delectable series of loamy turns and sneaky gaps, as I know what the Epic Trail holds next.

The climbing has to begin somewhere, and it does so abruptly with the infamous Stonefly trail. While this one is technical and slow going, the surroundings are soul nourishing. Thick rows of ferns and creek crossings are repeated through the climb, and reward my efforts through every tight switchback. With so much singletrack already, there hasn't been an ideal time to break out the snacks. Thankfully, Stonefly culminates with a long section of undulating firetrail, giving me a moment to chow down on cookies while admiring more magnificent views over the hazy blue mountains.

Whether I'm ducking beneath ferns or perching on a boulder while surveying the heights of Australia, the Epic Trail makes me feel miles away from civilisation. I would describe it as one of the most accessible ways to feel remote and removed – just you, your bike and miles of pristine mountains. After tackling the firetrail from Telephone Box Junction –

© Georgina Von Marburg

ALPINE SHELTER

The Australian Alps are dotted with time- and weather-worn huts, and Mt Buller is no exception. Originally built to shelter the early cattlemen or loggers, these rudimentary structures are made with log walls and iron roofs, containing little more than a fireplace and shelves. But to this day, they stand to provide lifesaving shelter to lost campers and hikers. Riders on the Epic Trail go past the Howqua Gap Hut, built in 1968 to accommodate working loggers during inclement weather.

Clockwise from left: climbing and descending on the Alpine Epic Trail; Mt Buller resort. Previous spread: big berms keep riders on the track

the physically hardest section of the Epic – the sweetest compensation awaits my weary legs. In my view, this next section is what makes the trail so iconic: the 10km (6 mile) Epic Descent. I know we've reached this final pièce de résistance of singletrack by the log on the ground with 'Enjoy :)' engraved on it, greeting riders as they enter this heavenly dirt. The next 10km are filled with a variety of features designed to carry you all the way to the base of Mt Buller. The carefully crafted waves of dirt generate the perfect speed for each optional jump, while every loamy corner inspires confidence for the next.

My 160mm enduro bike requires some pedal strokes throughout the descent, each of which are absolutely worth it. However, a 120–140mm dual-suspension bike would be the ideal partner on the trail, and would provide comfort and assurance on descents, while remaining efficient on the climbs.

After the 10km descent, we find ourselves at Mirimbah, where a Blue Dirt shuttle is ready to take us and our bikes back to the Buller village square. After a quick dip in the shimmering Delatite River, I load my bike onto the trailer and reminisce about the journey. The Epic Trail is not something I'm content to do once; there are so many features and sections I'm eager to master, and lookouts I want to witness at different times of the day. We'll meet again soon, Buller! **GVM**

TOOLKIT

Start/Finish // Mt Buller Alpine Village / Mirimbah
Distance // 51km (31 miles)
Getting there // Mt Buller is a 3.5-hour drive from the Melbourne CBD, or a 2.5-hour drive from Albury.
When to go // December to February. This is the dry season, when the trail is often cleared and maintained.
What to pack // A backpack with a hydration bladder is essential as there are no drinking water stations. Bring a multi-tool, spare tube, tube repair kit, first-aid kit and plenty of snacks. Wear a base layer and summer riding kit, but bring a wind or rain jacket in case the skies turn grey.
Where to stay // Buller Chalet is a well-appointed hotel in the village. Shuttle company Blue Dirt offers backpacker-style accommodation for those on a budget.
Tours // Local bike shop All Terrain Cycles offers various tours and skills coaching from its Buller store.
More info // www.ridehighcountry.com.au

Opposite: the top of Lake Mountain overlooks Marysville

MORE LIKE THIS
HIGH IN THE VICTORIAN ALPS

INDIGO EPIC

If you're seeking High Country mileage, Beechworth's own Epic Trail is set to open in the autumn of 2023. The Indigo Epic Trail will connect the neighbouring historic towns of Beechworth and Yackandandah, through a combination of pre-existing and brand-new singletrack. This world-class loop will be open year-round, through the luscious ferns and dense pine forests that characterise this region. Both Beechworth and Yackandandah are home to various breweries and distilleries, acclaimed restaurants and boutique accommodation. The Indigo Epic Trail is accessible from either location, letting you choose which direction to tackle the loop. The climate is quite temperate, but be prepared for damp and cold conditions in winter and spring.
Start/Finish // Beechworth Historic Park or Yackandandah Sports Park
Distance // About 50km (31 miles)
More info // www.indigoshire.vic.gov.au

BIG HILL MOUNTAIN BIKE PARK, MT BEAUTY

For purist mountain bikers eager to get lost in singletrack, look no further than Big Hill Mountain Bike Park on Mt Beauty. A sprawling maze of singletrack webs itself across the hill – be sure to refer to a map on your phone, or better yet, hail down a local rider for directions. It's the country's oldest mountain bike park, and arguably where the sport itself was born in Australia. The local mountain bike club prides itself in preserving the original trails, allowing nature to deepen the ruts and create new lines. Big Hill sets itself apart from the modern trend of machine-built 'flow' trails, forcing riders to get imaginative with line choice and sharpen their skills. The town itself lies in the shadow of Mt Bogong, a sharp peak visible from almost every street. There's a grocery store, several motels, a famous bakery, and a coffee roaster that will give any inner-city cafe a run for its money.
Start/Finish // Big Hill Mountain Bike Park trailhead, Bogong High Plains Tourist Drive
Distance // Over 40km (25 miles)
More info // www.tmb.org.au

LAKE MOUNTAIN CASCADES TRAIL

Lake Mountain offers a magical trail just 1½ hours from Melbourne's CBD. The 30km (19 mile) Cascades descent runs from the tiny alpine resort to the charming town of Marysville. While it drops over 1500m (4900ft), it also climbs a total of over 500m (1640ft) – so be prepared for a solid three to five hours in the saddle. The Cascades trail can be broken into five main descents, each with a distinctive flavour. The top section contains classic alpine boulders and white gums, while the lower sections weave through gigantic ferns and ancient trees. There are some highly technical but optional lines along the trail, making it a playground for bikes with 140-160mm suspension. Marysville provides ample accommodation options. The local watering hole, The Duck Inn, serves up some brilliant meals and is known for being cyclist friendly. The Lake Mountain Information Centre will shuttle you to the top of the resort, where you can ride the entire Cascades trail back down to Marysville.
Start // Lake Mountain Resort
Finish // Marysville
Distance // About 30km (19 miles)
More info // www.lakemountainresort.com.au

LAKE MOUNTAIN SUMMIT
1433 METRES ABOVE SEA
Emergency Marker
Call 000 and quote
LMT007
MAXXIS
roval
FOX

- EPIC BIKE RIDES OF AUSTRALIA & NEW ZEALAND -

ALONG THE ACHERON WAY

Take a challenging day-ride among some of the world's tallest trees, encountering unique wildlife and witnessing the rebirth of a town in the state of Victoria.

- EPIC BIKE RIDES OF AUSTRALIA & NEW ZEALAND -

Saturday dawns on a winter weekend in Warburton, Australia. The former logging town, an end of the (paved) road sort of place, lies in a steep-sided forest valley; low clouds streak the green-grey treetops. The Yarra River, which broadens as it reaches Melbourne, runs through its centre.

I carry my road bike down from my motel room and make my final checks: pump, two tubes, puncture-repair kit, multi-tool, water, cake. Before I set off, I see Franz, the barrel-chested owner of the motel, who has cycled and photographed this part of Victoria for decades. I tell him where I'm planning to go and he lets me in to a couple of local secrets.

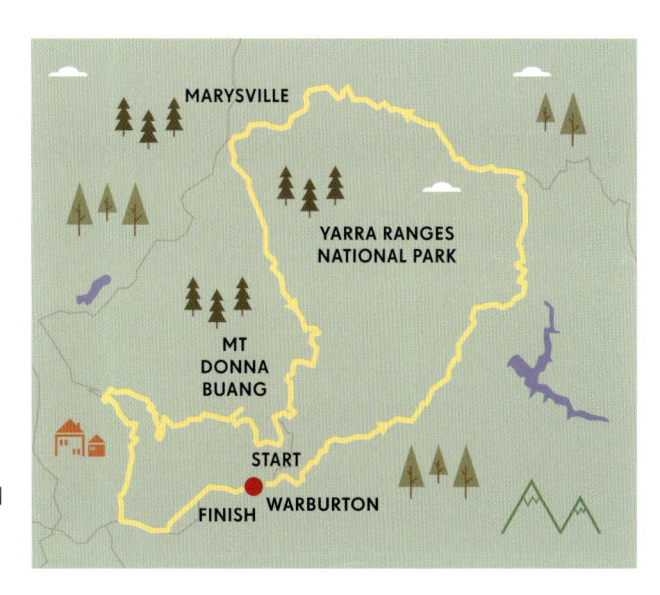

In the cool air, I follow the Woods Point Rd east out of Warburton along the valley floor. It undulates through a couple of townships before turning left about 30 minutes later. As I round the corner, the road pitches up. It's a steady gradient, so I settle into a comfortable gear – I know this is a big climb. The sparsely populated valley floor has been replaced by the dense forest of the Yarra Ranges National Park. On either side are mountain ash trees, manna gum trees, mountain grey gums and myrtle beeches, rising above an understory of 3.5m (12ft) ferns. The mountain ash eucalypts are among the tallest flowering plants in the world, topping out at over 100m (330ft). It's common to feel dwarfed by the Australian landscape, but here I'm dwarfed by the trees. The road curves round the contours of the Reefton Spur. I pedal higher. At breaks in the trees, on corners, I glimpse wave after wave of green, as far as I can see. Another sort of wave breaks over me – trepidation. What if I break my chain and can't fix it? What if I tear a tyre, or simply run out of steam?

A pair of crimson rosellas, foraging on the verge, provide a distraction. They burst upwards and fly alongside me – streamlined red bodies, straight blue wings a blur – before peeling off into the undergrowth, like vivid Spitfires. These raucous and social parrots are common companions on these roads. Higher in the tree canopy, large flocks of white cockatoos flap haphazardly from ridge to ridge, cawing loudly. A rarer sight are yellow-tailed black cockatoos; larger birds, they fly slowly and purposefully, like WWII bombers.

I'm breathing deeply but steadily. This is a 20km (12.5 mile) climb and eventually it levels out before meeting a junction. I turn left to Marysville. This road (slightly busier, meaning one or two cars, or a logging truck) runs along the spine of a ridge, dipping and rising, never straight. Up here I get a glimpse of something terrible but curiously beautiful: entire hillsides of dead trees, the colour of grey-white bone. This is the aftermath of Black

"From June to October this gravel road is a traffic-free treat for cyclists; great scrolls of bark are strewn across it"

Saturday. On 7 February 2009, after days of withering heat (in Melbourne the temperature exceeded 46°C) bush fires ignited. Fanned by 100km/h winds, fires measuring 1,200°C – with flames 100m (330ft) tall – roared through the Kinglake-Marysville region, where 159 people died. The surviving trees are now bursting with new life, green shoots growing from charred trunks. Birds and animals are returning.

Through this landscape in transition, the road begins to drop into Marysville. This is a long, fast descent – I check brake pads, cables and quick releases first. As I slalom round the bends, I shift my weight to the outside pedal for grip, raising the inner pedal and leaning my knee towards the tarmac. The road steepens before Marysville and then tilts uphill into the main street. When the fire swept through, only 33 houses remained habitable, 400 were destroyed. For personal accounts of Black Saturday, stop by the Phoenix Museum in the tourist information centre.

After topping up my water bottles at Fraga's Cafe and wolfing down a baguette, I continue south on the main road. This is the busiest stretch of the route but it doesn't last long – I'm looking for a left turn onto the Acheron Way. Off the highway here you're back in the shady forest. A couple of years ago, when I first rode this logging road that runs beside the Acheron River, I saw a red-bellied black snake, hunting for frogs. Now if I stop, I watch where I put my feet.

The Acheron Way turns into a gravel road as it climbs up over the Acheron Gap at 756m (2480ft) and down the other side. After a dusty, helter-skelter descent, I rejoin the tarmac at the Rainforest Gallery, a 15m/49ft-high walkway through the forest canopy. Warburton is a short descent away, but if you've still got some zip left in your legs, turn right to head up Mt Donna Buang, one of Australian cycling's iconic climbs. It's another long but gradual ascent, with views over the Yarra Valley. About one kilometre from the summit, I follow Franz's first tip and turn left onto the C505. There's a gate across the entrance – in the winter Parks Victoria closes this gravel road, which means that from June to October it's a traffic-free treat. Scrolls of bark are strewn across the descent, and the wildlife has grown unaccustomed to people. I watch as a lyrebird, a famous mimic, disappears into the undergrowth.

After a 10km (6 mile) descent, I turn left at the next junction towards Launching Place, keeping an eye out for Franz's second suggestion. It's easy to miss: on a fast descent I spot the crossing point for the O'Shannassy Aqueduct Trail. This little-used track for walkers and cyclists follows the route of a now-disused aqueduct that was opened in 1914 to deliver water from Warburton's reservoir to Melbourne, 82 km (51 miles) away, and I follow the flat track back to Warburton for 10km (6 miles): fire and water in one day. **RB**

LEADBEATER'S POSSUM

One forest resident that you probably won't spot is the Leadbeater's possum, also known as the fairy possum. This mini-marsupial, weighing between 100g and 160g, fitting into the palm of a hand, is one of the world's most endangered creatures. The mountain ash forests of the Central Highlands are its habitat – it lives in colonies of about a dozen, but only one pair will breed – where the possum makes its home in high-rise hollow trees.

Left to right: the Yarra River; the O'Shannassy Aqueduct Trail and giant mountain ash trees; a Leadbeater's or fairy possum in the wild. Previous spread: the gravel descent on the Acheron Way

TOOLKIT

Start/Finish // Warburton
Distance // 150km (93 miles)
Getting there // Warburton is about a 90-minute drive northeast from Melbourne. Even better, the Lilydale-Warburton Rail Trail allows you to cycle 40km (25 miles) from Lilydale train station (on the Melbourne line).
Tour // You can take some of the hard work out of the ride by signing up with Soigneur (www.soigneur.cc), a Melbourne-based tour operator that escorts cyclists on rides, including this route.
Where to stay // There's a motel and two hotels in Warburton. If you break the ride at Marysville there are a couple of new hotels in the town.
What to take // Carry spare inner tubes, food, water (to be replenished at Marysville), tools and sunscreen.

Opposite: The Great Ocean Road along Victoria's south coast

MORE LIKE THIS
VICTORIAN ROAD RIDES

THE 7 PEAKS RIDE

Every year, Parks Victoria challenges cyclists to climb seven of the toughest road climbs in Australia, all of them in Victoria's High Country. At the top of each you can get your 7 Peaks passport stamped, and riders who have completed more than four are entered into a prize draw. Four of the climbs are close to the beautiful town of Bright: Mt Hotham, Mt Buffalo, Falls Creek and Dinner Plain. Mt Buller (see p104CKCK) near Mansfield is another. The sixth climb is Lake Mountain, which starts from Marysville. And the final climb is short but very steep Mt Baw Baw to the southeast. All are achievable for a fit cyclist and riders generally have five months of warm weather to attempt all seven.
Distance // Individual climbs range from 10km to 30km (6 miles to 19 miles), but would typically be part of a longer ride.
More info // www.ridehighcountry.com.au/7-peaks

AROUND THE BAY IN A DAY

Australia's largest mass participation bike ride was first held in 1993. Although much of the route around Melbourne's Port Phillip Bay is rideable throughout the year (the Mornington Peninsula, the eastern end of the croissant-shaped route, is particularly popular with weekend cyclists), this is the only time you will ride in the company of 15,000 other cyclists. The full loop is 250km (155 miles), with participants catching the ferry between Sorrento at the tip of the Mornington Peninsula to Queenscliff at the tip of the Bellarine Peninsula. Groups start and finish at Alexandra Gardens in Melbourne, but head off in different directions, east and west. Many of the roads are closed to cars for the ride.
Start/Finish // Alexandra Gardens
Distance // 250km (155 miles)
More info // www.bicyclenetwork.com.au/around-the-bay

GREAT VICTORIAN BIKE RIDE

The GVBR was founded in the mid-1980s and has grown to become an annual fixture on the cycling calendar. Think of it less as a quiet, solitary ramble through the countryside and more of a travelling jamboree on wheels, with thousands of other cyclists. The ride covers approximately 550km (340 miles) over eight or nine days, so distances aren't daunting; nobody cares much what you ride (or wear). The GVBR ranges over a different corner of Victoria each year, with luggage being carried on ahead in dozens of trucks, leaving you free to enjoy the ride. Tent cities spring up in every host town, which compete to offer the warmest welcome.
Start/Finish // The route varies
Distance // Typically around 550km (340 miles)
More info // www.bicyclenetwork.com.au

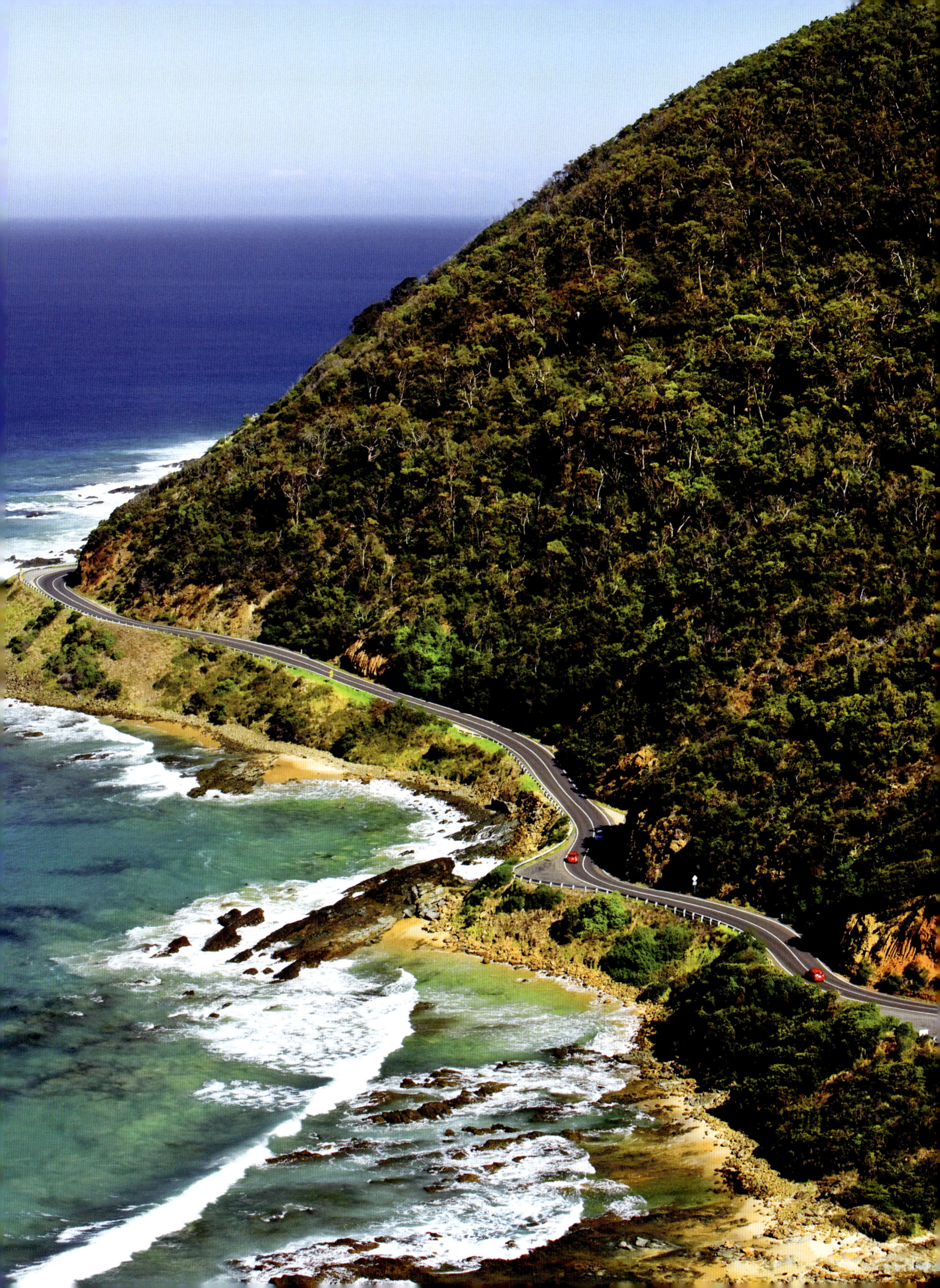

— EPIC BIKE RIDES OF AUSTRALIA & NEW ZEALAND —

BIKEPACKING ON THE GOLDFIELDS TRACK

Few off-road routes in Victoria are as perfect for beginner bikepackers as the Goldfields Track between Ballarat and Bendigo.

'Psssht'... Two thirds of the way along the Goldfields Track, I've not just punctured my tyre on some sharp shale, I've slashed it. It's fixable with the tyre boot that I always carry but it's also bad enough to force a rethink of my ride. Do I want to be nursing a weakened tyre on a loaded bike through bushland on a searingly hot day? Perhaps not. Time to consider the options.

Rewind 170 years. In the 1850s, gold fever swept the state of Victoria and nowhere was it more acute than in the swathe of hills northwest of Melbourne. The goldfields fed the local economy as prospectors streamed north, and such towns as Ballarat, Castlemaine and Bendigo built grand avenues and buildings on the back of the gold rush. Around four million ounces of gold was unearthed here and by 1860 the population of Victoria had grown ten-fold to 540,000. The prospectors left behind not only the machinery and watercourses of mining, but also the paths they took across the hills. Those paths – specifically the Eureka Track from Mt Buninyong to Creswick, the Wallaby Track from Creswick to Daylesford, the Dry Diggings Track from Daylesford to Castlemaine and the Leanganook Track from Castlemaine to Bendigo – now form all 210km (130 miles) of the Goldfields Track.

I started at Ballarat, an easy train trip from Melbourne if you avoid the peak commuting times. Staying overnight allowed for an early start the following day and also a meal of spring rolls and steamed fish at Vietnamese restaurant Saigon Allee.

The Goldfields Track officially starts (or ends, it can be ridden in both directions) on Mt Buninyong, but this involves doubling back for a few kilometres, so I decided to crack on towards Creswick. One way that the Goldfields Track makes life easier

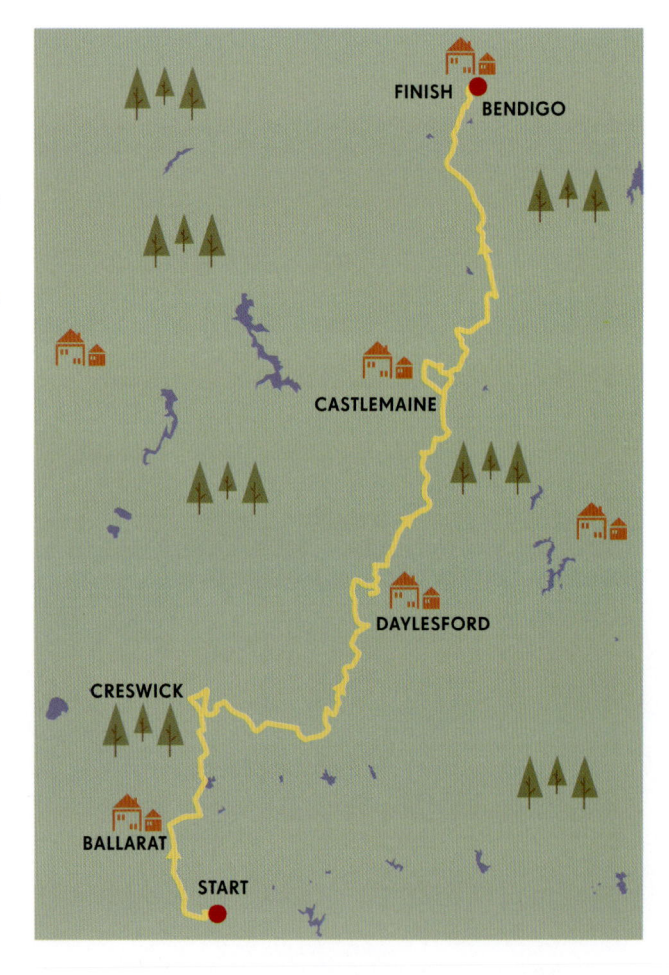

TAS – VIC

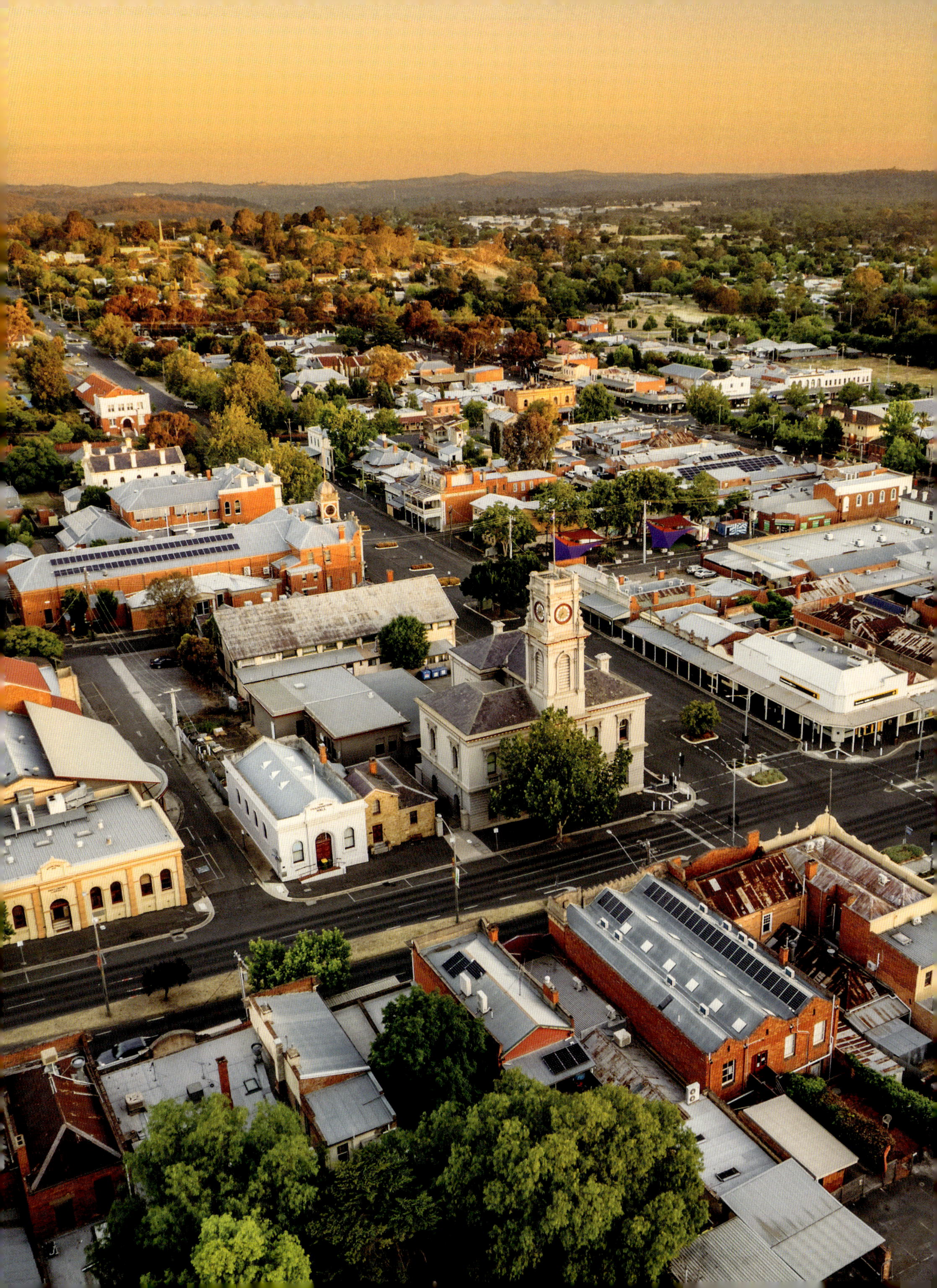

for novice bikepackers is that it is signposted its whole length. After a couple of missed turns, I learned to look behind trees and bushes for the gold-topped posts. I'd also uploaded maps as GPX files to my phone for reassurance, which was invaluable.

From Ballarat, the route takes in some stiff climbs through plantation forest, but things improved as I approached Creswick: forest roads gave way to rougher doubletrack and then purpose-built singletrack that flowed into gullies and around trees. Creswick has its own network of mountain biking trails, built by the Dirt Art collective, which merit more exploration, but I pressed onwards with 25km (15 miles) under my belt. After Creswick, the Eureka Track segues into the Wallaby Track, which bounds along all the way to Daylesford. At first the terrain is fertile farmland, but old-growth forest began to appear on the approach to the spa town, where large grey kangaroos bounced along in front of me. If you listen carefully you can sometimes hear the rustling of echidnas at the foot of the tall trees.

Before entering Daylesford, watch for signs to Sailors Falls, one of the mineral springs for which the resort town is renowned. Water tumbles over basalt columns and into a fern-filled gully. But rather than overnight in Daylesford, which is very much budgeted to weekending Melburnians, I pedalled a few more minutes up the road to quieter Hepburn Springs.

The next stretch of the Goldfields Track is the Dry Diggings section. This started with a couple of steep climbs to wake up the legs, but soon settled into some fun singletrack, with a rocky and rooty descent as a reward. Evidence of the gold mining boom became more apparent around every corner of the Castlemaine National Heritage Park. Here, I began to learn about the impact the mining had on the Dja Dja Wurring Country and its traditional owners. Topsoil was removed, destroying ecosystems,

SPRINGS TO SAVOUR

Victoria's spa capital, Daylesford, and the adjoining town of Hepburn Springs are about midway along the Goldfields Track and make for a refreshing place to stop. This is a volcanic area, about 750m (2,460ft) above sea level. In fact, there could still be magma below the surface. Several million years ago, lava flows filled valleys, and where the resulting basalt lava meets a fault, mineral springs bubble up, each with a different taste – Tipperary Spring is even fizzy.

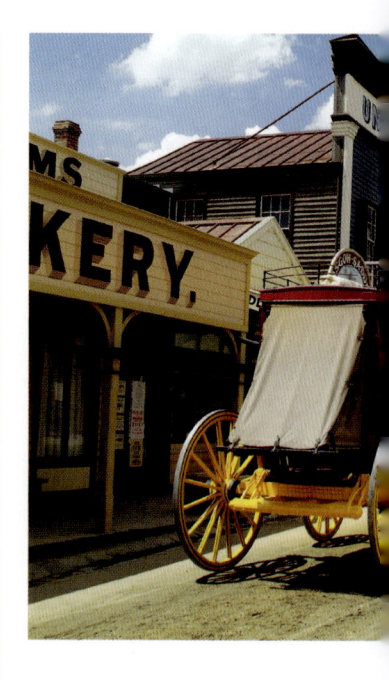

Clockwise from top: Sovereign Hill, an open-air gold-rush museum in Ballarat; view from Mt Alexander National Park; parked up in gold mining country. Previous page: the town of Castlemaine

and the mining also displaced Aboriginal people. In Australia, it doesn't take much to start unpicking history.

In 1851, gold was discovered near Castlemaine and within weeks thousands of miners had moved to the fast-growing town, which became an administrative centre of the goldfields. Today, there's still a pick and a shovel on the town's flag.

I followed a watercourse built by miners into the town, which is my second overnight stop. Although Castlemaine's good fortunes faded as quickly as they arrived, it remains a handsome town with sturdy Victorian architecture and a railway station. On the north side of town, a new development near the Botanical Gardens on the site of a former mill has attracted brewers, bakers and winemakers. I stayed nearby in an earthen home in a permaculture community, where I was welcomed with a bowl of cherries from the orchard. My host, Ellen, cooked us a meal from veggies she has grown and we watch the kangaroos loiter at the edge of the garden: 'The big males can be a bit unpredictable,' she advised. 'Don't look them in the eye.'

The fourth section of the Goldfields Track is the Leanganook Track from Castlemaine to Bendigo, which heads north through Mt Alexander Regional Park. But it was about 5km (3 miles) out of town that I had the deflating experience. A puncture is usually not a problem for tubeless tyres: the rubber solution seals most holes but it can't cure an inch-long gash in a sidewall. So I stuck a tyre boot inside the damaged tyre and installed a tube. It worked well enough to ride on, but what if it failed 25km (15 miles) from town on a 35°C day? I returned to Castlemaine and mulled it over in Saff's Cafe. My decision was to not take a risk: I'd take the train to Bendigo instead, replace the tyre and then ride the last leg of the Goldfields Track in reverse back to Castlemaine. Sometimes discretion is the better part of valour.

"Evidence of the gold rush became more apparent around every corner of the Castlemaine National Heritage Park"

TOOLKIT

Start // Ballarat
Finish // Bendigo
Distance // 210km (130 miles)
How to get there // Direct trains run from Melbourne to and from Ballarat and Bendigo, making travel exceptionally easy. Check when you can bring a bike on board.
What to take // Pack clothing for three days and nights, but there's no need to carry a lot of food as you're never far from a town. A mountain bike is best on this route.
When to go // Winter can be quite dark and wet, and summer potentially very hot. Better to aim for late spring or autumn and enjoy the blossom and fall foliage.
Where to stay // Breaking the ride in Daylesford or Hepburn Springs and Castlemaine suits most people, but you can make the sections shorter still. There are plenty of campgrounds in the parks, forests and towns here, or book a B&B.
More info // www.goldfieldstrack.com.au

Opposite: wild emus in Victoria's Grampians National Park

MORE LIKE THIS
BEGINNER BIKEPACKING

THE GEYSERLAND CLASSIC, NEW ZEALAND

This relatively straightforward route revolves around the hub of all things thermal in New Zealand's North Island: Rotorua. The city is also into biking in a big way, with a mountain bike park on its doorstep and several long-distance routes nearby. The Geyserland Classic began as a three-day bikepacking event, taking place each spring. But you can follow the route in your own time. It heads out to coastal Matata on the Kaikokopu Cycle Trail, turns inland to the Waikite Valley and loops back to Rotorua via the Te Ara Ahi cycle path. The surface is mostly gravel and there are stores and campsites along the way.
Start/Finish // Rotorua
Distance // 240km (150 miles)

ATTACK OF THE BUNS, NEW SOUTH WALES

The route was created by Adam Lee of Endless Cycle with the intention of sharing some of his beautiful backyard of the Southern Tablelands, part of the Great Dividing Range. It cruises north from the outskirts of Canberra towards Sydney, dropping in on a number of country towns and rural cities and a couple of national parks, never gaining or losing any great elevation and never far from a comfortable campsite. That makes it an ideal trip for a long weekend of riding bikes with buddies and also a great trip for soloists and first-timers. One challenge is getting to and from the start and finish with your bike using NSW's decidedly bike-unfriendly public transport. More than half the route is off-road, but typically on moderate gravel tracks. You may wish to carry camping gear, but there's plenty of accommodation along the way.
Start // Bungendore
Finish // Bundanoon
Distance // 323km (200 miles)

GRAMPIANS LOOP, VICTORIA

Starting from the vibrant country town of Ararat, set on a direct train line west of Melbourne and the gateway to the Grampians region, this gravel circuit cuts across the Grampians National Park twice. It passes through Moyston and close by Halls Gap, the park's hub, before arriving at the Jimmy Creek campground for the night. The next day takes you south for another night under the stars (there are various options depending on the distance you want to ride), before you turn around for Ararat. There are a couple of steep climbs midway but the full route is relatively flat (for Victoria). Much of it is on gravel roads with a few interludes on tarmac, so a gravel bike will be fine. Find the complete route (designed by Stephanie Quinceton) and downloadable mapping at www.adventurecyclingvictoria.com.
Start/Finish // Ararat
Distance // 155km (96 miles)

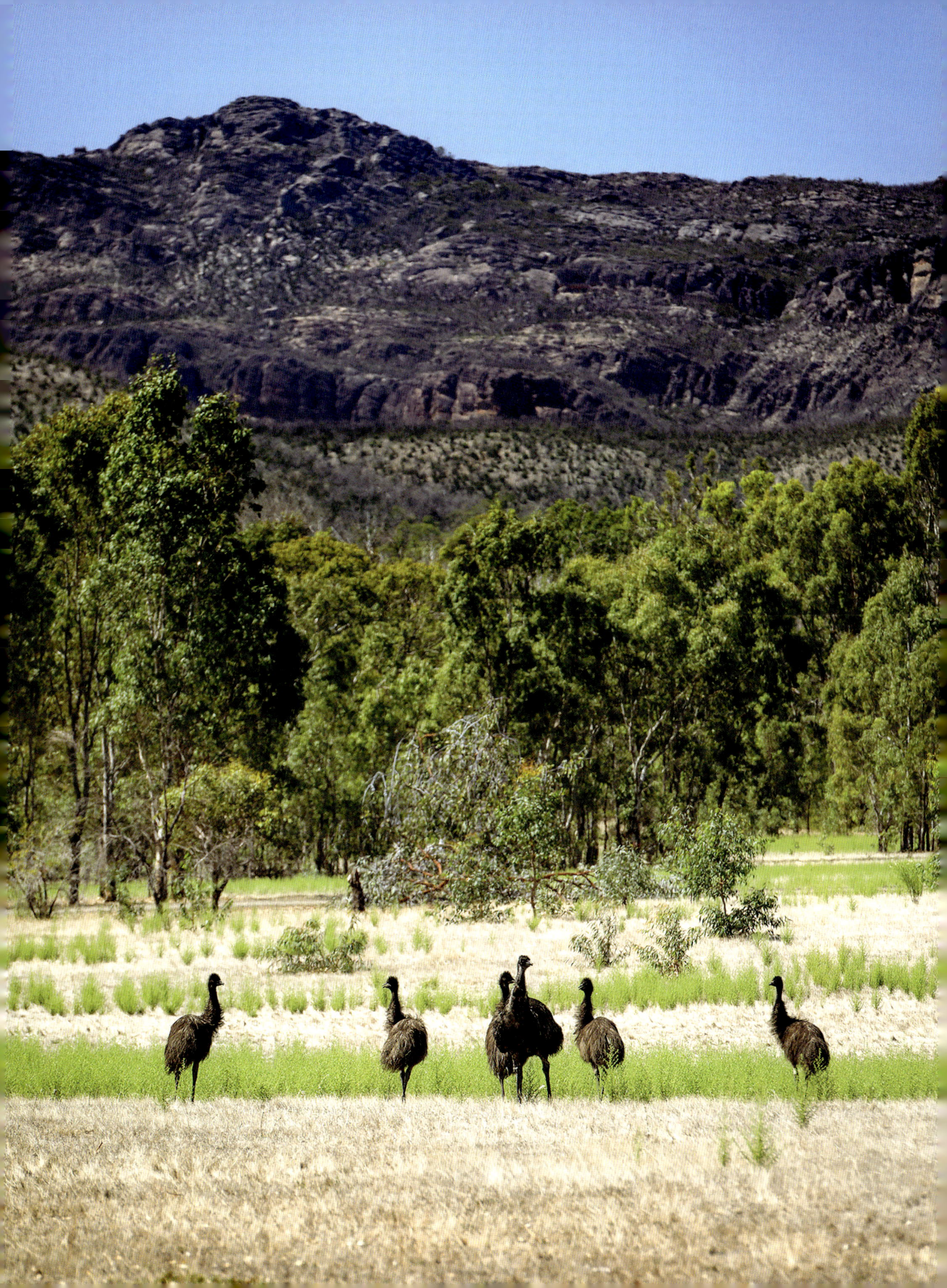

ON THE ROAD TO NOWHERE

The building of a road through one of Tasmania's greatest wildernesses was hugely controversial, but the result is a cycling adventure on the edge.

It's a beautiful calm evening after a raging storm over the Central Highlands, which didn't seem like the likely outcome for the day when we left home on a summer's morning. So as we sit on the banks of the Pieman River, looking across the black, watery void, we take mental inventories of what we might have forgotten to bring for this type of weather.

A lonely figure sits on the opposite shore, his bike lying on the road, so near to us and yet so far. There is no bridge – will the barge collect him tonight, or will he sleep there, just out of reach of the small cluster of houses that makes up Corinna?

Welcome to the beginning of the edge of the world. Welcome to the Road to Nowhere. Tonight, we will be eating warm food and drinking cold beer. But there are no rooms left in town, so a warm bed has been swapped for a wild camp under the stars.

Corinna is on the border of the Tarkine, a region of wilderness in the northwest of Tasmania, between the Pieman River and the Arthur River. This land represents Australia's largest remaining single tract of temperate rainforest. Add to this dry sclerophyll forest, buttongrass moorland, coastal sand dunes, wetlands, grassland and communities of sphagnum moss, and it provides a habitat for rare species, including Tasmanian devils, eastern quolls and giant freshwater lobsters.

In the 1990s, the Tasmanian government bulldozed a road right through the middle of this untouched area, with even the federal government calling it an 'act of environmental vandalism'. Although the road was billed as a way to bring better access to the isolated northwest of the island, it would have been an easy prelude to mining and logging in the area. Campaigners fought to stop further road-building, and to bring recognition and protection to the Tarkine, just as was done in the 1980s for the Tasmanian Wilderness World Heritage Area to the south and east.

What remains from this turbulent happening is a stunning path though temperate rainforest and rolling foothills of bushland. There are few more remote stretches of gravel in Australia than the roughly 100km unsealed road that connects Arthur River with Corinna. The Road to Nowhere is also known

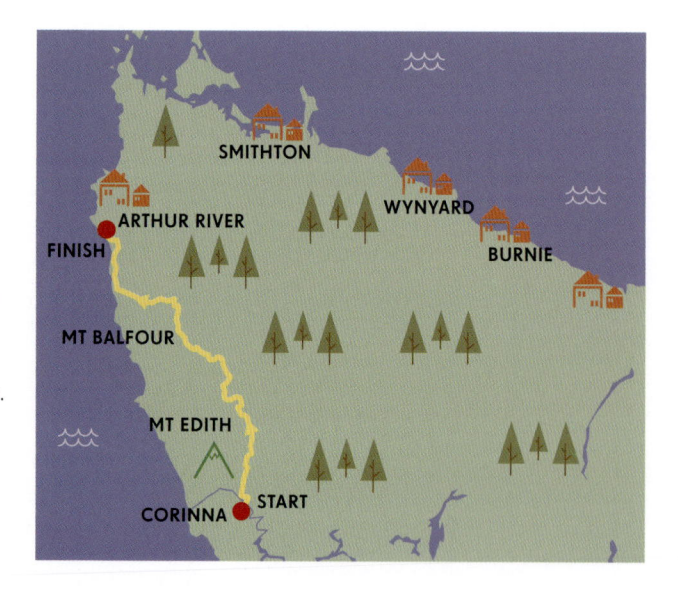

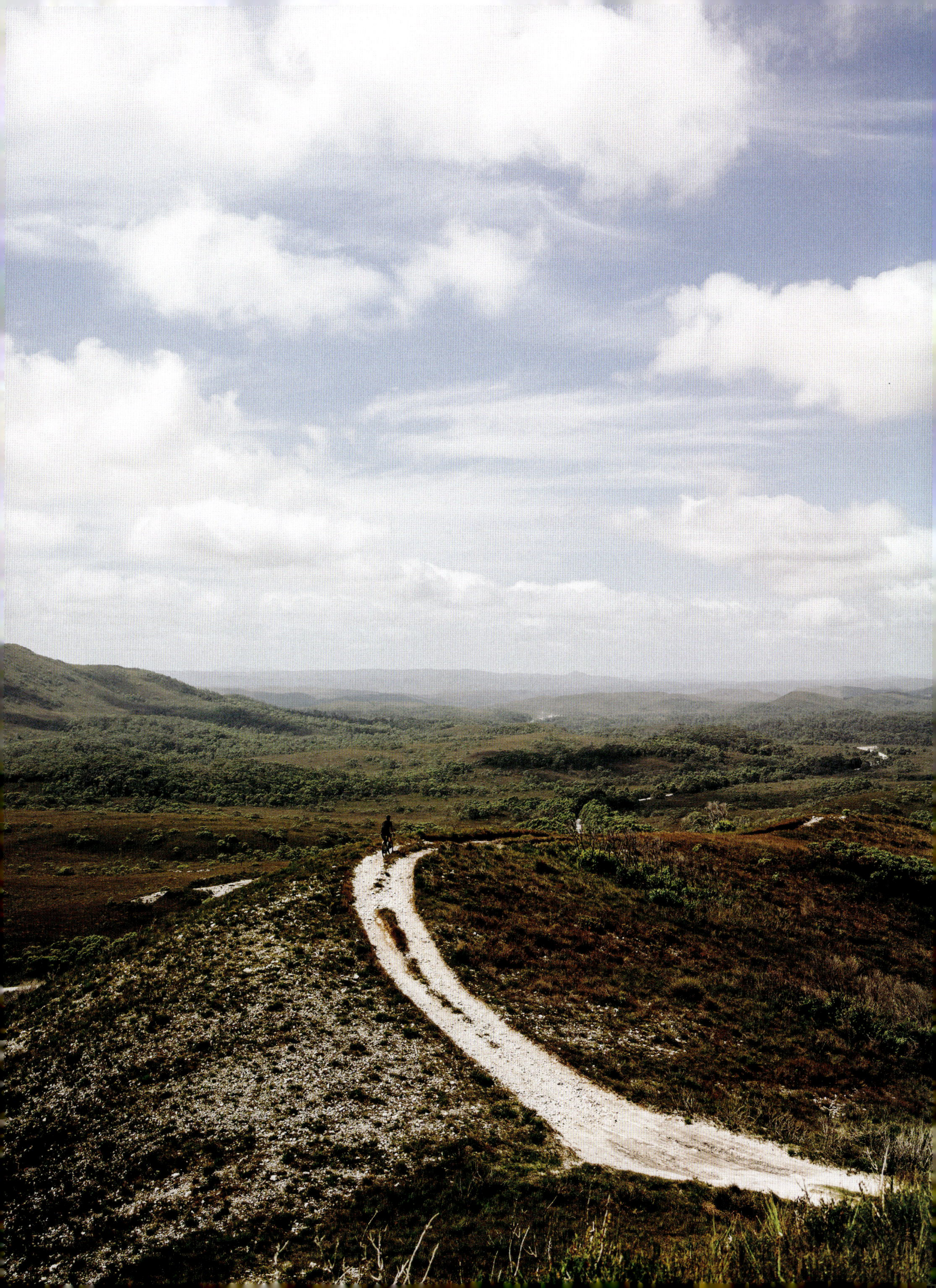

on maps as the C249, and on travel blogs as the Western Explorer Road. Either way, it has the feel of true adventure.

We leave Corinna, discovering that the 'nowhere' promised by this road can change swiftly from dense rainforest to open buttongrass plains and coastal grasslands. The west coast weather shows a similar tendency to vary dramatically over relatively short distances. This is the region of the Roaring Forties, with no landmass at this latitude between us and South America, half a world away, to catch the westerly winds before they hit this wildest shore of Tasmania.

The gravel squeaks and grinds under our tyres as Mt Edith and the peaks of the Norfolk Range loom in the distance, beyond fire-blackened forest. At this point, we're more than 40km (25 miles) past Corinna, the last clear sign of humanity in this wilderness besides the road itself. Satisfaction washes over us like the fickle golden light and warm, salty breeze.

It turns out you can get to somewhere from nowhere – if you're open to leisurely side trips from the road. We follow a boggy and desperately steep track to the top of Mt Balfour. Drivers often try to get around the deep, water-filled potholes by going off-road onto the buttongrass plains, but it's not recommended. So we find ourselves with wet socks as we grind uphill. Standing at the end of the road, taking in the unending views from Mt Balfour towards the Southern Ocean, it's easy to see why this could be considered the edge of the world. That description has specifically been attached to Gardiner Point, a headland at the sandy mouth of the Arthur River.

LOST AND FOUND

Corinna was once called Royenrine. Both names are thought to have come from Aboriginal terms for the Tasmanian tiger or thylacine, a species that probably became extinct in the 1930s, although some people claim it still lives on in remote regions like the Tarkine. Corinna – a former mining settlement born when prospectors pushed overland south from Waratah to Zeehan – was also the location of the discovery of Tasmania's largest gold nugget, at 7.5kg (265oz).

Clockwise from top: overnight accommodation; preparing food; gravel bikes like Specialized's Diverge are ideal on this terrain

Life goes on in this wilderness, almost ignoring our passing, including the ground parrots that dance among clumps of buttongrass. We don't see many cars, although the ones that do approach are made obvious by the plumes of dust that engulf us with their passing. At the end of the C249, it's back to a sealed road surface, and as we turn west to reach the coast, around the sandy coves at Couta Rocks, we find the first cluster of houses since Corinna. We reach the northern boundary of the Tarkine at Arthur River, and for us this represents the end of nowhere – or perhaps the start of somewhere.

'We're on a ride to nowhere
Come on inside
Taking that ride to nowhere
We'll take that ride
Maybe you wonder where you are, I don't care
Here is where time is on our side, take you there
We're on a road to nowhere'

These are the words to a song by American band Talking Heads, who wanted to capture a resigned, even joyful look at doom. Cycling this road through the beautiful region of the Tarkine may be just what Talking Heads were getting at, and I can't help but consider that the lyrics fit my feelings about this area's history, and my experience of riding it. The Tarkine still remains under threat of logging and mining. In May 2021, there was further destruction of forest in order to build roads for exploratory drilling, to test the potential for a new tailings dam. The campaign to declare the Tarkine a World Heritage Site continues. **SM**

TOOLKIT

Start/Finish // Corinna/Arthur River
Distance // 108km (67 miles)
Getting there // From the northern city of Launceston, Corinna is a 3.5-hour drive through the Central Highlands. If approaching from the south, remember the car ferry only crosses the Pieman River in daylight.
When to go // Late spring and early autumn are ideal. The region can be subject to extreme wet and cold conditions in winter, or potential wildfires in summer.
What to wear // Weather in the west coast is unpredictable, so always pack for rain and cold winds.
What to pack // This region is remote, so a level of self-sufficiency is required. Small towns will only have the basic items available, at best.
Where to stay // Corinna and Arthur River have camping and other accommodation. These are limited and book up quickly during peak tourist season.
Where to eat // The Corinna Pub has good warm food and nice cold beer, with vegan options on the menu.
Tours // There are private tailor-made options with companies such as www.tasmaniancyclingtours.com.
More info // www.discoverthetarkine.com.au

Opposite: Cradle Mountain and Dove Lake

MORE LIKE THIS
BEYOND THE ROAD TO NOWHERE

CLIMIES TRACK

The Road to Nowhere begins at Corinna on the north shore of the Pieman River. Just as spectacular are the roads south of the river, running to Granville and Trial Harbours – a pair of small settlements on the craggy west coast, to the north and south of Mt Heemskirk. If a few jagged edges is more your speed, consider the 4WD Climies Track, which runs between the two. It's a hilly, muddy and rutted ride around 20km (12 miles) in length, with rocky river crossings, clifftop waterfalls and full-on coastal scenery. Camping is available at Trial Harbour. If you finish this ride in Zeehan, you can do so on the singletrack at Oonah Hill.
Start // Corinna
Finish // Zeehan
Distance // 75km (47 miles)
More info // www.parks.tas.gov.au

THE LORAX ROUTE

If you need a little more, and are perhaps looking to complete a loop from Devonport or Launceston, consider this tour of the Tarkine and the wider northwest (not to be confused with a climbing and base-jumping route on the peak of Frenchmans Cap in southwestern Tasmania). With the major exception of the Road to Nowhere, this route runs predominantly on sealed highways and well-kept back roads. Before you enter the Tarkine, you'll pass through the sub-alpine highlands at the foot of Cradle Mountain, one of Tasmania's scenic calling cards. The northern continuation includes a lasso loop around more upstream forest reaches of the Arthur River, and a close track of the north coast and its small towns.
Start/Finish // Launceston
Distance // 843km (524 miles)
More info// www.ridewithgps.com/routes/36573615

THE TASSIE GIFT

A route thought up in 2019 by long-distance, all-terrain cycling enthusiast Emma Flukes, the Tassie Gift may or may not be fated to become a regular event, but it's already legendary by its very nature. At almost 1800km (1120 miles), with more than 30,000m (98,000ft) of climbing, the route represents a serious undertaking. The figure-of-eight loop traces two butterfly wings towards the northwest and northeast corners of the island, hinging at Miena in the centre. The Tarkine figures strongly, but so too do the mountains around Queenstown, the Bay of Fires, Cradle Mountain Rd, the surroundings of Hobart, and countless more places that show the diversity of Tasmania. The precise route includes some portions on private land, with permissions given for specific events, but at other times you may need to make modifications.
Start/Finish // Hobart
Distance // 1,780km (1,100 miles)
More info // www.ridewithgps.com/routes/40968891

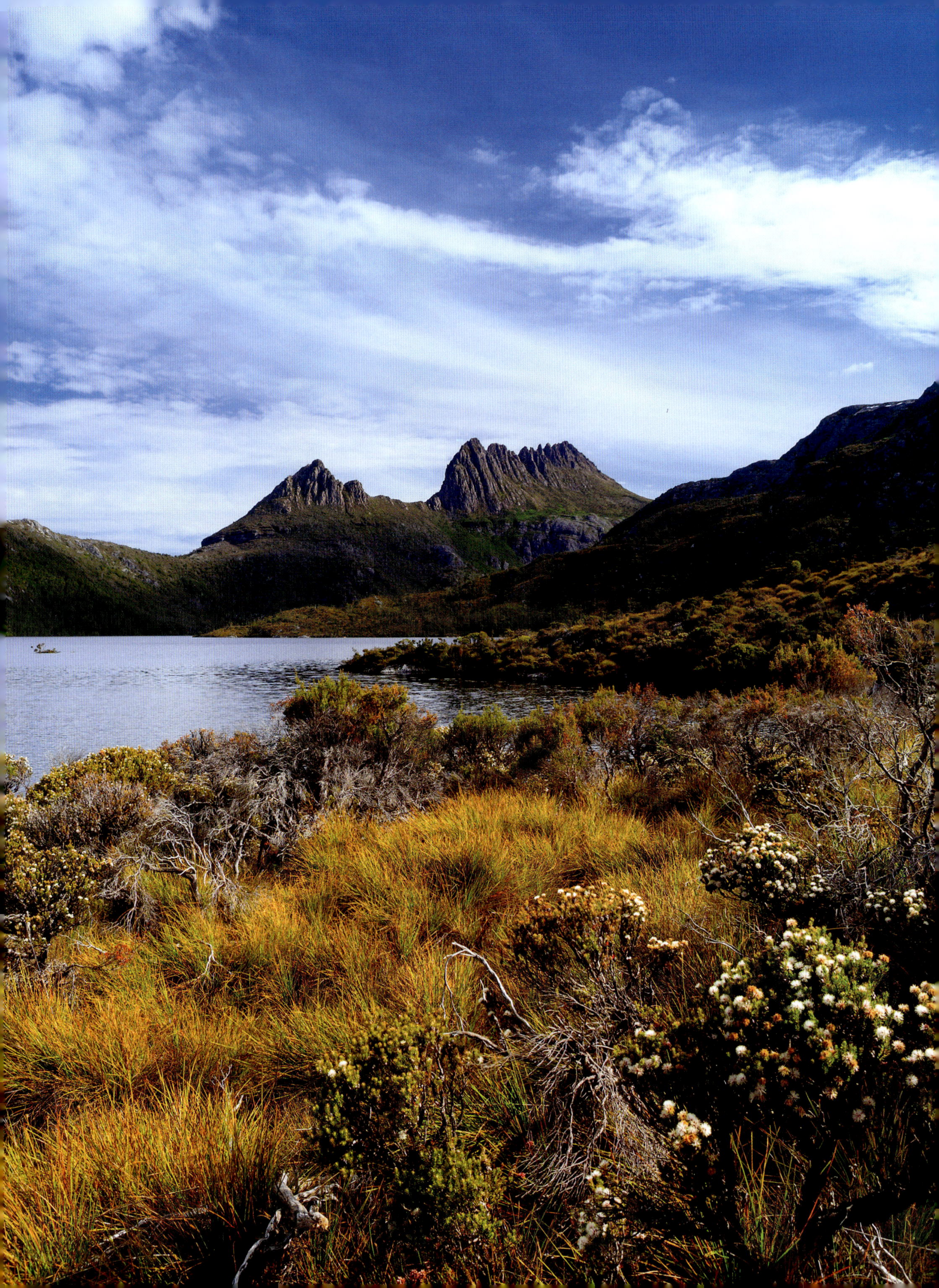

- EPIC BIKE RIDES OF AUSTRALIA & NEW ZEALAND -

MURRAY TO THE MOUNTAINS

Follow this former railway from Wangaratta to the alpine resort town of Bright, a traffic-free route that becomes more scenic with every kilometre.

The question that ran through my mind as the two Great Pyrenees dogs pelted down the field towards me, barking and baring their teeth, was: I wonder if that gate is open? It always is. So began one of the slowest sprints in cycling history: uphill and into a headwind with two snarling sheepdogs at my heels. With even a lightly laden bike, I didn't think I'd have much in the tank, but thankfully I outlasted the older of the two dogs who, believing his day's job was done, trotted triumphantly back to his farm. And after my lively diversion at Myrtleford, I returned to the relative safety of the Murray to the Mountains rail trail.

I'd joined this cycle path, which is almost entirely separated from traffic, at Wangaratta. From here, the main route follows the former Bright Railway along the Ovens River valley to the High Country hub of Bright. Somewhat confusingly, the Murray to the Mountains rail trail has several offshoots, one of which leads north from Wangaratta to Rutherglen (mostly sharing roads), where it reaches the grand Murray River that lends its name to the route. Australia's longest river flows from the Australian Alps all the way to the ocean just east of Adelaide in South Australia. Other diversions meander to Milawa (at the top of King Valley), Beechworth, Yackandandah and

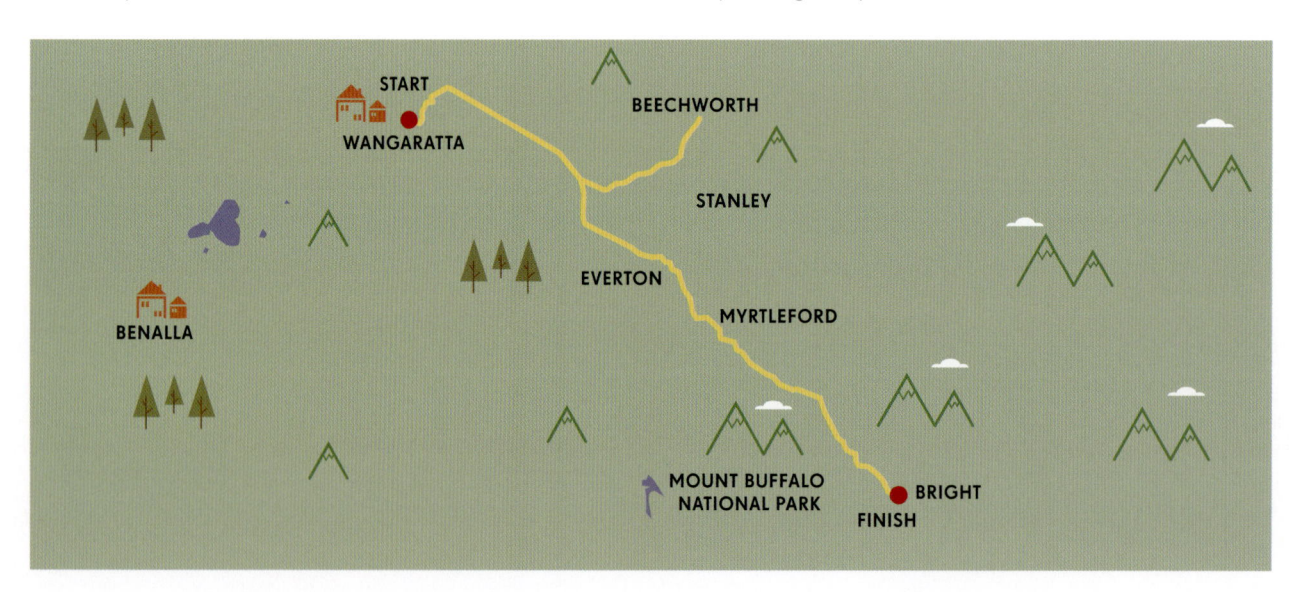

TAS – VIC

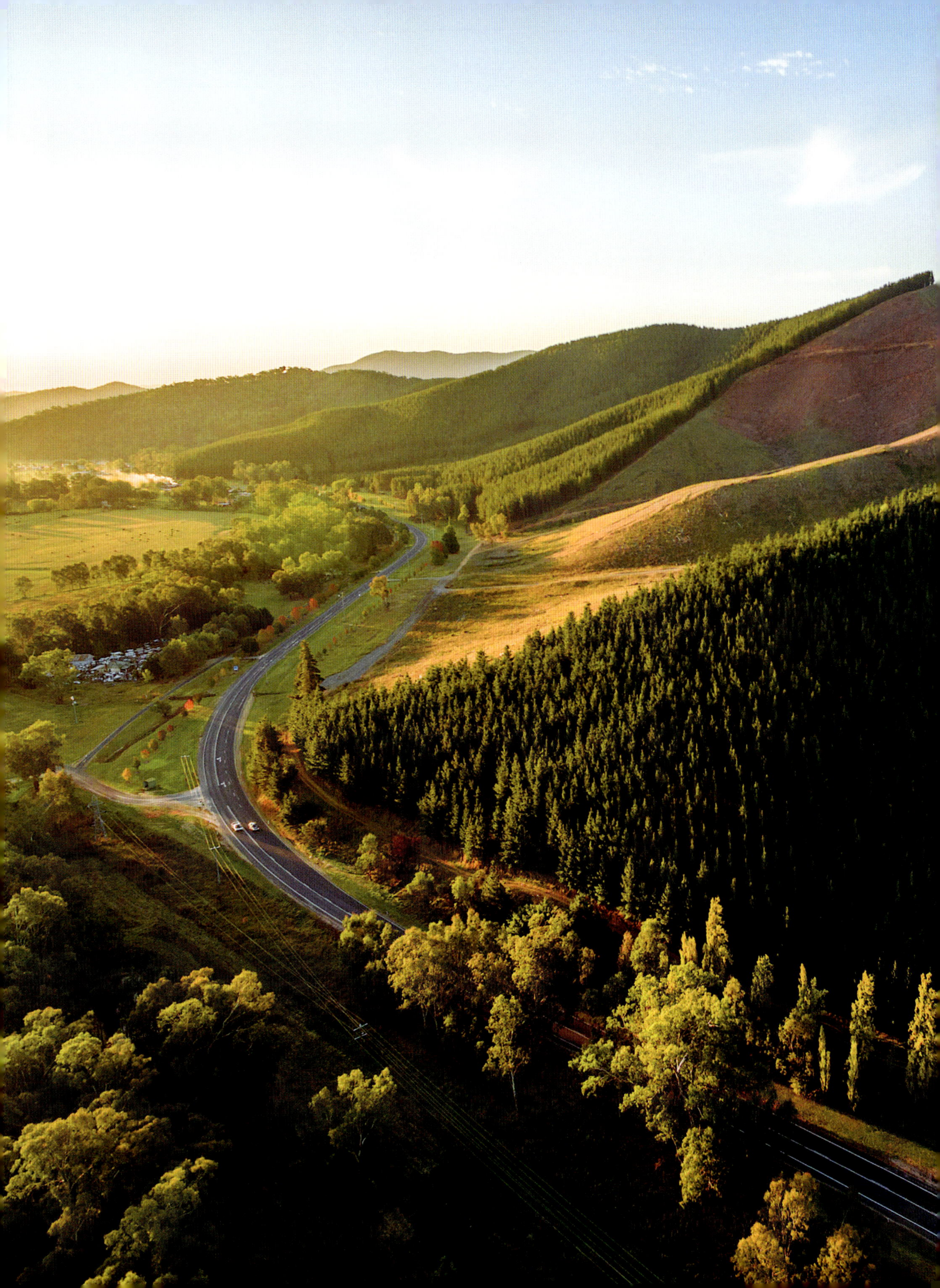

Harrietville. But for a straightforward A to B bike ride, the Wangaratta to Bright route is the one to do (or in reverse).

Having picked up the first signposts at Wangaratta's Apex Park, just a five-minute ride east of the town's train station, I set off through the suburbs before reaching more open countryside around Bowser. This is the first of the stations that was part of the old Bright Railway. The line had linked the High Country with the agricultural area of Wangaratta for almost a century, ferrying holidaymakers to the alpine resorts, including the railway's own chalet on Mt Buffalo, but the service stopped in 1983. Perhaps due to the increased ownership of cars? It must have been a sad loss for the outlying communities in the High Country, but in 2002 it gifted cyclists a gently ascending path to the mountains.

From Bowser, the route cuts east across to Everton, always rising at a very easy-going gradient and often shaded by trees. Two more former stations passed by – Londrigan and Tarrawingee – their platforms and sidings still standing. Most of the former stations now feature shelters, loos and sometimes drinking water for refilling water bottles. This first stretch of the Murray to the Mountains is the least spectacular so don't feel bad about rushing it. However, at the next one-time station, Everton, I had already decided to take my first scenic diversion.

At Everton, the rail trail divides: the main route continues towards Myrtleford, but there's a tempting trail that leads up to the beautifully preserved town of Beechworth. This is the former

"The eating and drinking options along the way set the Murray to the Mountains apart from most rail trails"

Beechworth to Everton railway. Unlike the rest of the route, it is a constant climb all the way, for around 16km (10 miles). This will feel like it goes on forever. The forest on either side, filled with wildlife, offers some distraction from the grind, but the real reward lies at the top: one of Australia's most charming towns. The heritage architecture is reason enough to visit, but you can also discover some of the legend of Ned Kelly, the 19th-century bushranger, who was tried and imprisoned here.

After the purgatory of the ascent, I exited the Murray to the Mountains rail trail on the south side of Beechworth, opposite Lake Sambell and within coasting distance of a good motel. With the bike stowed and having showered, I revisited one of my favourite places in the state, Bridge Road Brewers on Ford St. Ben and Maria Kraus brew some great beers and make delicious pizzas with local ingredients to accompany them. I settled down with a Bling IPA and an apple and gorgonzola pizza and watched the sun set at the top of the street.

The eating and drinking options along the way set the Murray to the Mountains apart from most rail trails. If, like me,

MT BUFFALO

There are some superlative cycle rides around Bright, such as the short extension of the rail trail to Wandiligong, or a lovely loop along the Kiewa valley. But for fit cyclists or those on e-bikes, the climb up to the summit of Mt Buffalo is a must. At about 21km (13 miles) and a moderate gradient, it's still a serious challenge, but the views from the top are wonderful and you can take a breather at the chalet formerly owned by the Bright Railway.

Left to right: Cathedral Rock, Mt Buffalo National Park; a Great Pyrenees welcome; view from Huggins Lookout over Bright; the rail trail is well marked. Previous spread: the Great Alpine Rd and rail trail on the left, south of Myrtleford

this is important to you, then allowing for an extra day or two in Beechworth is recommended. Some great wineries are within reach of the town by bicycle, with a favourite, Pennyweight, lying alongside the rail trail itself. Elizabeth and Stephen Morris have been making biodynamic wines in their Arcadian setting for many years. 'We came up here because it's cooler,' explained Elizabeth. Their tree-shaded winery, like most in Beechworth, is at a higher elevation, meaning a zestier grape at harvest time.

The next day, after stocking up on pastries from Beechworth's renowned bakery, it was time to rejoin the trail. Fatefully, rather than return the way I'd come, down to the Everton turn-off, I followed a beautiful undulating road to the town of Stanley for the simple reason that it is the apple-growing capital of Victoria with a farmshop that sells chilled apple juice. After gulping down a bottle and stashing another for later, I made the steep descent off the Beechworth plateau. It was at the junction with the Myrtleford road that I met the two unwelcoming guardians.

Having evaded the dogs, I turned right and soon met the Great Alpine Road, where a left turn put me back on the Murray to the Mountains rail trail, my cargo of apple juice and pastries intact. Once more, the route followed the Ovens River, towards Eurobin and Porepunkah and its backdrop grew more mountainous. From the Everton turn-off to Bright it's about 60km (37 miles), every one enjoyable. And at Bright, another great brewery awaited, next to an icy river in which to dangle hot feet. **RB**

TOOLKIT

Start // Wangaratta
Finish // Bright
Distance // About 100km (62 miles)
How to get there // Wangaratta is on the Melbourne to Albury train line. You can get a V/Line bus back from Bright with your bike.
Where to stay // There's abundant accommodation throughout the route for every budget (except perhaps for the free camper). Beechworth makes for a good overnight stop.
When to ride // Winter will bring rain and sometimes snow to the region so it's better to ride from spring (September) onwards. Autumn is a spectacular time.
What to bring // You can be as self-supporting as you like or not bring anything beyond a credit card and a change of clothes.
More info // www.ridehighcountry.com.au

Opposite: The peloton heads past Bells Beach near Geelong

MORE LIKE THIS
BIG VIC BIKE RIDES

GREAT VICTORIAN RAIL TRAIL

Stretching from Tallarook to Mansfield (with a short diversion down to Alexandra), the Great Victorian Rail Trail covers similar ground to the Murray to the Mountains, although in a more agricultural setting. Instead it offers a number of beguiling country towns and villages, including Yea, Yarck and legendary Bonnie Doon, famous for its serenity since the 1997 comedy *The Castle*. Also along the route lies the longest rail trail tunnel in Victoria (bring bike lights!) and several big bridges, including one across Lake Eildon that's 385m (1263ft) in length. Mansfield itself, at the foot of Mt Buller, is a thriving country town, but since the coaches to Melbourne don't carry bicycles you might be here for some time. Tallarook is on the train line to Melbourne, so you might prefer to ride it in reverse.
Start // Tallarook
Finish // Mansfield
Distance // 134km (83 miles)

AMY'S GRAN FONDO

Victoria's most famous road is closed for this epic sportive in support of the Amy Gillett Foundation, which works to improve the safety of cyclists with the goal of zero cyclist fatalities. Amy's Gran Fondo takes place over a loop from Lorne to Apollo Bay via rural Birregurra, covering some of the most spectacular stretches of the Great Ocean Road. The route descends through the Otways' forest and returns along the coast with sweeping views of the ocean over your right shoulder. Distances range from 45km (28 miles) to 130km (80 miles) for the competitive race. And talking of competition, you'll need to get your application in early for this popular once-in-a-lifetime cycling experience, which typically takes place in September.
Start/Finish // Lorne
Distance // 130km (80 miles)
More info //
www.amysgranfondo.org.au

HUNT 1000

This epic mostly-offroad route starts (or ends) in Melbourne and crosses the entire state of Victoria and enters New South Wales and the Australian Capital Territory to finish in Canberra. It was devised in 2016 by Dan Hunt as a way to explore Victoria. As a race, it's extremely tough, with fewer than half the entrants completing it. But you can also ride sections in your own time and discover regions such as the High Country and the Yarra Ranges between Melbourne and Mt Hotham. The route usually sticks to 4WD tracks via the very occasional town or cattle drovers' hut, so self-sufficiency is a must. The elevation gain and conditions are definitely not to be underestimated. A highlight is the Jagungal Wilderness Area, which has some great biking trails.
Start/Finish // Melbourne/Canberra
Distances // 1000km (621 miles)

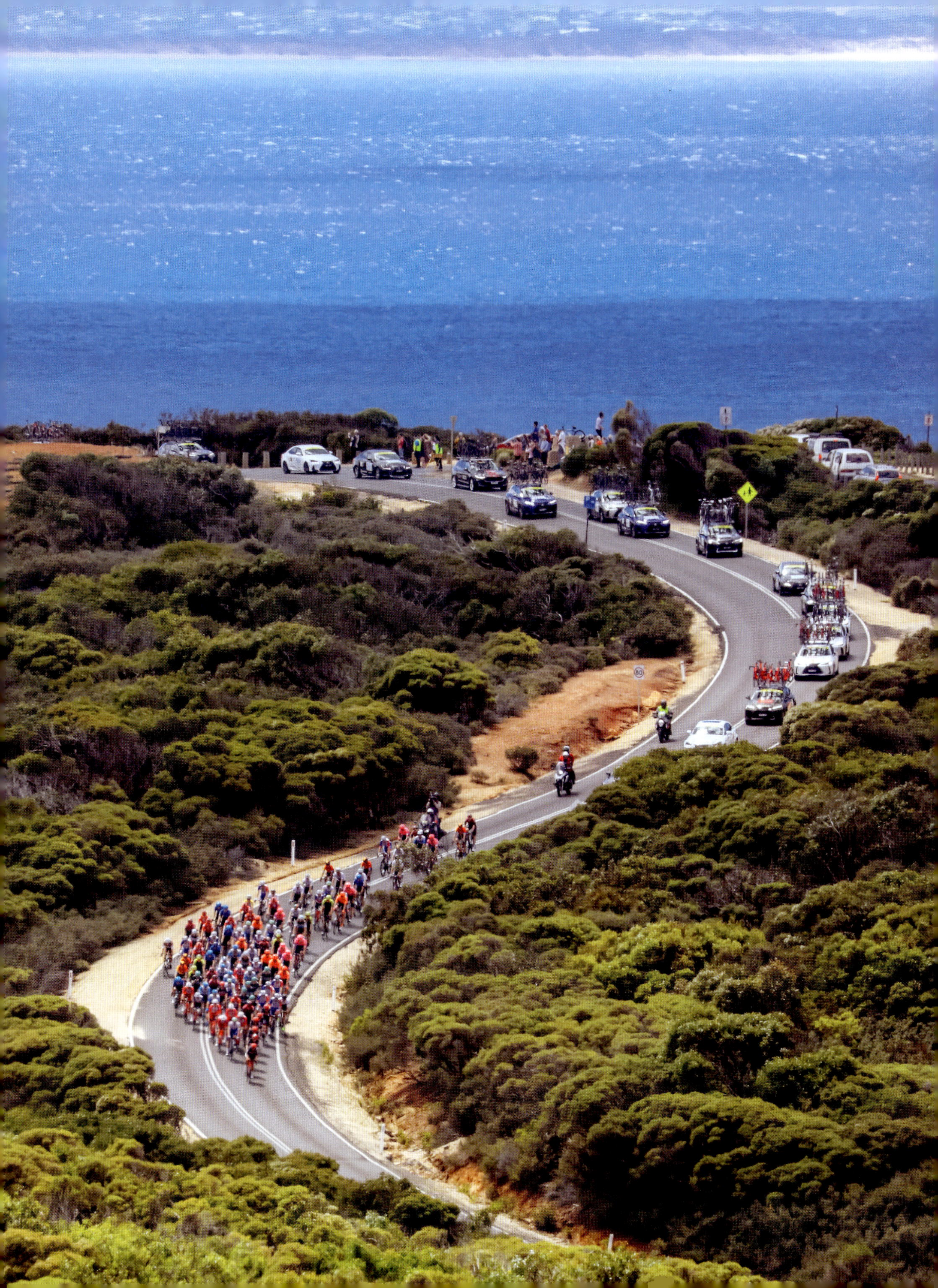

VICTORIA'S OTWAY ODYSSEY

Set back from the Great Ocean Road, the gorgeous Otway forests are best explored by bicycle — an annual event is an ideal excuse to reconnoitre the region.

Even in late summer, there was a chill in the air at 6am in Victoria's Otway forest. I'd set my alarm earlier, but there was no need: the excitement at racing the best-known mountain bike marathon in Australia had me wide awake before the birds. The Otway Odyssey was first staged in 2007, offering 100km (62 miles) of riding along the dirt roads around the settlement of Forrest, set just north of the beach town of Apollo Bay on the Great Ocean Road. From Apollo Bay, the road to Forrest climbs steadily into the fog-shrouded folds of the Otways, where giant mountain ash, myrtle beech trees and Dickson ferns thrived in the damp gullies. I don't know whether Forrest was named before or after the logging started, but for a while there was money to be made hewing the huge hardwood trees here, some with trunks 12m (40ft) around. Of course, the boom didn't last forever and the community declined when logging ceased, at least until the mountain bikers arrived.

I raced the Otway Odyssey in 2013. By that time, a couple of things had changed at the event. It no longer started on the coast or demanded a gruelling climb up to the off-road tracks. Instead, it started from playing fields just on the north side of town. And in the intervening half-dozen years, the mountain bike trails around Forrest had blossomed. With investment from the local shire, trail-builders had created two distinct networks, north and south of the town. The trails were huge fun and more natural than most other mountain bike parks. Trails to the south extended down to Lake Elizabeth and dove into lush gullies and over streams. To the north, the Yaugher trailhead accessed sandier singletrack that twisted around spiky grass trees and through drier woodlands. By the year that I lined up at 7am on

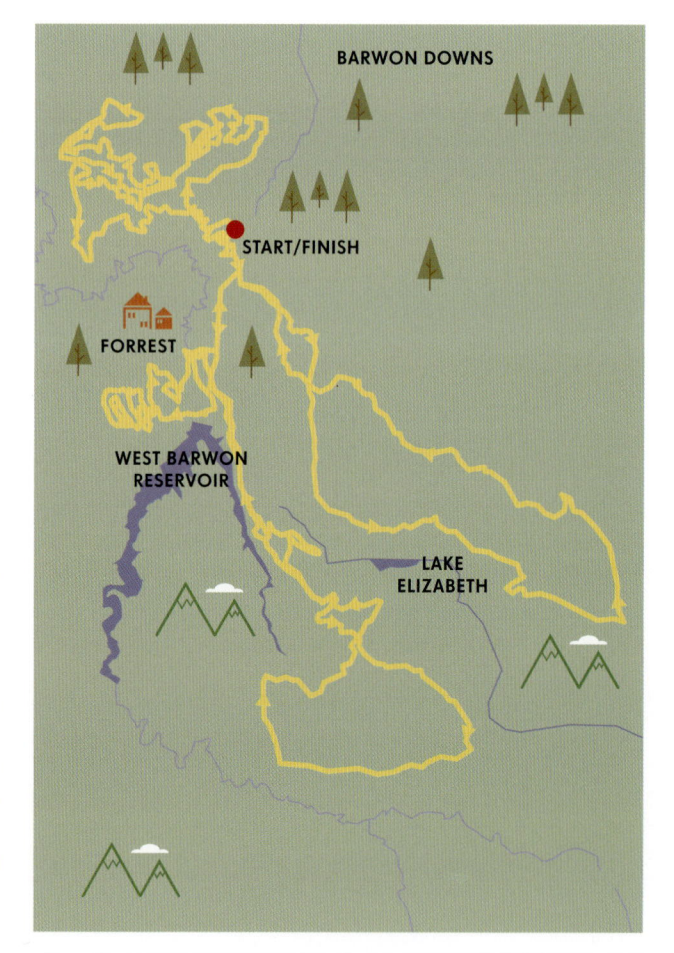

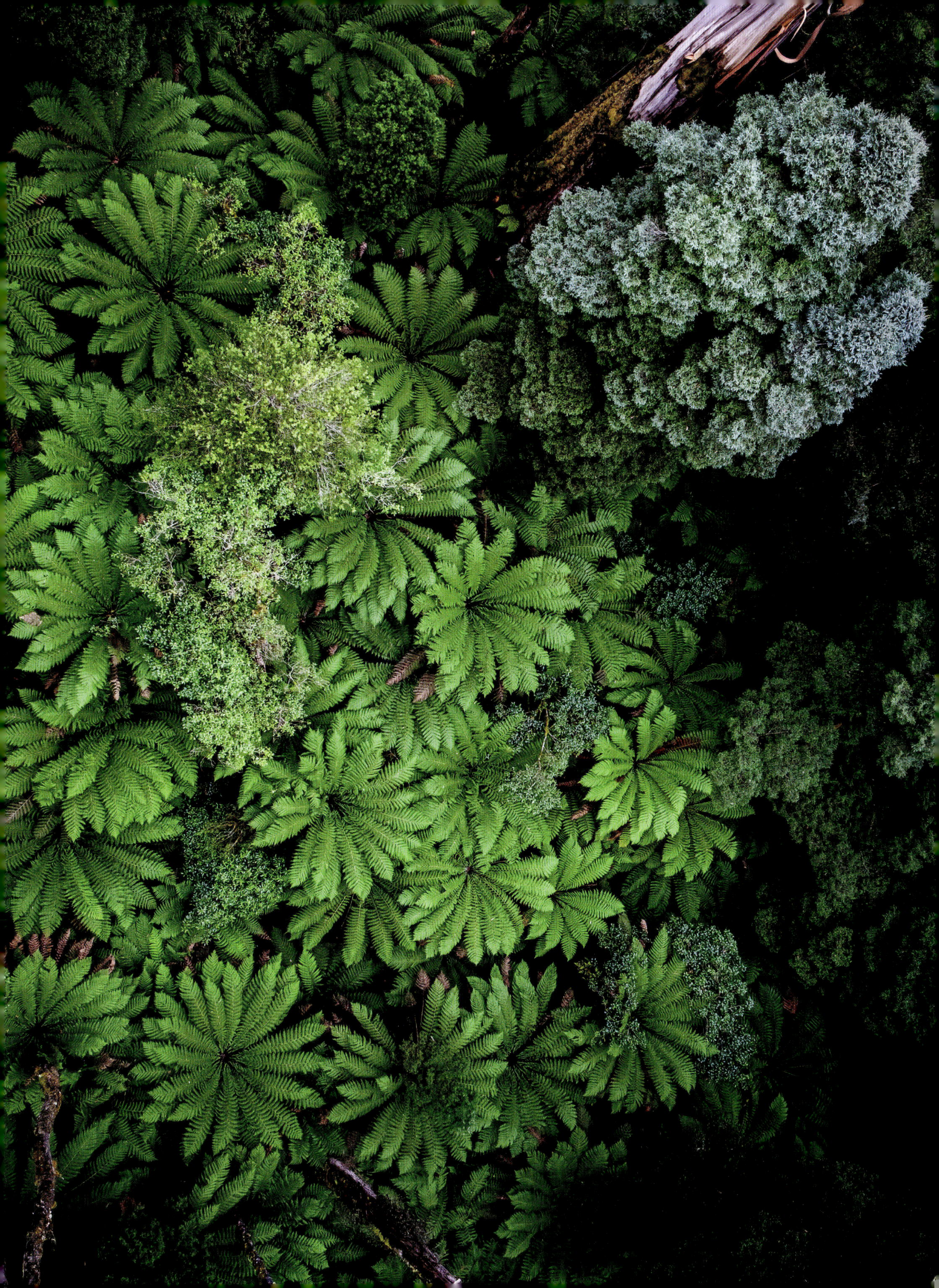

a dry, sunny morning, the Odyssey's route had absorbed many of these fun sections of singletrack.

A year previously, I had rented a mountain bike from Norm and Jess Douglas in Forrest for my first foray onto the trails. Jess was an Australian national champion and three-time world 24hr solo mountain bike champion, which is to say that she was the best in the world at riding relentlessly for a very long time without the help of a team. Now a cycling coach, she had agreed to show me around some of Forrest's trails and give me some tips for taking on some of the features, such as log rolls and drops.

'We focus on demystifying mountain biking,' said Jess. 'Each technique is broken down into three or four steps, which work on bigger terrain and at higher speeds. The skills are repeatable: I can negotiate a log in the same way at hour 24 as at hour one.'

We headed out to the Follow the Dog trail, which weaved around the eucalypt forest south of town, and practised tight turns, steep descents and hopping over logs. 'People think that they have to lift with their arms to get over a log, but what they should be doing is moving back in the cockpit and unweighting the front wheel,' said Jess. 'Some people assume mountain biking is all about grunt, but it's quite a Zen sport, once you find your groove.

'Our typical customer is a 30-something professional woman who just wants to be confident when they go out on a ride.'

At the Odyssey, before I get to try out my skills on the singletrack, there's the small matter of a large loop of gravel roads for the 100km (62 mile) competitors to ride before the route returns to Follow the Dog and Yaugher forest. Those who

ADVENTURE CENTRAL

There's lots to do in the region other than mountain biking, making the Otway Ranges a great weekending destination. Wake early enough and you can join a trip to Lake Elizabeth to spot wild platypus. A little further out, Otway Fly Treetop Adventures offers a zipline and a canopy walk in the mountain ash forest. There are several waterfalls in the region and even more walking routes.

Clockwise from top: friends take on the Odyssey; gravel roads connect singletrack trails; the womens' race gets underway. Previous page: forest ferns in the tranquil Otways

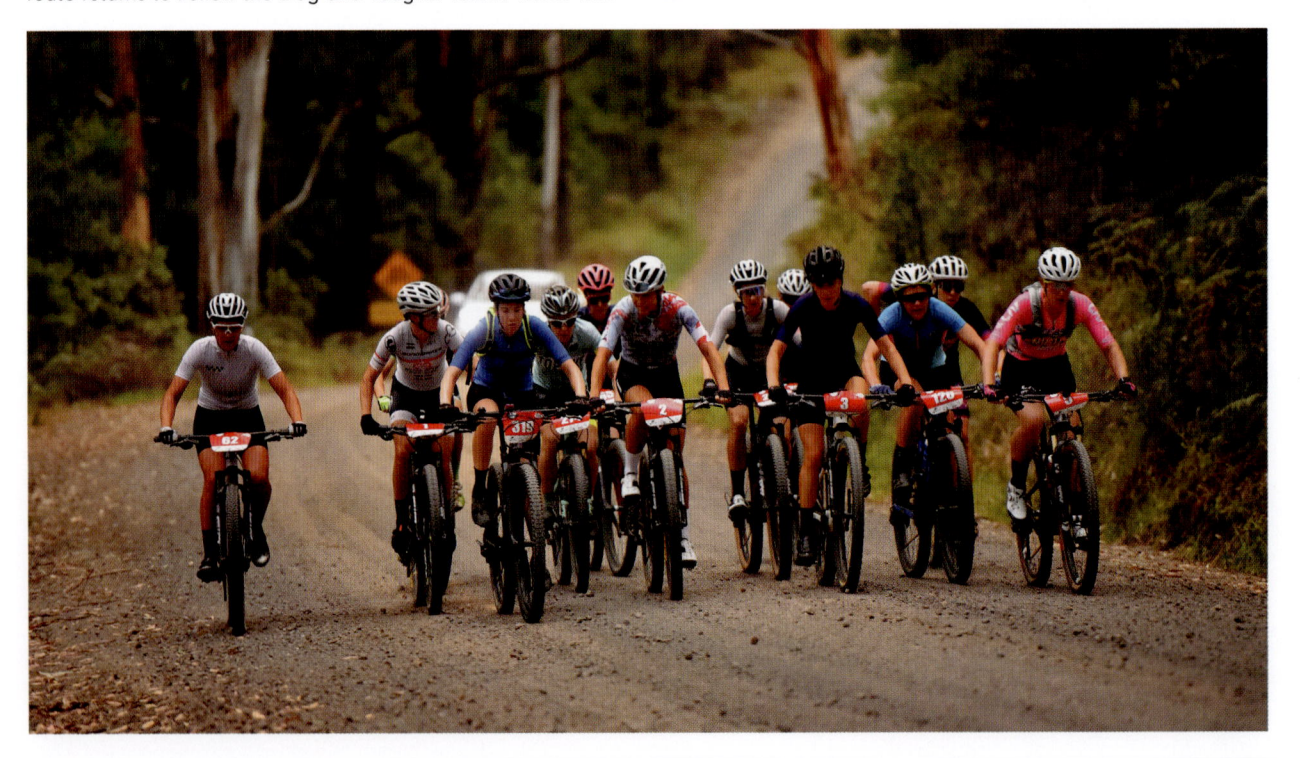

opt for the 50km (30 mile) or 30km (18 mile) races get to skip straight to the fun stuff.

At the start, dust was kicked up into the cool air by the tyres of 700 riders. The serious racers shot to the front, but behind them were a wide range of riders of different abilities. Most of the time, mountain biking is a social occasion. As I passed one rider on a fat bike, its three-inch tyres going squirrelly in the sand, I learned that he had cycled across Australia on his bike, putting our odyssey in perspective. At the first fast descent, down towards the coast before the slog back uphill to Forrest, I heard a yelp as one rider cartwheeled into the bush.

As the sun climbed into the blue sky on a scorching late summer day, we turned around and pedalled back to Forrest, passing through the event village again, where I took the chance to fill up my hydration pack with water, reapply sunscreen and wolf down an energy bar or two. The second half of the Odyssey was all about the engaging trails that had made the town one of my favourite escapes from Melbourne, about three hours' drive away.

The Red Carpet descent near Lake Elizabeth was a highlight of the finale, as tyres chattered over rocks and the giant ferns provided some shade overhead. Then it was back to Yaugher to tackle Marriners Run and other trails to the north, before crossing the line in almost exactly twice the time it took the winner.

Forrest's artful, natural trails and the Otway Odyssey, now with a sister event, the Great Otway Gravel Grind, put the region on the mountain biking map in the 2010s. But time doesn't stay still, and with more competition from bike parks across Australia, the local government approved another investment in Forrest's trails in 2023 to keep the mountain bikers coming back. **RB**

© Courtesy of Rapid Ascent

"Some people assume mountain biking is all about grunt, but it's quite a Zen sport, once you find your groove"

TOOLKIT

Start/Finish // Forrest
Distance // 100km (62 miles)
Getting there // Forrest is about three hours' drive west from Melbourne. There's a bus to Apollo Bay from Geelong, but you'd have to cycle the rest of the way.
When to ride // The Otways are fine all year round, but the Odyssey is held in late February.
Where to eat and stay // The Forrest Brewing Company offers food, beer and a couple of rooms. The excellent Forrest Guesthouse is the pick of the accommodation and there's also a campground.
What to take // Just the usual biking kit: water, tools and spares. There are maps at the trailheads and the network is relatively compact and close to town.
More info // www.rapidascent.com.au; www.visitotways.com

Opposite: tackling the trails of the You Yangs Mountain Bike Park

MORE LIKE THIS
MELBOURNE AREA MTB

WOODEND

Woodend is one of several charming country towns, along with Kyneton, Mount Macedon and Gisborne, that lure Melburnians north, either for a weekend of wine-tasting and walks or a longer-term life change. The mountain biking action centres on the wooded trails in Wombat State Forest to the south of town. There are a couple of loops, totalling about 17km (10 miles), enough for an afternoon of riding before retiring to the Holgate Brewhouse in Woodend for home-produced beer and food (try the Temptress chocolate porter). Woodend is about an hour from Melbourne by train on a direct line.
Start/Finish // Woodend
Distance // 17km (10 miles)

YOU YANGS

Sitting between Melbourne and Geelong to the west, the You Yangs were where many local mountain bikers cut their teeth. This range of granite slopes offered good grip and natural contours for trail building. Over time, the trails evolved into two networks: the Kurrajong area for easier, flatter riding suitable for first-timers; and the Stockyards, accessed from Drysdale Rd, for more experienced mountain bikers to tackle rock gardens and jumps. There's now about 50km (30 miles) in total, with tracks like Turbulence and Bandages and Glory being for experts only. Access is easiest by car and the You Yangs are about an hour's drive from Melbourne.
More info //
www.youyangsmtbinc.com.au

WARBURTON

The most exciting news in mountain biking in Victoria – and potentially Australia as a whole – is the development of trails around the former logging town of Warburton in the Yarra Ranges, northeast of Melbourne. Except, it's not really news: state-backed plans and funding have been in place for years, but the project has taken time to progress as stakeholders seek to assuage local concerns. Finally, in November 2022, the planning minister gave the green light for up to 180km (112 miles) of cutting-edge trails to be crafted in the temperate forest in these mountains. The biggest descent, down Mt Donna Buang, is on hold, but there's enough to excite every mountain biker and Warburton will be a world-class destination. Keep an eye on www.rideyarraranges.com.au for more.
Start/Finish // Warburton

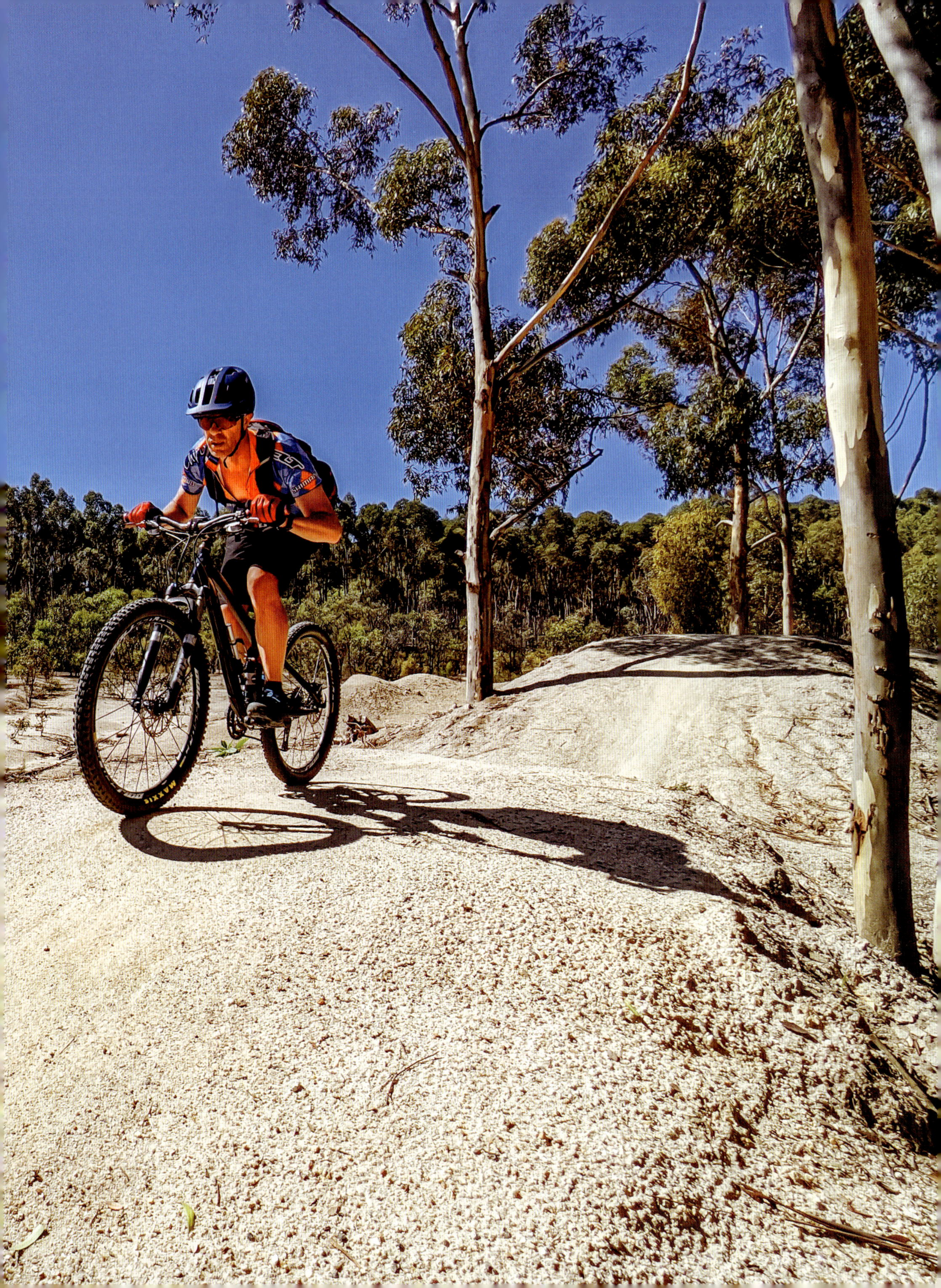

- EPIC BIKE RIDES OF AUSTRALIA & NEW ZEALAND -

THE BAY OF FIRES TRAIL

Ride this rollercoaster mountain bike trail, descending through northeast Tasmania's forest to the beautiful lichen-covered boulders of Binalong Bay, near St Helens.

'It always feels wild down here. We come twice a year from Queensland and love the landscape. It's very different.' I'm in the back of a shuttle van, talking to Queenslanders Julie and Chris. We're part of a group of mountain bikers being ferried to the start of a new trail in Tasmania's northeast corner called the Bay of Fires Trail. There's an air of anticipation because the trail has only been open a couple of weeks and, at more than 40km (25 miles) in length, it promises to be quite an adventure.

The Bay of Fires Trail is part of the network of mountain bike tracks around the town of Derby. Typically, these trails start up in the hills around the town and descend back to the valley. The Bay of Fires Trail is a bit different. It starts from the same trailhead on the Blue Tier plateau as many of the other tracks, but it heads off in a wildly different direction: east towards the coast.

Since 2015, a large group of dedicated and creative people has been working on developing Derby as a hub for mountain biking in the region. Some have lobbied officials and secured funding and approvals, others galvanised local businesses, gained goodwill or built trails. The result is that, by any international yardstick, this half-forgotten corner of Australia's

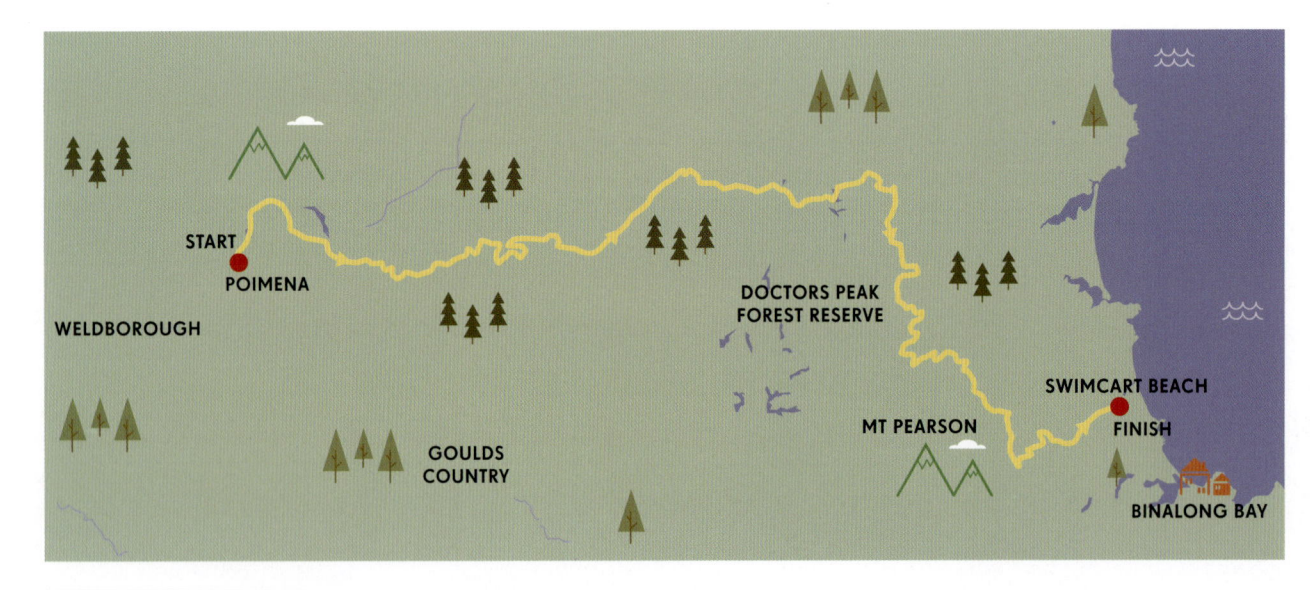

Opposite: log rides on Hobart's North-South trail

MORE LIKE THIS
TASMANIAN MTB

NORTH-SOUTH TRACK, HOBART

Skirting the foothills of kunanyi/Mt Wellington, which provides the mountain backdrop to Hobart, this purpose-built trail descends towards Glenorchy Mountain Bike Park. Fit riders can pedal out to the start in Wellington Park from Hobart, passing Cascade, the oldest brewery still operating in Australia. But with the road climb to the start you might prefer catching the Explorer bus (it's $10 to bring your bike). The trail, rated by IMBA as moderate, takes up to an hour to complete but there are plenty of fun sections to play on, including log rides and drops. When you get to Glenorchy's bike park, there are more mountain bike trails to explore, of varying difficulty, then it's another hour's ride back to the city.
Start // The Springs, Wellington Park
Finish // Glenorchy Mountain Bike Park
Distance // 11km (7 miles)

MAYDENA BIKE PARK

Tucked just south of Mount Field National Park, around an hour's west of Hobart, Maydena is one of Tasmania's top-rated bike parks. Unlike some of the others on the island, its focus is more on the gravity-fed side of the sport, with the more difficult, black-graded downhill tracks aimed at experienced and expert mountain bikers. The park also hosts a round of the Enduro World Cup series plus Australian national championships in all mountain biking disciplines. There are around 100 separate uplift-accessed trails, totalling up to 80km (50 miles) challenging singletrack, despite the park's relative youth (it was opened in 2018). Big things are planned for the next five years, including more trails and accommodation, a skills park and a possible chairlift.
More info // www.maydenabikepark.com

ST HELENS

Out on Tasmania's east coast, and near the end point of the Bay of Fires Trail, St Helens' mountain bike trails offer something slightly different. With the beach being so close, the trails are dry, hard-packed sand that weave around large, lichen-covered boulders and sparse trees. There's a wide variety of easy greens and blues, including some longer routes, such as the 27km (16km) Dreaming Pools trail. Some black-graded trails feature more airtime. The trails radiate out from a couple of trailheads, including Flagstaff and Loila Tier, and you can piece together several trails to make a more demanding day out. And at the end of the afternoon there's always the beach on which to chill out, with free camping or accommodation in St Helens.
More info // www.sthelensmtbtrails.com.au

THE THYLACINE

The emblem of Blue Derby is the thylacine, also known as the Tasmanian tiger, a striped, meat-eating marsupial that was about the shape of a medium-sized dog. Once widespread across Australia, the thylacine's territory became reduced to Tasmania due to persecution by people. The last known example died in Hobart Zoo in 1936 but there have been sightings ever since, none of them convincing. But if there are thylacines still surviving, this is exactly the sort of place they'd be hiding.

Left to right: the Blue Derby trailhead; lichen-covered boulders in Binalong Bay; the trout paintwork by Trouty the trail; riding the Bay of Fires Trail. Previous spread: iron bark trees and button grass on the lower levels of the Bay of Fires Trail

We unload the bikes into a cold, damp fog. The trailhead is at an elevation of 800m (2625ft) and the Bay of Fires Trail flows all the way down to sea level. This means that riders pass through several different ecosystems and it's rewarding to spot the transition from one to another. At the top, the trail is at its most obviously constructed, with banked corners that catapult you into the next turn at ever greater speeds. Or at least they would if the trail wasn't so wet and had bedded in properly. With so few tyres rolling over it, the track is still soft and slippery. Thick foliage at least gives me some cushioning as I slide off the path several times. But as the elevation drops, the trail dries out and the plants become more widely spaced. Melaleuca, a honey-scented myrtle, flowers in gullies. A little further, and a cinnamon scent suggests I'm passing pepper trees – this is one of the few areas in Tasmania they grow. Their leaves and berries make for pungent flavouring. Golden bottlebrush flowers of the banksia brighten the bush.

After about a third of the way, the descent levels out and the surface changes from a grippy mulch to sand and grit. As the glaciers retreated from Tasmania, they shifted and deposited huge granite boulders and ridges and it is these that the trail now winds up and down and around. Button grasses and wildflowers proliferate and birds flash through the more open woodland. As the coast approaches, a bit of navigation is required and the route becomes a doubletrack for vehicles. Reaching Swimcart Beach, under a hot sun, I park the bike and clamber over the lichen-covered boulders to soak in the sea. **RB**

TOOLKIT

Start // Blue Tier trailhead
Finish // Swimcart Beach, Binalong Bay
Distance // 42km (26 miles)
Getting there // Most riders take a shuttle with a local operator from Derby to the trailhead. The shuttle will meet you at the beach and take you back to Derby. Derby can be reached by car from Launceston and Hobart but there's limited public transport.
When to ride // Winters are wet and the trail can suffer so summer or autumn may be best.
What to take // Tools for repairs and punctures, sunscreen, water and snacks. If you want to swim at the beach then swimwear too. Navigation is not strictly required but always recommended.
More info // www.ridebluederby.com.au; www.vertigomtb.com.au

island state is one of the world's most respected and enjoyable mountain biking destinations. It's up there with the best Europe and the Americas can offer thanks to the quality and variety of the trails and their one-of-a-kind setting. It's a success that some of Derby seem unsure of how to respond to.

The town has never had it easy. A tin mine was dug here in the 1870s and it brought prosperity: Derby's population exceeded 3000 (for comparison, Australia's 2021 census showed 109 residents with an average age of almost 50 years). But in 1929, a dam burst and flooded the mine, killing 14 people and damaging the town. Although the mine reopened after five years, things were never the same and Derby dwindled. In later years, income came from logging the incredible old-growth eucalyptus reglans or mountain ash trees growing in the temperate forests around the town. These forests of immense trees are known to store more carbon than any other kind of forest. And the tallest of the mountain ash still stands in Tasmania, Centurion, at 102m (334ft) tall. A government business called Sustainable Timbers currently makes woodchips from trees logged from parcels of forest around Derby and adjoining the trails. All of which makes for quite a complicated dynamic in Derby. Tasmania has long been torn between conservation and the jobs provided by environmentally damaging industries.

As one of the tens of thousands of people now visiting Derby each year to ride mountain bikes in the forests (and spending on average $250 per day), I made it my mission to

"Riders pass through several different ecosystems and it's rewarding to spot the transition from one to another"

try as many of the tracks as possible. They're in two groups. Close to town, a large number of trails descend into Derby and include many challenging classics, such as the jump-filled Air-Ya-Garn; Detonate, which slides through a crack between two giant granite buttresses; and Trouty, which passes a trout painted on a rock face, visible from the road below. Further away are a handful of longer, more mellow trails that come off the misty Blue Tier plateau and finish conveniently close to the Weldborough pub. I warm up on the 20km (12-mile) Blue Tier trail, which gives a preview of what to expect on the Bay of Fires Trail as it makes fast, sweeping turns through the fern-filled forest.

The next day I take the shuttle for the 50km (30 miles) to the Blue Tier trailhead. Driver Mike Bretz, an ecologist, shares some background on the area. Around 20,000 years ago, inland Tasmania was locked beneath ice sheets but there was a land bridge across Bass Strait. As the ice melted, the bridge disappeared and Tasmania was separated from mainland Australia, along with all the creatures living on the island. That's why there are rare beetles and other species that are found only in certain gullies here.

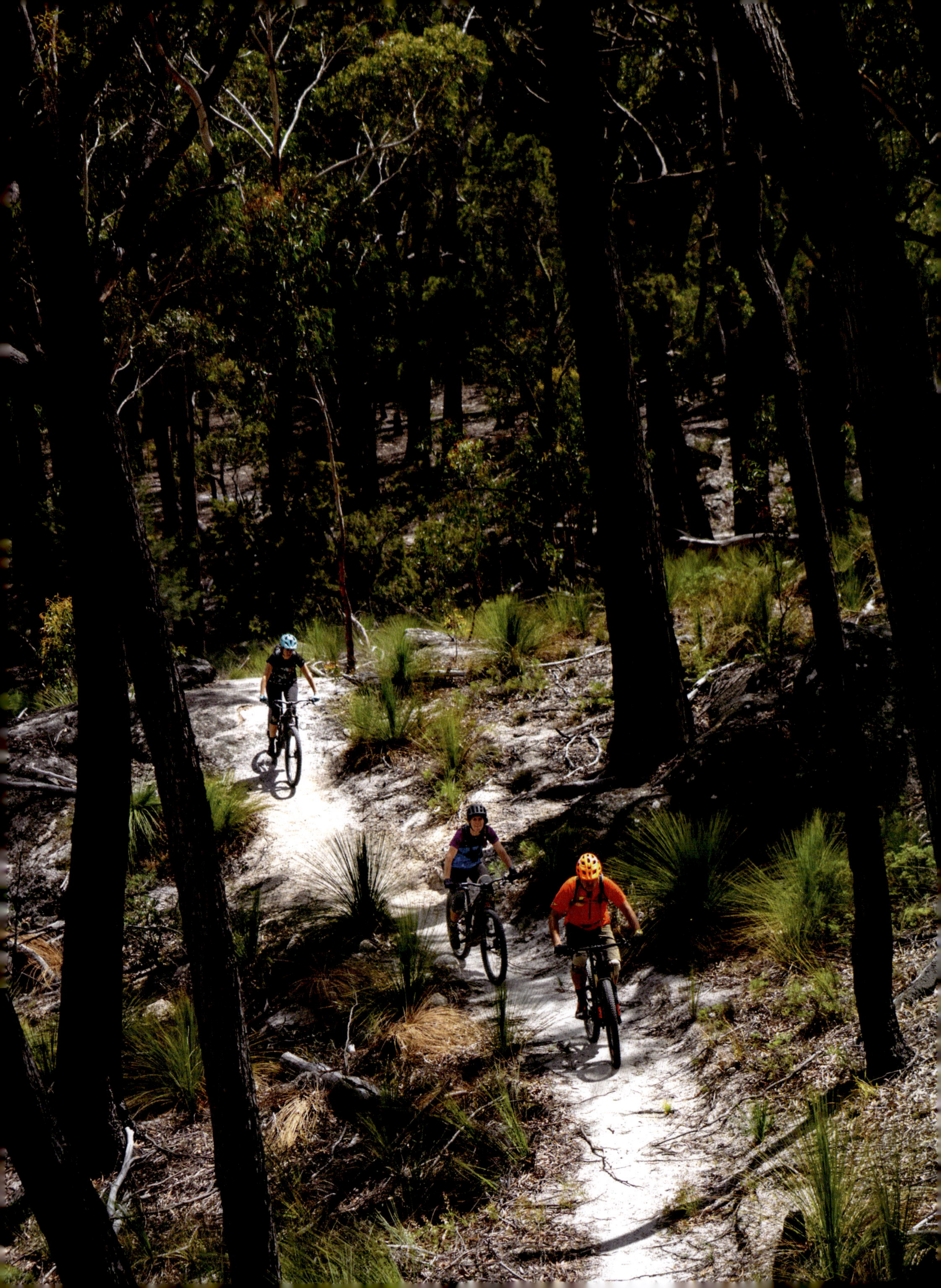

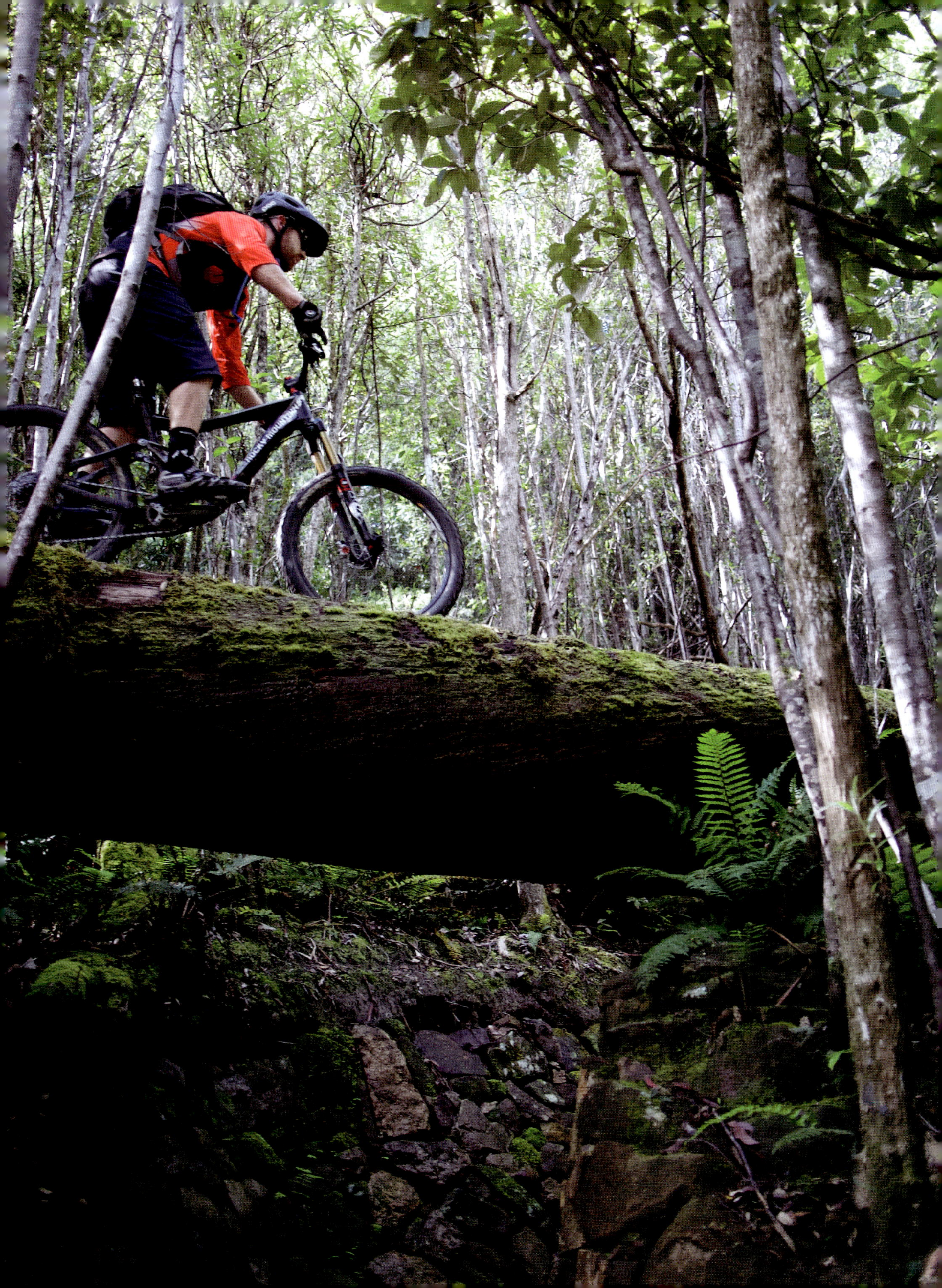

- EPIC BIKE RIDES OF AUSTRALIA & NEW ZEALAND -

THE SILVER CITY OF THE WESTERN WILDS

The untamed west coast of Tasmania has been long associated with mining. But the new Silver City trails are bringing mountain bikers to this rough land too.

'Silver City' sounds like the title of a classic John Wayne movie. This, however, is not a story about the Wild West, but a tale about the Western Wilds, Tasmania's sparsely populated far frontier. Instead of horses of flesh and blood there will be mountain bikes of carbon and steel, with men and women to ride them. But it still has a sweeping cinematic backdrop of high mountain country, unforgiving weather in a remote wilderness and raw mining towns. Tasmania's west coast is a place where searchers go.

I was in Zeehan during December 2022 for the opening of a new network of mountain bike trails in Mt Heemskirk Regional Reserve. The Silver City trails are set on the hillsides surrounding this historic mining town. Silver, lead and tin were discovered here in the 1870s and 1880s, and the mines supported a population of more than 10,000 people and 150 mining companies. The decline started after WWI and the last mine closed in the 1960s. With parcels of land changing hands for just a few thousand dollars, Zeehan had had its day. But tourism and mountain biking offered an opportunity

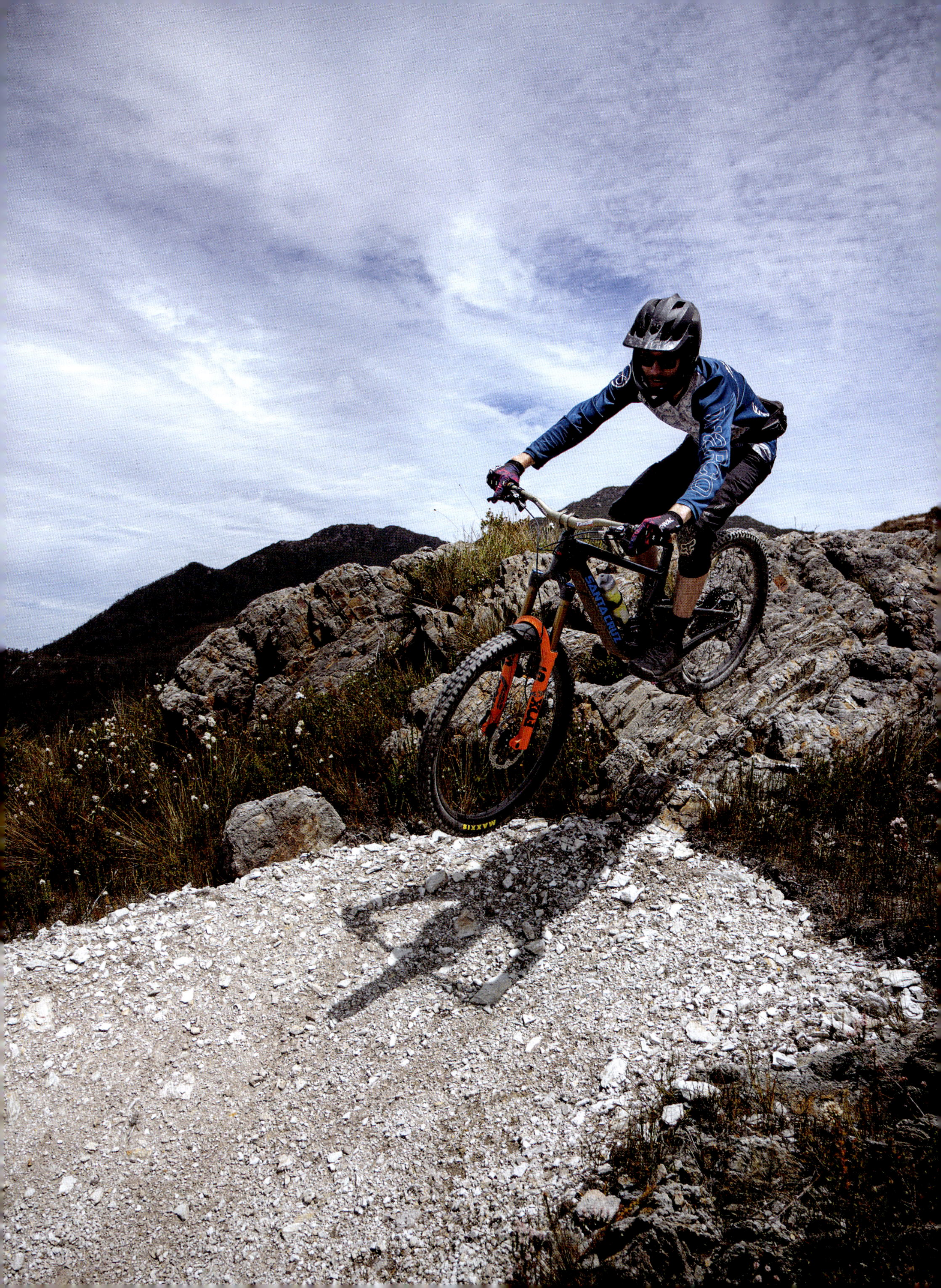

for revival. The trails have been designed as a series of ever more expansive loops, starting easy and getting progressively more challenging the further you rode from Zeehan. And government-funded Silver City was intended to connect with other trail networks that are part of the West Coast Mountain Bike Project at Queenstown, Montezuma Falls and beyond.

On the opening day of the Silver City trails, the first question was: 'What's the weather going to do?' As any local will tell you, the weather on this coastline is a fickle beast. It had been the wettest spring on record with roads washed out by landslips, lost bridges and newly formed lakes. With early predictions of snow down to 700m (2300ft), everyone was nervous. Nights under the stars were swapped for sturdier accommodation, but the opportunity to place fresh tyre marks on a new trail kept us motivated.

Don't let the Silver City trail's 35km (22 mile) length fool you into thinking it is a gentle roll. There is one way in and one way out, quite literally up the side of a mountain. The landscape is rugged with buttongrass plains over the lower hills, cut through by small river crossings, leading to granite slabs and steep climbs. It is rare in this modern age of mountain biking that the ascent is as well-crafted as the descent, so it was refreshing to put in the climb up the mountain, punching up switchbacks and granite slabs. There was even a small hike section near the top where the last of the trail waited to be linked.

The morning was spent leap-frogging with another crew of riders, who included some trail builders testing their finished product. The weather turned out to be a bluebird day. That's not to say there was no breeze; keep in mind that the previous piece of land that the wind – affectionately known as the Roaring Forties – had seen prior to us was South America.

One of the aims of this ride was a recon mission to check the trail for future plans for an overnight exploration, so we paused for lunch in what we hoped might be a good location to visit for a longer stop in the future. We noted that the access to fresh running water on this trail was genius. The ability to plan your ride and refills around a single water bottle without the need to lug 3-litres around on your back is a small detail that you might not have considered, but it is one that changes the experience completely.

From our pitstop, there were views across the sawtooth skyline of mountains to the west coast. This was followed by a brief race across the high plateau that helped to explain why this route needs to be ridden. Long hours leading up to the opening of this trail were spent daydreaming of the white zigzag stitching of the descent off the Heemskirk Range. Once we were stood before it, looking over at how high it was, we couldn't help but feel a bit intimidated. Its black rating is well earned: it's a long limp out if you get it wrong. The ride is steep with some nice features to navigate, but it's predictable.

© Josh Frith

MIND THE MINES

Zeehan's first boom came when prospector Frank Long discovered silver-lead deposits near Mt Zeehan. This find brought miners to the area and kicked off a boom that resulted in Zeehan growing to become the third-largest town in Tasmania, gaining the name Silver City. Care needs to be taken at the beginning of the ride to stick to the rail as mine shafts still exist, sometimes directly adjacent to where your tyres roll.

Left to right: what goes up, must come down (Oonah Hill). Previous spread: intermediate and advanced features on the Silver City trails

"Despite the trail's 35km length, it is no gentle roll. There is one way in and one way out, up the side of a mountain"

The berms have been expertly dug to catch and wash off speed and, just when you need a break from the concentration of navigating a safe route, a brief flattening out is provided to compose and then resend down the next section.

The rest of the ride had us hooting and hollering down, grinding back up through unending grass fields. The legs got weary, but the next layer of the trail revealed itself. Black went back to blue, and on the final portion of the trail back to green. Labelling Oonah Hill as a green trail is belittling the artistry achieved when building this loop. It can only be described as dirt paradise. As the grass gave way to temperate forest, the real fun began. By then, tired was an understatement and the fast pace that data had to be processed at when howling down this trail began to become almost overwhelming – if it wasn't so much fun. Faster and faster, tyres ripped to hold on against the terrain like a six-shooter stand-off at the end of a western. Westerns are about dramatic adventures, wild backdrops and honest storytelling. And they're sometimes about second chances for towns like Zeehan. **SM**

TOOLKIT

Start/Finish// Heemskirk Rd, Zeehan
Distance// 35km (22 miles)
Getting there// The west coast can be accessed via Tasmania's two major domestic airports at Launceston and Hobart. Both airports are a 3- to 4-hour drive.
When to go // Late spring to early autumn.
What to wear // A packable raincoat/windbreaker is a must regardless of the forecast. Tasmanian weather conditions are changeable and potentially dangerous.
What to pack // Water is available on the trail at various points, drinkable in free-flowing creeks. Food to support a 6- to 8-hour ride is required. A snake bite bandage is advisable given the tour's remote nature.
Where to stay // Zeehan has a handful of hotel, motel and camping options.
Where to eat // Heemskirk Motor Hotel in Zeehan has bistro dining.
Tours // Shuttle options are available for Oonah Hill. For a complete connection from airport to trails, check out Into The Wild (www.gointothewild.com.au).

Opposite: a rope bridge spans the creek at Montezuma Falls

MORE LIKE THIS
WEST COAST TASMANIA TRAILS

MT OWEN

Mining for copper, silver and gold from the 1880s turned the hills around Queenstown into a moonscape, and despite some regrowth, there are still stretches of exposed rock and earth in vivid oranges and pinks, which continue to tint the Queen River. Rising 1146m (3760ft) above the newly arts-focused town, Mt Owen has a series of gravity-based descent trails (mostly intermediate) with a 800m (2625ft) vertical drop. The scarcity of vegetation does mean that views from the top of the mountain as you ride are almost unobstructed.
Start // Mt Owen
Finish // Queenstown
Distance // 36km (22 miles)
Details // mtb.westcoasttas.com.au

MONTEZUMA FALLS

Tasmania's highest waterfalls, at 104m (341ft), would have been much harder to access among the dense temperate rainforest of leatherwood and giant tree ferns, had a narrow-gauge tramway not been built past it in the 1890s to assist with mining operations. Although the rails are long gone, a 5km (3 mile) multi-use trail runs to the falls from the trailhead south of Rosebery. If you want to continue from this easy-graded trail, carry your bike across the rope bridge that now spans the creek beneath the waterfall to reach more testing 4WD tracks that finish at the Murchison Highway.
Start // Montezuma Falls trailhead
Finish // Murchison Highway
Distance // 19km (12 miles)
Details // www.trailforks.com

STERLING VALLEY

If you prefer your MTB trails largely unreformed, the Sterling Valley trail is a classic of the kind, running at the foot of Mt Murchison, north of Queenstown. The intermediate-to-difficult trail runs through moss-covered myrtle forest, climbing steadily from the Murchison Highway near the south end of Lake Rosebery, up to a 500m (1640ft) saddle, then down more steeply to the mining town of Rosebery. The route was once part of the multi-day Wildside race held every two years, but since that seems to have stopped in 2016, there has been less regular maintenance to clear fallen trees and the like. The dense canopy makes this track a dark, slippery and raw riding experience in the middle of nowhere – ensure you leave details of your whereabouts.
Start // Murchison Highway, near Tullah
Finish // Rosebery
Distance // 11km (7 miles)
Details // www.trailforks.com

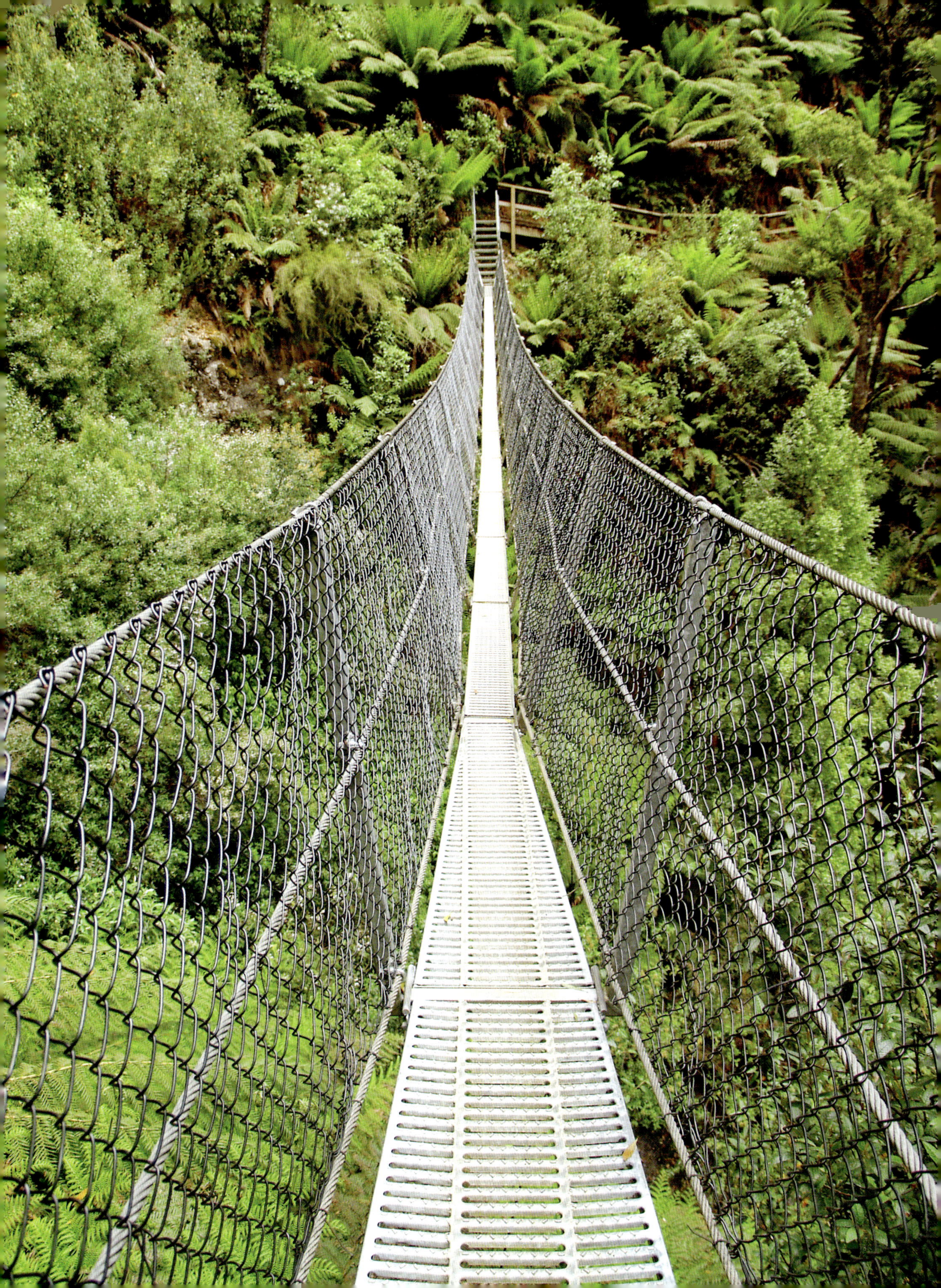

THE NORTH ISLAND, NEW ZEALAND

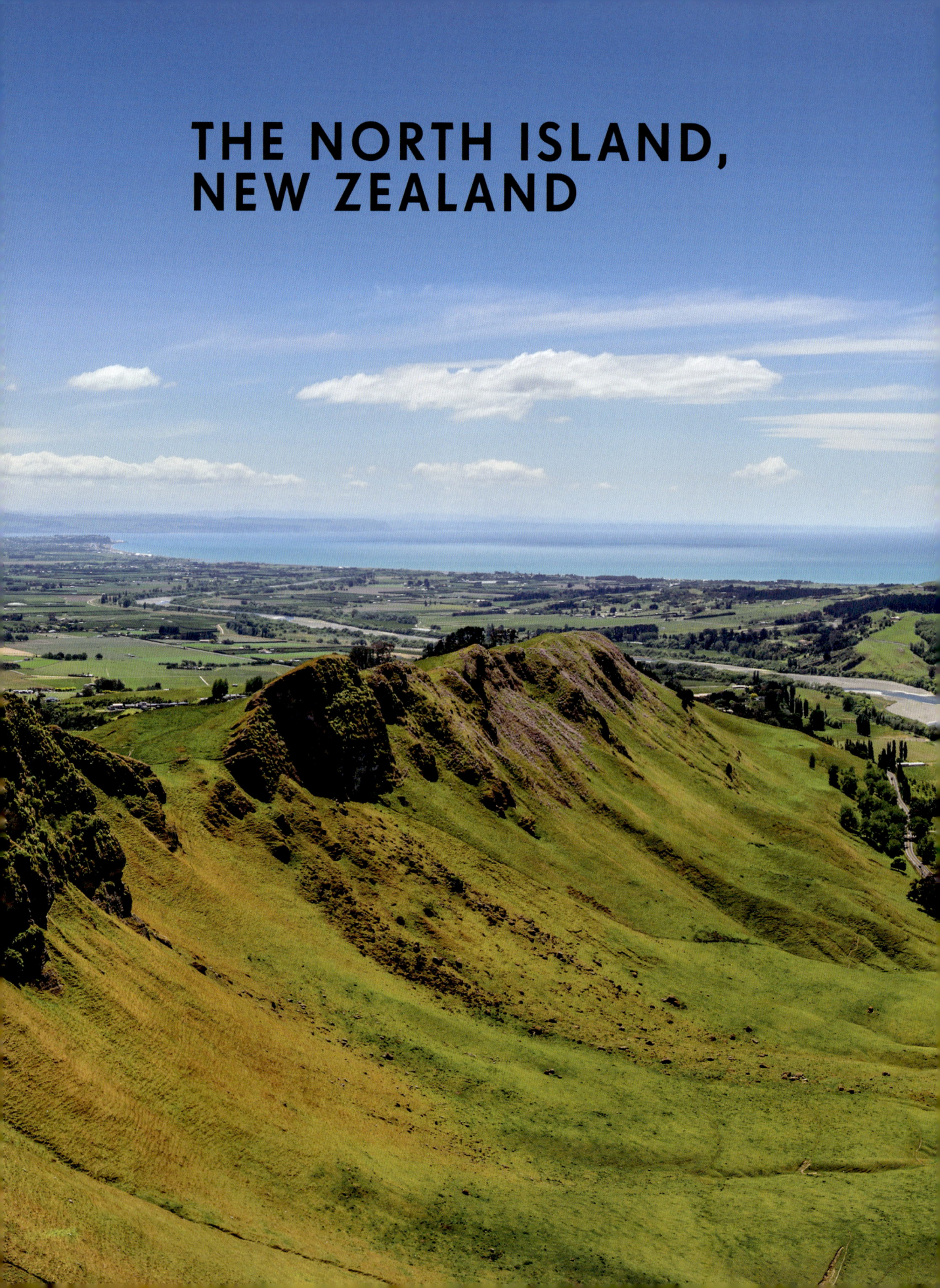

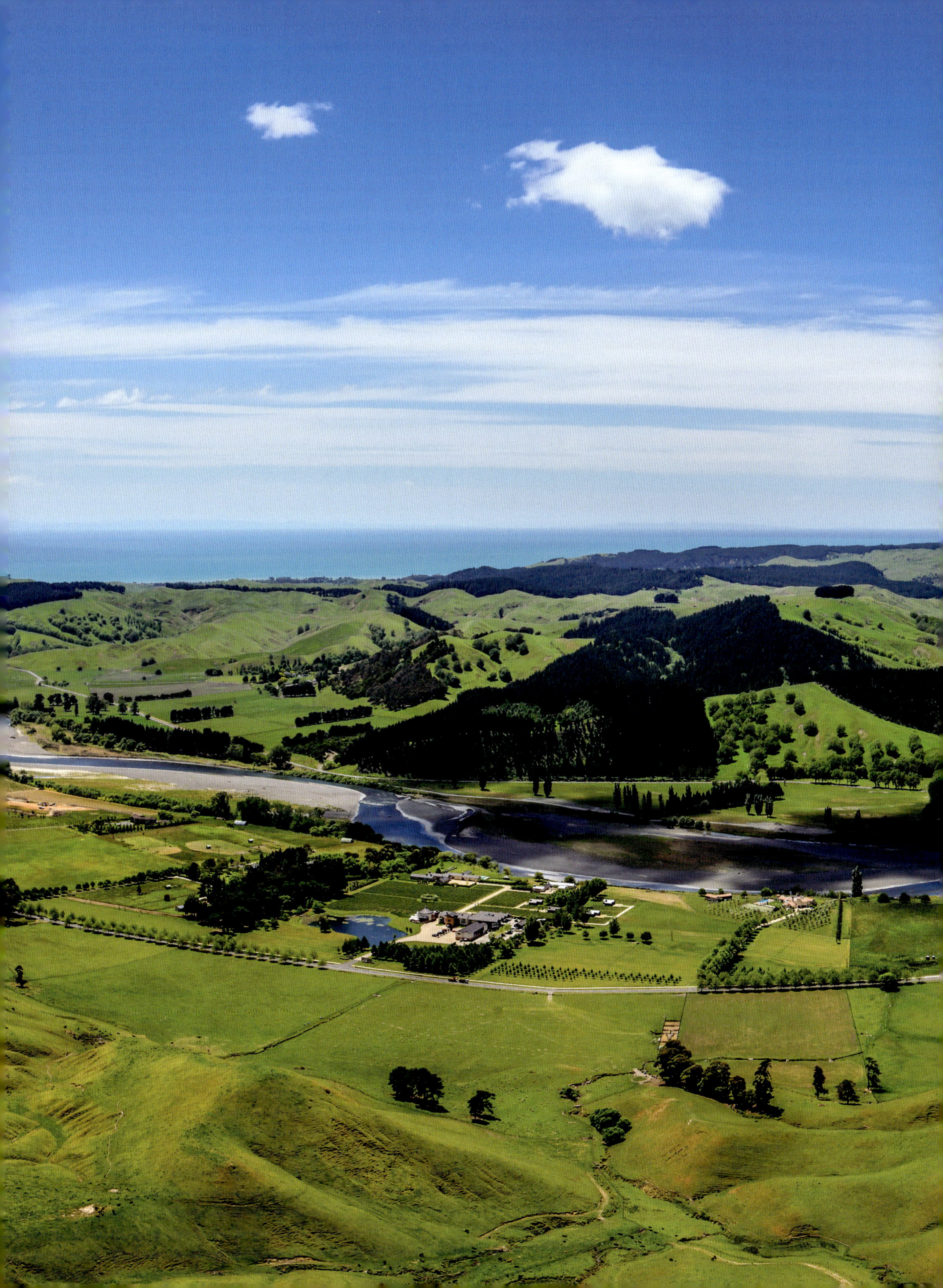

THE HAURAKI RAIL TRAIL

Cycle through gentle dairy country to one of New Zealand's most dramatic gorges on this relaxed ride of immense contrast.

On the Hauraki Plain, south of Thames, I have only cows for company. Pasture stretches out lush and green, and the only bends in the trail seem to be around paddocks rather than land features. There's gold ahead, or at least some highly visible reminders of the gold rushes that transformed the area, but on this grassy plain it's all about these dairy cows as I cycle out of Thames on the Hauraki Rail Trail.

One of the great promises of rail trails is gentle gradients – trains, like weary cyclists, avoided climbs – but few are as faithfully flat as these first hours along the Hauraki Plain. Hills rear up from its edges, but there's barely a rise along the trail and across this valley with a cow obsession. Through the green paddocks, the animals blithely watch me pass, and I pedal past an organic cheesemaker and the Convenient Cow Cafe, which milks the bovine theme with the likes of cow clocks and painted milk jugs.

The cows are good company, watching me with their doe eyes, but they're not the reason I'm here. The standout feature of the Hauraki Rail Trail, which follows one of New Zealand's oldest rail corridors, is Karangahake Gorge, a deep and dramatic groove in the earth that harbours a section of cycling as beautiful as any in the country.

Since the Hauraki Rail Trail was launched in 2012, it has grown a couple of new arms, extending out from Thames along the bird-rich shores of the Firth of Thames to Kaiaua; and south from Paeroa, past the North Island's tallest waterfall (153m-high Wairere Falls) to Matamata, famously home to the Hobbiton movie set from Lord of the Rings. Combine every arm of the rail trail – riding out and back through Karangahake Gorge before pedalling south to Matamata – and you can puzzle together a 197km bike ride spread over up to five days. But always it's the gorge that beckons most spectacularly.

Karangahake Gorge begins to make its presence known as I pedal out of Paeroa, where this most dramatic section of the trail turns off the Hauraki Plain. Paeroa, New Zealand's furthest inland port, is a town known throughout the country for the uniquely Kiwi carbonated drink Lemon & Paeroa, aka L&P,

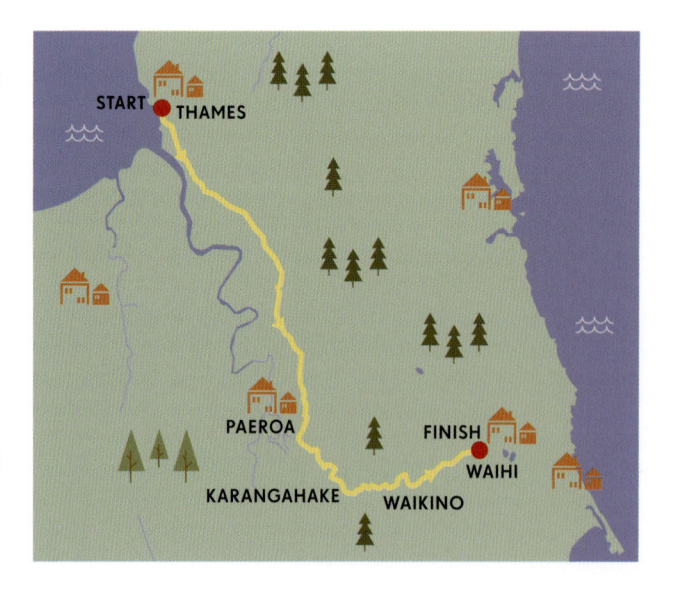

THE NORTH ISLAND, NEW ZEALAND

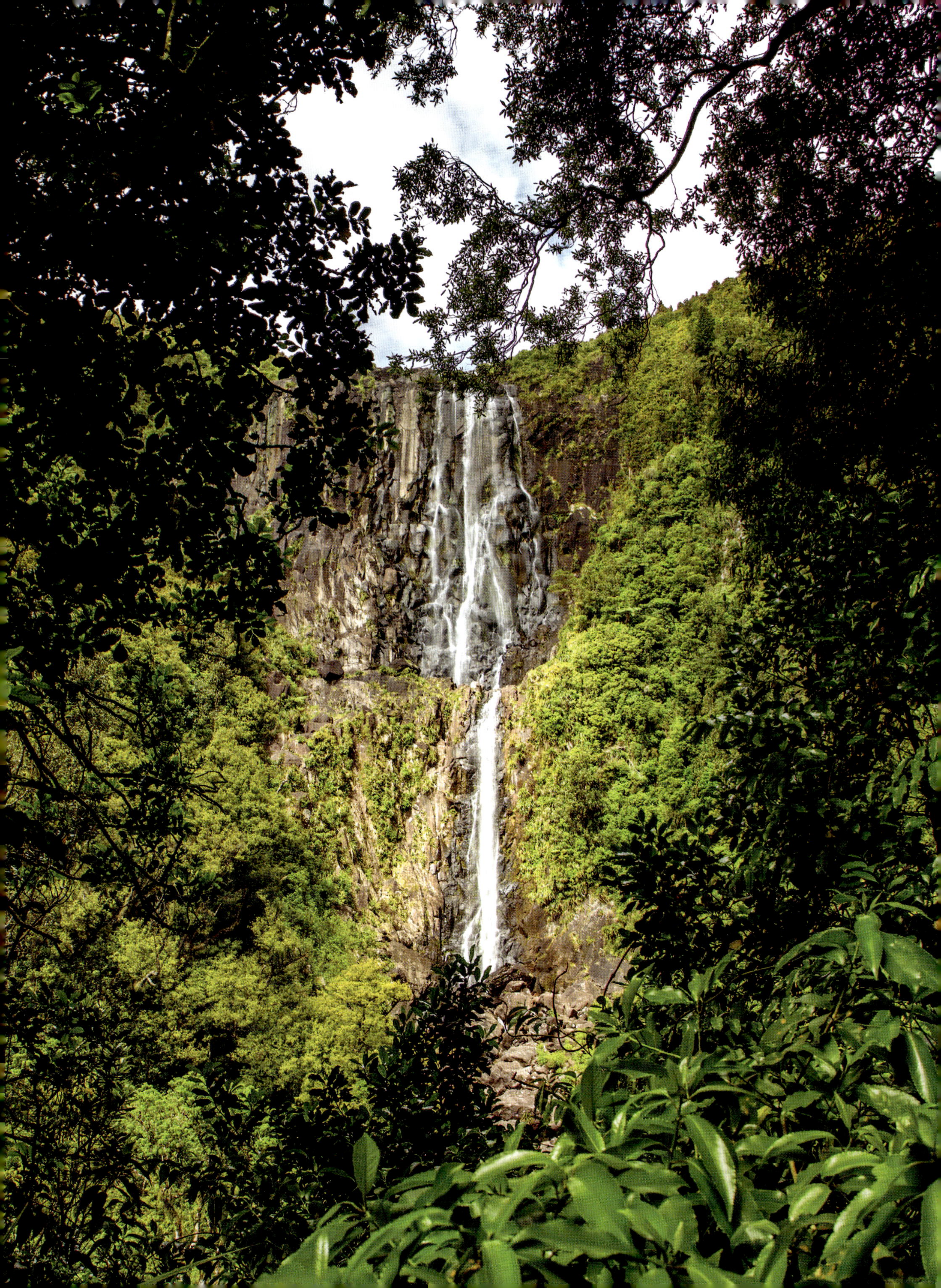

first created here in 1907 from lemons and mineral water from a local spring. I cycle past the town's landmark 7m-high (23ft) brown L&P bottle and begin the squeeze into the gorge.

The change in the landscape is almost instantaneous as the slopes of the hills narrow around me, pressing the trail tight against the Ohinemuri River. For the first time, I can feel a gradient knotting my thighs and slowly, like a building drama, the hills close in further until the trail rises onto a bridge over the river and State Highway 2 and enters a tunnel. At 1km in length, this former rail tunnel is now the longest cycling tunnel in New Zealand. It's faintly lit, but still the darkness is disorientating. A few metres into the tunnel, I stop, strapping a headtorch to my helmet to light my way through this temporary night.

The tunnel signals more than a transition; it's an abrupt revolution in the landscape. As I emerge back into daylight, the world has been transformed. The walls of the gorge have almost clamped together, with their high cliffs split by the fast-flowing Ohinemuri River. The highway runs along one bank, with the trail on the other, and the small town of Karangahake rising up the slopes.

I've seen a few cyclists up till now, but suddenly the path is crowded with bikes. Karangahake Gorge has been dubbed one of New Zealand's natural wonders (a big call in a country with such an abundance of spectacle), and the presence of such an easy but dramatic trail – along with proximity to

THAMES GOLD RUSH

Though gold was first discovered in New Zealand on the nearby Coromandel Peninsula in 1852, the first big gold strike, and the country's first major gold rush, came at Thames in 1867. The town's grand streetscape reflects the scale of this heady gold rush. Home to the longest main street in New Zealand, Thames was for a time the largest town in the country, home to 18,000 people and more than 100 pubs.

Clockwise from top: bike parking; old rail bridges; Karangahake Gorge. Previous: Wairere Falls

THE NORTH ISLAND, NEW ZEALAND

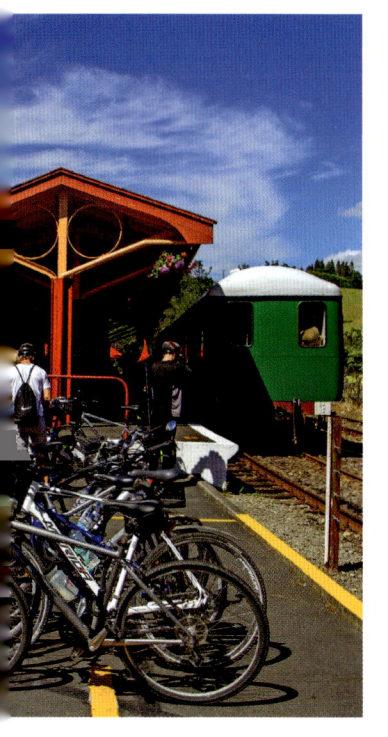

Auckland, 90 minutes' drive away – has transformed the gorge into a major recreational cycling destination, with around 40,000 people pedalling here each year.

To get the best from the gorge, however, you also need to get off the bike. Walking tracks radiate into the slopes and tributaries, most notably the Windows Walk. I park up my bike by the river and set out on this 2.5km (1.5-mile) loop, which bores through the cliffs on a trail carved by gold miners. Four 'windows' were also cut to allow miners to dump tailings through them into the Waitawheta River, spectacularly visible below.

Pedalling on, the trail follows the wriggles of the river, bending and twisting beside it, riding against the flow. A detour of just a couple of hundred metres leads off the trail to Owharoa Falls, fanning down across a black cliff, and then it's on to the Victoria Battery, the haunting remnants of the world's first cyanide gold-mining operation. The concrete arches still standing held 15m-high (50ft) tanks that were filled with crushed ore and potassium cyanide.

Just a few minutes ahead, after another river crossing, is Waikino and the chance to end this rail trail on the rails. The final operating section of the railway, now known as the Goldfields Railway, connects Waikino to Waihi, with bikes able to be transported to the trail's end, just a few kilometres ahead. But I ride on. The gorge falls behind me, and the land opens wide again as the trail meanders beside the river into Waihi, where gold is still mined from an open pit. It's a fitting finish to a golden ride. **AB**

"A detour leads off the trail to Owharoa Falls, fanning down across a black cliff"

TOOLKIT

Start/Finish // Thames/Waihi
Distance // 58km (36 miles)
Duration // 1-2 days
Getting there // Thames is 115km south-east of Auckland. InterCity buses run from Auckland to Thames and Waihi.
When to go // It's good year-round, but the gorge – and its waters – come into their own in summer.
Where to stay // If breaking the ride into two days, try accommodation options in Paeroa and Karangahake.
Tours // Jolly Bikes (www.jollybikes.co.nz) runs Hauraki Rail Trail tours from half-day to five days. Paeroa-based Hauraki Bike Hire (www.haurakibikehire.co.nz) does exactly what the name on the tin suggests, while Biking Hiking Shuttles (www.bikinghikingshuttles.co.nz) offers transport and pick-ups along the trail.
More info // www.haurakirailtrail.co.nz

Opposite: jumping off Kawarau Bridge

MORE LIKE THIS
GORGE RIDES

SIMPSONS GAP BIKE PATH, NORTHERN TERRITORY

Cross desert sands to one of Tjoritja/West MacDonnell Ranges' most impressive gorges on this sealed bike path out of Alice Springs. Beginning at the roadside grave of John Flynn, founder of the Royal Flying Doctor Service, it skirts dunes and hills beneath the mountain range as it makes a largely flat approach towards Simpsons Gap. Most of the ride is inside Tjorita/West MacDonnell National Park, with ghost gums and desert bloodwoods for floral company (and rare shade). The West Macs are a constant presence to the path's immediate north and slowly the break in them that is Simpsons Gap draws nearer. After a final approach on a roadside bike lane, park up at bike racks beside the visitor car park and make the 400m walk to the mouth of the gorge. Swimming in the pool inside the gorge isn't permitted.
Start/Finish // John Flynn's Grave, Alice Springs
Distance // 17km (10.5 miles)
Duration // 1-2 hours
More info // www.discovercentralaustralia.com

ONKAPARINGA RIVER NATIONAL PARK, SOUTH AUSTRALIA

Flowing along Adelaide's southern suburban fringe, the Onkaparinga River has carved a beautiful gorge dotted with waterholes and lined with trails, several of which are open to mountain bikers. Get one of the best gorge views on the easy Punchbowl Lookout Trail (2km return) to the namesake lookout platform above the gorge. Continue along the intermediate Punchbowl Link Trail to complete a 6km loop with regular gorge views. On the opposite side of the river, the intermediate Chapel Hill Lookout Trail (1.5km) leads to another gorge lookout. Greater challenges come on the rim-to-rim Gorge Link Trail (3km), which descends steeply into the gorge, crosses the river and climbs just as steeply back out; and the Old Coach Link Trail (3km one way), with its steep pinches along the Old Coach Road Track.
More info // www.parks.sa.gov.au/parks/onkaparinga-river-national-park

KAWARAU GORGE, NEW ZEALAND

Queenstown's long moment in the adventuring sun began at Kawarau Gorge, where the world's first commercial bungee jump was opened in 1988. The gorge, and the bungee bridge, are now part of the Queenstown Trail, a tentacle-like collection of trails that radiate out from Queenstown. To reach the gorge, take to the Twin Rivers Trail from Kawarau Falls, near Queenstown Airport. This remote trail heads along the bank of the Kawarau River, turning briefly up another famous waterway – the Shotover River – crossing it on the restored 1871 Old Lower Shotover Bridge. Skirting the town of Lake Hayes, the trail climbs Thompson's Hill to a lookout high above Kawarau River before meeting with the Arrow River Bridges Trail at Morven Ferry Road – turn south onto this trail and you'll quickly arrive at the Kawarau's suspension bridge and its bungee. Now, to jump or not to jump?
Start/Finish // Kawarau Falls Bridge
Distance // 55km (34 miles) return
Duration // 5-8 hours
More info // www.queenstowntrails.org.nz

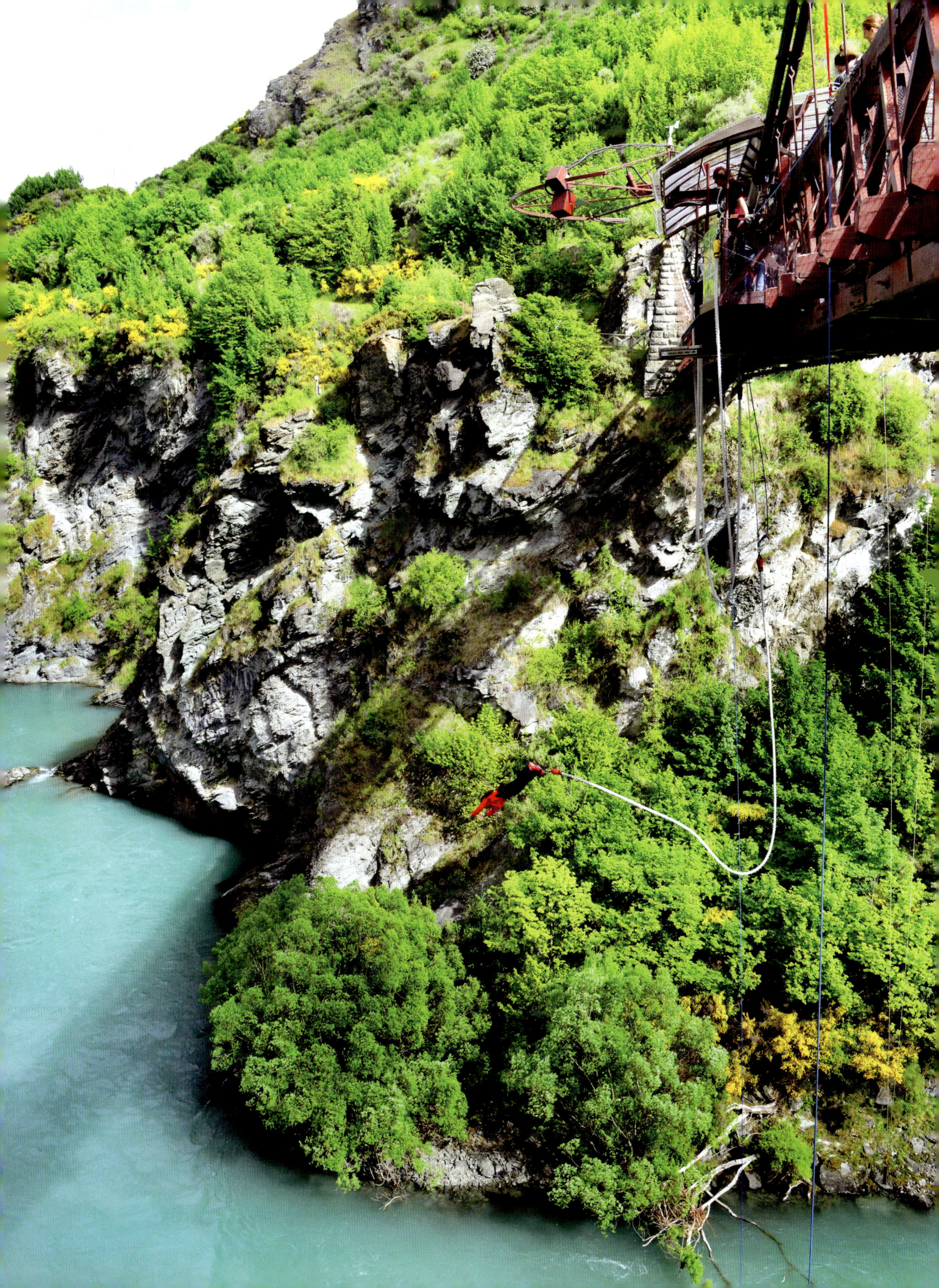

OVERNIGHT ON THE MOERANGI TRACK

Less renowned than its singletrack adventure counterparts in the South Island, this remote trail in the East Coast region is every bit as special and worth slowing down for.

Warm breaths swirl in the crisp morning air around concentrating faces. There is fussing and faffing as we each focus on the challenge of attaching overnight gear to full-suspension bikes with cold fingers.

Our group of four are on a mountain biking road trip of the central North Island, which – among visits to more groomed and purpose-built mountain bike parks – includes this little bikepacking overnighter. With covid restrictions recently easing, the fact that it's mid-winter isn't going to dampen our enthusiasm for adventure. Though winter in these parts is mild, the promise of sleeping indoors at one of the charming huts on the trail is still a welcome drawcard, as is the visit to the thermal hot springs at Waikite – the suitable treat we decided on for our return.

Low-hanging cloud casts a haze over the landscapes as we set off, adding an extra dash of mystery to exploring an area that's new to us all. Moments later, I've already paused pedalling, the wild horses roaming the roadsides deemed worthy of a photo stop. Shortly after, the group drops me again while I admire a *marae* (Māori meeting place) and its *pou whenua* (carved wooden posts).

After a stretch of quiet, winding tarmac we veer off onto a lovely, narrowing ribbon of gravel. It leads us through forested hills draped in the remains of the dissipating clouds, punctuated by a few more appearances from wild horses (which have been outnumbering cars), before delivering us to the start of the singletrack. We're swallowed up by a tunnel of lush forest, and my eyes take a moment to adjust. Dense ferns and mosses blanket the forest floor, leaving only the sliver of dirt that guides the way. It would take quite a special effort to go off track and get lost here.

Following old hiking trails, the route has a few upgraded sections purpose-built to make it bike-friendly. Rather than any bermed corners and built features, it offers a more natural style of riding, with roots, ruts, the odd slip and treefalls

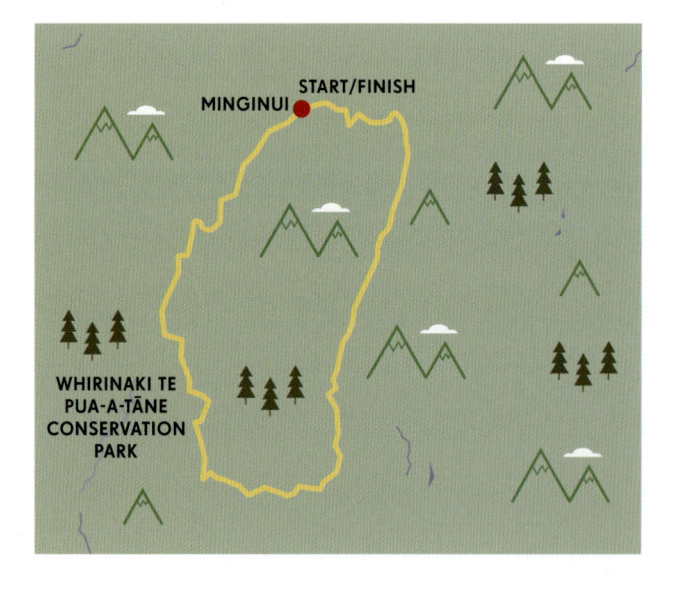

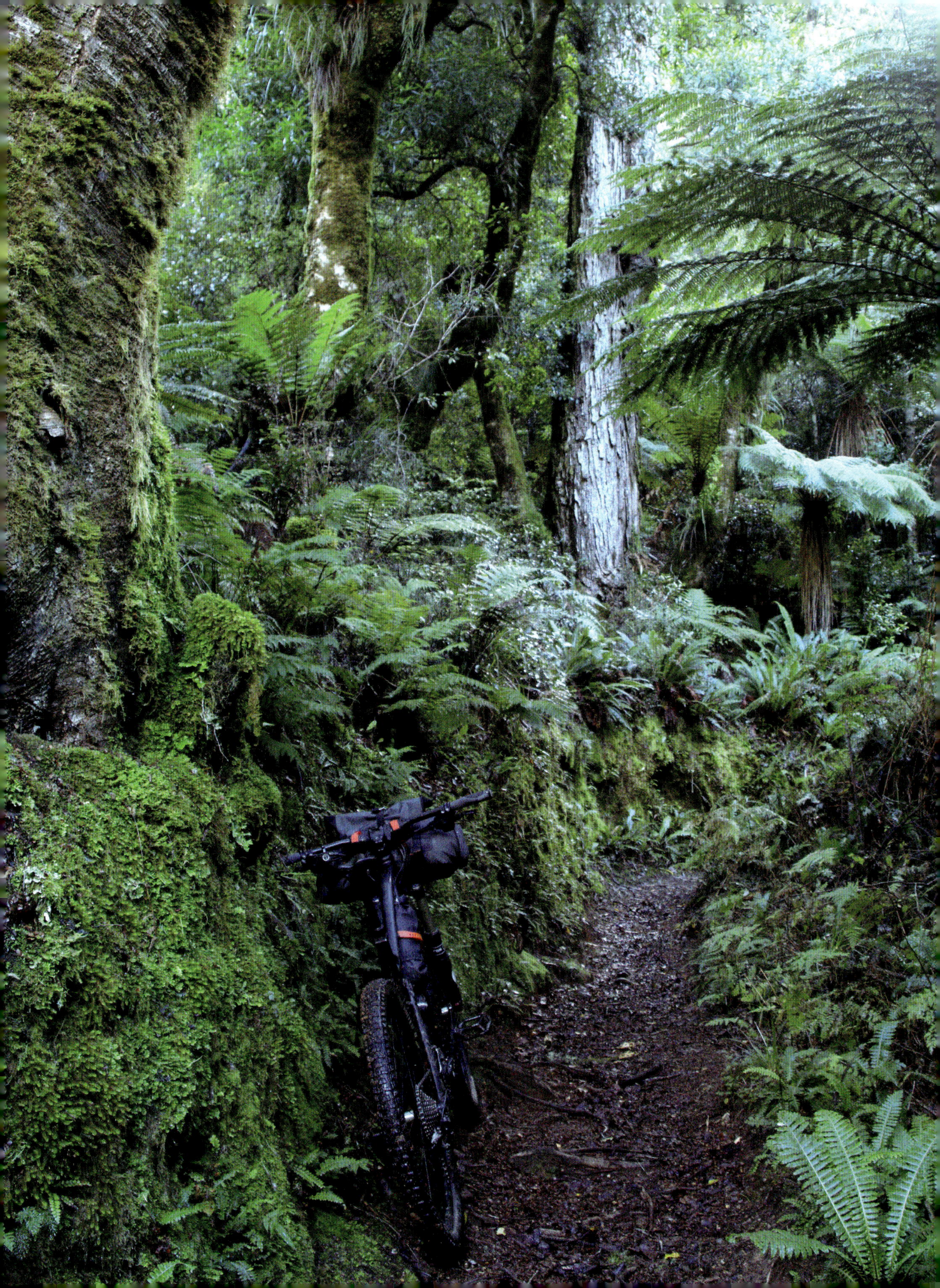

to negotiate, keeping things interesting and decidedly backcountry.

Before long we reach Skips / Whangatawhia Hut, a simple, green corrugated iron building with a welcoming veranda and fire-engine-red door, occupying a clearing on a riverbank. The picnic table makes a perfect spot for a long lunch break, helping us maintain an optimal ratio of equal parts riding and relaxing.

With bikes a little lighter and energy levels replenished, we continue up the valley. Soon, I hear a flap and a splash, and catch the briefest glimpse of a pair of rare whio, blue ducks, in the river below us. It's the first time I've seen them in the wild, and serves as a good reminder to stay alert to the treasures hiding in this ancient forest. This is more easily done along those stretches where I have to resort to pushing – the climbs, though never long, have a definite bite to them. We squiggle through the forest, enjoying the changing scenes and riding. Each climb is rewarded with a fun descent, another hut full of character and history, bridges spanning the sparkling, clear streams, and some sections of trail that battle it out with rampant plant growth. A sign to the just-off-trail Moerangi Hut appears and, taking stock of the group, it looks like great timing.

As a closet hut-bagger (those who dedicate themselves to visiting as many as possible of New Zealand's 950-ish backcountry huts) there is a giddy moment of discovery when arriving at a new hut – what's it like inside, how's the view, is anyone there? Nestled in a sloping clearing, the simple one-

SOUNDS OF THE FOREST

The ancient rainforest of the Whirinaki Te Pua-a-Tāne Conservation Park is a highlight of this ride. Until the 1980s the forest was still being logged, but thankfully this area was spared as a result of conservation battles. It offers the chance to see wonderful, ancient native forest and birds along the route, including kākāriki, kākā, whio (blue duck) and kārearea (New Zealand falcon). With some luck and an overnight stay, you could hear the distinctive call of kiwi after dusk, too.

Clockwise from top: watch for slippery boardwalk and bridges; a New Zealand falcon; the Whirinaki Forest. Previous spread: Moerangi's forested trail

room, nine-bunk sanctuary sits empty, and will be our home for the night. Of course, you could go unloaded and ride the route in a longer day, but with the challenge of getting here in the first place, why rush through?

A leisurely overnighter brings with it the joy of spending time in one of these shelters and observing the forest come to life at all hours of the day and night. Gathering firewood, crowding around the log-burner, flicking through the old entries in the hut logbook by candlelight, striking the right balance between warming cups of tea and minimal journeys to the long-drop toilet outside.

Waking up to the dawn chorus of birdsong as morning brews are prepared and sunlight begins to filter through the trees is, to me at least, one of life's great pleasures. If not for the enticing descent to come and the lack of extra food, it'd be easy to spend a lazy day here reading in my sleeping bag.

Rested legs grind up the last hearty climb to the high point of the Moerangi Saddle. We settle in for the long, thrilling descent, following a ridgeline to the Whirinaki River, with plenty of noisy outbursts of surprise, joy and general approval accompanying us all the way down. Emerging at the carpark, we're surprised to see a few picnicking visitors. I realise we haven't seen another soul on the trail until now, so after our brief but immersive escape this marks a return to civilisation. The road back is straightforward, though it would be rude not to ride the 16km Whirinaki Forest track while here too – a lovely, mellow loop that was the Department of Conservation's first foray into purpose-built mountain bike trails.

With the best now behind us, hot food and hot pools beckon, and keep the legs spinning. **ES**

TOOLKIT

Start/Finish // Minginui village
Distance // 64km (40 miles), plus 16km (10 miles) for the Whirinaki Forest Mountain Bike Track
Getting there // Drive or pedal – the track is 90km southeast of Rotorua. The Waikaremoana road is a scenic, hilly tour in its own right, and is part of the coast-to-coast Kōpiko Aotearoa bikepacking route.
When to go // This region has a mild climate compared to other parts of the country, making this ride possible year-round with a good forecast.
What to pack // Sleeping bag, spares and repair kit, food. Come prepared with everything you'll need, as the closest places to buy food are at least 20km off route.
Where to stay // Moerangi Hut or Skips Hut. Buy a backcountry hut ticket from the Department of Conservation.
Things to know // Some technical riding skills are required. The heart of this route is the 35km (22-mile) singletrack section, which is rated an intermediate–advanced trail. You can also organise a shuttle if you just want to ride this section.
More info // www.doc.govt.nz

Opposite: Reefton's main street; riding the Otago Central Rail Trail back from Big Hut

MORE LIKE THIS
RIDES WITH CHARMING HUTS

BIG HUT, SOUTH ISLAND

The Rock and Pillars is a distinctive range in Otago, its broad ridge covered in hardy tussock and sub-alpine shrublands, and studded with rock formations. A thousand metres above the plains, the unobstructed views from the ridge make it a great spot to spend the night. The unimaginatively but aptly named Big Hut is just the place for it, with solar lighting, a table tennis table, and entertaining tales of its ski hut origins. For an overnighter from Ranfurly or Waipiata on gravel roads, 4WD tracks and cycle trails, link up Paerau Road, Old Dunstan Road, and Rock and Pillar Ridge Road, then descend Kinvara Road just beyond Big Hut, to close the loop with the Otago Central Rail Trail north of Middlemarch. Be sure to stop in at the excellent Waipiata pub to sample one of their famous pies. The ridge is extremely exposed, so this trip will need a reasonable weather forecast.
Start/Finish // Ranfurly
Distance // 120km (75 miles)
More info // www.doc.govt.nz

WAIHĀHĀ HUT, NORTH ISLAND

In the central North Island's Pureora Forest Park, the Waihāhā Track is a shared hiking and mountain biking track, leading to the cute Waihāhā Hut. From a middle-of-nowhere spot on Western Bay Road, the trail heads west, loosely following the river upstream as it travels along singletrack through re-growth forest, grass clearings through shrubland, and mature forest. A great section traverses steep hillsides high above the river, looking out over sheer slabs of rock framed by native forest, and there are occasional views over the treetops into the distance. The wood-clad, cabin-like hut appears as you emerge from the forest into a small, grassy clearing near the river. It can easily be visited as a short out-and-back day ride, or an overnight trip, and makes an adventurous addition to the Waihāhā section of the Great Lakes Trail, which is better served by transport options.
Start/Finish // Western Bay Rd at Waihāhā River bridge / Waihāhā Hut
Distance // 9km (6 miles)
More info // www.doc.govt.nz

BIG RIVER HUT, SOUTH ISLAND

The historic goldmining town of Reefton has a network of tracks in the Victoria Forest Park. Many of them date back to mining days, so rusting relics and signs of former glory lie amid regenerating forest. Just south of Reefton, Soldiers Road leads into the park and eventually turns into the 4WD Waiuta Track. It's a bumpy but beautiful route winding through the forest, and opens up at the clearing of the old Big River mining settlement. Big River Hut is just a little beyond, perched on a small hill – it's a lovely and comfortable hut, with wooden panelling, a log burner, and views out over the hills. From the hut you can return the same way to Reefton (24km each way), or continue south to Waiuta on a more challenging and wild mountain biking trail (a further 11km). Reefton is an hour's drive from Greymouth or Westport.
Start/Finish // Reefton / Big River Hut
Distance // 24km (15 miles)
More info // www.doc.govt.nz

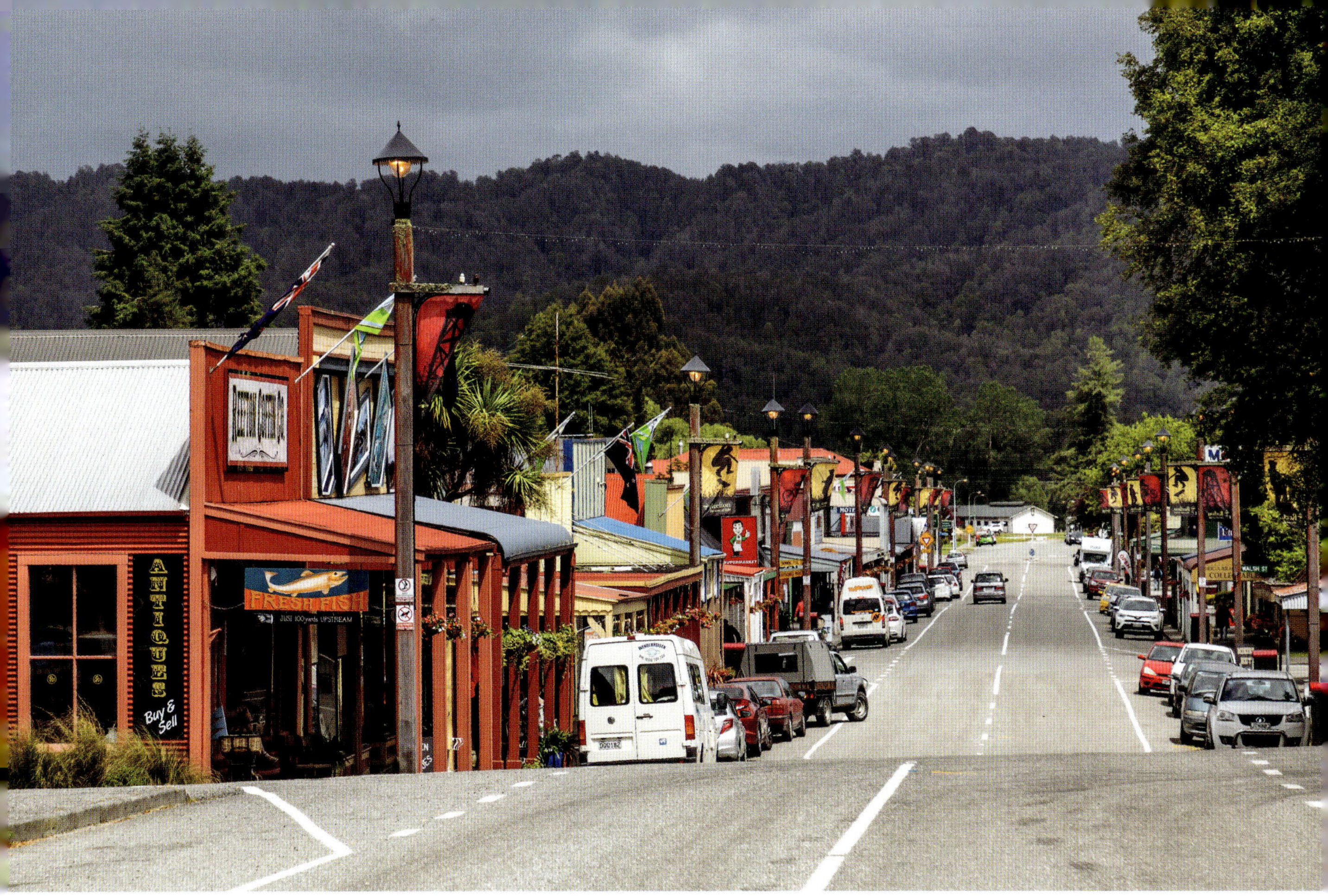
ANTIQUES
Buy & Sell
FRESH FISH
JUST 100 yards UPSTREAM

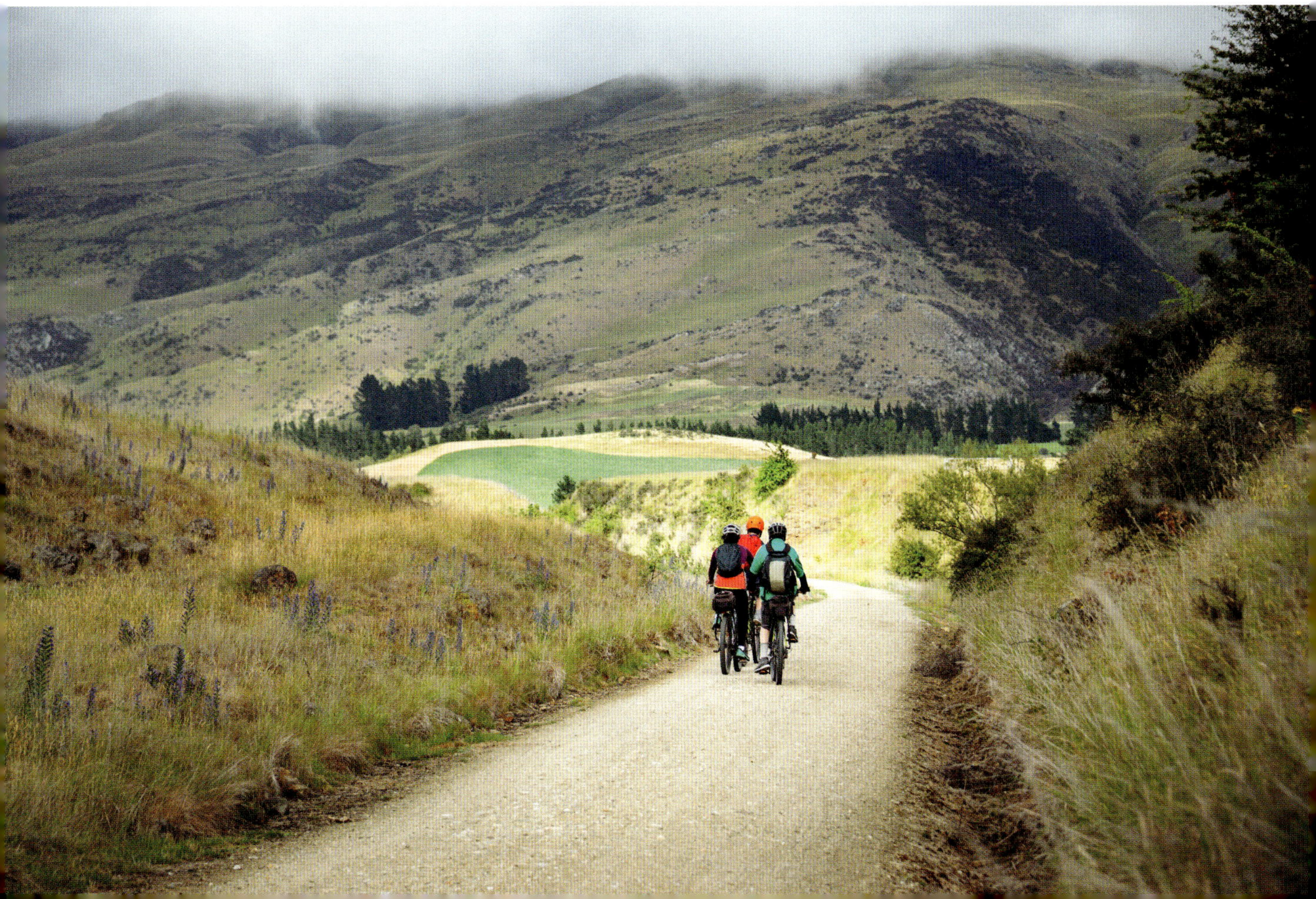

MOUNTAINS TO SEA EXPLORER

With the Mountains to Sea cycle route at its heart, this extended loop explores rivers treasured in Māori culture, two national parks and a bridge to nowhere.

I've often thought Whanganui is an underrated town. Its restored historic buildings, weekend farmers market and thriving arts community all make it a worthwhile place to start a ride. Although New Zealand isn't known for having a long written history, the town and its surroundings have some rich stories to tell, and bikes can sometimes take you to the heart of these tales when other modes of transportation can't.

We caffeinate and fuel up by the riverside, before heading out of town over Durie Hill. This hill features the country's only public transport elevator – for just $2 you can cut 66 vertical metres (216ft) from your ride. If that was an option on all my rides, I suspect I'd be a fair bit poorer. We're soon swooping down into the Whangaehu River valley – a typical snapshot of rural New Zealand, with grass creeping over the edges of the tarmac, more cows than cars on the road, and sparsely dotted farm buildings. The hills undulate gently (and sometimes less gently, I'm looking at you, Burma Hill), with always a little more up than down, taking us from near the coast towards Mount Ruapehu and the volcanic landscapes of the Central Plateau.

Ohakune is the only town on the route, so we stop to get our fill of food and sleep, and check out the novelty-sized root vegetable characters at the Ohakune Carrot Adventure Park (yes, this is a real place). Making an inexplicably enthusiastic detour, we decide to take an unloaded trip up the Ohakune Mountain Rd to tackle New Zealand's only 'hors catégorie' climb. As I ascend more than 1000 metres (3280ft) over 17km (10.5 miles), I have plenty of time to question this decision, but the road is delightfully deserted on a fine summer's day, with sweeping views as far as Mt Taranaki. The swimming holes on the way are a welcome spot to cool off.

Excited to get onto some trails, we head next for the Old Coach Rd, which follows an 1880s route and visits the impressive remains of old railway viaducts. The bone-rattling cobbles at the beginning have no doubt prompted a litany of complaints, but eventually the trail takes a smoother turn, winding through beautiful native forest. Emerging to more mountain views, we reap the rewards of the climb to the Central Plateau. The backroads that follow are largely downhill, touring through some lovely countryside before arriving at the Mangapurua Track.

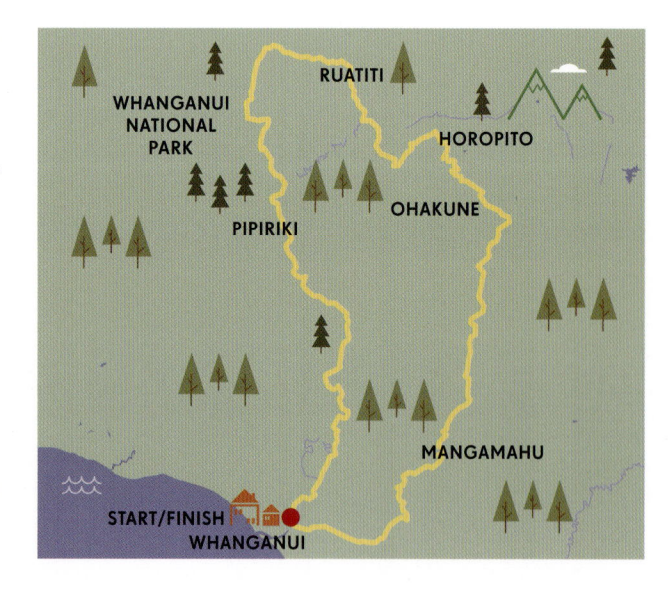

THE NORTH ISLAND, NEW ZEALAND

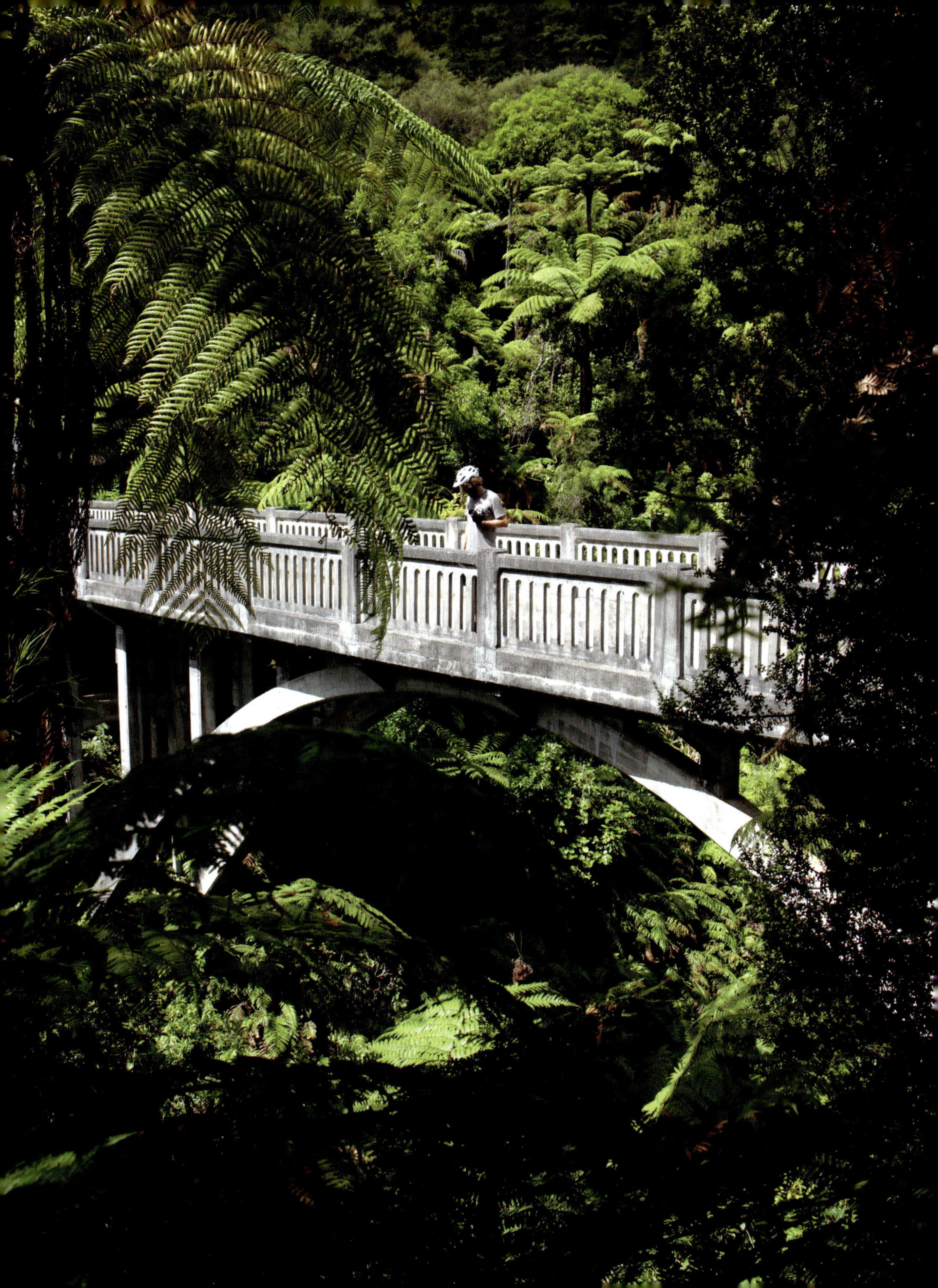

On the fringes of Whanganui National Park, we wind our way up to the summit of the track, taking in views over the forest canopy. A memorial marks this spot, with a glimpse into the lives of the valley's settlers. From 1917, soldiers returning from the First World War were offered parcels of land here by the government, but it would prove to be no easy place to make a life. Despite the modest height of this hill, the terrain is rugged and inhospitable. The settlers battled to clear farmland amid the dense native forest, and at its peak there were around 35 farms and even a school in the Mangapurua Valley. Over the years though, remoteness, difficult access, erosion of the steep land and economic hardship made living here nearly impossible, and eventually most of the settlers were forced to abandon their farms.

From the summit at Mangapurua Trig, the most adventurous stretch of riding begins. The steady descent passes through lush forest and along sheer bluffs. Known as 'papa rock', the soft mudstone of the area is often on the move, and at times the crumbling cliffs expose the trail to dizzying drops to the river below. We catch up to an older man, wrestling the weight of his e-bike through an awkward bridge obstacle. Alarmingly, he seems to be bleeding from every limb, and tells us how he was touring around in his motorhome with his e-bike, tackling many of New Zealand's Great Rides. Though his bike-handling skills may be questionable, he looks unfazed by any injuries – he is having a blast, just like us.

Hints of the past remain all the way along the trail. Humble wooden signs bearing the surnames of settlers mark the old parcels of land, and there are grassy clearings, brick chimneys and exotic trees left behind. But nothing is as jarring as arriving at the Bridge to Nowhere. Its geometric concrete form, with no roads at either end, looks remarkably out of place among the bursts of ponga ferns. Finished in 1936, the bridge was built for vehicle access to the Whanganui River and to link with the riverboat service. But only a few families remained in the valley, and they too would leave in 1942. Following a major storm, despite the recent efforts on the bridge, the government refused to maintain the road.

We arrive at the river's edge, slightly relieved to find our pre-arranged boat waiting for us. Granted, a jet-boat journey feels a like a lavish addition to a bike ride, but how often does one get to strap one's bike aboard, and explore the remote reaches of a beautiful river? The only downside is that this method of travel feels too fast, and I look longingly at the people paddling canoes, pottering around the camps and huts that are only accessible from the water.

LIVING RIVER

The Whanganui River has a long history and significance for Māori pre-dating any European arrival. In 2017, New Zealand passed a ground-breaking law granting the river legal personhood. The law declares that the river is a living whole, incorporating all its physical and metaphysical elements. This was part of a settlement with the Whanganui Iwi, who consider the river to be a living force. In their telling: 'Ko au te awa, ko te awa ko au' (I am the river, and the river is me).

Left to right: the Whanganui River Road; taking the jet-boat downriver; local amenities. Previous spread: the Bridge to Nowhere

At the Whanganui River Road in sleepy Pipiriki, we rejoin the populated world, albeit gently. We jump off the boat and back into the saddle, and after a little pedalling, stop to look at the old convent in Jerusalem. Begun when a young French missionary woman was invited here by the local Māori in 1883, it's still run by the Sisters of Compassion, but the beds are now available for visitors. On seeing it, we can't pass up the opportunity to spend the night. One of the things I relish about bike touring is that the random spots one winds up sleeping can be unique and wonderful, and this counts as both. With mint-green walls, rows of pink single beds, and crocheted hot water bottle covers, it feels like stepping into a place that time forgot, and we spend the evening exploring the building and its artefacts.

Continuing on the peaceful road back to Whanganui, the most notable traffic consists of a family crammed atop a four-wheel motorbike. We notice the river's transformation from the previous day, where wild growth clung to the sheer cliffs framing the dark, narrow, ribbon of water. Gradually, the density of buildings and people increases, the river widens, and as we arrive back where we started, it takes on a wholly different identity, with riverside parks and boardwalks and people out strolling along its banks. **ES**

TOOLKIT

Start/Finish // Whanganui
Distance // 285km (177 miles)
Getting there // Whanganui can be reached by car or bus (2.5 hours from Wellington).
When to go // This ride is best from spring to autumn.
What to pack // Being self-sufficient is recommended, as some areas are remote.
Where to stay // Find accommodation in Ohakune, Ruatiti, Pipiriki, Jerusalem at the old convent, and Whanganui. Campgrounds are in Ohakune, on the Bridge to Nowhere track, and on the Whanganui River Road.
Things to know // The Mangapurua Track is an intermediate grade mountain bike trail. It has steep drop-offs, best walked, and is slippery when wet. The Mountains to Sea route officially begins at the top of the Ohakune Mountain Road – shuttle providers can save you the climb.
More info // www.mountainstosea.nz

Opposite: Lake Ohau on the Hopkins Valley route; autumn in Arrowtown

MORE LIKE THIS
EXPLORING RIVERS

ARROW RIVER BRIDGES TRAIL, SOUTH ISLAND

Part of the Queenstown Trails network, this route connects charming Arrowtown to the vineyard-filled Gibbston Valley. It's an easy-grade, family-friendly cycle trail, traversing fantastic scenery as it follows the Arrow River downstream to where it meets the Kawarau River. Begin at the historic Chinese Settlement at the end of Arrowtown, which was established in the late 1800s gold rush and has been restored to take you back in time to mining days. The tree-lined trail opens up to river and mountain views, crossing the Arrow four times on bridges, including the 80m-long (262ft) Edgar Suspension Bridge looking over Arrow Gorge. It's 13km to the Kawarau Gorge Suspension Bridge, made famous as the world's first commercial bungy jumping operation. Return the same way, or add on the Gibbston River Trail to seek out a winery or the Gibbston Tavern before heading back.
Start/Finish // Arrowtown / Kawarau Bungy Bridge
Distance // 13.7km (8.5 miles)
More info // www.queenstowntrails.org.nz

WAIKATO RIVER TRAILS, NORTH ISLAND

Rambling alongside lakes created by a series of hydro dams, the Waikato River Trails combine five sections, each named after the lake it runs next to. If tackling the whole 103km length, you'll explore flowing trails through native forest, boardwalks wiggling over wetlands, quiet country roads, impressive dams and bridges, volcanic rock outcrops and flourishing birdlife. The small communities dotted along the trail keep you well fed, caffeinated and sheltered. They also provide access points to tackle shorter sections as day rides. The northern Karapiro section is popular for its brilliant river views, wetlands and the 152m Arapuni Suspension Bridge. Between Waipapa Dam and Atiamuri, the trail runs away from the road and mostly follows the river's edge, making this southern stretch particularly peaceful.
Start/Finish // Pokaiwhenua Bridge car park / Ātiamuri Village car park
Distance // 103km (64 miles)
More info // www.waikatorivertrails.co.nz

HOPKINS VALLEY, SOUTH ISLAND

Stretching north from stunning Lake Ohau, the Hopkins Valley is a wildly different flavour of river journey and makes a memorable overnight bikepacking trip. Grassy trails through meadows give way to rougher 4WD tracks criss-crossing the wide, braided riverbed. Wet feet are guaranteed on the way up this spectacular alpine river valley into the foothills of the Southern Alps, but the views make up for it. Choose your own adventure, exploring just the start of the valley, or head all the way up to Erceg Hut, 33km away. You'll pass half a dozen backcountry huts (historic Red Hut is especially photogenic) and endless camping spots to pick from. Though not hilly, this is a bumpy ride best suited to mountain bikes and wider tyres, and some navigation skills will come in handy. Start at the northern end of Lake Ohau Road, which is most easily reached by car.
More info // www.doc.govt.nz

© N. Minton/Shutterstock; Hyunja/Shutterstock

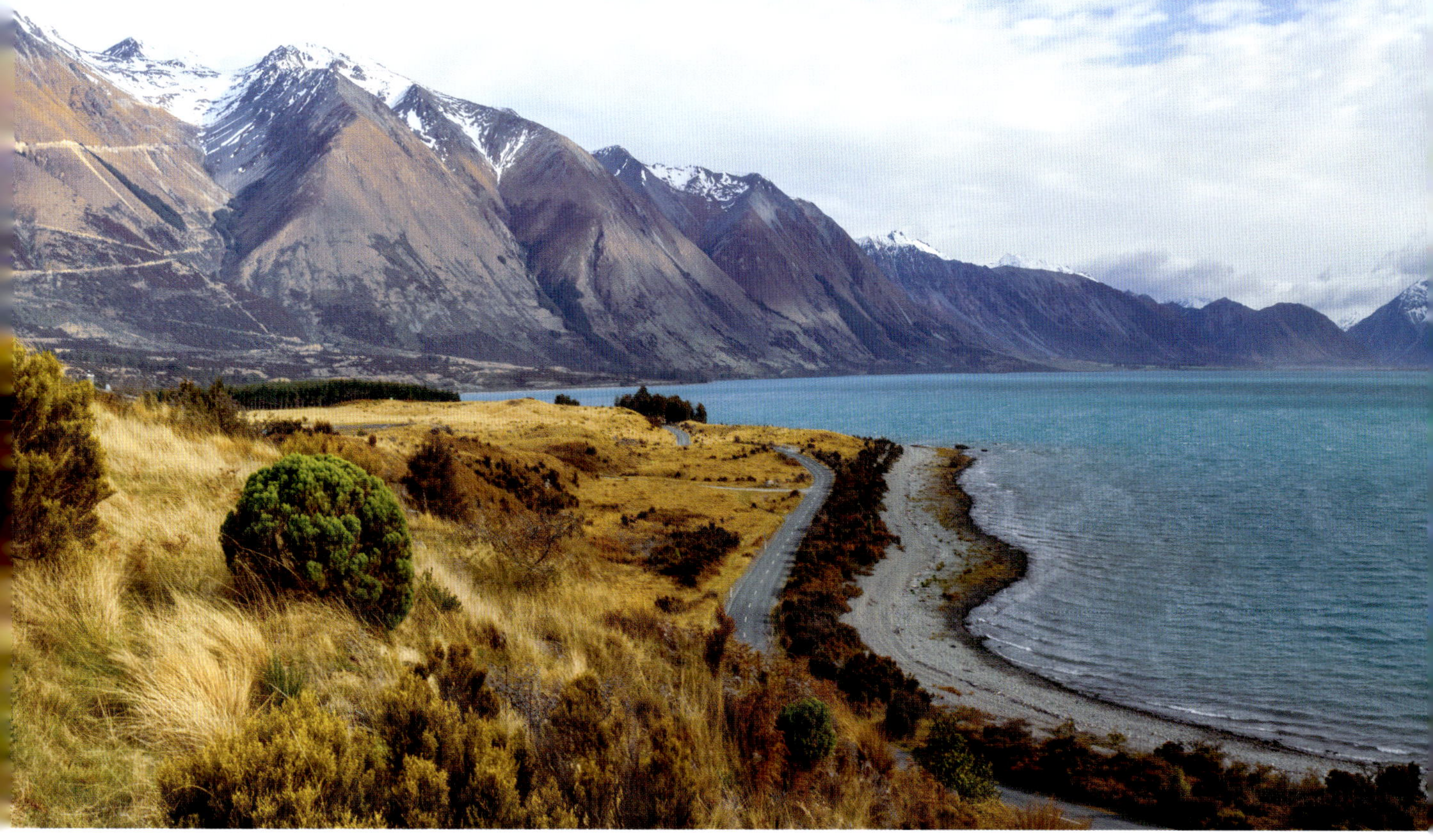

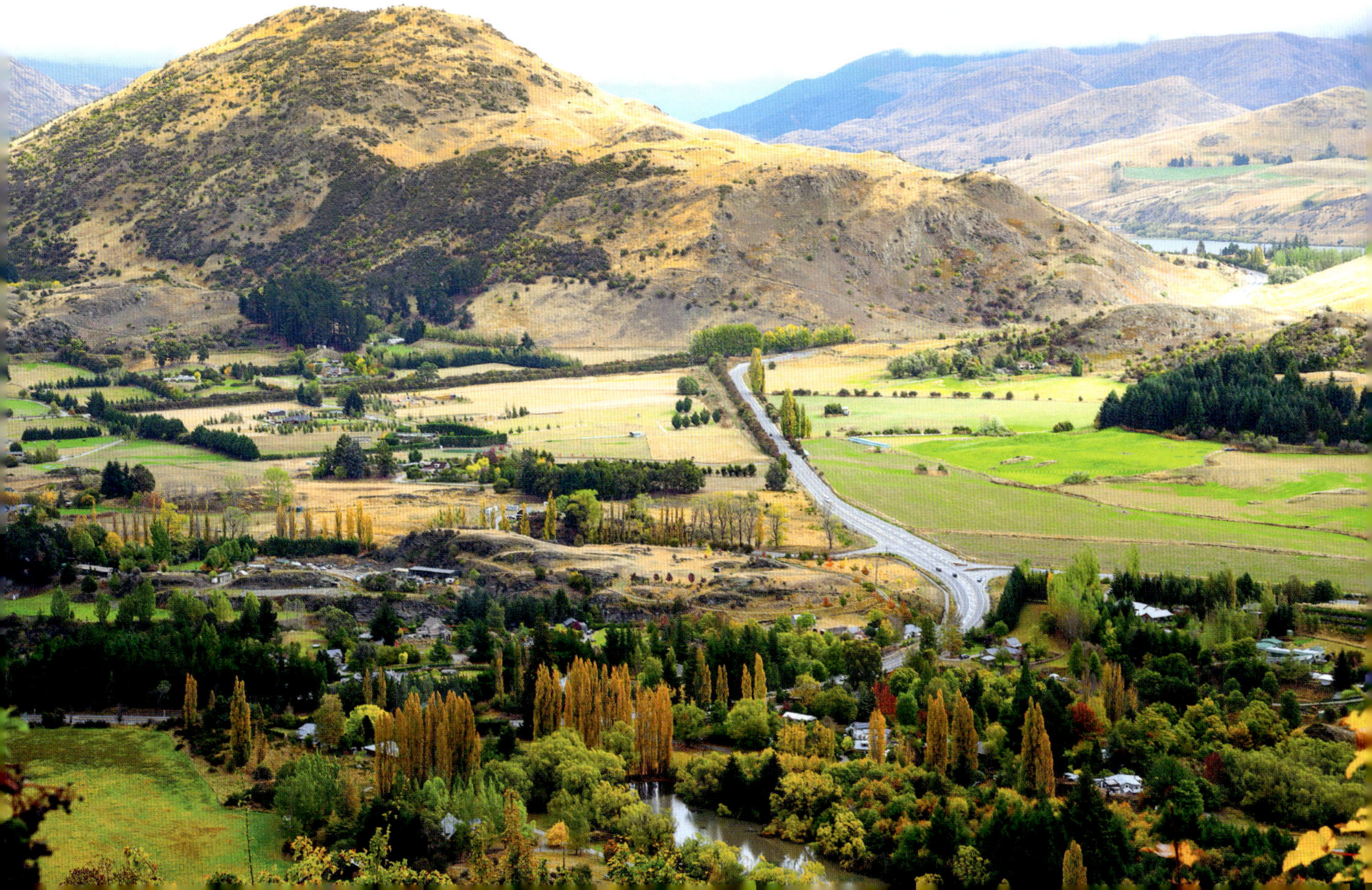

PAKIHI CIRCUIT ON THE MOTU TRAILS

The interplay of weather and land in the northeast of New Zealand's North Island is a reminder of our physical and temporal connections to the world.

A west wind chased us along New Zealand's Pacific Coast Highway at Waiotahe Beach, as the rugged massif of Eastland's Raukūmara Range rose into view. The road led under pohutukawa trees, between coastal escarpment to the right and surf to the left. We rolled into a layby where twin *pouwhenua* (carved posts) mark the gateway to the lands of the Iwi (tribe) Te Whakatōhea. Another 336km would get us around East Cape to Gisborne. For a shorter route we could take our chances with state highway traffic over the Waioeka Gorge, 149 km. But in a case of 'the journey is the destination', we were here for the Motu Trails.

Thanks to the Motu Trails Community Trust, these hinterland tracks are kept open and signposted, with re-supply and accommodation. It's an example of how communities enable and benefit from long-distance cycle touring. The trails' northern hub is the township of Ōpōtiki, population 5350, the capital of Whakatōhea.

Ōpōtiki-mai-Tāwhiti in its full name, is 'the place of the pets from far away'. I feel this loses some force in translation. The Whakatōhea founding ancestor Tarawa brought two domesticated freshwater tānahanaha fish from the far-off homeland of Hawaiki, and released them into a spring near Waiotahe.

What's in a name? Especially in the Māori world, a name is a continuity from past to present. 'In this place are imported domesticated fish'. To me, that says something about the people, their practicality and inventiveness, and readiness to merge new with ancient thinking. Such a mindset was borne out on the arrival of *Pākehā* (European New Zealanders). Whakatōhea

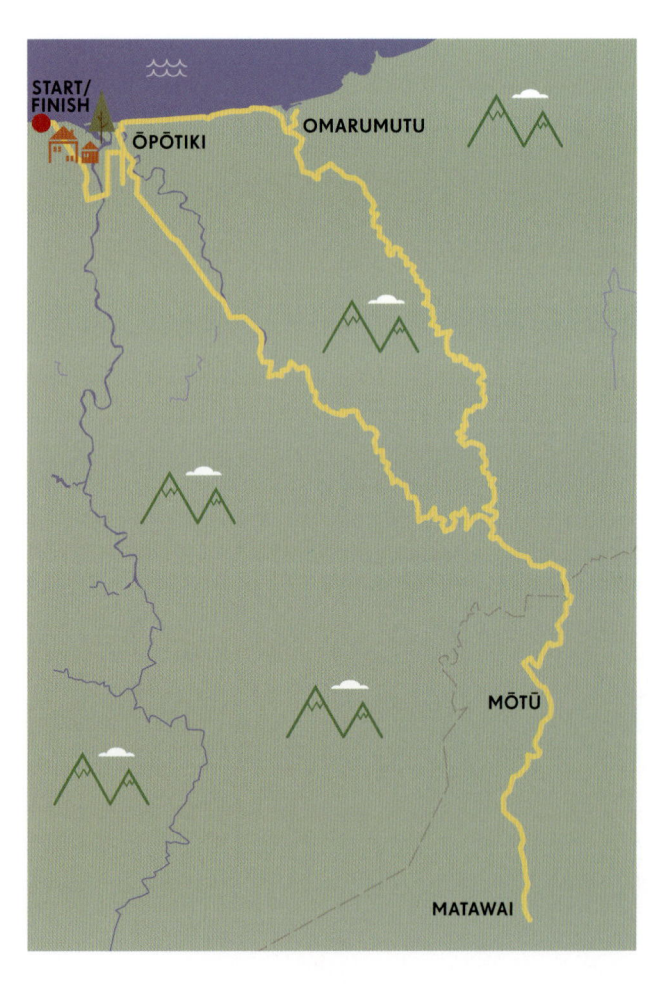

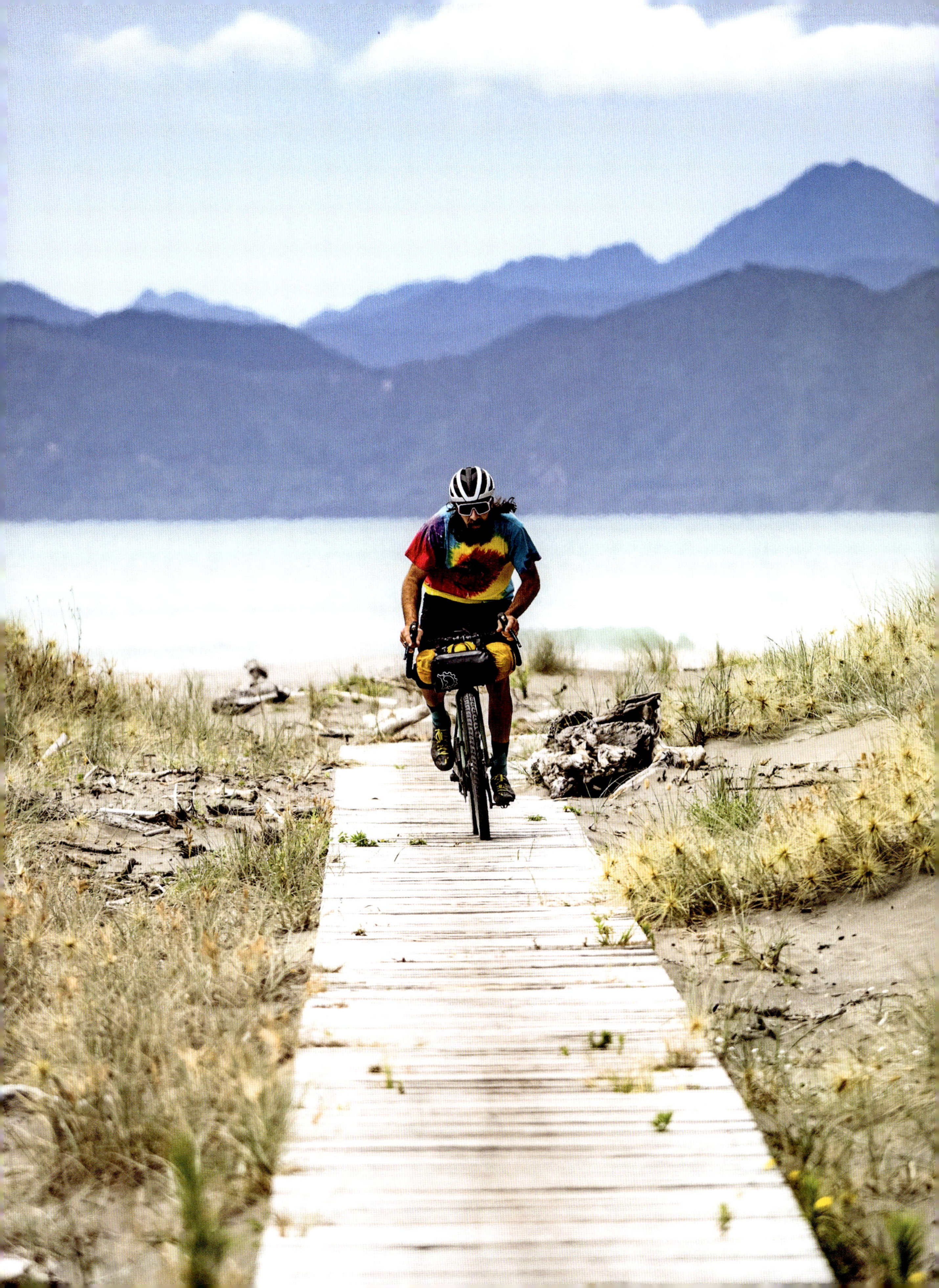

"Rolling down the maunga, the dirt and water become forest and plantation, that in turn become us"

were early economic participants, sending barges of marine and agricultural produce to supply the nascent settlement at Auckland.

The relationship soured after 1865, with the murder in Ōpōtiki of Lutheran missionary Carl Völkner. That in itself was a spill over from British atrocities in the war in Waikato. Although it was not Whakatōhea who killed the reverend, it did not stop the British from reprisal killings of Whakatōhea's *rangatira* (chieftains) and the confiscation and transfer of the most productive land to settlers. Much of the Iwi was internally exiled to a de facto reservation on its northeastern border at Ōpape.

In 1993 the Crown apologised to Whakatōhea, and in 2022 the Iwi accepted a $100 million settlement. A proud example of Iwi economic revival is New Zealand's largest offshore marine farm, growing the green-lipped Perna mussel. Even so, since the bulk of productive lands remain expropriated, any settlement can only be seen as partial.

After re-stocking in Ōpōtiki, we followed the sandy coast eastward on the Dunes Trail. We could find our bearings via the Bay of Plenty's landmark *maunga* (mountains). Behind us to the west was the rounded profile of Moutohorā / Whale Island; 50km (31 miles) out to sea, the active volcanic plume of Whakaari / White Island; and ahead to our right was Mākeo, the distinctively trapezoidal ancestral maunga of Whakatōhea.

In Māori understanding, rivers and mountains are ancestors. Nowadays, many default to DNA as ancestry. But the DNA itself, and the cells and tissues that hold it, have atoms with their own story. Rolling down the maunga, the dirt and water become forest and plantation, that in turn become us.

At Tirohanga we were met by carved pou representing two Whakatōhea *tīpuna* (ancestors), Tamaariki and Ngātorohaka. These are littoral ancestral lands, as the dunes harbour ancient *urupā* (graveyards). It was a sensitive point in trail design, that was resolved with advice from Whakatōhea kaumatua (elders), who ensured the track was routed over safe paths. The corollary is a request to stay on the path.

After leaving the Dunes Trail, we stopped for lunch at the Waiaua crossing, on a flat riparine stretch of the Motu Road under the western side of Mākeo. A lone horse grazed on the berm, as a dairy herd filed up the valley. From 16km (10 miles) on, the road is all about the grunt, winding almost 800m (2625ft) upwards through regenerating native forest. In 1914 it was said

FORAGING ON THE TRAIL

Supplementing your diet with what is found along the way can really add appeal to the outdoors. In late summer and autumn, fruit trees on public verges supply apples, plums and peaches. Wild thyme goes well in a cream sauce with mushrooms, and among new growth at the edges of landslips you may find the reddish-tinged leaves of the NZ pepper tree, horopito. Another traditional staple is pūhā (Sonchus oleraceus) or sow thistle. For a thorough look at this topic you could refer to The Forager's Treasury by Johanna Knox.

Clockwise from top: covering ground on the Motu Road; campfire cookery at Whitikau Forks campsite; a shelter near the end of the trail at Waiwhero. Previous spread: riding the Dunes Trail

to be 'the most dangerous trip in New Zealand', but today's mountain bike is surely more nimble than a Model T or even a Toyota Hilux.

Along the way we passed more than one bus or truck that did not make it, and was left to rust and lichen. Who knows where its metals will go – magnesium into chlorophyll and iron into hemes. Maybe there's some bus or bicycle in my own ancestry. There's almost certainly some plough and stirrup. At the top of Meremere Hill, the bush cleared and we stopped for a snack. A herd of beefstock spotted us on the skyline and started to head our way. Alas we were the wrong humans, the ones not bringing silage.

Pakihi Track was the payoff, an exhilarating downhill plunge, kept rideable only by the diligent work of the Motu Trails Trust. Riders should either keep right or bring a parachute, some of those slips yawn into nothingness. At the foot of the hill we stayed at the Department of Conservation's Pakihi Hut, wedged in its defile. Come sunset, two deer traversed the opposing valley wall, just 50m (164ft) away. I supplemented my dinner with plantain leaves foraged from the campsite lawn.

The final run took us along Pakihi Stream, with its clear pools and periodic rockslides. Here I chased a goat along the track for a couple of kilometres. On the ground were nectar-rich rewarewa flowers, with their striking red spikes. Overhead, tūī flitted from tree to tree. We returned along country roads to the capital.

What to take from this circuit? History does not repeat, so much as it comes back to correct itself. Recycling and correction is built into the world, from hydrological cycles, via carbon and metal cycles, down to bicycle cycles. Empires come and go and are consumed and something new grows from the wreckage. How to chase the infinite when our timeline is so short? You could do worse than go in a circle. Tēnā tātou katoa, greetings to us all. **GL**

TOOLKIT

Start / Finish // Ōpōtiki (Bay of Plenty) / Gisborne (Tairāwhiti)

Distance // 174km (108 miles)

Getting there // There are scheduled flights to Gisborne and Whakatāne. Bus operator Intercity is hit and miss in terms of readiness to take bicycles.

When to go // The most settled weather is usually in February and March. Torrential rain is possible at any time.

What to take // Sunscreen, sunglasses, and insect repellant are a priority. Apart from that, consider camping gear, cooking gear and food, bicycle maintenance gear, a first aid kit, and electronics including GPS and a PLB.

Where to stay and where to eat // The official Motu Trails website keeps a current list of affiliated providers, including the Weka Nest in Motu, and Mokonui Farmstay at Rere Falls. There are supermarkets at Ōpōtiki and Gisborne, and a small store at Matawai. Bush tucker possibilities (with appropriate permits) include deer, goats, pigs, trout, and foraged greens.

Things to know // Although the loop from Ōpōtiki has been done on road bikes, 2" tires better manage the sand, gravel, and mud. The Rere Falls Trail is mostly sealed road. The biggest thing that might try to eat you is a mosquito, or a logging truck on the stretch of State Hwy 2 at Matawai.

More info // www.motutrails.co.nz

Opposite: Te Rerenga Wairua, where two oceans collide; Rere Falls near Gisborne

MORE LIKE THIS
ANCESTRAL TRAILS

RERE FALLS TRAIL, NORTH ISLAND

If you don't go down the Pakihi, but instead continue from Motu to Matawai, the onwards path is the Rere Falls Trail (pronounced 'Rreh-Rreh'). You soon meet the phenomenal 7m (23ft) painted steel pou that is Hinetapuarau, the ancestral mother of Whakatōhea's southeastern neighbours, Te Aitanga a Māhaki. Rere Falls Trail is a backroad route to Gisborne (population 37,700), the largest East Coast settlement north of Napier. A main attraction is the Rere Rockslide, a natural rock waterslide. Sadly, European livestock farming has rendered the water hazardous to consumption. Although that does not stop people having a lot of fun, the fun might not be consequence-free. A short distance downstream, Rere Falls spill neatly over a ledge like the doorstep of some tidy giant.
Start // Matawai
Finish // Gisborne
Distance // 100km (62 miles)

TE RERENGA WAIRUA, NORTH ISLAND

If you're thinking about where you've come from and where you're going, you should visit Te Rerenga Wairua, the leaping-off place of spirits at Cape Reinga at the extreme north end of the North Island. It's the starting point for the Tour Aotearoa cycle journey. In Māori tradition it is also the gateway to Rarohenga, the underworld, where those who die are called back by their ancestors. The two available routes are via State Highway 1, or via te Oneroa-a-Tōhē (the Long Beach of Tohe, 90 Mile Beach, actually only 90km). You can spend the night at the DoC campsite at Tāpotupotu Bay. There is limited shopping after Te Kao. Do bring insect repellent and long sleeves, to protect against the vigorous local mosquitoes.
Start // Ahipara
Finish // Cape Reinga
Distance // 100km (62 miles)

ALICE SPRINGS, AUSTRALIA

Under big skies, the red desert around Alice Springs opens up to mountain bikers, thanks to 200km (125 miles) of singletrack. The trails are rideable from the centre of town, with networks on either side of the Stuart Highway. Cyclists can also use sections of the Simpsons Gap bike path and the Larapinta Trail, which passes through Arrernte country – Indigenous guides can share some of the dreamtime stories of the land. Discover more Indigenous history in Uluru-Kata Tjuta National Park, including rock art (you can also rent a bike from the cultural centre to ride around the base of Uluru). Winter is the best time to ride here when the temperatures are mild(er). The Redback mountain bike stage race, based out of Alice Springs, is held every August.
Start/Finish // Alice Springs
More info // nt.gov.au; redback.rapidascent.com.au

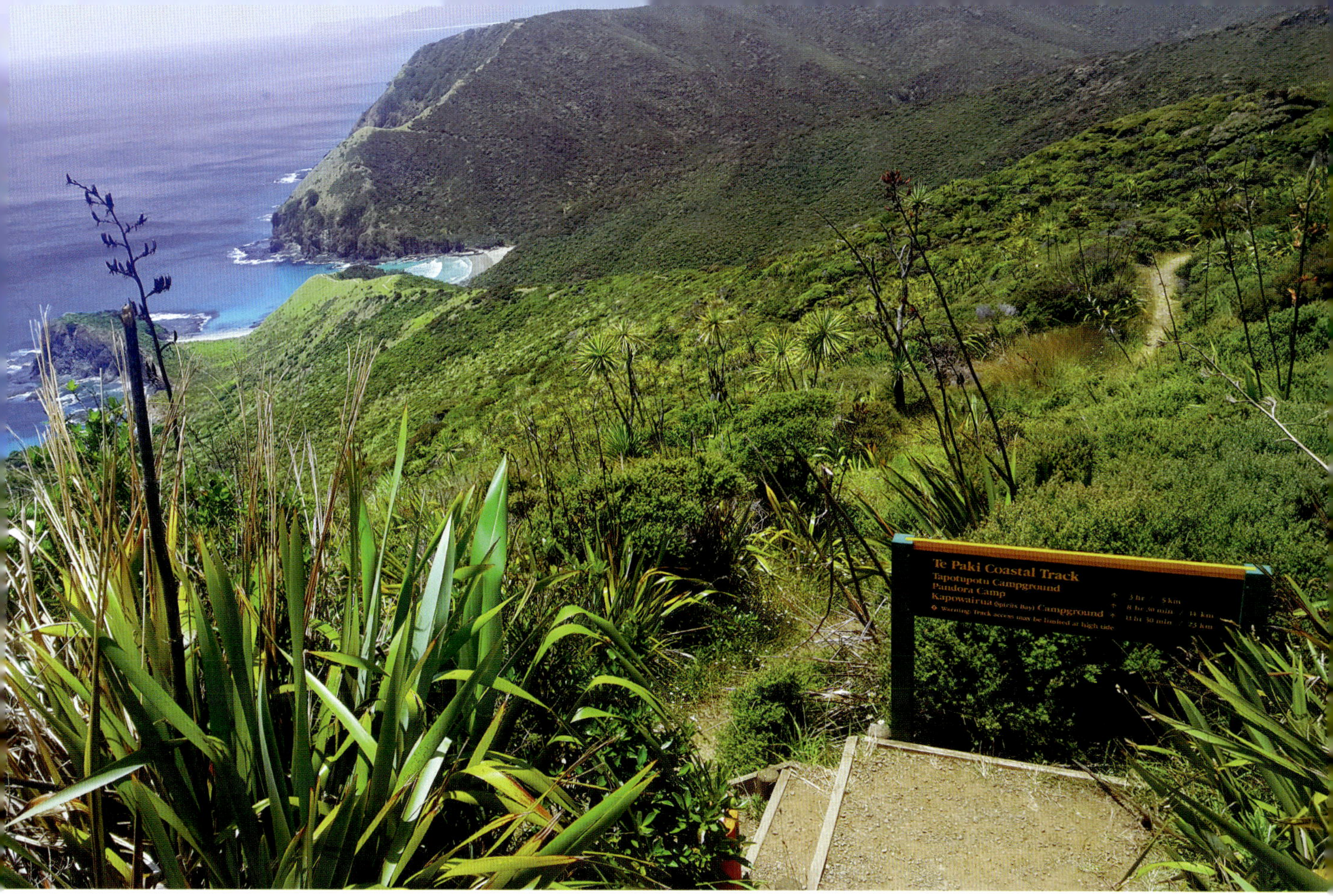
Te Paki Coastal Track
Tapotupotu Campground
Pandora Camp

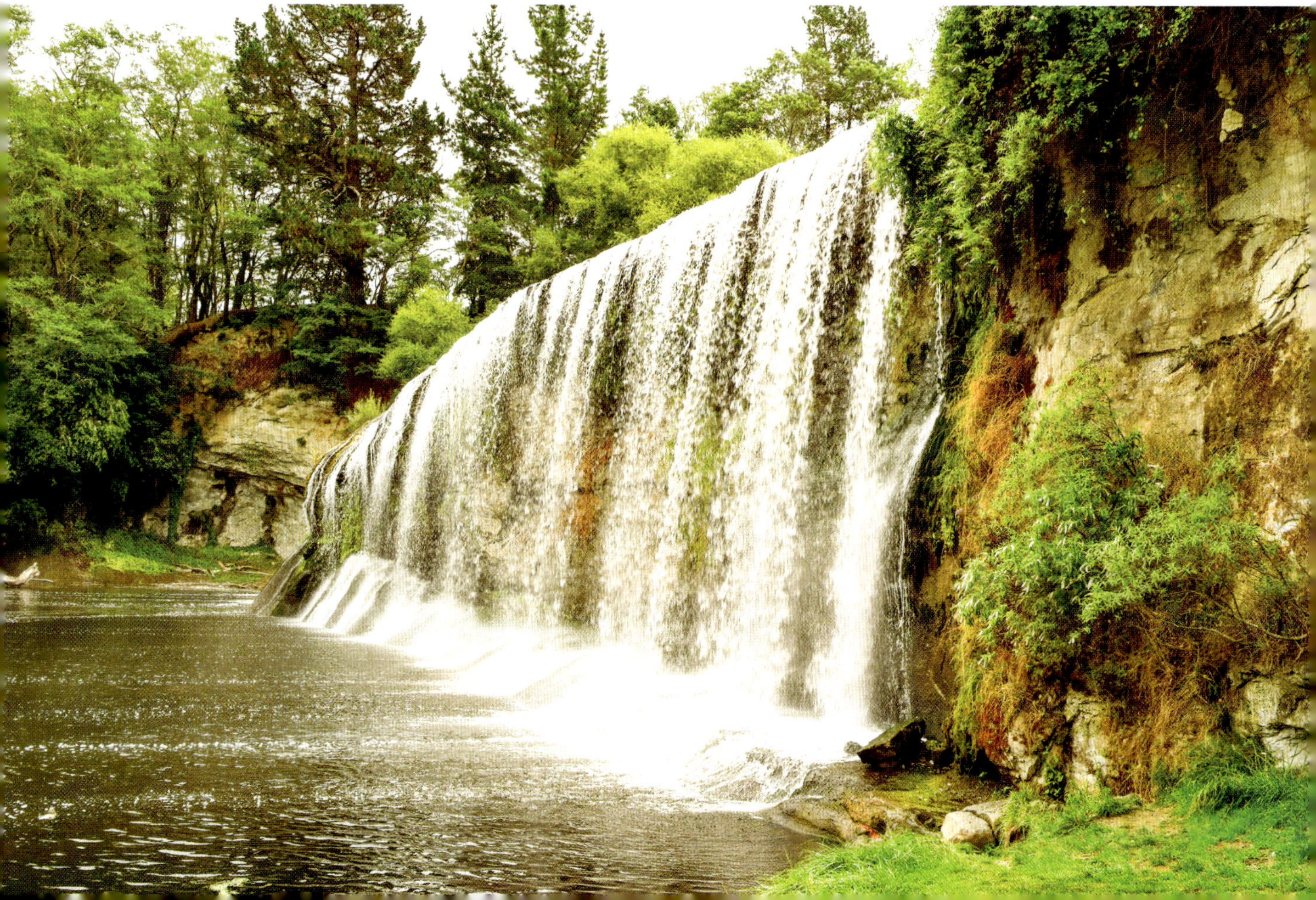

WHAKAREWAREWA FOREST LOOP

Redwood trees, blue lakes and hot pools: this loop of Rotorua's forest is a fun and family-friendly day out in a place packed with bike trails.

Always read the instructions. In my eagerness to get out on the Whakarewarewa Forest Loop, the freshest of New Zealand's Ngā Haerenga Great Rides, I zoomed off in the reverse direction – it's a one-way trail – and then kept on going and going. Just before reaching Lake Tarawera, I realised my error, but it was too late: Whakarewarewa would have to wait another day.

But it was worth the wait. Opening in 2021, this trail was built during the covid pandemic and circles the perimeter of Whakarewarewa Forest, just south of Rotorua. Inside the loop are some 200km (125 miles) of mountain biking trails that started in secret in this working forest many years ago but are now officially sanctioned and certainly among the very best in the country. The Forest Loop is slightly different: it's a circuit that takes some existing trails and connects them to create a longer, more laidback route suitable for families and novices. And because it visits each part of the whole park, riders will experience some of the beautiful lake scenery and the surprising forest of redwood trees.

Yes, there's a grove of giant redwood trees in Whakarewarewa, a little corner of northern California in New Zealand. They were planted in the early 20th century when foresters were figuring out which trees were the most suitable for commercial use in New Zealand. As it happened, redwoods didn't work out and the foresters decided on radiata pine (also known as the Monterey pine), which matures in a mere 20 years and explains why large tracts of New Zealand are now sterile pine plantations.

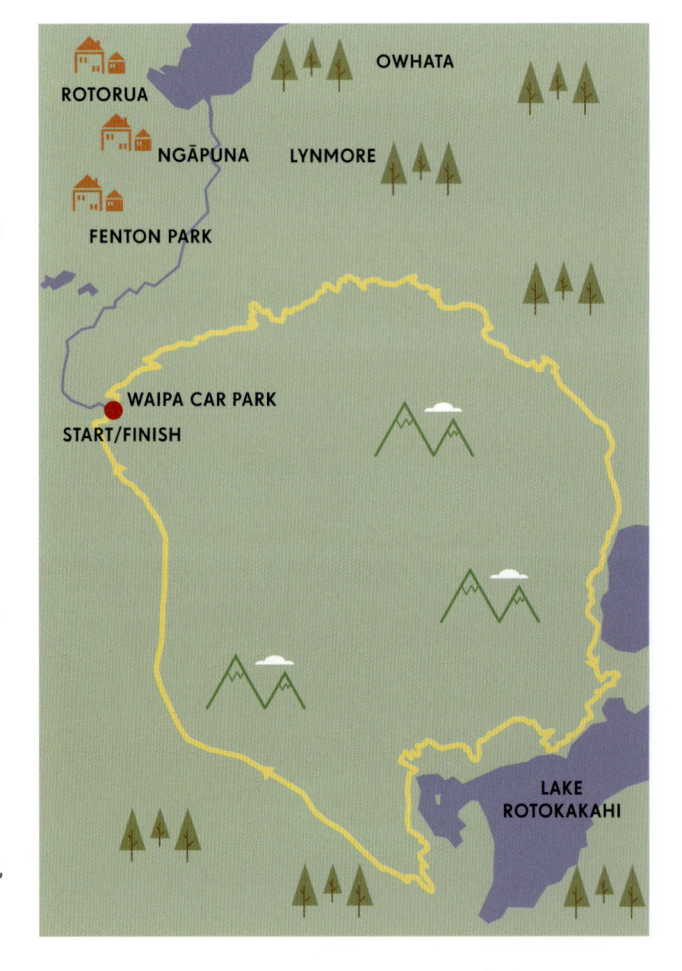

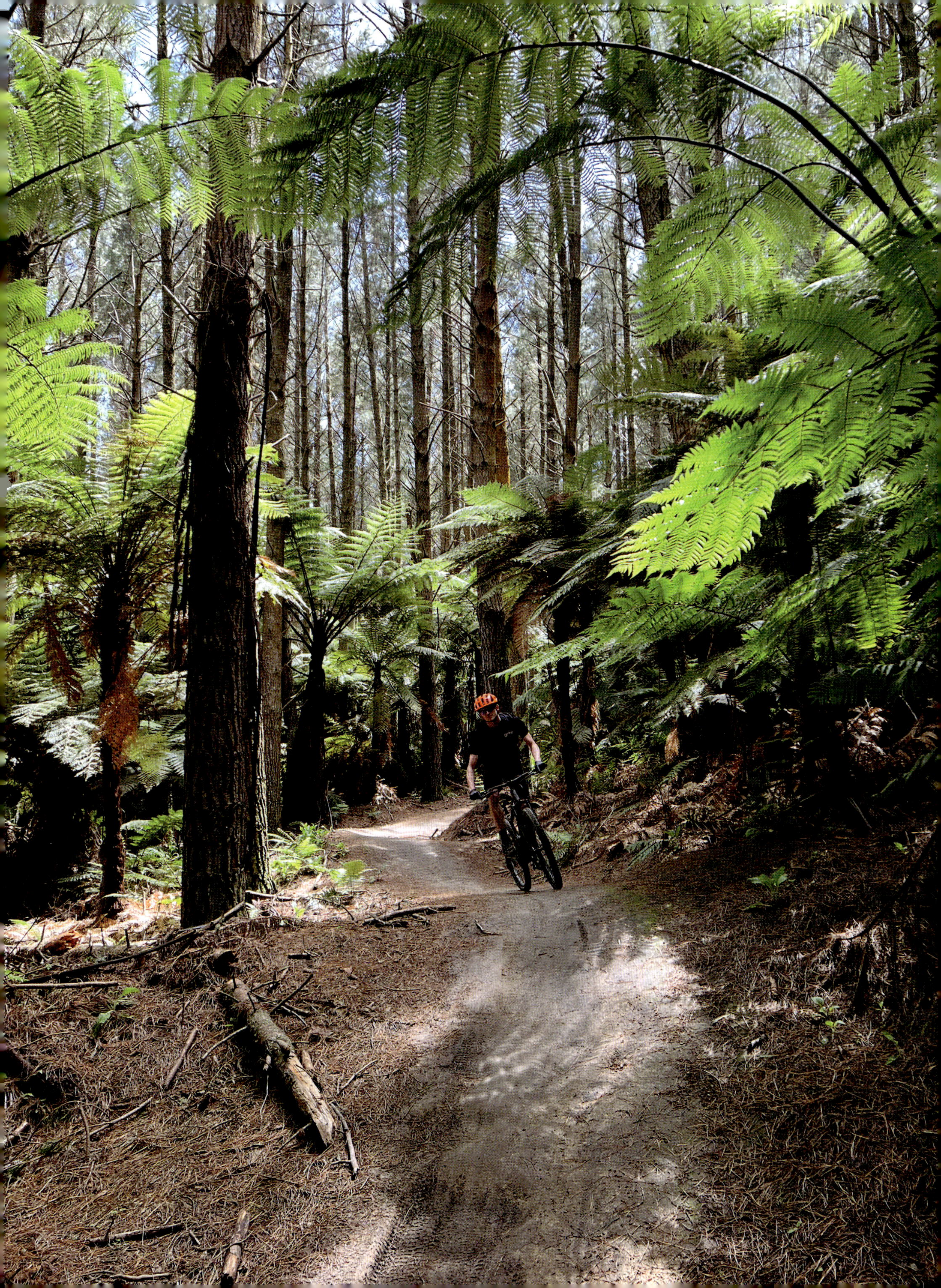

First impressions of Whakarewarewa (pronounced: fa-kuh-ree-wuh-ree-wuh) are fantastic. The outdoor area behind the large bike shop and cafe is thronged with people, aged from six years to 60. A group of silver-haired female riders, kitted out with elbow and knee pads, rolled up after shredding the mountain bike trails. Beneath an awning, riders received some free maintenance checks and tweaks to their bikes.

The entrance to the forest loop is opposite and I pedalled into the trees. The first section climbs up through a redwood grove on a path springy with fallen needles. The trees are well spaced with a high canopy, giving a wonderful sense of space and serenity. At the top, the surroundings switched to a logged landscape, through which the trail twisted. Down the hill to the left is an area of large eucalyptus trees, with a skills park and multi-use trails for families. But I continued ascending along the Forest Loop towards Lake Tikitapu, or Blue Lake. Large punga ferns signalled that the ground was getting wetter and the dirt track provided the perfect level of grip – because this is a one-way route, it's possible to let the brakes off with confidence.

The ferns are also known as silver ferns, due to the silver underside to their fronds. Back in the day, the leaders of Māori war parties would pick leaves at intervals and leave them silver side up on the trail in order to show the rest of

"I was still surprised to see a wallaby hop across the trail in front of me (like the redwoods and the pines, also not native)"

the group the right direction when travelling at night. The last warrior in the party would then turn over the fern leaf, hiding the silver from the moonlight and their passage.

Soon I arrived at the first of the two lakes on the Forest Loop. Tikitapu is named after the greenstone necklace the daughter of a Māori chief lost in the lake. No word as to whether it was eventually recovered. This lake is open to the public and particularly popular for swimming, fishing, boating and barbecuing with mates and some beers. Consequently, the trail gets a bit more crowded here, so ride responsibly.

The next lake is Rotokākahi, or Green Lake, which is privately owned by the local Māori *Iwi* (tribe). An island in the lake is the burial place of many Māori ancestors and therefore *tapu*, or sacred. But, hugging the edge of the forest, with views of the lake over my shoulder, this is the prettiest stretch of the route and the furthest point from the start. It's quiet, with no other people around, but I was still surprised to see a wallaby hop across the trail in front of me

MĀORI ROTORUA

Rotorua has some of the richest and most accessible Māori culture in New Zealand. It's thought that the region was first settled in the 14th century and there's plenty of history to read up on, including New Zealand's 19th-century Land Wars between colonists and Māori. Once the conflicts had subsided, Rotorua quickly developed into a geothermal spa town. But at cultural centres like Te Puia you can meet Māori, ask about local stories and enjoy traditional dishes.

Left to right: looking over Rotorua; shuttles take riders to the top of the mountain bike trails; there's a variety of forest activities; take a break by the lake. Previous spread: riding the Whaki trail

(like the redwoods and the pines, also not native). Savour this section along the lakes: stop, take a dip in Tikitapu, have some food.

The final stretch is less interesting. The route turns right onto a surfaced bike path that runs beside the highway to Napier. But at least it's all downhill so the next 8km (five miles) flies by and I soon arrived back at the Waipa hub, just two hours after setting off but feeling invigorated and ready for my next adventure.

Having enjoyed a great introduction to Whakarewarewa, it seemed essential to explore some of the mountain bike trails in the heart of the forest. Shuttle driver Brian dropped me at the top of the hill to ride the Eagle vs Shark trail. He took up mountain biking after his knees gave out at the age of 60. He's now 80 and rides an e-bike. It must be all the hot springs here. Eagle vs Shark, then Whaki, Te Poaka and finally the long run of Split Enz into Rollercoaster and then Moonshine are all very engaging trails, with sweeping banked turns under a canopy of giant ferns.

The whole forest is owned by Māori groups, Brian explained, and although logging still takes place, the owners are very aware of the responsibility to pass such a mountain biking treasure to the next generation. And after a long day on the bike, I've earned a soak in some of Rotorua's sulphurous springs.

TOOLKIT

Start/Finish // Waipa car park
Distance // 33km (20 miles)
Getting there // Rōtorua is centrally located in the North Island with easy access by road from Auckland in around 3hrs. There's a bus service that may accept boxed or dismantled bikes (carriage not guaranteed). It's possible to pick up the trail from the south side of town or park in the Waipa car park off Waipa State Mill Rd.
When to ride // The trails are open all year and the trails are quite sheltered from sun or rain.
Where to stay // The Rydges hotel on Tryon St (www.rydges.com) has secure bike storage and is on the edge of the forest and a short ride from the start.
What to take // A map of the trail and maybe a GPX file loaded on your phone will be enough. You can ride the trail on either a gravel or mountain bike.
More info // www.rotoruanz.com

Opposite: riding the Glendhu Bay track along Lake Wanaka

MORE LIKE THIS
KIWI MOUNTAIN BIKE TOWNS

WELLINGTON, NORTH ISLAND

The Kiwi capital's low-key charm continues with its affinity for mountain bikers, who don't mind contending with steep hills, strong winds and sideways rain (sometimes). Right in the heart of the city, Victoria Peak has several tricky trails. Take a breather to view the streets below. Also in the centre, the Waimapihi Reserve offers a long climb on the Transient trail and a sinuous descent on Ikigai. Just east of the city, Makara Peak Mountain Bike Park is Wellington's main mountain biking attraction, with more than 40km (25 miles) singletrack, much of it beginner-friendly. Longer loops in the park, from 8km (five miles) or more, piece together some of the popular trails. There are more trails across the water at the Wainuiomata Mountain Bike Park, set up by a local non-profit. From here you can also embark on much longer bikepacking rides around the Wainuiomata coast.
More info // www.wellington.govt.nz

NELSON, SOUTH ISLAND

Just across Cook Strait, at the top of the South Island, Nelson is a hotbed of mountain bike action and also one of the sunniest spots in New Zealand. Not only is it a convenient gateway for the Heaphy Track and the Old Ghost Road, both longer trails that can be linked together, but there are several excellent mountain bike parks in the area. Perhaps the most storied is Wairoa Gorge, which came into existence as the private playground of American billionaire Ken Dart (heir to a foam cup fortune). He commissioned some very challenging trails in 'the Gorge' but later opened up access to local mountain bikers and then gifted a long-term lease of the land to New Zealand's Department of Conservation. Even closer to town are the Codgers Trails, created in partnership between Nelson City Council and Nelson Mountain Bike Club.
More info // www.nelsonmtb.club

WANAKA, SOUTH ISLAND

Set on a sublime lake deep in the South Island, Wanaka is a low-key alternative to Queenstown's bright lights. Several riding spots are within reach of the town. First, Sticky Forest, with around 20 trails for intermediate riders through a pine plantation. Then there's the 11km (seven-mile) Deans Bank Track, packed with berms and jumps, to the north of Wanaka. Finally, Cardrona ski resort opens its lifts to mountain bikes for the summer months, providing access to more than 20 downhill tracks, ranging from easy-going greens such as Sweet As to black runs like Mile High Club. Bike rentals, lift passes and shuttles from Wanaka and Queenstown are available.
More info // www.lakewanaka.co.nz

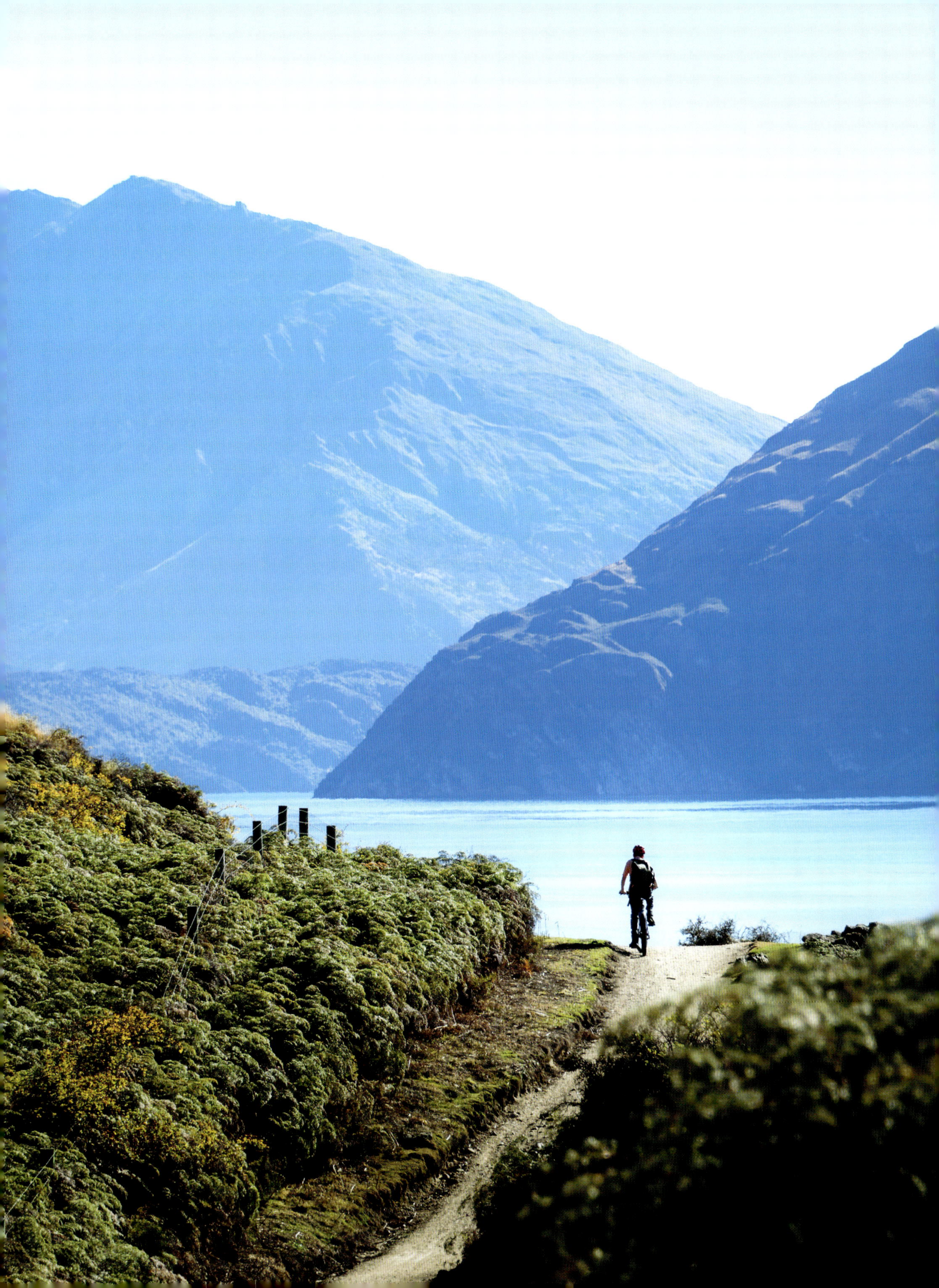

- EPIC BIKE RIDES OF AUSTRALIA & NEW ZEALAND -

REMUTAKA
CYCLE TRAIL LOOP

Escape Wellington for a two- or three-day ride along the Wild Coast and over the Remutaka Range via a rail trail on this simple but enjoyable route.

Wellington is one of the world's more diminutive capital cities, with a population one tenth that of Paris or Havana and just one eighth the size of its big sibling Auckland at the other end of the North Island. But what it lacks in size it makes up for with personality. Its Parliament (the first to give the vote to women) sits in a quirky Brutalist building called the Beehive. There are as many cafes per head of population as New York, almost certainly serving better coffee. And Wellington, rather than Chicago, is arguably the windiest city in the world, thanks to its position on the north side of the Cook Strait, which funnels the oceanic winds known as the Roaring Forties through a narrow channel.

That last fact explains why I averaged over 35km/h (22mph) on the road down from the neighbourhood of Wainuiomata to the mouth of the Orongorongo River. I had just started a 145km (90-mile) loop of the Remutaka Cycle Trail so it was good to make time.

If you stand on Wellington's waterfront and look east, the Remutaka Cycle Trail loops around the broad peninsula of land opposite. It's named for the Remutaka Range of mountains along its spine. To the north, at the top of the loop, the route uses the popular Remutaka Rail Trail to cross the Range. And to the south, along the bottom of the loop, it follows the windswept Wild Coast. I'd set off from Wainuiomata, a town just beyond Lower Hutt, a city-suburb of Wellington. You can start from the city itself but it means following a roadside bike path up to the Hutt River mouth for about 16km (10 miles).

Flying down the quiet road to the Wild Coast, on what is known as the Wainuiomata Connector cycle route, it was exciting to be a short ferry ride from a capital city and heading into its rugged backyard. When I arrived at the Orongorongo River carpark, there were just a couple of utes parked up, overlooking a beach of shingle and driftwood. The air had that refreshing energy you only find at the edge of an ocean. Signposts pointed me toward a gate, beyond which there was a rough doubletrack through a boulder field. And on the gate was a temporary sign, notifying people that the way along the coast may be impassable due to landslips. Still, nothing ventured.

By chance, I met a solo bikepacker was coming the other way soon after passing the gate. She reassured me that the trail was passable, if exhausting. But this was a glorious stretch of the loop, covering more than 20km (13 miles) and crunching through sand, shingle and rocks on my gravel bike. A mountain bike would have been more suitable but I'd have still had to walk the washed-out sections of the path at the foot of the hills and parts of the Kotumu Stream Shingle Fan. There was one fast-flowing river crossing where I spent half an hour scoping out the most shallow part only to slip over and get wet anyway.

WAIRARAPA WINE

Many bikepackers will spend a couple of nights somewhere along the Remutaka Cycle Trail. Staying down by the beach is a good option but you could also extend the route a little and ride up the east side of Lake Wairarapa and overnight in the pretty town Martinborough, the heart of the Wairarapa wine region and source of some fine pinot noir and sauvignon blanc. You'd then have to swing over the top of the lake and rejoin the Remutaka Rail Trail south of Featherston.

Clockwise from top: the Wild Coast lives up to its name; you may need to push your bike in places; you'll probably have the place to yourself. Previous spread: climbing into the Remutaka range; descending the rail trail to Upper Hutt

Eventually, however, I made it back to a semi-civilisation at Ocean Beach, a ramshackle collection of bachs backed by sand dunes and blasted by the elements. There's a campground at Corner Creek and other accommodation, if you're travelling at a sensible pace. And it would be a fantastic view to wake up to. But I had to press on and turned inland towards Lake Wairarapa.

The good news about this next stage of the loop, up the east side of the oblong, is that it was on a tarmac road. But the bad news was a headwind that made me work for each metre. Since the road was straight, there was no escape from the wind on my way towards Featherston. I recovered with a peanut butter-and-jelly sandwich before reaching the turn-off to the left that I'd been waiting for. This was the junction of Western Lake Rd with Cross Creek Rd that heralded the start of the Remutaka Rail Trail.

Back in 1878, the Remutaka Railway from Wellington was extended to Featherston, which meant building one of the world's steepest rail lines. It was one of just a handful of 'Fell' railways in the world, named after designer John Barraclough Fell (you can learn more at the Fell Locomotive Museum in Featherston). The Remutaka Railway snaked up to the summit of the Range via more than 60 cuttings and embankments, crossed several precarious bridges and chugged through a 221-metre (725ft) tunnel. Since 1987, cyclists have been able to follow the 18km (11-mile) rail trail past the Kaitoke Regional Park, which was used as the set for Rivendell in Peter Jackson's *Lord of the Rings* films.

I plodded up to the summit of the Remutaka Rail Trail, where old railway sheds still stand, and then descended through beautiful scenery toward Te Mārua and Upper Hutt. Here I picked up the Hutt River Trail, keeping to the east bank of the river, which I followed all the way to Petone. The end was in sight with just one obstacle remaining: Wainuiomata Hill. If you've pedalled 130km (80 miles) along beaches and over mountain ranges, it's not a welcome finale but the view from the top of Wellington was generous reward. The entire loop was a great ride, with very little traffic and some soul-stirring scenery along the Wild Coast. But you definitely don't have to do it in a day.

TOOLKIT

Start/Finish // Lower Hutt (or Wellington or anywhere else along the loop)

Distance // 145km (90 miles)

Where to stay // Riders pass by several suitable spots for overnight stops, at Ocean Beach, Petone, Wainuiomata and Upper Hutt, where there's a Kiwi Holiday Park.

What to take // Sections of the route are quite remote so be prepared with tools and spares. But you're not usually far from a shop with snacks. A gravel bike is a good compromise but you won't enjoy the Wild Coast on fragile tyres.

When to ride // Wellington experiences strong winds so winter weather is best avoided. November to March is ideal and check the forecast before setting off.

More info // The route is one of New Zealand's 23 Great Rides (www.nzcycletrail.com) and is also featured in the Kennett brothers' Bikepacking Aotearoa book (www.kennett.co.nz).

Opposite: Nugget Point on the Catlins coast; Otaki Beach on Wellington's Kapiti coast

MORE LIKE THIS
COASTAL ESCAPES

KĀPITI COAST CYCLE ROUTE, NORTH ISLAND

On the Wellington region's west coast, known as the Kāpiti Coast, cycling and walking paths connect the communities of Paekākāriki and Peka Peka via a series of sandy beaches. It's a relaxed region to explore by bicycle, with the main attraction being this easy-going 25km (15 miles) route along cycleways, with several coffeeshops for pitstops. But there are several short mountain bike trails in the steep hills behind the coast if you're looking for a more vigorous workout. The Kāpiti coast can be reached by train from Wellington in just over an hour and is also on the Northern Explorer scenic railway line from Auckland to Wellington, which stops at Paraparaumu (check the latest bicycle policy).
More info // www.kapiticoastnz.com/explore/walk-cycle-ride/trails/

CATLINS COAST, SOUTH ISLAND

The relentless wind has sculpted trees along this Antarctic-facing shore of the South Island into streamlined shapes so you'd best hope that it's at your back. This is the wild south edge of New Zealand, where yellow-eyed penguins and fur seals share space on beaches untroubled by sun umbrellas. It's a great place for cycling adventure with few roads but little traffic. Following the coastline from Invercargill to Balclutha, along some of the Southern Scenic Route, is a ride of around 180km (112 miles) that takes in such highlights as Nugget Point, Cathedral Caves and Curio Bay. The Kennett brothers have mapped a long route in their books or the local tourism offices have maps of shorter day rides.
More info // www.catlins.org.nz

NORTH WEST COASTAL PATHWAY, TASMANIA

This is a work in progress that will hopefully come to fruition in the near future: it's a 110km (68-mile) traffic-free route along Tasmania's northwest coastline from Latrobe towards Wynyard. Sections currently exist intermittently, such as parts of the 33km (20 miles) between Devonport and Penguin, but more financial support is required to finish the job (see Bicycle Network's funding campaign). The rewards will be a safe and visitor-friendly way of exploring this less-frequented corner of Tasmania, pedalling through flat, bucolic farming land and laidback beach-side towns. Check out the fairy penguins on Burnie's main beach. Devonport makes for a great base, being the port for the ferry from Melbourne.
More info // www.cradlecoast.com

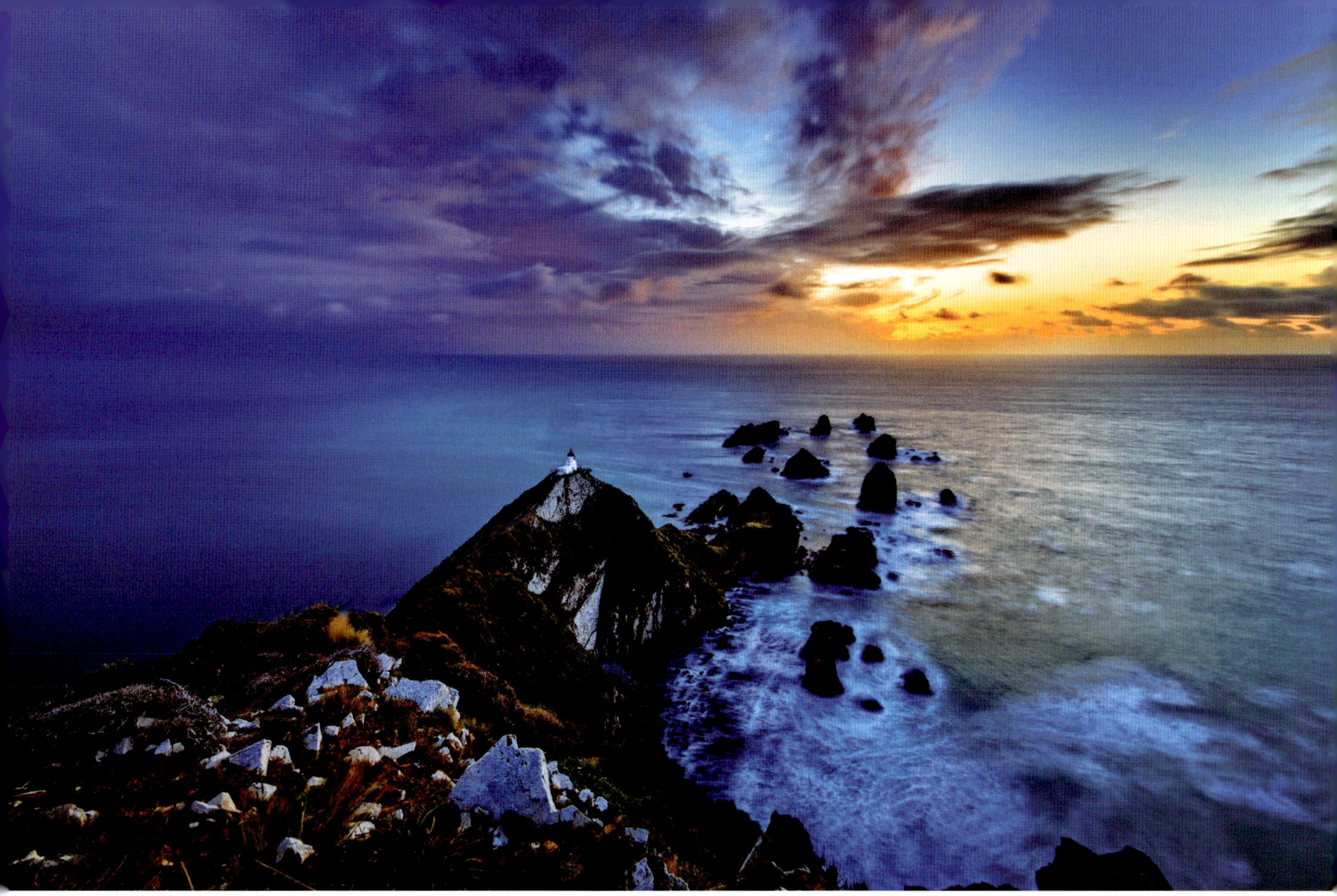

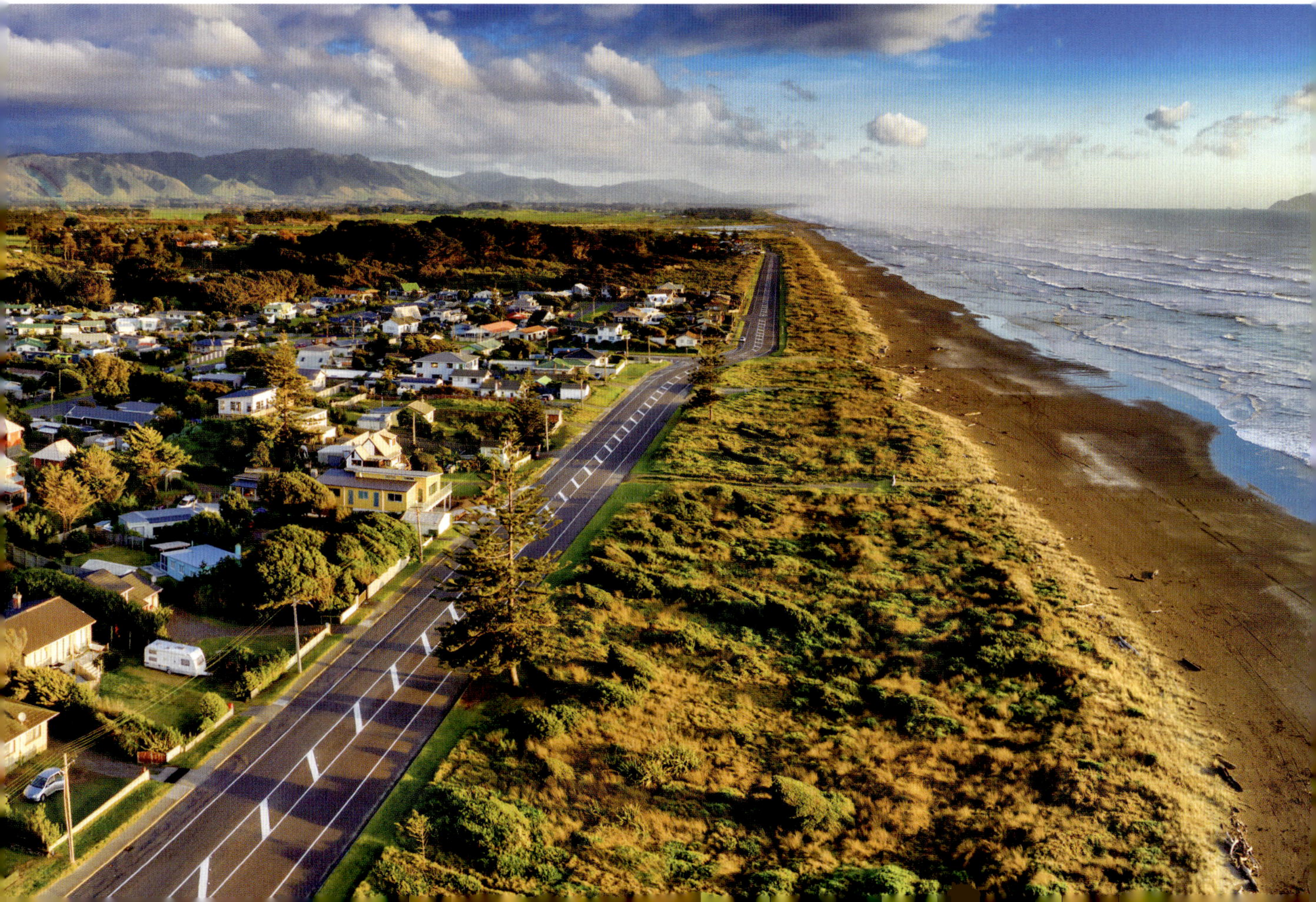

- EPIC BIKE RIDES OF AUSTRALIA & NEW ZEALAND -

THE HEART OF THE OCTOPUS

The Heart of the Octopus is a five-day (or more) bikepacking loop along the east and west coasts of Northland, discovering giant trees and beautiful beaches.

Before each solo bikepacking trip my mind is a whirlwind of increasingly irrational worries: what if I can't fix a mechanical problem? What if I'm chased by a pack of wild dogs over a cliff? Prior to embarking on this loop of Northland's east and west coasts, these anxieties were compounded by the conveyor belt of El-Niño-fuelled storms that were hitting New Zealand's North Island for weeks. On most days the rain and the trees were horizontal in the wind. I'd decided to start from near Opua on the east coast, because it was close to Russell in the Bay of Islands, a place I knew from my childhood. But, from the comfort of my Airbnb near Opua, the skies were dark and the wind was difficult to stand upright in.

The route I wanted to follow was developed by New Zealand's mountain biking pioneers, the Kennett brothers: Jonathan, Paul and Simon. They've been devising bike races and routes since the 1980s and were project managers on the Ngā Haerenga New Zealand Cycle Trail. The Kennett's Heart of the Octopus bikepacking route follows the Pou Herenga Tai / Twin Coast Cycle Trail, one of New Zealand's 23 Great Rides, from the east coast of the North Islands northern tip to Horeke near the west coast. Then it turns south onto the Kauri Coast Cycleway and passes through the North Island's kauri forests, one of the world's arboreal wonders. After returning to the east coast via farm roads, the final stretch hugs the coast back to the Bay of Islands.

THE NORTH ISLAND, NEW ZEALAND

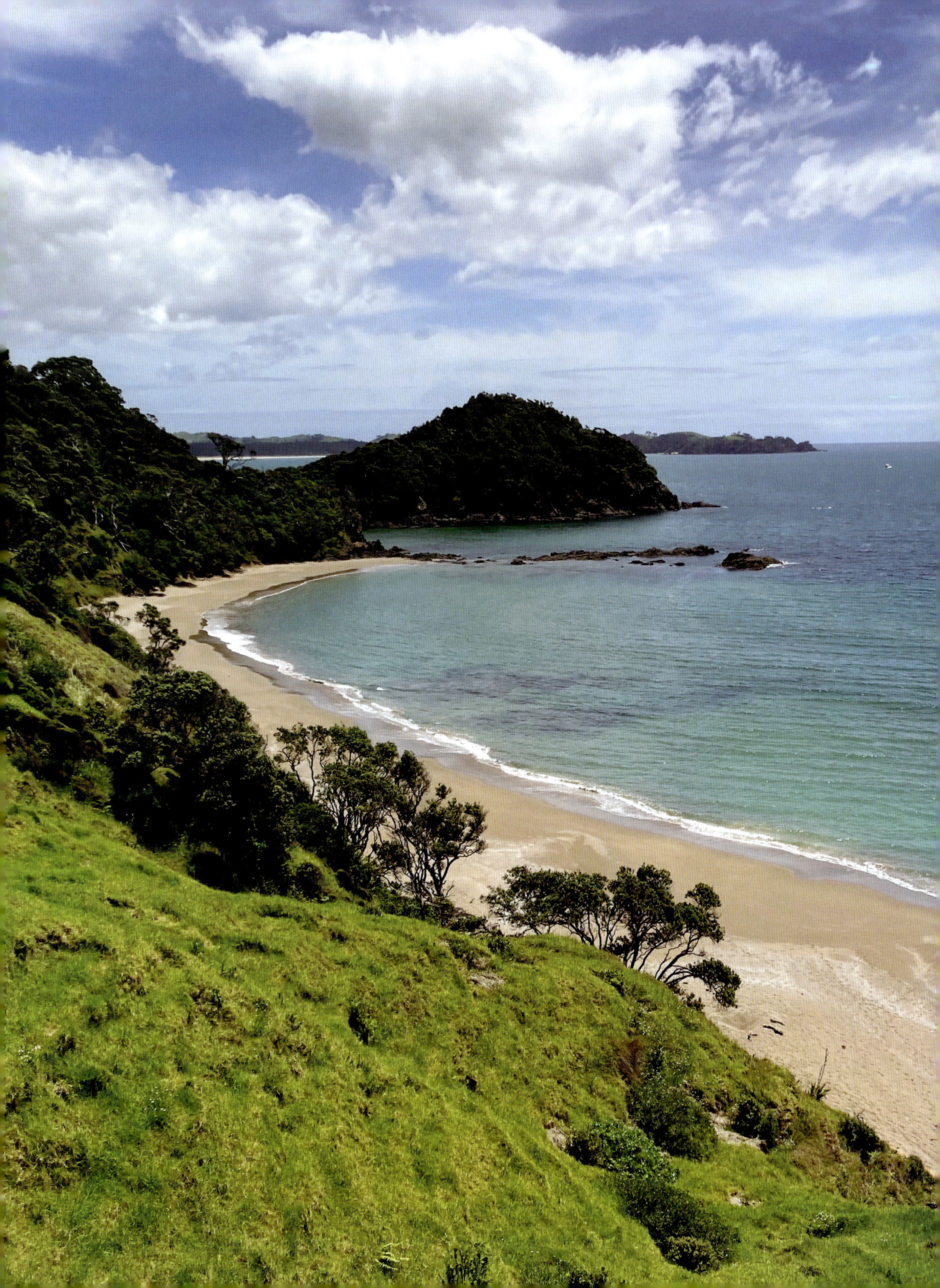

'You'll see two sides of Northland,' my Airbnb host Jarrad assured me. 'Extreme wealth and some of the most deprived communities in the country.' The east coast of Northland is where celebrities, such as Dame Kiri Te Kanawa, and billionaires buy beachfront property. And the west coast has long lacked investment.

When a day dawned with sunshine instead of storms, I set off. As always, once I was on the road for 30 minutes, every anxiety dissipated. Life got very simple: if I kept pedalling, I kept going forward. Soon, I'd joined the gravel bike path that forms most of the Pou Herenga Tai / Twin Coast Cycle Trail. The total distance of this Great Ride is 87km (54 miles) to Horeke so I'd planned to do that leg in one day and stay at the only hotel in Horeke, a hamlet on the shore of huge Hokianga harbour. From here, riders only wanting to ride the cycle trail need to book a shuttle van back to their starting point, which defies the point of being independent on a bicycle. A better schedule would be to break the journey in the township of Kaikohe, skip the hotel in Horeke, which is difficult to recommend, and continue to Rawene.

Regardless, I followed the largely flat and straight cycle trail across the top of Northland. Towards the end of that first day, the storms returned. Wind and rain bombarded me before I made the strange sanctuary of Horeke's hotel. The forecast didn't look great for the following day but there was little option but to commit and continue. So, I pulled on my waterproofs and set out towards the west coast under a heaving sky. Squalls of rain stung my skin but once you're wet, you're wet, and I dried quickly under the hot sun before the next drenching. This was an enjoyable day on quiet roads. I ate some excellent fish and chips at the takeaway in Opononi with views of sand dunes across the harbour mouth, before Haraena refilled my water bottles.

TĀNE'S TALE

Ranginui, the Sky Father, and Papatūānuku, the Earth Mother, clasped each other tightly, such was their love. Not a shaft of sunlight squeezed between them. But their children tired of darkness and their son, Tāne, used his broad shoulders to prise his parents apart. He pushed Ranginui upwards until light and life flooded throughout, creating the world. The rain that falls from the sky is Ranginui's grief but Tāne, the god of the forests, is still braced against Ranginui and Papatūānuku.

Clockwise from top: an audience with Tane Mahuta; fish and chips in Opononi; post-ride relaxation at the Wild Forest Estate; riding the gravel roads of the kauri forest

The Heart of the Octopus now adopts part of the Kauri Coast Cycleway as it heads south into Waipoua Kauri Forest, where the giant tree Tāne Mahuta stands just off the road. I chatted to the warden who ensured that visitors disinfected their shoes. Kauri are among the largest and longest-lived trees in the world and Tāne Mahuta is 2000 years old and the largest of his kind at around 51m tall (167ft) and a chunky 13.8m (45ft) in circumference.

This is a sublime section of riding, especially on an off-season weekday. My overnight stop in a hut at the Wild Forest Estate, hosted by Joanna and Nigel, was just as glorious. I bathed outside and listened out for kiwis calling in the dusk.

The next stretch took me back across Northland to Whangārei on a mix of gravel and tarmac roads. A navigational error sent me along State Hwy 14 but, with a breeze behind me, it was over quickly. After a night in Whangārei, I rejoined the Heart of the Octopus for two more legs up the east coast. This was another fantastic couple of days' riding. I passed through Glenbervie Forest on mountain bike tracks, into highland farming country, then reached the coast at Helena Bay before pitching up at the Whangaruru Beachfront Camp for the night. That section was harder and hillier than expected but I spent my last evening swimming and beachcombing at Whangaruru. The final stretch back to Opua was a short one at just 48km (30 miles) but it took me past several Māori *marae* and along the Russell-Whakapara Rd high into a cloud forest. Is the Pou Herenga Tai / Twin Coast Cycle Trail by itself a great ride? Not in my opinion. But the full Heart of the Octopus loop is a brilliant experience.

Previous spread: overlooking a beach near Woolley's Bay on Northland's east coast

TOOLKIT

Start/Finish // Opua (or anywhere along the loop)
Distance // 450km (280 miles)
Getting there // The standard start is from Whangārei, which is about a 2hr drive from Auckland. You should be able to take a bike on the InterCity bus service if it has both wheels removed, the handlebars turned and the chain covered but check in advance.
Where to stay // Airbnb can offer options for most schedules, such as the Wild Forest Estate (www.wildforestestate.com) in the Waipoua Kauri Forest.
What to take // Tools, spares and navigation kit – you won't pass many bike shops. A gravel bike is perfect.
When to ride // Northland has a mild climate so it's possible to ride the route all year round. Some of the gravel roads might become muddy in winter.
More info // www.kennett.co.nz has maps and route directions in their *Bikepacking Aotearoa* book.

Opposite: Ninety-Mile Beach in New Zealand's Far North; cross Kaipara Harbour on the Missing Link route

MORE LIKE THIS
NORTHLAND RIDES

GLENBERVIE FOREST

A tentacle of the Heart of the Octopus reaches out Glenbervie Forest via the Old Coach Road just northeast of Whangārei but doesn't linger. If you wish to explore the mountain bike trails here more deeply, you'll need to budget an extra day in the area. You'll find a network of old-school, slippery singletrack trails through tight-spaced trees but don't expect signposting or other amenities – local knowledge from the Whangārei Mountain Bike Club goes a long way. Glenbervie Forest is rideable from town (in 30 to 40 minutes) but most people will drive to ride. Gravel forest roads link the off-road trails so riders can piece together longer routes.
More info // www.whangareimtb.nz/trails-glenbervie

FAR NORTH CYCLEWAY

This route is a key component of the Tour Aotearoa, the once-in-a-lifetime ride along the length of New Zealand. The well-travelled cycleway starts from Cape Reinga, the country's most northern point, complete with a lighthouse and endless beaches. It bears south along Ninety-Mile Beach towards the charming historic town of Rawene, sitting on the south bank of the Omanaia River, where it joins up with the Twin Coast Cycleway and the Heart of the Octopus extended loop of Northland. To reach Rawene you will take a ferry across the river from Kohukohu. It's a fine end to a wind-swept 100-mile (160km) ride. Rawene has good options for food and accommodation and actually it makes a better base than Horeke on the Heart of the Octopus for several reasons.
More info // www.nzcycletrail.com

KAIPARA MISSING LINK

If you've ridden half of the Heart of the Octopus from the east coast but would prefer to ride all the way to Auckland rather than complete the loop through Whangārei, then this is the cycle route for you. You'll need to continue a little further south down the Kauri Coast to Dargaville rather than turn east to Whangārei. Then you pick up the Kaipara Missing Link from Dargaville and follow it for 120km (75 miles) to Auckland across fertile farmland and through some Victorian-era towns to New Zealand's largest city. A highlight is a lengthy boat trip across beautiful Kaipara Harbour from Pouto Point to Parakai. Many riders opt to spend a night in historic Helensville nearby.
More info // www.nzcycletrail.com

THE NORTH ISLAND, NEW ZEALAND

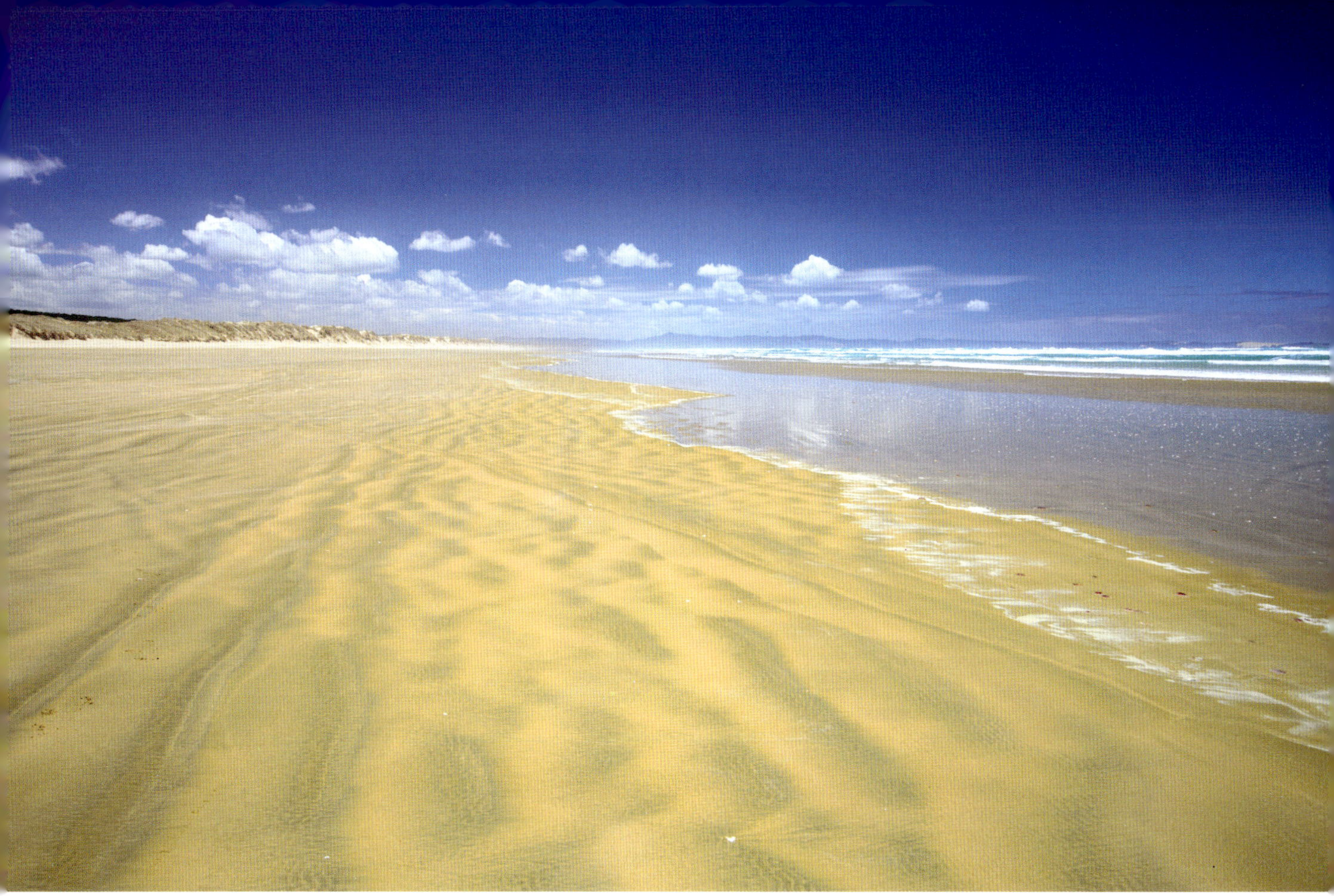

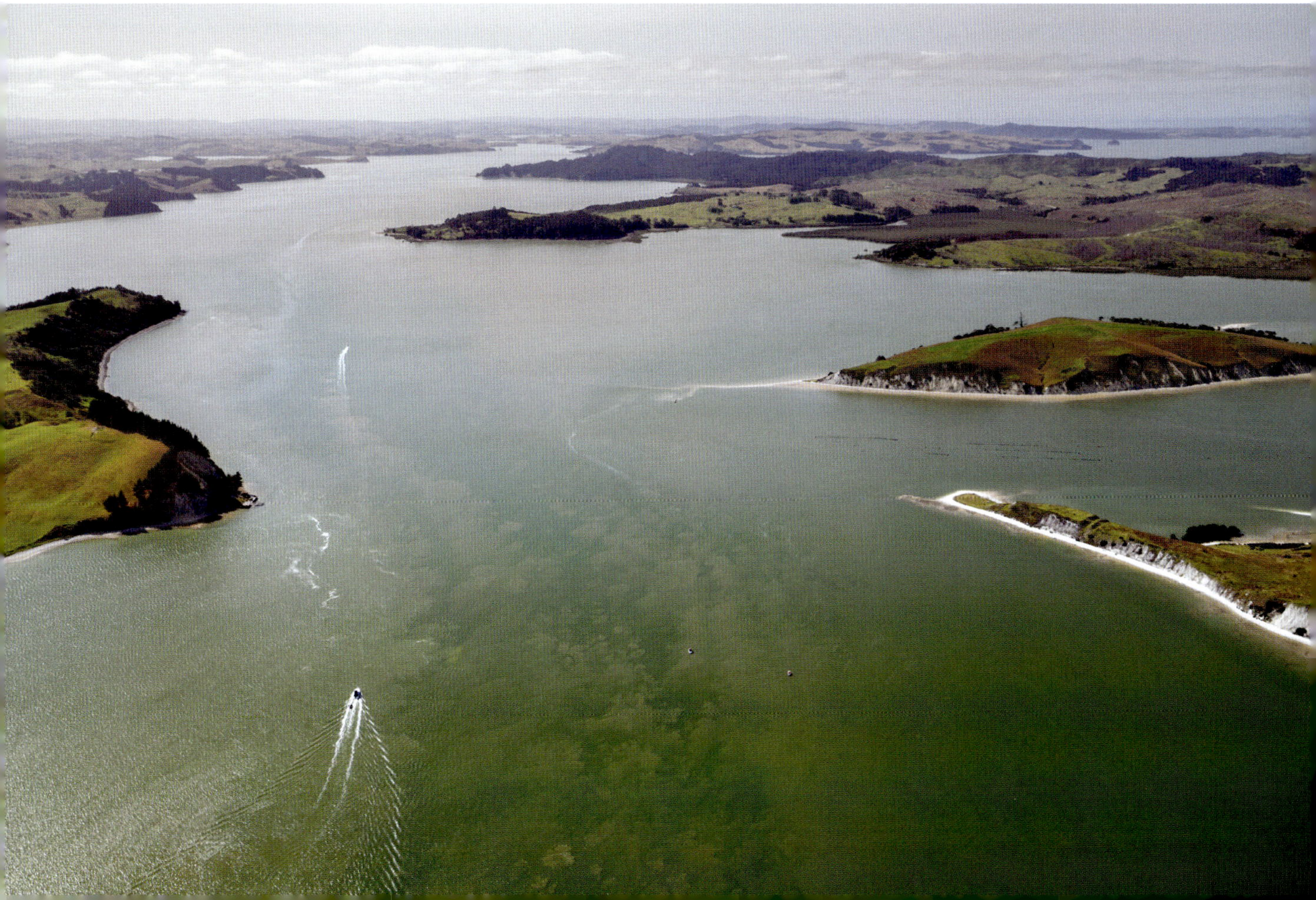

A NORTHERN COROMANDEL LOOP

A great weekender ride within easy reach of Auckland, this has singletrack, gravel and hike-a-bike, kākā and kauri, stunning views of the Hauraki Gulf and a good meal at the end.

With just over 1.5 million people, Auckland isn't a large city in international terms. But most of it is built on a narrow isthmus, and most Aucklanders live in freestanding houses, so the urban sprawl along State Highway 1 runs for the best part of 70km from north to south. And those kilometres can feel slower when everybody is driving to and from work.

All that means that having an easy overnighter cycling adventure requires a bit of cogitating for us Aucklanders. For my group, it turned out that the correct answer is a 118km loop around the very top of Coromandel Peninsula. Cycling through remote, bush-covered coastlines for two days with barely a car in sight wrenched us out of our dull, suburban lives.

A pre-dawn start with a BP coffee got two cars full of bikes and cyclists onto the beautiful, winding coastal road from Thames to Coromandel as the sun came up and into Colville for second breakfast (a key feature of any good cycling expedition). What a breakfast! The Hereford 'n' a Pickle Café fed us on their home-bred beef, with mince on toast and pies, then let us leave our cars in the paddock next door. A few sandwiches and bars were stuffed in pockets, as we knew that this could be the last food stop before dinner.

It would have been an easy 23km back to the turnoff at Driving Creek Road, but we chose the path less travelled – starting as a farm track, turning into some tricky singletrack (so tricky I manage to fall into a thankfully smallish ravine), and finally we were pushing our bikes up out of a creek. We were not unhappy to arrive back on the road, and then see the turnoff to Driving Creek Road.

This is the bottom station for the Driving Creek Railway. Established by the late Barry Brickell, potter and one-of-a-kind creator, this small-gauge mountain railway line shuttles between pottery studios and regenerating kauri forest. It's worth a visit, not just for its cafe open on weekends, toilets and fresh water.

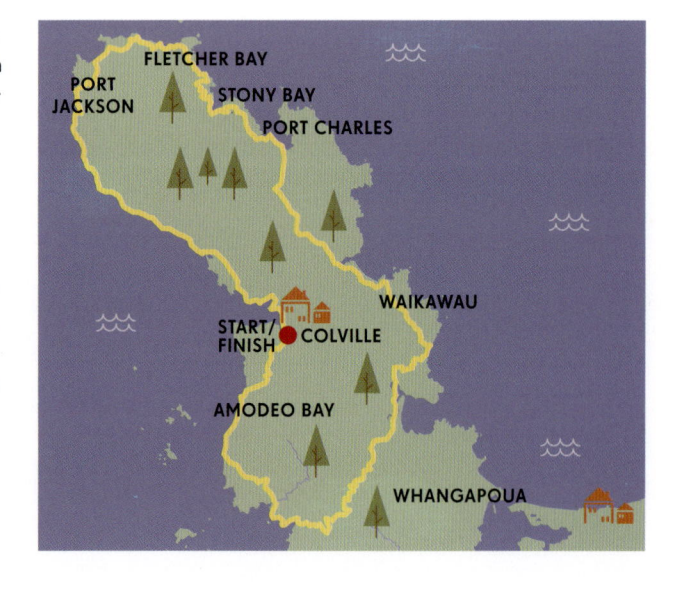

THE NORTH ISLAND, NEW ZEALAND

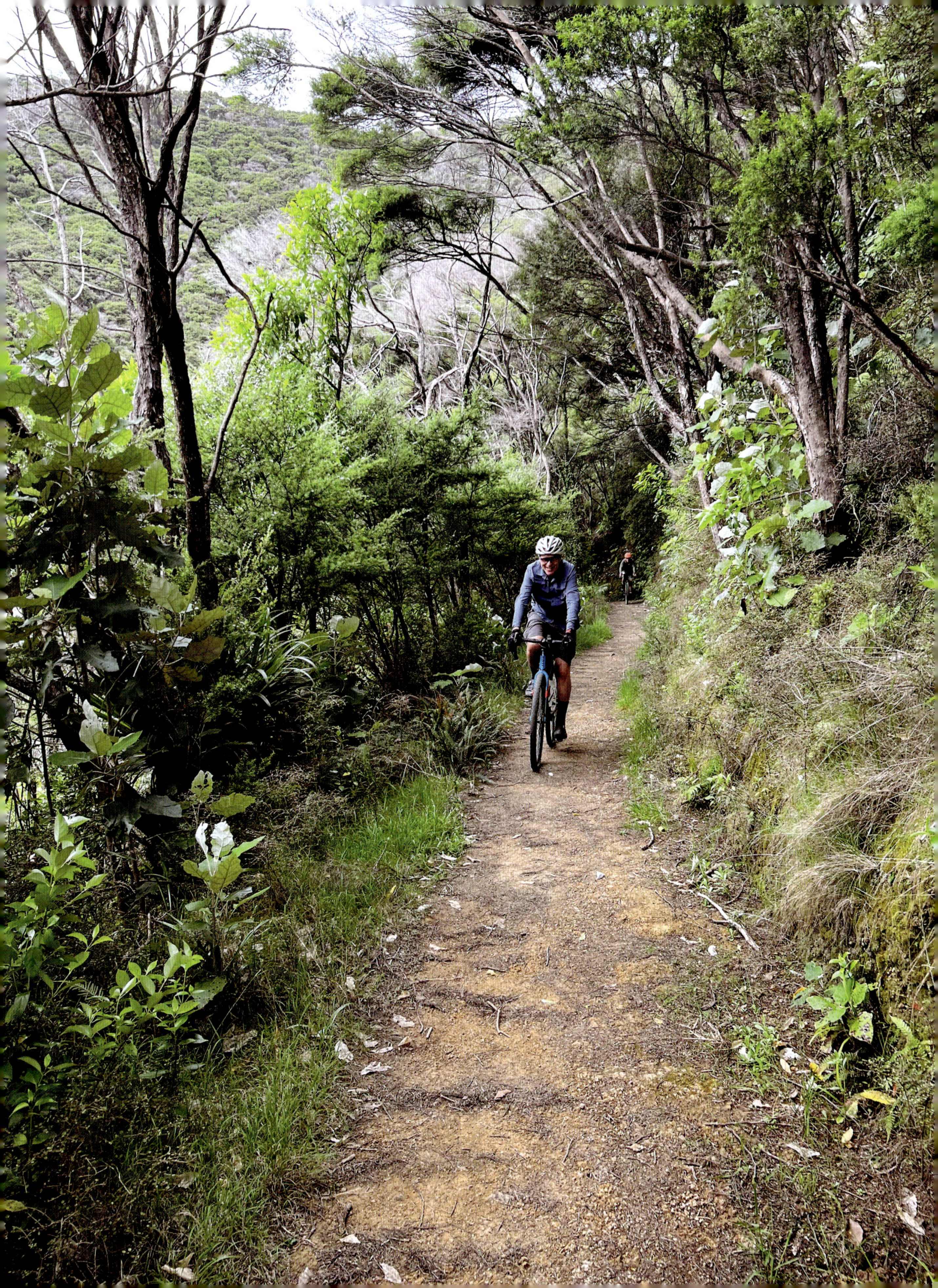

But it had been a slow ride from Colville, so we took on water and kept going. And going. Up 400m vertical at 10% gradient to the top of the spine of the Coromandel, with views out to the Mercury Islands and the Pacific Ocean to the east, and back to Waiheke Island and Auckland to the west. Rolling on down at speed, we passed through Kennedy Bay and stopped at the coast at Tuateawa, a rocky bay full of happy fishermen. 'I don't really even like snapper,' one said, as they laughed and hauled in fish after fish from the clear, calm water.

One more steep climb, and a swim in the sea for some at the long, white sands of Waikawau Bay, came before a final climb to roll into Tangiaro Kiwi Retreat, concealed in the bush just before Port Charles. Sixty-two kilometres is not that far for some of us, but we all felt the 1400 metres of climbing in the legs, and were ready for a shower, cold beer, hot pool and some huge, hearty meals before hitting the hay.

Day one was beaches, vistas and the rise and fall of long gravel roads. By day two, we had reached the pointy end of Coromandel Peninsula. This was a day of rocky shorelines, tiny bays and short but very sharp climbs.

Up early, with a packed lunch from our accommodation, it didn't take us long to roll through the little settlement of Port Charles and arrive at Stony Bay – literally the end of the road. To get from Stony to Fletcher Bay (the end of another road on Coromandel's western side), we could choose either an

THE PULL OF COROMANDEL

The Coromandel Peninsula comes alive in the New Zealand summer. Close to key population centres, it includes towns that explode with surfers and swimmers (Whangamatā is popular), beaches like New Chums and Cathedral Cove, hikes through its native forest-covered heart, and campers everywhere – some in town campgrounds cheek-by-jowl with young people, others in remote Department of Conservation facilities up north.

Left to right: a pitstop in the jungle; Cathedral Cove beach; local accommodation; come to Colville, stay for the steaks. Previous spread: the natural habitat for gravel bikes

8km Grade 5 mountain bike track (steep and slippery) or the 10km coastal walkway (big drop-offs over cliffs). We took the latter and survived. The track hugs the coast overlooking deep rocky bays and is mostly rideable – with caution – except for a steep, hike-a-bike section into and out of Poley Bay.

For an early lunch, we dropped our bikes and walked up a steep, short track to a lookout on the Sugar Loaf promontory. Looking north, we could almost touch the green peaks of Great Barrier Island / Aotea. Looking down, outside the shelter of the Hauraki Gulf, the Pacific Ocean roiled and churned. Looking up, one of us spotted a kākā, a native parrot still at risk. We felt a very long way from the home.

Across some farmland, we rejoined the road to meet modern life again at Fletcher Bay (a few walkers) and Port Jackson (a few campers). As we started to smell the finish (and the beef!), we formed into a peloton to drive ourselves against the rising headwind and occasional squalling shower, to finish the ride with five kilometres of tarmac back into Colville.

Where the Herefords and the cars and the cafe were all waiting for us. Mince on toast, burgers, pies. Frozen steaks and ribs to take home to families. Some snores in the car as we wound our way back down the Coromandel Coast, onto Highway 1, and finally back to the traffic and high rises of Auckland. We had only left town 36 hours before. But this overnighter had taken us a long way from home. **SE**

TOOLKIT

Start/Finish // Colville
Distance // 118km (73 miles)
Getting there // Colville is about three hours' drive from Auckland, Hamilton or Tauranga.
When to go // Ride any time in the 'winterless north'.
What to pack // Don't forget to bring daytime food. There are almost no food options en route. Swimming togs and sunscreen.
Where to stay // Tangiaro Kiwi Retreat in Port Charles has outstanding food and accommodation. Or there are beautiful DOC campgrounds and some cabin options in Waikawau Bay, Stony Bay, Fletcher Bay and Port Jackson that would all break up the ride slightly differently.
Where to eat // Start and finish with some of the home-raised beef at the Hereford 'n' A Pickle in Colville – the mince on toast, the pies, in fact all the food is recommended. Bring home a few frozen steaks too.
More info // www.doc.govt.nz, www.hikeandbike.co.nz/coromandel-bike-trails

Opposite: fragrant lavender on Waiheke Island

MORE LIKE THIS
AUCKLAND'S DOORSTEP RIDES

PUKEKOHE TO RAGLAN

Strike south from Pukekohe to Onewhero on a sealed road before hitting the challenging Klondyke Road gravel descent, down to Port Waikato for a coffee, and then along a spectacular coastal gravel road through limestone country all the way to Te Ākau Wharf just across the estuary from Raglan. A local boatman will deliver you across the estuary to dinner and a bed in surfy, alternative Raglan. Do the same in reverse the next day, or forget the ferry and head back around Raglan Harbour for more sealed road and a few more kilometres. Don't forget to stop at Nikau Cave and Café either direction – it produces beautiful lunch, and is the only food between Pukekohe and Raglan (you can also take a tour through a limestone cave and stay the night).
Start/Finish // Pukekohe
Distance // 210km (130 miles) return

PUHOI TO LEIGH

At the bohemian village of Puhoi, 40 minutes north of Auckland, grab a coffee (or oysters and chips) then head on mostly shingle country roads northwest to Port Albert, with outstanding views of the huge Kaipara Harbour on the west coast. After a quick lunch, head northeast through Te Hana, Pākiri and (after an epic final climb) arrive in the beautiful fishing port of Leigh – home to the Leigh Sawmill, which offers excellent craft beer, food and live music. Stay overnight there, or elsewhere in Leigh. Return the same way, or more quickly through Matakana (beautiful bakery), Warkworth and the backroads to Puhoi.
Start/Finish // Puhoi
Distance // 200km (124 miles) loop

WAIHEKE CIRCUIT

Catch a ferry with your bike (one-hour trip) over to Waiheke Island from Downtown Auckland or Devonport. From Matiatia Wharf where the ferry lands, hug the north coast to take you through Oneroa, Palm Beach and Onetangi until you hit Man O' War Bay Road. This gravel road basks in views of the Hauraki Gulf, and takes you to Man O' War where, at the vineyard of the same name, you can eat, drink, swim and watch the yachties anchored in the beautiful bay. Then ride back along the southern coast to the ferry. The ride isn't long, but don't underestimate the hills. This one can be completed in a day, but better to stay overnight somewhere on Waiheke and enjoy the island.
Start/Finish // Matiatia Wharf, Waiheke
Distance // 60km (37 miles)

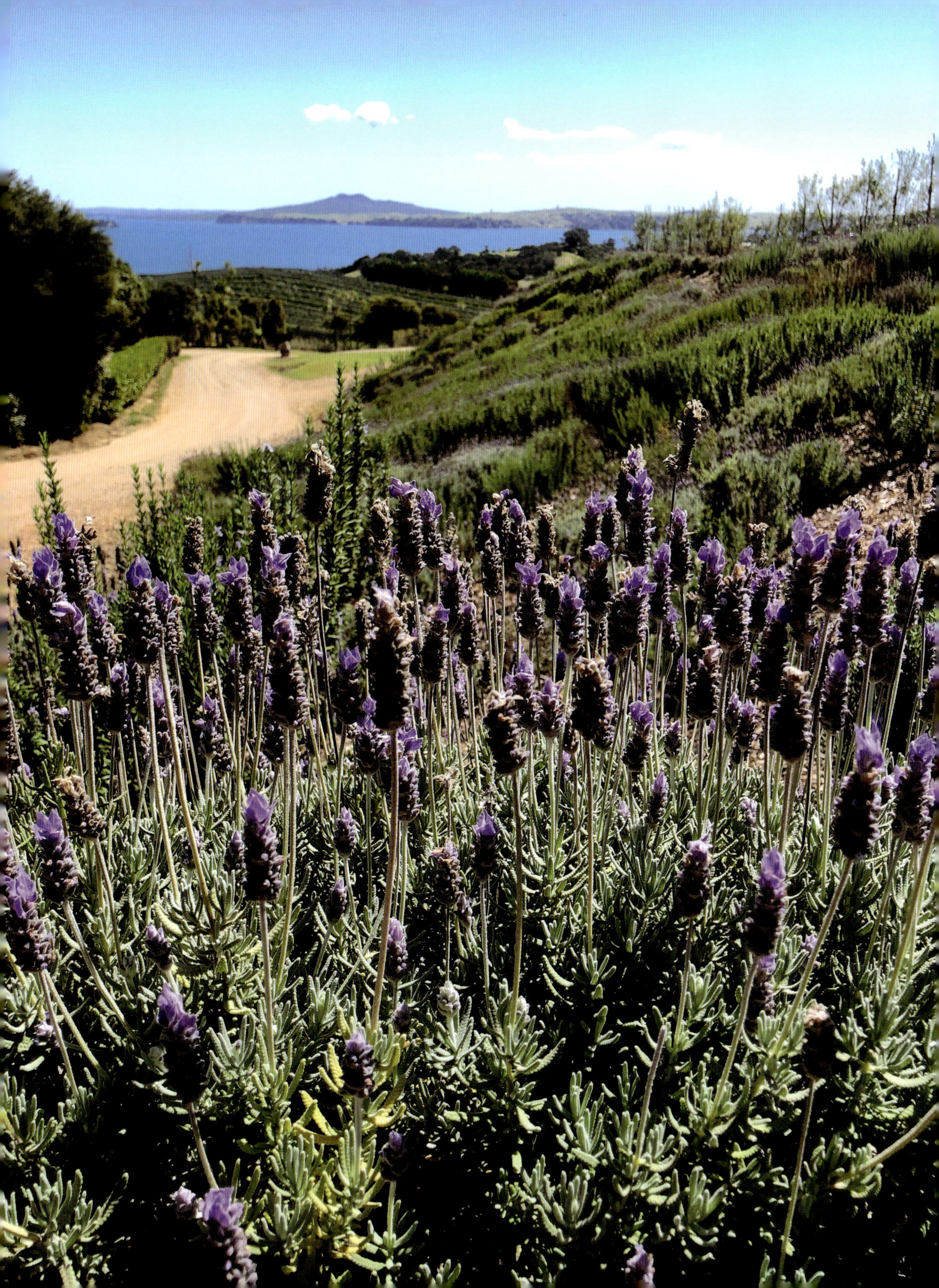

TOURING HAWKES BAY WINERIES

Pedal to cellar doors, farmers' markets and cafes on the laidback trails around Napier and Hastings in Hawkes Bay, with a beautiful ocean backdrop.

Sometimes planning bike rides is as much fun as actually doing them, which is how I found myself talking to Tigs Conran over a glass of Tony Bish's Heartwood chardonnay in Tony's Urban Winery. It was a Saturday night and Tigs, the general manager of this working winery and bar in a side street of Napier's Ahuriri neighbourhood, was preparing for a local jazz band to take to the stage, while spinning some of the winery's collection of 2400 vintage vinyl records.

The Urban Winery served not only its own highly regarded wines but also some of the best of the region and I wanted to glean some tips from Tigs on the best cellar doors at which to stop during my ride the following day. 'Askerne,' he answered. 'Good prices, good wine and good people.' Tigs poured a taste of Smith & Sheth's Cru albariño from Havelock North. 'And Craggy Range – it's one of the top five wineries in the country and spectacular.'

I already had a sense of the geography of Hawkes Bay. This was New Zealand's first wine region and has 150 years of grape-growing history. It lies low on the east coast of the North Island and is reputed to have some of the best weather in the country, earning it the reputation as the fruit bowl of New Zealand.

Napier is the largest city in Hawkes Bay and is set behind some broad, sandy beaches. It's famous for its art deco architecture, which came about due to a devastating earthquake in 1931. The city was rebuilt (it wouldn't be the last New Zealand city to be rebuilt after a natural disaster, indeed Hawkes Bay was hit hard by Cyclone Gabrielle in early 2023) and by the end of the decade it was the most contemporary city in the world. Today, its art deco buildings, painted in beautiful pastel shades, are celebrated globally.

Inland and slightly south of Napier are the adjoining country towns of Hastings and Havelock North. All three are within cycling distance of each other, for stronger cyclists. But for those wishing to do some leisurely wine

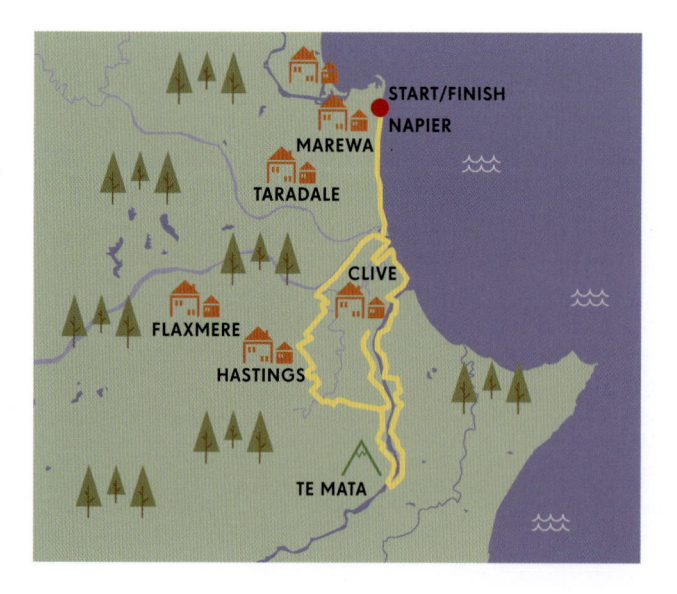

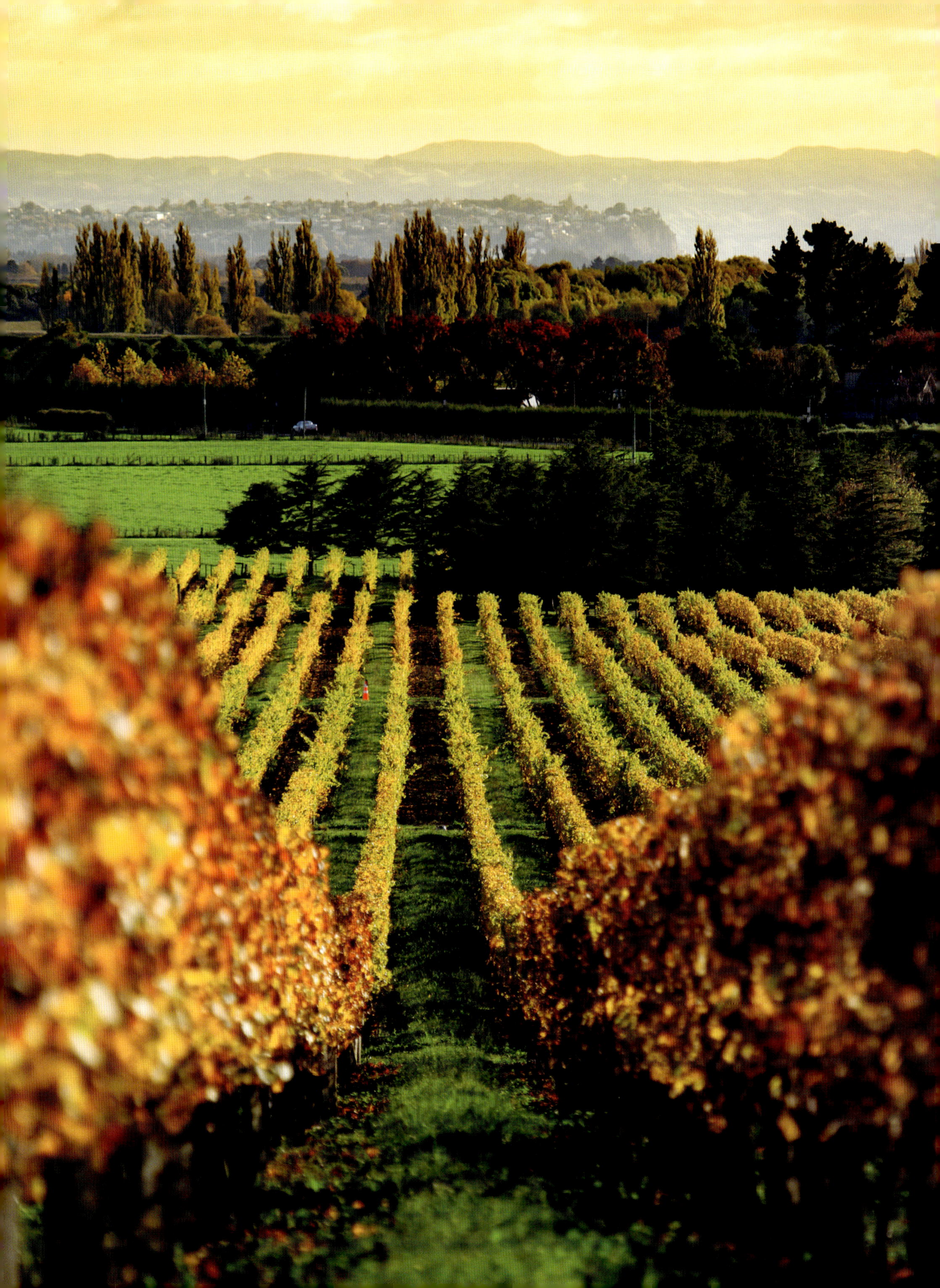

touring by bicycle, it would be better to focus on one of the three areas. Fortunately, the Hawkes Bay tourist board has developed three interlinked cycling routes that, between them, cover the highlights.

Heading north from Napier, the 'Water Ride' covers the Ahuriri coast and estuary. In the middle of Hawkes Bay, the 'Wineries Ride' takes in some of the key roads north of Hastings, along which many of the cellar doors are set, such as in the Bridge Pā district. And, finally, the 'Landscapes Ride' follows the Tukituki river towards Havelock North and the Te Mata peak.

Conveniently, Askerne winery is located along the Tukituki River and Craggy Range is overlooked by Te Mata's tectonic ridge. So, as Tigs brought out some oysters to accompany the albariño, and a barefoot jazz saxophonist prowled the audience, a plan for the next day's ride was shaped. I walked back to my hotel on Napier's Marine Parade via the steep, San Francisco-like streets of Bluff Hill.

The next day, I woke to a still ocean and the Norfolk pine trees outside untroubled by wind. Perfect cycling conditions. I'd concocted an ambitious route of around 80km (50 miles) that combined some of the Wineries and Landscapes routes but made a point of passing by the weekly farmers' market at Hastings, held every Sunday. The route would be too long for those solely interested in visiting cellar doors under their

"I made several wrong turns before I found Hastings Showgrounds and a sun-drenched farmers' market"

own steam, but it allowed me to see as much of Hawkes Bay as I could in a day.

Weaving in and out of the Sunday strollers along the shared bike path beside the beach, I reminded myself that this wasn't a race. The crowds quickly thinned out and I cruised south to Clive, where I picked up the gravel path to Hastings alongside the Ngaruroro River. Although there's a comprehensive network of bike paths, either separate from roads or running along their hard shoulder, the signposting is ambiguous in places and it's easy to lose your way: even with the route loaded into my phone and a paper map in my pocket, I made several wrong turns before I found Hastings Showgrounds and a sun-drenched early summer market where local producers were selling delicious things such as olives, berries, honey and cheese under the shade of trees.

A snack of blueberry gelato refreshed me and I was soon making my way through Hastings towards Havelock North.

THE NORTH ISLAND, NEW ZEALAND

HAWKE'S BAY WINES

Hawkes Bay has a huge range of terroirs with mild winters, long summers and high sunshine hours make great conditions for ripening grapes, explains local Master of Wine and expert guide on wine-tasting bike rides, Simon Nash. The key wines are the world-class chardonnays and the Bordeaux varieties that thrive in the stony soil. Most of the cycling routes for wine tours are flat but, Simon notes, 'a 25km round trip is quite long when visiting wineries'.

Left to right: the Sunday farmers' market in Hastings; Craggy Range winery and the craggy range itself; Napier is known for its art deco architecture. Previous spread autumnal vines in Hawkes Bay

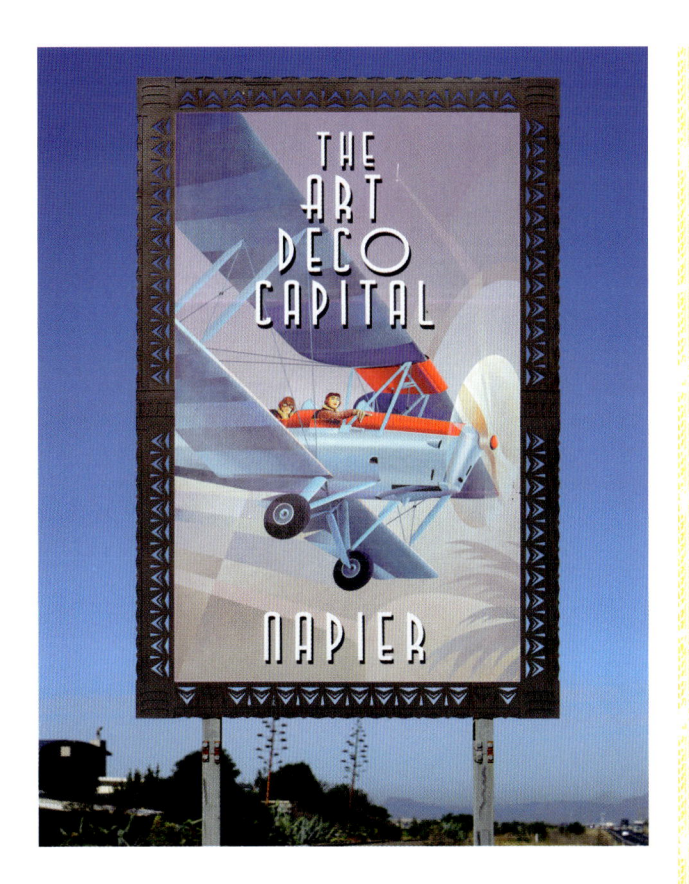

Second note: New Zealand's drivers, as is mentioned elsewhere in this book, are not very considerate towards cyclists, so beware of car doors being opened in front of you and don't expect much space on the roads without bike lanes. But, reaching Havelock North, I was soon back on the car-free path along the Tukituki River.

My plan was to ride south to visit the boutique, family-run Askerne winery and then turn around and head up to Craggy Range before returning to Napier along the coast. But even the most carefully plotted plans can have a flaw. In this instance, it was that Askerne winery and the other cellar doors along the Tukituki River, are not actually accessible from the river-side bike path, only from the busy road on their far side. This meant no sampling of their sauvignon blanc for lunch.

So, I turned around for Craggy Range, consoled slightly by the swallows swooping low around me as I pedalled upriver towards Te Mata. This distinctive ridge was formed two million years ago when the seabed tilted skywards. In its shadow, Craggy Range is one of New Zealand's star cellar doors, with great views of the ancient hills from its modern building. After a brief stop, I rode on up to Red Bridge, crossed the river and pedalled back towards the coast via a quiet, undulating road. Retracing the route to Napier was a chance to reflect on a wine tour without any wine.

TOOLKIT

Start/Finish // Napier
Distance // various
Getting there // The car is the most convenient mode of transport to Napier, which is on the southeast coast of the North Island. It takes about five hours to drive from Auckland and four from Wellington. There's no direct train and buses take even longer.
What to take // There are several places renting bicycles in Hawkes Bay but they tend to be heavy, cruiser-type bikes. If you want something sportier, bring your own. For the rides, this isn't wilderness so basic tools, a phone, water and sunscreen will suffice.
When to ride // Spring to autumn is a delight but winter on the east coast is also mild enough for cycling.
Where to stay // The Scenic Hotel Te Pania in Napier is right on the cycling route and has great waterfront views.
More info // www.hbtrails.nz

Opposite: a wine dog waits for a fuss; vines at Mornington Peninsula's Western Port

MORE LIKE THIS
WINE TOURS

MORNINGTON PENINSULA, VICTORIA

For serious Melbourne cyclists, riding Beach Rd towards the Mornington Peninsula on the weekend, clad in Lycra, is a rite of passage. But if you tend towards the sybaritic rather than the streamlined (or perhaps both), there are several tasty routes on the peninsula itself, without having to pedal there. The 25km (15-mile) Bay Trail covers the coastline from Safety Beach to Sorrento, passing gourmet stops like the Provincia Food Store. But to better explore the region's cellar doors and breweries, you'll need to go inland, up to the Red Hill area where a 13km (eight-mile) rail trail connects Merricks and Red Hill. Classic Mornington pinots and chardonnays can be sampled at Stonier Wines near Merricks and Main Ridge Estate near Red Hill. Look out too for fungi in the autumn.
More info // www.visitmorningtonpeninsula.org

CLARE VALLEY, SOUTH AUSTRALIA

There are some rules for wine touring by bicycle: quiet roads or preferably bike paths. Lots of shade. And as few hills as possible. The Clare Valley ticks all three boxes. Best of all there are many great cellar doors offering refreshing riesling to taste or purchase. The 33km (20-mile) Riesling Trail runs through the centre of the valley from Barina, just north of Clare down a slight gradient to Auburn via Sevenhill and Watervale. There's bike hire available near Clare and then some very well-regarded wineries, including, north to south, Tim Adams, Shut the Gate Wines, Skillogalee and finally Grosset. Skillogalee, set down a tree-lined lane, offers lunches and snacks on the deck of a cottage built by a Cornish miner in 1851. From Auburn, cyclists can extend their trip by taking the Rattler rail trail to Riverton.
Start // Barina
Finish // Auburn
Distance // 33km (20 mile)
More info // www.clarevalley.com

TASMAN'S GREAT TASTE TRAIL, SOUTH ISLAND

For a multi-day epicurean epic, however, look to the Nelson region of New Zealand. The Tasman's Great Taste Trail offers a number of different options out of the city of Nelson, but the highlights are the town of Motueka, best known for its hop cultivation, reached around the Tasman Bay coast path and a ferry at Māpua. Yes, there are craft breweries in the town. From Motueka, head towards the fruit stalls and cafes of Riwaka and then follow the Motueka River inland to Woodstock, where you can decide whether to brave the longest rideable railway tunnel in the southern hemisphere, Spooners Tunnel, or take the off-road route to Wakefield. Along the road from Wakefield to Brightwater and Richmond are numerous wineries to casually drop into.
Start/Finish // Nelson
Distance // 177km (110 miles)
More info // www.nzcycletrail.com

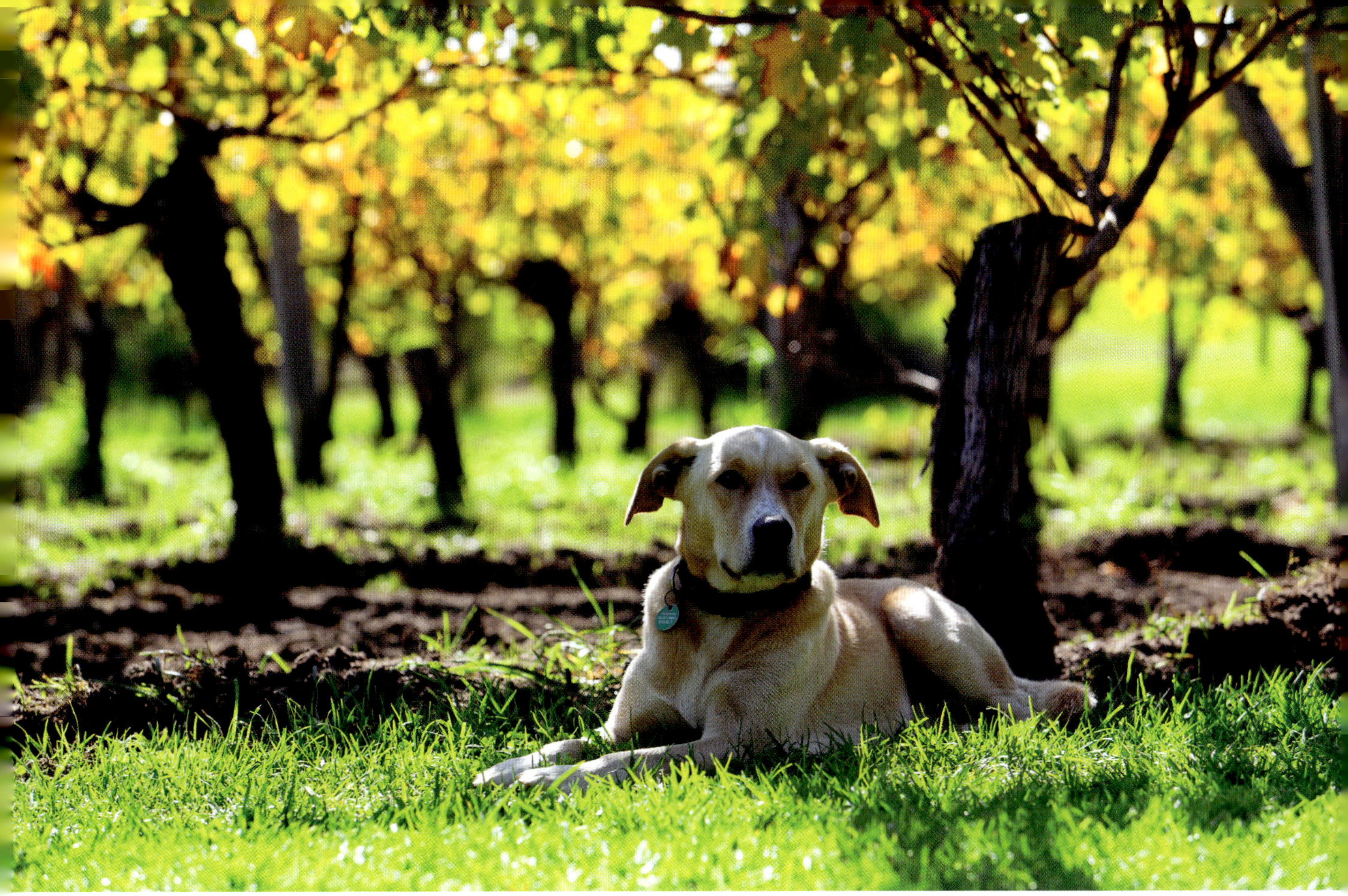

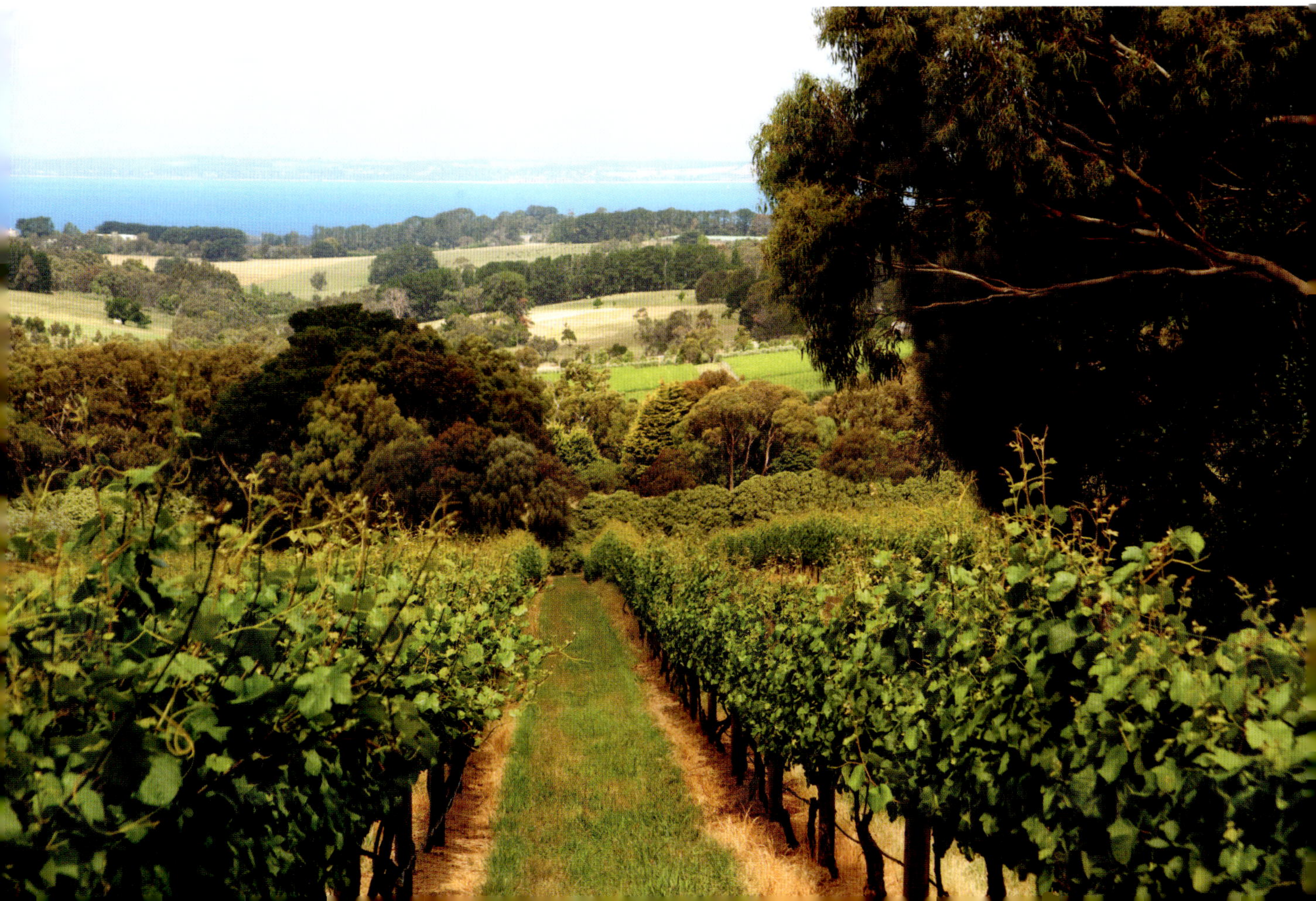

THE TIMBER TRAIL

Take a couple of days to explore the reclaimed Timber Trail and discover local history and natural wonder deep in rural Waikato.

Don't look down, I think, but I can't resist. I'm halfway across one of the highest and longest suspension bridges in New Zealand, the Maramataha Bridge, which spans 141m (462ft) across the gorge of the same name. About 53m (175ft) below, the river rushes around boulders and giant ferns explode from the forest like green fireworks. Then I raise my eyes to focus on the far side of the gorge and try to ignore the gentle bounce as I wheel my bike across the rest of the bridge.

The Maramataha Bridge is one of the spectacular suspension bridges along the Timber Trail, which itself is a highlight of the 23 Great Rides of the New Zealand Cycle Trail. The entire project is intended to bring visitors to overlooked corners of the country and the Timber Trail does exactly that. It's set in the centre of the North Island, but beyond the traditional attractions of Lake Taupo and Tongariro National Park. The trail repurposes some of the logging tramways of the Waikato's working forests and takes in native broad-leaf podocarp forest, as well as regenerating tracts of land.

I'd started my ride from the trailhead in Pureora Forest, at the eastern end of the route. Most people ride from here to the end in Ōngarue, 85km (52 miles) west, because it's largely downhill. But there's nothing stopping you from cycling in the opposite direction, which is what bikepackers riding the cross-country Kōpiko Aotearoa route typically do. Logistics can be a challenge:

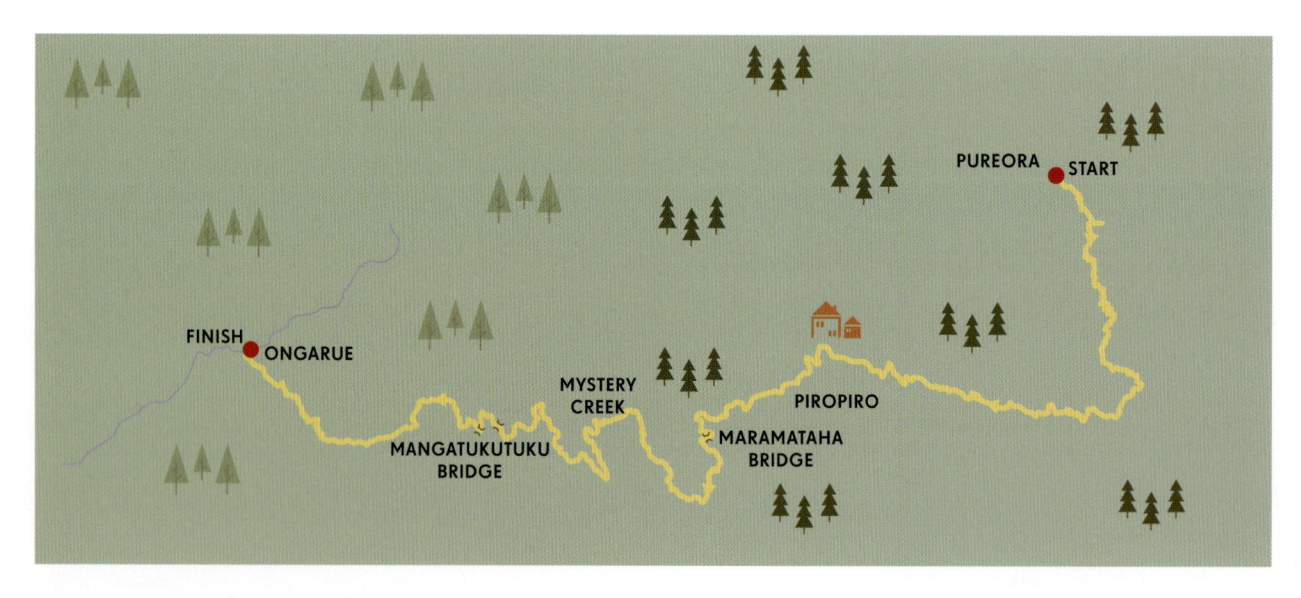

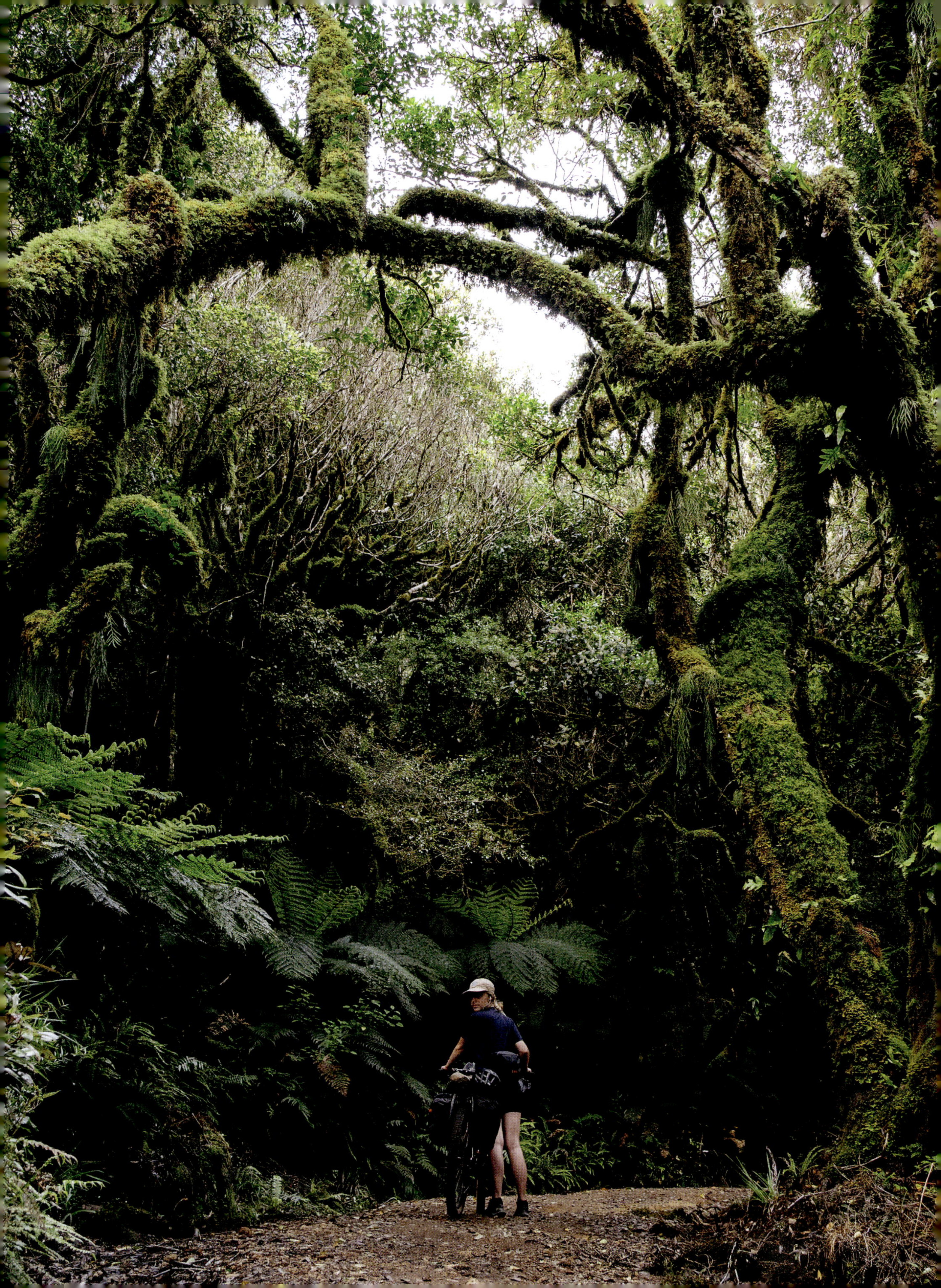

the town of Taumarunui recently became a more regular stop on the Northern Explorer railway line between Auckland and Wellington but generally a vehicle is required. Most people on the Timber Trail will have parked at Ōngarue and taken a shuttle to the other end of the trail. Midway along the trail, deep in the bush at Piropiro, the Timber Trail Lodge (or nearby campsite) is a popular overnight spot for most riders, although I planned to complete the whole route in one go, after a night at the lodge.

The night before the ride, I'd chatted with the Timber Trail Lodge's manager, Russ Malone, during the communal dinner: 'After the global financial crisis of 2008, John Key [New Zealand's then-Prime Minister], asked what could be done to make use of the opportunity,' Russ explained. 'The government invested millions in creating the Great Rides program, which provided work for New Zealanders and would draw travellers to the less obvious regions of the country for years to come.'

The Timber Trail was one of the projects: 'About ten years ago, some local business folk got together, applied for a grant, and built the Timber Trail lodge. A lot of good thinking went into the project, which employs local people.'

According to Russ, the Timber Trail Lodge was modelled more on a ski lodge than a motel, hence the decking from which to enjoy the sunset with a Panhead pale ale, and the comfortable rooms. The lodge provide rental bikes, including e-bikes, which makes the trail as accessible to casual cyclists as it can be.

After plundering the breakfast buffet, I jumped in the shuttle bus and was ferried to Pureora with 15 other people. Once the bikes are unloaded, we set off up to the highest point of the trip. The trail has been surfaced with pumice, evidence of the volcanic past of the region. Lake Taupo to the east is the colossal caldera of the Taupo supervolcano, responsible for some of the world's most powerful eruptions, which sent boulders flying over the area.

KING COUNTRY

Covering 25,000sq km (9650sq miles) of central North Island, the Waikato has played a key role in New Zealand's history and economy, due to industries including, farming, forestry and mining. It was also where the Māori people realised that they would have to unite to face settlers and soldiers. In 1858, Waikato chief Pōtatau Te Wherowhero became the first Māori king. Some land was eventually returned to Māori iwi in 1995.

Clockwise from top: unloading the shuttle; post-ride pizza; crossing one of several suspension bridges; the Timber Trail Lodge. Previous spread: exploring old-growth forest

THE NORTH ISLAND, NEW ZEALAND

The trail zigzagged upward through misty old-growth forest, topping out at almost 1000m (3275ft). Gnarled trees are draped with strands of moss, all a beautiful shade of green. This is the Pikiariki Conservation Area. Soon evidence of the logging industry appeared in the rusting shape of a Caterpillar tractor from the 1920s. It was a surprise to learn that logging was as prevalent on Māori-owned land as government or private land and that few places outside of the national parks have escaped being logged or mined, but land use is gradually changing. There's a long tradition of environmental activism in New Zealand and Australia; in 1978 protesters halted the logging of old-growth trees here.

Once at the top, near Mt Pureora, the Timber Trail turns downhill, still on a durable, gravel surface, and speeds towards the first of the suspension bridges across Bog Inn Creek and then the Orauwaka bridge. During the construction of the trail, which opened in 2013, the weight-bearing strength of the bridges was tested to check that they could carry ten people at a time. But it's still a bit nerve-wracking to ride or walk a bike over something that sways high above the ground.

After about 40km (25 miles), I reach the lodge at Piropiro in time for a quick lunch. On the approach, white manuka blossom is out. Local beekeepers move their hives in time with the bushes that provide a lucrative New Zealand product, manuka honey. Most riders pause for the night here, but I continue for the next 45km (27 miles) to the end. The second stretch has less virgin forest but you'll see more remnants of the logging industry: tunnels, camps and the engineering wonder of the Ōngarue Spiral and the Maramataha Bridge soon after leaving Piropiro. At one point a huge red deer melts into the pine forest. The final few kilometres to Ōngarue curve around hills stripped of trees and grazed by sheep. Even in a country that prizes nature as much as New Zealand, almost no landscape is untouched by people.

TOOLKIT

Start // Pureora
Finish // Ōngarue
Distance // 85km (52 miles)
Where to stay // Most riders staying at the lodge will park at Ōngarue and be shuttled to the start or to the lodge. Campsites are at the start and middle of the trail.
What to take // The route is signposted. Bring water or a purification system if refilling along the route.
Getting there // You'll need your own transport. The start is just off Hwy 30 near Barryville but most people use shuttles. Taumarunui train station, 20 minutes from Ōngarue, is on the Northern Explorer rail line (bicycles accepted if dismantled). .
More info // www.timbertraillodge.co.nz; www.timbertrail.nz

Opposite: Tawhai Falls in Tongariro National Park, near the 42 Traverse Trail

MORE LIKE THIS
NORTH ISLAND MTB RIDES

42 TRAVERSE

Just north of Mt Ruapehua and Tongariro National Park is Tongariro Forest, a conservation area with greater access for bike and horse riders and other recreational users than the national park. Chief among the attractions for mountain bikers is the 42 Traverse multi-use trail, which covers 46km (28 miles) of rough terrain. Access is via the Kapoors Rd carpark, which maximises the amount of descent as you ride down to Owhango. You can leave a car at the end and take a local shuttle to the start. The route is also used by 4WDs for half the year (December to May) so there will be ruts along this former logging track. Expect some river crossings and to get your feet wet. Listen out for native birdlife, including brown kiwis.
Start // Kapoors Rd off State Hwy 47
Finish // Owhango off State Hwy 4
Distance // 46km (28 miles)
More info // www.doct.govt.nz

MARTON SASH & DOOR TRAMWAY

For a shorter and easier ride, the Marton Sash and Door Tramway is a family-friendly loop along a former tramway on the volcanic plateau between Tongariro National Park and Whanganui National Park to the west. For some of the route, the tramway runs beside the main railway line that serves National Park Village with infrequent trains from Auckland and Wellington (three days per week each). Then the trail dives into sub-alpine bush, rich with native birdlife. The tramway was originally operated by the Marton Sash and Door logging company (which presumably made windows and doors) and there are remnants of both the locomotives and the logging industry to see. It's also part of the larger Mountains to Sea / Ngā Ara Tuhonu route.
Start/Finish // National Park Village
Distance // 19km (12 miles)
More info // www.mountainstosea.nz

CRATERS MOUNTAIN BIKE PARK

On the north shore of Lake Taupo, Craters is a mountain bike park with around 55km (34 miles) of purpose-built trails spread throughout a commercial pine plantation. There are trails for a wide range of abilities, with several tracks filled with jumps and berms. It's a good place for a quick fix of fat-tyred fun, although there are no big adventure rides available: black-rated tracks such as Outback or Waipouawerawera are less than 10km (six miles) in length. Thanks to the quick-draining terrain, Craters Mountain Bike Park is suitable to ride all year. However, the park sustained some damage during a cyclone during 2023 and repairs were underway at the time of writing.
Start // Wairakei Drive, Taupo
Distance // 55km (34 miles)
More info // www.biketaupo.org.nz

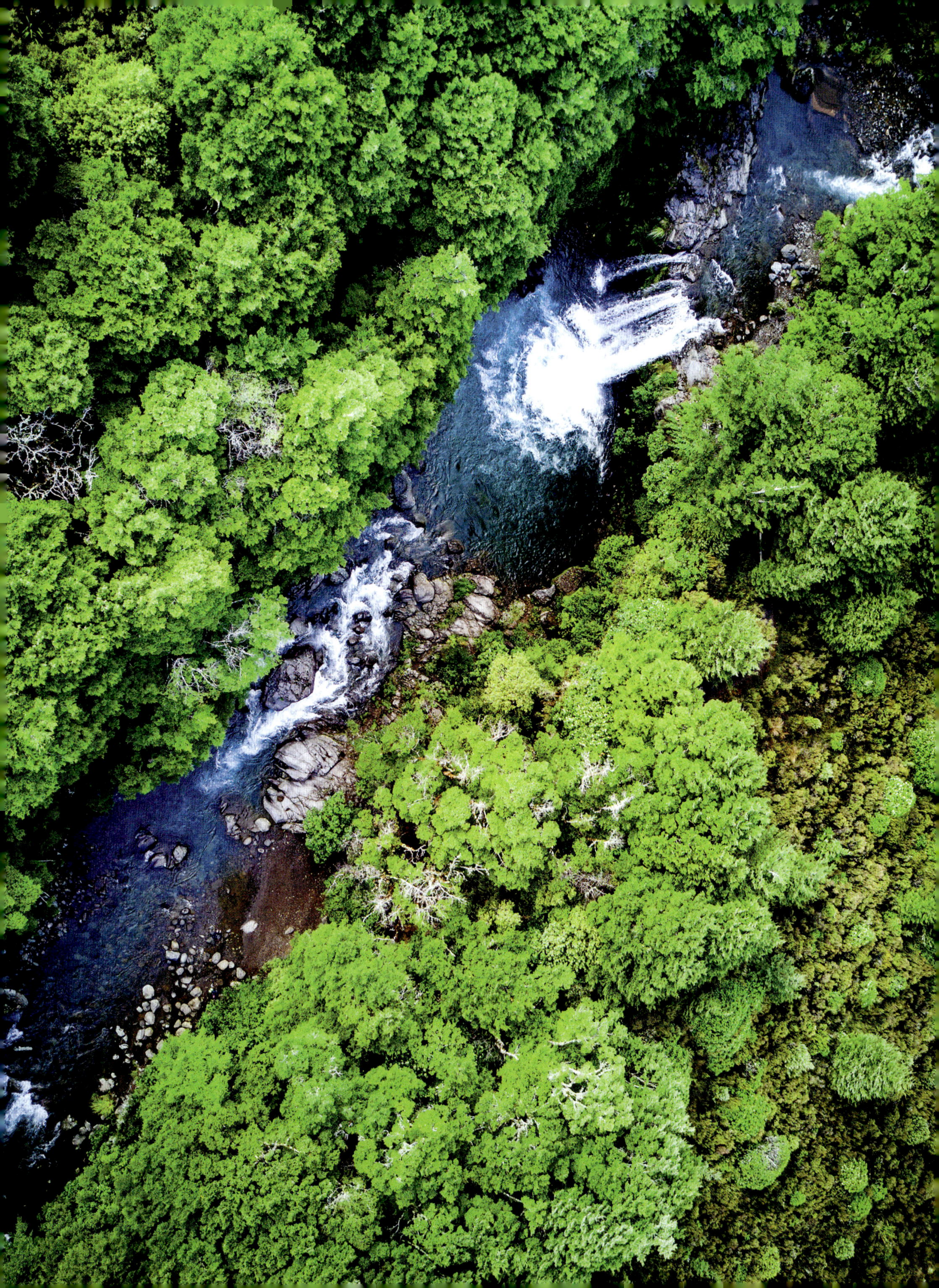

- EPIC BIKE RIDES OF AUSTRALIA & NEW ZEALAND -

KŌPIKO AOTEAROA

Kōpiko is an epic 1000km trip across the centre of New Zealand's North Island. How many mistakes could 12 middle-aged Kiwi men make on one bike ride?

If our Māori language skills had been better, we might have taken the name as a warning: *Kōpiko* – to go alternatively in opposite directions, go back and forth, meander, wander, ramble. But instead, the Irishman and I – regular road cycling friends – thought 'why not?'. Get a few mates together, ride across the island, enjoy sights and swims, evening meals and a beer.

Our enthusiasm was infectious. Ten more friends signed on. They bought gravel bikes and bags, a few even did some training. We looked over the course: a new epic ride by the famous Kennett Brothers, running for 1071km through some very hilly, remote country in the centre of the North Island. A lot of hills – 17,000 metres of climbing all told. And not much else – a few settlements but no supermarket across those thousand kilometres.

Some of the terrain is legendary to New Zealanders. The gravel roads and one-way, hand-built tunnels of the Forgotten World Highway from Stratford to Taumarunui; 80km of single on the Timber Trail through the ancient Pureora Forest; and the bush and hills of Te Urewera, a place where the Māori language is spoken as frequently as English.

As we arrived at Cape Egmont lighthouse before dawn one

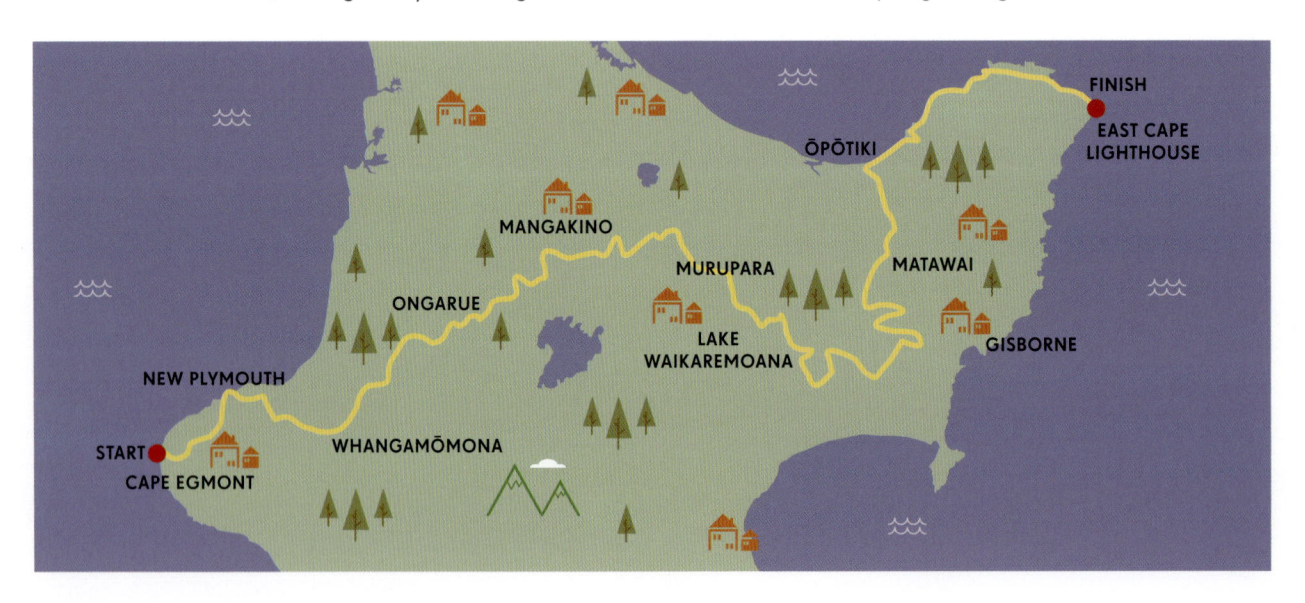

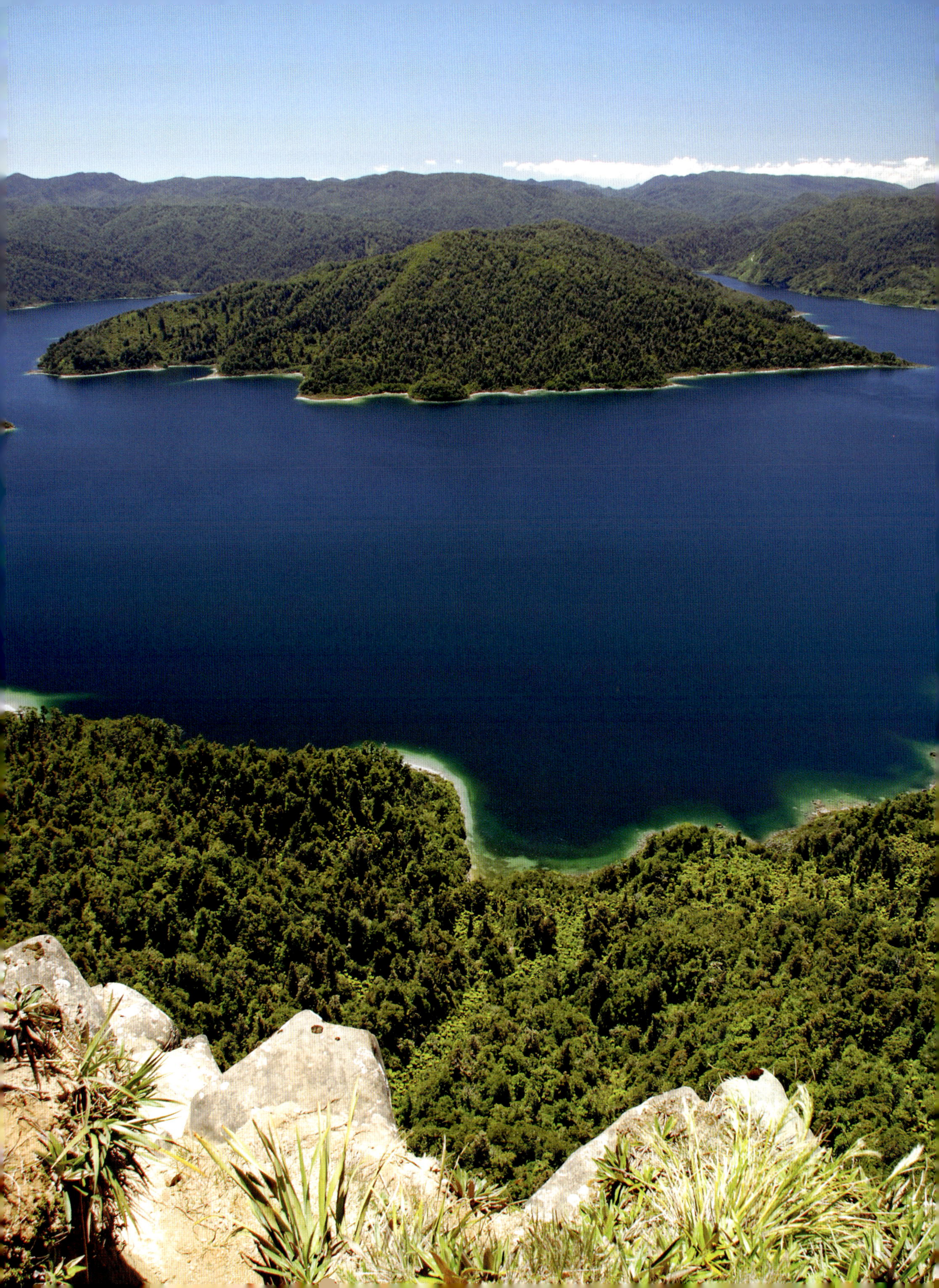

> *"The call and response of cows and dogs (and the occasional snorer) serenaded us as we curled up"*

January morning with a dozen or so other Kōpiko hardies, the anticipation was electric.

Less so a few days later. After putting our wet gear back on and cycling 40km on the Timber Trail in the wrong direction, we held on through the 'trauma trail' – a greasy, narrow piece of singletrack – only to battle 100km/h crosswinds into Whakamaru by 3pm. We were a ragged band by that point. The Builder's blisters meant he couldn't sit down, the mountain-biking Saffa had taken a couple of falls, loose pages from our trail guide blew over State Highway 32, and the Accountant was talking about calling a friend for a pickup. We still had 70km to ride to reach our hotel ('dark, dank and filthy' said TripAdvisor, but how bad could it really be?).

What had gone so wrong?

Perhaps it was the planning. Seven days with 150km (90 miles) distance and a bit over 2000m of climbing each day seemed reasonable to some road cyclists. Much less so when you are four hours into the Timber Trail and are averaging 10km/h. Perhaps it was the weather. The Ngāi Tūhoe people of the central North Island are called 'the children of the mist' and we soon understood why. Perhaps it was our equipment. Broken panniers hurled over cliffs in disgust, narrow shoes leaving feet in agony, tubeless tyres leaking day after day. Or perhaps it was our slightly haphazard accommodation plans. 'Can you give me the key to the cabin?' 'What cabin?'

But of course, it is out of such adversity that legends arise. And there were many legends on this trip.

That first idyllic day. Dawn slowly lighting up the faces of our fellow riders. (The Kennett Brothers limit the starts to 100 a day so there are enough places to sleep and eat.) The climb up to the narrow, bush-covered road circling Mount Taranaki. A sprint around an outdoor velodrome north of New Plymouth. The group erupting into Bon Jovi's 'we're halfway there' 70km in. Our first shingle roads leading us to a beer sitting outside the pub in the famously independent Republic of Whangamōmona.

The ride through Murupara, Minginui, Ruatāhuna and on to Lake Waikaremoana and Te Urewera, one of the remotest parts of Aotearoa and now back under the *rangatiratanga* (chiefly autonomy) of local iwi Ngāi Tūhoe. Soaring native podocarps, wild horses grazing on the side of the road, a hunter with a wild pig on the back of the truck giving his sage advice ('tell the guy Crocodile Candee sent you and he'll give you a beer').

The brilliant country hospitality. Arriving on a dry, sunlit evening to Taaheke farmstay. Hot soup waiting for us, one lasagne and – when we demolished that – a second. The call and response of cows and dogs (and the occasional snorer) serenading us as we curled up in the old shearers' quarters. Winding our way the next morning through the cold, clear light to be greeted every few hours by 'trail angels' – locals who just like having us in their neck of the woods. We drink up the water, the fresh fruit from the trees, the hospitality.

On the seventh morning, I woke up before dawn with my head out the end of my bivvy bag, and was stunned by the blazing galaxies beaming through the clear coastal air. We packed up our gear one last time, and set off on the long but flat day up the East Cape from Ōpōtiki to the lighthouse at the end. After the usual double breakfast, we enjoyed a proper lunch beside the clear water in Waihau Bay as the locals showed up in utes for a big fishing competition. A few hills around Te Kaha and then there we were on the white gravel road along the shoreline taking us to East Cape Lighthouse. There were nearly tears when two friends surprised us with champagne and a BBQ – and almost some more as we saw other friends, about to start in the opposite direction, being welcomed with kai and manaakitanga (food and hospitality) by the local Māori community.

Would we do it all again? For sure. Would we do it differently? Definitely. Our key insights? Cycling with a big group of friends is awesome. (We still liked each other at the end of the trip, though perhaps don't mention 'pizzagate' to the one who missed out on a slice). Take the time to smell the roses. (We should have slid down the Rere Rockslide, lain in the hot pools at Waikite, cycled the Pakihi track, and much more.) Oh, and of course, always wear double bib shorts. **SE**

INDEPENDENCE DAY

When the government decided that the settlement of Whangamōmona was actually part of Manawatu-Wanganui rather than Taranaki, locals rebelled. Different rugby teams, different beers, different people – no way! The town declared itself the 'Republic of Whangamōmona' and you can still get your passport stamped or buy a Whangamōmona passport for a couple of dollars.

Clockwise from top: shacking up for the night; on the open road. Previous spread: Lake Waikaremoana translates as 'sea of rippling waters'

TOOLKIT

Start/Finish // Cape Egmont / East Cape Lighthouse
Distance // 1071km (665 miles)
Getting there // Cape Egmont is around 50km from New Plymouth, which has an airport. East Cape Lighthouse is 190km from the nearest airport in Gisborne. Shuttles are available during Kōpiko season.
When to go // You can ride it any time, but the Kennett Brothers run it as a sociable event each January (free with donation to a good cause).
What to wear // It can be wet, and you gain altitude on the Timber Trail, so it can be cold even in summer.
What to pack // There are no bike shops or supermarkets or much else on the way, so carry tubes, tyres and tools to last you until the finish.
Where to stay // Unless you take a tent, accommodation options are limited, so book in advance. The Kennett Brothers Kōpiko Guides have good advice. Farmstays are recommended, plus old country pubs.
Where to eat // Everywhere you can! Food supplies are limited, so you need to plan and carry some.
More info // www.touraotearoa.nz/p/kopiko.html

Opposite: dawn breaks at Milford Sound; touring near Lake Tekapo

MORE LIKE THIS
SOUTH ISLAND BREVETS

THE KIWI BREVET

Kōpiko is one of a number of organised bikepacking events (or 'brevets') run around the country over the New Zealand summer. They all have a pretty similar ethos. At 1000kms or so they'll likely take you a week or more and they aren't races (well, for most riders!). Riders are on their own – the organisers don't provide food, accommodation or mechanical help but riders are expected to carry a tracker and to donate to a relevant charity. Taking part will put you on the road with a few dozen or a few hundred others, young and old, men and women, locals and travellers, all keen on a challenge. The Kiwi Brevet is probably the oldest bikepacking multiday event, starting and finishing in Blenheim in February, taking in Molesworth Station, Hanmer Springs, Arthurs Pass and coming back up the West Coast.
More info // www.greatkiwigravel.com/kiwi-brevet

THE TUATARA 1000 AND GREAT SOUTHERN BREVET

This brevet departs from Gore and moseys around the deep South in February. The philosophy? 'Is there a gravel option? Take it. Can we visit the coast? Go on. Can we avoid the main road? Please. If we go down this dead end road, will it be worth it? For sure.' Also on the South Island, in January, the Great Southern Brevet takes off from Tekapo, 'possibly the most stunning and inspirational 1100km ride you can find on our little planet' according to bikepacking.com and I wouldn't argue. Routes vary but can include a steamer trip across Lake Wakatipu, the mighty Nevis Valley (highest public road in New Zealand), closeups of Mount Cook, and miles of gravel roads and farm tracks. Some riders (including some Tour Divide bikepacking legends) do race this one.
More info // https://www.facebook.com/groups/greatsouthernbrevet
https://www.greatkiwigravel.com/tuatara-1000

SOUND TO SOUND

And a new ride rolls from Marlborough Sounds down to Milford Sound called, appropriately, Sound to Sound. This one starts a little later (1 March to allow riders on to the Queen Charlotte Track in the Marlborough Sounds) and goes a little longer (1500kms including some hike-a-bike – you are really not going to want to do this in a week). A big ride that brings some of the highlights of the Kiwi Brevet and the Great Southern Brevet together in one ride. Maps are freely available online and 'trail angels' will cheer you along and farmstays will have meals ready during the event.
More info // http://www.touraotearoa.nz/p/sound-to-sound.html

© Southern Lightscapes-Australia/Getty Images; Klanarong Chitmung/Shutterstock

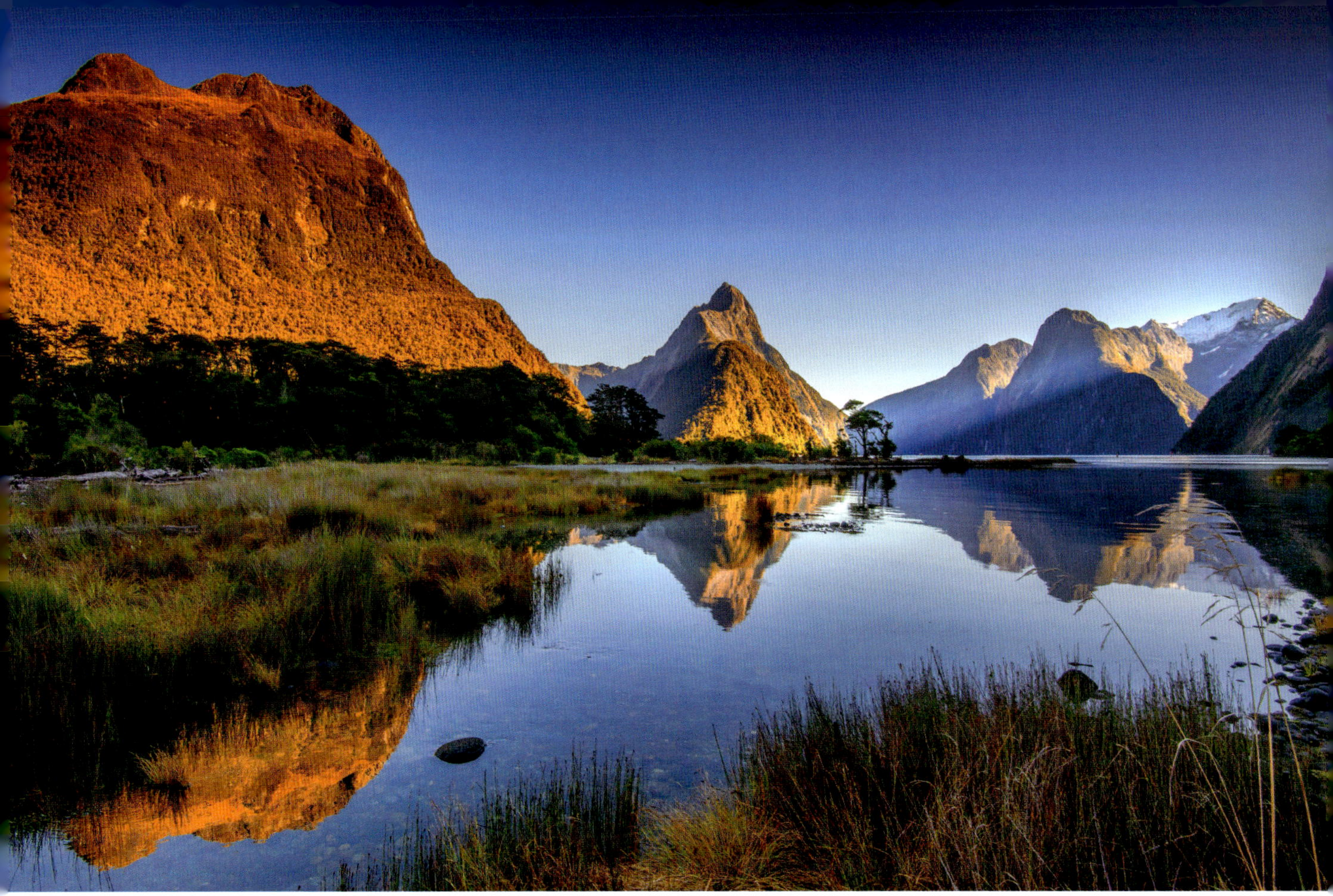

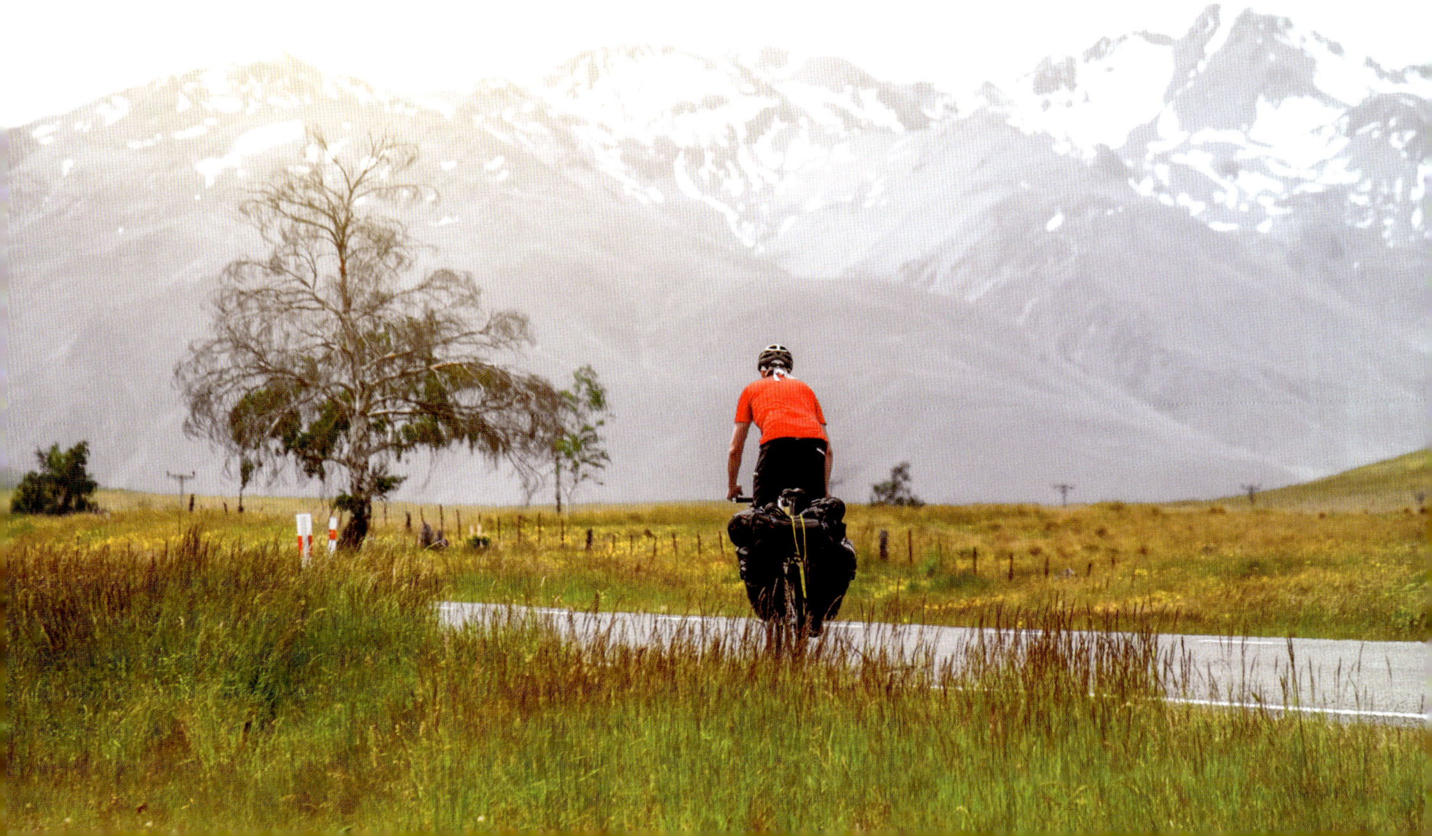

THE SOUTH ISLAND, NEW ZEALAND

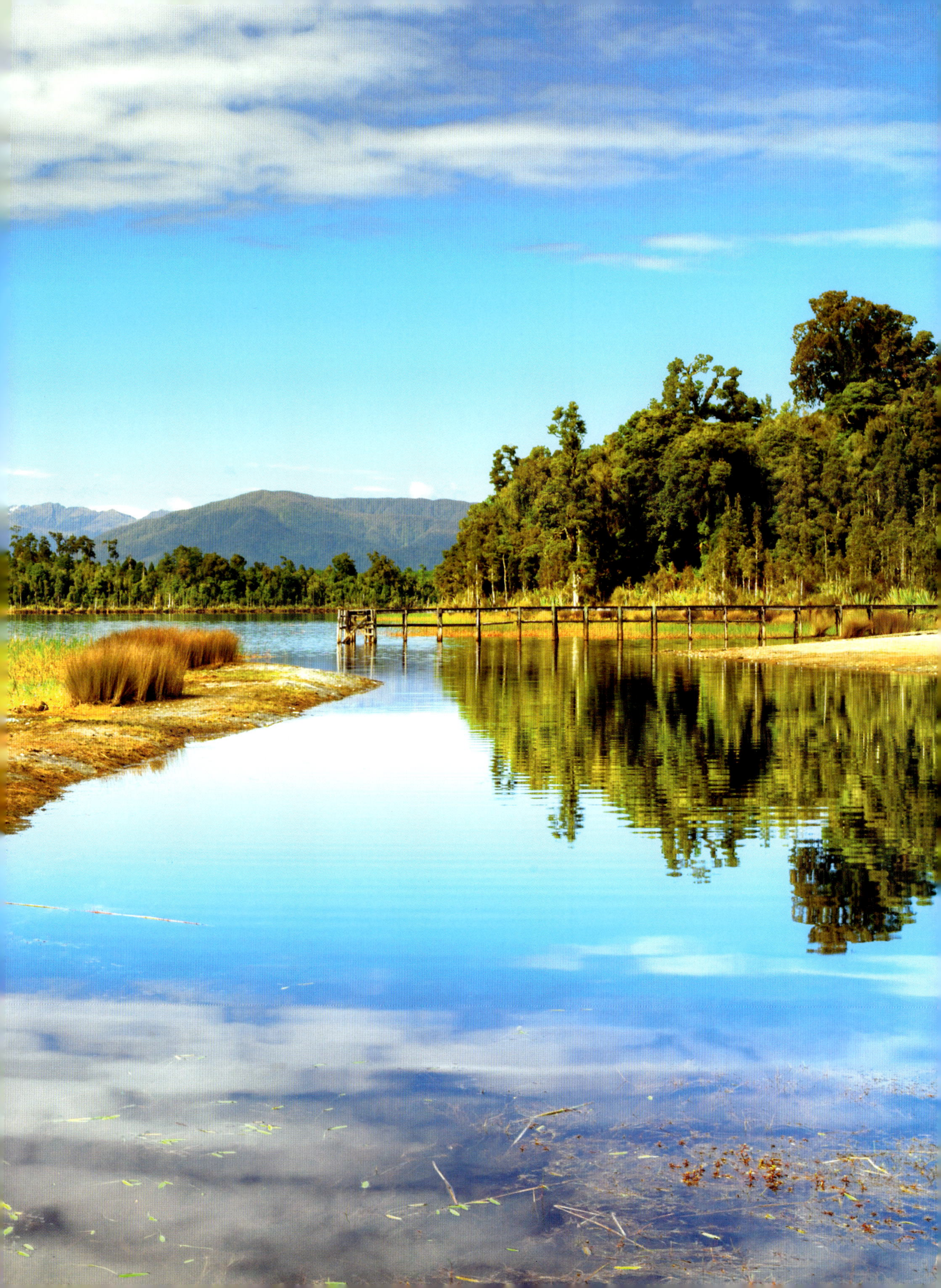

THE MOLESWORTH MUSTER

As little fluffy clouds float above you and speckle the surrounding landscape of Marlborough, take a two-wheeled tour of vast sheep stations on this brilliant bikepacking route.

Molesworth Station is the largest working farm in New Zealand at 1800 sq km (695 sq miles). It sits about 900m (2900ft) high, behind the inland Kaikoura range, two hours north of Christchurch. A farm may not sound like the most glamorous of bikepacking destinations, but the topography of the Marlborough High Country really makes this place special. So, drawn by the promise of empty gravel roads with ranges in every direction, I set off into this hidden yet totally characteristic part of New Zealand.

I'd decided on a loop that could be ridden through the southern section of Molesworth, connecting through the adjoining Rainbow Station to St Arnaud, then back down to Hanmer via the St James Cycle Trail, one of New Zealand's Great Rides. My only real unknown was a river crossing with a missing bridge. But it was summer and I hadn't seen rain in weeks, so how much of a problem could one river crossing really be?

I packed four dinners and enough oats for an emergency day or two. I had a shelter, water filter and stove, so the rest was down to me. Leaving the small village with another bikepacker I'd met in town the day before, we made the first climb up 700m (2300ft) into the valley.

This was big, open country that felt like a micro-Andes: wide-view gravel roads and glacially formed mountains on both sides, with the occasional farm vehicle as the only traffic. It was the type of landscape that you almost can't believe still exists. The dusty gravel road hugs the Acheron River for most of this section, and after a day of awe-filled riding in high summer sun, we recharged our weary bodies in the cool currents before scoping out a spot to camp for the night.

One of my favourite things about riding in New Zealand is the generally harmless wildlife. The largest things you're likely to encounter are wild pigs or deer, but what people forget to warn you about are the sandflies – tiny black insects that arrive in swarms and bite as soon as they find an exposed piece of skin, quite often unaffected by bug spray. The most effective deterrent is just to keep on riding.

After a day of progress with light tailwinds, it wasn't until we stopped and lost the breeze that we realised quite what we'd be up against. As we set up our shelters for the first night's camp, the presence of the sandflies quickly became apparent, but not enough to distract us from the last golden rays of sun catching the peaks. This place felt equally beautiful and

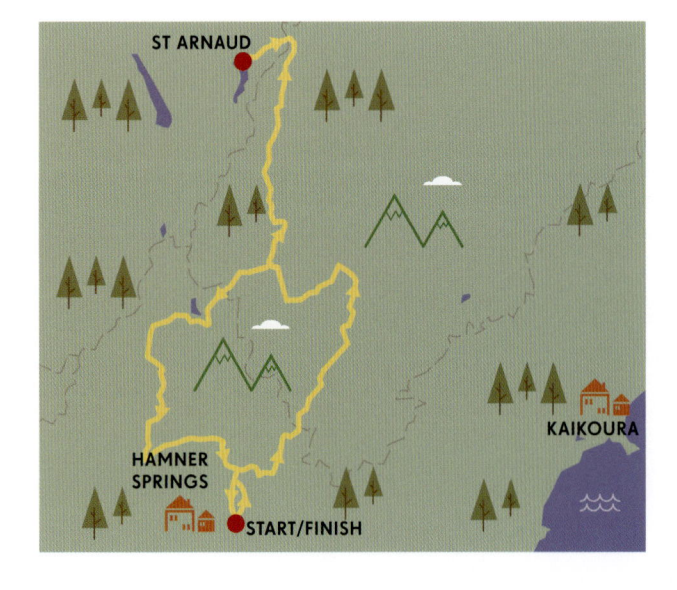

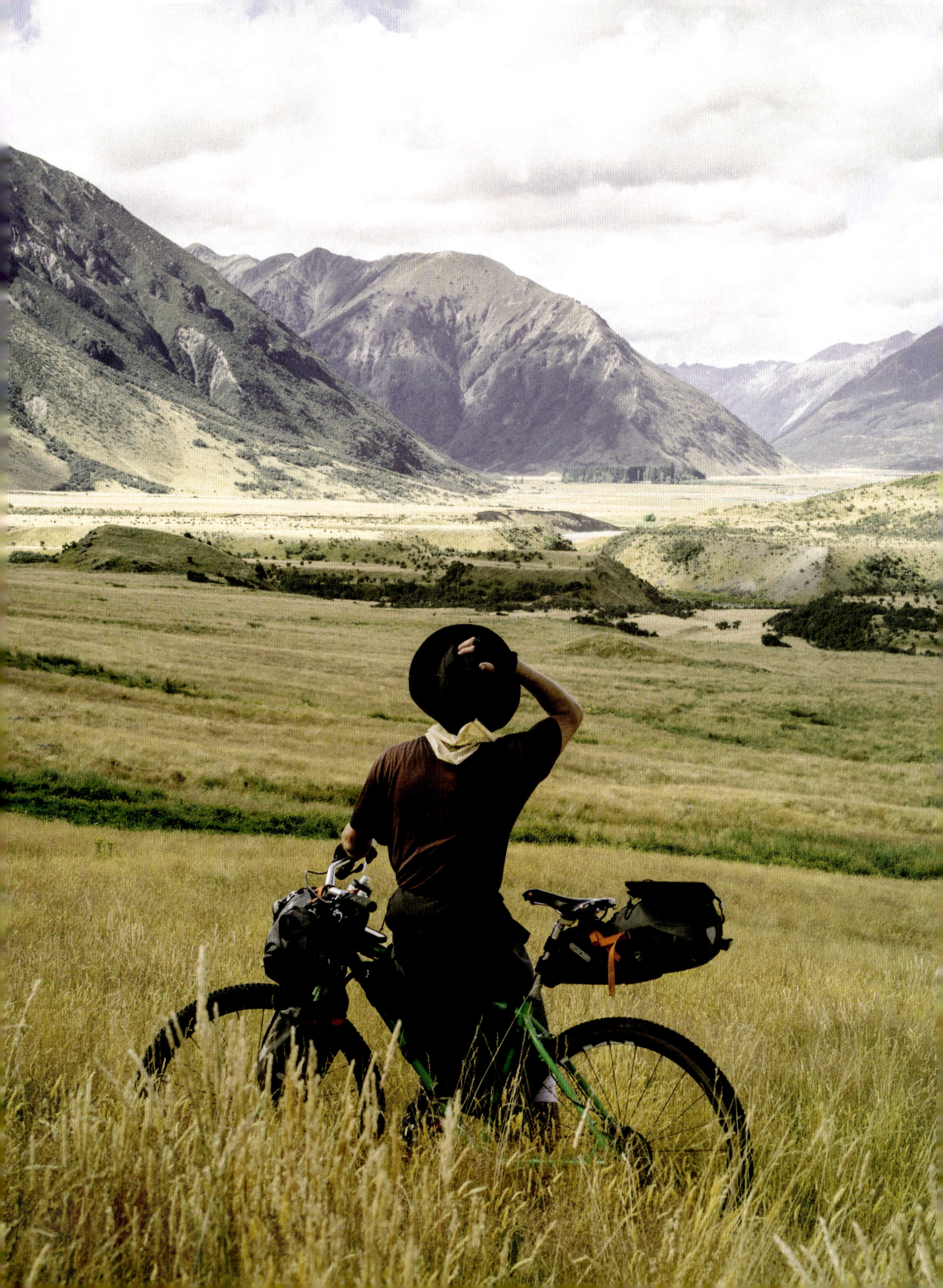

remote, with nothing but the sound of the river and our pots boiling to make our dehydrated meals for the night, which would be a well-rested one.

After a rushed departure to avoid the morning swarms, we arrived at the entrance to Rainbow Station. A road that is only open to the public for a couple of months each year winds down from 1100m (3600ft) through colourful canyons. This is a working farm now used for honey instead of cattle, and is supported partly by the toll paid by passing overlanders, bike tourers and motorcycles. We escaped another sandfly attack thanks to the tollgate volunteer who kindly boiled his billie for us and let us shelter in the mustering hut while we had our lunch. It was a very welcome rest, and one that would not be repeated until we reached St Arnaud that night.

Lake Rotoiti, on the outskirts of St Arnaud, was where I left my riding partner. We made the most of being in civilisation and celebrated with pizza at the local tavern. After parting ways, I turned back up the Rainbow Valley, stopping at a shelter just off Lake Sedgemere, where the lure of a bed and a hut with dry firewood proved too much of a draw to push on. As the wind and rain picked up, my rest was partially disturbed by worries of how this unexpected downpour might affect the upcoming river crossing. But the sound of rain on the tin roof and the crackle of firewood proved far too soothing to let this distraction last for long.

Lake Tennyson to Maling Pass takes you up to 1300m (4260ft), with captivating views into the valley beyond. Riding down this potholed 15% 'road' with its steep drop-off on my right was one of the most satisfying parts of the trip, with technical sections that had my disc brakes screeching all the way to the valley floor.

With nothing but flat grasslands in a beautiful valley surrounding me, it seemed like the obvious place for a lunch break. But once again, such plans were soon foiled by the swarming sandflies. It was as if they were determined to keep me on my feet and not waste a minute of this incredible riding.

Towards the bottom of the valley, the river crossing fears in the back of my mind were reignited by signs warning of the out-of-service bridge just beyond Pool Hut. It was decision time. I could choose to take a detour that would guarantee a safe passage home but cut off half of the St James Trail, or I could continue and take my chances with the crossing. Having taken the safe route on previous journeys and often wondered what might have been, I opted for the latter. Regret would have been a far worse option than a day of scenic backtracking if the river proved impassable.

On what would be my final night on the trail, I arrived at Pool Hut, having been on my bike since 8am with nothing more than a few fleeting breaks. My excitement about a good night's rest was soon put to an end, as the hut offered no protection from the flies, with fist-sized holes in the walls. Instead, I set up camp next to the hut and watched the sun disappear behind the Southern Alps. I could only imagine

THE SOUTH ISLAND, NEW ZEALAND

what morning would bring. Would the river be passable or would I be riding back? Or would I lose my belongings to the rapids? My dreams of river crossings were disturbed only by rats in the hut next to me, rifling through the makeshift kitchen. It's times like these that you have to love bikepacking, when your only concerns are river crossings and wildlife, and you're surrounded by nature and feel very present.

The next morning, I woke with nerves at this moment of truth. Minutes after leaving camp, I was tasked with finding a way across the Waiau Uwha River with no bridge. I followed signs of trodden grass – where previous wanderers must have faced the same prospects – to the riverbank, where the rapids seemed fast and deep, and offered little chance to cross.

As with any solo adventure, the voices in my head were loud and playing havoc with my decisions: 'I should have taken the detour.' 'Is this a stupid thing to do solo?' It took me nearly an hour of cautious attempts, emergency PLB close by, with shaky legs and cleats on wet boulders. The water was up to my waist and the strong current pulling me off balance made carrying my loaded bike on my shoulders a necessity. Dry bags become flotation devices and water flowing through the spokes created so much drag that getting washed downstream felt like a very real hazard. Once I'd found an island, there was no going back, so I made the final push and collapsed, wet up to my armpits, on the other side. I was laughing with exhilaration because what had been in the back of my mind this whole journey was now over, and I was grateful not to have listened to those doubtful inner voices.

The only thing left to do now was complete the last section back to St James Homestead, then on into town to the nearest bakery. I sat there in Hanmer Springs, covered in pastry, as I finished off my second pie, strangely missing the company of the sandflies and everything they represented to me – living off my bike in the wilderness. The bites on my legs served as beautiful souvenirs of an adventure I'd happily relive in an instant. **TP**

ONCE BITTEN

Sandflies breed in running water and are most often found near damp bush, beaches, lakes and rivers, especially on the west coast of the South Island. They don't like wind, and are most numerous during first and last light in humid, overcast conditions, and just before it rains. They also don't like smoke, so fire can be more useful than just for heat. Sandflies evolved to prefer penguins as their main source of food. This is perhaps why they are attracted to the colour black. They can also bite through clothes.

Clockwise from top left: riding with friends; looking out over Lake Rotoiti; planning the route; campground cookery. Previous spread: travel through broad, glacial valleys.

TOOLKIT

Start/Finish // Hanmer Springs
Distance // 295km (183 miles)
Getting there // The nearest airport is Christchurch. From there, head north to Hanmer Springs junction.
When to go // November to March.
What to wear // Conditions are changeable, so pack for cold, rain and heat: base layers, shell and puffer.
What to pack // Water filter, personal location beacon (PLB) and, of course, bug spray and bug net for your head.
Where to stay // There are many camping options and backcountry huts that need to be booked. Hanmer Springs has options for hotels, Airbnb and campgrounds.
Tours // www.hanmeradventure.co.nz
Things to know // Eat at PJ's Pies in Hanmer Springs. At the end of the trip take a dip in Hanmer's hot springs.
More info // www.nzcycletrail.com; www.komoot.com/tour/1030017345?ref=wtd

Opposite: which way now? An Otago sign points riders in the direction of both Nevis Valley Back Country and Mt Cook

MORE LIKE THIS
SOUTH ISLAND ACTION

AROUND THE MOUNTAINS

Serving up some of the most dynamic mountain vistas in New Zealand, this intermediate cycling adventure begins with a scenic lake cruise from Queenstown. From there, the stellar views just keep on coming as the trail heads around the Eyre Mountains, passing though the Von Valley and south of the Mavora Lakes, which is a good spot to break for an incredible night's camping. The route can be linked back to Queenstown or on to Southland and Te Anau.
Start // Walter Peak Station, Lake Wakatipu
Finish // Kingston
Distance // 186km (115 miles)
More info //
www.aroundthemountains.co.nz

NEVIS VALLEY

On the borders of Central Otago and Northern Southland, the Nevis is a cycle ride that runs on the highest public road in New Zealand, though at 1300m (4260ft), it isn't recommended for cars. On top of that, it's closed in the winter, and at other times the weather is very changeable. The gravel road has multiple fords to ride through, as well as two steep climbs, taking you through sparse landscapes that are a complete contrast to the shores of Lake Wakatipu, just 10km (6 miles) over the peaks to the west. After a long downhill into Bannockburn (going northbound), you'll find a great coffee truck waiting.
Start // Garston
Finish // Bannockburn
Distance // 67km (42 miles)

RAINBOW TRAIL

If you don't want to do the full loop here, including part of the St James Cycle Trail (especially if the bridge at the Waiau Uwha River remains down), consider this one-way itinerary on the trail that connects St Arnaud with Hanmer Springs via the original stock route between Marlborough and Canterbury. It passes through two working farms – Rainbow Station, which is privately owned, and Molesworth Station, managed by the Department of Conservation. It's a remarkable high-country wilderness experience, complete with craggy mountains, beech forest and beautiful open tussock lands, as well as remote campsites and backcountry huts.
Start // St Arnaud
Finish // Hanmer Springs
Distance // 115km (71 miles)
More info // www.nzcycletrail.com

© Kym McLeod/Shutterstock

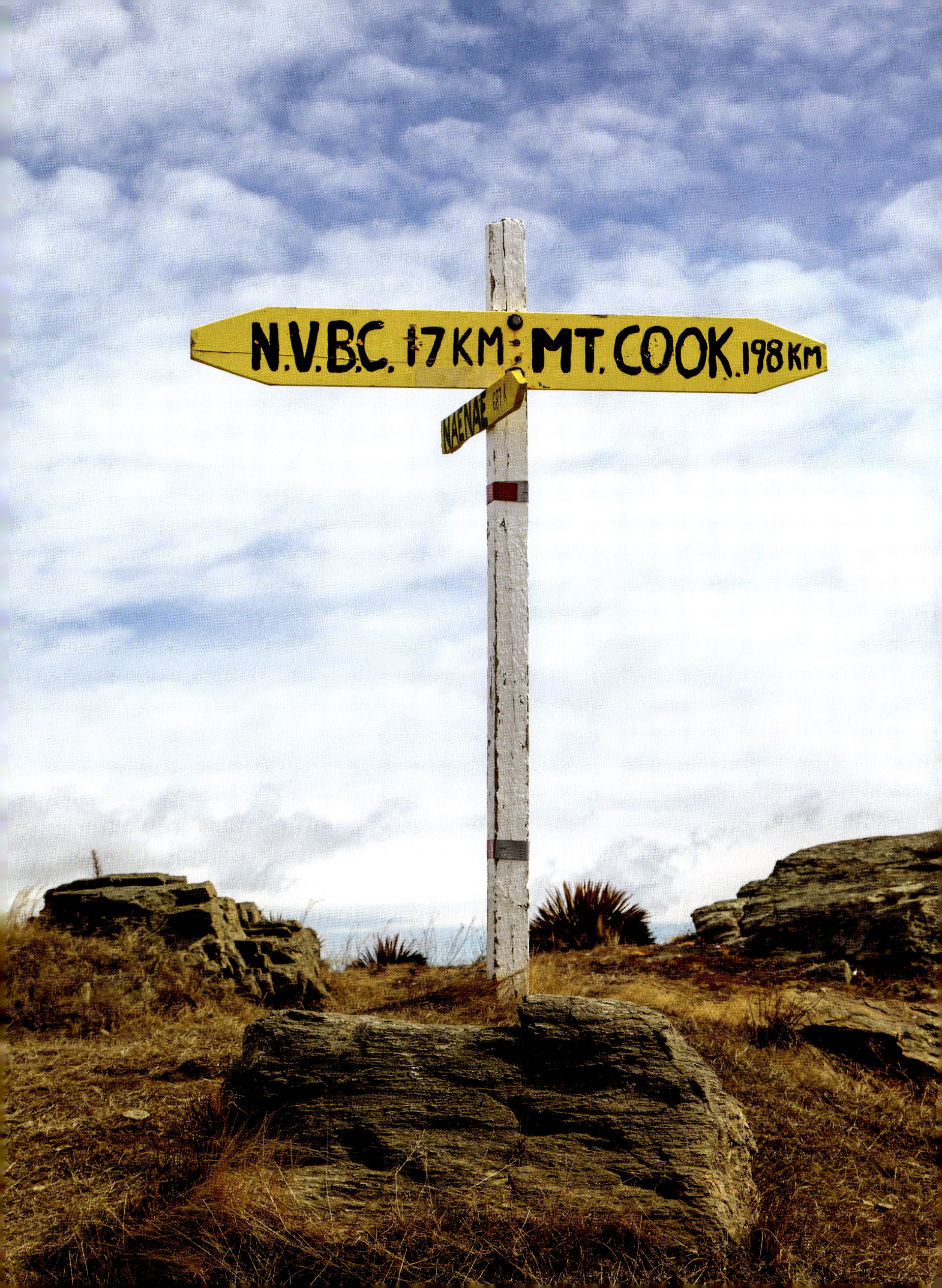
N.V.B.C. 17 KM
MT. COOK. 198 KM
NAENAE 687 K

- EPIC BIKE RIDES OF AUSTRALIA & NEW ZEALAND -

THE WEST COAST WILDERNESS TRAIL

Pedal through gold-rush history on the South Island's damp west coast as you ride squeezed between the sea and Southern Alps on this Great Ride.

The northwest coast of the South Island is New Zealand's original gold coast. In the 1860s, a gold rush boomed to such proportions that the town of Hokitika almost instantaneously became New Zealand's most populous settlement, home to thousands of prospectors and their hangers-on, with dozens of pubs furnishing its streets. Today, it's not prospectors that roll into town, but cyclists, with Hokitika one of a string of former gold towns threaded together by the West Coast Wilderness Trail (WCWT).

Fittingly, the ride begins (or ends) in Ross, the WCWT's southern trailhead and the scene of New Zealand's largest-ever gold strike – the 3.09kg Roddy Nugget, which was unearthed in 1909 and gifted to King George V on his coronation a year later, only to be melted down into a royal tea set.

More than gold, however, it's green that defines the southern end of the trail as I set out pedalling from Ross, burrowing into rainforest and passing the West Coast Treetop

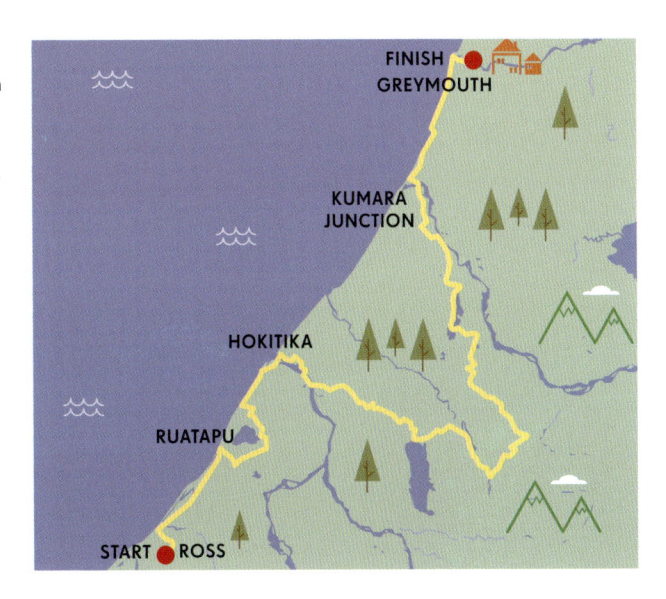

Walk, an elevated walkway and tower rising up to 47m (154ft) above the forest floor.

The 'wilderness' component of the trail's name is a reference to this thirsty rainforest, fed by some of New Zealand's biggest rains, and the fierce west coast beaches along the journey. At times, the bush leans permanently with the prevailing winds, and New Zealand's highest mountains serrate the sky to the east. True to form, it's raining as I first enter the forest, though it's just a hint of this region's potential to pour – Hokitika averages around 3m (10ft) of rain a year, while the Cropp River, little more than 20km (12 miles) inland from Ross, was once deluged by 18m (60ft) of rain in a year.

Though the trail is wild in its surrounds, it's largely mild in terrain terms. It resembles a classic rail trail, even if it is more of a cycling jigsaw puzzle; a connecting series of former tramlines and railways, old packhorse trails, roads, historic bridges and newer singletrack. Even the towns – Ross, Hokitika, Kumara, Greymouth – are well spaced, a day's ride apart.

Out of Ross, the trail follows the old railway line along the coast before swinging onto the Maranui Tramline, a former logging tramway still stitched in parts with sleepers as it skirts the shores of Lake Mahinapua. Curling through dense rainforest, it's a tangible reminder that timber felling took over once gold fever had faded (though the latter never entirely disappeared: in 2019, a 177g nugget was found near Hokitika).

This first day is a simple one – just 33km (20 miles) into Hokitika, where there's a classic gold-rush grandeur to the town

> *"At times the only human mark is the trail, as I cycle past hillsides tangled with rainforest, bare mountain slopes and translucent rivers"*

architecture. Even more impressive is the surrounding skyline, with the snow-capped Southern Alps hovering over the town's rooftops. The black sands of the town beach are so littered with driftwood that Hokitika has turned them into a semi-natural art gallery of bare-bones sculptures, stretching for hundreds of metres.

Hokitika is the point where the WCWT leaves the coast, not to return until the final stretch into Greymouth. A longer day awaits me – a 72km (45 mile) haul into Kumara – flirting with the foothills of the Southern Alps, but mercifully never quite entering them. Instead, I set out across a coastal plain dotted with glacial lakes and wide braided rivers that formed much of the setting for Eleanor Catton's 2013 Booker Prize-winning novel, *The Luminaries*.

Etched into this plain is the hand-dug Kaniere Water Race, a gold-rush-era channel that the WCWT follows to Lake Kaniere, riding on a trail as narrow as the Water Race itself. I ride deep in rainforest again, popping out into bright light only as I reach the shores of the lake, which, on a breathless morning, is cast in near-flawless reflections of the mountains.

This Wilderness Trail has never felt wilder than here, behind Hokitika's back. At times the only human mark is the trail, as I

HOKITIKA GORGE

It's worth building in an extra day for a detour out to one of this region's most spectacular natural features: Hokitika Gorge. From the town of Hokitika, it's roughly a 30km (19 mile) ride on roads through the farmland of the Kokatahi Valley to the mouth of the gorge. Inside the gorge, a 2km (1.2 mile) loop walk crosses a couple of swing bridges high above the river's impossibly blue glacial waters.

Left to right: a scenic spot to park up; a farmer musters sheep along the road; treetop walk at Hokitika Previous spread: swing bridge across Hokitika Gorge; the West Coast's wonderful shoreline

cycle past hillsides tangled with rainforest, bare mountain slopes and translucent rivers, including the Arahura, which was a rich source of *pounamu* (greenstone) for Māori – the green that came before the gold. Kererū (New Zealand pigeons) burst out of trees, and there's the chance to park up the bikes and walk into the slanderously named Cesspools, which are actually perfect glacial-blue pools dotted between rapids on the upper Arahura River.

Even the human features along this section have a wild edge. Leaving the Cesspools, the WCWT begins a cleverly designed climb, almost tying itself in knots as it coils through a series of tight switchbacks to Cowboy Paradise, a replica Wild West town.

The climbs grinds on, but not for long. Crossing 317m (1040ft) Kawhaka Pass, the coast, now almost 40km (25 miles) away, begins to beckon again. The long descent follows dams, water races and lakes – water hurrying towards water – and I pause for the night in Kumara before rolling on to the coast the next morning. I cross the Taramakau River and ride towards Greymouth, with the Tasman Sea for company along the WCWT's home straight.

Entering the largest town on the west coast, I turn up onto the bank of the Grey River, riding atop a floodwall built in 1988 after a series of floods. I am once again – momentarily – riding towards the mountains, from which Aoraki/Mt Cook, the highest peak in New Zealand, now rises, but my finish is far closer at hand. Along the floodwall, an installation straddles the path like a victory arch, heralding the end of the trail. My ride through green and gold has ended beside the Grey River. **AB**

TOOLKIT

Start // Ross
Finish // Greymouth
Distance // 133km (83 miles)
Duration // 3-4 days
Getting there // Greymouth is connected to Christchurch by the TranzAlpine railway, as well as East West Coaches. Ross has no public transport, but the Wilderness Trail Shuttle (www.wildernesstrailshuttle.co.nz) can transport you between Greymouth and Ross (and points in between).
When to go // Rainfall in this region is spread across the year – February is the driest month, and December the wettest – so this ride is less seasonal than it might appear at first glance. The crisp winters can bring a stunning backdrop of snow-smothered Southern Alps peaks.
Tours // Adventure South (www.adventuresouth.co.nz) runs five-day tours along the WCWT, including transport to/from Christchurch.
More info // www.westcoastwildernesstrail.co.nz

Opposite: precipitous accommodation on the Old Ghost Road

MORE LIKE THIS
GOING FOR GOLD

GOLDFIELDS TRACK, VICTORIA

As the name suggests, the Goldfields Track is the ultimate showcase of Australia's most celebrated gold region. Following unsealed roads, firetrails and sections of singletrack, it's a challenging off-road journey through the big names of Australian gold: Ballarat, Creswick, Daylesford, Castlemaine and Bendigo. Between towns, it winds through gold diggings, follows the Great Dividing Range as it nears its southern end, traces the route that Creswick gold miners walked to join the Eureka Stockade, and passes the Garfield Water Wheel, the largest ever built in Victoria. Towns are spaced no more than 60km (37 miles) apart, breaking the ride into manageable portions, and there's even the chance to indulge in a therapeutic treatment at Hepburn Springs at around the midpoint of the ride.
Start // Mt Buninyong
Finish // Bendigo
Distance // 207km (128 miles)
More info // www.goldfieldstrack.com.au

OLD GHOST ROAD, SOUTH ISLAND

In the 1870s, gold miners set out to build a road between two isolated gold fields on New Zealand's west coast. The mountain country in between was so rugged that it ultimately defeated them, and the road was never completed. In 2007, a map of its proposed path was discovered, and the idea for the Old Ghost Road was seeded. The shared-use (mountain biking and walking) trail reflects the difficulties of the original route: a 1,200m (3,940ft) vertical climb from Buller Gorge into the Lyell Range to begin; narrow, vertiginous, cliff-hugging stretches once you reach the mountaintops; and a tight, exposed balancing act through the Mokihinui Gorge to finish. The views are stunning and the elevation is exhilarating. Four purpose-built huts (and two other basic huts) provide shelter and accommodation, including two private 'summer sleepouts' at each main hut.
Start // Lyell Historic Reserve
Finish // Seddonville
Distance // 85km (53 miles)
More info // www.oldghostroad.org.nz

WAIKAKAHO/CULLEN CREEK WALKWAY, SOUTH ISLAND

Following an old gold-mining trail near the Marlborough Sounds, this mountain-biking traverse packs plenty of punch into a short ride. From the Waikakaho Valley, it's a long climb to Waikakaho Saddle, about 800m (2,600ft) above sea level (and 700m/2,300ft above the Waikakaho Valley), passing an intriguing collection of gold-mining relics, from a tunnel burrowed beneath the Waikakaho River to a drive dug more than 100m (330ft) into the rock at remote Village Clearing, which was once a town of 200 miners. The first 2km (1.2 miles) beyond the saddle are rough enough to be largely unrideable – enjoy the walk! – before descending steeply to Prospector Creek. The miner-cut trail hacked into the cliffs above this creek is a truly spectacular section. Note that there are unbridged streams that become impassable after heavy rain at both ends of the track.
Start // Waikakaho Valley
Finish // Cullensville
Distance // 33km (20.5 miles)

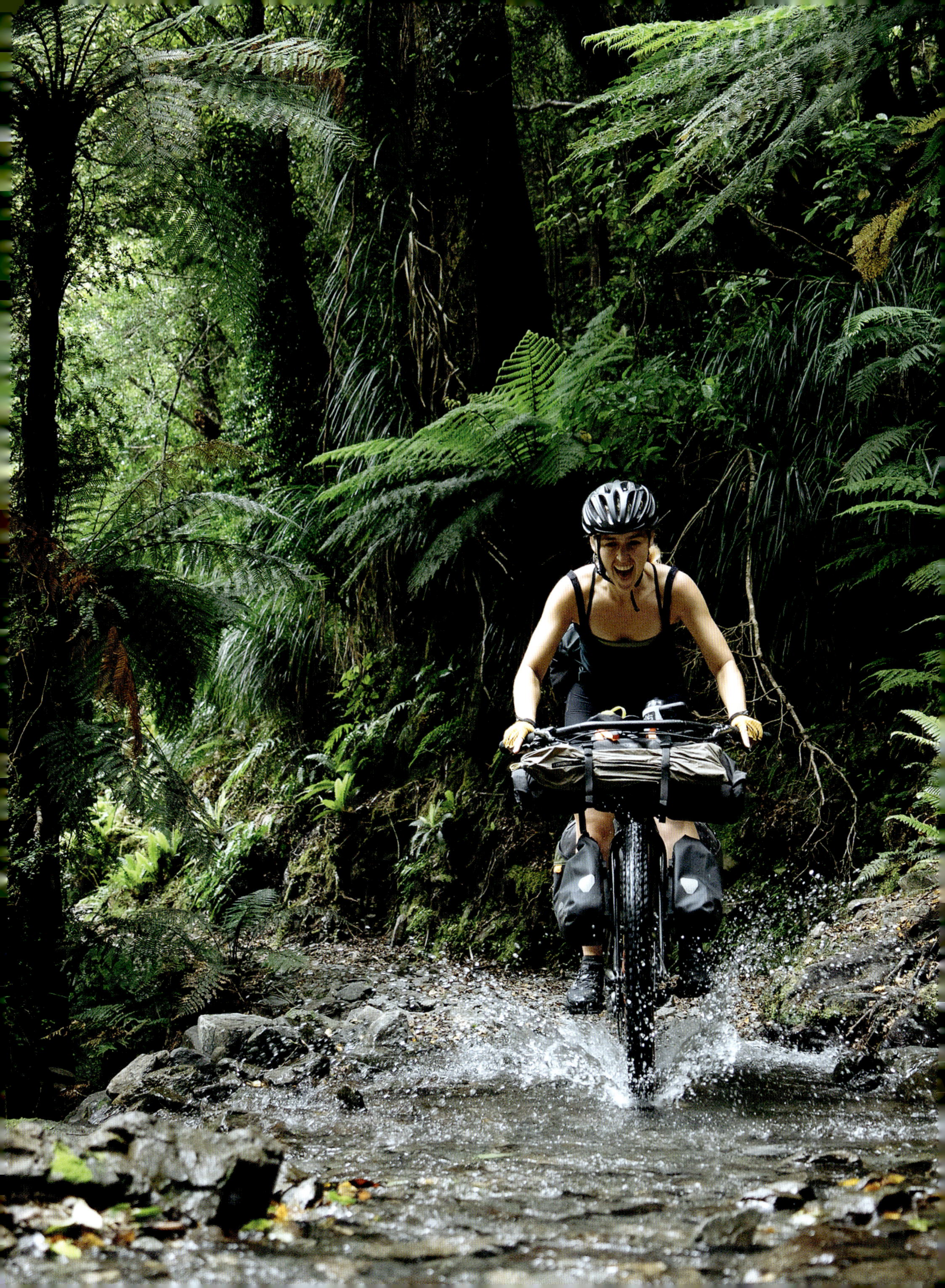

good night's sleep after all that climbing today.' We unravel our sleeping bags in preparation for our forty winks.

The next morning, the wakening hut booms to the sound of Phil's voice, as he waves off the first set of early risers. Semi-conscious, I reach for my coffee kit and begin the daily grind. As the coffee blooms, Tom rushes over, distressed.

'You won't believe it, mate. Someone's stolen the head torch and protein bars from my frame bag!' He heads outside and shows me the crime scene. As we inspect the frame bag for clues, I catch a swish of movement in my peripheral vision.

'Over there, Tom – is that your head torch?' I ask, trying desperately to hold back my laughter. 'Come back, you little bastard!' Tom cries out, as a thieving weka retreats into the bush, Tom's head torch flailing around its speckled neck. The next 10 minutes feel like something out of a Monty Python sketch, as we try to catch the feathered bandit. After a few bumps (and bruised egos) we admit defeat, retreating to the hut. I pour Tom a coffee to help cushion the blow and we set about packing the bikes, ready for day two.

'This is epic! I feel like I'm riding in the European Alps,' Tom screams out as he negotiates a series of tight, off-camber switchbacks in the subdued morning light. Down 300m (984ft), we plummet through the morning mist and the landscape changes in an instant. Gnarled beech forest lines the trail, with long branches bowing under the strength of the wind. Burnt oranges, rusty yellows and lurid greens pop from the forest canopy as we snake our way down the beautifully treacherous trail ahead.

HUT-PACKING

Complete with fully equipped kitchens, campsites and even helipads, the huts of Old Ghost Road are almost as impressive as the trail itself. Don't miss a night's sleep at the Ghost Lake Hut: sitting at 1200m (3940ft) above sea level, its spectacular views are a highlight of the trip. From a standard self-supported bikepack, to a leisurely multi-day cruise with chopper drops of cheese and wine, the huts make almost anything possible.

Clockwise from top: Ghost Lake hut; packing for the day on the trail. Previous spread: expect some water crossings on the route

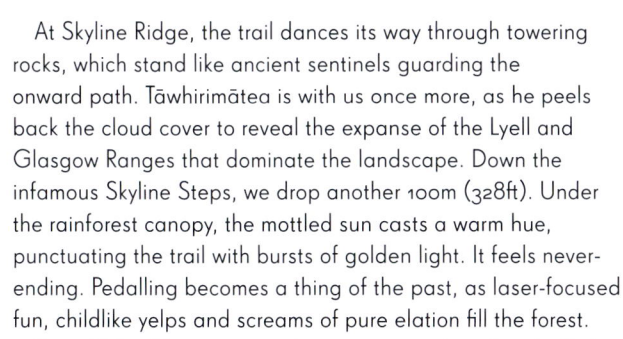

At Skyline Ridge, the trail dances its way through towering rocks, which stand like ancient sentinels guarding the onward path. Tāwhirimātea is with us once more, as he peels back the cloud cover to reveal the expanse of the Lyell and Glasgow Ranges that dominate the landscape. Down the infamous Skyline Steps, we drop another 100m (328ft). Under the rainforest canopy, the mottled sun casts a warm hue, punctuating the trail with bursts of golden light. It feels never-ending. Pedalling becomes a thing of the past, as laser-focused fun, childlike yelps and screams of pure elation fill the forest.

Stern Valley Hut comes and goes as our adrenaline-fuelled second wind carries us onwards. With full exposure, we soak up the harsh UV rays and sweat as the temperature soars to 32°C. We begin the climb through the earthquake-scarred Boneyard as the searing midday sun continues to sap our energy. Progress is slow, but we grind on through the lunar landscape, draining our water bottles until we taste their plastic.

One final pinch climb to crest the Solemn Saddle and we're fading fast. 'That's the last climb of the route, guys. It's pure downhill from here to pizza!' Bec announces, as she shovels peanut butter in her mouth. 'We've got plenty of light left, so I vote we go for it,' Tom gushes as the promise of pizza ignites the fabled third wind and we set off for one final flurry.

The group dynamic is at an all-time high as we pull into Rough & Tumble Lodge. Laughter fills the air as we replay the morning's antics with the naughty trail weka and tuck into our pizzas. After two months riding the South Island together, this would mark the end of our time with Tom. With new friendships forged on the trail, we part ways, thankful that our last ride was the Old Ghost Road. **SR**

TOOLKIT

Start/Finish // Lyell/Seddonville
Distance // 84km (52 miles)
Getting there // The best way to get to the Old Ghost Road is to use one of the round-trip van services, usually running out of Westport. There are also some great services that will drive your vehicle from the start to the end of the trail, with key-drop boxes at each end. Another option is to ride a loop from Westport.
When to go // October to April. February traditionally has the best weather.
What to wear // Be prepared for cold and wet weather. Long sleeves and trousers are essential as the sandflies can be pretty treacherous.
What to pack // Bug spray and wet weather gear are vital, along with some essential bike tools. Emergency kit items are also important as the ride is technical.
Where to stay // You can either choose huts or basic tent sites along the trail. Book your stays in advance, as it's a very popular ride year-round.
Good to know // We suggest starting at Lyell and riding in a south-to-north direction. Due to the technical nature and gradient of 4km (2.5 miles) of trail north of Ghost Lake, this section is easier to descend than ascend.
More info // www.oldghostroad.org.nz

Opposite: descending the Paparoa Track

MORE LIKE THIS
EPIC MOUNTAIN BIKING

ALL-MOUNTAIN TRAIL, NEW SOUTH WALES

Thredbo is Australia's best year-round alpine destination. In winter, it's home to the country's longest ski runs and its only alpine gondola. In summer, the resort switches into MTB gear – it has Australia's only lift-accessed mountain bike park, and more than 35km (22 miles) of trails, including downhill, flow and cross-country, plus a pump track and skills park. The trails are tucked into the side of Kosciuszko National Park, weaving around the highest peak in Australia, Mt Kosciuszko (2228m/7310ft). With beginner, intermediate and advanced level trails, bike rental and even an MTB school, Thredbo has something for every rider no matter your skill level. The All-Mountain Trail is an intermediate-level descent in two parts, running 9km (5.6 miles) from the topmost lift station back down to the resort.
Start/Finish // Thredbo, Kosciuszko National Park
Distance // 35km (22 miles)
More info // www.thredbo.com.au

THE PAPAROA TRACK, SOUTH ISLAND

Tucked away on the same coastline as the Old Ghost Road, the Paparoa Track showcases more of what riding the wild west coast has to offer. The first new Great Walk in 20 years, the track is a 55km (34 mile) purpose-built hiking and mountain biking route. Weaving its way past mine sites and through some of the most remote and untouched parts of Paparoa National Park, it stitches together an area that was inaccessible for 150 years. Lurid green ferns, spiky tropical nikau palms and northern rātā crowd around this epic trail, with abundant flowing singletrack and views that stretch across the Tasman Sea.
Start // Blackball
Finish // Punakaiki
Distance // 55km (34 miles)

AUSTRALIAN ALPINE EPIC TRAIL, MT BULLER, VICTORIA

The Australian Alpine Epic Trail is both tough and thrilling, with some calling it the jewel in Mt Buller's crown. Offering 40km (25 miles) of unique riding in the Australian Alps, the trail is the first in the Southern Hemisphere to be designated 'epic' by the International Mountain Bicycling Association (IMBA). You'll wind through a thick green canopy, showcasing terrain and landscapes that exist nowhere else in the world. With huge vistas, flowing singletrack and juicy descents galore, the Alpine Epic is a trail-building masterpiece – living up to its name as the 'best trail in Australia'.
Start // Mount Buller Alpine Village
Finish // Mirimbah
Distance // 40km (25 miles)
More info // www.ridehighcountry.com.au

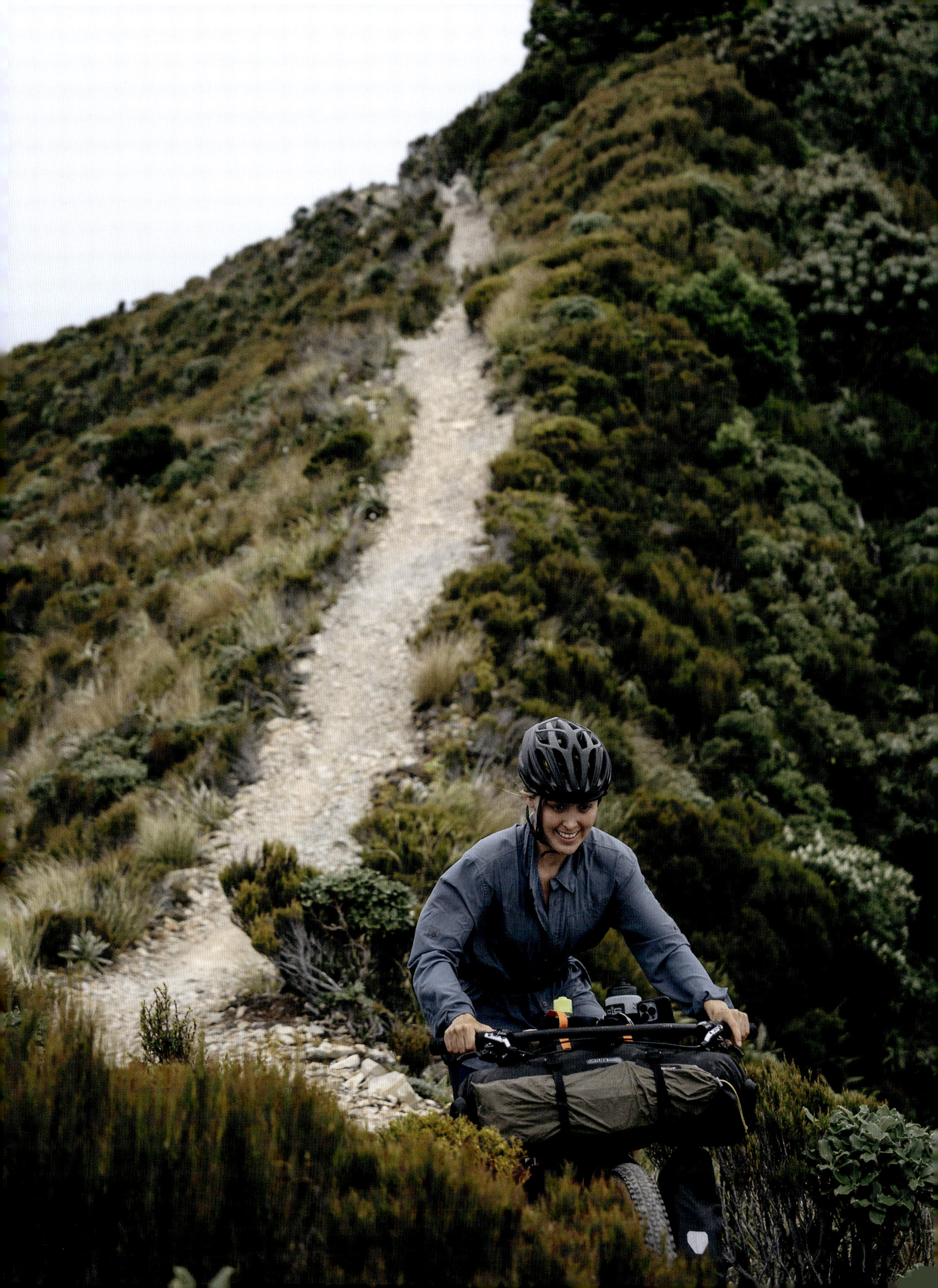

- EPIC BIKE RIDES OF AUSTRALIA & NEW ZEALAND -

THE QUEEN CHARLOTTE TRACK

Mountain bike through New Zealand's Marlborough Sounds on this popular walking track that doubles as an off-road cycling route high above the waters.

At Resolution Bay, I am indeed in need of resolve. It is my first morning on the Queen Charlotte Track, and I've cycled less than 5km (3 miles) since setting out from Meretoto/Ship Cove. Rain has been falling, and the clay surface has turned into a slippery slide. I've pushed, pulled, pedalled, slipped and sworn my way between these two bays near the mouth of Queen Charlotte Sound/Tōtaranui. I'm so covered in mud that I look as though I've been dipped in caramel. It's been dirty, tiring and at times painful, but it somehow seems more fun this way. And there are now only 67km (42 miles) to go…

The Queen Charlotte Track was a watershed in off-road cycling in New Zealand. Constructed as a pure tramping trail in 1983, it became, 30 years later, the first major walking path to open to bikes, a trend that has since extended to the likes of the Heaphy Track and Old Ghost Road. Mainly following the hilly spine of a spit of land that separates Queen Charlotte Sound/Tōtaranui from Kenepuru Sound, it's a rollercoaster ride through a tangle of forest that would be impenetrable were it not for this track, carved across the hillsides and along the rise and fall of the ridge.

In Resolution Bay, only the first of the climbs is behind me, with far greater ones ahead. Around the bay, at least, things

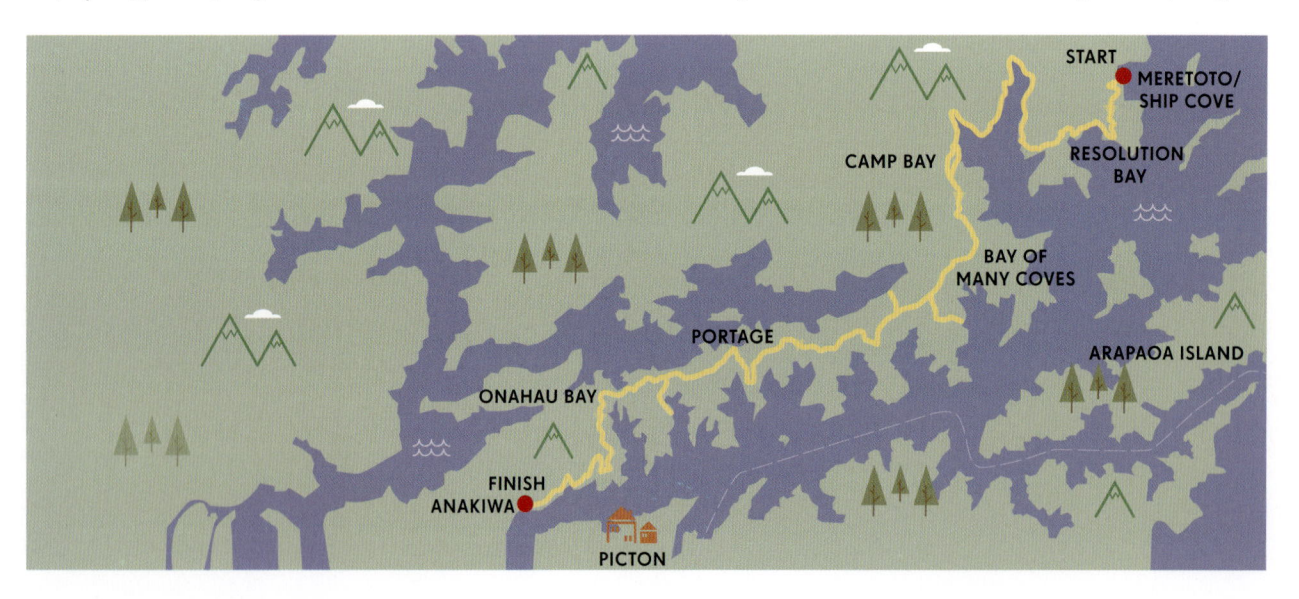

THE SOUTH ISLAND, NEW ZEALAND

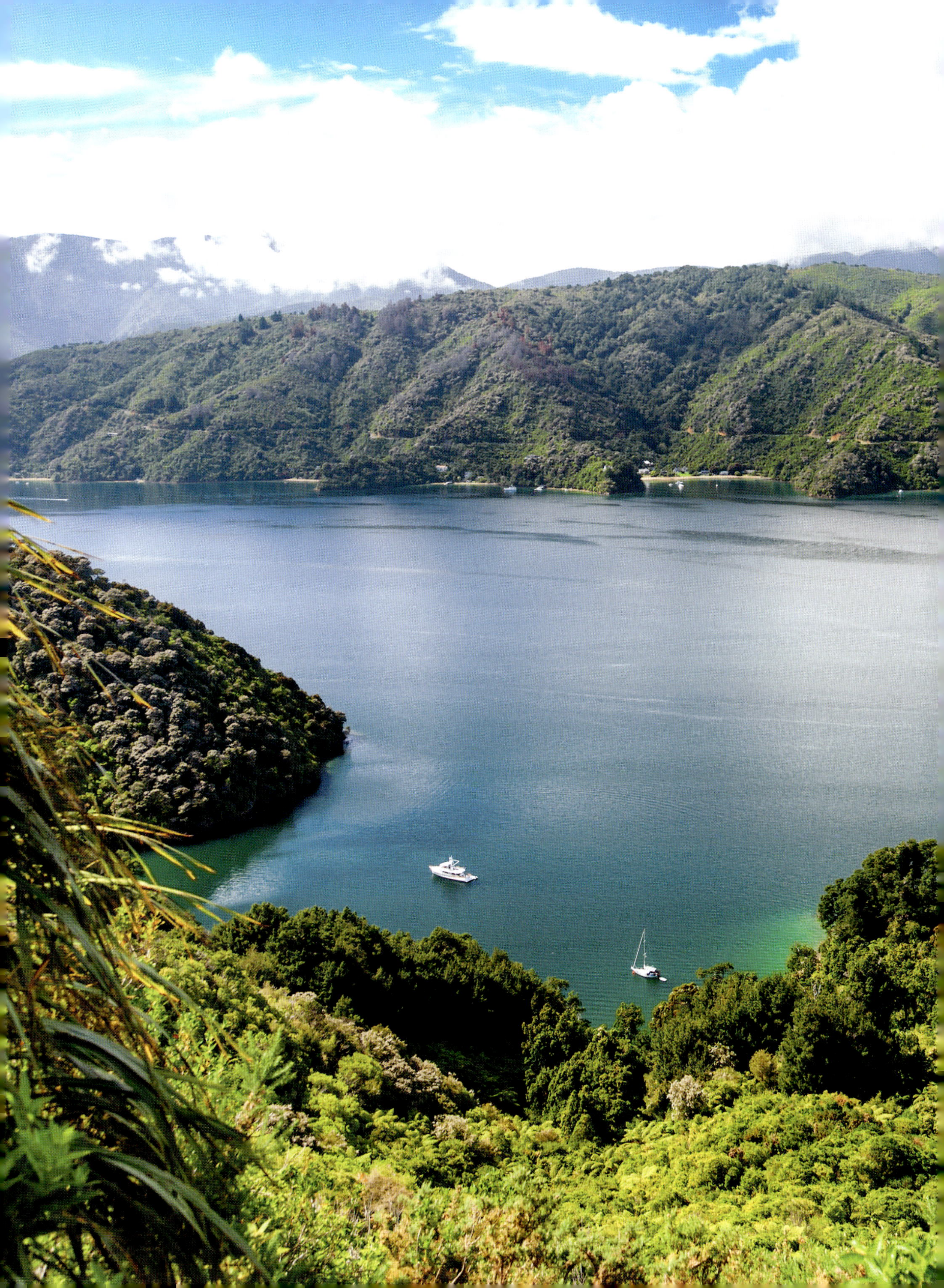

briefly flatten and 12km/h (7mph) has never seemed so fast after the slowness of the headland crossing to get here. Then the climbing begins again.

Another headland separates Resolution Bay from Endeavour Inlet, and as I continue to find my climbing legs, my speed is negligible – there are even wekas popping out of the bush, watching me like avian spectators at the world's slowest bike race. More welcome is a fantail that flits around my wheels, devouring the sandflies that are trying to devour me.

Endeavour Inlet is the largest bay along Queen Charlotte Sound's heavily frayed coastline, and as I reach its edge, with my bike slipping and sliding down the track once again, my day's goal of Camp Bay is visible across the water. To get there, however, requires another 15km (9 miles) or so of cycling – more than half my day in the saddle – as the track clings to the shores of the bay, which has more arms than an octopus.

At Camp Bay, the Queen Charlotte Track turns off the shores and up onto the main ridge. It's the track's longest climb, rising to its highest point, almost 500m (1,640ft) above sea level. It's a solid start to my second day on the bike, especially as it's raining again as I set out in the morning. Wet days like these on the Queen Charlotte Track are at least the exception, not the norm. Blenheim, less than 50km (30 miles) from Camp Bay, is regularly

"*The track skirts a precipitous edge as I roar down through beech forest, past waterfalls and over streams*"

touted as NZ's sunniest town, with an average of some 2,500 hours of sunshine a year – about seven hours a day. It's only poor timing and bad luck that has rain tapping at my helmet again.

The climb from Endeavour Inlet ascends to the tip of the forest-smothered ridge that splits the sounds. Even inside this murky soup of cloud and rain, it's clear that this hard-earned ridgetop is one of the Queen Charlotte Track's most beautiful sections. Ferns crowd the trail and there are glimpses into Queen Charlotte Sound/Tōtaranui to my left and Kenepuru Sound to my right, as though I'm riding a high, green tightrope between the two.

Nearly 20km (12 miles) from Camp Bay, the track slips off the ridge for a whooping, winding descent to Torea Saddle, the slopes around me still thick with ferns and beech forest. At the saddle, the Queen Charlotte Track crosses the rarity of a road. When breaking the ride into three days, this saddle is the logical point at which to depart the track for the day. To the north, the road deviates down to seaside Portage, which contains the likes of the Cowshed Bay campsite and The

IN COOK'S TRACKS

The first day on the Queen Charlotte Track is dominated by reminders of the presence of Captain James Cook. Endeavour Inlet and Resolution Bay are named after two of the ships in Cook's fleets, while Meretoto/Ship Cove – the track's starting point – was like a second home to the British explorer. Cook anchored in this bay five times during his various voyages through the Antipodes, staying for about 100 days in total. A large monument at the cove marks his visits.

Left to right: fully loaded touring cycle; sailing in the Sounds; a sign on the track shows its place in the world Previous spread: view from the Queen Charlotte Track over Queen Charlotte Sound

Portage hotel. It's just a 1km (0.6 mile) detour, but it does come at a price – a 100m (330ft) vertical climb back up to Torea Saddle the next morning.

My way is onwards and ahead, continuing along the ridge and into the Queen Charlotte Track's final big climb. After resorting, at times, to pushing my bike on the hills behind me, I have determined to stay on the bike for the entirety of this climb, at least until I look behind me to see another cyclist pushing his bike and still moving at the same speed as me.

I rise into open clearings, and dip back among ferns and beech forest, squeezing between Te Mahia and Onahau bays, where this spit of land on which I ride is little more than 600m (1,970ft) wide. Six kilometres (3.7 miles) on, and the same distance from the track's end, the final major descent begins. The track narrows and skirts a precipitous edge as I roar down through beech forest, past waterfalls and over streams that often don't flow but are in full force after the rains of the last couple of days. I reach the coast 3km (1.9 miles) from the track's end at Anakiwa, riding back beside Queen Charlotte Sound/Tōtaranui for the first time since leaving Camp Bay 44km (27 miles) ago.

As civilisation nears, the landscape flits between forest and fields. A dog comes running up the track from Anakiwa, then a jogger. The end is nigh. **AB**

TOOLKIT

Start/Finish // Meretoto/Ship Cove/Anakiwa
Distance // 72km (45 miles)
Duration // 2-3 days
Getting there // Cougar Line (www.queencharlottetrack.co.nz) and Beachcomber Cruises (www.beachombercruises.co.nz) run water transfers from Picton and Anakiwa. Picton is 335km (208 miles) north of Christchurch.
When to go // The opening section is open to bikes only from 1 March to 30 November.
Where to stay // There are six campsites along the track, and private accommodation at Resolution Bay, Endeavour Inlet, Bay of Many Coves, Portage, Te Mahia and Anakiwa.
Tours // Wilderness Guides (www.wildernessguidesnz.com) runs self-guided trips, with transfers, accommodation and bike hire. Marlborough Sounds Adventure Company (www.marlboroughsounds.co.nz) runs similar trips.
More info // www.qctrack.co.nz

Opposite: looking out over Picton, one of the main towns on Marlborough Sounds

MORE LIKE THIS
MARLBOROUGH SOUNDS RIDES

NYDIA TRACK

Another Marlborough Sounds mountain-biking classic, the challenging Nydia Track connects three bays while crossing two saddles in between. From Duncan Bay, the shared-use (cycling and walking) track follows the coastline around a headland into Ngawhakawhiti Bay before ascending to 347m (1138ft) Nydia Saddle, which provides views north over Tennyson Inlet. It's a damp, shaded descent from here to Nydia Bay, where there's a campsite. A little further around the bay, a Department of Conservation lodge has bunkrooms. The bay is about halfway along the track, making it the perfect stop if you want to break the ride into two days. Crossing farmland, the track begins the second of its climbs, rising through beech forest to 387m (1270ft) Kaiuma Saddle and views (on a good day) all the way to the Inland Kaikoura Range. The ride ends back beside the water at Kaiuma Bay.
Start // Duncan Bay
Finish // Kaiuma Bay
Distance // 27km (17 miles)

QUEEN CHARLOTTE DRIVE

Welcome to the road cyclists' equivalent of the Queen Charlotte Track. This winding coastal road, which passes near the finish of the Queen Charlotte Track, links two of Marlborough Sounds' main towns: Picton and Havelock. Running along the shores of Queen Charlotte and Pelorus sounds, it also makes a 5km (3 mile) overland crossing between the sounds, blessedly picking a flat path through the hills that surround the road – the hilliest sections of the ride are elsewhere, along the shores of the sounds. Dense native forest lines the road (along with several artists' studios), and you'll likely be slowed by the beauty of the surrounds rather than the terrain – the lookout at Cullen Point, in particular, provides an eyeful of brilliant Pelorus Sound water.
Start // Picton
Finish // Havelock
Distance // 40km (25 miles)

WAKAMARINA TRACK

Immodestly described by local tourism authorities as one of 'the world's greatest natural mountain bike trails', this technical route (shared with walkers) crosses the peaks of Mt Richmond Forest Park before settling into a gentler finish along Wakamarina River. The former gold-mining track makes a steady climb along a ridge to Fosters Clearing before descending through technical rocky sections and tight switchbacks to a creek crossing. This heralds the start of another climb to the track's highest point – a 1066m (3497ft) summit – where the fun truly begins. Over the next 2.5km (1.5 miles), the track descends 800m (2625ft) through beech forest to Devils Creek, bumping downhill over tree roots and other small drops before following the Wakamarina River and eventually an old water race to Butchers Flat. There are huts at Fosters Clearing and Devils Creek if you're breaking the ride into two days, and shuttle services can return you from Butchers Flat to Onamalutu.
Start // Onamalutu
Finish // Butchers Flat
Distance // 45km (28 miles)

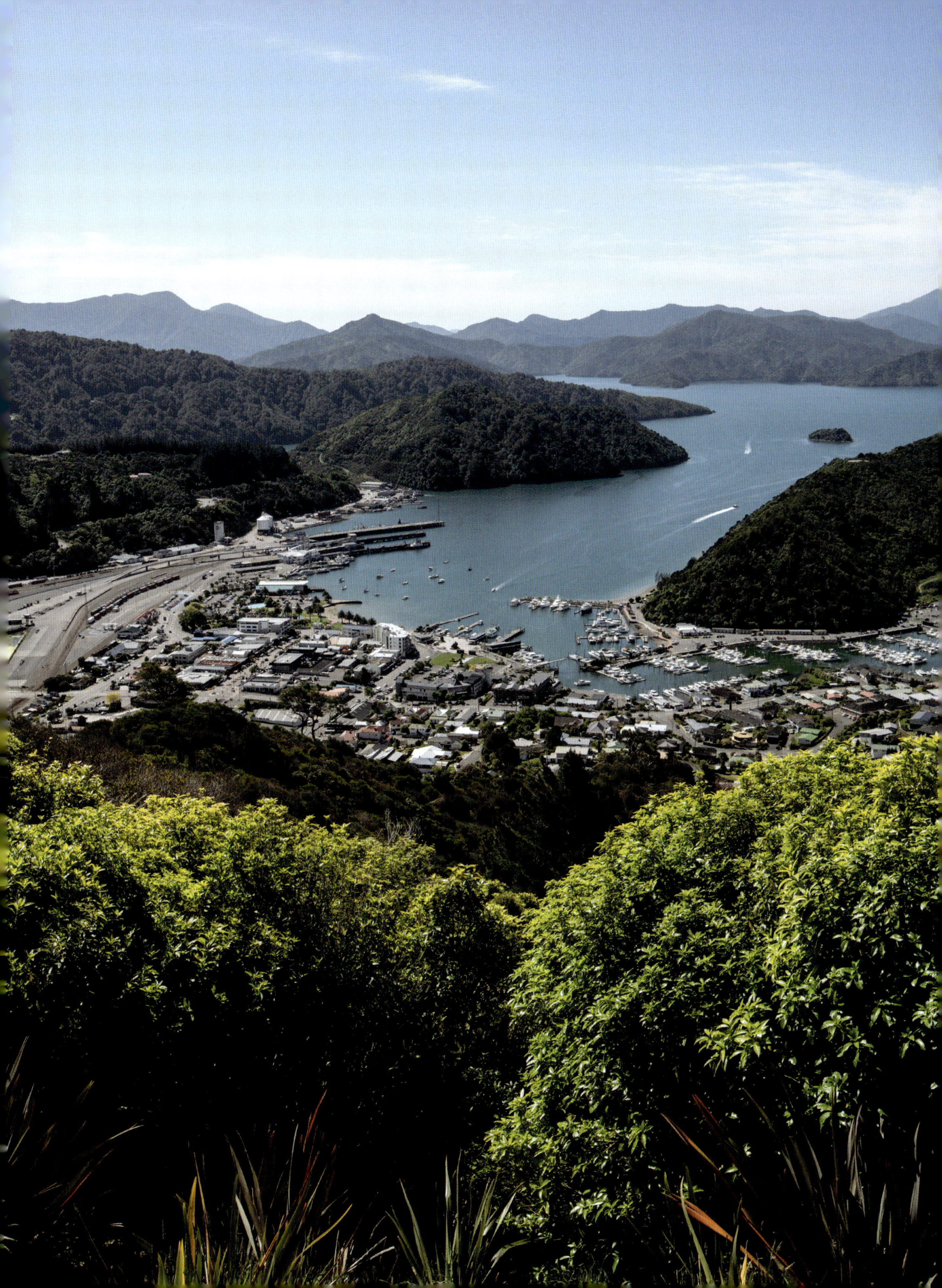

OTAGO'S CENTRAL RAIL TRAIL

Take a virtual pub crawl along New Zealand's first and most famous rail trail, packed with history, barren landscapes, gentle gradients and an assortment of character-filled hotels.

Outside the Otago town of Alexandra, the landscape is straight from a spaghetti western. Across the bare schist hills, the earth is serrated with rock and old rail lines have been repurposed as fenceposts. Ahead, largest of all, is the scarily named Tiger Hill, the toughest climb on the Otago Central Rail Trail, although 'toughest' here is relative. It is the trail's steepest section, but Tiger Hill has an average gradient of just 2%. I later hear a cyclist mock it as 'Pussycat Hill'. There's nothing to fear here.

Australasia's love of a good rail trail was born on this ride. When a trail through this largely forgotten tourist region, pinched between Dunedin and Queenstown, was first mooted, the idea was met with opposition and indifference. But from the moment it opened as New Zealand's first rail trail in 2000, it was a hit, attracting more than 10,000 cyclists every year and resuscitating towns, pubs and accommodation providers along its horseshoe-shaped route. It's the kind of trail that a seasoned cyclist might attempt in a day, but it's just as friendly to those who come with little or no cycle-touring experience.

At its western end, the ride begins in the town of Clyde, cut into the bank of the Clutha/Mata-au River, which, during the Central Otago gold rush in the 1860s, was the richest gold-bearing river in the world. What gold remains as I set out riding is in the colour of the seasons. It's autumn, and every tree-lined waterway is a meandering yellow line through the bare landscape, as though a child has scribbled across this part of New Zealand with a crayon.

There's a symmetry to the Otago Central Rail Trail, which ascends gently for the first half (whichever direction you begin), and descends just as gradually through the second half. The climb is barely noticeable, ascending only 450m (1,480ft)

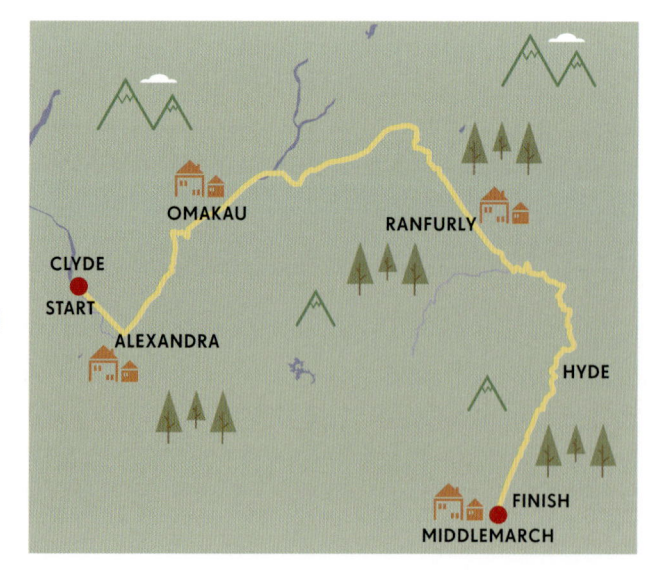

THE SOUTH ISLAND, NEW ZEALAND

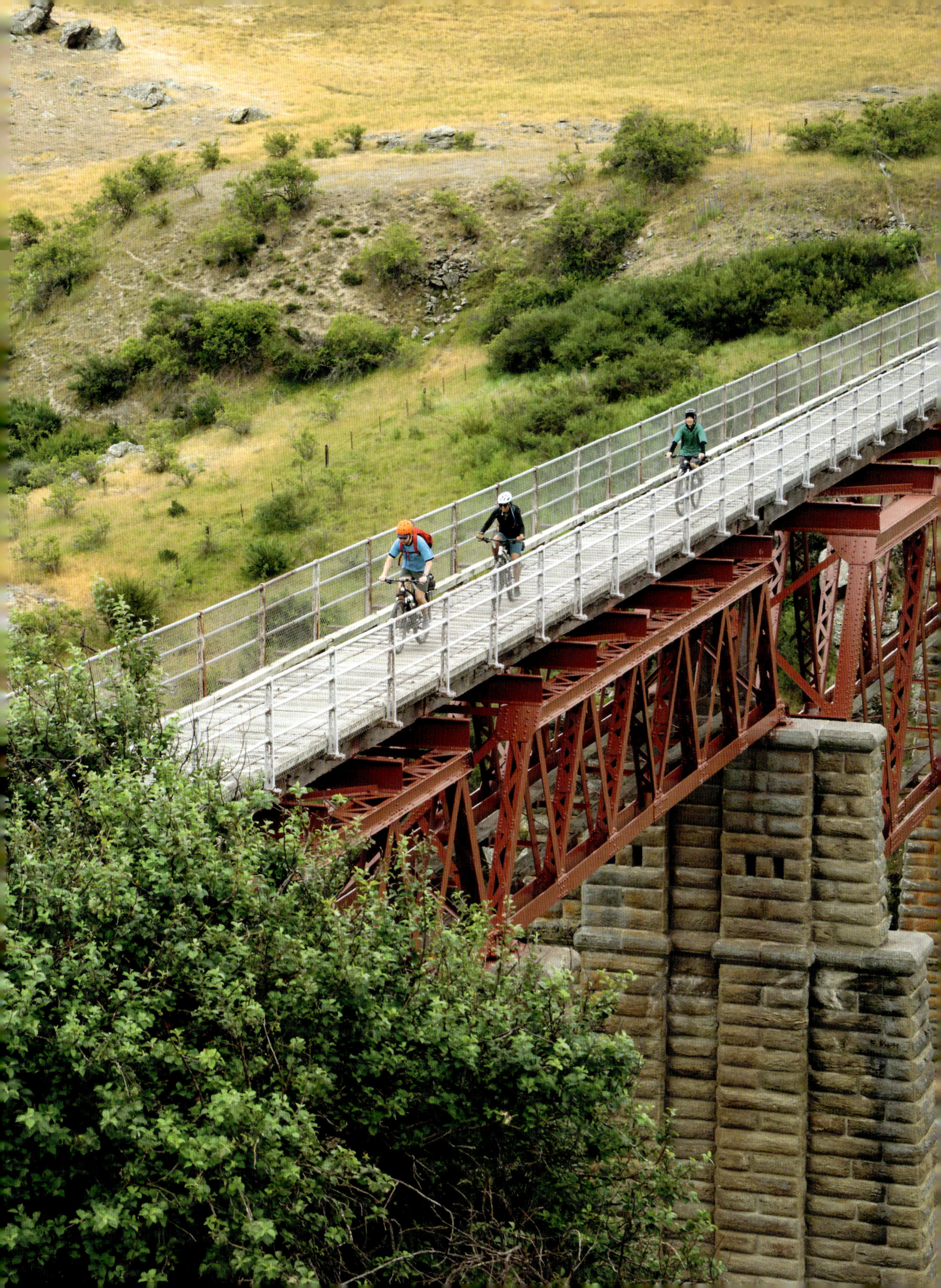

across more than 70km (44 miles), even if somebody gave part of it a name as falsely fearsome as Tiger Hill.

The Tiger is quickly tamed, however – I pedal up the hill beside a newcomer to cycling who doesn't even change a gear for the entire climb – and the land beyond opens out into a broad, bucolic valley, with the frayed schist slopes of the well-named Raggedy Range to one side and the taller Dunstan Mountains to the other. Pinched between them is my first night's stop, Lauder, a settlement so small that it seems more of a glorified pub than a town. It's a common feeling on the Otago Central Rail Trail, which is dotted with so many hotels – about one pub every 12km (7.5 miles) on average – that it's also been christened the Ale Trail.

The one thing that outnumbers pubs on this trail is bridges, with the ride crossing almost 70 old railway bridges. The most spectacular of these – coupled with the trail's most dramatic section – are through skinny Poolburn Gorge, just outside Lauder. To enter the gorge, I cross the 110m/360ft-long Manuherikia Viaduct, while inside the gorge is the Poolburn Viaduct, the ride's highest bridge, poised a heady 37m (120ft) above the creek.

Around these bridges, the hills and cliffs of the Raggedy Range close in to create a spectacularly narrow and rugged gorge. The tenacity of the Otago Central Branch Railway builders becomes clear as I ride over bridges and through a pair of 200m/650ft-long railway tunnels so dark that I hear another bike crash into the wall ahead of me.

Through the gorgeous Ida Valley, the ride begins to make its long, slow turn for home, swinging south and crawling up to

MAKE A GAME OF IT

A popular detour along the Otago Central Rail Trail is the Southern Hemisphere's only indoor curling rink. Located in Naseby, the Olympic-standard rink is a 13km (8 mile) side trip from Ranfurly (one of the logical stops on the second night along the rail trail). Hotels can often arrange shuttles if you don't fancy the extra ride. Book a sheet and deliver a few stones, or come in winter to try out the adjoining, 360m/1,180ft-long ice luge through the Naseby Forest.

Clockwise from top: the Wedderburn goods shed on the Otago Central Rail Trail; truck outside a railway shed on the route; a Middlemarch hotel Previous page: cycling along the 37m-high Poolburn Viaduct

a subtle pass that is the trail's highest point at 618m (2,028ft) above sea level). Along the way, I twice cross the 45th parallel: for these two brief moments, I am exactly halfway between the Equator and the South Pole. As cyclists universally like to chant (usually erroneously, though correctly in this case), 'It's all downhill from here.'

On a day of strong northerly winds, I blow south like a hurricane, moving quickly to my day's end in Ranfurly, before setting out the next morning on the final stage to Middlemarch. For the first hour of this new day, I cross the wide Maniototo Plain, a flat land of sheep and tussocks, wool and wind, before wriggling into the second of the trail's gorges: the Upper Taieri.

Fighting its way through this gorge is New Zealand's fourth-largest river, the 200km (124 mile) Taieri River. Fighting along beside it were once those 19th-century railway builders, carving another section of line where no line rightly belonged. Where the cliffs intruded, the workers built more viaducts and blasted a 150m (490ft) tunnel. As I ride through the darkness of a tunnel again, I listen for bikes hitting rock, but there is only the crunch of tyres on the earth. Things are improving.

A quick stop in Hyde brings the railway's darker history into focus, for it was here in 1943, midway through the Otago Central Railway's eight decades of operation, that a train derailed, killing 21 passengers. A memorial marks the site of what was New Zealand's second deadliest railway disaster.

It's not the only late reminder of the trail's railway origins. Along this last afternoon into Middlemarch, there are lone railway sleepers beside the trail, sections of old railway track and, as I coast to a finish at the Middlemarch train station, a railway turntable. My ride is done; I'm off the rails. **AB**

"I twice cross the 45th parallel: for these two brief moments, I am exactly halfway between the Equator and the South Pole"

TOOLKIT

Start/Finish // Clyde/Middlemarch
Distance // 152km (94 miles)
Duration // 2-4 days
Getting there // Clyde is a 2.5-hour drive northwest of Dunedin, and little more than an hour east of Queenstown. Middlemarch is an hour's drive northwest of Dunedin, and three hours southeast of Queenstown. Buses run from Dunedin and Queenstown to Clyde.
When to go // Autumn is the most colourful time on the trail, while winter rides offer an often crisp, frosty difference to the scenery.
Where to stay // There is accommodation along the trail's length. The official trail website has full listings.
Tours // Of the many tour operators along the trail, try Adventure South NZ (www.adventuresouth.co.nz), Trail Journeys (www.trailjourneys.co.nz) or Central Cycle Trail Co (www.centralcycletrail.co.nz).
More info // www.otagocentralrailtrail.co.nz

Opposite: taking the jetboat along the Roxburgh River with Clutha River Cruises

MORE LIKE THIS
CENTRAL OTAGO ROUTES

LAKE DUNSTAN TRAIL

Launched in 2021, the Lake Dunstan Trail spins off the Otago Central Rail Trail at Clyde, making it now possible to cycle almost 200km (124 miles) from Middlemarch to Cromwell purely on bike paths. Even as a standalone ride, there's a lot to like about the Lake Dunstan Trail, which follows the shores of its namesake lake for the entire journey between Cromwell and Clyde. At times it does so on sections of boardwalk clipped onto cliffs, while also crossing an 89m/290ft-long suspension bridge. This trail is more remote than the Otago Central Rail Trail – there's a 25km (16 mile) section with no road access – and your thighs can anticipate a greater workout, with 580m (1,900ft) of ascent along the journey. But then there are the appeasing pleasures, such as the wineries around Bannockburn, and a floating cafe on the lake at Cairnmuir Gully.
Start // Cromwell
Finish // Clyde
Distance // 41km (25.5 miles)

ROXBURGH GORGE TRAIL

Another ride that branches off the Otago Central Rail Trail, the easy Roxburgh Gorge Trail clings to the Clutha/Mata-au River as it scours a deep gorge through the Otago landscape. The ride breaks away from the Otago Central Rail Trail in Alexandra (8km/5 miles along the trail from Clyde), following the river as it wraps around bluffs rising up to 350m (1150ft) above the river and old gold diggings. Schist huts remain as relics of the golden days, as does the thyme that was planted on the slopes – sniff the breeze to catch a scent. One unusual aspect of this ride is the need to break it with a jetboat transfer; book ahead (www.clutharivercruises.co.nz; www.beaumontjet.co.nz) to meet the boat at Doctors Point, taking a 40-minute spin to rejoin the trail 13km (8 miles) downstream at Gorge Creek. The boat ride provides a whole new angle and perspective on the miners' huts and rock shelters inside the gorge.
Start // Alexandra
Finish // Roxburgh Dam
Distance // 21km (13 miles)

CLUTHA GOLD TRAIL

Continuing the journey along the Clutha/Mata-au River from Roxburgh Dam is this trundle deeper into Central Otago. From New Zealand's largest gravity-fed dam, it makes a gentle journey downstream. Pause just beyond Roxburgh town for a cooling dip at Pinders Pond, a rare tranquil moment on the Clutha/Mata-au (keep an eye out later for the sunken gold dredger in the river). Detour out to the Lonely Graves – unmarked graves from the gold rush – and Horseshoe Bend Bridge, an impressive, century-old pedestrian suspension bridge straddling the river, before climbing to Big Hill Tunnel, a 440m/1444ft-long railway tunnel that also mark's the trail's highest point. The descent that follows brings you to the trail's end at Otago's very first gold-rush town, Lawrence.
Start // Roxburgh Dam
Finish // Lawrence
Distance // 73km (45 miles)

800 CLUTHA

NEW ZEALAND

PAPAROA & PIKE29 MEMORIAL TRACKS

A heady mix of South Island scenery and serenity, unique flora and fauna, and meaningful trail-building, the Paparoa Track is a well-placed tribute.

As the warm, humid air that welcomed our first pedal strokes begins to shift, great plumes of cumulus fill the sky. Mesmerised, we watch as a patch of thick cloud dances along the main Paparoa ridgeline, ebbing and flowing with the sun in a delicate ballet of light and shade. There's a real sense of weather in motion up here, and it feels like a show that's all for us.

Between momentary breaks in the cloud, I catch a glimpse into the deep channels of Pike River valley, which once held the Pike River Mine. On 19 November 2010, a gas explosion at the mine trapped and killed 29 coal miners. It was one of the most devastating days in New Zealand's history, and one for which final answers are still being sought. The miners' bodies have never been recovered. But in 2020, with investment from the Department of Conservation, the Paparoa & Pike29 Memorial Track was built in their memory.

The first new Great Walk in 20 years, the Paparoa Track is a 55km (34 mile) purpose-built hiking and mountain biking route. Weaving its way past the mine site and through some of the most remote and untouched parts of Paparoa National Park, it stitches together an area previously inaccessible for 150 years. As part of our tour of NZ, my partner Bec and I decided to ride the trail, with a little help from our friend Bernie.

'Are you sure they're going to fit, Bernie?' I ask, struggling to hold back the doubt in my voice. 'Yeah, she'll be right, we've had four bikes on this beauty in the past,' she reassures me as I hoist our bikes onto the back of her toy-sized Toyota Yaris. 'We made this bike rack ourselves and we've only had one accide...'

She pauses, noticing the dread that floods across my face.

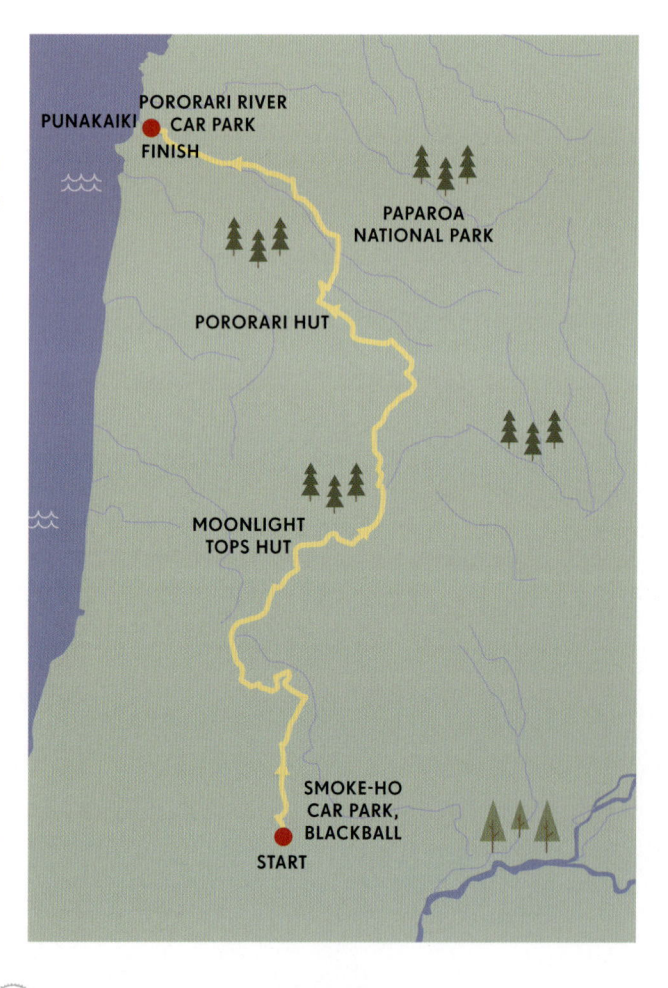

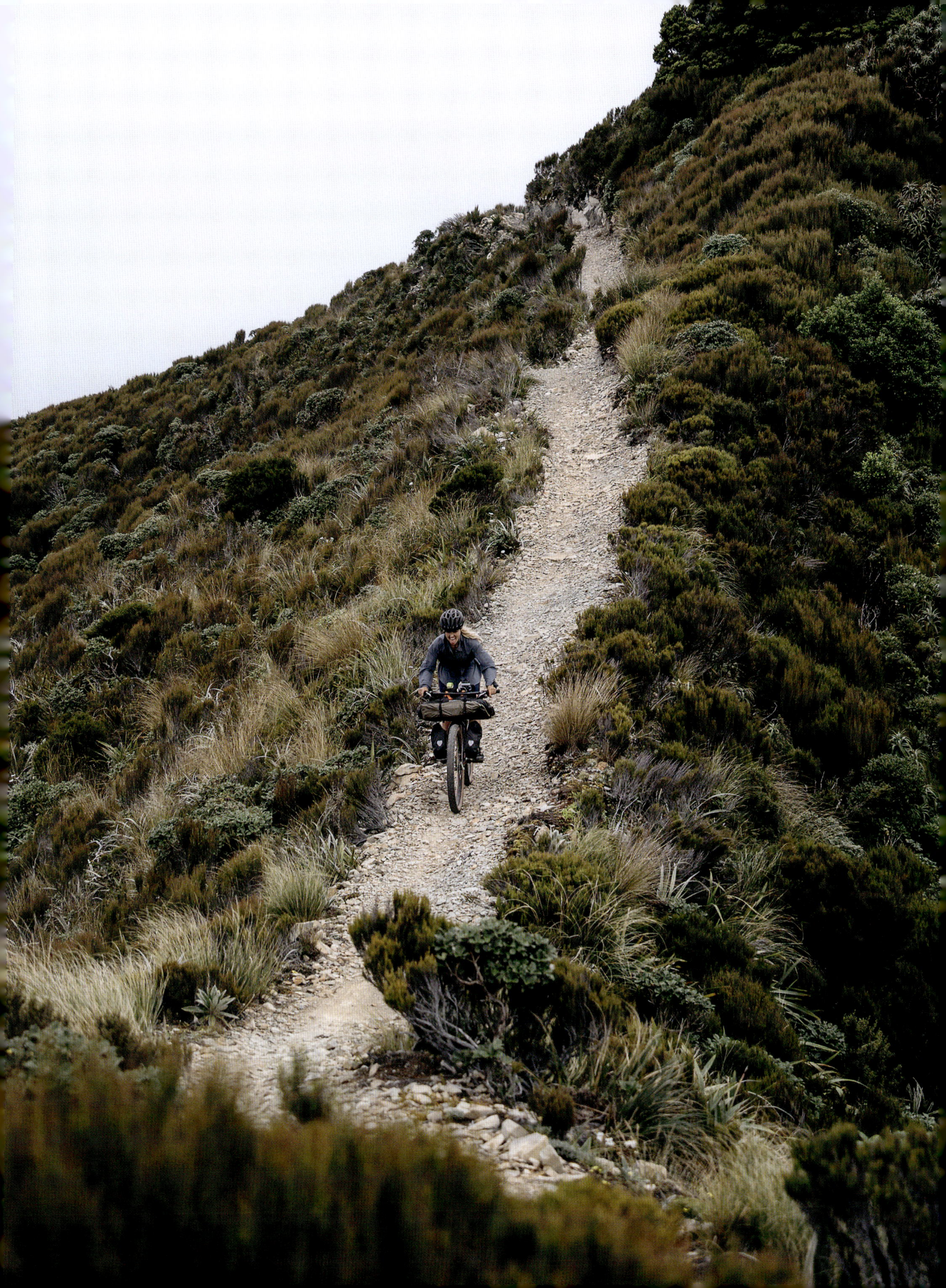

'Oh stop looking so worried, Sam, and get in the car. I've made you guys some fruit leathers and a ginger slice for your ride.' We pile into the Yaris and rattle our way to the trailhead at Smoke-ho car park.

Over-caffeinated and under-prepared, we fly out of the car and immediately begin climbing up the historic Croesus Track. Under the dense beech and gnarled native forest, the bright summer sun is barely visible. With coffee still swirling in our bellies, this section of the trail is rough going. The jagged rocks, baby-head boulders and slippery leaf litter mean it feels more like a Ninja Warrior course than a mountain bike trail. 'It's not all like this, is it?' Bec asks, as she lifts her bike over another rock feature and begins to push. 'Nah, it's just this first section to Ces Clark Hut,' I reply, trying desperately to veil the bonk goblins already breathing down my neck.

Bernie's fruit leathers get inhaled swiftly and our bagels – meant for lunch – get reduced to crumbs as we rush to fill our rapidly dwindling fuel tanks. Just as the calories kick in, we crest the high point of the ride and are swallowed whole by the mountains. The mighty Grey Valley dominates the backdrop as the vast Tasman Sea shimmers beneath a thin ribbon of surf. 'I've never ridden a trail where you can see the mountains and the sea at the same time,' I yell out to Bec. 'Welcome to New

> "We crest the high point and are swallowed by the mountains. The mighty Grey Valley dominates as the Tasman Sea shimmers beneath a ribbon of surf"

Zealand, Sam!' she gloats, as she bombs down the next section of the track, hugging the gravel tightly.

Buoyed by the scenery, we whip past Moonlight Tops Hut, the suggested stop at the end of day one. So with our tent in tow, we push on a further 9km (5.6 miles), eager to continue enjoying the pace and flow of the trail. Time ticks by at a breakneck pace and we're forced to stop riding by the natural alarm clock of fading light. As we rush to set up our tent, the sky is on fire. Its tangerine tones bounce light into the surrounding valleys and deep ravines. With the adrenaline of the day starting to wane, our legs come back online as we feel every metre of elevation. Tired and sweaty, we climb inside our sleeping bags and instantly pass out.

Dawn comes, and Bec beams excitedly as she nudges me awake: 'Yesterday was tough. But the GPX says it's all downhill

KIWIS OF THE WEST

Paparoa National Park has an abundance of native New Zealand wildlife, including the famous great spotted kiwi (roroa). Because of pests like stoats, possums and pigs, their numbers have been rapidly declining, but conservation efforts by the Department of Conservation across the park are increasing the size of existing populations, delivering significant gains for the largest of the five species of kiwi, and protecting many other creatures whose survival depends on this coastal region.

Left to right: morning rituals; a great spotted kiwi scours the forest floor; cool temperate forest shrouds the slopes. Previous spread: some the trail is surfaced for durability

today. Let's pack up quickly and get this show on the road.' She tears Bernie's ginger slice in half, gulps down her share, and begins packing her bike. Straight into the action, we snake our way down the exposed trail. With every metre of elevation loss, the temperature rises and the salty coastal air clings to our skin, humid and moist.

As the trail transforms into what feels like a pump track, the rainforest is a riot of colour and noise. Lurid green ferns, spiky tropical nikau palms and northern rātā explode around us. Birdsong fills the air as we spot wekas, fantails, pipits and kererūs enjoying the abundance of the forest alongside us. Before we know it, we hit the final two crossings, over a suspension bridge and out to the finish line at the Punakaiki River, where a familiar face and pint-sized Yaris lies waiting.

With bikes strapped once more to Bernie's rack of death, we bundle into the car and head towards home. Usually, after a ride, my brain's awash with thoughts of French fries and chocolate milk. But this time, I can't help but ruminate around what we just experienced. Riding this landscape feels like such a privilege. The Paparoa Track is so much more than 'just' a mountain bike trail. Having ridden it, having learned its story, I know it's a genuine celebration of both the land, and the lives of the 'Pike29' miners. May they rest in peace. **SR**

TOOLKIT

Start/Finish // Blackball/Punakaiki
Distance // 56km (35 miles)
Getting there // The best way to get to the trail is to use one of shuttle services to the track from the towns of Punakaiki or Greymouth. Most people start the track at the Smoke-ho car park at the end of Blackball Rd.
When to go // October to April, with February traditionally having the best weather.
What to wear // You can expect to use rain jackets all year round. Always prep for cold conditions.
What to pack // Bug spray and wet weather gear, along with some essential bike tools. Pack your own food. Note that e-bikes are not allowed on this route.
Where to stay // There are three Great Walk huts. These need to be booked on the Department of Conservation website in advance.
More info // www.doc.govt.nz

Opposite: Tasmania's Montezuma Falls

MORE LIKE THIS
ROAMING REGIONS OF OZ

ATHERTON TABLELANDS, QUEENSLAND

Filled with waterfalls and waterways, the Atherton Tablelands is a natural wonderland 50km (31 miles) southwest of Cairns. Surrounded by rainforest and eucalypt woodlands, the area is known for its geological wonders, diversity of wildlife and classic Australian trails. A favourite spot is the Atherton Forest Mountain Bike Park, with a 54km (34 mile) network of purpose-built, singletrack mountain bike trails in the Herberton Range State Forest. The 17 trails weave through an open forest of gums bloodwood, mahogany, she-oak and cycads, and some old experimental plots of teak, blackbutt and tallowwood.
More info //
www.tablelandstrails.com

TASMANIA'S WILD WEST

Offering trails from easy to extreme, the wild west coast of Tasmania is the spot for adventurous riding. Home to ancient rainforests, untamed rivers and deep gorges, there are countless trails here including the tough Sterling Valley track near Rosebery, or the beginner-friendly Montezuma Falls ride. There are also some great bike-adjacent activities to be explored: you can cruise the waterways, race down the rapids, catch some serious surf or climb one of the many rock faces. So, if you're after towering mountains, waterfalls and riding alongside 1,000-year-old Huon pines, the west coast of Tasmania is the place for your next ride.
More info //
www.discovertasmania.com.au

JAGUNGAL WILDERNESS, NEW SOUTH WALES

Located in Kosciuszko National Park, the Jagungal Wilderness has some incredibly remote backcountry riding. Best ridden between October and March, the trails take you through a beautiful sub-alpine habitat, with a range of different dirt routes that span its large landscape, past backcountry huts such as Derschko's or O'Keefe's. Mt Jagungal (2061m/6762ft) is omnipresent. The trail surroundings are also home to some amazing wildflowers – keep your eyes peeled for buttercups, billy buttons, waxy bluebells and daisies.
More info //
www.nationalparks.nsw.gov.au

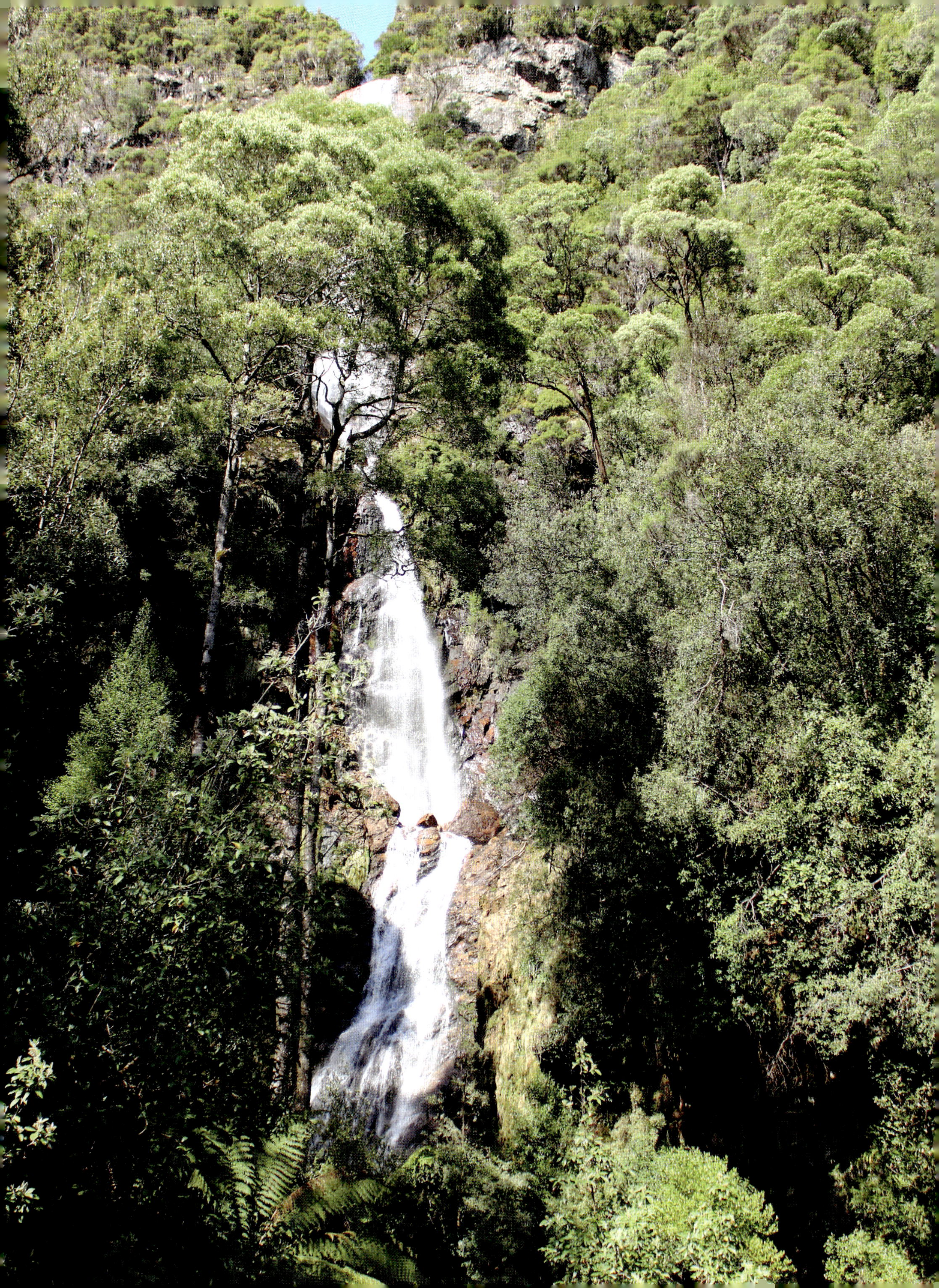

TOURING THE WAKATIPU RANGES

Discover the high country of Otago and Southland on this challenging but spectacular loop, as it traverses high saddles, follows alpine valleys and visits dazzling lakes.

We're only 15 minutes into the long climb up the legendary Nevis Road, and already our group are strung out down the gravel, with everyone settling into their own pace. We started the day in Cromwell, a lakeside orchard town where the temperature was in single digits, but now with the sun high in the bluebird sky we're down to T-shirts. Although autumn brings cold mornings to Otago, the reward is a vibrantly coloured landscape as the region's deciduous trees turn golden, and the valley below us is alive with colour. The Nevis Road climbs for a steady 900m (3,000 ft) and, as we ascend, it leads us through a characteristic Otago landscape of lofty tussocks, spiny spear grass and schist tors.

The route we've planned for this tour covers nearly 400km (248 miles) and includes over 6,000m (19,685 ft) of elevation as it undulates over picturesque Otago high country, traversing high saddles and visiting three lakes. This day is one of the biggest, with 73km (45 miles) and over 1,800m (5,900ft) of climbing, but we've got a perfect day for it. Duffers Saddle is the high-point on the road where the view of the craggy mountains to our west reminds us that we're cycling on the other side of the peaks of Queenstown's justly named Remarkables.

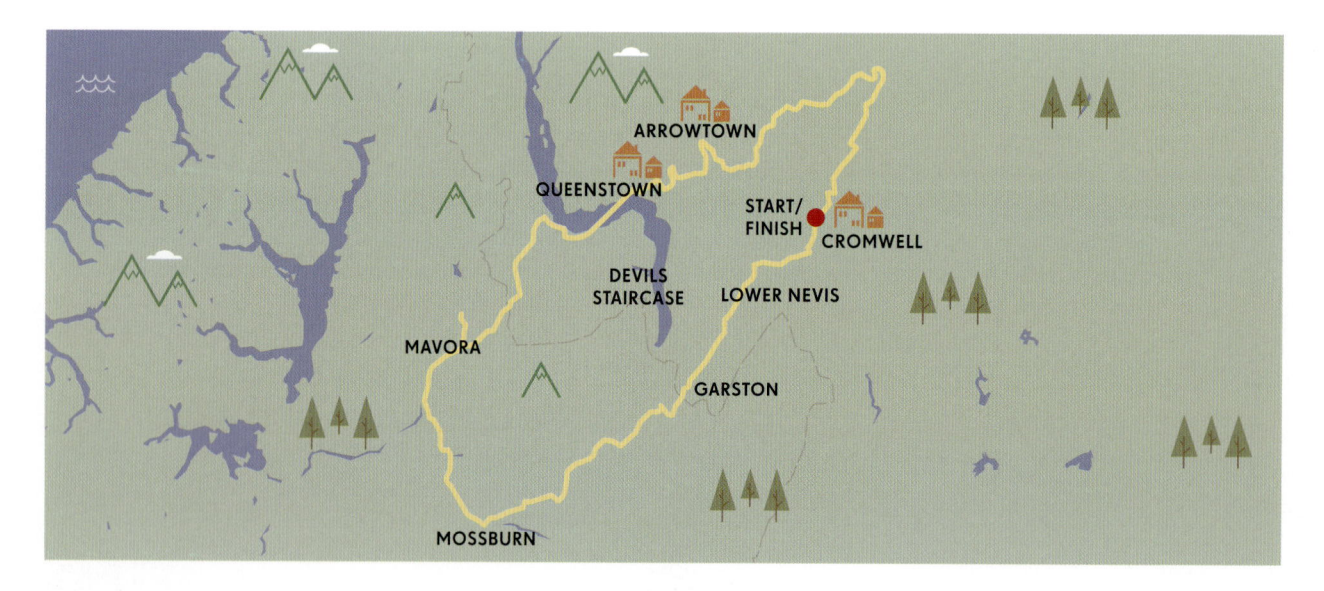

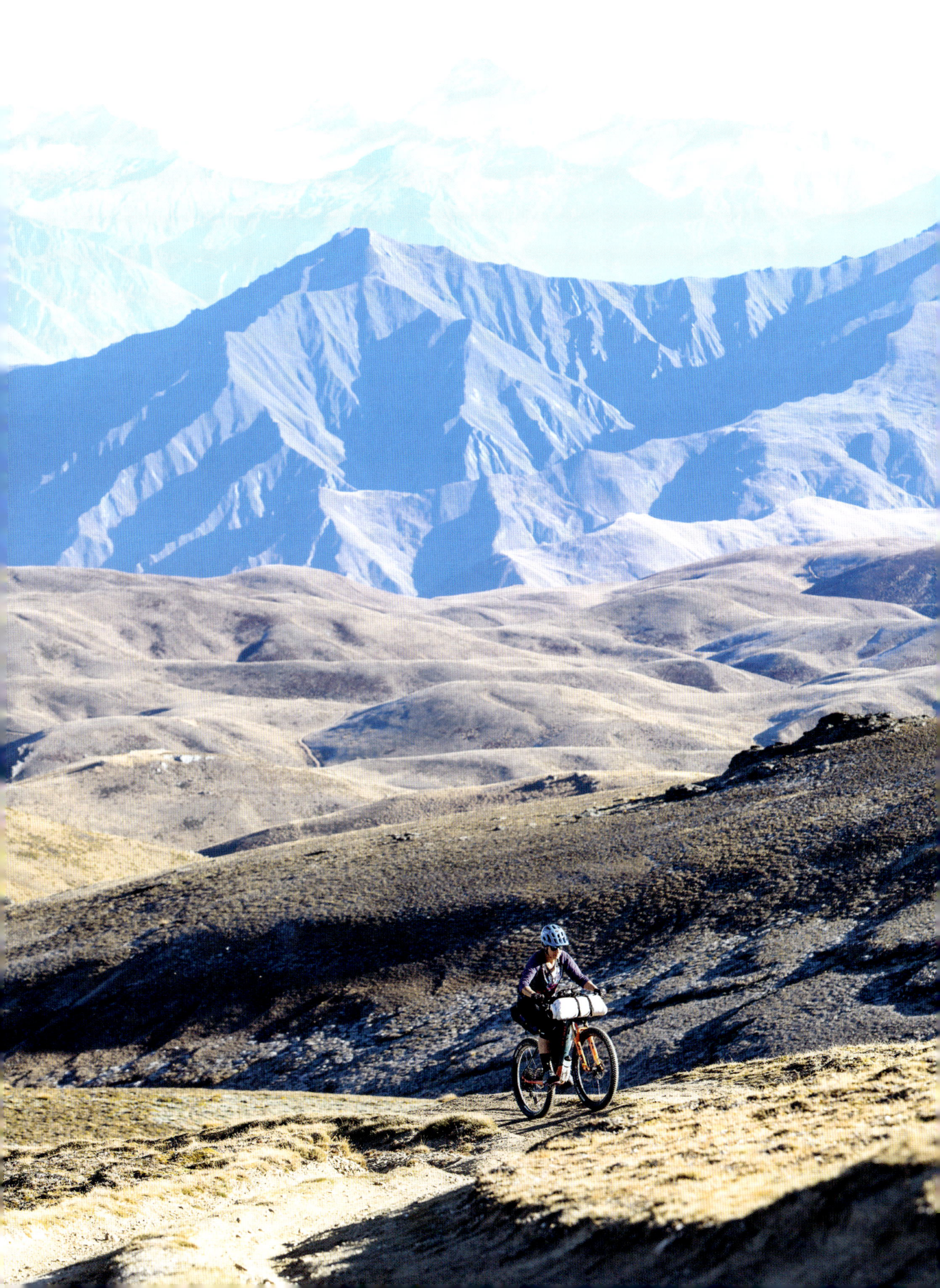

"It's dusk when we arrive at South Mavora Lake and stop to camp. With practised efficiency, tents go up, stoves come out and soon we're debriefing the ride so far"

It's a fast and windy descent down into the Nevis Valley and we soon feel more remote. Aside from a single homestead, this valley is unpopulated, but 19th-century pioneers made it home for their farming and mining endeavours. These days, there's little trace of this history, but we're content with the views of the Otago backcountry as we climb the long valley to the day's finish at Garston Ski Hut. This rustic building was once a ski base for the New Zealand Alpine Club. Legend has it that the hut was supposed to be sited elsewhere, but the truck transporting it broke down, so it had to be unloaded where it was. But some might say the hut is in the perfect spot – high on a mountain ridge, with expansive views across the Eyre Mountains.

The Mavora Lakes are our goal for the following day, which starts with a cold but beautiful downhill to Garston. There's a throng of other travellers around the village's famous food cart, and we can't resist a bacon butty and coffee for second breakfast. The morning passes with a fast ride along a section of the Around the Mountains Cycle Trail, a purpose-built cycleway that funnels us through sheep and dairy country hemmed in between rugged ranges. A cafe lunch in Mossburn fuels us for the next leg to Mavora, and we push on into the wide plains and rolling hill country of the Ōreti Valley. While a stiff headwind takes some of the fun out of the ride, we're looking forward to the beech forest and lakes that await.

It's dusk when we arrive at South Mavora Lake and stop to camp on the lake edge. With practised efficiency, the tents go up, stoves come out and soon we're debriefing the ride so far and sipping tea. It's an early start the next morning to make the ferry we have booked to cross Lake Wakatipu, but as we head into the Von Valley, still in the dark, it's raining steadily and we ride heads-down through the moody landscape. Once over the saddle, we descend into better weather and by the time we reach Walter Peak Station on the lake edge, the sun's out and we can appreciate the post-glacial landscape that Queenstown is famous for. Bold ridges rise from the lake and isolated patches of forest decorate the valleys.

We cross the choppy lake as a crisp southerly blows away the clouds. After lunch in Queenstown, we're back in the saddle heading towards Arrowtown. It's an easy and pleasant afternoon amble along cycle trails flanked with autumn colour. The Arrowtown campground is home for the night and a pub dinner fortifies us for what will be the queen stage of this tour: crossing the Pisa Range. Although the Crown Range Road

ICY LEGACY

Occupying a glacially deepened valley, Lake Wakatipu – one of this route's main features – is a narrow 'finger lake' that forms a dog-leg shape, making it New Zealand's longest lake at 80km (49 miles). It's also one of the deepest, at 380m (1,246ft), with its floor below sea level. The lake is a typical feature of a landscape shaped by glaciers. Other classic landforms you might notice include *roches moutonnées* (resistant domes of rock, buffed into smooth shapes by the glacier), moraine humps and kettle lakes.

Clockwise from top: Mountain vistas make for hearty appetites; crossing Lake Wakatipu. Previous spread: conquering another climb

might be considered one of New Zealand's cycling challenges, for us it's just the warm-up for day four, and from Crown Saddle we climb steadily on 4WD tracks that wind over the alpine landscape. As the road climbs steeply to Quartz Knoll with its high-point at 1592m (5223ft), we're forced to push for a while, but some rock outcrops on the ridge make an irresistible lunch stop and we soak up the views.

An icon of Otago, the long and broad Pisa Range stretches between Wanaka, in the north, and Cromwell. Snowcapped in winter, it's a distinctive feature that would not be out of place in Montana or Wyoming, with its treeless slopes and crags. We follow the top of the range for the rest of the day, dipping in and out of saddles, swooping down some incredibly fun tracks and engaging our legs on the climbs. After we pass the commercial area of the Snow Farm, the terrain mellows and we wind through shallow valleys. At this height, icicles dangle alongside small streams and the tussock is golden in the late afternoon light. Kirtle Burn Hut is our home for the night. Well insulated, it's soon warm from our stoves, and we have the place to ourselves on this pristine autumn evening, high on the range with views across to Mount Aspiring.

Our final day starts with more climbing to the range's high-point at 1963m (6440ft), but from there it's an Andean-scale 1600m (5249ft) descent down to the valley. It's one of those downhills that just keeps on giving as it winds its way on. A short highway ride and calmer lakeside cycle trail conclude the ride back to Cromwell and close our epic loop. **MW**

TOOLKIT

Start/Finish // Cromwell
Distance // 397km (247 miles)
Getting there // Queenstown has an international airport and the route is accessible at several points by road.
When to go // Late spring, summer and early autumn.
What to wear // This is an alpine route, requiring clothing suitable for cold, stormy weather.
Where to stay // There are two public huts on the route: Garston Ski Hut and Kirtle Burn Hut. Meadow Hut, near the Pisa Range Snow Farm, can be booked. There are campgrounds and rooms available in Cromwell, Queenstown and Arrowtown, and campsites at Mavora Lakes.
Good to know // The route is best ridden in a clockwise loop. Cromwell makes a logical start and finish, saving the best section (Pisa Range) for last, but you can choose your starting point to suit the weather forecast.
More info // www.doc.govt.nz

Opposite: the TSS Earnslaw steamship ferries passengers across Lake Wakatipu

MORE LIKE THIS
SUPER-SCENIC SOUTH ISLAND

CORONET LOOP TRAIL

Rapidly gaining classic status, this spectacular mountain bike track can be ridden as a standalone loop (4–8 hours) or incorporated into the Wakatipu Ranges Tour for an extra day of Otago bikepacking. You'll experience singletrack traversing in an expanse of backcountry that's rich in mining and pioneering heritage. Historic water races, dams and old huts are as much a feature as bush and tussock-covered ranges and Wakatipu Basin views. The route is well marked as it climbs initially to Bush Creek Saddle, before dropping and climbing to Skippers Saddle at 949m (3,114ft). A long downhill leads to two smaller climbs before the big haul up to Deep Creek Saddle and a final epic descent. Suspension, at least on the front, is recommended, as is a light load.
Start // Butler's Green
Finish // Arrowtown
Distance // 50km (31 miles)
More info // www.queenstowntrails.org.nz

AROUND THE MOUNTAINS CYCLE TRAIL

Queenstown's famous entry-level cycle trail is well suited to first-time bikepackers or 'credit card' tourers who prefer a bed at night. The route follows purpose-built cycle trails and gravel roads, with just one significant climb through the Von Valley. The route can be cycled in either direction, but is commonly initiated in Queenstown, with the memorable crossing of Lake Wakatipu on the century-old steamship *TSS Earnslaw*, a start which is bookended in Kingston – home to the historic steam train, the Kingston Flyer. Highlights are the Wakatipu Basin scenery, Von Valley, Mavora Lakes, Mossburn cafes and rugged Otago landscapes.
Start // Walter Peak Station, Lake Wakatipu
Finish // Kingston
Distance // 186km (116 miles)
More info // www.aroundthemountains.co.nz

OTAGO CENTRAL RAIL TRAIL

New Zealand's original Great Ride is well deserving of its status, providing an accessible cycling route that's steeped in rail history and which links a series of Central Otago heartland towns. When it launched, the railway line connecting Clyde and Middlemarch opened up Central Otago for farming opportunities. These days, the rail corridor provides a rich cycling experience as the route makes a gentle excursion through one of New Zealand's most widescreen landscapes. It's typically cycled in three to four days, and there are plenty of opportunities for accommodation and refreshments along the way. Poolburn and Upper Taieri Gorges are two particular highlights, but the route is peppered with points of interest, from the historic Gilchrist's Store in Oturehua (great pies), to abundant rail infrastructure and farming history.
Start/Finish // Clyde/Middlemarch
Distance // 152km (94 miles)
More info // www.otagocentralrailtrail.co.nz

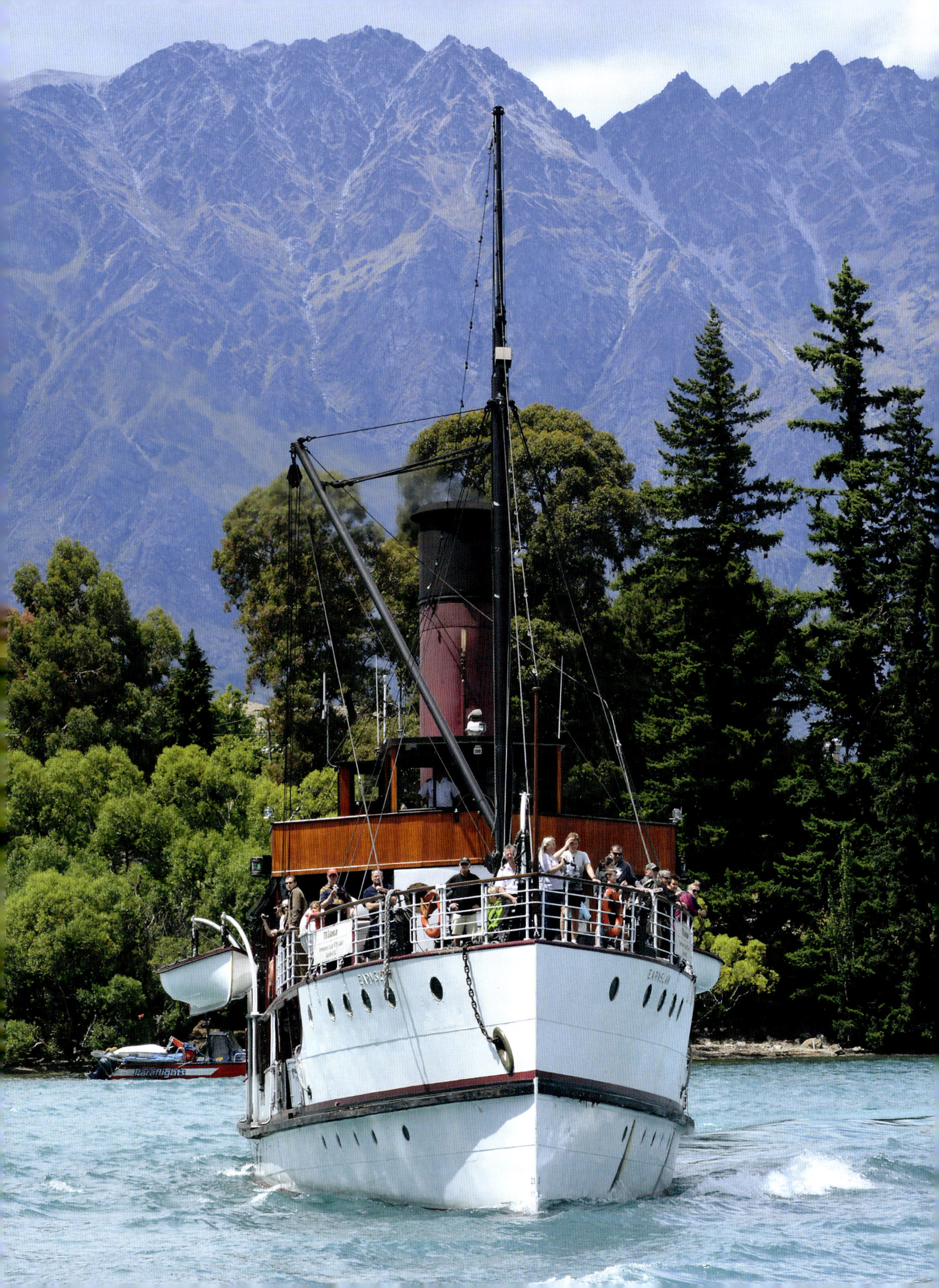
Paraflights

THE HEAPHY TRACK

A roadless tract of the South Island's west coast is home to one of New Zealand's premier singletrack rides, through a national park full of abundant plants and birdlife.

My experiences on the superlative Heaphy Track have been many and varied, from five-day excursions with four panniers on the bike, to racing through in less than seven hours. I've done it in both directions, with various groups of friends, and in all sorts of weather. It's a place so diverse and enchanting that you can visit it repeatedly and not tire of it. Every time I visit, I experience a previously missed detail or a different aspect of Kahurangi National Park's character.

On this occasion, I'm riding from east to west with a group of friends. Like many people we took a light plane from Karamea to the ride's start at Brown Hut. This simplifies logistics, because from the end of the ride it's just 18km (11 miles) back to our vehicles. But the flight also provides an amazing view of the coastline and interior of Kahurangi National Park as it traces the rugged shore and then the Heaphy River, giving us views of Gouland Downs and the route's high-point before we descend to land.

My friends have regrouped at Perry Saddle Hut after the near 900-vertical-metre (2950ft) climb up from Browns Hut. Although completely rideable for moderately fit cyclists, it's a long, sustained climb through beech forest, and we're all glad of a breather while we take stock of our position. The hut site offers a fantastic vista across to Dragons Teeth and Anatoki Peak over the densely wooded valleys below us. Already, we have transitioned from tall lowland forest to montane beech, tussock and alpine plants.

The cooler air up here bites a little, so we saddle up and head off to regroup at the next hut. It's a mostly downhill ride to the edge of Gouland Downs, splashing through creeks and picking lines down the sometimes-rough track. Gouland Downs Hut is historic and provides a reminder of the human history along this corridor, which has been used by Māori as a *pounamu* (greenstone) route long before European exploration of the area. During the mid-1840s, explorers Charles Heaphy and Thomas Brunner traversed the coast north of Karamea. Although Heaphy never crossed the route of the track, it has taken his name, as has the river. Later in the 1800s, prospectors began to explore the route as a connection between Golden Bay and the West Coast, but it didn't become popular for tramping until the 1970s.

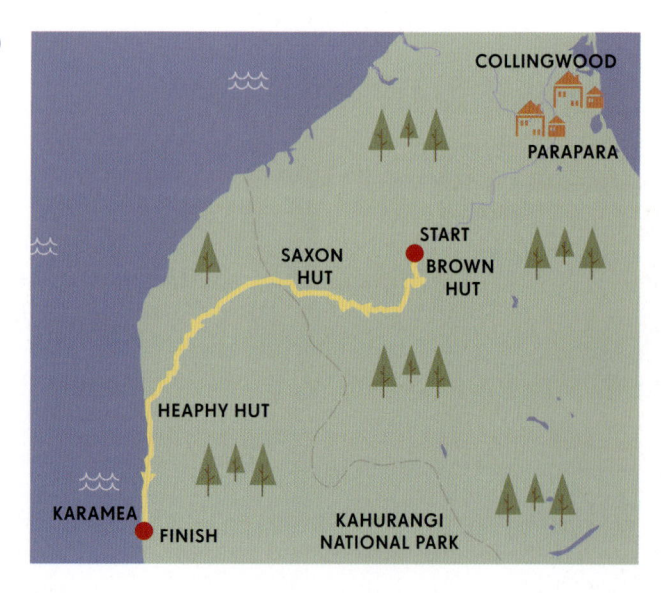

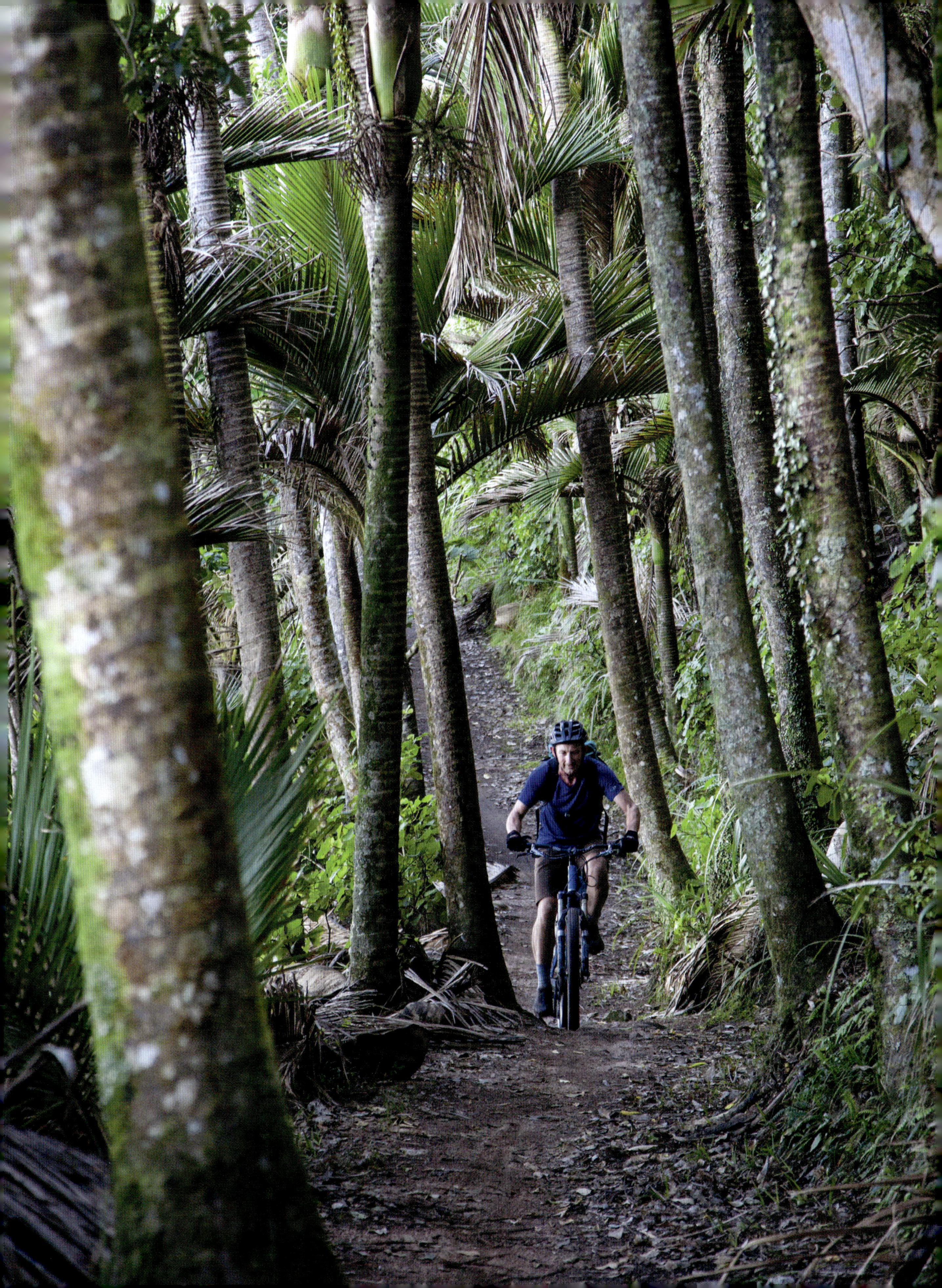

"Being by the sea after starting the day in the mountains brings a strong sense of contrast and journey"

Gouland Downs provides a contrast to the rest of the Heaphy Track with its swampy ground, tea-coloured streams and low-lying alpine scrub. Just past the hut, we pass some limestone caverns that reveal the karst massif that lies under our feet. We're lucky, and spot a couple of endemic whio (blue ducks) feeding in the rapids of a creek – given away by their shrill call. Saxon Hut lies on the western side of the downs and is our stopping point for the night. It's a beautiful spot, with the hut close to the beech forest, surrounded by tussock that turns golden with the late afternoon sun. Takahē, nationally vulnerable flightless birds that were thought extinct until their rediscovery in 1948, have been reintroduced to this area, and can sometimes be seen near Saxon Hut and about the downs.

From Saxon, Heaphy Hut will be our destination. The day is relatively short, but it packs in some fantastic riding as we undulate over the terrain, swoop around corners and stop sometimes to take it all in. Our surroundings are a mixture of beech forest with thick carpets of moss, leafy astelias, and pockets of tussock and tufty dracophyllum that could be right out of a Dr Seuss book.

We take lunch in the sun at James Mackay Hut, another popular overnight stop. The view looks out to the Tasman Sea, and down to the Heaphy River mouth, where the river makes a final elegant S-bend before issuing into the churning surf. That's where we're headed, and between us and the sea is an outrageously good 700m (2300ft) descent that snakes its way

AT A CRAWL

Giant carnivorous snails might sound like something from a fantasy novel, but they're just another of the curiosities you might discover on the Heaphy Track. The powelliphanta snail likes to snack on earthworms, but while you're unlikely to see a live one, it's quite common to encounter their shells lying in the forest. It's prohibited to remove them, but their aesthetic forms make great photos.

Clockwise from top: crossing Kohaihai River; Flanagans Corner; downhill stretch; Heaphy Beach Previous page: riding through nikau palms on the Heaphy Track

© Mark Watson

THE SOUTH ISLAND, NEW ZEALAND

through luxuriant forest. The air warms as we drop and, once we've pedalled the final few flattish kilometres to the hut, the flora changes again. Lowland coastal forest is the theme now, but the main characters are the uniform nikau palms which, like many of the other plants we've seen, are endemic to New Zealand. These palms lend an island paradise feel to the rest of the ride.

One can't visit Heaphy Hut without a short walk down to the beach for sunset. We zigzag through mounds of driftwood and pīngao grass, and stand on the sand watching waves pound the shore. Being by the sea after starting the day in the mountains brings a strong sense of contrast and journey, and that's one of the aspects that makes the Heaphy so special.

When we return to the hut, there's a group of curious weka stalking the bikes, looking for anything loose or some food they can snatch. These cheeky, flightless birds are sometimes mistaken for kiwi, but they're much bolder and provide endless entertainment as they prey on the property of careless cyclists.

The final stretch of the ride out to Kohaihai takes just the morning, and we stop often to enjoy the views of golden sandy beaches and steep mountain streams that cut their way between granite boulders. The riding flows nicely, hugging the coastline, dipping and climbing, twisting through the trees. It's perfect singletrack. The final descent to the Kohaihai river mouth has everyone smiling, before the warm-down along the road to Karamea where we're looking forward to a cafe lunch. **MW**

TOOLKIT

Start // Brown Hut
Finish // Karamea
Distance // 78km (48 miles)
Getting there // Collingwood is the closest town to the eastern end, while Karamea services the west. Pre-booked shuttle or flight options are available at either end.
When to go // The Heaphy is a Great Walk, within Kahurangi National Park. It's only open to cyclists between 1 May and 30 November. The track is wetter during the winter months.
What to wear // Rain is common on the Heaphy and Gouland Downs is exposed. Bring suitable clothing.
Where to stay // Booking is mandatory for the huts and campsites throughout the route, except Brown Hut at the eastern end of the track. There is accommodation in Collingwood and Karamea.
More info // www.doc.govt.nz/heaphytrack

Opposite: the tropical beach at Totaranui

MORE LIKE THIS
WOODLAND AND WAVES

QUEEN CHARLOTTE TRACK, SOUTH ISLAND

In 1770, explorer Captain James Cook moored his ship, *Endeavour*, in Ships Cove for rest and reprovision. It was the first of four times this sheltered bay was used by the ship and its crew. These days, water taxis from Picton stop at the scenic cove to drop cyclists at the start of one of New Zealand's best multi-day rides. Typically mountain-biked over two to three days, the Queen Charlotte Track dives into scenic bays and follows ridges with panoramic views of the sounds, much of the time under the shelter of coastal forest. You can ride self-sufficiently, staying at designated campsites, or have the water taxi transport your luggage while you cycle unencumbered between accommodation. Riding in from the Anikiwa end for a full or half day's ride is also a great way to see the area.
Start/Finish // Meretoto/Ships Cove/Anikiwa
Distance // 71km (44 miles)
More info // www.qctrack.co.nz

TASMANIAN TRAIL, TASMANIA

An unparalleled traverse of the Tasmanian high country, the Tasmanian Trail runs from north coast to south following gravel roads and sections of rougher track through the heart of the island. The route offers a backcountry experience, but passes through or close to numerous small towns that provide a cultural contrast and opportunities for resupply. But it's perhaps the diversity of the landscapes, from fertile farming country to high plateau and ancient forests, that make this route really special. You might spot some of Tasmania's unique wildlife too.
Start/Finish // Dover/Devonport
Distance // 465km (289 miles)
More info // www.tasmaniantrail.com.au

GIBBS HILL, SOUTH ISLAND

Offering a taste of Abel Tasman National Park's beach-and-forest charm with some grade-3 mountain biking on singletrack, the Gibbs Hill circuit is well worth doing if you are in the area. The trail is accessible to the public from 1 May to 30 September. The route starts in Wainui Bay and crosses the Gibbs Hill track to the long beach at Tōtaranui on the east-facing shore, before returning to the start via a 13km (8 mile) gravel road. From the route's high point on a clear day, you can see into Golden Bay, out to the tip of the South Island at Farewell Spit and back towards Tōtaranui.
Start/Finish // Wainui Bay/Tōtaranui
Distance // 23km (14 miles)
More info // www.doc.govt.nz

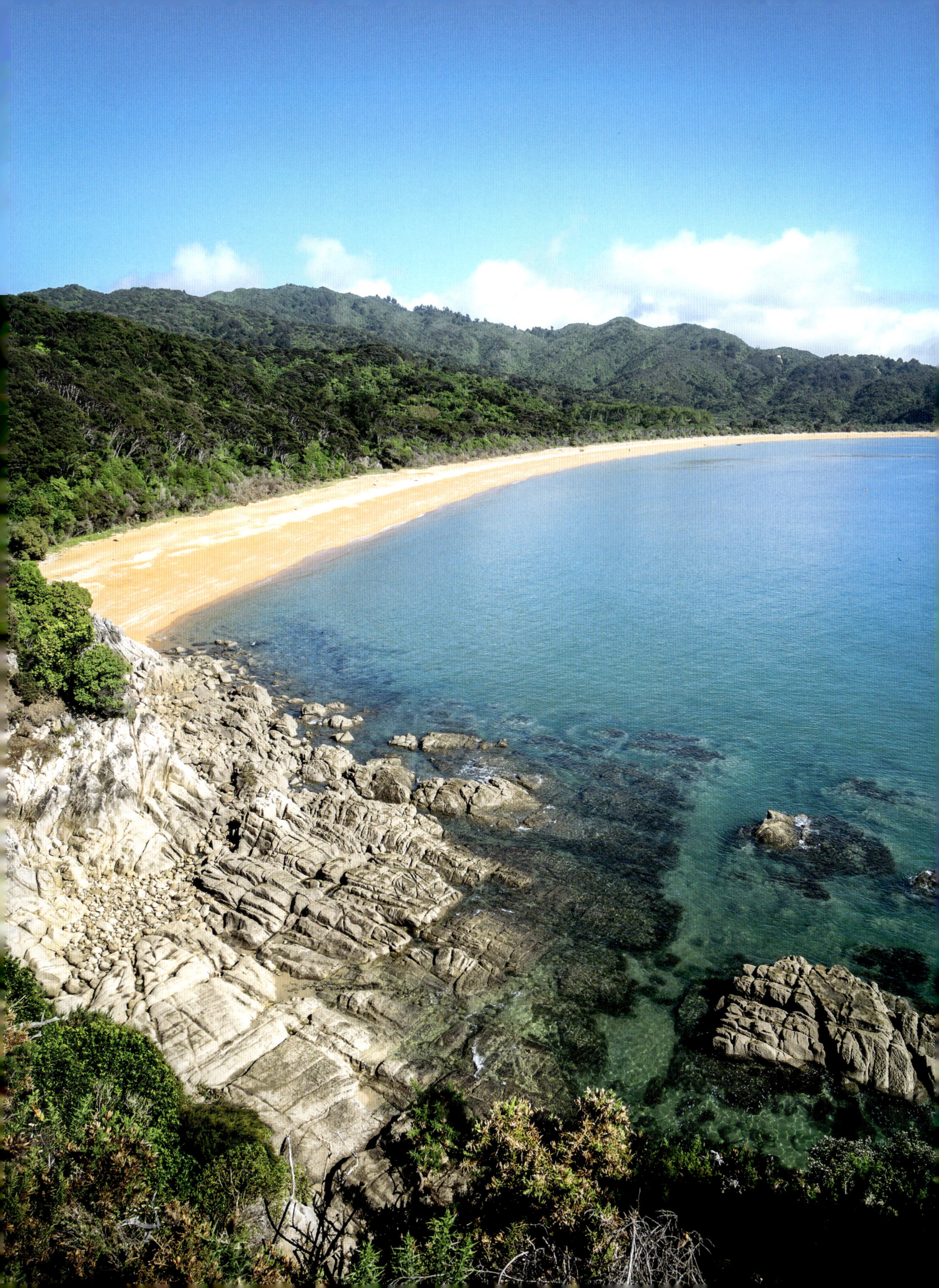

- EPIC BIKE RIDES OF AUSTRALIA & NEW ZEALAND -

THE CORONET LOOP

In a region not short on outdoor attractions, the Coronet Loop is an epic singletrack adventure that opens up a fresh way to explore a treasured New Zealand landscape.

- EPIC BIKE RIDES OF AUSTRALIA & NEW ZEALAND -

If Paris is known as the home of art, and Bangkok the capital of street food, then Queenstown has made 'adventure' its mission. On the edge of the Southern Alps, its mix of snow-capped mountains, roaring rivers and cinematic vistas make it an adrenaline junkie's promised land. From skiing, snowboarding and ski touring in the winter, to bungee jumping, paragliding, whitewater rafting and mountain biking in the summer, the town is a magnet for stoke-seekers the world over.

Tracing its namesake mountain, the Coronet Loop takes riders on a 56km (34.5 mile) adventure through previously unreachable sections of the majestic Wakatipu Basin. It's a land of wild contrasts: from rock-face waterfalls and deep river gorges to brake-melting flow trails along reclaimed water races and distant gullies. The trail was finished in March 2022, and I was lucky enough to ride it with my friend Sophie on its opening weekend.

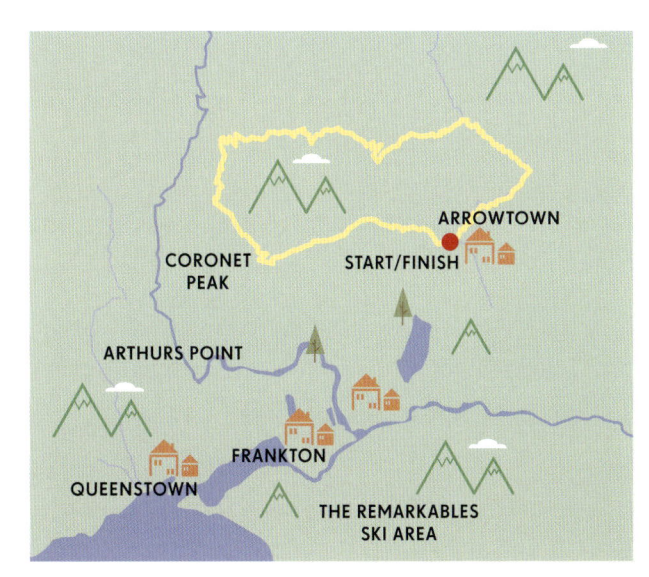

Arrowtown is on the cusp of autumn as we arrive at the trailhead and begin unloading our bikes. Towering oaks, sycamores and ash trees tease their golden tones as the first of their leaves start to turn. Beneath a canopy of native beech forest, the trail snakes 500m (1,640ft) up a series of tight switchbacks, before spitting us out onto the southern face of Coronet Peak.

Blanketed in thick snow between the months of June and October, Coronet Peak transforms into the region's most famous ski resort. Its stunning alpine environment, wide-open runs and natural roller-coaster terrain attract thousands of people each year. But as the snow begins to melt and the hot summer days of Central Otago kick in, skis are replaced with rubber, and the dusty landscape morphs into a mountain biker's playground.

At the top of the climb, Queenstown's splendour is on full display. The cloud-crowned Remarkables flank the town as paragliders hunt for thermals over the steel-blue waters of Lake Wakatipu. The views are so good, we almost don't want to leave. But with another 150m (490ft) of climbing left, and the promise of a ripping downhill just ahead, we push on.

'I can't believe I've never ridden a full-sus before!' I scream out to Sophie as I throw myself into the tight berms of the 'Pack, Track & Sack'. With dropper post down, it's just me and the trail – a unity of focus and fear, where the hypnotic sound of gravel crushing under tyre seduces me to ride faster. It's an assault on the senses and I'm well and truly hooked. But in the blink of an eye, the trail ends and we're climbing once again.

"Before I know it, Sophie chucks her bike to the ground and immerses herself head-first in the glacial run-off"

Blonde mountain grass and billowing tussocks dance in the mountain breeze as the dusty trail leads us through a juxtaposed landscape of life and death. Non-indigenous pine trees brought to NZ in the 1800s (but now considered pests, and sprayed with herbicides) stand lifeless like grey tree-skeletons, haunting the landscape. 'Eventually, they'll be felled, with native beech and matagouri replanted in their place,' Sophie tells me as we tumble down a ribbon of descending trail to Greengates Hut.

Perfectly placed at the 25km (15.5 mile) mark, Greengates Hut is a prime spot for our first lunch. Legend has it the hut was once run as a piggery, serving bacon sandwiches to groups of hungry miners in search of their fortune. Still standing today, its schist stone walls and corrugated-iron roof show the decades of revolving seasons through their storm-scarred patinas.

Fuelled by falafel, we continue upstream and over Picnic Rock before a long and steady descent towards the valley floor. Sophie's in her element as we traverse the numerous fresh creek crossings and ride alongside tumbling waterfalls. The mountains wear the scars from winter's deep freeze, and with their meltwater channels provide a path for gallons of water to barrel

ARROWTOWN IN AUTUMN

As summer fades, Arrowtown erupts in autumnal foliage that attracts visitors from all over the world. When gold was discovered in Arrow River in 1862, a township was quickly established and non-native, deciduous trees were planted by the settlers. The magnificent display of oaks, sycamores, willows and birch trees engulfs the town with russet tones from March to May.

Left to right: the trail weaves through the dark schist rock; there are multiple creek crossings to make. Previous spread: riding the Coronet Loop

off the high cliffs. Before I know it, Sophie chucks her bike to the ground and immerses herself head-first in the glacial run-off. 'It's beautiful, but it's bloody cold!' she yells out between intermittent bouts of teeth chatter, rushed breathing and the Om mantra.

With Sophie's quota of Wim Hof philosophy well and truly smashed, we head off for the final section of the loop. Although the hustle and bustle of Queenstown is just 25km (15.5 miles) away, there's a genuine sense of remoteness out here. 'I've been exploring this part of Queenstown for 25 years and I've never seen this side of the mountain,' Sophie muses as her face lights up with an explorer's excitement. Sharing the new landscape – both of us for the first time now – every pedal stroke feels pioneering. Savouring each moment, we slow the pace and appreciate the final kilometres of the trail while snacking on wild blackberries.

The summer light begins to gently fade as we merge with Macetown Rd. Its potholed jeep tracks signal that Arrowtown is close. One final corner and the road ahead is a kaleidoscope of colour. Pockets of russet brown and crimson red pop from the autumnal scene like a Monet painting. We were back in Arrowtown, where we'd left just five hours earlier. Sun-kissed, hungry and full of smiles, we jump in the car and head home.

On the face of it, the Coronet Loop is just a day ride of four to six hours. But for me, it represents the very best of what Queenstown has to offer. The capital of adventure has a new jewel in its crown. **SR**

TOOLKIT

Start/Finish // Arrowtown
Distance // 50km (31 miles)
Getting there // Parking is available next to Dudley's Cottage or in the car park at Ramshaw Lane.
When to go // The best time is October to April. The weather can change rapidly, so check the forecast.
What to wear // Bring layers in case of a weather change. In summer, pack a long shirt – the NZ sun is no joke!
What to pack // Bring lunch, bike tools and chain lube. Water is limited, but there are plenty of mountain streams for a refill along the way (treating the water first).
Where to stay // This route is intended to be done in a day. You can shorten it by starting at Skippers saddle off Coronet Peak Rd and skip the big climb of the day. There are two basic backcountry shelters on the trail that are used on a first come, first served basis.
Where to eat // Arrowtown has plenty of options for food to go, or fill up on before and after your ride.
Things to know // The trail is best ridden clockwise up Bush Creek track.
More info // www.queenstowntrails.org.nz

Opposite: morning mist settling over Moke Lake

MORE LIKE THIS
QUEENSTOWN AREA LOOPS

DEVILS CREEK TRACK

The Devils Creek Track is a lesser-known trail located near Coronet Peak. The track starts at Skippers Saddle (shortly after Skippers Rd turns off from Coronet Peak Rd), and begins with a steady 370m (1214ft) ascent to Mt Dewar (1310m/4298ft). From here, the anti-clockwise loop continues with a descent on the Shotover Canyon Track, crossing Devils Creek in a hidden valley before one last uphill push over the shoulder (930m/3050ft) on Devils Creek Track to finish down on Coronet Peak Rd above the more open valley of the Shotover River. It's steep in places and can be challenging, but it's a fairly short ride, and the rewards are well worth it with panoramic views of Wakatipu Basin. In winter, this area can get a good dump of snow and can be pretty slippery going down.
Start // Skippers Saddle
Finish // Coronet Peak Rd
Distance // 12km (8 miles)
More info // www.doc.govt.nz

MOKE LAKE LOOP

Shaped like a pair of baggy trousers, Moke Lake is set in a valley just north of Lake Wakatipu's middle zigzag, and feels remote even though it's only a 15-minute drive from Queenstown. A hiking and mountain biking trail traces its shores, with the Moke Lake Rd on the east bank completing the loop. The tussock-covered peaks of Ben Lomond, Ben More and Mt Hanley frame the scene in the tranquil Moke Lake Reserve. The route is perfect for beginners, families or simply those wanting to have a short trip and a dip in fresh water. In the autumn and winter months, the surrounding mountains are dusted with snow, making the trail magical in all seasons. Other activities at Moke Lake include fishing (with a licence), kayaking and camping, so you're likely to see other people while out adventuring.
Start/Finish // Moke Lake Road
Distance // 7km (4 miles)
More info // www.doc.govt.nz

THE MOONLIGHT CIRCUIT

This epic half-day MTB loop shows off the best of the rugged Queenstown backcountry. Riding up dramatic gorges on challenging singletrack, this sometimes steep route is for skilled riders tackling rocky and exposed areas, along with gnarly hike-a-bike necessary on some sections. The first bit (if going anti-clockwise) is a straightforward run up the road from Queenstown to Arthurs Point, but joining the Moonlight Track changes the equation to grade 4. Follow the trail round the north shoulder of the Ben Lomond massif until you reach Moke Lake, where you can take the track round its west side. From there it's a descent to Lake Wakatipu and back to Queenstown. Although a hard path at times, the scenery is unbeatable: panoramas of towering peaks, winding rivers, deep blue lakes and wild terrain.
Start/Finish // Lake Esplanade, Queenstown
Distance // 40km (25 miles)
More info // www.singletracks.com

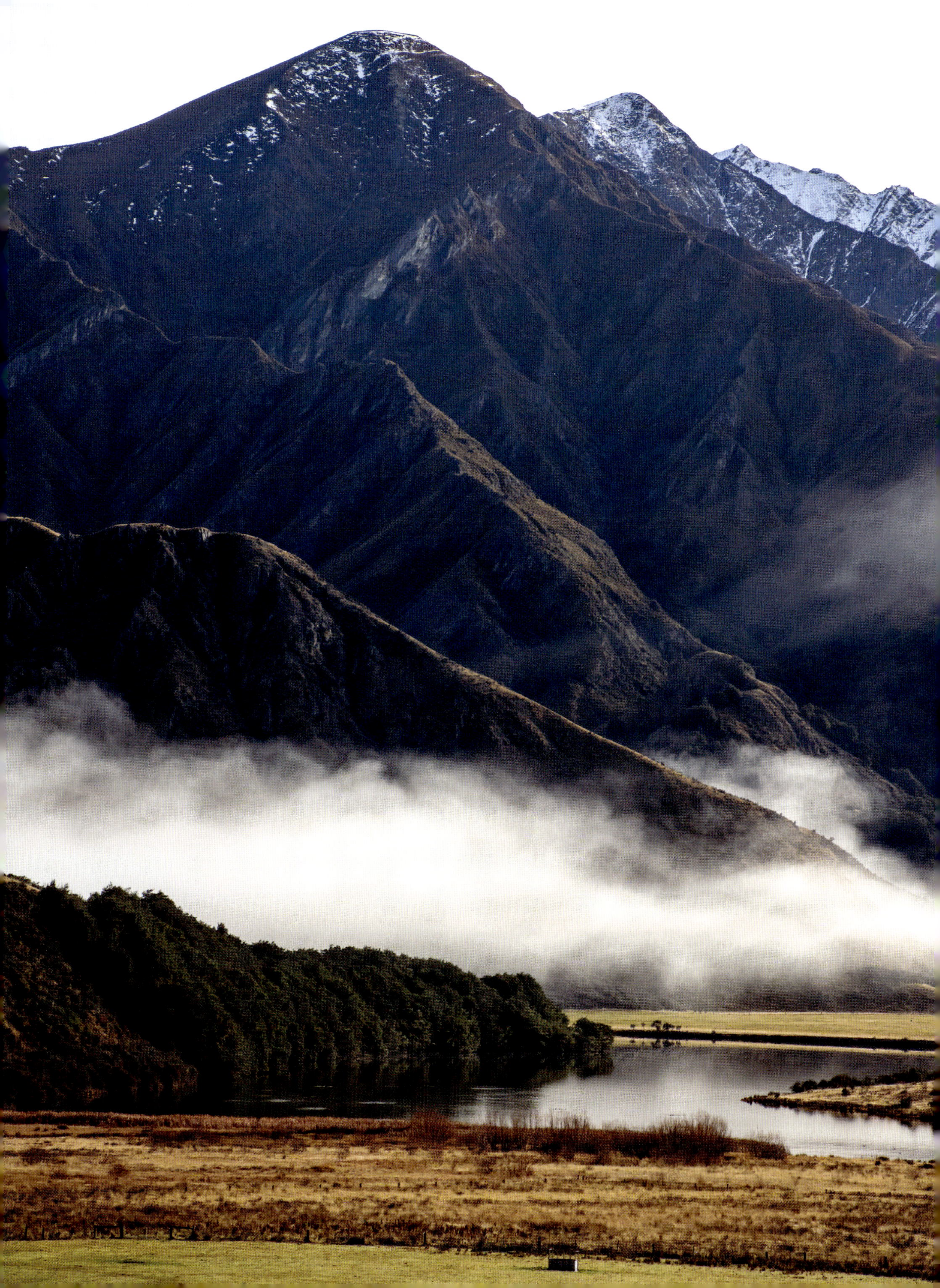

CANTERBURY'S BANKS PENINSULA

On one of New Zealand's most unusually shaped landforms, a network of scenic rural roads climb and hug once-volcanic hills. Welcome to the Banks Peninsula.

Early in the morning, Lyttelton Harbour/Whakaraupō is mirror-calm, disturbed only by the bow of the small ferry as it cuts across the placid water. We catch a glimpse of the distant harbour mouth and open ocean, and a few minutes later we're mooring at Diamond Harbour in the shadow of Mount Herbert. At 919m (3015ft), it's the highest point in Banks Peninsula/Te Pātaka o Rākaihautū, a crinkled outlier poking from the Canterbury Plains.

For the next three days, we're going to be exploring these eroded remnants of two large volcanoes, whose eruptions more than five million years ago left the peninsula incised by two deep harbours and countless bays and coves. The hills are studded with craggy spurs, and it's hills that this place is famous for. Seldom flat, the Banks Peninsula is a climber's paradise of long routes that wind from sea level up to the high ridges, followed by fast descents on quiet rural roads.

We've come prepared with easy gears on our bikes and we're already using them as we climb steadily away from Diamond Harbour and Purau. This over-the-shoulder ride to Port Levy is the 'entrance' climb, made easier by being on asphalt, and from the top there's a panoramic view back to Lyttelton and Christchurch city's Port Hills. Barely have we reached the flat at the bottom of the descent before we begin climbing again on a dirt road. Western Valley Road snakes its way up past small farms and forest, until it reaches a high saddle. We only saw two cars on the 640m (2100ft) climb, but now we're heading properly off road on the classic Double Fence Line mountain bike ride.

After a short climb and descent on a grassy track, we reach another saddle that has a mysterious copse of remnant totara forest. The branches have been blown skewwhiff by the prevailing winds that howl up from the Pacific Ocean,

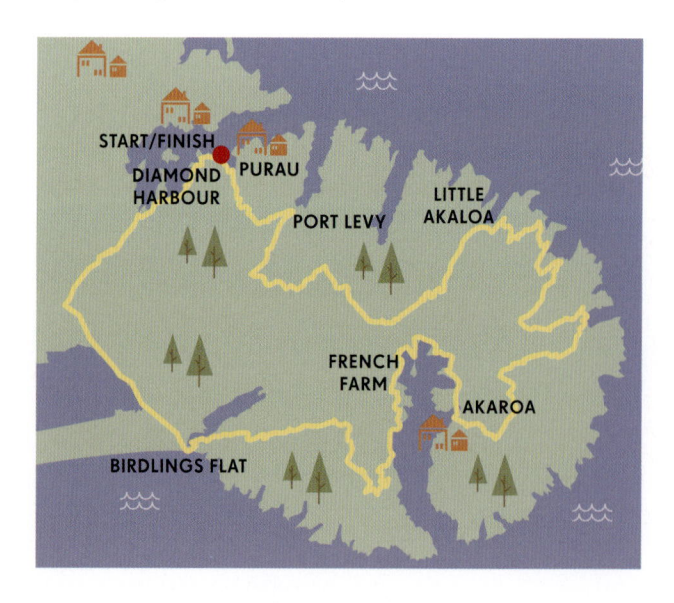

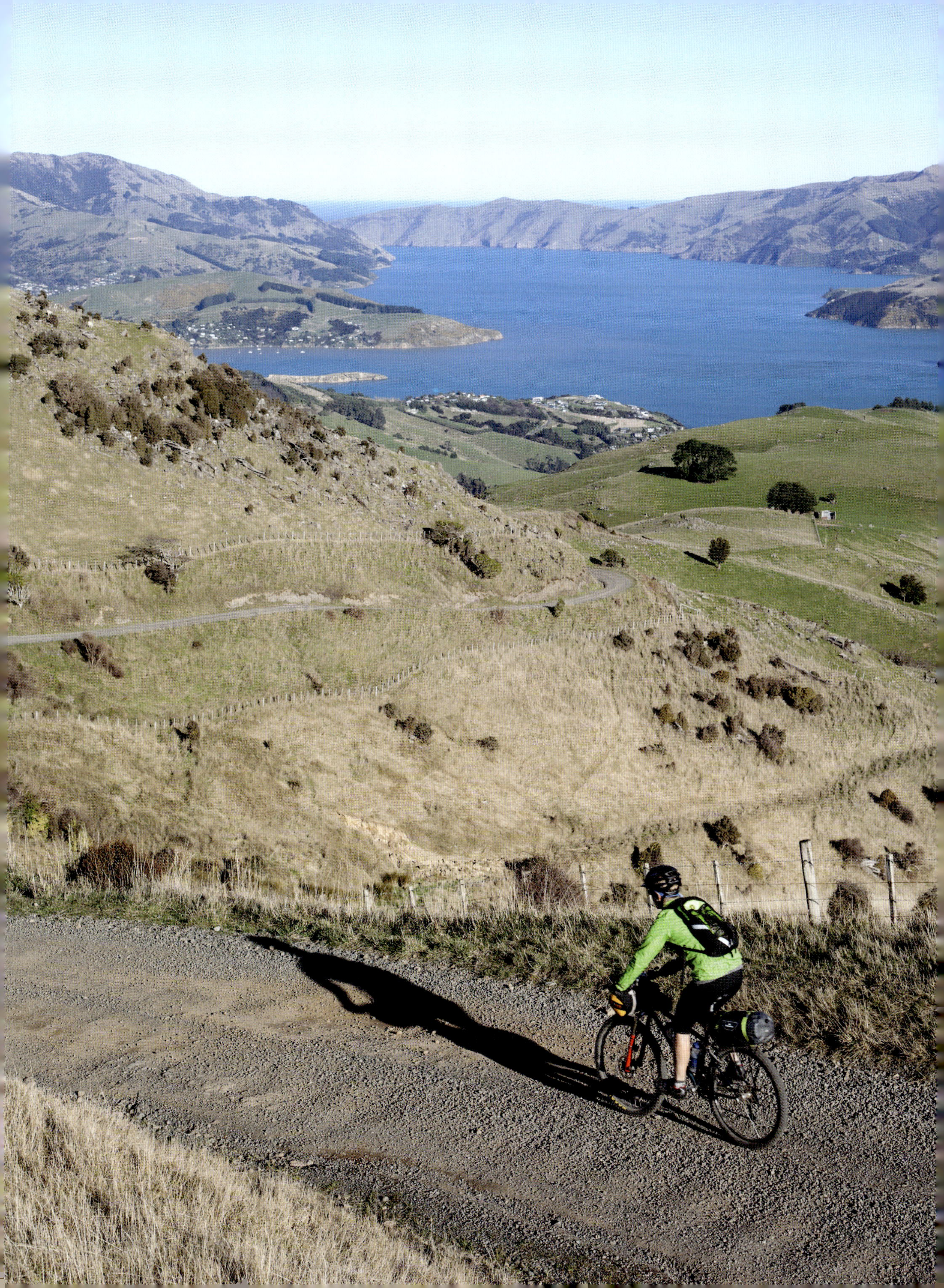

making the trees look as if they were melting in a Salvador Dalí painting. It's one of the most photogenic spots on the ride and we linger for a while, appreciating the scene.

Wide-open views of the peninsula's endless hills and ridges, and out to the ocean are the flavour of the morning, as we ride a rolling single- and doubletrack route along broad, grassy ridges. Just below the top of Mt Fitzgerald, we stop for lunch in the sunshine, happy to rest our legs after what has already been a lot of climbing.

Later, we cross Mt Sinclair and emerge onto a hillside that's covered with the ghostly, white skeletons of long-dead trees, bleached by the sun and polished by the wind. Though interesting, this scene is a sad reminder that the entire peninsula was once covered in mature forest. Were it still covered in such forest now, it would surely be a national park, but pioneers logged the peninsula of endemic tree species long ago, mostly for the construction of Christchurch. These days, mature forest on the peninsula is confined to a few small pockets, although in many places it's slowly regenerating.

After a farm track downhill, we reach a gravel road and then climb on the tarmac Summit Road to the turn-off to Little Akaloa. From here, forest, farms and old homesteads speed by in a blur as we coast down a long descent to the inlet of Little Akaloa. There's a small community campground here, but we ride on to Okains Bay to make the next day shorter.

"The peninsula's climbs are hard, but they always reward you with expansive vistas and fun downhills"

The view from the climb out of Little Akaloa is a mandatory photo stop – the long, narrow bay being a classic Banks Peninsula landscape. This section of the ride over to Okains Bay is on tarmac, but although the road is modern, the rustic cottages have an aura that takes us back to bygone farming times. The shadows are lengthening as we roll down the final hill into Okains Bay and find a spot at the beachside campsite.

In the morning we're away early and, of course, the road heads straight uphill. This climb is one of the route's longest, up the aptly named Big Hill Road, and we spin up the sometimes-steep gravel road from sea level to over 500m (1640ft). This part of the ride has a more remote feel than the previous day. There's no one around, and no traffic on the sinuous dirt roads. Lavericks Ridge Road provides a high-speed descent towards Le Bons Bay, and an epic view east over empty ocean as far as the eye can see. The peninsula's climbs are hard, but they always reward you with expansive vistas and fun downhills.

We're looking forward to the cafe in Akaroa, so we push on through Le Bons, back up to the Summit Road and then along

THE ISLAND THAT WASN'T

Attached to the 'mainland' with just narrow coastal plains and a low ridge, Banks Peninsula has an island-like feel, and that's just what Joseph Banks, the naturalist sailing in 1770 aboard Captain Cook's *Endeavour*, believed it to be. The ship's crew were too far away to see the low-lying connection, and thus this remarkable landform appeared as Banks Island on the earliest maps of New Zealand.

Left to right: plotting the route during a pitstop at Le Bons; the top of the route near Hinewai Reserve; the coastline of the Banks Peninsula. Previous spread: descending the gravel track to the coast

towards Hinewai Reserve, a forest restoration project. Purple Peak is our target, as we turn off onto singletrack and climb steeply up to a short saddle. From here, a fun singletrack and farm road drops steeply towards Akaroa, with postcard views of Akaroa Harbour to absorb.

Settled by the French in 1840, Akaroa is Canterbury's oldest town. It brims with quirky charm due to its timber cottages, picket fences and pier, but we're more interested in food and make a beeline for the cafe. We resupply for the final night and day at the store, and ride around the scenic bays to Wainui where there's a campground that's alive with birdsong from tui and bellbirds.

The notorious Bossu Road is the final big climb of this route, but it's also the best. This rugged corner of the peninsula is exposed to storms from the south, and is the least populated section. We're lucky to have a calm, clear morning, and as we climb the road towards the day's high-point, we can see a large swathe of the terrain we traversed over the previous two days. The road turns to gravel and undulates along the range through a sub-alpine environment, until we plunge down towards Birdlings Flat, a small coastal community. It's the start of a beach that sweeps away southwest, almost unbroken for 135km (84 miles). But after the rail trail that provides a respite from climbing until Gebbies Pass, we must turn back on one last road through this peninsula to catch the ferry home. **MW**

TOOLKIT

Start/Finish // Diamond Harbour
Distance // 184km (114 miles)
Getting there // Lyttelton (where you catch the ferry to Diamond Harbour) can be reached from Christchurch by car or bus (bikes allowed) through the Lyttelton Tunnel, or by bicycle over the Port Hills.
When to go // Summer, autumn and spring. Winter can also allow great riding on fine days, but the roads can be wet and muddy in places.
What to wear // Banks Peninsula is very exposed to the wind and incoming weather. Carry appropriate clothing.
What to pack // Basic camping equipment and stove.
Where to stay // There are campgrounds at Little Akaloa, Okains Bay, Akaroa, Duvauchelles, Wainui and Okuti Valley (off-route). Some B&B/motel options are also available, but these are very limited outside Akaroa.
More info // www.christchurchnz.com; www.ridewithgps.com/routes/41752938

Opposite: Tangarakau Gorge, one of the highlights along the Forgotten World Highway

MORE LIKE THIS
SHORT MULTI-DAY VENTURES

REMUTAKA CYCLE TRAIL, NORTH ISLAND

Typically done as a multi-day ride, the Remutaka Cycle Trail loops through and around mountains northeast of Wellington. It has multiple access points, and can be picked up at various points or cycled in sections easily. The heart of this Great Ride is the historic Remutaka Incline, a 25km (15 mile) section of rail trail that gradually ascends to the route's high point at Summit, an old railway station site, and down to Cross Creek. This section of the ride features extensive rail history, with interpretation panels that tell the story of building and maintaining the railway in rugged terrain. There are various tunnels along the route between Maymorn and Cross Creek, with the longest being over half a kilometre (bring a torch). In contrast to the Remutaka Rail Trail section, the section from Ocean Beach to the mouth of the Orongorongo River provides a raw and remote coastal experience, upping the grade of the ride from 3 to 4.
Start // Petone
Finish // Orongorongo River
Distance // 115km (71 miles)
More info // www.wellingtonregionaltrails.com

FORGOTTEN WORLD HIGHWAY, NORTH ISLAND

This hilly North Island heartland ride is usually incorporated into a longer tour, such as Kōpiko Aotearoa, but it makes a great multi-day point-to-point ride too. A once-forgotten tract of remote farming country has been rediscovered in recent years as one of New Zealand's best gravel and quiet tarmac experiences, with such highlights as the richly forested Tāngarākau Gorge, the quirky rural settlement of Whangamōmona, and views of the perfect cone of Taranaki/Mt Egmont as you approach New Plymouth. Historic road tunnels, such as the Hobbit's Hole – combined with old homesteads and sprawling native forest – lend the region a frontier flavour, creating a ride that's full of mystique and points of interest at every turn.
Start // Taumarunui
Finish // New Plymouth
Distance // 183km (113 miles)
More info // www.nzcycletrail.com

BUNDEENA TO KIAMA, NEW SOUTH WALES

Kicking off in New South Wales' Royal National Park, the one- to two-day ride from Bundeena to Kiama hugs the coastline, combining coastal roads and bike paths. Epic ocean views, surf beaches and the cliffs of the Illawarra Escarpment are the flavour of this outing. After cycling through the national park, the route picks up sinuous coastal roads and bike paths as it heads south to Wollongong, with plenty of opportunities for beachside refreshments along the way. The start of the ride can be reached by ferry from Cronulla to Bundeena. There's a train from the finish at Kiama back to Sydney.
Start // Bundeena
Finish // Kiama
Distance // 120km (75 miles)
More info // www.weareexplorers.co

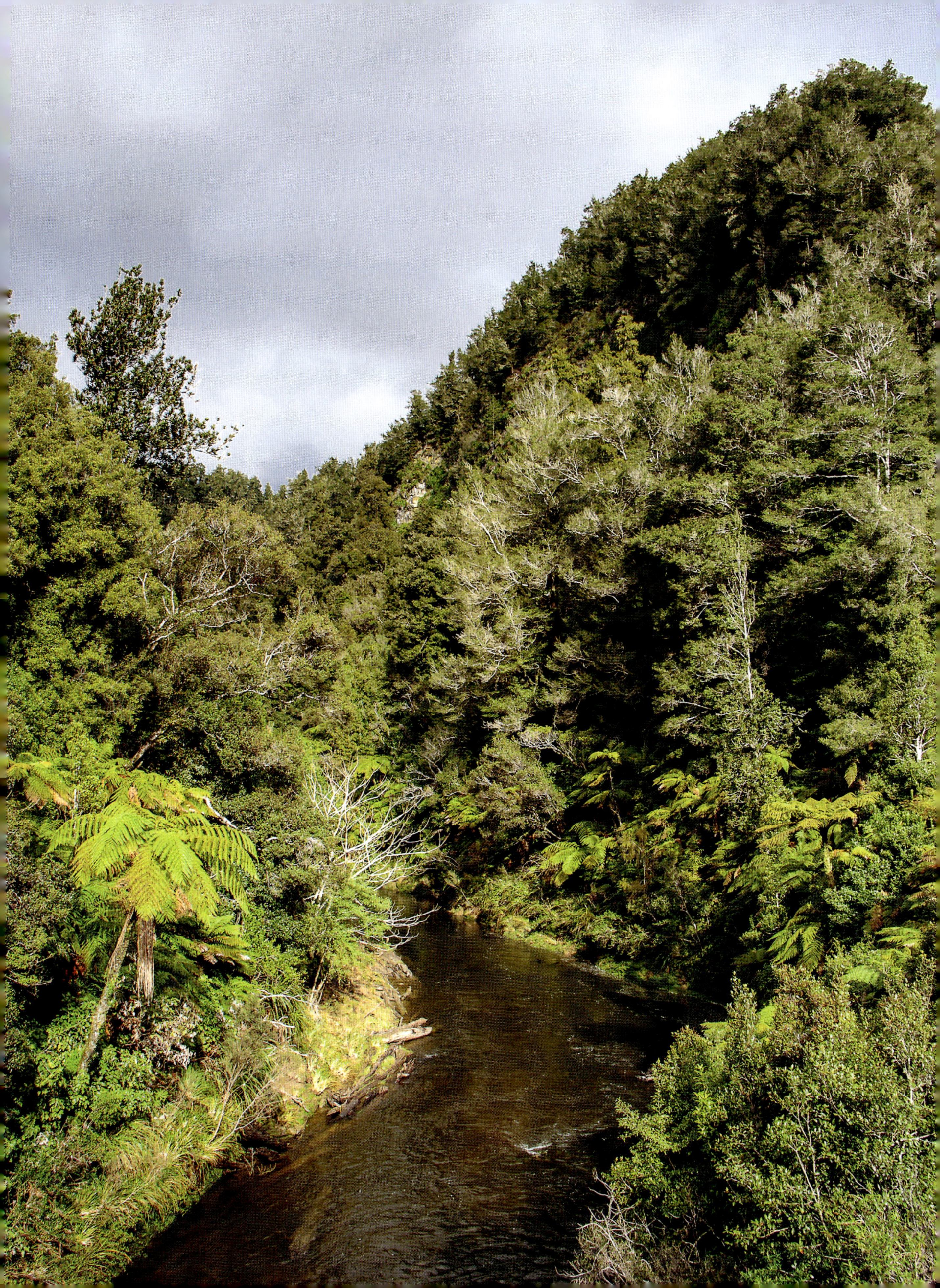

ALPS 2 OCEAN CYCLE TRAIL

New Zealand's longest cycle trail serves up colossal, colourful vistas on its way from the Southern Alps to the Pacific Coast town of Oamaru.

New Zealanders have long been mad for mountain biking. But when, in 2009, the government injected NZ$50m (AU$47m) to build a nationwide cycle trail network and it was matched by another NZ$50m from community groups, it was diggers at dawn in the battle to become the world's ultimate off-road cycling destination.

The fruits of this funding are the New Zealand Cycle Trail's 23 Great Rides, ranging from day-trips to multi-day epics, some following old byways and others cutting new paths through previously inaccessible wilderness. I have now ridden 22 and while there's the odd lemon among them, the majority are fat, juicy cherries on a riding pie that already boasted such internationally renowned trail centres as Rotorua's Redwoods and Wellington's Makara Peak.

The South Island's Alps 2 Ocean (A2O) is one of the best – an instant classic that can be enjoyed by almost anyone. Stretching more than 300km (186 miles) from mountains to sea, divided into nine sections ridden individually or in full over four to six days, its merits are many and varied. First up, there's the starting point at the foot of New Zealand's highest peak, 3724m (10741ft) Aoraki/Mt Cook, amid the splendour of the Southern Alps.

The A2O heads down the lower Hooker Valley and soon meets an impasse at the Tasman River. It's a quick helicopter hop to the other side, from where the trail recommences through fairly rocky terrain along the Tasman delta. The broad, braided river channels are a spectacular sight, backdropped by the Ben Ohau Range that remains in view downriver to Lake Pukaki, where the trail follows the smoother Braemar Rd towards Twizel.

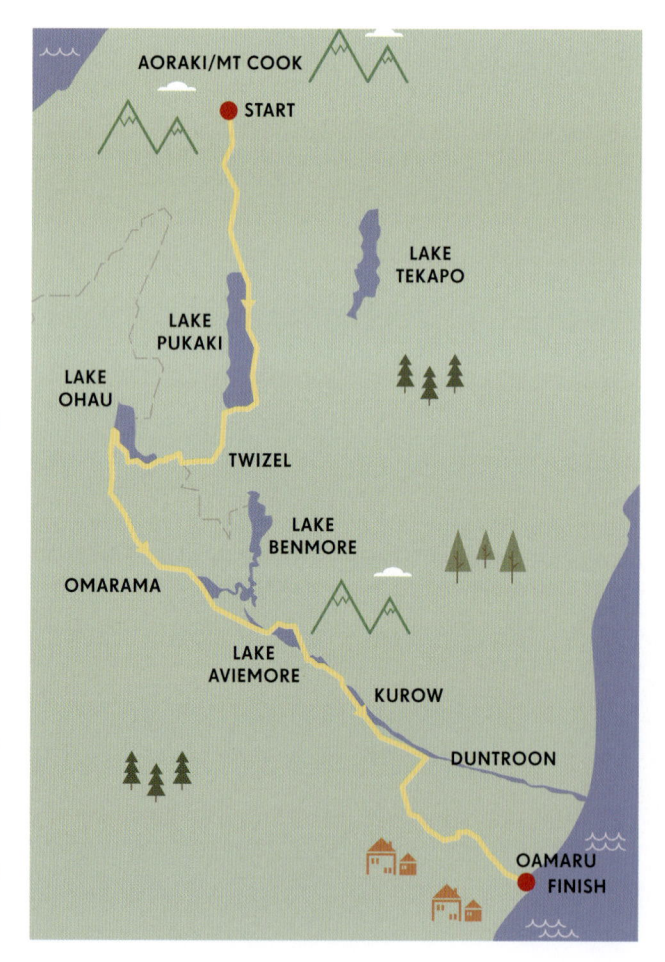

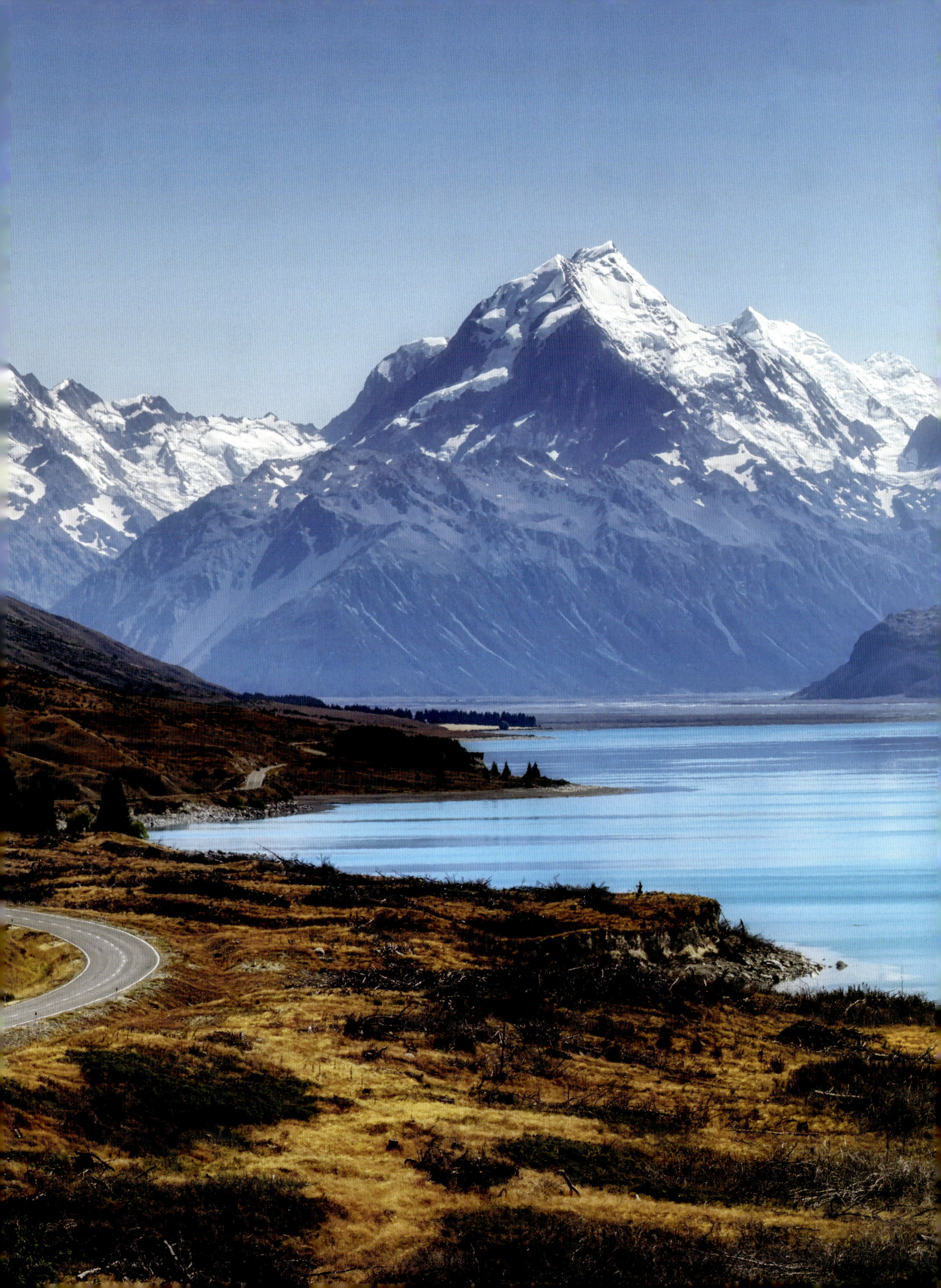

There's an alternative start at Lake Tekapo, from where the trail parallels the first of many powder-blue hydropower canals through golden tussock-land, past the Tekapo B Power Station, to meet the main trail on Braemar Rd. Lake Tekapo itself is a must-see, the turquoise jewel in the heart of Mackenzie Country. Above it is Mt John Observatory, the focal point of the Aoraki Mackenzie International Dark Sky Reserve, a magnet for astronomers and amateur stargazers alike. Big skies, day and night, are a constant on the A2O.

The town of Twizel was established in 1968 for workers on the Waitaki hydroelectric power station. Defiantly surviving beyond its use-by date only to play second fiddle to the national park village of Aoraki/Mt Cook, today it's undergoing a bit of a micro-boom. Close to major crossroads, more or less in the middle of everything, it's a solid service town for passing A2O riders, and also a pleasant home base for day rides on and around the trail.

One of the A2O's best day rides is from Twizel to Lake Ohau: a leisurely cruise along pretty country roads and another intensely blue canal, then beside the lake to longstanding Lake Ohau Lodge, with an atmospheric restaurant, bar and killer mountain views.

From there, the A2O heads up and over an old moraine terrace, then down the quintessentially rural Quailburn Rd towards the town of Omarama. The climb over the hill is a bit of a grind, but rewards with panoramic views over one of New Zealand's most celebrated landscapes.

As well as a merino ram sculpture on the main highway, Omarama has benign skies, encouraging glider flying for which it is famous. Scenic flights are all go, as are the town's wooden hot tubs, tucked into tussocky gardens. Around the A2O's halfway point, a therapeutic soak holds considerable appeal.

ELECTRIFYING VIEWS

The Waitaki Hydro Power Scheme is a constant companion for nearly two-thirds of the A2O journey, imbuing it with considerable colour and texture. Lakes and canals brim with surreal blue waters, contrasting starkly with the surrounding golden tussock and flinty grey ranges, while eight powerhouses and dams lend industrial elegance. The power stations also offer elevated vantage points over the landscape. Two particularly spectacular lookouts are Benmore, near Otematata, and Tekapo B overlooking Lake Pukaki.

Clockwise from top: lake country; be prepared for all sorts of weather. Previous page: parts of the route are roughly surfaced and mountain bikes might be advisable

Omarama signals the start of the trail's gentle descent down the Waitaki Valley, funnelling riders towards the sea. The upper valley is home to three pretty hydro lakes, the first of which is Benmore, New Zealand's largest manmade lake. Benmore Dam is an awesome place for a picnic and a few snaps with the camera.

A picturesque road follows the shore of Lake Aviemore, where we stopped for a cooling dunk and lingered in the shade of the willows. Beyond the much smaller Lake Waitaki is Kurow, another logical overnight stop with warm hospitality and the bonus of the Vintner's Drop. Home to boutique Ostler winery, it offers a rare opportunity to try wines from the Waitaki's propitious but tricky terroir. And then there are the medicinal benefits, of course.

Near Kurow, the Waitaki River is released from its concrete confines and flows in its naturally braided fashion over broad alluvial plains, all the way to the ocean. Down the line, though, at Duntroon, the Alps 2 Ocean detours away from the river into rolling hills with hidden delights. What could be merely a gentle pedal through idyllic countryside quickly ramps up with a series of unexpected limestone boulders and escarpments. One particular cluster, Elephant Rocks, lie like oddly cast, oversized knucklebones scattered across a paddock, filled with nibbling sheep. By the time you've worked out a few more camera angles, scoffed your sandwich, and had a lie-down in one of the rocks' warm, smooth cradles, a good hour will have whiled away.

From here it's only around 50km (31 miles) to Oamaru, with the trail tracking hither and thither along an old railway line and passing through a spooky tunnel. Then it's a swooping downhill cruise to Oamaru's manicured public gardens, emerging through them to the town's waterfront. The harbourside park, along the town's magnificent Victorian Precinct, is a great place to savour a cold beer after a celebratory toe-dip in the Pacific Ocean. **SB**

"Mt John Observatory, in the Dark Sky Reserve, is a magnet for astronomers and amateur stargazers"

TOOLKIT

Start // Aoraki/Mt Cook Village or Lake Tekapo (4 hours' drive from Christchurch; 3 hours' drive from Queenstown)
Finish // Oamaru (3.5 hours' drive from Queenstown; 90 minutes' drive from Dunedin)
Distance // 301km (187 miles)
Getting around // The trail is well supported by tour companies offering bike hire, shuttles, luggage transfers and accommodation, many of which are detailed on the trail's website.
What to take // A mountain bike with knobbly tyres.
Terrain // Varied, but predominantly wide and smooth with some rougher, hilly stuff.
Weather // Changeable, particularly around the Southern Alps and high country, which may be blanketed with snow in winter. Check the forecast and track conditions before setting off, and take clothing for all eventualities.
More info // www.alps2ocean.com

Opposite: riding through Queenstown Mountain Bike Park

MORE LIKE THIS
PARKS, PEAKS AND PATHS

MOUNTAINS TO SEA, NORTH ISLAND

The North Island's version of the Alps 2 Ocean is the similarly named Mountains to Sea, which starts on the slopes of Mt Ruapehu in volcanic Tongariro National Park. Altogether it's a much more gnarly adventure, taking riders through hilly backcountry, remote valleys in Whanganui National Park and along the Whanganui River all the way to the Tasman Sea. The journey is rich in natural and cultural heritage, featuring such sights as an old cobbled road, towering bluffs, Māori meeting houses and the isolated Bridge to Nowhere. Off-the-bike activities include hiking, kayaking and a jet boat ride down the river. Completing the full trail requires good planning, dry conditions, reasonable fitness and off-road bike skills.
Start // Mt Ruapehu
Finish // Tasman Sea
Distance // 297km (184.5 miles)

GREAT LAKE TRAIL, NORTH ISLAND

Skirting the shores of New Zealand's largest lake not far from downtown Taupo, this trail dishes up an enviable mix of lush forest and wetlands, waterfalls and beaches, plus panoramic views of Tongariro National Park's volcanoes. Although most of the trail is smooth and flowing, some moderate hill climbs make it most suitable for reasonably fit riders. The ride can be spread over two days, or broken into shorter sections of various lengths and difficulty using local shuttles and a water taxi. Starting at pretty Kinloch, the deservedly popular W2K Track climbs around a bushy headland between Whangamata and Whakaipo Bays, with the option of a return ride known as the Headland Loop. Both options take around half a day.
Start/Finish // Kinloch
Distance // 71km (44 miles)

QUEENSTOWN TRAILS, SOUTH ISLAND

Proving the saying that getting there is half the fun, this extensive trail network is a richly rewarding way to reach many of the Queenstown region's must-see attractions while soaking up sublime Central Otago scenery. Linking Queenstown, Arrowtown and the Gibbston Valley, trails range from easy lakeside jaunts to ambitious cross-country treks, offering adventures for cyclists of almost every ability and interest. Options include the family-friendly Lake Hayes Loop, and the Gibbston River Ride, an easy wine-tour through the 'Valley of the Vines', beginning at the Kawarau bungee-jump bridge. Handy bike hire depots, open terrain and clear signage make planning and navigation a breeze, while wide, smooth paths means riders can keep eyes front and cameras ready.
Start/Finish // Queenstown
Distance // 120km (75 miles) of trails
More info //
www.queenstowntrail.co.nz

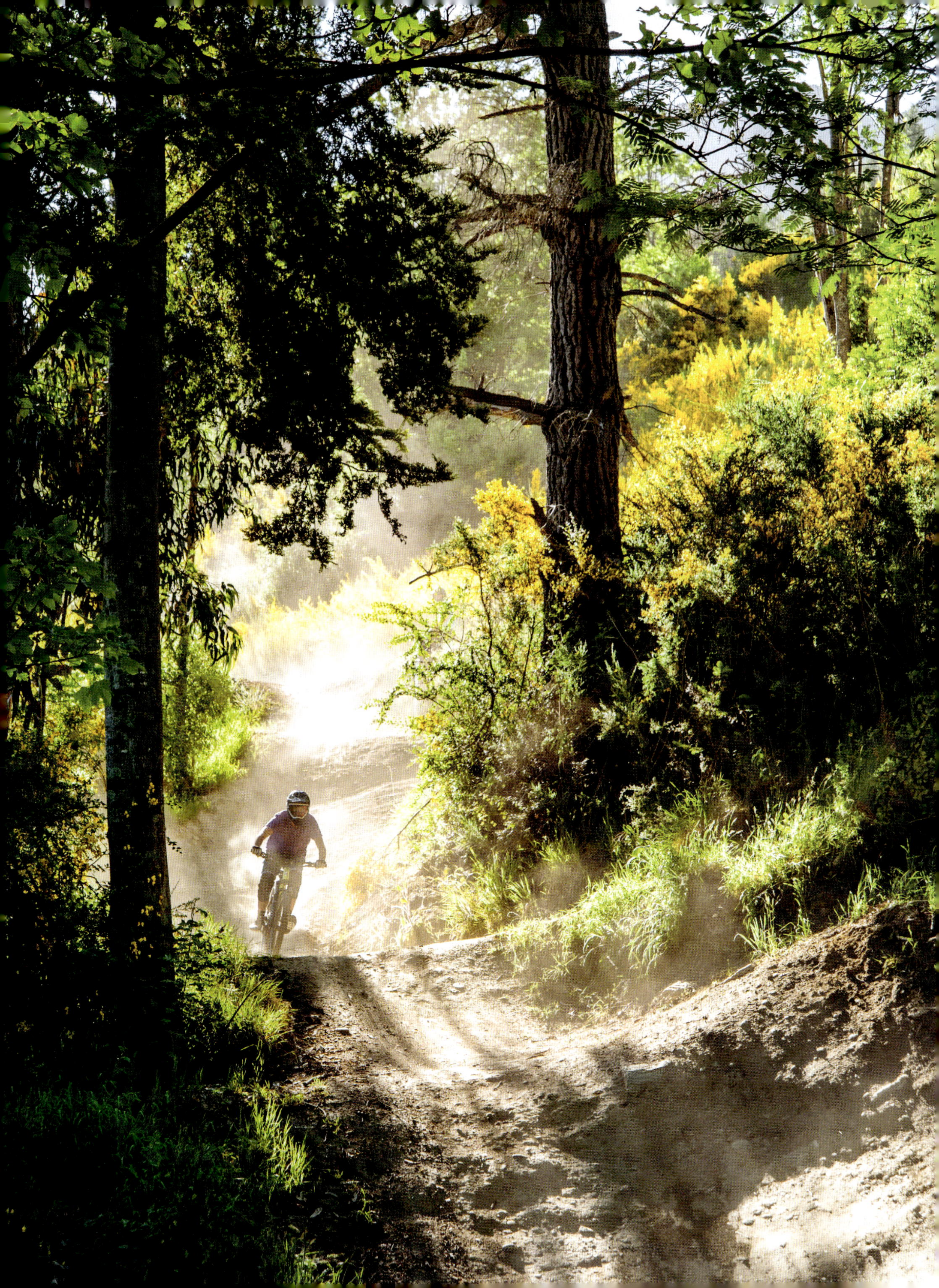

THE OLD DUNSTAN ROAD

Less like the New Zealand of many imaginations, but as near to a fantasy setting as it gets, the Old Dunstan Road follows forgotten gold-rush tracks in deserted landscapes.

Open this book on any route in New Zealand and you're sure to find the pages heavy with beautiful landscapes, from snow-capped mountains, pristine beaches and ancient volcanic craters to verdant native forests, crystal lakes and mesmerising fjords. But, hidden among this rich biodiversity, there is a secret landscape. One that's far off the beaten track and almost abandoned to history.

As New Zealand's only high-mountain desert, the Old Dunstan Road has a rugged beauty found only in this region. Pioneered by gold miners in the 1860s, the 175km (108 mile) route links Clyde – known until 1865 as Dunstan – to the bustling city of Dunedin, via a crocheted network of ancient wagon-wheel roads and dusty doubletrack. So, when Central Otago local Sophie invited me on a multi-day adventure to ride the trail, it was an easy yes from me.

Under a banner of cloudless blue sky, we pick up the Otago rail trail out of Alexandra. Gravel cracks under tyres and the scent of wild thyme fills the air. Past the trail-side pub, we narrowly escape the lure of hot chips and start the ascent through the Crawford Hills. It's our first climb of the day and even though it's only 400m (1313ft), the landscape changes dramatically. Trees, once glowing with life and autumn's vibrant colour palette, shrivel under the blistering sun like dehydrated vegetables. It's tough going, and our pace reflects the mood as we crawl up the mountain, battling blast-furnace winds en route to Poolburn Dam.

Poolburn is a place where life and death coexist in a strange harmony. Strewn across the scorched earth, thirsty tussocks and rust-coloured spear grasses stand lifeless, gasping for water. The landscape is offset perfectly by a sapphire-blue lake that shimmers elegantly under the sun. Its calm waters are a locus of life in an otherwise barren moonscape. It's no wonder Peter Jackson chose this location for the kingdom of Rohan in *The Lord of the Rings* trilogy.

'Do not trust to hope. For hope has forsaken these lands!' I boom at the top of my voice. The famous line ricochets off

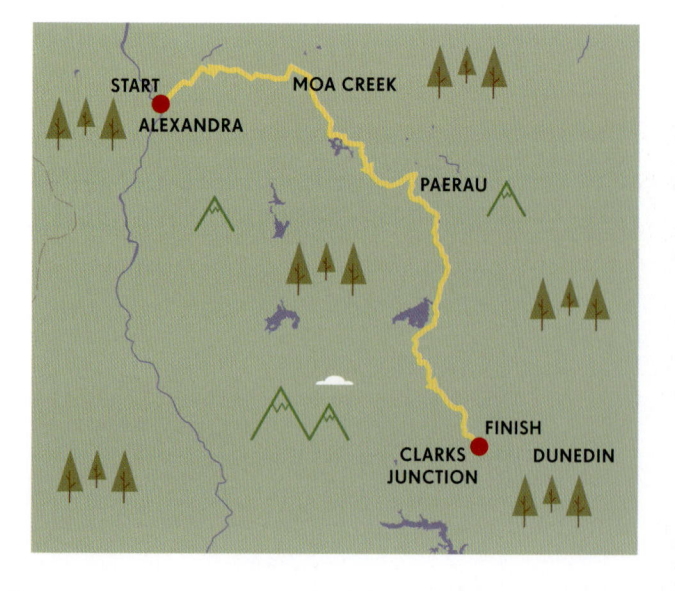

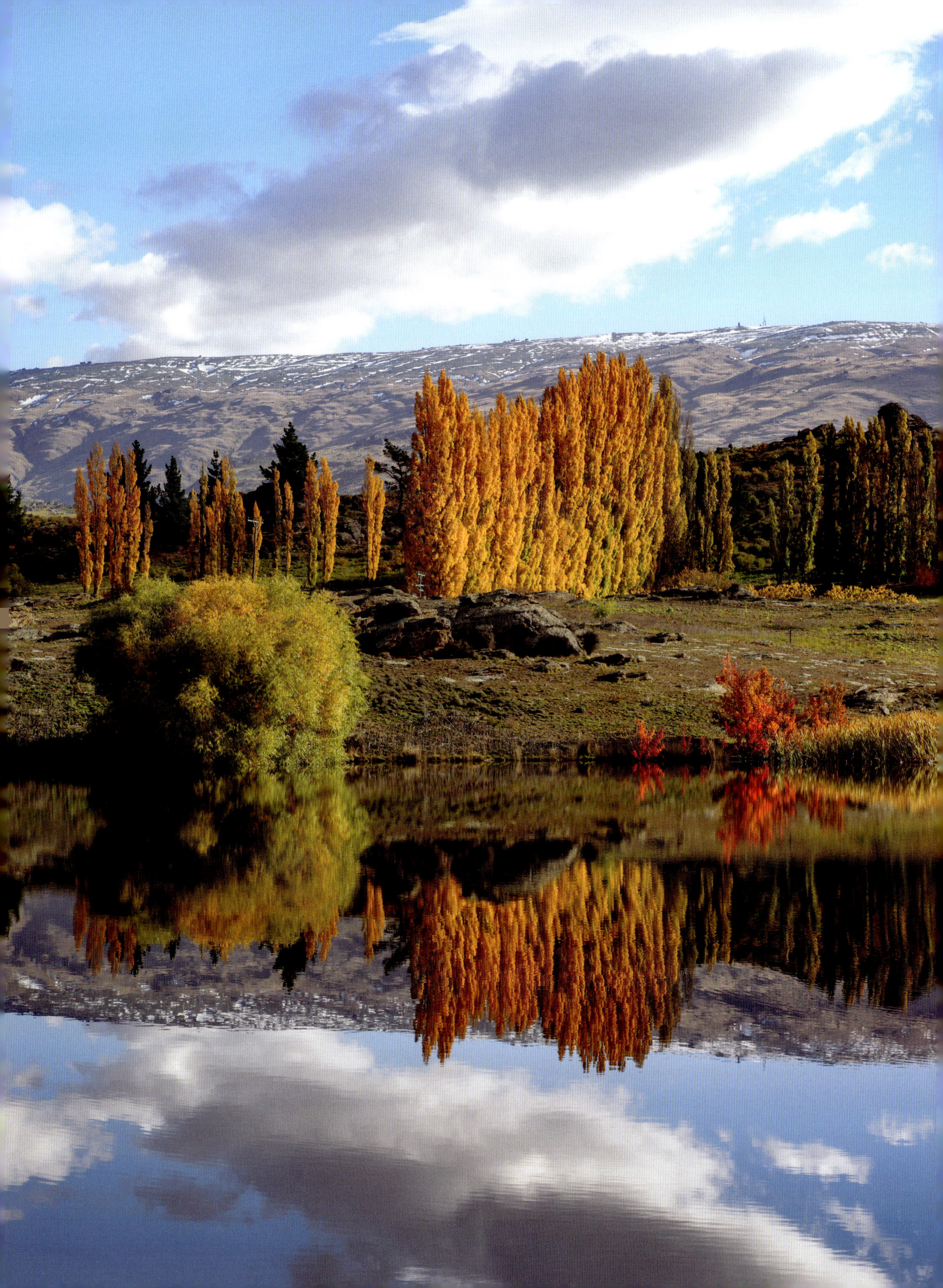

> *"The scene looks like a fantasy wasteland and, as I reach for my camera, I half expect a gang of orcs to come charging through the fog"*

the beaten-up old fishing shacks that cluster by the lake. In retrospect, it probably wasn't the most helpful thing to do while Sophie scouted for our campsite.

Amused by my performance, Sophie heads towards one of the more salubrious huts. 'That's Trev's place,' she says, pointing. 'I remember a Christmas Eve party here about a decade ago. I woke up the next morning sleeping outside on the deck.' She unlocks the years-old memories and chuckles to herself. 'It's a beautiful night and there's no rain forecast – do you want to sleep under the stars?' Her excitement is so captivating, it's impossible for me to say no. So, we brush our teeth, inflate our mats and climb inside our sleeping bags, ready for the stars to shine across Middle Earth.

At 5.30am I'm woken by the rhythmic drip of water. Above me, morning mist clings to Trev's satellite dish and the gathering dew drips onto my forehead. As I crawl out of my sleeping bag semi-conscious, I'm greeted with a sunrise I'll never forget. Stretched-out strands of cirrus clouds bloom and fill the air. Their ghostly shapes cast Martian tones of russet, carmine red and coral across the morning sky. The tussocks that littered the landscape just yesterday are gone, drenched in thick fog and cool moist air. The scene looks like a fantasy wasteland and, as I reach for my camera, I half expect a gang of orcs to come charging through the fog, hungry for man flesh.

Eventually, my overactive imagination cools off enough for us to start the day's riding. Legs refreshed, we put our heads down and rumble through the open desert plains at pace. With all-day cloud cover, we make light work of the morning pinch climb and enjoy the long descents. The rough, rocky hills stretch out in all directions, making the vacant landscape feel infinite. Good in places, horrific in others, the corrugated doubletrack thrashes our bodies and turns our bikes into wooden boneshakers as we rattle towards Loganburn Reservoir.

As we arrive at the dam, I'm suddenly hit by a wave of knowing fear. 'Sophie – you're not going to believe this,' I say, trying desperately to veil my anxiety. 'I think I've left my tent poles at home!' Sophie bursts into a mix of laughter and disbelief at my words. But with zero phone reception, rapidly reducing light and lingering rain clouds above, I have no choice but to accept my fate and practice some good old Kiwi ingenuity.

GOLD IN THEM HILLS

In August 1862, Central Otago changed forever when 40kg of pure gold thumped down on the assay office desk in Dunedin. For months, two veteran prospectors, Horatio Hartley and Christopher Riley, battled amid sub-zero temperatures and thick snow. Their haul sparked fevered curiosity and global headlines. Within a month, the new Dunstan Goldfield (present-day Clyde) was declared and a second major gold rush began in New Zealand.

Clockwise from top: dams and dirt tracks on the Old Dunstan Road. Previous spread: autumnal poplars

Pocket knife in hand, I whittle some makeshift tent stakes out of the dry twigs that rest on the ground. Sophie makes a cuppa, grinning to herself as I stomp around the campsite, suddenly buoyed by the life-or-death situation now at hand. I'm taking it all far too seriously. But, as I proceed to flip my bike upside down, toss the flysheet over the wheels and tension it down with my homemade stakes, I realise that this might actually work. It's not going to win any design awards, but it might just keep me dry.

The rain starts and we're forced inside. Now's the moment of truth for me and my primitive nylon palace. Specks turn to splashes and the rain drums down on us with force. 'Sophie, it's working – kind of,' I yell out as she giggles at me through her bivvy bag and bids me goodnight.

The rain continues all night, and between the regular rain-to-the-face wakeups and flysheet flooding intermissions, the next morning isn't easy. But with just 21km (13 miles) before we hit the smooth tarmac at Clarkes Junction, we launch into action and mount our bikes. Pavement isn't usually something I long for, but with a soggy sleeping bag and a drenched flysheet stuffed in my seat pack, as soon as we hit the road it feels almost biblical. The smooth, silky asphalt propels us past Outram, through Mosgiel and into the hustle of Dunedin. Tired, wet and in serious need of caffeine, we pull into Sophie's favourite coffee shop and celebrate the end of our adventure with a perfect piccolo. **SR**

TOOLKIT

Start // Alexandra
Finish // Dunedin
Distance // 174km (108 miles)
Getting there // Buses run regularly from major cities to Alexandra and several of the country's rail trails connect up here.
When to go // October to March. The Old Dunstan Road is closed during winter due to cold weather.
What to wear // In the summer months, it's essential to be fully covered up to protect yourself from the sun.
What to pack // Bug spray and wet weather gear, along with a sun shirt and hat. Don't skimp on water either, it's pretty dry up there.
Where to stay // There's plenty of accommodation at the start and end of the trail, but during your ride, you'll need to carry a tent and overnight essentials.
Where to eat // You'll need to pack all your own food. There are big supermarkets in both Alexandra and Dunedin for the start and end of the route.
More info // www.centralotagonz.com

Opposite: watch for the giant weta in the Old Man Range

MORE LIKE THIS
OTAGO BACKCOUNTRY

NEVIS ROAD

Deep in the tussock-covered backcountry east of Queenstown's famous Remarkables, the Nevis Road runs through very rugged terrain – and is prone to cold, impassable conditions in winter. In the summer months it's a real joy to ride, its open doubletrack dirt road seems to flow and keep going forever (especially with a tailwind). There is fresh water from streams along the entire route, making camping up top a breeze. The trail starts at Garston in Northern Southland and finishes in Bannockburn in Central Otago, but can be easily ridden either way. At 1,300m (4,265ft), it's the highest public road in New Zealand, although it isn't recommended for 2WD cars (a win for cyclists).
Start // Garston
Finish // Bannockburn
Distance // 67km (42 miles)

OLD MAN RANGE

High above Central Otago are the rolling tops of the Old Man Range. Characterised by sub-arctic landforms, this range is home to native high-altitude plants and insects including giant wētāpunga, as well as the famous 26.6m/87ft-high rock known as the Obelisk, or Kopuwai. These mountains, reaching up to 1,680m (5,512ft) hide some seriously great dirt roads. The area is steeped in mining history, and you'll find various backcountry huts such as Boundary or Nicholsons dotted throughout the Kopuwai Conservation Area, along with fresh water for all your hydration needs. There are many start and finish points across the range, with longer rides beginning or ending in the towns of Alexandra or Roxburgh. For a grade 4 MTB taster, go up the Symes Road to reach the Obelisk and Old Man Range 4WD ridge road, then descend by Waikaia Bush Rd.
Start // Fruitlands
Finish // Shingle Creek
Distance // 13km (8 miles)
More info // www.doc.govt.nz

ROCK & PILLARS RANGE

Running east of the Old Dunstan Road, in parallel with the Taieri River that flows past Middlemarch, the Rock and Pillars Range was created by the movement of two parallel faults. Its distinctive flat top with steep escarpments on either side make it an interesting landscape to ride, filled with hills that feel like they roll on forever, and with rocks you may have seen before in a *Lord of the Rings* film. A rare lenticular cloud formation, dubbed the Taieri Pet, tends to stick around atop the range. For a clockwise MTB loop from Middlemarch, one option is to take the Stonehurst Track to reach Old Dunstan Rd by Loganburn Reservoir, then link up to the Rock and Pillar Ridge Rd up to its 1,450m (4,757ft) high point, descending by Kinvara Rd.
Start/Finish // Middlemarch
Distance // 65km (40 miles)
More info // www.doc.govt.nz

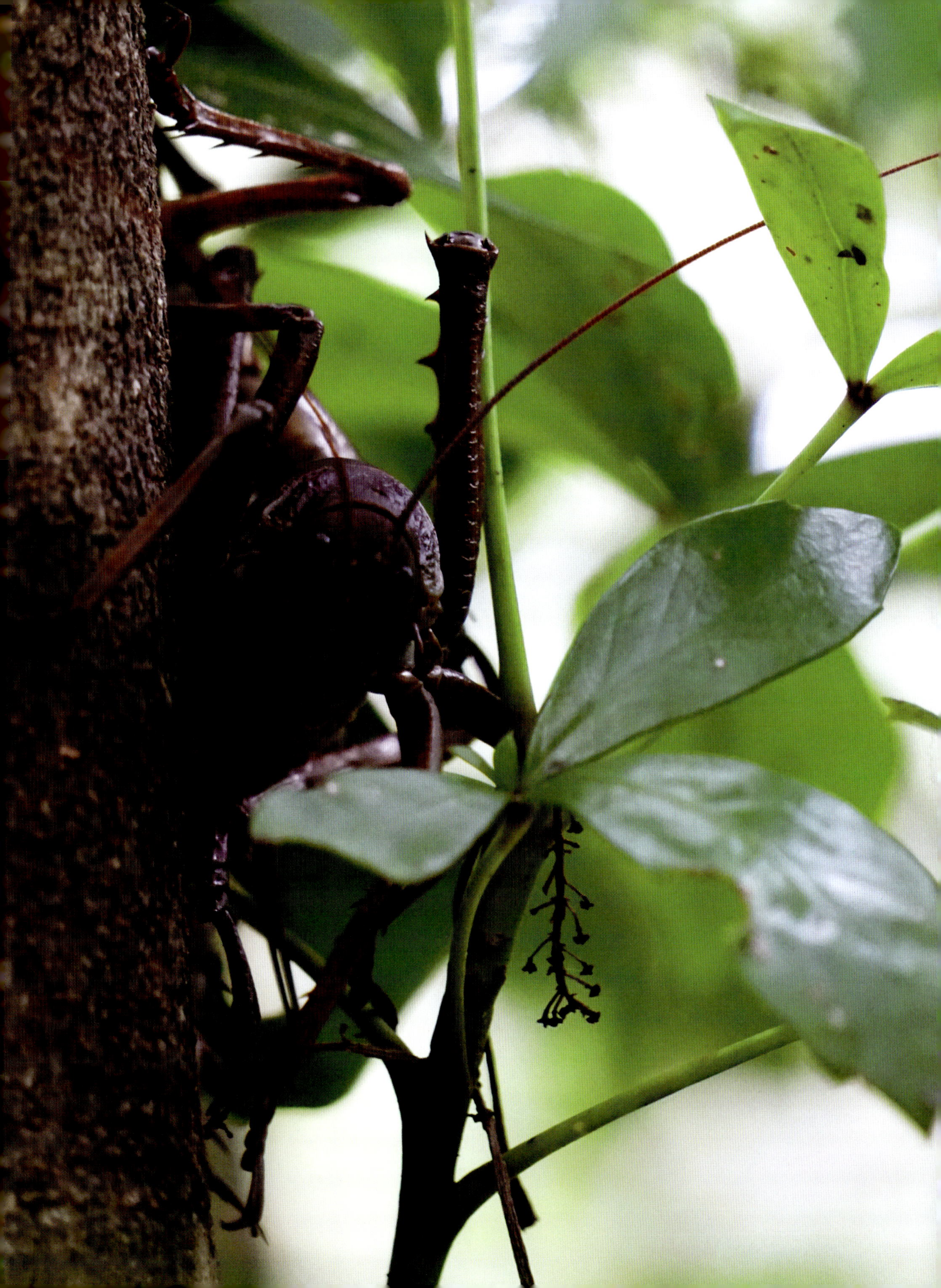

INDEX

A
adventure rides
Atherton Tablelands, QLD 38–41
Australian Alpine Epic Trail, VIC 126–129
Blue Mountains, NSW 32–35
Destination Cape York, QLD 8–11
Mawson Trail, SA 82–85
Mereenie Loop, NT 80
Moerangi Track, NZ 182–185
Molesworth Muster, NZ 244–247
Mountains to Sea, NZ 308
Munda Biddi Trail, WA 88–91
Old Dunstan Road, NZ 310–313
Rainbow Trail, NZ 248
Road to Nowhere, TAS 144–147
Sandstone Wilderness Outback Adventure, QLD 44–47
Tanami Track, NT 92
Tasmanian Trail, TAS 290
Top End, NT 76–79
Western Wilds, TAS 278
Australian Capital Territory
Bicentennial Trail 92
Canberra Centenary Trail 20–23
Lake Burley Griffin Circuit 14–17
Majura Pines 42

B
bikepacking
Around the Mountains, NZ 248, 284
Attack of the Buns, NSW 142
Bicentennial Trail, Australia 92
Bluff, NZ 12
Brisbane Valley Rail Trail, QLD 24, 56–59
Cape Reinga, NZ 12
Cockle Creek, TAS 12
Destination Cape York, QLD 8–11
Geyserland Classic, NZ 142
Gibb River Road, WA 80
Goldfields Track, VIC 138–141
Grampians Loop, VIC 142
Great Southern Brevet, NZ 240
Heart of the Octopus, NZ 212–215
Hopkins Valley, NZ 192
Kahurangi 500, NZ 92
Kiwi Brevet, NZ 240
Kōpiko Aotearoa, NZ 236–239
Lavender Cycling Trail, SA 86
Maria Island National Park, TAS 54
Mawson Trail, SA 48
Mereenie Loop, WA 80
Minjerribah Island, QLD 50–53
Moerangi Track, NZ 182–185
Molesworth Muster, NZ 244–247
Munda Biddi Trail, WA 88–91
Oodnadatta Track, SA 48, 80
Queen Charlotte Track, NZ 262–265, 290
Remutaka Cycle Trail, NZ 206–209
Road to Nowhere, TAS 144–147
Sandstone Wilderness Outback Adventure, QLD 44–47
Sound to Sound, NZ 240
Tanami Track, NT 92
Tasmanian Trail, TAS 24, 290
Top End, WA 76–79
Tuatara 1000, NZ 240
Wakatipu Ranges, NZ 280–283

C
coastal rides
Bass Coast Rail Trail, VIC 118
Bay Trail, VIC 228
Bluff, NZ 12
Bundeena to Kiama, NSW 302
Cape Reinga, NZ 12
Catlins Coast, NZ 210
Cockle Creek, TAS 12
Coromandel Peninsula Loop, NZ 218
Far North Cycleway, NZ 216
Flinders Island, TAS 114–117
Hawkes Bay wineries, NZ 224–227
Heart of the Octopus, NZ 212–215
Kāpiti Coast Cycle Route, NZ 210
King Island, TAS 118
Maria Island National Park, TAS 54
Minjerribah Island, QLD 50–53
North West Coastal Pathway, TAS 210
Nydia Track, NZ 266
Puhoi to Leigh, NZ 222
Pukekohe to Raglan, NZ 222
Queen Charlotte Drive, NZ 266
Queen Charlotte Track, NZ 262–265, 290
Remutaka Cycle Trail, NZ 206–209
Wadjemup/Rottnest Island, WA 54
Waiheke Island, NZ 54, 118, 222
West Coast Wilderness Trail, NZ 250–253
culture-rich rides
East Gippsland Rail Trail, VIC 18
Fremantle Public Art Trail, WA 18
Lake Burley Griffin Circuit, ACT 14–17
Silo Art Trail, VIC 18

F
family-friendly rides
Arrow River Bridges Trail, NZ 192
Barossa Trail, SA 86
Bass Coast Rail Trail, VIC 118
Dirty Deeds CX, VIC 112
Fremantle Public Art Trail, WA 18
Jack Bobridge Track, SA 86
Kangaroo Island, SA 86
Kāpiti Coast Cycle Route, NZ 210
Kilkivan to Kingaroy Rail Trail, QLD 60
Lake Burley Griffin Circuit, ACT 14–17
Lake Dunstan Trail, NZ 272
Lavender Cycling Trail, SA 86
Maria Island National Park, TAS 54
Mawson Trail, SA 82–85
Melburn-Roobaix 108–111
Moke Lake Loop, NZ 296
Queenstown Trails, NZ 308
Ride around the Rock, NT 48
Riesling Trail, SA 86
Roxburgh Gorge Trail, NZ 272
Simpsons Gap Bike Path, NT 180
Wadjemup/Rottnest Island, WA 54
Wagga Wagga Gears & Beers, NSW 26–29
Whakarewarewa Forest Loop, NZ 200–203

G
gravel rides
Acheron Way, VIC 132–135
Ben Lomond & the Barrow, TAS 120–123
Big Hut from Ranfurly/Waipiata, NZ 186
Brisbane Valley Rail Trail, QLD 24, 56–59
Central West Cycle Trail, NSW 62–65
Climies Track, TAS 148
Coromandel Peninsula Loop, NZ 218–221
Devil's Gullet, TAS 124
Girls Go Gravel, QLD 30
Grampians Loop, VIC 142
Gravelista, VIC 30
Great Otways Gravel Grind, VIC 30
Heart of the Octopus, NZ 212–215
Kōpiko Aotearoa, NZ 236–239
Molesworth Muster, NZ 244–247
Mt Albert Rd, TAS 124
Mt Lofty to Mt Osmond Lookout 104
Mt Victoria Rd, TAS 124
Myponga Beach Loop, SA 100–103
Nevis Valley, NZ 248, 314
Old Dunstan Road, NZ 310–313
Oodnadatta Track, SA/NT 48, 80
Remutaka Cycle Trail, NZ 302
Road to Nowhere, TAS 144–147
Sugarloaf Reservoir Loop, VIC 104
Wagga Wagga Gears & Beers, NSW 26–29
Willunga Hills, SA 104

H
history-rich rides
Arrow River Bridges Trail, NZ 192
Brisbane Valley Rail Trail, QLD 24
Goldfields Track, VIC 138–141, 254
Otago Central Rail Trail, NZ 268–271, 284
Paparoa Track, NZ 274–277
Remutaka Cycle Trail, NZ 302
Waikakaho/Cullen Creek Walkway, NZ 254
West Coast Wilderness Trail, NZ 250–253

I

Indigenous culture
　East Gippsland Rail Trail, VIC 18
　Motu Trails Pakihi Circuit, NZ 194–197
　Mountains to Sea, NZ 188–191, 308
　Rere Falls Trail, NZ 198
　Ride around the Rock, NT 48
　Te Rerenga Wairua, NZ 198
　Top End, NT 76–79
　Whakarewarewa Forest Loop, NZ 200–203

M

mountain biking
　42 Traverse, NZ 234
　Acheron Way, VIC 132–135
　Alps 2 Ocean Cycle Trail, NZ 304–307
　Atherton Forest Mountain Bike Park, QLD 278
　Atherton Tablelands, QLD 38–41, 278
　Australian Alpine Epic Trail, VIC 126–129, 260
　Banks Peninsula, NZ 298–301
　Bay of Fires Trail, TAS 162–165
　Ben Lomond & the Barrow, TAS 120–123
　Bicentennial Trail, Australia 92
　Big Hill Mountain Bike Park, VIC 130
　Big Hut from Ranfurly/Waipiata, NZ 186
　Big River Hut/Waiuta Track, NZ 186
　Blue Mountains, NSW 32–35
　Bluff, NZ 12
　Canberra Centenary Trail, ACT 20–23
　Cape Reinga, NZ 12
　Cardrona, NZ 204
　Climies Track, TAS 148
　Codgers Trails, NZ 204
　Coromandel Peninsula Loop, NZ 218–221
　Coronet Loop, NZ 284, 292–295
　Craters Mountain Bike Park, NZ 234
　Deans Bank Track, NZ 204
　Destination Cape York, QLD 8–11
　Devils Creek Track, NZ 296
　Eagle Mountain, SA 42
　Flinders Island, TAS 114–117
　Gibbs Hill, NZ 290
　Glenbervie Forest, NZ 216
　Goldfields Track, VIC 138–141, 254
　Great Lake Trail, NZ 308
　Heaphy Track, NZ 286–289
　Heart of the Octopus, NZ 212–215
　Indigo Epic, VIC 130
　Jagungal Wilderness, NSW 278
　Kahurangi 500, NZ 92
　King Island, TAS 118
　Kōpiko Aotearoa, NZ 236–239
　Lake Mountain Cascades Trail, VIC 130
　Majura Pines, ACT 42
　Makara Peak Mountain Bike Park, NZ 204
　Mangapurua Track, NZ 188
　Marton Sash & Door Tramway, NZ 234

Mawson Trail, SA 48
Maydena Bike Park, TAS 166
Mereenie Loop, NT 80
Mittagong to Wombeyan Caves, NSW 36
Moerangi Track, NZ 182–185
Moke Lake Loop, NZ 296
Montezuma Falls, TAS 172, 278
Moonlight Circuit, NZ 296
Mountains to Sea, NZ 188–191, 308
Mt George, TAS 166
Mt Owen, TAS 172
Munda Biddi Trail, WA 88–91
Narrow Neck Peninsula, NSW 36
Nevis Valley, NZ 198
North-South Track 166
Nydia Track, NZ 266
Old Coach Road, NZ 188
Old Dunstan Road, NZ 310–313
Old Ghost Road, NZ 254, 256–259
Old Man Range, NZ 314
Onkaparinga River National Park, SA 180
Otway Odyssey, VIC 156–159
Paparoa Track, NZ 260, 274–277
Queenstown Trails, NZ 308
Remutaka Cycle Trail, NZ 302
Rock & Pillar Range, NZ 314
Royal Ramble, NSW 36
Sandstone Wilderness Outback Adventure, QLD 44–47
Silver City, TAS 168–171
Sterling Valley, TAS 172, 278
Sticky Forest, NZ 204
Tanami Track, NT 92
Tasmanian Trail, TAS 24
Tassie Gift, TAS 148
Thredbo All-Mountain Trail, NSW 260
Thredbo Mountain Bike Park, NSW 260
Thredbo Valley Track, NSW 24
Timber Trail, NZ 230–233
Top End, NT 76–79
Victoria Peak, NZ 204
Waihāhā Track, NZ 186
Waiheke Island, NZ 54
Waikakaho/Cullen Creek Walkway, NZ 254
Waikato River Trails, NZ 192
Waimapihi Reserve, NZ 204
Wainuiomata Mountain Bike Park, NZ 204
Wairoa Gorge, NZ 204
Wakamarina Track, NZ 266
Wakatipu Ranges, NZ 280–283
Warburton, VIC 160
Whakarewarewa Forest Loop, NZ 200–203
Woodend, VIC 160
Yack Tracks, VIC 42
You Yangs, VIC 160

multi-day rides
　Alps 2 Ocean Cycle Trail, NZ 304–307
　Around the Mountains, NZ 248, 284
　Attack of the Buns, NSW 142
　Banks Peninsula, NZ 298–301

Bicentennial Trail, Australia 92
Big Hut from Ranfurly/Waipiata, NZ 186
Big River Hut/Waiuta Track, NZ 186
Bluff, NZ 12
Brisbane Valley Rail Trail, QLD 24, 56–59
Bundeena to Kiama, NSW 302
Canberra Centenary Trail, ACT 20–23
Cape Reinga, NZ 12
Catlins Coast, NZ 210
Central West Cycle Trail, NSW 62–65
Clutha Gold Trail, NZ 272
Cockle Creek, TAS 12
Coromandel Peninsula Loop, NZ 218–221
Destination Cape York, QLD 8–11
Far North Cycleway, NZ 216
Flinders Island, TAS 114–117
Forgotten World Highway 98, 302
Geyserland Classic, NZ 142
Gibb River Road, WA 80
Girls Go Gravel, QLD 30
Goldfields Track, VIC 138–141, 254
Grampians Loop, VIC 142
Great Lake Trail, NZ 308
Great Southern Brevet, NZ 240
Great Victorian Bike Ride, VIC 136
Hauraki Rail Trail, NZ 176–179
Heart of the Octopus, NZ 212–215
Hopkins Valley, NZ 192
Kahurangi 500, NZ 92
Kaipara Missing Link 216
Kangaroo Island, SA 86
Kilkivan to Kingaroy Rail Trail, QLD 60
Kiwi Brevet, NZ 240
Kōpiko Aotearoa, NZ 236–239
Lavender Cycling Trail, SA 86
Lorax Route, TAS 148
Mawson Trail, SA 48, 82–85
Mereenie Loop, NT 80
Minjerribah Island, QLD 50–53
Mittagong to Wombeyan Caves, NSW 36
Moerangi Track, NZ 182–185
Molesworth Muster, NZ 244–247
Motu Trails Pakihi Circuit, NZ 194–197
Mountains to Sea, NZ 188–191, 308
Munda Biddi Trail, WA 88–91
Murray to the Mountains, VIC 60, 150–153
Old Dunstan Road, NZ 310–313
Old Ghost Road, NZ 254, 256–259
Oodnadatta Track, SA/NT 48, 80
Otago Central Rail Trail, NZ 268–271, 284
Paparoa Track, NZ 274–277
Puhoi to Leigh, NZ 222
Pukekohe to Raglan, NZ 222
Queen Charlotte Track, NZ 262–265, 290
Rainbow Trail, NZ 248
Remutaka Cycle Trail, NZ 206–209, 302
Road to Nowhere, TAS 144–147
Sandstone Wilderness Outback Adventure, QLD 44–47
Sound to Sound, NZ 240

Swallow Tail Pass Loop, NSW 66
Tanami Track, NT 92
Tasmanian Trail, TAS 24, 290
Tasman's Great Taste Trail, NZ 228
Te Rerenga Wairua, NZ 198
Timber Trail, NZ 230–233
Top End, NT 76–79
Tour Down Under, SA 94
Tuatara 1000, NZ 240
Wagga Wagga Gears & Beers, NSW 26–29
Waihāhā Track, NZ 186
Waikato River Trails, NZ 192
Wakamarina Track, NZ 266
Wakatipu Ranges, NZ 280–283
West Coast Wilderness Trail, NZ 250–253
Windsor to Gosford, NSW 66

N

nature-rich rides
Acheron Way, VIC 132–135
Atherton Tablelands, QLD 38–41, 278
Australian Alpine Epic Trail, VIC 260
Bay of Fires Trail, TAS 162–165
Blue Mountains, NSW 32–35
Bluff, NZ 12
Canberra Centenary Trail, ACT 20–23
Catlins Coast, NZ 210
Coromandel Peninsula Loop, NZ 218–221
Coronet Loop, NZ 284, 292–295
Destination Cape York, QLD 8–11
Flinders Island, TAS 114–117
Great Lake Trail, NZ 308
Hauraki Rail Trail, NZ 176–179
Heaphy Track, NZ 286–289
Jagungal Wilderness, NSW 278
Kangaroo Island, SA 86
Kawarau Gorge, NZ 180
Kōpiko Aotearoa, NZ 236–239
Lake Burley Griffin Circuit, ACT 14–17
Maria Island National Park, TAS 54
Marton Sash & Door Tramway, NZ 234
Mawson Trail, SA 82
Minjerribah Island, QLD 50–53
Mittagong to Wombeyan Caves, NSW 36
Moerangi Track, NZ 182–185
Motu Trails Pakihi Circuit, NZ 194–197
Mountains to Sea, NZ 188–191, 308
Munda Biddi Trail, WA 88–91
North West Coastal Pathway, TAS 210
Old Dunstan Road, NZ 310–313
Old Ghost Road, NZ 256–259
Old Man Range, NZ 314
Onkaparinga River National Park, SA 180
Otago Central Rail Trail, NZ 60
Paparoa Track, NZ 260, 274–277
Royal Ramble, NSW 36
Simpsons Gap Bike Path, NT 180

Tasmanian Trail, TAS 24, 290
Timber Trail, NZ 230–233
Top End, NT 76–79
Tour Down Under, SA 94–97
Wadjemup/Rottnest Island, WA 54
Wakatipu Ranges, NZ 280–283
West Coast Wilderness Trail, NZ 250–253
Whakarewarewa Forest Loop, NZ 200–203

New South Wales, Australia
Attack of the Buns 142
Bicentennial Trail 92
Blue Mountains 32–35
Bundeena to Kiama 302
Central West Cycle Trail 62–65
Jagungal Wilderness 278
Mittagong to Wombeyan Caves 36
Moss Vale to Nowra 66
Narrow Neck Peninsula 36
Newcrest Orange Challenge 98
Royal Ramble 36
Swallow Tail Pass Loop 66
Thredbo All-Mountain Trail 260
Thredbo Valley Track 24
Wagga Wagga Gears & Beers 26–29
Windsor to Gosford, NSW 66

Northern Territory, Australia
Mereenie Loop 80
Oodnadatta Track 48
Ride around the Rock, Uluru 48
Simpsons Gap Bike Path 180
Tanami Track 92
Top End 76–79

North Island, New Zealand
42 Traverse 234
Auckland to Piha 98
Cape Reinga 12
Coromandel Peninsula Loop 218–221
Craters Mountain Bike Park 234
Far North Cycleway 216
Forgotten World Highway 98, 302
Geyserland Classic 142
Glenbervie Forest 216
Great Lake Trail 308
Hauraki Rail Trail 176–179
Hawkes Bay wineries 224–227
Heart of the Octopus 212–215
Kaipara Missing Link 216
Kāpiti Coast Cycle Route 210
Kōpiko Aotearoa 236–239
Makara Peak Mountain Bike Park 204
Mangapurua Track 188–191
Marton Sash & Door Tramway 234
Moerangi Track 182–185
Motu Trails Pakihi Circuit 194–197
Mountains to Sea 188–191, 308
Old Coach Road 188
Puhoi to Leigh 222
Pukekohe to Raglan 222
Remutaka Cycle Trail 206–209, 302
Rere Falls Trail 198

Sticky Forest 204
Te Rerenga Wairua 198
Timber Trail 230–233
Victoria Peak 204
Waihāhā Track 186
Waikato River Trails 192
Waimapihi Reserve 204
Wainuiomata Mountain Bike Park 204
Whakarewarewa Forest Loop 200–203

Q

Queensland, Australia
Atherton Tablelands 38–41, 278
Bicentennial Trail 92
Brisbane Valley Rail Trail 24, 56–59
Destination Cape York 8–11
Girls Go Gravel 30
Kilkivan to Kingaroy Rail Trail 60
Minjerribah Island 50–53
Sandstone Wilderness Outback Adventure 44–47

R

races, events, brevets & sportives
7 Peaks Ride, VIC 136
Amy's Gran Fondo, VIC 154
Around the Bay in a Day, VIC 136, 154
Beechworth Granite Classic, VIC 112
Dirty 130 (Wagga Wagga), NSW 26–29
Dirty Deeds CX, VIC 112
Girls Go Gravel, QLD 30
Goldfields Cyclassic, WA 74
Gravelista, VIC 30
Great Otways Gravel Grind, VIC 30
Great Southern Brevet, NZ 240
Great Victorian Bike Ride, VIC 136
Kiwi Brevet, NZ 240
Kōpiko Aotearoa, NZ 236–239
Newcrest Orange Challenge, NSW 98
Otway Odyssey, VIC 156–159
Perth City Criterium, WA 74
Sound to Sound, NZ 240
Tassie Gift, TAS 148
Tour Down Under, SA 94–97
Tour of Margaret River, WA 70–73
Tuatara 1000, NZ 240
Wagga Wagga Gears & Beers, NSW 26–29
Weekender, VIC 74

road rides
7 Peaks Ride, VIC 136
Acheron Way, TAS 132–135
Amy's Gran Fondo, VIC 154
Around the Bay in a Day, VIC 136, 154
Auckland to Piha, NZ 98
Cockle Creek, TAS 12
Destination Cape York, QLD 8–11

INDEX

Flinders Island, TAS 114–117
Goldfields Cyclassic, WA 74
Great Victorian Bike Ride, VIC 136
King Island, TAS 118
Lorax Route, TAS 148
Melburn-Roobaix, VIC 108–111
Perth City Criterium, WA 74
Queen Charlotte Drive, NZ 266
Tour Down Under, SA 94–97
Tour of Margaret River, WA 70–73
Wagga Wagga Gears & Beers, NSW 26–29
Weekender, VIC 74
Windsor to Gosford, NSW 66

S

South Australia
Banks Peninsula 298–301
Barossa Trail 86
Clare Valley wineries 228
Eagle Mountain 42
Jack Bobridge Track 86
Kangaroo Island 86
Lavender Cycling Trail 86
Mawson Trail 48, 82–85
Mt Lofty to Mt Osmond Lookout 104
Myponga Beach Loop 100–103
Onkaparinga River National Park 180
Oodnadatta Track 48, 80
Riesling Trail 86, 228
Tour Down Under 94–97
Willunga Hills 104

South Island, New Zealand
Alps 2 Ocean Cycle Trail 304–307
Around the Mountains 248, 284
Arrow River Bridges Trail 192
Banks Peninsula 298–301
Big Hut from Ranfurly/Waipiata 186
Big River Hut/Waiuta Track 186
Bluff 12
Cardrona 204
Catlins Coast 210
Clutha Gold Trail 272
Codgers Trails 204
Coronet Loop 284, 292–295
Deans Bank Track 204
Devils Creek Track 296
Gibbs Hill, Abel Tasman National Park 290
Great Southern Brevet 240
Heaphy Track 286–289
Hopkins Valley 192
Kahurangi 500 92
Kawarau Gorge 180
Kiwi Brevet 240
Lake Dunstan Trail 272
Moke Lake Loop 296
Molesworth Muster 244–247
Moonlight Circuit 296

Nevis Valley 198, 248, 314
Nydia Track 266
Old Dunstan Road 310–313
Old Ghost Road 254, 256–259
Old Man Range 314
Otago Central Rail Trail 60, 268–271, 284
Paparoa Track 260, 274–277
Queen Charlotte Drive 266
Queen Charlotte Track 262–265, 290
Queenstown Trails 308
Rainbow Trail 248
Rock & Pillar Range 314
Roxburgh Gorge Trail 272
Sound to Sound 240
Tasman's Great Taste Trail 228
Tuatara 1000 240
Waikakaho/Cullen Creek Walkway 254
Wairoa Gorge 204
Wakamarina Track 266
Wakatipu Ranges 280–283
West Coast Wilderness Trail 250–253

T

Tasmania, Australia
Bay of Fires Trail 162–165
Ben Lomond & the Barrow 120–123
Climies Track 148
Cockle Creek 12
Devil's Gullet 124
Flinders Island 114–117
King Island 118
Lorax Route 148
Maria Island National Park 54
Maydena Bike Park 166
Montezuma Falls 172, 278
Mt Albert Rd 124
Mt George 166
Mt Owen 172
Mt Victoria Rd 124
North-South Track 166
North West Coastal Pathway 210
Road to Nowhere 144–147
Silver City 168–171
Sterling Valley 172
Tasmanian Trail 24, 290
Tassie Gift 148
Western Wilds 278

U

urban rides
Dirty Deeds CX (Melbourne), VIC 112
Fremantle Public Art Trail, WA 18
Lake Burley Griffin Circuit (Canberra), ACT 14–17
Melburn-Roobaix 108–111
Perth City Criterium, WA 74
Victoria Peak (Wellington), NZ 204
Waimapihi Reserve (Wellington), NZ 204

V

Victoria, Australia
7 Peaks Ride 136
Acheron Way 132–135
Amy's Gran Fondo 154
Around the Bay in a Day 136, 154
Australian Alpine Epic Trail 126–129, 260
Bass Coast Rail Trail 118
Bay Trail 228
Beechworth Granite Classic 112
Bicentennial Trail 92
Big Hill Mountain Bike Park 130
Dirty Deeds CX 112
East Gippsland Rail Trail 18
Goldfields Track 138–141, 254
Grampians Loop 142
Gravelista 30
Great Otways Gravel Grind 30
Great Victorian Bike Ride 136
Great Victorian Rail Trail 154
Indigo Epic 130
Lake Mountain Cascades Trail 130
Melburn-Roobaix 108–111
Mornington Peninsula wineries 228
Murray to the Mountains 60, 150–153
Otway Odyssey 156–159
Silo Art Trail 18
Sugarloaf Reservoir Loop 104
Warburton 160
Weekender, The 74
Woodend 160
Yack Tracks 42
You Yangs 160

W

Waiheke Island, NZ 54, 118, 222
Western Australia
Fremantle Public Art Trail 18
Gibb River Road 80
Goldfields Cyclassic 74
Munda Biddi Trail 88–91
Perth City Criterium 74
Tour of Margaret River 70–73
Wadjemup/Rottnest Island 54

Epic Bike Rides of Australia & New Zealand
August 2023
Published by Lonely Planet Global Limited
www.lonelyplanet.com
10 9 8 7 6 5 4 3 2 1

Printed in China
ISBN 978 1 8386 9604 7
Text & maps © Lonely Planet 2023
Photos © as indicated 2023

Publishing Director Piers Pickard
Senior Editor Robin Barton
Designer Jo Dovey
Editors Rory Goulding, Nick Mee
Index Polly Thomas
Print Production Nigel Longuet

Although the authors and Lonely Planet have taken all reasonable care in preparing this book, we make no warranty about the accuracy or completeness of its content and, to the maximum extent permitted, disclaim all liability from its use.

All rights reserved. No part of this publication may be reproduced, stored in a retrieval system or transmitted in any form by any means, electronic, mechanical, photocopying, recording or otherwise except brief extracts for the purpose of review, without the written permission of the publisher. Lonely Planet and the Lonely Planet logo are trademarks of Lonely Planet and are registered in the US Patent and Trademark Office and in other countries.

Lonely Planet Global Limited
Digital Depot, Roe Lane (off Thomas St),
Digital Hub, Dublin 8,
D08 TCV4
Ireland

STAY IN TOUCH lonelyplanet.com/contact

Authors (AB) Andrew Bain; (BM) Bella Molloy; (DM) David Mark; (ES) Eileen Schwab; (GL) George Laking; (GVM) Georgina von Marburg; (HS) Hans Schmidt-Harms; (IT) Iain Treloar; (MW) Mark Watson; (MC) Matthew Crompton; (PE) Peter English; (RB) Robin Barton; (SE) Sam Elworthy; (SR) Sam Rice; (SP) Sarah Pendergrass; (SM) Scott Mattern; (TP) Tom Powell

Cover illustration by Ross Murray (www.rossmurray.com).

Acknowledgement of Country

Lonely Planet would like to acknowledge all Aboriginal nations throughout Australia, who have nurtured and maintained the land since time immemorial. This book was written on, and is written about, the lands of many diverse nations.
We recognise the unique and ongoing connection that Aboriginal peoples have to land and waters and thank them for their efforts to preserve them. We pay our respects to Elders past and present and extend this respect to any Aboriginal or Torres Strait Islander people who may be reading this guide. We also recognise the ongoing efforts of Aboriginal peoples for reconciliation, justice, and social, cultural and economic self-determination. Sovereignty was never ceded. Australia always was, and always will be, Aboriginal land.